Majumder's

Laws Relating to

NOTICES

Notice means an information, an advice or a written warning in more or less formal shape, intended to apprise a person of such proceeding in which his interest is involved or informing him of some fact which is his right to know and the duty of the notifying authority to communicate. To protect the rights guaranteed by the Constitution of India or laid down in other statutes or contractually agreed, one may have to receive or issue notice from or to persons or authorities.

In the instant edition of this utility oriented work, care has been taken to cover the relevant areas as much as possible with emphasis on recent legislations and/or amendments thereof. Attempt has been made to incorporate all the important decisions of the apex court and various High Courts to present an up to date state of the law, without making any departure from the compact character of the book. It has made room for a wide variety of laws and Acts under which notices are to be served, catering to the various segments of society.

The present edition provides a comprehensive account of the subject by dealing with the definition and purpose, their classes and requirements, their service and such other broad features. While incorporating the new issues or legislations, this edition eliminates the obsolete ones to reduce the unnecessary bulk. It is devoted to notices coming under several recent Acts of the Central Government. It also contains model forms to render the work useful from the practitioners' point of view.

This edition deals with all the current aspects of the subject will surely be treated as helpful as, if not more than, it was in its earlier editions.

Kolkata
Eastern Law House Private Ltd.
54 Ganesh Chunder Avenue
Kolkata 700 013

New Delhi
Eastern Law House Private Ltd.
36 Netaji Subhash Marg, Daryaganj
New Delhi 110 002

Majumder's

Laws Relating to NOTICES

EIGHTH EDITION

by

Purnendu Bhattacharyya MA, LLM
Former District & Sessions Judge and
Director, West Bengal Judicial Academy

Kolkata New Delhi
EASTERN LAW HOUSE

Published and processed by
EASTERN LAW HOUSE PRIVATE LTD.
54 Ganesh Chunder Avenue
Kolkata 700 013
Tel: (033) 2215-1989
Email: mail@elh.co.in
www.elh.co.in

First Edition 1966
Second Edition 1968
Third Edition 1972
Fourth Edition 1978
Fifth Edition 1982
Sixth Edition 1993
Seventh Edition 2005
Eighth Edition 2022

ISBN 978-81-7177-370-1

Printed at
Dey's Offset, Kolkata

Preface

Majumdar's *Notices* has for more than five decades been accepted as a standard treatise on the subject. Indeed, its utility and immense popularity has been apparent from the earlier editions. The current version of the book (Eighth edition) is marked by inclusion of up to date and new statutes and exclusion of obsolete laws. For example, the chapters on the Arbitration and Conciliation Act, the Companies Act, the Consumer Protection Act and the Employees Compensation Act have been revamped and completely re-written. Obviously, recent pronouncements of the Supreme Court and various High Courts have been included. In refashioning and re-designing the book, however, we have taken due care to retain its compact and comprehensive character.

Notice is almost of everyday use to persons of legal profession. It is used preceding judicial proceedings, during judicial proceedings and at times following judicial proceedings. Its importance, therefore, cannot be over-emphasised in matters of law. The questions of its legality, sufficiency, validity and service often come up for judicial determination.

I appreciate the active co-operation extended by Eastern Law House Private Ltd., in particular its Director Mr. Asok De and Mr. Somnath Chakraborty, in preparation of this edition.

I shall be grateful if any suggestion is received from the legal fraternity for improvement of the book.

Kolkata
2nd January 2022

PURNENDU BHATTACHARYYA

Contents

		PAGE
Preface		[5]
CHAPTER		
1	Introduction	1
2	Classification of Notices	7
3	Requirements in a Notice	25
4	Service of Notice	36
5	Persons Competent to Issue Notice	64
6	Persons Competent to Accept Notice	77
7	Effects of Notice of Joint-interest Holders	89
8	Waiver of Notice	94
9	Savings of Limitation where Notice is Statutory (Section 15(2) of the Limitation Act 1963)	105
10	Miscellaneous Facts about Notices	116
11	Notices under the Code of Civil Procedure 1908	131
12	Notices under the Railways Act 1989	188
13	Notices under the Indian Partnership Act 1932	225
14	Notices under the Sale of Goods Act 1930	243
15	Notices under the Arbitration & Conciliation Act 1996	252
16	Notices under the Indian Contract Act 1872	262
17	Notices under the Constitution of India, Law of Wrongful Dismissal and the Law of Torts	271
18	Notices under the Negotiable Instruments Act 1881	299
19	Notices Relating to Tenancy	321
20	Notices under the Companies Act 2013	416
21	Notices under the Consumer Protection Act 2019	466

CHAPTER		PAGE
22	Notices under the Code of Criminal Procedure 1973	493
23	Notices under the Securities and Exchange Board of India Act 1992 (SEBI)	537
24	Notices under the Industrial Disputes Act 1947	548
25	Notices under the Factorie's Act 1948	571
26	Notices under the Employee's Compensation Act 1923	578
27	Notices under the Industrial Employment (Standing Orders) Act 1946	586
28	Notices under the Municipalities, Municipal Corporations and other Body-corporates	611
29	Notices under the Labour Laws	615
30	Notices under other Central Acts	623
31	Miscellaneous Notices	667
Index		717

CHAPTER 1

Introduction

SYNOPSIS

1 Notice—meaning
2 Notice of a fact
3 Object of a notice
4 When a notice is given
5 Laws relating to notices—adjective laws
6 Notice and notification
7 Scheme of the work

1 Notice—meaning

To a man of the legal profession, the word 'Notice' is almost of everyday use. The legal meaning of notice is intimation, instruction, warning, announcement, news, a written paper or placard conveying these matters. Notice is given to a person to inform, instruct or intimate something which has happened or is about to happen and of which the noticee may or may not be fully aware.[1] A notice is a legal notification required by law or agreement, or imparted by operation of law as a result of some fact. It may also mean a definite legal cognizance, actual or constructive, of an existing right or title.[2] In other words, as Mozley and Whitelay's *Law Dictionary* (10th Ed.) says, notice is a word which means knowledge either actual or imputed by construction of law, sometimes a formal notification of some fact or some intention of the party giving the notice, sometimes the expression of a demand or requisition.

Notice is a word which involves that knowledge may be imparted by notice, but 'notice' and 'knowledge' are not the same thing, although loosely one sometimes talk as if to act with notice and to act with knowledge were indeed the same.[3] In some circumstances it may mean a caution. Notice means information, an advice or written warning in more or less formal shape intended to apprise a person of some proceeding in which his interests are involved, or informing him of some fact which it is his right to know and

1 B.C. Sarma, *Fair Hearing and Access to Justice,* Ed. 2012, p. 160.
2 Black's *Law Dictionary,* 10th Ed.
3 *Cresta Holdings Ltd.* v *Karlin* [1959]3 All ER 656.

the duty of the notifying authority to communicate.[4] While a notice specifying the date, time and venue of a meeting announces as well as intimates a programme of the meeting, a notice preventing thoroughfare on a road under repairs serves as a caution to unwary pedestrians or the like against dangers involved in using the road recklessly. Notices that we come across in legal texts or in courts of law have had the same import, and, in addition, an information of something to be. It is not synonymous with knowledge but knowledge may as well be imparted by a notice.

2 Notice of a fact

Notice means bringing a fact to a person's knowledge. A person is said to have notice of a fact when but for wilful abstention from an enquiry, he would have known it and that in equity a man who ought to have known a fact should be treated as if he actually does know it.[5] A person has notice of a fact if the person knows the fact, has reason to know the fact, has received an effective notification of the fact, or should know the fact to fulfil a duty owed to another person.[6] It has been held in the context of s. 3 of the Transfer of Property Act 1882 that the word 'notice' is of wider import than the word 'knowledge'. A person may not have actual knowledge of a fact but he may have notice of it.[7]

A notice to a partner for dissolution of a partnership firm or a notice asking the debtor to meet the claim of the notice-giver or a notice asking the tenant to quit the leasehold premises after expiry of a certain time is an announcement, while a notice of an intended suit is a timely caution, made known to the addressee, to meet the claim and/or to make amends lest a suit should follow.

Despite the fact that notices generally have for their object one common idea, to wit, to enable the proposed defendant to meet or resist the claim of the notice-giver, each particular type of notice has its object peculiar to it.

Public notice is a *sine qua non* before the partners can escape their joint liability in respect of any act of a partner and where there is no proof that a public notice of dissolution was given, any creditor advancing money to a partner for the purposes of the firm would be entitled to seek remedy against all the partners. But the public notice is not the only mode of notifying the fact of dissolution. If the creditors have notice of the dissolution *aliunde*; they cannot hold the partners liable.[8]

4 Tapash Gan Choudhury, *Penumbra of Natural Justice,* 3rd Ed., pp. 155-156.
5 *Canara Bank* v *Canara Sales Corporation* (1987)2 SCC 666.
6 *Restatement of the Law,* Third, s. 1.04(4), Agency, vol. 1, Ch. 1, p. 70.
7 *Ram Niwas (dead) through LRs* v *Bano (Smt.)* (2000)6 SCC 685; AIR 2000 SC 2921.
8 *Manjunatha Nayak* v *Ullal Dayananda Hanumantha Nayak* AIR 1984 Kant 55; *Ratanji* v *Prem Shankar* AIR 1938 All 619; *Central United Bank Ltd.* v *Venkatarama* AIR 1963 Mad 302; *Rama Rao* v *Venkateswara Rao* AIR 1963 AP 154.

3 Object of a notice

Notice is the first limb of natural justice more specifically *audi alteram partem*. It is essential that a party should be put on notice of the case before any adverse order is passed against him. The laws of both God and man recognize the opportunity to make defence, if a party has any. Even God Himself did not pass sentence upon Adam before he was called upon to make his defence.

The object of a notice under s. 78B of the Indian Railways Act (New s. 106 of Railways Act 1989) is to enable the Railway Administration to have an opportunity of settling the claim by making an enquiry into the claim in time with a view to preventing dishonest claims being put up all of a sudden by unscrupulous persons after a long time.[9] Section 106 of the Railways Act 1989 contemplates a notice of claim in writing to be served. The effect of s. 106 of the Act is to bar the plaintiff's claim unless he can show that he has complied with the requirements of law as regards notice of claim.[10]

Again, the object of a notice under s. 80, CPC is manifestly to give to the Government or the Public Officer sufficient time and notice of the case which is proposed to be brought against it or him so that it or he may consider the position and decide for itself or himself whether the claim of the plaintiff should be accepted or resisted.[11]

The object of a notice to quit under s. 106 of the Transfer of Property Act is to make the tenant aware of the intention of the Lessor to terminate the lease.[12] Similarly, a valid notice to quit upon the tenant is a condition precedent in a suit for eviction [vide s. 6(1)(*e*) of the W.B. Premises Tenancy Act 1997]. Section 7 of the W.B. Premises Tenancy Act 1997 has saddled the tenant with an imperative obligation in an eviction suit filed before civil Judge on any ground stated in s. 6 of that Act to perform the rent liability as specified in that section in order to be entitled to get the protection offered in s. 6 of the W.B Premises Tenancy Act 1997. If provisions of s. 7 of the Act are not complied with, the tenant would be deprived of his right to contest the eviction suit under s. 7(3) of the W.B. Premises Tenancy Act 1997.

Reasonable notice

Reasonable notice is a notice or information of a fact as may fairly and properly be expected or required in the particular circumstances.

9 *Oudh and Tirhut Rly.* v *Karamchand Paras Ram* AIR 1958 All 234.

10 *Mahadeva* v *S.I. Railways Co.* 45 Mad 135.

11 *State of Andhra Pradesh* v *Suryanarayana* AIR 1965 SC 11; *State of Madras* v *C.P. Agencies* AIR 1960 SC 1309; *Sudhir Ranjan Halder* v *State of West Bengal* AIR 1961 Cal 626; *Union of India* v *Landra Engg. & Foundry Works* AIR 1962 Punj 262; *Hazi Jamal Noor Mohammad* v *Governor General in Council* AIR 1947 Cal 26.

12 *Gurdit Singh* v *Tata Iron & Steel Co. Ltd.* AIR 1965 Pat 311.

What constitutes a reasonable notice (by an arbitrator) has been considered by the Supreme Court in *Sohanlal Gupta* v *Asha Devi Gupta*.[13] For constituting a reasonable opportunity, one of the conditions required to be observed that each party must have notice that the hearing before the arbitrator is to take place. A party does not have unfettered right. The arbitrator has a right of managing the hearing, therefore, he would be entitled to give directions to the parties to be present on the particular date at a particular time and particular place which would be sufficient compliance with the requirements of law.

4 When a notice is given

When is a notice given? The direction to issue a notice is not equivalent either to the issue of a notice or to service of a notice to the addressee. In *Mahammed Tahsin Khan* v *Seth Basant Rai*,[14] Sen, J. observed: "A notice can be said to be given when such party receives the notice". Observations of Adams, J. in *Ram Gopal Marwari* v *B. & N.W. Railway*,[15] gave rise to a controversy whether posting of a letter containing the notice was a service of the notice. Section 77 (now changed to s. 106) of the Railways Act requires that a letter containing the notice of claim against a Railway Administration must reach the addressee within six months' time from the 'date of delivery for carriage by railway'. In *Ram Gopal Marwari* v *B. & N.W. Railway*,[15] the letter containing the notice had been posted within six months but too late to reach the addressee within six months. Adams, J. held: "The question is whether this posting complies with the terms of s. 77, that is to say, whether the posting of the letter containing the notice was a proper service of notice as contemplated by s. 77 ...... Reading however, s. 140(*c*) it would seem quite plain that the preferment of the claim has to be made by forwarding the letter by post, that is to say, by posting a registered letter ...... It seems clear also that when the letter was posted the claim was preferred as contemplated in s. 77." The section only means that the claim should be preferred within the period of six months and not that it should also reach the Railway Administration before its expiry.

Therefore, a notice cannot be said to be given or served until it reached the addressee and was tendered to him and was either accepted or refused by the addressee. 'Giving' of anything as ordinarily understood in the English language is not complete unless it has reached the hands of the person to whom it has to be given. In the eye of law, however, 'giving' is complete in many matters where it has been offered to a person but not accepted by him. Tendering of a notice, is in law, therefore, giving of notice even though the person to whom it is tendered refuses to accept it. There is no authority or

13 (2003)7 SCC 492.
14 AIR 1930 All 477.
15 AIR 1927 Pat 241.

principle for the proposition that as soon as the person with a legal duty to give the notice despatches the notice to the address of the person to whom it has to be given, the giving is complete.[16] A notice takes effect from the date of service and not from the date of issue.[17]

5 Laws relating to notices—adjective laws

Laws on notices are procedural laws and, therefore, have to be followed rigidly. Law does not excuse laches in drawing up notices, particularly with regard to those which are statutory and mandatory. It is needless to say that notices failing to satisfy requirements of a statute are fatal for the suit to follow. It must not be understood that *bona fide* errors, honestly made, stand on the same footing. It is also true that mistakes which do not violate the provision of law or affect the cause of action may be ignored.

Of late, there is a tendency to have a liberal view on the construction and interpretation of a notice. Even with regard to a notice under s. 80, CPC, the earlier pedantic view point has been condemned. Although strict compliance with the terms of s. 80, CPC is necessary, it is not necessary to scrutinize a notice under s. 80, CPC in a pedantic manner or in a manner devoid of common sense.[18] Similarly, a notice to quit under s. 106 of the Transfer of Property Act is to be construed not with a desire to find fault with it which would render it defective but to be construed in such a manner that it may prevail *ut res magis valeat quam pereat* (i.e. an act may prevail rather than perish).[19]

Though a notice is not a technical matter, precision, clarity and definiteness can be reasonably demanded of any notice. It has been the tendency of the law to minimize the field of uncertainty and the progress of law in various directions points to the substitution of the fixed for the fluid. Terse but brief, certain yet simple, should be the character of a notice.

6 Notice and notification

There are many statutes under which publication of notification is a prerequisite for taking action under the law. For example, publication of notification under s. 4 of the Land Acquisition Act 1894 (corresponds to s. 11 of the Right to Fair Compensation and Transparency in Land Acquisition, Rehabilitation and Resettlement Act 2013) is *sine qua non* for any proceeding under the Act.[20]

16 *K. Narasimhiah* v *H.C. Singri Gowda* AIR 1966 SC 330.
17 *Pooran Chand Joshi* v *Union of India* AIR 1971 Raj 12.
18 *Dhian Singh* v *Union of India* AIR 1958 SC 270; *State of Madras* v *CP Agencies* AIR 1960 SC 1309.
19 *Harihar Banerjee* v *Ramsashi Roy* AIR 1918 PC 102.
20 *R.L. Jain* v *DDA* (2004)4 SCC 79; AIR 2004 SC 1904.

7 Scheme of the work

The work is complete in three parts.

Part I covering first 10 Chapters, deals with general observations on laws relating to notices—their definition and purpose, their classes and requirements, their service, and such other broad features.

Part II is devoted to notices coming under several Acts of the Union Government with reference to laws governing those.

And, Part III contains model forms of notice to render the work useful from the practitioners' point of view.

CHAPTER 2

Classification of Notices

SYNOPSIS

1 Oral (or verbal) and written notices
2 Mandatory, statutory and directory notices—notice when condition precedent
3 Public and private notices
4 Actual (or express) and constructive (or implied) notices
5 Reasonable and defective (or invalid) notices
6 Composite notices
7 Statutory notice
8 Personal notice

1 Oral (or verbal) and written notices

By a 'notice' we generally mean a written notice issued under one or the other provision of law. We are reminded of notices under s. 80 of the CPC or under s. 106 of the Railways Act 1989 or under s. 106 of the Transfer of Property Act. Provisions of law requiring the issue of like notices also require that a notice contemplated therein should be in writing. Even where a notice is not statutory but merely optional in character, the notice is generally in writing; for, a written notice is easy to prove; its contents, being reduced to writing, are certain, leaving hardly any scope for speculation or dispute.

Even then, a notice may be oral or verbal. A notice to quit may be given orally. But oral notice to dispossess or terminate possession of the tenant upon acquisition by the Government is not sufficient.[1] Generally speaking, where there is no statutory provision for the determination of a tenancy by a written notice, a notice to quit may be oral.[2] A verbal notice is quite sufficient to determine a tenancy[3] unless there is express provision requiring a notice in writing.[4] When the Legislature used the word "notice" it must be presumed to have borne in mind that it means not only a formal intimation

1 *State of West Bengal* v *Vishnunarayan & Associate Private Ltd.* (2002)4 SCC 134.
2 *Deonundan Pershad* v *Meghu Mahton* ILR 34 Cal 57; 11 CWN 225.
3 *Zingu* v *Ramji Mahadu* AIR 1929 Nag 169.
4 *Jhagru Mian* v *Raghunath Singh* AIR 1929 Pat 630.

but also an informal one. Similarly, it must be deemed to have in mind the fact that the service of a notice would include constructive or informal notice. It is enough if it is orally given to the parties when they are present by themselves or by their authorised agents at the time of filing the award.[5] Section 94 of the Negotiable Instruments Act, amongst others, provides for oral notice.

2 Mandatory, statutory and directory notices—notice when condition precedent[6]

In case a condition precedent is not fulfilled, there is no right to sue.

(i) *Prescribed by Statute*

Notice under s. 80, CPC is a condition precedent to the institution of a suit against the Government or Public Officers in their official capacity.

The provision under s. 80, CPC is mandatory but the right can be waived by the party for whose benefit it has been provided; and no suit can be instituted without service of notice under s. 80, CPC which is required statutorily as a condition precedent.[7] If the notice has been given to the concerned necessary party in a proper way, the requirement of service of notice upon the other parties may be waived.[8]

Notice to the Railway Administration claiming compensation for loss, destruction, determination of animals or goods under s. 106 of the Railways Act 1989 is a condition precedent.

Section 106 of the Railways Act 1989 provides a precondition that no claim for compensation and refund of over charge can be preferred against a railway administration without serving a notice in writing by the claimant within six months from the date of entrustment of the goods.

A legal termination of the monthly tenancy requires two conditions to be fulfilled, viz. that there must be a notice terminating the tenancy giving 15 days' notice and it must expire with the end of the tenancy month. A notice giving mere 15 days' time by itself will not answer the requirement of s. 106.[9]

Section 114A of the Transfer of Property Act requires two conditions to be fulfilled before a suit for ejectment could lie—(1) that a notice should be given to the lessee specifying the particular breach complained of; and

5 *Sayed Mahbub Hussain Shah* v *Anjuman Imdad Quarza* AIR 1942 Lah 129.

6 Conditions precedent may be imposed either by the provisions of some statute or by the parties, either expressly or by necessary implication arising out of the construction of the document or agreement or they may be implied by law according to the nature of the transaction—Wharton's *Law Lexicon,* 14th Ed., p. 228.

7 *Dayanand* v *State* AIR 2001 Raj 257; *Municipality* v *Gas Authority of India Ltd.* AIR 2006 MP 17.

8 *Mavindra Ch. Paul* v *State of Tripura* AIR 2007 Gau 103; 2008(1) Civ CC 771.

9 *F.J. Fernandis* v *A.P. Cardoza* AIR 1984 Kant 226.

(2) that the lessee should be called upon to remedy the breach. If these conditions are fulfilled, then alone the lessor would be entitled to bring a suit for ejectment of the lessee.[10]

In a suit for ejectment by the lessor against a lessee for breach of an express covenant, a notice under s. 106, Transfer of Property Act or a notice under s. 6(4) of the West Bengal Premises Tenancy Act 1997 is a must. Under s. 6(4) of the West Bengal Premises Tenancy Act 1997, except where the tenant has given notice to quit but has failed to deliver vacant possession of the premises to the landlord in accordance with such notice [s. 6(1)(*e*)], in all other cases mentioned in s. 6(1) of the said Act, notwithstanding anything in any other law for the time being in force, no proceeding for the recovery of possession of any premises shall be initiated by the landlord unless he had given to the tenant one month's notice expiring with a month of the tenancy.

The above list is illustrative, not exhaustive.

(ii) *Enjoined by agreement between parties*

Where the agreement specifically enjoins that notice has to be served it is known as contractual notices.

When a notice has to be served pursuant to a provision of a statute (Central or State), the notice is a statutory one; for example, a notice as enjoined under s. 80 of the Code of Civil Procedure.

When the suit is against government notice is mandatory unless the court dispenses with such notice under s. 80(2), CPC. In respect of suits against a public officer notice is also mandatory.[11] When a suit has been instituted against the government and its authorities without compliance with the provisions of s. 80(2), CPC, such suit is not maintainable.[12]

A statutory notice may again be sub-divided into mandatory (or obligatory) and directory (or recommendatory) notices. Mandatory notices are those which must have to be served, otherwise, the suit following should itself fail. There is a legal obligation to serve a notice and, as such, it is mandatory.

Directory notices are those which the law directs. If the direction was not followed, certain consequences were to follow to the detriment of the interest of one who ought to have followed the direction of the law. The law recommends the issue of a notice in such cases in the interest of the notice-giver. Hence such a notice is recommendatory in character.

All mandatory notices are statutory. But all statutory notices are not necessarily mandatory. There is a common belief that a statutory notice is

10 *Basant Lal* v *State of UP* (1980)4 SCC 430.

11 *Amalgamated Electricity* v *Ajmer Municipality* AIR 1969 SC 227; *Sibananda* v *Janaki* AIR 1985 Ori 197.

12 *Bajaj Hindustan Sugar & Industries Ltd.* v *Balrampur Chini Mills* AIR 2007 SC 1906; (2007)9 SCC 43.

invariably mandatory and a statutory notice has practically come to mean a mandatory notice. It is submitted that though there is some sense in the belief but it is not wholly correct; for some notices are statutory but not mandatory.

A few illustrations of mandatory notices are:

(a) *A notice under s. 80 of the CPC*

Section 80 was enacted as a measure of public policy with the object of ensuring that before a suit is instituted against the government or a public officer, the government or the officer concerned is afforded an opporunity to scrutinise the claim in respect of which the suit is proposed to be filed.[13]

In respect of suits to which s. 80 applies (i.e. suits against the Government or the Public Officer) compliance with it is mandatory. Therefore, a suit which does not satisfy its terms is liable to be dismissed. There should be identity of the person who issues the notice with the person who brings the suit. Where suit has been filed against the Government after notice duly issued under s. 80, and that suit is withdrawn with permission of court to file a fresh suit and when a fresh suit is filed, fresh notice under s. 80 before such suit is not necessary.[14]

But notice under s. 80, CPC is to be served before filing a suit against the Administrator of Union Territory,[15] Commissioner of Calcutta Corporation,[16] or any officer of Food Corporation of India.[17] No notice is necessary when Government is a formal party.[18] Similarly, a claim petition under Motor Vehicles Act 1988 against the Government for compensation for death in motor accident by a Government vehicle, no notice under s. 80, CPC is necessary.[19]

(b) *A notice under s. 106 of the Railways Act 1989*

A notice of claim for compensation and refund of overcharge under s. 106 of the Railways Act 1989 is a condition precedent to the maintainability of a suit.[20] Non-service of a notice is fatal to the claim.[1] Notice must be given within six months from the date of consignment of the goods to the railways.[2]

13 *Bihari Chowdhary* v *State of Bihar* AIR 1984 SC 1043; (1984)2 SCC 627.
14 *S.N. Dutt* v *Union of India* AIR 1961 SC 1449; *Amarnath Dogra* v *Union of India* AIR 1963 SC 424; *State of Jammu and Kashmir* v *Lucky Glass Works* 72 CWN 795; *R. Kamalan* v *State of Tamil Nadu* AIR 1980 Mad 86.
15 *Kanhaiyalal* v *Government of India* AIR 1975 Gau 37.
16 *Govardhan Das* v *Calcutta Corporation* AIR 1970 Cal 539.
17 *Kanta Prosad* v *Regional Manager, FCI* AIR 1974 Pat 376.
18 *Zakiruddin* v *Asst. Commissioner* AIR 1963 Pat 11.
19 *Manilal Ganpat* v *Union of India* AIR 1974 MP 159.
20 *Governor General in Council (Union of India)* v *Musaddilal* AIR 1961 SC 725.
1 *Niranjan Lall Agarwalla* v *Union of India* AIR 1962 Cal 42.
2 *Union of India* v *Lakshmi Textile* AIR 1968 Ker 23.

(c) *A notice under s. 10 of the Carriers Act 1865*

If a common carrier has to be sued for the loss of, or injury to, goods entrusted to him for carriage, a notice in writing of the loss or injury must precede the institution of a suit.[3] Such notice should be given within six months from the date on which the plaintiff first learned of the loss or injury. Notice has to be given even where the carrier knows of the loss.[3] The period of six months as prescribed by s. 10 cannot be reduced.[4]

(d) *A notice under s. 54(2) of the Sale of Goods Act 1930*

Statutory power of resale under s. 54(2) arises if the property in the goods has passed to the buyer subject to the lien of the unpaid seller.[5]

A notice by an unpaid seller to the buyer of his intention to resell is mandatory inasmuch as the giving of notice is a condition precedent to the lawful exercise of the power of resale by the vendor.[6] Section 54(2) cannot be invoked if notice of intention to resell is not served.[7]

OTHER MANDATORY NOTICES

A notice under s. 154 of the Delhi Municipal Corporation Act 1957 is mandatory before effecting seizure of cattle.[8] No recovery proceedings could be instituted unless a notice of demand had been served on the legal representative under s. 8 of the U.P. Sales Tax Act 1947.[9] No proceeding for the recovery of possession of any premises shall be started by the landlord unless he has given the tenant one month's notice expiring with a month of the tenancy in terms of s. 6(4) of the West Bengal Premises Tenancy Act 1997. A notice under s. 148 of the Income Tax Act 1961 on the assessee is mandatory for assessment of the income which has escaped assessment.

DIRECTORY NOTICE

Issue of notice to the Board of Auqaf under s. 89 of the Waqf Act 1995 is a condition precedent to the filing of a suit against the Board. The requirement as to notice applies to suits against the Central Board in respect of their acts as well as to suits for any relief in respect of any waqf.[10] The defect of want

3 *Br. B. Foreign Marine Ins. Co.* v *India etc. Rly. Co.* AIR 1918 Cal 896; ILR 38 Cal 50.
4 *M.G. Bros. Lorry Service* v *Prasad Textiles* (1983)3 SCC 61; AIR 1984 SC 15; (1983)2 SCR 1027.
5 *PSNS Ambalavana Chettier & Co.* v *Express Newspapers Ltd., Bombay* AIR 1968 SC 741.
6 *Narayandas* v *Kunjilal* AIR 1924 Nag 162.
7 *Endupuni Narshimham* v *Mahadevram Udinram* AIR 1974 Ori 98; *Kanhaiyalal* v *Kasturchand* AIR 1957 MB 168.
8 *Keshoram* v *Delhi Administration* (1974)4 SCC 509.
9 *Homely Industries* v *The Sales Tax Officer* (1976)3 SCC 705.
10 *Siraj Ul Haq* v *Board of Wakfs* 1959 SCJ 367.

of notice cannot be equated to a formal one as it is a redical defect going to the root of the claim.[11]

A few illustrations of directory notices are:

(a) *Notice of accident under s. 161 of the Electricity Act 2003*

Section 161 of the Electricity Act provides for giving of notice of accident occurring in connection with any part of electric lines or electrical plants to Electrical Inspector or any other persons holding an inquiry under sub-sec. (2) and such other authorities as the Appropriate Government may direct.

(b) *A notice for revocation or renunciation of agency under s. 206 of the Contract Act*

Section 206 enjoins that a reasonable notice must be given for revocation or renunciation of agency, otherwise the damage thereby resulting to the principal or the agent, as the case may be, must be made good to the one by the other. Where an agency has been created for a fixed period, a reasonable notice would be necessary to terminate it. A reasonable notice is one that is fairly to be expected or required under the particular circumstances. The requirement of reasonable notice is mandatory under s. 206 for termination of agency.[12] A termination without notice is ineffective.[13] The length of notice will depend, among other things, upon the length for which the agency has continued.[14] When reasonable notice is the condition precedent for terminating the jural relationship of principal and agent, it necessarily follows that renunciation of agency without notice would be clearly illegal.[15] As termination of agency by the principal is inequitable or works an unjust hardship on the agent, the law requires a reasonable notice.[16] Where an insurance agent had acted as an agent for a long period of time and had to maintain a large establishment of staff, there three and half months' notice was not reasonable and that the notice ought to have been at least of two years in the circumstances.[17] If the Agency is determined without reasonable notice "the damages thereby resulting to the agent must be made good by the principal". Where an agency has been created for a fixed period, compensation would have to be paid for premature termination, if the termination is without sufficient cause. Reasonable notice for premature termination of agency was not given and the compensation of three months' earning was allowed.[18] No compensation is payable where the agency has

11 *Shamsuddin* v *Tuticorin Jamia Masjid* AIR 1984 Mad 276; *M.S. Abdul Hamid* v *S.M. Sheik Mohamed* AIR 2003 Mad 179.
12 *Popular Shal Mart* v *K. Srinivasa Rao* (1989)2 Andh LT 541.
13 *Om Prakash Pariwal*, re AIR 1988 Cal 143.
14 *Shipping Corporation of India* v *Machadeo Bros* (1996) AIHC 3869 (Mad).
15 *Popular Shal Mart*, re AIR 1990 NOC 87 (AP); (1989)2 Andh LT 541.
16 *International Oil Co.* v *Indian Oil Co. Ltd.* AIR 1969 Mad 423.
17 *Sohrabji* v *Oriental Government Security Assurance Co.* AIR 1946 PC 9.
18 *J.K. Sayani* v *Bright Bros* AIR 1980 Mad 162.

not been created for any definite period or where, though created for a specified length of time, reasonable notice for its termination has been given or the termination is otherwise based upon a sufficient cause. Absence of notice would merely penalise the defaulting party in the shape of damages to the other.[19]

The above list is not comprehensive but is illustrative of above types of notices.

(c) *Contractual and optional notices*

Where a provision is made by parties, by entering into a contract, for the issue of a notice and a notice is eventually issued under the terms of the contract, the notice is a contractual notice. For example, a licence is revocable at the will of the grantor but there is a provision in the licence that the licensee would be entitled to a notice before being required to vacate and notice is, in fact, issued under the said provision of the licence: the notice is a contractual notice.

Other common illustrations of a contractual notice are:

(*a*) a notice for determining partnership after a particular period of time agreed to in the partnership deed;

(*b*) a notice by party to arbitration proceedings to concur in the appointment and in supplying vacancy of Arbitrator, Umpire, when agreed;

(*c*) a notice for revocation or renunciation of agency if the agreement for agency provides for issue of a notice;

(*d*) a notice for termination of service when service conditions contemplate issue of a notice;

(*e*) a notice for termination of tenancy or lease where agreement provides for issue of a notice;

(*f*) a notice by tenant for repairs of leasehold premises where lease agreement provides for issue of a notice;

(*g*) contractual service of temporarily recruited employees could be terminated at any time without notice.[20]

Optional notices, on the contrary, proceed from volition of the notice-giver. Though not obliged by any provision of law the notice-giver voluntarily issues notice as a warning for the threatened litigation. Optional notices have two objects in view—(*i*) Direct: to have the claim of the notice-giver settled out of a court of law; (*ii*) Indirect:,to give a pressure on the addressee for meeting the demand of the notice-giver in time.

19 *S. Rm. S.T. Narayana Chettiar* v *The Kaleswarar Mills Ltd.* AIR 1952 Mad 515.
20 *Surendra Kr. Gyani* v *State of Rajasthan* (1992)4 SCC 464.

The notice of this category is optional; for, neither the law enjoins nor he is bound to issue the notice. It is up to his option. A notice claiming arrears of rent, a notice claiming money on a handnote, a notice claiming dues on credit accounts are optional notices. It may be added that there is no bar to bring a suit for claims without prior notice in such cases.

3 Public and private notices

Public notice means notice to the public concerned.[1] Notice given to the public or persons affected, usually by publishing in newspaper of general circulation.[2] Public notices are meant to be issued when members of the general public are concerned and are likely to be interested in or affected by such a notice. Public notice is a notice given to the public or persons affected usually by publishing in a newspaper of general circulation. A notice issued under s. 116(3) of the Delhi Municipal Corporation Act 1957, for example, is a public notice.[3] Under s. 149(1) of the Patna Municipal Corporation Act 1951, requirement of giving public notice for publication of assessment list, is mandatory.[4] Private notices relate to interests affecting individuals. A notice under s. 184(2), Kolkata Municipal Corporation Act to determine annual valuation of land & building, for enhancement of such valuation and for revision should be given as it is mandatory under the statute.[5]

A public notice carries with it an intention of largest possible circulation of contents of such a notice. Hence, it is no wonder that the legislature would enjoin publication of such notices (as a notice of retirement or expulsion of a partner, or a notice of dissolution of a registered firm) through the Gazette as provided for in s. 72 of the Indian Partnership Act.

Following are some illustrations of public notices:

(*a*) A notice of sale of a business;

(*b*) A notice for termination of an agent's authority;

(*c*) A notice of dissolution of a registered firm;

(*d*) A notice of retirement or expulsion of a partner.

The following are illustrations of common private notices:

(*a*) Notice by a landlord to a tenant to quit;

(*b*) Notice by a tenant to determine lease;

(*c*) Notice by tenant to repair;

(*d*) Notice to tenant to attorn;

1 *Barfoot* v *Goodall* 3 Campbell 149.

2 Mitra, *Legal & Commercial Dictionary,* 6th Ed.

3 *Krishna Mohan (P) Ltd.* v *Municipal Corporation of Delhi* (2003)7 SCC 151.

4 *Ravimal Krishna* v *State of Bihar* (2003)6 SCC 401.

5 *Auro Impex (P) Ltd.* v *Calcutta Municipal Corporation* (2003)2 CHN 469.

(*e*) Notice of claim to a debtor;

(*f*) Notice of dishonour of a cheque, etc.;

(*g*) Notice by vendor to complete purchase;

(*h*) Notice of assignment of lease;

(*i*) Notice to appoint an Arbitrator.

Mode of giving public notice

Different enactments specify the mode of giving of public notice. Usually such notice is given in a newspaper of general circulation to the public or persons affected by publication.

Public notice under the Partnership Act

Section 72 of the Partnership Act deals with the mode of giving public notice. A public notice under the Partnership Act is given—

(*a*) Where it relates to the retirement or expulsion of a partner from a registered firm, or to the dissolution of a registered firm, or to the election to become or not to become a partner in a registered firm by a person attaining majority who was admitted as a minor to the benefits of partnership, by notice to the Registrar of Firms under s. 63, and by publication in the Official Gazette and in at least one vernacular newspaper circulating in the district where the firm to which it relates has its place or principal place of business; and

(*b*) in any other case, by publication in the Official Gazette and in at least one vernacular newspaper circulating in the district where the firm to which it relates has its place or principal place of business.

The formalities in the case of a registered firm are these—

(1) Notice to the Registrar;

(2) Publication in the Official Gazette;

(3) Publication in the vernacular newspaper circulating in the district where the firm to which it relates has its place or principal place of business.

In the case of an unregistered firm a public notice is necessary in the following circumstances:

(1) When a partner retires;

(2) When a firm is dissolved;

(3) When a minor has been admitted to the benefits of the firm and on attaining majority has to give public notice of his election to become or not to become a partner. In the case of an unregistered firm, first formality of informing the Registrar is not necessary because the name of the firm is not in the register.

In a case, what was relied on as a public notice was a publication in a Sunday edition of a Malayalam daily. The court held that this alone would not satisfy the requirement of public notice. The conclusion of the court was that the Bank could not be presumed to have had notice of acknowledgment against a retired partner also until all the requirements of s. 72 regarding the registered firm were complied with.[6]

Public notice under the Contract Act

Section 208 of the Contract Act deals with the termination of agent's authority. Revocation by the act of the principal takes effect as to the agent from the time when the revocation is made known to him and as to third parties when it is made known to third parties and not before. To bring this into effect, the principal revokes of an agency expressly, by direct and formal writing advertised, i.e. public notice so that it comes to the knowledge of all concerned.

4 Actual (or express) and constructive (or implied) notices

A notice may be actual (or express) or constructive[7] (or implied).[8]

A notice may be actual notice where the party has actual knowledge of the fact. It would be constructive where the party is deemed to have knowledge of the fact.

Actual notice as is positively proved to have been given to a party directly and personally, or such as he is presumed to have received personally because the evidence within his knowledge was sufficient to put him upon inquiry.[9]

Section 3 of the Transfer of Property Act speaks of the equitable doctrine of notice. One may have notice of a fact in two ways. He may have notice—actual (or express) or the notice may be imputed to him. In the latter case, the notice is implied. A notice may be imputed to a man by reason of his wilful abstention from an enquiry which he ought to have made or by reason of his gross negligence. Likewise, a notice may be imputed to a man by reason of his agent's knowledge. Implied notice is a notice that is inferred from facts that a person had the means of knowing and that is thus imputed to that person.

'A person is said to have notice' is defined in s. 3 of the Transfer of Property Act. A person is said to have notice of a fact when he actually knows that fact, or when, but for wilful abstention from an enquiry or search which he ought to have made, or gross negligence, he would have known it. In terms of Explanation II to the said definition actual possession is notice

6 *C. Assiamma* v *State Bank of Mysore* AIR 1990 Ker 157.
7 *Sahadul Mia Jan Mahamad Mian* v *Union of India* AIR 1968 Pat 188; *State of Andhra Pradesh* v *G. Venkata Suryanarayana* AIR 1965 SC 11.
8 *Ramniwas* v *Bano* (2000)6 SCC 685.
9 Tapash Gan Choudhury, *Penumbra of Natural Justice*, 3rd Ed., p. 156.

of the title of the person in possession.[10] A statutory presumption of 'notice' arises against any person who acquires any immovable property or any share or interest therein of the title, if any, of the person who is for the time being in actual possession thereof.[11]

In case of actual notice, knowledge of the fact is brought directly home to the party by sending to him or by giving him a notice. Such information must be definite; for, a person is not bound to attend to vague rumours. Actual notice, in order to be binding, must focus a definite information given by a person interested in the property, in the same transaction "so that a reasonable man, or an ordinary man of business, would act upon the information and would regulate his conduct by it.[12]

Constructive notice

Constructive notice is information or knowledge of fact imputed by law to a person, although he may not have actual notice of facts by which he is sought to be affected, because the person concerned could have discovered the fact by proper diligence, and his situation was such as to cast upon him the duty of inquiring into it.[13] Notice arising by presumption of law from the existence of facts and circumstances that party had a duty to take notice of, such as a registered deed or pending law suit, is known as a constructive notice. Refusal to receive registered letter is an example of constructive notice. A person refusing to receive a registered letter sent by post must be deemed to have constructive notice of its contents.[14] In a constructive notice, notice is presumed by law to have been acquired by a person and thus imputed to the person. Constructive notice has been defined as knowledge which the court imputes to a person from the case upon a presumption so strong that it cannot be allowed to be rebutted, that the knowledge must be presumed though it may not have been formally communicated. A constructive notice is a notice arising by presumption of law from the existence of facts and circumstances that a party had a duty to take notice of, such as a registered deed or a pending law suit; notice presumed by law to have been acquired by a person and thus imputed to that person.[15] Again, a constructive notice arises "in those circumstances under which the court concludes either that the notice must be imputed on grounds of public policy to an innocent person, or that the person has been guilty of such negligence by not availing himself of the means of acquiring it, as, if permitted, might be a check to

10 *R.K. Mohammed Ubaidullah* v *Hajee C. Abdul Wahab* (2000)6 SCC 402.
11 *Ramniwas* v *Bano* (supra).
12 *Ashiq Husain* v *Chaturbhuj* AIR 1928 All 159; *Barnhart* v *Greenshields* (1954)9 Moore's PC 18.
13 Tapash Gan Choudhury, *Penumbra of Natural Justice,* 3rd Ed., p. 157.
14 *Pakhar Singh* v *Kishan Singh* AIR 1974 Raj 112.
15 Black's *Law Dictionary,* 10th Edition.

fraud, and which, therefore, in the common interests of society, should, in its consequences, be treated as equivalent to actual notice."[16]

A transferee of an immovable property may be fastened with the constructive notice of any prior transaction affecting the title of the transferor, if he wilfully refrains from making any enquiry when circumstances are such as would lead a prudent and reasonable person to embark on an enquiry regarding the title of the transferor. But a subsequent transferee cannot be fixed with constructive notice of the prior transaction, where the circumstances do not require him to make an enquiry.[17]

Knowledge which the law implies a party to have had—whether he actually had it or not: thus the law implies that an under-lessee has knowledge of the contents of the head lease, whereas very frequently he has not.[18]

Constructive notice, properly so called, is the knowledge which the courts impute to a person upon a presumption so strong of the existence of the knowledge, that it cannot be allowed to be rebutted, either from his knowing something which ought to have put him upon further inquiry or from his wilfully abstaining from inquiry, to avoid notice.[19] If one by exercise of reasonable care would have known a fact, he is deemed to have had constructive knowledge of such fact, e.g. matters of public records. Notice means bringing it to a person's knowledge.[20]

Cases in which constructive notice have been recognized are two-fold:

(*a*) Actual notice of a fact which would have led to notice of other facts. The court presumes that the addressee of the actual notice has had knowledge of such other facts.

(*b*) Knowledge imputed by the court from the evidence that the party has designedly abstained from inquiry for the very purpose of avoiding notice. This latter class has been extended to cover those cases which follow from the duty of (*i*) investigating title as well as of (*ii*) requiring production of title-deeds.

Constructive notices arise in the following circumstances:

(*a*) Registration as notice;

(*b*) Possession amounting to notice;

(*c*) Notice to agent is notice to principal; and

(*d*) Knowledge of the broker.

16 *Radha Rai* v *Ram Rekha Rai* AIR 1964 Pat 144; *Hewett* v *Loosemore* (1851)9 Hare 449.
17 *Radha Rai* v *Ram Rekha Rai* AIR 1964 Pat 144.
18 Wharton's *Law Lexicon*.
19 *Espin* v *Pemberton* (1859)3 DeG&J 547 quoted from Mitra's *Legal & Commercial Dictionary*, 5th Ed., p. 167.
20 *Canara Bank* v *Canara Sales Corporation* (1987)2 SCC 666.

(I) REGISTRATION AS NOTICE

Registration of a document relating to a transaction with regard to immovable property which requires to be registered under the Registration Act is constructive notice of the transaction. Explanation I to s. 3 of the Transfer of Property Act reads: "Where any transaction relating to immovable property is required by law to be and has been effected by a registered instrument, any person acquiring such property or any part of, or share or interest in, such property shall be deemed to have notice of such instrument as from the date of registration......".

It would at once appear that when the transaction is not required to be effected by a registered instrument, registration, in fact, would not amount to constructive notice. Accordingly, a document which needs no registration, registration of such a document would not raise a constructive notice. Prior to insertion of sub-sec. (1A) in s. 17 of the Registration Act 1908 by the Registration and Other Related Laws (Amendment) Act 2001 effective from 24th September 2001, an agreement to sell immovable property was not required to be effected by a registered instrument. In such a case, registration of such an agreement *per se* would not amount to constructive notice of the agreement.[1] When there is no duty cast to make a search in the Registration office to see whether there was any encumbrance, such Registration should be treated as no notice.[2] When the property in question is situated in several sub-districts, or if registration has been effected in another district, such registered deed will not be treated as notice unless and until memorandum of such registration has been received and filed by the sub-registrar of the sub-district in which the property is situated.[3] An agreement for sale of an immovable property will not fall under s. 17(1)(*b*) of the Registration Act as it does not create, declare, assign, limit or extinguish any right, title, or interest in immovable property. But an exception to this settled law has been made by the insertion of sub-sec. (1A) in s. 17 which *inter alia* provides that the document containing contract to transfer for consideration any immovable property for the purpose of s. 53 of the Transfer of Property Act shall be registered. Where there is no evidence that the mortgage bond or its memorandum was filed anywhere in the district 'B', the registration in district 'A' of the mortgage bond does not amount to a notice to the purchasers of the property situated in the jurisdiction of the Sale Register of district 'B'.[4]

Where the builder had actual notice of partition of the partnership property effected by registered deeds of partition and rectification and rectification deed having been referred to in the agreement with the builder, the

1 60 IC 986.
2 *Backer Khorasanee* v *Ahmed Ismail* AIR 1928 Rang 28.
3 *Rajo Kuer* v *Brij Bihari Prasad* AIR 1962 Pat 236.
4 *Mt. Rajo Kuer* v *Brij Bihari Prasad* AIR 1962 Pat 236; *Ganga Singh* v *Santosh Kumar* AIR 1963 All 194; *Mst. Bhoridevi* v *Mst. Sua* AIR 1963 Raj 141.

rectification deed being registered document it was a constructive notice under s. 3 of the Transfer of Property Act, the builder cannot be said to be a *bona fide* purchaser for consideration without notice.[5]

(II) Possession amounting to notice

Possession in certain circumstances amounts to constructive notice. The principle is embodied in Explanation II to s. 3 of the Transfer of Property Act which reads: "Any person acquiring any immovable property or any share or interest in any such property shall be deemed to have notice of the title, if any, of any person who is for the time being in actual possession thereof." When any property which is to be sold, is not in possession of the vendor but was possessed by a third party, it is the duty of the purchaser to make enquiry from that person and he is bound by all the equities which the party is possession may have in the property.[6] Possession of property by a person other than the vendor which indicates that the vendor is not entitled to present possession, at once puts the purchaser on enquiry as to the interest the occupier holds.[7] No purchaser can protect himself merely by registering his document of title against the title of person in possession of the property. Actual physical possession itself is notice.

(III) Notice to agent is notice to principal

Next we come to the third circumstance where a notice to the agent is deemed a constructive notice to the principal. Explanation III to s. 3 of the Transfer of Property Act reads:

"A person shall be deemed to have had notice of any fact if his agent acquires notice thereof whilst acting on his behalf in the course of business to which that fact is material:

Provided that, if the agent fraudulently conceals the fact, the principal shall not be charged with notice thereof as against any person who was a party to or otherwise cognizant of the fraud."

Section 229 of the Indian Contract Act enjoins: "Any notice given to or information obtained by the agent, provided it be given or obtained in the course of the business transacted by him for the principal, shall, as between the principal and third parties, have the same legal consequences as if it had been given to or obtained by the principal." It, therefore, appears that a notice to the agent is a notice to the principal of such agent. The agent must have acquired the knowledge during the period when he was actually acting as the agent.[8] Therefore, knowledge of an agent not acquired in the matter

5 *Bina Murlidhar Hemdev* v *Kanhaiyalal Lokeram Hemdev* (1999)5 SCC 222.

6 *Balchand Mahton* v *Bulaki Singh* AIR 1929 Pat 284; *Pravathathammal* v *Sivashankara* AIR 1952 Mad 265.

7 *Baba Sah* v *Hajee Md. Akbar Sahib* AIR 1923 Mad 563.

8 ILR 11 Mad 419.

for which he was agent, cannot be imputed to a principal and used to upset transaction of a date before the agency commenced.[9] The fact that the principal is the Government does not render the doctrine of constructive notice inapplicable.[10] If the agent has not fraudulently communicated his knowledge to the principal, benefits of proviso to Explanation III come in. Where the act done by the agent is such that it cannot be said to be done by him in his character of agent but is done by him in the character of a party to an independant fraud on his principal, that is not to be imputed to the principal as an act done by his agent.[11] Then fraudulent concealment or representation on the part of the agent exempts the principal from the rigour of imputed notice.

To effect the principle with the notice to an agent, five things are necessary, namely:

(*i*) the agent must have received knowledge during the agency;

(*ii*) the knowledge must come to him as agent;

(*iii*) it must be in the same transaction;

(*iv*) it must be material to the transaction;

(*v*) it must not have been fraudulently withheld from the principal.[12]

In order that a notice to agent will be a notice to principal the notice received by the agent must be in course of the business transacted by him with the principal.[13]

(IV) Knowledge of the broker

Whether a broker is acting as an agent of the assured or the insured, depends on the facts of each case. If a broker has the authority or power to bind the insurer (i.e. bonder) he will be an agent of the insurer and his knowledge will be deemed to be the knowledge of the insurer. Thus, where a member of the broker's firm knows of the criminal past of the assured, the insurer was not permitted to any liability on the ground that the past had not been disclosed.[14]

5 Reasonable and defective (or invalid) notices

Reasonable notice is a notice or information of a fact as may fairly and properly be expected or required in the particular circumstances.[15] When a statute does not enjoin issue of a notice but principles of justice, equity and good conscience recommend issue of a notice, a reasonable notice is issued.

9 *Chabildas Laloo Bhai* v *Dayal Mowji* 11 CWN 1109.
10 ILR 26 Bom 271.
11 *Cave* v *Cave* 15 ChD 639 at p. 644; *Texas & Co.* v *Bombay Banking Co.* 44 Bom 139 (PC).
12 *Kettelwell* v *Watson* 21 ChD 685.
13 *State of Orissa* v *Goyenka Investment* AIR 1983 Ori 438.
14 *Wovleatt* v *Excess Insurance Co. Ltd.* [1978]1 Lloyd's Rep 633.
15 Tapash Gan Choudhury, *Penumbra of Natural Justice,* 3rd Ed., p. 158.

Though not statutory it has come to have sanction of law, being customary and conventional.

A reasonable notice may be viewed from another angle as well. We have noticed that some provisions of law enjoin certain requirements in a notice contemplated therein. A notice under s. 80, CPC requires cause of action and reliefs to be stated. A notice under s. 106 of the Transfer of Property Act requires termination of lease to be stated in express language, and, so on. There may be occasions where in a notice no definite requirements are prescribed. In such cases a question arises whether the notice is a reasonable and sufficient one. Requirements of a section as to validity of a notice will not apply to such cases.[16] The question of sufficiency and adequacy in such cases will have to be determined according to principles of justice, equity and good conscience.

What constitutes a reasonable notice is essentially a question of fact. In *Sohanlal Gupta (Dead)* v *Asha Devi*,[17] Supreme Court has considered the question of reasonableness in the light of s. 14(2) of the Arbitration Act 1940.[17] Reasonable notice is that which is fairly to be expected or required under the particular circumstances.[18]

Section 106 of the Transfer of Property Act provides for issue of a notice for termination of a lease. The only change that has been brought about in para 1 of pre-amended section is the words "expiring with the end of a year of tenancy" and expiring with the end of months of tenancy have been deleted. The requirement of the notice period expiring with the end of year or month has been omitted, the tenancy can be validly terminated from any date. There are certain cases which are not governed by provisions of s. 106 of the Transfer of Property Act. Nevertheless, a sufficient and reasonable notice, in the absence of a contract, local law or usage to the contrary, would be required even in such cases for a lease to be determined. And, lease in such cases will not be determinable without such notice.[19] What, then would be the nature of such a notice? Though requirements of s. 106 of the Transfer of Property Act as to the validity of a notice in such cases will have no application,[20] the exact synchronising of the date fixed in the notice, with the termination of the period of lease is not necessary. Notice to quit must be reasonable yet that may be kept in view as a guide to what may be a reasonable notice.[1] In each case it will have to be seen whether the notice given is a reasonable one with regard both to the length of such notice and

16 *Ramnath* v *Badrinath* AIR 1928 Lah 348.
17 (2003)7 SCC 492.
18 Black's *Law Dictionary*, 10th Edition.
19 *(Penubarti) Gurumurti* v *Vemalapati Rangiah* AIR 1933 Mad 165.
20 *Ramnath* v *Badrinath* AIR 1928 Lah 348; *Janu Poojari* v *Somakke* AIR 1925 Mad 346.
1 *(Gummideli) Anantapadmana Bhaswami* v *Official Receiver of Secunderabad* AIR 1933 Lah 134.

the time at which it is to expire.[2] In the case of a tenancy not governed by the Transfer of Property Act, a six months' notice calculated according to the Bengali Calendar was held to be a reasonable notice to terminate the tenancy.[3]

It is not reasonable to give a short notice. It is more unreasonable and opposed to principles of equity that a man should be thrown out in the middle of a season. Necessarily, the question will depend on facts and circumstances of each case.[4] For obvious reasons, local custom, if there be any, will have to be given due consideration in determining the reasonableness of a notice. A notice purporting to terminate an agricultural tenancy should either ask for possession at the end of the agricultural year or at least when the crop of the year has been harvested.[5]

Section 206 of the Indian Contract Act speaks of a reasonable notice for revocation or renunciation of agency. There is no indication in the section itself as to what would be the degree of reasonableness of a notice under s. 206. Broadly speaking, that would constitute a reasonable notice which did not violate our notions of justice and equity. In a notice under s. 206, a very important element to be taken into consideration is the nature of employment of the agent. A two years' notice was held reasonable for termination of a chief agency of an Insurance Company which had done good business ranging over 47 years.[6]

The equitable right of redemption is dependant on the mortgagor giving the mortgagee reasonable notice of his intention to redeem and on his fully performing his obligations.[7]

Reasonable notices are also issued prior to termination of service where there is no specific obligation for issue of a notice prior to such termination.

A notice which does not satisfy the requirements of law under which it is purported to have been issued, or a notice which is not a reasonable notice is a defective (or invalid) notice. Any and every defect will not invalidate a notice; for, "every venial error or defect cannot be permitted to be treated as a peg to hang a defence to defeat a just claim."[8] A material defect which affects the cause of action and cannot be condoned by any stretch of leniency

2 2 IC 656; ILR 26 Cal 751; *Damodar Prasad Tewari* v *Lachimi Prosad Singh* AIR 1928 Pat 354; *Debendranath Bhowmik* v *Shyam Prosana Bhowmik* 48 IC 354.

3 11 CWN 1124.

4 *Aiyanars & Kaniyala Swamigal Koli Devasthanam, Kochadai* v *Pariakaruppa Thevan* AIR 1929 Mad 617.

5 *Badrinath Upadhay* v *Baijnath Mandal* AIR 1930 Pat 134; 6 CWN 69; ILR 20 Cal 720.

6 *Sohrabji Dhunjibhay Medora* v *Oriental Government Security Life Assurance Co. Ltd.* AIR 1944 Bom 166.

7 *Achaldas Durgaji Oswal (dead) through LRs* v *Ramvilas Ganga (dead) through LRs* (2003)3 SCC 614.

8 *State of AP* v *Gundugola Venkata Suryanarayana Garu* AIR 1965 SC 11.

necessarily invalidates a notice. Mistake in mention of section, held, did not invalidate a notice (the notice was intended to be issued under s. 106 of the Transfer of Property Act read with s. 13(6) of the W.B. Premises Tenancy Act 1956, erroneously mentioning s. 102 of the Transfer of Property Act instead of s. 106, but tenant was not misled thereby).[9]

When the contract is for the sale of immovable property the vendor must give reasonable notice requiring the specific performance of the contract within a definite time.[10]

6 Composite notices

When notices under two separate enactments or under various sections of one enactment or more are issued in a combined form, it is a composite notice. For example, a notice under s. 106 of the Transfer of Property Act read with s. 6(4) of the West Bengal Premises Tenancy Act 1997 or a notice under s. 106, Railways Act 1989 read with s. 80 of the CPC.

7 Statutory notice

It is a notice made by legislative enactment. Many statutes impose, either absolutely or sub modo, a duty to give notice of certain matters.

8 Personal notice

It is a notice that involves, according to circumstances, communication of notice orally or in writing directly to the person affected or to be charged.

9 *Bal Kissen Shaw* v *Kanupada Bhowmick* AIR 1985 Cal 129.

10 *Devendra Basappa* v *Smt. Sounbai* AIR 1971 Mys 217; *Narayana Swami Pillai* v *Dhanakoti Ammal* AIR 1967 Mad 220 relied on.

CHAPTER 3

Requirements in a Notice

SYNOPSIS

1 Forms and contents of a notice–mention of 'section' in a notice
2 Name, description and address of parties should be stated in the notice
3 Wrong particulars or variation in plaint—effect
4 Date, place of issue and place of hearing should be indicated
5 Recital in a notice–'cause of action'–expression explained
6 Recital in a notice–'reliefs claimed'–principal and incidental reliefs
7 Notice without containing any date of appearance, etc.

1 Forms and contents of a notice—mention of 'section' in a notice

Except notices prescribed under several Orders under the Code of Civil Procedure and under ss. 24 and 145 of the Code for which the Code itself provides Forms[1] and except certain Public Notices, generally issued at the Government level, there is no particular form for any particular notice. Whether it is a notice under s. 80, CPC or a notice under s. 43(1) of the Indian Partnership Act or a notice under s. 106 of the Railways Act 1989 or a notice under s. 106 of the Transfer of Property Act—no particular or technical form is necessary.

1 Notices with prescribed forms under the Code of Civil Procedure:
(1) Notice to produce document (Or. 11, r. 16); (2) Notice to inspect document (Or. 11, r. 17); (3) Notice to admit documents (Or. 12, r. 3); (4) Notice to admit facts (Or. 12, r. 5); (5) Notice to produce (general form) (Or. 12, r. 8); (6) Notice to show cause why a payment or adjustment should not be recorded as certified (Or. 21, r. 2); (7) Notice to show cause why execution should not issue (Or. 21, r. 16); (8) Notice to state objections to draft of document (Or. 21, r. 34); (9) Notice to show cause why warrant of arrest should not issue (Or. 21, r. 37); (10) Notice of attachment of a decree to the court which passed it (Or. 21, r. 53); (11) Notice of attachment of a decree to the holder of the decree (Or. 21, r. 53); (12) Notice to attaching creditor (Or. 21, r. 58); (13) Notice of the day fixed for settling a sale proclamation (Or. 21, r. 58); (14) Notice to person in possession of movable property sold in execution (Or. 21, r. 79); (15) Notice to show cause why sale should not be set aside (Or. 21, rr. 90 to 92); (16)

A notice would not be bad if it does not refer in its body to the specific section of the Act under which it is issued. A combined notice under s. 106 of the Transfer of Property Act and s. 13(6) of the West Bengal Premises Tenancy Act 1956 [now s. 6(4) of the West Bengal Premises Tenancy Act 1997], without reference to section or sections, was held good.[2] Conversely, mere mentioning the section would not make an otherwise invalid notice a valid one. Section 106 of the TP Act does not obviate the necessity of terminating the tenancy either in express or implied terms. A notice under s. 80, CPC was sent by registered post to Railway authority within six months from date of booking the goods for claim of compensation for non-delivery of those goods. Purpose of notice is to give an opportunity to opposite party to consider claim of plaintiff. Mere non-mention of provision regarding notice, i.e. s. 106 of the Railways Act 1989, would be of no consequence.[3] A mere mention of s. 106 of the TP Act in the notice without there being a recital, express or implied, terminating the tenancy of the person to whom the notice is addressed, is not sufficient in law to bring about the termination of tenancy.[4]

A notice under s. 80 of the Code of Civil Procedure need not be in any particular or technical form.[5] But notice under s. 80 of that Code is a requirement of law and not a mere formality.[6] In a Rajasthan case it is *held*: "No particular form of notice has been prescribed. If, therefore, the notice gives reliefs and cause of action and the names and addresses of parties claiming the reliefs, the conditions of s. 80 of the Code of Civil Procedure are satisfied."[7] A joint notice given by all the plaintiffs of different suits mentioning the total amount payable by the Secretary of State is proper when the sum total demanded in the separate suits does not exceed the amount mentioned in the notice. There is no particular form of the notice

---

Notice to respondent (Or. 41, r. 2); (17) Notice to respondent of the day fixed for hearing of the appeal (Or. 41, r. 14); (18) Notice to a party to a suit not made a party to the appeal but joined by the court as a respondent (Or. 44, r. 20); (19) Notice of appeal *forma pauperis* (Or. 44, r. 1); (20) Notice to show cause why a certificate of appeal to the Supreme Court should not be granted (Or. 54, r. 3); (21) Notice to respondent of admission of appeal to the Supreme Court (Or. 45, r. 8); (22) Notice to show cause why a review should not be granted (Or. 47, r. 4); (23) Notice of payment into court (Or. 24, r. 2); (24) Notice to parties of the day fixed for examination of a witness about to leave the jurisdiction (Or. 18, r. 1); (25) Notice to minor defendant and guardian (Or. 32, r. 3); (26) Notice to O.P. of the day fixed for hearing of evidence of pauperism (Or. 33, r. 6); (27) Notice of application for transfer of a suit to another court (s. 24); and (28) Notice to surety of his liability under a decree (s. 145).

2 *Santosh Kumar Gupta* v *Chinmoyee Sen* AIR 1966 Cal 615.

3 *Bharat Kumar* v *Union of India* AIR 2005 Raj 124; (2004)4 Raj LW 2074.

4 *Sunder Lal* v *Yokoob Ali* AIR 1979 NOC 38 (All).

5 ILR (1954) Mys 465.

6 *New India Assurance Co.* v *Delhi Development Authority* AIR 1991 Del 298.

7 *Ramanand* v *Union of India* AIR 1958 Raj 23.

prescribed anywhere and so long as the notice satisfies the conditions provided in s. 80, the mere splitting up of notified claims into different suits does not render suits non-maintainable for want of notice.[8]

If an amended plaint is based on a completely new cause of action (facts and events which took place after filing of the original plaint), a fresh notice under s. 80, CPC would be required to be given. The same not having been given, the suit on the new cause of action was not maintainable.[9]

If a suit wherein Government is involved is filed but without prior service of notice, the suit can be dismissed for non-compliance of that provision. But if the plaintiff had taken leave of the court to file such suit by satisfying the court that urgency is involved, compliance of s. 80 of the Code of Civil Procedure may be exempted.[10] But if the court is of the opinion that there is no urgent or immediate need, it can refuse the leave and in that case, plaint is to be returned for presentation after complying with the requirements of s. 80(1) of the Code of Civil Procedure.[11]

The object of the notice under s. 80, CPC is to give the Government or the public servant concerned an opportunity to reconsider its or his legal position and, if that cause is justified, to make amends to settle the claim out of court. The section is imperative and must undoubtedly be strictly construed. Failure to serve a notice complying with the requirements of the statute will entail dismissal of the suit. But the notice must be reasonably construed. Every minor or venial error or defect cannot be permitted to be treated as a peg to hang a defence to defeat a just claim. If on a reasonable reading but not so as to make undue assumptions, the plaintiff is shown to have given the information which the statute requires, any incidental defects or errors may be ignored. In each case, in considering whether the imperative provisions of the statute have been complied with, the court must see whether prescribed requirements are present.[12] Mistakes which do not violate the provisions of law or affect the cause of action are excusable.

In *Ghanshyam Das* v *Dominion of India*[13] Supreme Court reiterated that the whole object of serving a notice under s. 80 is to give the Government sufficient warning of the case which is going to be instituted against it and that the Government, if it so wished, can settle the claim without litigation or afford restitution without recourse to a court of law. Though the terms of s. 80 have to be strictly complied with, that does not mean that the notice should be scrutinised in a pedantic manner divorced from common sense. The point to be considered is whether the notice gives sufficient information

8 *Kashinath Singh* v *Nawab Alam Ara Begum* AIR 1934 Pat 346 (348).
9 *Bishan Deyal* v *State of Orissa* (2001)1 SCC 555.
10 *W. Thanthianga* v *State of Mizoram* AIR 2018 Gau 143.
11 *State of A.P.* v *Pioneer Builders* AIR 2007 SC 113; (2006)12 SCC 119.
12 *State of AP* v *Gundugola Venkata Suryanarayana Garu* AIR 1965 SC 11.
13 (1984)3 SCC 46.

as to the nature of claim such as would enable the recipient to avert the litigation. If the notice substantially fulfils its object of intimating the parties concerned generally of the nature of suit intended to be filed, it would be sufficient compliance of the section. When interpreting the pre-amended section the courts must have due regard to the change in law brought about by sub-sec. (3) of s. 80, which shows legislative acceptance of the rule of substantial compliance. The question as to whether a notice under s. 80 is valid or not is a question of judicial construction. Section 80 of the Code is but a part of the procedure enacted to provide the regulation on machinery by means of which the courts may do justice between the parties. It is, therefore, merely a part of the adjective law and deals with procedure alone and must be interpreted in a manner so as to subserve and advance the cause of justice rather than to defeat it. As far as possible no proceeding in a court of law should be allowed to be defeated on mere technicalities. This is the principle on which our laws of procedure are based. Supreme Court overruled *S.N. Dutt* v *Union of India* AIR 1961 SC 1449 and affirmed *Raghunath Dass* v *Union of India* AIR 1969 SC 674; *State of Madras* v *C.P. Agencies* AIR 1960 SC 1309; *Amarnath Dogra* v *Union of India* AIR 1963 SC 424.

Section 78B of the Indian Railways Act 1890 (now s. 106 of the Railways Act 1989), similarly, does not prescribe any particular form or words which would guide a notice under this section.[14] A notice under s. 78B (now s. 106) would be sufficient if it indicates clearly the intention of the notice-giver to inform the Railway Administration of his claim within six months from the date of delivery of goods for carriage by the railway. The notice must satisfy the requirements of s. 78B (now s. 106) of the Indian Railways Act 1890.[15]

A notice for revocation or renunciation of agency under s. 206 of the Indian Contract Act 1872, merely says that a 'reasonable notice must be given of such revocation or renunciation; otherwise the damage thereby resulting to the principal or the agent, as the case may be, must be made good to the one by the other'. It, by the use of the expression 'reasonable', refers to a reasonable period which must expire before there is actual revocation or renunciation. No particular form is needed: no particular language is obligatory.

There is no specific form for a notice under s. 10 of the Carriers Act 1865. A notice under this section must state in a clear language the alleged loss of or injury to the goods and the circumstances leading to such loss or injury, i.e. the cause of action has to be stated, reliefs desired may or may not be (at the option of the notice-giver) stated. For such statement of the cause of action the notice-giver is at liberty to use the language of his choice.

14 *Samrathnal* v *Union of India* AIR 1959 MP 305.

15 See *Salem Dayalbagh Stores Ltd.* v *Governor General in Council* AIR 1947 Mad 362; *Jutmull Bhojraj* v *Darjeeling Himalayan Rly.* AIR 1962 SC 1879; (1963)2 SCR 832.

The statutory provision under s. 138 of the Negotiable Instruments Act indicates in unmistakable terms as to what should be clearly indicated in the notice and what manner of demand it should make. In the absence of a specific demand for payment of the cheque amount, the notice would be imperfect and bad in law.[16] It is a well settled principle of law that the notice has to be read as a whole. Whether notice issued under proviso (*b*) to s. 138 of the Negotiable Instruments Act will be bad would depend on the language of the notice. If in a notice apart from cheque amount, any other sum is indicated it will not invalidate the notice.[17]

2 Name, description and address of parties should be stated in the notice

A notice should contain the name, description and address of the party who serves a notice. When a notice is issued by the authorised representative, the notice should contain those particulars of the notice-giver on whose behalf the notice is thus sent. This would enable the addressee to know for certain the identity of the notice-giver. Except in the case of a notice under s. 80, CPC, in all other cases, whether such notice be statutory or optional, the description of the notice-giver is not a must feature. Mere name and residence is sufficient to establish the identity of the notice-giver.

When the issuance of a notice is prescribed by law as a condition precedent to the commencement of proceedings, it must be addressed correctly for want of which it will be treated as an invalid one. It must be remembered that all proceedings initiated under an invalid notice would be *ultra vires* and without jurisdiction.[18]

Similarly the name and address of the addressee should be correctly stated in the notice to ensure its safe delivery. In other words, a notice should be properly addressed; for that is the instruction under s. 27 of the General Clauses Act. If in a notice under s. 148, Income Tax Act 1961, the name of the assessee was wrongly mentioned, such a notice is invalid.[19]

The publication of the substituted service in a local news paper other than the one indicated by the court but equally widely circulated would constitute sufficient notice to the defendants, though it would be an irregularity in the service of the summons.[20]

Section 27 of the General Clauses Act 1897 can be profitably imported in a case of s. 138 of the Negotiable Instruments Act read with s. 114 of the Evidence Act where the sender has despatched the notice by post with the correct address written on it.

16 *K.R. Indira* v *Dr. G. Adinarayana* AIR 2003 SC 4689; (2003)8 SCC 300.
17 *Suman Sethi* v *Ajay K. Churiwal* AIR 2000 SC 828.
18 Tapash Gan Choudhury, *Penumbra of Natural Justice,* 3rd Ed., p. 164.
19 *Commissioner of Income Tax* v *Bibhuti Bhusan Mallick* (1987)165 ITR 107 (Cal).
20 *Basant Singh* v *Roman Catholic Mission* (2002)7 SCC 531.

Notice to be served in sufficient time

If the reason to give notice is to provide an opportunity to make representations, the notice should be served in sufficient time to enable representations.[1] Disclosure of charge or of opposing the case must be made in reasonable time to allow the person to prepare his defence or his comments.[2]

3 Wrong particulars or variation in plaint—effect

Section 80, CPC, enjoins that a notice under this section should mention amongst others, the name, description and place of residence of the plaintiff. A strict compliance of such procedural law is necessary. Where notice was given by one individual, a group of plaintiffs could not sue. The Supreme Court observed that when the notice under s. 80, CPC was given only on behalf of the first plaintiff and the plaint was in the names of both the plaintiffs, it could not be held that s. 80 was complied with.[3] There should be identity of the person who issues the notice with the person who brings the suit. Where a notice has been given on behalf of one plaintiff stating his cause of action, his name, description and place of residence and the relief which he claims, a suit cannot be instituted by him and another. If the notice under s. 80 did not state the name, description and residence of the plaintiff who brought the suit, the notice was not in accordance with law and was invalid. No suit could have been filed without service of valid notice under s. 80.[4] In *Beohar Rajendra Sinha* v *State of MP*[5] the Supreme Court reiterated and applied the following principles laid down in *State of Andhra Pradesh* v *Gundugsla Venkata Suryanarayana Garu.*[6] A notice under s. 80, CPC must be reasonably construed. Any unimportant error or defect cannot be permitted to be treated as an excuse for defeating a just claim. In considering whether the provisions of the statute are complied with the court must take into account the following matters in each case:

(1) whether the name, description and residence of the plaintiff are given so as to enable the authorities to identify the person serving the notice;

1 *R.* v *Liverpool Corporation ex. p. Liverpool Taxi Fleet Operators' Association* [1972]2 QB 299; [1972] WLR 1262 (CA); [1972]2 All ER 589.

2 *R.* v *Thames Magistrate's Court ex. p. Polemis* [1974]1 WLR 1371.

3 *Union of India* v *Eastern Market Co.* AIR 1964 AP 172. See *Haridas Mondal* v *Anath Nath Mitra* AIR 1961 SC 1419.

4 AIR 1947 PC 197. Also see *Dominion of India* v *Purushottam Das* AIR 1927 PC 176; *Bhaychand* v *Secretary of State* AIR 1931 Mad 175; *Government of Madras Province* v *Vellayan Chettear* AIR 1944 Mad 544; *Dominion of India* v *Purushottam Das* AIR 1961 All 176. See also the following cases: *S.N. Dutt & Co.* v *Union of India* AIR 1961 SC 1449; *Raghunath Das* v *Union of India* AIR 1969 SC 674; *Union of India* v *Mangilal Janakiprasad* AIR 1979 Gau 17.

5 (1969)1 SCC 796 at 799-800 (para 5).

6 AIR 1965 SC 11; (1964)4 SCR 945. See also *Raghunath Das* v *Union of India* AIR 1969 SC 674.

(2) whether the cause of action and the reliefs which the plaintiff claims are set out with sufficient particularity;

(3) whether a notice in writing has been delivered to or left at the office of the appropriate authorities mentioned in the notice;

(4) whether the suit is instituted after the expiration of two months next and after notice has been served and the plaint contains a statement that such a notice has been so delivered or left.

If in a notice under s. 148 of the Income Tax Act 1961 for reassessment of tax, the name of the assessee is not correctly mentioned such a notice is invalid.[7]

If on a reasonable reading of the notice the plaintiff is shown to have given the information which the statute requires him to give, any incidental defect or irregularity should be ignored. It is, therefore, a settled law that notice should be given by all the intending plaintiffs.[8]

Where an individual carries on business in some name and style, the notice has to be given by the individual in his own name for the suit can only be filed in the name of the individual. Though an individual may, in certain circumstances, be sued in the name of the firm of which he is a proprietor, he would not, however, have any right to sue in that name.[9]

In some cases, the description of the notice-giver is of vital importance where the plaintiff is not an individual but is a corporate body, such as a firm, society, corporation, company and the like. When the notice is given by a firm it should be so stated. But a notice describing the plaintiff as a partnership firm is not invalid simply because it omits to state that it is a registered partnership.[10] A question still hangs: is the description correct? Notice given on behalf of a trust without specifying names and addresses of all Trustees is not sufficient compliance with s. 80, CPC.[11] Notice issued in the name of the family firm cannot be deemed a notice by the managing member of the family firm.[12] Again, a notice issued by a person in his own name will not be sufficient for suit instituted by him and cannot be said to be the same as a notice issued by him as a manager of the Hindu joint family.[13] Notice given by a private firm is bad in a suit brought by a proprietor in his individual capacity.[14] In other words, the notice-giver and the person or the body corporate which brought subsequently a suit must be identical.

7 *CIT* v *Bibhuti Bhusan* (1987)165 ITR 107 (Cal).
8 *State of A.P.* v *Gundugsla Venkata Suryanarayana* AIR 1965 SC 11.
9 *Mohanlal Saraf* v *The Cuttack Electric Supply Co. Ltd.* AIR 1964 Ori 198.
10 *State of Madras* v *C.P. Agencies* AIR 1954 Nag 342.
11 *Government of the Province of Bombay* v *Pestonji Ardeshir Wadia* AIR 1949 PC 143.
12 *K. Dhondoji Rao* v *Dominion of India* AIR 1957 Mys 94.
13 AIR 1949 Mad 416.
14 *Surajmal Jain* v *Union of India* AIR 1956 Pat 478; *Naseema Textiles* v *Union of India* AIR 1971 Ker 192; *S.N. Dutt* v *Union of India* AIR 1961 SC 1449.

All that s. 80 requires is 'residence' and not address but mention of the address in the cause-title of the plaint does not render the notice invalid.[15]

4 Date, place of issue and place of hearing should be indicated

A notice should contain the date of issue to indicate whether the noticee got reasonable time to meet the charges brought against him and to attend the hearing. The respondent should get a reasonable notice of the date, place and time where the proceedings are intended to be held by the authority exercising judicial or quasi-judicial function.[16] If the date, time or place of hearing intimated in a notice is such that the noticee cannot be reasonably expected to attend or even if he attends, he would not be able to prepare his defence, the authority may not be justified to proceed with the hearing.[17]

5 Recital in a notice—'cause of action'—expression explained

The expression 'cause of action' occurs in three broad situations, to wit, s. 20(*c*), s. 80 and Or. VII, r. 1(*e*) of the Code of Civil Procedure.

Section 20(*c*) of the Code of Civil Procedure enjoins that every suit shall be instituted in a court within the local limits of whose jurisdiction the 'cause of action', wholly or in part, arises. Section 80, CPC prescribes that a notice under this section should state the 'cause of action.' Again, Or. VII, r. 1(*e*) states that a plaint should state the facts constituting the 'cause of action' and when such cause arose.

Now, what is this 'cause of action'? A cause of action, broadly speaking, is a bundle of facts which inform encroachment on rights giving the aggrieved a right to sue. We may proceed to see how. The most oft-quoted explanation comes from Madras: "The cause of action means the bundle of essential facts which is necessary for the plaintiff to prove before he can succeed in the suit or, to put it differently, it refers to the media upon which the court arrives at a conclusion in his favour."[18] When used in a restricted sense, the expression means the circumstances informing infringement of the right or the immediate occasion for the action.[19] In the wider sense, it means the necessary conditions for maintainability of the suit, including the infraction coupled with the right itself. The right to sue and 'cause of action' are the same and the cause of action is synonymous with the right to sue.[20]

It should be understood that the expression 'cause of action' is not a technical word. It has to be given a meaning which is not technical. The words mean nothing more than the reason which impels a plaintiff to seek

15 *State of Madras* v *C.A. Agencies* AIR 1954 Nag 342.

16 *Dhian Singh Khazan Singh* v *Dy. Secretary to Govt. of Punjab* AIR 1960 Punj 41. See also *Priecco Lawrie Ltd.* v *State of W.B.* (2009)2 SCC (L&S) 729.

17 *Hanson* v *Church Commissioners for England* [1978] QB 823.

18 In re, *D. Lakshminarayana Chettiar* AIR 1954 Mad 594.

19 AIR 1950 Pep 211; AIR 1942 Cal 407.

20 AIR 1958 AP 451.

his remedy against the defendant in a suit, or, in other words, that which, according to the plaintiff, gives him a right to sue the defendant. The expression does not necessarily mean or refer to the facts which constituted a cause of action. The cause of action is something which arises either out of a bundle of facts and circumstances or out of a single fact or incident which, so to speak, provides the plaintiff with the animus or motive to go to court for the purpose of seeking relief'.[1]

When s. 80, CPC enjoins that the notice under the section should state the cause of action, it means that the notice-giver must state the fact or facts which entitle him to go to a court of law. On this principle, notices generally are to state the cause of action. If it substantially informs the defendant of the grounds of complaint, the cause of action would have been amply stated within the meaning of s. 80, CPC.[2] This principle covers notices as well.

It should be remembered that the expression 'cause of action' should not be construed in a narrow sense, be it a notice under s. 80, CPC[3] or under other enactments.

The expression (stating the cause of action) in a notice under s. 80, CPC should not be narrowly construed, the object of this section being to bring to the knowledge of the defendant of the ground of complaint.[4] Cause of action gives right to sue for certain reliefs. In the notice the relief proposed to be claimed was for declaration that employee's resignation was invalid on ground that it was obtained by coercion and undue influence. In the suit the relief claimed was for declaration that the order of acceptance of resignation was invalid—*Held* notice was invalid as relief claimed in the suit and cause of action of such relief were not specified in the notice.[5] Where notice under s. 56 of the Wakf Act 1954 and notice under s. 80, CPC are required to be given as well, both the notices must be valid.[6] If a new cause of action is being introduced, a fresh notice under s. 80, CPC would be required and if the same is not given, the suit on this cause of action is not maintainable.[7] If the tenor of the section such as s. 11 of Madras City Tenants' Protection Act 1921, which provides a mandatory provision to issue three months' notice for institution of a suit for ejectment of a tenant, and unless plaintiff mentions in the plaint that he had given due notice, which is a condition precedent, no suit can be validly instituted. Section 11 of the said Act cannot be compared with s. 80, CPC so far as waiver of notice is concerned.[8]

1 *Dominion of India* v *Babulal* AIR 1962 All 461.
2 *Samrathmal* v *Union of India* AIR 1959 MP 305.
3 *State of Madras* v *C.A. Agencies* AIR 1954 Nag 342.
4 8 CWN 913.
5 *Jonardan Misra* v *State of UP* AIR 1981 All 213.
6 *AP State Wakf Board, Hyderabad* v *All India Shia Conference (Branch), AP* (2000)3 SCC 528.
7 *Bishandayal & Sons* v *State of Orissa* (2001)1 SCC 555.
8 *S.A. Ramchandran* v *S. Neelavathy* (1997)1 SCC 767.

6 Recital in a notice—'reliefs claimed'—principal and incidental reliefs

As a corollary to 'cause of action', the question of 'relief' comes up. 'Cause of action' gives right to sue for certain 'reliefs'.

We are led to a discussion whether any or all notices should have recital of the relief or reliefs the notice-giver seeks. Where law enjoins that the notice has to state the reliefs, as in a notice under s. 80, CPC, the recital of reliefs is a 'must' feature in such notice. A notice under s. 80, CPC is to state the reliefs which the intending plaintiff claims. "......the details which it (a notice under s. 80, CPC) contains should be sufficient to inform the party, on whom it is served, of the nature and basis of the claim and the relief sought."[9] Should the term 'relief' include the person against whom relief is sought?[10] Necessarily, not.[11] The cause of action and the relief which the plaintiff claims should be set out in the notice with sufficient particularity.[12] All forms of relief need not be given in detail.[13] Reliefs which are ancillary to principal reliefs may be admitted though not mentioned in the notice. In appropriate cases, the court can grant relief not claimed in a notice under s. 80, CPC.[14]

Section 106, Transfer of Property Act in a sense recites the relief, i.e. the notice-giver desires as a relief termination of tenancy and consequent quittance from the leasehold premises.

But where law does not require that a notice should state the reliefs, absence of mentioning of reliefs in a notice would not make the notice defective. If the notice-giver mentions reliefs in the notice, even then that would not make the notice bad.

Recital of reliefs in a notice is not necessary in that type of notice which by itself is not capable of reciting any relief, e.g. a public notice by a partner after attainment of majority under s. 30(5) of the Indian Partnership Act 1932, or a notice of stoppage in transit by an unpaid seller under s. 52 of the Sale of Goods Act 1930, or a notice on the Collector of the district by a finder of treasure under s. 4 of the Indian Treasure Trove Act 1878 and so on.

Where a notice is not statutory or where a notice is mere recommendatory in nature or where a notice is optional, it is usual that a notice contains reliefs sought for as in a notice of demand for arrears of rent or as in a notice for money for goods purchased on credit.

9 *Amarnath Dogra* v *Union of India* AIR 1963 SC 424.
10 *Governor-General-in Council* v *Krishnaswami Pillai* AIR 1946 Mad 366.
11 *A. Sankunni Menon* v *South Indian Railway* AIR 1952 Mad 502.
12 *State of AP* v *Gundugsla Venkata Suryanarayana* AIR 1965 SC 11.
13 *Sourendra* v *Secretary of State* AIR 1934 Pat 701.
14 *State of Rajasthan* v *Associated Stone Industries Kota Ltd.* AIR 1971 Raj 128; *New Chumtia Coal Co.* v *Union of India* AIR 1959 Cal 585 dissented from.

Reliefs which would necessarily be admissible if principal reliefs be granted need not be specifically recited in a notice nor reliefs which would be granted under operation of law, e.g. costs of suit, etc.

Where a statutory notice under s. 80, CPC is required to be given the period of 60 days would be added to the period of limitation prescribed by Art. 58 of the Limitation Act.[15] A suit against the Government or a public officer, to which the requirement of a prior notice under s. 80, CPC is attracted, cannot be validly instituted until the expiration of the period of two months next after the notice in writing has been delivered to the authorities concerned in the manner prescribed in the section and filed before the expiry of the said period, the suit has to be dismissed as not maintainable. The language of s. 80, CPC is express, explicit and mandatory and it admits no implication or exception.[16] In *Beohar Rajendra Sinha* v *State of Madhya Pradesh* the Supreme Court laid down the contents and requirements of the notice under s. 80, CPC. If on reading of the notice the plaintiff is shown to have given the information, which the statute requires him to give, any incidental defect or irregularities should be ignored.[17]

7 Notice without containing any date of appearance, etc.

If any notice contained neither date for appearance before the concerned authority nor it is mentioned that if reply is not given within a stipulated time, it would be presumed that the person concerned has no objection in that regard.[18]

15 *Mohd. Quaramuddin (dead) by LRs* v *State of AP* (1994)5 SCC 118; *S.S. Rathore* v *State of MP* (1989)4 SCC 582.

16 *Bihari Chowdhury* v *State of Bihar* AIR 1984 SC 1043; (1984)2 SCC 627.

17 *Beohar Rajendra Sinha* v *State of MP* AIR 1969 SC 1256; (1969)1 SCC 796.

18 *Scheduled Castes Co-op. Society* v *State of Punjab* AIR 2005 P&H 100; (2005)1 Punj LR 665.

CHAPTER 4

Service of Notice

SYNOPSIS

1 Introduction
2 Service of a notice—meaning of
3 Modes of service of a notice
4 Personal service including vicarious services
5 Service by post
6 Notice to old address
7 Notice sent by registered post—presumption
8 Distinction between non-service and irregular service of notice
9 Service of notice under the West Bengal Premises Tenancy Act—provisions of s. 106, T.P. Act may be invoked
10 Service of notice under Income Tax Act 1961
11 Authentication of notices
12 Service of notice under Negotiable Instruments Act
13 Service of notice under Railways Act
14 Endorsements—'refused', 'left', 'not found', 'not-claimed' etc., by postal peon—meaning thereof
15 Presumption as to time of delivery of notice
16 Inordinate delay in service of notice—effect
17 Rebuttal of presumption—how made—illustrative circumstances
18 Notice sent by registered post—onus of proof
19 Presumption of service when notice sent under a certificate of posting—difference, when sent by registered post
20 Knowledge of contents of refused notice
21 Contractual mode of service
22 Statutory mode of service—personal tender affixation of a copy of notice
23 Affixation of copy on residential house
24 Service of notice through electronic form
25 Service of notice—interpretation of terms 'to give', 'to deliver', 'to issue', 'to serve', 'to send' and 'to prefer' in relation to a notice
26 Service of notice on illiterate person
27 Service of notice through phonogram

1 Introduction

Service of notice means lawful delivery of a notice or process. It also includes the formal delivery of writ, summons or other legal process. It is also applicable in case of formal delivery of some other legal notice. Publication of notice in a newspaper or other public medium is also deemed to be service by publication. Any method of service allowed by law in place of personal service, such a service by mail, can be treated to be substituted service. It is also termed constructive service.[1] The object of all service is of course only to give

1 Black's *Law Dictionary*, 8th Ed., p. 1399.

notice to the party on whom it is made, so that he may be made aware of, and may be able to resist, that which is sought against him: and when that has been substantially done, so that the court may feel perfectly confident that notice has reached him, everything has been done that is required. Broadly speaking, delivery of a notice to the addressee constitutes service of a notice.[2] The act of making a notice available to the addressee of the notice is known as service of notice. Terms such as 'to give', 'to deliver', 'to issue', 'to send' and 'to prefer' in relation to a notice carry the same import. All the terms are synonymous. It would be sufficient if such expression used the intention to serve the notice.[3] The period allowed in a notice is never arbitrary. In some cases, the period is fixed by an enactment while in other cases, where law is silent; the period is a reasonable period depending on facts and circumstances of each case. When a notice is statutory and is, therefore, mandatory in nature and is made a condition precedent for institution of a suit due service of such notice is required. Notices which are statutory but the enactment does not prescribe any particular period, the notice has to allow a reasonable period. Another class of notice is the optional notice which, from equitable considerations, allows reasonable period for compliance. The date of posting but not the date of writing or signing the notice is an important factor for obvious reasons.

2 Service of a notice—meaning of

Service, according to the meaning given in the *Oxford Dictionary* is 'legal serving of writ etc.'—delivery with announcement of contents to person affected. In *Chaturbhuj Sohanlal* v *Clive Mills Co. Ltd.*,[4] D.N. Sinha and A.C. Sen, JJ. referred to observations in *Hope* v *Hope*[5] where it was held: "The object of all service is of course only to give notice to the party on whom it is made, so that he may be made aware of and may be able to resist that which is sought against him: and when that has been substantially done, so that the court may feel perfectly confident that service has reached him, every thing has been done that is required. Broadly speaking, delivery of a notice to the addressee constitutes a service of a notice."

Of course, modes of delivery differ.

3 Modes of service of a notice

There are known five direct modes and one indirect mode of service of a notice.

2 *Hope* v *Hope* 1854(4) Dc GM & G 328; *Chaturbhuj Sohanlal* v *Clive Mills Co. Ltd.* AIR 1964 Cal 241.
3 *Sushil Kumar Chakravarty* v *Ganesh Chandra Mitra* AIR 1958 Cal 251.
4 AIR 1964 Cal 241.
5 1854(4) De GM and G 328 at p. 342.

The direct modes are:

(*i*) Personal service (including vicarious service);

(*ii*) Service by post;

(*iii*) Contractual mode of service;

(*iv*) Statutory mode of service;

(*v*) Service through electronic form.

Indirect mode of service—service by implication.

(i) *Personal service*

A notice may be served on the addressee personally which is commonly known as personal service. In other words, delivery of a notice to the person on whom it is to be served constitutes what is known as 'personal service'. When a personal service is effected, a receipt acknowledging delivery of the notice in writing should be insisted from the addressee.

(ii) *Service by post*

The most commonly adopted mode of service of a notice is 'service by post', i.e. sending a notice to the addressee, addressed at his usual place of abode or the last known place of abode or business, by post. A notice may be sent by ordinary post; it may be sent under a Certificate of Posting or it may be sent per registered post. Dispatch of a notice by ordinary post is not free from risks inasmuch as the notice-giver has had left with him nothing to prove service of the notice if the addressee denied of having received the notice. Dispatch of a notice by post under a certificate of posting places the notice-giver in no better position. A certificate of posting, issued by the post office of dispatch, certifies posting of a letter containing a notice but it is not a guarantee that the letter must have reached the addressee. But sending a notice per registered post places the notice-giver on a better and surer footing and the law will presume that a notice, sent under registered post, was duly served on the addressee.

When a notice is sent by registered post and when the notice is admittedly sent to correct and proper address with pre-paid stamp a statutory presumption arises that the notice has been received by addressee.[6]

A notice was served by registered post and the envelope with endorsement was 'refused' or 'not claimed'. Presumption of due service of notice arises by reason of s. 27, General Clauses Act read with s. 114(*e*), Evidence Act; to prove service plaintiff is not to examine the postal peon. But if the addressee denies on oath the tender of notice and the denial is believed, the onus

6 *Harihar* v *Ramsashi* 23 CWN 77 (PC); *Kulkarni Patterns* v *Vasant Babu Ram* AIR 1992 SC 1097; (1992)2 SCC 46; *A. Valliammal* v *Jayanthi* AIR 2009 Mad 182.

springs back on the sender to prove by some evidence that the registered cover was tendered and this may include the examination of the postal peon.[7]

(iii) *Contractual mode of service*

The contractual mode of service adopts the mode as agreed to by the parties thereto. When an agreement or a contract contains a term as to the mode of service of notice (e.g. as in partnership or arbitration agreement), the notice should be served conforming strictly to such mode.

(iv) *Statutory mode of service*

When a particular provision of law directs a particular manner as to how a notice has to be served (e.g. in a case of a notice under s. 80 of the Code of Civil Procedure directing the notice "to be delivered to or left at the office of the Secretary to the Union, Provincial Government. General Manager of a railway or the Collector of a district as the case may be)—the notice-giver has to follow the mode. The last direct mode of service of a notice is the special mode which may be enjoined by an enactment, for example, leaving a notice in a conspicuous part of the premises of the addressee and so on.

(v) *Service through electronic form*

A FAX or facsimile transmission, is a method of transmitting over telephone line an exact copy of a printed matter through a machine termed telecopier. This method may be used for sending a notice in accordance with the Evidence Act as amended by the Information Technology Act.

Now-a-days a practice has developed, of sending or receiving of notices by e-mail without signature or acknowledgement of the addressee. Nobody can deny it because of the mechanism of keeping record of such service. Section 88A of the Evidence Act which was inserted by the Information Technology Act 2000 provides for presumption of electronic message by the originator through e-mail server to the addressee.

Indirect mode of service—service by implication

The indirect mode, referred to at the beginning, lies in service by implication. It arises when a notice was duly tendered by the notice-giver or bearer or the postman as the case may be, but was refused by the addressee. Refusal, by implication, is as good as service thereof.

4 Personal service including vicarious services

When a notice is not sent by post, the delivery or tender of the notice must be made to the addressee personally. Notice under s. 106 of the Transfer of

7 *Puwada Venkatesware* v *C.V. Ramana* AIR 1976 SC 869.

Property Act to a person through whom a tenant was inducted is not a notice to the tenant[8] except when such delivery or tender is made at his residence, in which case it may be made to one of his family-members or servants.[9] Delivery or tender to a member of family or servant at the residence is enough, though there is no proof of prior tender or delivery to the tenant personally.[10]

Personal service may be effected on the duly authorised agent such as an officer of a corporation or the solicitor of the party concerned.[11] When a notice is sought to be delivered personally to the tenant who refuses to accept the notice, it is a valid service.[12]

Again, where a notice is desired to be served at the residence of the addressee, it must be delivered or tendered to him or to one of his family or servants. In the absence of such delivery or tender, merely beating a drum and affixing the notice to the wall of the house wherein the addressee resides will not be enough.[13]

In a case where a notice cannot be served personally but is served upon the servant of the family, it is known as 'vicarious service'. Whether it is residence or not, personal service on the addressee can be effected at any place where the addressee is available but vicarious service can be effected only at the residence of the addressee.[14] Therefore, a notice to quit, sent by post and delivered by the postal peon to a person other than the defendant at the shop from which the defendant was sought to be evicted, but where the defendant did not reside, is not a good notice within the meaning of s. 106 of the Transfer of Property Act.[15]

The tender and refusal of a notice is as good as delivery of the notice for the purpose of s. 106 of the Transfer of Property Act. This principle applies also to cases where the refusal is not by the addressee himself but by one of his family-members or servants at his residence.[16] Certain notices under s. 106 of the Transfer of Property Act were sent by post; and the postal peon went to the family dwelling house of the tenants with notices for all the tenants; several of the latter were present; they saw the covers but refused to accept them—*Held* that the requirements of s. 106 had been fulfilled.[17]

8 *Parshotam Lal* v *Kalayan Singh* AIR 1971 J&K 20.
9 *Kedarnath Sadhukhan* v *Madhu Sudan Das* AIR 1923 Cal 628.
10 75 IC 105.
11 *Bhojabhai* v *Haymen Samuel* (1898) ILR 22 Bom 754.
12 *Paritosh Bhowmick* v *Nandadulal Kar* alias *Goswamy* AIR 2012 NOC 192 (Cal).
13 51 IC 44 (*per* Walmsly, J.).
14 48 IC 277.
15 13 IC 59.
16 5 IC 783.
17 16 IC 213.

5 Service by post

Various laws recognize the mode of service of a notice by post. Service by post may again be in three ways, i.e. dispatch of a notice by ordinary post; dispatch of a notice under certificate of posting; and lastly, dispatch of notice by registered post, as noted earlier.

Service of notice by registered post with acknowledgement due is the best method as such mode of service ensures the service and it helps doing away with lot of litigation challenging the action for want of service.[18]

Certificate of posting

Certificate of posting is regarded as an acknowledged method of dispatch. Yet, sending a notice under certificate of posting does not inspire judicial confidence.[19] In *M.S. Madhusoodhanan* v *Kerala Kaumudi Pvt. Ltd.*[20] Supreme Court considered the general rule regarding certificates of posting. Judicial notice has been taken that certificates of posting are 'easily' available. What was seen as a possible but rare occurrence in 1981[1] is now seen as common. In *Shiv Kumar* v *State of Haryana*[2] Supreme Court said: "We have not felt safe to decide the controversy at hand on the basis of the certificates produced before us, it is not difficult to get such postal seal at any point of time".

In *Saleema's* case (supra) Supreme Court held that a certificate of posting might lead to a presumption if the letter was properly addressed and was posted, that it in due course, reached the addressee. But that is only a permissible and not an inevitable presumption. This general rule regarding certificates of posting has not been changed under s. 53 of the Companies Act 2013 although it does provide that if a document is sent by post in the manner specified, "service thereof shall be deemed to be effected". The word 'deemed' literally means 'thought of' or in legal parlance presumed. There is a distinction between 'presumption' and 'proof'. Raising a presumption does not by itself amount to proof. The words 'shall presume' in sub-sec. (2) of s. 53 must raise a rebuttable presumption, provided the basic facts, namely the due posting of the document is proved, the onus being on the addressee to show that the document referred to in the certificate of posting was not received by him.

Section 106(4) of the Transfer of Property Act enjoins: "Every notice under s. 106(1) must be in writing, signed by or on behalf of the person giving it, and either be sent by post to the party who is intended to be bound by it or be tendered or delivered personally to such party, or to one of his

18 *Hiranyaprava Samantray* v *Orissa State Financial Corporation* AIR 1995 Ori 1.
19 *Godakh Yashwantrao Kankarro* v *E. Valias Balasaheb Vikhe Patil* AIR 1994 SC 678.
20 AIR 2004 SC 909; (2004)9 SCC 204.
1 *Mst. L.M.S. Ummu Saleema* v *B.B. Gujral* (1981)3 SCC 317.
2 (1994)4 SCC 445.

family or servants, at his residence, or (if such tender or delivery is not practicable) affixed to a conspicuous part of the property." A notice under s. 106, Transfer of Property Act need not necessarily be sent by registered post. It can be sent under certificate of posting as well. When notice is sent by post and correctly addressed as evidenced by certificate of posting, a presumption arises that there was proper service of notice.[3]

On analysis, s. 106, T.P. Act allows the modes of personal service, service by post and a special mode of service by affixture. Briefly stated, a notice under s. 106 has to be served in one or other of the four modes prescribed by the section, namely, (*a*) by post; (*b*) by delivery or tender to the addressee personally, even when sent by post; (*c*) by delivery or tender to one of his family or servants at his residence; and, (*d*) where modes in (*b*) and (*c*) are not practicable, by affixing the notice to a conspicuous part of the demised property. Notice sent by post in the name of the defendant-company who is the tenant is fully in accordance with the requirement of s. 106 of the Transfer of Property Act.[4] If a notice is sent by registered post—which is refused by the addressee—such notice must be presumed to have been served.[5] In the section under review, the law directs that the notice be sent by post. It does not qualify 'sending by post' anyway. But what the common law—rule desires is embodied in s. 27 of the General Clauses Act 1897.

The process of sending documents through private courier service and through registered post through postal department are qualitative different. The presumption of delivery which arises under s. 27 of the General Clauses Act is in such case strengthened by the presumption which arises under s. 114 of the Evidence Act. Several statutes have recognized the service of notice by registered post as safe and sure mode of service. The notice sent by registered post is well recognized and well accepted method of service in our country. Such mode of service cannot be equated with courier service run by a private courier agency.[6]

The legal position is different when the civil court sends a summons to the party. Summons too is a kind of notice in such circumstances. Order V, r. 9 (since 1.7.2002) recognizes service through courier services as an approved mode of service by the High Court or by the District Judge.

Section 27 of the General Clauses Act reads:

> "Where any Central Act or Regulation made after the commencement of this Act authorises or requires any document to be served by post, whether the expression 'serve' or either of the expressions 'give' or 'send' or any other expression is used, then, unless a different intention

3 *Santosh Kumar* v *Chinmoyee Sen* AIR 1966 Cal 615.

4 *Kulkarni Patterns* v *Vasant Baburao* AIR 1992 SC 1097.

5 *Jagdish Singh* v *Nathu Singh* AIR 1992 SC 1604.

6 *K.V. Joseph & Sons* v *Surya Constructions* AIR 2005 Ker 159.

appears, the service shall be deemed to be effected by properly addressing, pre-paying and posting by registered post, a letter containing the document, and, unless the contrary is proved, to have been effected at the time at which the letter would be delivered in the ordinary course of post."

On the face of it, s. 27 of the General Clauses Act relates to any Central Act or Centrally-framed Regulation and is confined to service of a document, letter, notice by post, no matter whichever expression of the three, viz., 'serve', 'give' or 'send' be used in the material Act or the Regulation. Service of a notice by post, therefore, requires three things: (*i*) the notice should be properly addressed; (*ii*) the notice should be sent per registered post; (*iii*) the proper postage should be prepaid. Section 42 of the Arbitration Act 1940 corresponded partly to s. 3 of the Arbitration and Conciliation Act 1996 dealing with the mode of service of a notice by a party under the Act lays down, *inter alia*—notice shall be served by sending it by post in a letter addressed to that person at his usual or last known place of abode or business in India and registered under Chapter VI of the Indian Post Office Act 1898.

When a notice, therefore, was posted properly addressed and prepaid and in a registered cover, a rebuttable presumption arises that the service of notice was effected at the time at which the letter would be delivered in the ordinary course of business.[7] A notice sent to an assessee firm by registered post properly addressed and postage prepaid and received by an employee of the firm would raise a presumption of due service of the notice under s. 27 of the General Clauses Act. The presumption, however, is rebuttable and it is open to the assessee to prove that the notice was not received by him.[8] But, there cannot be any irrebuttable presumption in favour of the proper service of notice simply because the notice had been sent as required by s. 27 of the General Clauses Act.[9] The presumption would be rebuttable and if the contrary proof is given, the landlord will not be able to bank upon the presumption for the purpose of contending that the tenancy of the defendant should be treated as validly terminated simply because the notice was sent by registered post.[10] Three several eviction notices under s. 106 of the Transfer of Property Act were sent by registered post acknowledgment due one of which was at the correct address of the tenant. Presumption of service of notice can be drawn in favour of sender-landlord. In rebuttal of the presumption the tenant produced an acknowledgment receipt and denied his signature therein. It was held that rebuttal can be treated as relating to receipt for one notice only and not for all three notices. Hence service of

7 AIR 1955 NOC 3022 (MB).
8 *M.X. de Norala* v *I.T. Commissioner* AIR 1952 All 137 (*per* Malik, CJ.).
9 *Sharad* v *Vishnu* AIR 1978 Bom 187; *Badriprasad* v *Lakshmi Narain* AIR 1964 All 426.
10 *Matadin Sharma* v *Upendra Sharma* AIR 1972 Pat 292.

notice to the tenant must be presumed in absence of any rebuttal to such presumption by the tenants.[11]

The prerequisite condition of service by post is that the notice should be properly addressed. If the address be defective, care taken in sending the same by registered post with bigger postage is of no avail. Under s. 106 of the Transfer of Property Act 1882, sending by post must mean sending by post to the tenant's proper address.[12]

The proviso to s. 11(1)(*i*) of the J&K Houses and Shops Rent Control Act insists that before any amount of rent can be said to be in arrear a notice has to be served through post office under registered cover. All that a landlord can do to comply with this provision is to post a prepaid registered letter (with acknowledgment due or otherwise) containing the tenant's correct address. This is the only method of service of the notice prescribed by the proviso. Once he has done this and the letter is delivered to the post office, he has no control over it. It is then presumed to have been delivered to the addressee under s. 27 of the General Clauses Act. Under the rules of the post office, the letter is to be delivered to the addressee or a person authorised by him. Such a person may either accept the letter or decline to accept it. The acceptance or refusal can be treated as a service on, and receipt by the addressee.[13]

Service of a notice by post delivered to a member of the addressee's family—even when such a member is a minor one—may be a good service. A notice may be issued by the Income-tax Officer by means of registered post with acknowledgment due. The notice was delivered by the postal peon to the assessee's son who was found to be a minor and possessed of ordinary intelligence. The son was living with his father and when on previous occasions notices had to be served on the assessee they were taken delivery of by his son. 'Mukherjee and Bennet, JJ. considered s. 184 of the Contract Act and treating the minor son as an agent of his father held that in proper circumstances a minor son might be an agent of his father and the service in the circumstances was a good service.[14]

A notice may be delivered at the residence to a member of the family of the person intended to be bound by it or to his servants. Where the adult male members on whom the notice was to be served were not to be found in the house and the servants refused to accept it—the service was effected by affixing the notice on the outer door of the house. And it was accepted to be a good service.[15]

11 *Kulkarni Patteras Pvt. Ltd.* v *Vasant Baburao Ashtaker* (1992)2 SCC 46; AIR 1992 SC 1097.

12 *Prahladrai Chooreewalla* v *Commissioners for the Port of Calcutta* AIR 1939 PC 11 (*per* Lord Macmillan, Lord Porter and Sir George Rankin).

13 *Madan & Co.* v *Wazir Jaivir Chand* (1989)1 SCC 264; AIR 1989 SC 630.

14 *L.C. Souza,* in the matter of AIR 1932 All 374.

15 5 IC 783.

In case of acknowledgment by someone other than the addressee at the other end, the presumption would be that it was received on behalf of the addressee.[16]

6 Notice to old address

A notice under s. 143(2) of the Income Tax Act 1961 was issued to the assessee's old address which was available as per PAN database. No application was made by the assessee to change his address in the PAN database. In absence of any intimation to the assessing officer relating to change of address, the assessing officer was justified in issuing the notice at the old address which was available as per the PAN database.[17]

7 Notice sent by registered post—presumption

The best method of service of a notice is to send it by registered post with acknowledgement due. This mode not only ensures the service but also helps doing away with lot of litigtion challenging the action for want. of notice.[18] Section 114 of the Evidence Act reads: "The court may presume the existence of any fact which it thinks likely to have happened, regard being had to the common course of natural events, human conduct and public and private business, in their relation to the facts of the particular case."

As many as nine illustrations have been appended to the section. *Illustrations* (*e*) and (*f*) are relevant for our purpose.

Illustrations

(*e*) The court may presume that judicial and official acts have been regularly performed;

(*f*) The court may presume that the common course of business has been followed in particular cases.

What do these presumptions mean? 'Presumption' ordinarily means supposition, balance of probability. It is generally an inference of existence of one fact from the existence of some other fact based upon previous experience of their relationship. When a man is quarrelling, it may be presumed he is agitated. The presumption as to his state of mind from the fact of outburst is a logical inference suggested by previous experience of causal relation. In the field of law, the word 'presumption' has had the same import. The word has not been defined anywhere. A.N. Bhandari, CJ. in *Fatah Gugan* v *Sardara*[19] interpreted the term by saying: "A presumption is a rule of law that attaches definite probative value of specific facts or

16 *Commissioner of Hazari Bagh* v *Fulchand* AIR 1966 Pat 434.

17 *Principal Commissioner of Income Tax, Mumbai* v *I-Ven Interactive Limited, Mumbai* (2019)10 SCC 13.

18 *Smt. Hiranyaprava Samantray* v *Orissa State Financial Corporation* AIR 1995 Ori 1.

19 AIR 1958 Punj 333.

directs that a particular inference as to the existence of one fact not actually known shall be drawn from a fact which is known and proved. It furnishes *prima facie* evidence of the matter to which it relates and relieves the party of the duty of presenting evidence until his opponent has introduced proof of rebutting the presumption. It raises such a high degree of probability in its favour that it must prevail unless clearly met and explained and overturned by explanatory proof to the satisfaction of the court. Presumptions hold the field in the absence of evidence, but when facts appear presumptions recede." A presumption has been defined as "an inference, affirmation or disaffirmation of truth or falsehood of a doubtful proposition drawn by a process of probable reasoning from something proved or taken for granted. They are rules of evidence which attempt to assist the judicial mind in the matter of weighing the probative or persuasive force of certain facts proved in relation to other facts presumed or inferred".[1]

Thus, with an idea what a presumption is, we would now proceed to examine the implications of Illustrations (*e*) and (*f*) under s. 114 of the Evidence Act. The meaning of Illustration (*e*) is that if an official act is proved to have been done, it will be presumed to have been regularly done; while Illustration (*f*) means that if some work has been done, the common course of business has been followed in doing the work. Conforming to above illustrations, the court is entitled to presume that all official acts have been regularly performed in the first case, and, that acts were done following the common method of doing such acts in the second case.

Relying on these presumptions of s. 114 of the Evidence Act, a notice sent duly by registered post should be presumed to have been served on the addressee.[2] The position has been nicely dealt with by K.C. Das Gupta and B.K. Guha, JJ.: Where a notice to quit, after being properly addressed, prepaid and posted by registered post is returned with endorsement "refused", two different presumptions are of assistance to the plaintiff. "One is the presumption as mentioned in Illustration (*f*) of s. 114 of the Evidence Act, namely, that the court may presume that the common course of business has been followed in particular cases." As soon as the court presumes that the common course of business has been followed, it is entitled to hold that the postal peon did go to the address and the return of the cover was due to one of two reasons, either that the man was not found or that, though found, he had refused. These circumstances entitled the court to hold, unless the contrary is proved, that the endorsement "refused" was made by the peon

1 *Izhar Ahmad* v *Union of India* AIR 1962 SC 1052 at 1060 referred to and relied on in *M.S. Madhusoodhanan* v *Kerala Kaumudi Pvt. Ltd.* AIR 2004 SC 909; (2004)9 SCC 204.

2 *Zakir* v *Mohammad Hussain Khan* AIR 1977 All 476. Also see *Commissioner of Hazari Bagh* v *Fulchand* AIR 1966 Pat 434; *Mrs. Achamma Thomas* v *E.R. Faizoman* AIR 1970 Mys 77; *Harihar* v *Ramsashi* 23 CWN 77; 71 CWN 282; *Matadin Sharma* v *Upendra Sharma* AIR 1972 Pat 292.

himself and that it was correctly made. Apart from this, the presumption mentioned in Illustration (*e*) of s. 114 of the Evidence Act is also of great assistance to the plaintiff. That illustration says that "the court may presume that judicial and official acts have been regularly performed". All that happens in the post office from the time of posting of a letter to the point of delivery to the addressee or return to the sender are official acts. As the law entitles the court to presume that official acts have been regularly performed, the court is entitled to hold that the endorsement was made by the peon and it was correctly made .... Even if there was no other evidence on record on which a decision that the endorsement was actually made by the peon and not by somebody else was available, the presumption that the court may make under Illustrations (*e*) and (*f*) of s. 114 entitles the court to hold, in the first place, that the endorsement has been made actually by the peon and then that the endorsement "refused" that has been made is a correct statement of fact. If the court chooses to make a presumption under s. 114, the court is entitled to hold that this is the correct statement subject to this that, if there is evidence to the contrary and that evidence is believed by the court, the presumption must be held to have been rebutted.[3]

If a notice is properly addressed, stamp is prepaid and sent by registered post then court may presume the service of such notice, under s. 27 of the General Clauses Act.[4] The presumption of due delivery to the addressee applies with still greater force to letters which the sender has taken precaution to register, and is not rebutted but strengthened by the fact that a 'receipt' for the letter is produced, signed on behalf of the addressee by some person other than the addressee himself.[5] Relying on the reported case, in *Sailabala Dasi* v *Atul Krishna Mandal*:[6] "Where notices are sent by registered post and returned with the endorsement 'refused', the courts are entitled to presume that they were tendered."[7] Again, relying on the above observations of Lodge, J. in *Sailabala Dasi* v *Atul Krishna Mondal*, Bapna and Gupta, JJ. held in *Kanraj* v *Vijay Singh*:[8] "The postal service in India is on the whole, fairly satisfactory and if an endorsement purports to be by an officer of the Post Office that the addressee had refused to receive the document, it can be presumed that the document was tendered and refused." Such presumption can be rebutted and in proper cases only by a denial by the addressee. Bare denial is sufficient.[9] *Contra*: Bare denial does not rebut the presumption.[10]

3 *Sushil Kumar* v *Ganesh Chandra* AIR 1958 Cal 251; 62 CWN 193.
4 *Har Charan Singh* v *Shiv Rani* AIR 1981 SC 1248; (1981)2 SCC 535; *Budha* v *Bedariya* AIR 1981 MP 76; *Gangaram* v *Phulwati* AIR 1970 All 446.
5 *Harihar Banerjee* v *Ramsashi Roy* AIR 1918 PC 102.
6 30 CWN 934.
7 *Sailabala Dasi* v *Atul Krishna Mondal* AIR 1948 Cal 63.
8 AIR 1951 Raj 74.
9 *Jagat Ram* v *Batti Mal* AIR 1976 Del 111.
10 *Mushiyat Ullah* v *Abdul Wahab* AIR 1972 All 539.

Where a notice by registered post is received by somebody in the house of the addressee, the presumption is that it was duly served unless it is shown that the person receiving it was neither a servant nor a member of the family nor its agent who had authority to receive it. In the absence of proof on this point, the presumption could not be rebutted.[11] Therefore, where the acknowledgment receipt of a notice, sent per registered post, is signed by the defendant-addressee, a presumption of due service of notice can be raised under s. 114 of the Evidence Act.[12] It is advisable, therefore, to send notice always by Registered Post with A/D.

The effect of sending a letter to the post office will, in general, be regarded as presumptively proved if the letter be shown to have been handed to or left with the person whose duty it was in the ordinary course of business to carry it to the post office.[13] Relying on a case reported in AIR 1920 Cal 387, it was held in *Mohanlal Kejriwal* v *Sunder Lal Nandlal Saraf*: when the registered letter addressed to the person was received back with the remark 'refused' a presumption arose that it was refused by the defendant himself even though the word 'refused' was not proved to be in his handwriting. A presumption of due service arose as soon as it was established that the cover containing the notice was transmitted by registered post to the defendant.[14] Due service of notice under s. 69, Embankments Act, should be presumed under s. 114 of the Evidence Act in absence of evidence to the contrary.[15] We may refer to yet another illustration of presumption under s. 114 of the Evidence Act. Where a notice of hearing of appeal is sent by registered post to the appellant but has come back with the endorsement 'refused' made by the postal authorities, the mere endorsement is sufficient in the eye of law to justify the presumption of service of the notice on the appellant.[16]

Where a notice or other document is served by post, it shall be deemed to have been served at the time when the letter containing it would be delivered in the ordinary course of post and in proving such service, it shall be sufficient to prove that the letter containing the notice or other document was properly addressed and registered.[17]

Evidence of actual tender and refusal to accept delivery is not necessary to bring about the presumption.[18] Presumption can be raised that attempt

11 *Balgovind Rastogi* v *Bhargava School Book Depot* AIR 1958 All 369 (*per* Randhir Singh, J.).

12 *Jagannath Upadhyay* v *Amarendra Nath Banerjee* AIR 1957 Cal 479.

13 *Chunilal Dwarka Nath* v *Hartford Fire Insurance Co. Ltd.* AIR 1958 Punj 440.

14 AIR 1949 East Punj 295.

15 *Sasi Sekhar Sen* v *Bir Bikram Kishore Manikya* AIR 1932 Cal 267 (*per* Mitter and Patterson, JJ.).

16 AIR 1952 All 856.

17 Section 194 of the Railways Act 1989.

18 *Jagat Ram* v *Bhatti Mal* AIR 1976 Del 111.

was made to deliver the notice to the addressee. No reliable evidence was produced to rebut such presumption. Defendant's bare denial is not sufficient. He must be deemed to have constructive notice.[1] Notice terminating tenancy by registered post returned with endorsement 'refused'. Tenant denied service of notice with a plea that they were out of station to perform a 'mooran' ceremony. The presumption of service was rebutted by denial. It was incumbent on landlord to lead further evidence or plead otherwise.[2]

Reference may be made to the following cases.[3]

Next, we shall proceed to discuss the presumption what s. 27 of the General Clauses Act raises.

Section 27 enacts that unless the contrary is proved, service shall be deemed to have been effected by properly addressing, prepaying and posting by registered post a letter containing the notice. As soon as it is proved that the letter containing the notice is properly addressed, prepaid and posted by registered post, service shall, under s. 27 of the General Clauses Act be deemed to have been effected. This 'deeming' has been held to amount to presumption which unless rebutted would prove the fact of service. Even if, therefore, the actual refusal by the addressee is not proved, service of notice may well be held to be proved.[4]

The contrary view is worth noting. The proof of fact that a letter correctly addressed has been posted and has not been received back through the Return Letter Office may justify the presumption that it has been delivered in due course of mail to the addressee; but proof of the fact that a letter has been duly posted and has been returned by the postal authorities does not justify the presumption that has been so returned because it has been refused by the addressee; for, it may well be that it has been returned because the addressee has not been found.[5] The answer to that is, let us believe that in such a case the postal peon will make an endorsement 'not found' or 'refused'. Beaumont, CJ. held in *Vaman Vithal Kulkarni* v *Kandera Ram Rao Sholapurkar*[6] that service was not sufficient even if the refusal was proved. His Lordship added: "Even if the refusal has been proved, I should not be

1 *Pakhar Singh* v *Kishan Singh* AIR 1974 Raj 112. Also see AIR 1989 SC 1433.

2 *Rama Devi* v *Ramprakash* AIR 1985 All 17.

3 AIR 1918 PC 102; AIR 1929 Cal 651/652; AIR 1938 All 388; AIR 1952 Cal 467; AIR 1924 Mad 214; AIR 1927 Pat 305; AIR 1926 Lah 520; AIR 1920 Cal 287; AIR 1930 Lah 439; ILR 15 Cal 681; AIR 1963 SC 822 [illustration to s. 114(*e*)]; *Sushil Kumar* v *Ganesh Chandra* 62 CWN 193; 65 CWN 690 and 71 CWN 282. Examination of postman not necessary (*M.P. Swami* v *Mangaram Agarwalla* AIR 1979 Ori 1; *Puwada Venkataswara Rao* v *Chidanana Venkata Ramana* AIR 1976 SC 869). Presumption—how rebuttable—*Shiv Dutt Singh* v *Ram Dass* AIR 1980 All 280.

4 *Sushil Kumar Chakravarty* v *Ganesh Chandra Mitra* AIR 1958 Cal 251; AIR 1938 All 388.

5 AIR 1915 Cal 313.

6 AIR 1935 Bom 247.

prepared to hold that a registered letter tendered to the addressee and refused and brought back unopened was well served. There are, I know, some authorities in this court to contrary, but it seems to me impossible to say that a letter has been served so as to bring the contents to the notice of the person to whom the letter is addressed if the agent for service states that, in fact, the notice was not served, although the reason may have been that the addressee declined to accept it. One cannot assume that because an addressee declines to accept a particular sealed envelope he has guessed correctly as to its contents. Many people in this country make a practice of always refusing to accept registered letters, a practice based, I presume, on their experience that such documents usually contain something unpleasant."

Admittedly, the observations of Beaumont, CJ. are a bold exposition of things. But the trend of judicial opinion in different High Courts over the matter is in favour of a quick presumption as to good and effective service. It has been held in a number of cases, as we have seen hereinbefore, that the postal endorsement of refusal is admissible in evidence even if the postman is not examined,[7] there may be cases where such examination of proof may be required and that unless rebutted, it would be sufficient proof of service of the letter.[8] It was held by a Division Bench of the Punjab High Court that the presumption equally attaches to the postal peon's report 'refused', because the report is made in the usual course of business and it is open to the court to presume that the usual course was followed in the particular case. When, therefore, a letter is duly addressed and posted, particularly when it is also registered, the presumption is that the postman did tender the letter to the addressee. The fact that the letter came back does not by itself rebut the presumption that it was tendered. The writing of endorsement 'refused' falls within the ambit of the common course of business of the postman and, therefore, even without any formal proof, involves the presumption that it was written on a refusal by the addressee.[9] The postman need not be examined.[10]

When a registered notice was returned with remark "addressee not known and not traceable"—it must be proved that notice was refused or the addressee gave a fictitious address—section 27 of the General Clauses Act, held, not applicable.[11]

8 Distinction between non-service and irregular service of notice

There is a distinction between non-service of notice and a notice though served but with some kind of procedural irregularities in serving. In the case of former category of cases, all consequential action, if taken would be rendered

7 *Saibalini Saha* v *Snehalata Bose* 65 CWN 690.
8 AIR 1953 Mad 884.
9 AIR 1957 Punj 284.
10 AIR 1966 Ass 104; for contra see *Parshotam Lal* v *Kalyan Singh* AIR 1971 J&K 20.
11 *Jitendra* v *Chairman, RTA Bolongir* AIR 1971 Ori 120.

bad in law once the fact of non-service is proved whereas in the case of latter category of cases, the consequential action, if taken would be sustained. It is for the reason that in the case of former, since the notice was not served on the person concerned he was completely unaware of the proceedings which were held behind his back thereby rendering the action "illegal" whereas in the case of latter, he was otherwise aware of the proceedings having received the notice though with procedural irregularity committed in making service of such notice on him. If a person has a knowledge of the action proposed in the notice, then the action taken thereon cannot be held as being bad in law by finding fault in the manner of effecting service unless he is able to show substantial prejudice caused to him due to procedural lapse in making service on him. It, however, depends upon individual case to find out the nature of procedural lapse complained of and the resultant prejudice caused.[12]

Whether service of notice is valid or not is essentially a question of fact. In a case regarding taxation, the Court held that non-issue of notice or mistake in the issue of notice or defective service of notice does not affect the jurisdiction of the assessing officer, if otherwise reasonable opportunity of being heard has been given. Issue of notice as prescribed in the Rules constitutes a part of reasonable opportunity of being heard. If prejudice has been caused by non-issue or invalid service of notice the proceeding would be vitiated. But irregular service of notice would not render the proceedings invalid; more so, if the assessee by his conduct has rendered service impracticable or impossible.[13]

9 Service of notice under the West Bengal Premises Tenancy Act —provisions of s. 106, T.P. Act may be invoked

Provisions of s. 106 being part of the General Law, i.e. the Transfer of Property Act may be invoked to the extent not repealed by the Special Law, i.e. the West Bengal Premises Tenancy Act for carrying into effect the purpose and provisions of the latter and this without any further legislation will automatically attract the presumption of service as per ss. 27/28 of the Central/Bengal General Clauses Act.[14]

10 Service of notice under Income Tax Act 1961

The service of a notice or summon or requisition or order or any other communication may be made by delivering or transmitting a copy thereof to the person by post or by such courier services as may be approved by the Board. Notice may also be sent in such manner as provided under the Code of Civil Procedure for the purpose of service of summons. Notice may be sent in the form of any electronic record as provided in the Information Technology

12 *Prabin Ram Phukan* v *State of Assam* (2015)3 SCC 605.
13 *Commissioner of Sales Tax* v *Subhash & Co.* (2003)3 SCC 454.
14 *Miss D. Ennis* v *Calcutta Vyaper Pratisthan* AIR 1991 Cal 152.

Act 2000 or by any other means of transmission of documents as provided by the rules made by the Board.[15] Service of notice is a condition precedent for making of an order of income tax assessment.[16]

11 Authentication of notices

A notice or other document to be issued by any income-tax authority, such notice or other document should be signed and issued in paper form or communicated in electronic form by that authority in accordance with such procedure as may be prescribed.[17]

12 Service of notice under Negotiable Instruments Act

Section 138 of the Negotiable Instruments Act does not require that the notice should be given only by post. The principles incorporated in s. 27 of the General Clauses Act 1897 can be profitably imported in a case where the sender has dispatched the notice by post with correct address written on it. Then it can be deemed to have been served on the sendee unless he proves that it was not really served and he was not responsible for such non-service.[18]

13 Service of notice under Railways Act

Section 192 of the Railways Act provides that any notice or other documents which is to be served in the case of a Zonal Railway, on General Manager or any of the authorisd Railway servant (*a*) by delivering it to him; or (*b*) by leaving at his office; or (*c*) by registered post to his office address.

A notice cannot be served on a subordinate officer like the Chief Commercial Superintendent where there is a Manager or General Manager.[19]

Service of notice by a railway administration on any person either of the following manners: (*i*) by delivering it to the person; (*ii*) by leaving it at the usual or last known place of abode of the person; (*iii*) by registered post addressed to the person at his usual or last known place of abode. Section 193 of the Railways Act (corresponding to s. 141 of the old Act) governs the manner of service of claims.[20]

14 Endorsements—'refused', 'left', 'not found', 'not-claimed' etc., by postal peon —meaning thereof

In some circumstances the endorsement 'refused' by postman means service of notice but not in all cases.[1] When a registered envelope is tendered by a

15 Section 282 of the Income Tax Act 1961.

16 *R.K. Upadhyaya* v *Shanabhai P. Patel* (1987)66 ITR 163 (SC).

17 Section 282A of the Income Tax Act 1961.

18 *V. Raja Kumari* v *Subbarama Naidu* AIR 2005 SC 109.

19 *Ram Padarath* v *Union of India* AIR 1974 All 465; *Union of India* v *H.N. Sugar Mills* AIR 1968 Pat 146.

20 *Union of India* v *Lakshmi Textiles* AIR 1968 Ker 23.

1 65 CWN 690; AIR 1953 Mad 884; 1957 Punj 284; *Saeed Ahmed* v *Syed Qumar Ali* AIR 1973 All 24.

postman to the addressee but he refused to accept it, there is due service effected upon the addressee. By refusal, the addressee must, therefore, be imputed with the knowledge of the contents thereof and then follows the presumption raised under s. 27 of the General Clauses Act and s. 114 of the Evidence Act.[2]

The endorsement 'left' does not warrant the presumption of service of notice.[3] Tenant leaving India without leaving behind foreign address nor authorising anybody to accept notices on his behalf service of notice by registered post with A/D coming back with endorsement 'left' notice was sought to be served manually. A copy thereof was affixed on front door—*Held*, notice was properly served on the tenant.[4]

The endorsement 'not found' does not always indicate service. Sufficiency of service is relative.[5]

The endorsement 'not-claimed' may mean service under exceptional circumstances as when the addressee refuses to accept the same as his letter.[6] In case of 'unclaimed' and not refused notice, the sender could opt for any of the two courses for the presumption of service of the notice: (*i*) to concede to the stand of the sender; or (*ii*) to contest the stand of the sender at the risk of proving that he, in fact, received the notice.[7]

When a notice to quit is returned with the postal endorsement 'not claimed', such postal endorsement is sufficient to hold that the notice is duly served if the defendant is unable to prove that the endorsement made upon the unserved notice cover is not correct.[8]

15 Presumption as to time of delivery of notice

The presumption as above, it may be noted here, is not only of service but the presumption extends further as to the time, actual or approximate, when the notice was delivered. Taking into consideration the period that is usual for transmission and delivery the approximate time of delivery can be presumed. In *Amulya Charan De* v *Corporation of Calcutta*,[9] Sinha, J., *held*: "The presumption is that the notice was served at the time when it would be delivered in the ordinary course of post."

2 *Harcharan Singh* v *Shiv Rani* AIR 1981 SC 1284; (1981)2 SCC 535.
3 *Sitanath Mandal* v *Soleman Molla* 51 CWN 650; AIR 1952 Cal 221; contra *Harekrishna Das* v *Hahnemann Pub. Co. Ltd.* 70 CWN 262; *Surajmall* v *Samadarshan Sur* AIR 1969 Cal 109.
4 *D. Ennis* v *Calcutta Vyapar Pratisthan Ltd.* AIR 1991 Cal 152.
5 *A.E.K. Keliappo* v *S.V.K.R. Amirthavalavandammal* AIR 1973 Mad 255.
6 70 CWN 676.
7 *Dalmia Cement (Bharat) Ltd.* v *Glaxy Traders & Agencies* (2001)6 SCC 462.
8 *Maniram Industrial Enterprises, Bangalore* v *B.S. Sathya Kumar* AIR 2006 Kant 262; 2006 AIHC 2669; 2006(4) Kant LJ 675.
9 AIR 1950 Cal 256.

16 Inordinate delay in service of notice—effect

When the summons on the defendant could not be served as the summons was returned with the endorsement that the defendant could not be found at the address given and thereafter that summons was sent to alternative address given for which inordinate delay occurred, it is held that there was no lapse on the part of the plaintiff in taking steps to serve the summons. Such inordinate delay in serving summons is not attributable to plaintiff and cannot be a ground for dismissal of the suit or rejection of plaint.[10]

17 Rebuttal of presumption—how made—illustrative circumstances

The law of presumption itself suggests that when the facts are known, there remains hardly any scope for a presumption. To quote A.N. Bhandari, CJ.: "Presumptions hold the field in the absence of evidence, but when facts appear presumptions recede".[11] Therefore, a presumption cannot be raised, it was held in *Uday Narayan* v *Radha Shyam*,[12] in the face of clear evidence to the contrary. A light-hearted jurist has been quoted (in *Fatah Gugan* v *Sardara* by A.N. Bhandari, CJ.) to have observed: "Presumptions may be looked on as the bats of the law flitting in the twilight but disappearing in the sunshine of actual facts."[13]

Section 114 of the Evidence Act uses the expression 'may presume' which means that the provision therein gives the court a discretionary power to make or not to make a presumption, implying thereby that presumption when made is rebuttable. Again, what s. 27 of the General Clauses Act provides for is only a presumption and a presumption of fact can be rebutted. It would depend upon the circumstances of each case whether or not the presumption had been rebutted by the proof of further facts.[14] In other words, whether such presumption has been rebutted depends on the acceptability of evidence denying tender or delivery offered by the defendant. Mere denial will not lead invariably to rebuttal of presumption properly raised.[15] The question whether the presumption under s. 114 of the Evidence Act or under s. 27 of the General Clauses Act is rebuttable or not is always a question of fact and the court should consider having regard to all the surrounding circumstances and the conduct of the parties concerned.[16]

10 *Apollo Tyres Ltd.* v *Transport Corporation of India* AIR 2007 NOC 2314 (Mad).
11 *Fatah Gugan* v *Sardara* AIR 1958 Punj 333.
12 AIR 1950 Ori 36. See also *Kishorilal* v *Chalti Bai* AIR 1959 SC 504.
13 *Fatah Gugan* v *Sardara* AIR 1958 Punj 333.
14 *Commissioner of Income-tax* v *Mulchand Surana* AIR 1956 Cal 537; *Radha Kishan* v *State of UP* AIR 1963 SC 822; (1963)1 Cr LJ 809.
15 *Chhaya Devi* v *Lahoriram Prashar* 67 CWN 819; *Sukumar Guha* v *Naresh Chandra Ghosh* AIR 1948 Cal 49.
16 *Smt. Sushila Devi* v *Manoharlal* AIR 1985 All 178.

When a notice, therefore, has been posted, properly addressed and prepaid and in a registered cover, the presumption raised even as regards the service is not conclusive but is rebuttable.[17] When the question was whether certain letter meant to be dispatched by post to the plaintiff by the office of an insurance company was in fact posted, in the absence of any evidence to establish that the letter in question was in fact delivered to the post office, no presumption can be drawn to the effect that it was in fact posted as provided in s. 114 of the Evidence Act and that the letter had reached the plaintiff.[18] Assuming it was so, the presumption of due delivery under Illustration (*f*) to s. 114, Evidence Act hardly arises if there is no evidence of posting the letter.[19] Where, however, the presumption to whom the notices were stated to have been tendered denies that they were tendered to him the court is competent to consider the circumstances and to hold that the denial under the particular circumstances was sufficient to rebut the presumption.[20] Statement on oath by the addressee that such letter was not tendered to him—presumption stands rebutted.[1]

18 Notice sent by registered post—onus of proof

When a notice-giver claims that he had sent the notice per registered post and that he complied with the requirements as provided for in s. 27 of the General Clauses Act, he can reasonably claim a discharge from obligation of proving the service of the notice though, where practicable, he, in his interest, should take all possible measures to prove the effective service thereof. In *Saligram Rai Chunilal Bahadur* v *Abdul Gani*,[2] relying on the principle of s. 27 of the General Clauses Act. Thadani, CJ., *held*: "There is no obligation upon a lessor to prove service of a notice upon the lessee if he sends a notice by registered post properly addressed." It was further held in the said reported case: "It cannot be said that 'because the postal peons were not called to prove the service of notices, the notices were not sent to the defendant."[3]

There may be cases where a registered notice did not come back to the sender being refused by the addressee. But when a notice came back being refused, the sender thereof has to discharge his obligation of proving refusal by the addressee. Who knows if anybody other than the addressee refused? "Where a notice is sent by registered post and it is alleged that it has been

17 AIR 1932 All 374 (*per* Mukherji and Bennet, JJ.); *Gour Sankar Pani* v *State of West Bengal* AIR 1996 Cal 13.
18 *Benarsi Dass* v *New India Assurance Co. Ltd.* AIR 1959 Pat 540.
19 AIR 1958 Cal 644.
20 *Sailabala Dasi* v *Atul Krishna Mandal* AIR 1948 Cal 63 (*per* Lodge, J.).
1 *Meghji Kaniz Patel* v *Kundamal Chaman Lal* AIR 1968 Bom 387; *Parshotam Lal* v *Kalayan Singh* AIR 1971 J&K 20; *Jagat Ram* v *Battumal* AIR 1976 Del 111.
2 AIR 1953 Ass 206.
3 AIR 1953 Ass 206; also see AIR 1966 Ass 104.

returned with the postal endorsement that the addressee refused to accept it, the endorsement has to be proved by calling in evidence the postman who tendered the registered letter to the addressee. Unless it is so proved, the endorsement is not admissible in evidence in proof of the allegation".[4] Preponderance of authority now is in favour of the view that even without a peon being examined a court was justified in holding that proper service was effected.[5] Where a notice sent by registered post has returned with an endorsement 'refused' it is not always necessary to produce the postman who tried to effect service. A denial of service by a party may be found to be incorrect from its own admission or correct.[6] A presumption of correctness of the postal endorsement of 'refusal' can also be drawn with the aid of ss. 16 and 114 of the Indian Evidence Act. In *Jogendra Chunder* v *Dwaraka Nath*[7] a notice to quit was sent by registered post and was returned with the postal endorsement of refusal. In holding that this was sufficient evidence, the learned Judges of the Calcutta High Court observed thus:

> "Upon the case cited before us,[8] and *Papillon* v *Brunton*,[9] and having regard also to s. 16(*b*) Illustration, Evidence Act, we think that only a cautious doubt could lead us to regard that service as insufficient."

Further in *Durganath* v *Rajendra Nath*[10] another Bench of the Calcutta High Court following the decision held that:

> "Service was sufficiently proved by the production of the postal endorsement." Similar view was taken in *Girish Chandra* v *Kishore Mohan*[11] wherein the view taken in AIR 1915 Cal 313 was treated as one on facts of that case and it was held that:
>
> "The production of postal endorsement would be a sufficient proof."

In *Sher Afzal* v *Mohanlal*[12] law on the point has been laid down thus:

> "Where a notice sent by post in a registered cover is returned by the postman with the note that the addressee refused to receive it, and the posting of the notice has been proved, the presumption under s. 114, that the addressee did refuse to receive it arises".

Once the presumption of service of notice by 'refusal' thereof by the defendant was raised the plaintiff need not further examine the postman concerned to prove the postal endorsement since such endorsement was itself proof of the fact of service by refusal. It was for the defendant to

4 AIR 1957 MB 151.
5 52 CWN 659; AIR 1958 Cal 251; AIR 1966 Ass 104.
6 *Puwada* v *C.V. Ramana* AIR 1976 SC 869.
7 ILR (1888)15 Cal 681.
8 *Lootf Ali* v *Pearee Mohun* (1871)16 WR 223.
9 (1860)5 H and N 518.
10 (1909)17 CWN 1073.
11 AIR 1920 Cal 287(2).
12 AIR 1926 Lah 520.

disprove the fact or presumption. Mere denial of the plaint-averment on the point was not sufficient.[13] The defendant deposing on oath that no notice was served on him and defendant's testimony was not challenged by plaintiff in cross-examination and the plaintiff did not produce postman or any other evidence to prove service—*Held*, presumption as to service of notice was rebutted by the defendant.[14] Where after a lapse of time the postman deposed about the tender and refusal of the letter by the addressee but could not identify her, the endorsement held did not lose effect. No adverse inference could be drawn since it did not mean that he had not gone to the place of the addressee or that it had not been refused by her.[15]

Presumption arises from the mere dispatch of letter to correct address. Non-production of acknowledgement does not affect this presumption otherwise.[16]

19 Presumption of service when notice sent under a certificate of posting—difference, when sent by registered post

Law favours service of a notice under registered post and discourages dispatch of a notice by ordinary post or under certificate of posting. For obvious reasons it is so.

Ordinary dispatch by post does not entitle the sender to any presumption. The Calcutta High Court is agreeable to give some value even when notice is sent by ordinary post.[17] Dispatch by post of a notice under a certificate of posting may help invoke the assistance of s. 114 of the Evidence Act in proper circumstances,[18] though not so weighty a presumption as a notice sent by registered post would carry.[19] A notice sent by registered post carries with it a presumption of law but a notice sent under a certificate of posting has to depend on the findings of facts. In any case, dispatch by post under a certificate of posting is permissible.[20] When a certificate of posting is put in evidence, the presumption is that the letter was posted and that it reached its destination unless something is shown to the contrary. It would not be just for a court to work on the presumption that the 'certificate of posting' was a forgery. In *Hemangini Dasee* v *Sarnalata Dasee*, Sen, J. *held*: "There

13 AIR 1976 SC 869.

14 AIR 1976 SC 869 and AIR 1970 All 446 (FB), foll. *Gur Bachan Singh* v *Dharam Samaj Society* AIR 1981 All 208.

15 AIR 1968 Bom 387; AIR 1976 SC 869 foll. *Smt. Ram Shree* v *Smt. Khadija Bibi* AIR 1981 All 5.

16 *Babu Khan* v *Nagar Palika, Lucknow* AIR 1963 All 111.

17 *Sukumar Guha* v *Naresh Chandra Ghosh* AIR 1968 Cal 49; *Jitendra Nath Das* v *Bijoy Lal Das* AIR 1976 Cal 478.

18 *Kanaklata Ghosh* v *Amal Kumar Ghosh* AIR 1970 Cal 328; *Achamma Thomas* v *E.R. Fairman* AIR 1970 Mys 77; *Fitter Peera Saheb* v *K. Balachandra Rao* AIR 1972 Mys 14.

19 51 CWN 650; AIR 1952 Cal 221; AIR 1968 Cal 49; AIR 1970 Mys 77.

20 *Santosh K. Gupta* v *Chinmoyee Sen* AIR 1966 Cal 615.

is the certificate of posting. The learned counsel on behalf of the petitioner mentioned a case where it was proved that the certificate of posting was forged. That may be so, but it would be entirely wrong for me to work on the presumption that the certificate of posting was a forgery. On the other hand, I should presume that the letter was posted and that it reached its destination unless something is shown to the contrary."[1]

A notice dispatched under certificate of posting though regarded as an acknowledged method, does not inspire confidence as certificate of posting is easy to procure.[2] Judicial notice has to be taken that the certificates of posting are notoriously easily available.[3]

In *B.L. Srivastava* v *M.M.L. Sridhar*,[4] it was held that by a certificate of posting presumption about posting arises, but no presumption as to receipt by the addressee. Again, where there is in effect no evidence regarding various steps that render service of notice valid such as that the cover contained the notice and that it was posted in the post office, the court cannot raise a presumption under s. 114 of the Evidence Act about service by certificate of posting.[5] A certificate of posting might lead to a presumption if the letter was addressed and was posted, and in due course, it reached the addressee. But that is only a permissible and not an inevitable presumption. Neither s. 16, nor s. 114 of the Evidence Act, compels the court to draw a presumption. The presumption may or may not be drawn.[6]

20 Knowledge of contents of refused notice

Refusal of acceptance of a notice can be construed as service of notice. Relying on this broad principle, a school of thought will not hesitate to penalise the maker of refusal as having knowledge of the contents of the refused notice. When a notice was served through registered post, a tenant refusing to receive the notice cannot plead ignorance of its contents.[7] After a couple of decades, the above view finds support. Where a closed envelope is tendered to a person and he refused to accept delivery of the same, he, of course, has no knowledge of the contents of that envelope, but when he does not care to accept delivery of the envelope, the law should impute knowledge of the contents thereof to him, and it is on that basis that refusal to accept delivery of a registered or unregistered notice is regarded as sufficient notice of the contents of the envelope to the addressee.[8]

1 AIR 1940 Cal 227.
2 *Godakh Yashwantrao Kankarrao* v *E. Valias Balasaheb Vikhe Patil* AIR 1994 SC 678.
3 *M.S. Madhusudanan* v *Kerala Kaumudi* (2004)9 SCC 204; AIR 2004 SC 909.
4 AIR 1975 MP 21.
5 *J. Mc. Gaffin* v *L.I.C. of India* AIR 1978 Cal 123.
6 *Mst. L.M.S. Umma Saleema* v *B.B. Gujral* (1981)3 SCC 317.
7 *Jogendra Chunder Ghose* v *Dwarkanath Karmoka* ILR 15 Cal 681.
8 *Srinath* v *Saraswati Devi Jaiswal* AIR 1964 All 52.

21 Contractual mode of service

When the terms of an agreement provide any particular agreed mode of service of a notice, irrespective of the provision of a law, such mode of service can be termed a contractual mode. When, for example, it is agreed in the partnership deed that leaving a notice at the residence of a partner will be and constitute a service, the notice has to be served that way.

22 Statutory mode of service—personal tender affixation of a copy of notice

The statutory mode of service of a notice is enjoined by this or that statute; for example, Rules 12, 14, 15 of the West Bengal Premises Tenancy Rules 1999, provide for service by registered post. Generally speaking, the most common statutory mode is to send a notice to the addressee duly addressed, postage prepaid and under registered post. Section 80, CPC, prescribes that a notice has to be delivered to or left at the address of the addressee. There is no harm if the notice is delivered to the addressee through a post office or left at the office of the addressee through postal peon.

In *Chaturbhuj Sohanlal* v *Clive Mills Co. Ltd.*, D.N. Sinha and A.C. Sen, JJ. discussed at length the service of a notice under s. 14(2) of the Arbitration Act 1940 (since repealed and replaced by the Arbitration and Conciliation Act 1996). Their Lordships' observations broadly outline statutory modes.

Sinha, J.: "The notice under s. 14(2) of the Arbitration Act has to be served like a writ of summons on the defendant. When the notice is sought to be served upon him, he is found present and the serving officer shows the original notice to him and he accepts a copy of the notice in the possession of the serving officer, but when he is asked to sign the acknowledgment he refuses to do so, the service is complete even without affixation ....

"It is true that serving officer should ask for an acknowledgement of service on the original summons, but the serving officer cannot compel the defendant to give such acknowledgement and his obligation to affix a copy only arises when the defendant refuses to accept service. When a copy of the summons has been delivered personally to the defendant and has been accepted by him, it cannot be said that he has refused to accept service. Therefore, in such a case affixation is not an essential part of the service and in its absence service will not be rendered illegal.

"Affixation becomes necessary only when the defendant does not accept delivery, that is to say, does not take the copy. If the serving officer comes back without affixation of the copy, then the defendant would not be left without any means of familiarising himself with the contents of the notice or summons if he is inclined to do so. Even when the serving officer has the copy and is in a position to affix it, the affixation must be made even when the defendant retains copy but without signing acknowledgement.

"To that extent, the provision for affixation is not a superfluity but is one that must be complied with. It is equally clear that if the defendant himself makes it impossible for a copy to be affixed, and this includes the case when he has received the only copy in the possession of the serving officer and does not return it, then he cannot be heard to say that the copy should have been affixed."[9]

In *Bisweswar Roy* v *Pitambar Nath*[10] Walmsley, J. observed: "The peon's report is that he found neither of the defendants at the house; he was told that the lady was indoors and that the boy had gone out to look after the cattle (the peon went to serve a notice under s. 106 of the T.P. Act upon two tenants, one of whom was a *pardanashin* lady and the other a minor boy), and that he beat a drum, read the notice aloud, and affixed a copy to a wall of the house. It appears, however, that there were servants present, but no attempt was made to tender the notice to the servants or to find the boy out and tender the notice to him, and on a literal interpretation of the words of the section I must hold that the service was not good; for the drum-beating and the affixing to a wall are of no avail unless tender or delivery is not practicable."

23 Affixation of copy on residential house

Fact about the debtor living in some other place known to process-server—affixation held not valid service.[11]

Under s. 106 of the T.P. Act the last alternative of an affixation of a notice does not contemplate refusal of personal delivery but envisages the situation where either the person concerned or his family members or his servants are not available at the premises and it is only then that the notice has to be affixed and therefore, if personal delivery is refused and that is proved by evidence then it would be lawful tender of notice and the service of notice would be held to be sufficient.[12]

Where the requisite namely, the defendant cannot be found, has not been established the service by affixation is not a good service.[13] A temporary absence or absence at an unusual time does not mean that the addressee 'cannot be found'. The officer should make enquires about his whereabouts and only when the officer is reasonably satisfied that the person cannot be found it can be said that the condition precedent to a substituted service has been satisfied.[14]

9 AIR 1964 Cal 241; *Acharna* v *E.R. Faisman* AIR 1970 Mys 77.
10 51 IC 44.
11 *Shashidhar Prasad Sinha* v *State of Bihar* AIR 1977 NOC 175 (Pat).
12 *Sambhu Dayal* v *District Judge, Rae Bareli* AIR 1977 All 447.
13 *Gopiram Agarwalla* v *First Addl. Income-tax Officer* AIR 1959 Cal 420.
14 *Narayanan Nair* v *State of Kerala* AIR 1980 Ker 153.

Where affixing copy of a notice on the land in dispute [under s. 145(3) of CrPC] is not denied, it would be legitimate to presume that requirements of the law have been duly complied with.[15]

24 Service of notice through electronic form

Where by provisions of a Special Act or under the terms of an agreement a special mode of service of a notice is enjoined, that particular mode has to be resorted to.

With the passing of the Information Technology Act 2000, and granting of legal recognition of electronic records, a notice may also now be sent in an electronic form.

According to Information Technology Act 2000 a notice may be sent through electronic form. Where any law provides that information or any other matter shall be in writing or in any typewritten or printed form, then, notwithstanding anything contained in such law, such requirement shall be deemed to have been satisfied if such information or matter is—(*a*) rendered or made available in an electronic form; (*b*) accessible so as to be usable for a subsequent reference.[16]

An electronic record shall be attributed to the originator— (*a*) if it was sent by the originator himself; or (*b*) by a person who had the authority to act on behalf of the originator in respect of that electronic record; or (*c*) by an information system programmed by or on behalf of the originator to operate automatically.[17]

Acknowledgement of receipt

Where the originator has not stipulated that the acknowledgement of receipt of electronic record be given in a particular form or by a particular method, an acknowledgement may be given by— (*a*) any communication by the addressee, automated or otherwise; or (*b*) any conduct of the addressee, sufficient to indicate to the originator that the electronic record has been received.[18]

Where the originator has stipulated that the electronic record shall be binding only on receipt of an acknowledgement of such electronic record by him, then, unless acknowledgement has been so received, the electronic record shall be deemed to have been never sent by the originator.[19]

Where the originator has not stipulated that the electronic record shall be binding only on receipt of such acknowledgement, and the

15 *Thounaojan Munal Singh* v *Karam Ibeyaima Singh* AIR 1971 Mani 1.
16 Section 4 of the Information Technology Act 2000.
17 Section 11 of the Information Technology Act 2000.
18 Section 12(1) of the Information Technology Act 2000.
19 Section 12(2) of the Information Technology Act 2000.

acknowledgement has not been received by the originator within the time specified, or agreed or, if no time has been specified or agreed to within a reasonable time, then, the originator may give notice to the addressee stating that no acknowledgement has been received by him specifying a reasonable time by which the acknowledgement must be received by him and if no acknowledgement is received within the aforesaid time limit he may after giving notice to the addressee, treat the electronic record as though it has never been sent.[20]

Admissibility of the notice sent through electronic records

Any information contained in an electronic record which is printed on a paper, stored, recorded or copied in optical or magnetic media produced by a computer shall be deemed to be also a document, if the conditions mentioned in this section are satisfied in relation to the information and computer in question and shall be admissible in any proceedings, without further proof or production of the original, as evidence of any contents of the original or of any fact stated therein of which direct evidence would be admissible.[21]

25 Service of notice—interpretation of terms 'to give', 'to deliver', 'to issue', 'to serve', 'to send' and 'to prefer' in relation to a notice

The act of making a notice available to the addressee of the notice is known as service of notice. Terms such as 'to give', 'to deliver', 'to issue', 'to send' and 'to prefer' in relation to a notice carry the same import. In other words, all the terms are nearly and almost synonymous.

Several Acts have used the expression 'serve' in preference to other words mentioned above. Sections 192 and 193 of the Railways Act 1989 and s. 21(4) of the Right to Fair Compensation and Transparency in Land Acquisition, Rehabilitation and Resettlement Act 2013, amongst others, use the term 'serve'. Section 206 of the Indian Contract Act 1872, ss. 93, 94 and 138 of the Negotiable Instruments Act 1881 and s. 21(1) of the Right to Fair Compensation and Transparency in Land Acquisition, Rehabilitation and Resettlement Act use the term 'give'. On the other hand, s. 80 of the Code of Civil Procedure and s. 3 of the Arbitration and Conciliation Act use the term 'deliver'. It may be mentioned that the Railways Act 1989 have also used the term 'delivered' in the same ss. 192 and 193, just as the Right to Fair Compensation and Transparency in Land Acquisition, Rehabilitation and Resettlement Act 2013 uses the terms 'give' [s. 21(1)], 'sent' [s. 21(5)]. Section 89 of the Waqf Act 1995, again, uses the term 'delivered'. According to s. 27 of the General Clauses Act, the term 'serve' has the same meaning as the terms 'give', 'send' etc., if so, the term 'prefer' cannot mean anything different.[22] Obviously the law is liberal as to the choice of the word, the only

20 Section 12(3) of the Information Technology Act 2000.

21 Section 65B of the Indian Evidence Act 1872.

22 *Union of India* v *Lakshmi Textiles* AIR 1968 Ker 23.

restriction being that whatever may be the term it should have the same shade of meaning.

We are incidentally referred to s. 27 of the General Clauses Act 1897, which provision, though relates to service by post, suggests that the terms identical in meaning serve the purpose of law, provided the intention in all the cases is the same. The relevant portion of s. 27 reads:

> "......... whether the expression 'serve' or either of the expressions 'give' or 'send' or any other expression is used, then, unless a different intention appears .... etc.".

By the expression "any other expression" the legislature, it is submitted, intended that all expressions conveying the same import as that of the expressions 'give', 'send', 'serve', would be sufficient if from such expression used the intention was to serve the notice. This has been dealt with in AIR 1958 Cal 251 and in *Sharad* v *Vishnu*[23] elaborately.

26 Service of notice on illiterate person

If a notice is served on an illiterate person who is unable to put his signature on the notice, but the signature on the notice belongs to some other person, such a notice cannot be said to have been served on him personally.[24]

27 Service of notice through phonogram

Notice to quit conveyed through phonogram by the Advocate of the landlord is not a valid notice under s. 106 of the Transfer of Property Act.[25]

23 AIR 1978 Bom 187.

24 *Orissa Industrial Infrastructure Development Corporation* v *Supai Munda* AIR 2004 SC 390; (2004)12 SCC 306.

25 *Shyam Narayan* v *Raghunath Prasad* AIR 1977 Pat 155.

CHAPTER 5

Persons Competent to Issue Notice

SYNOPSIS

1 Competency to issue a notice
2 Notice by a party direct
3 Notice by court
4 Notice by agent, constituted attorney, lawyer or solicitor
5 Notice by a receiver–by joint-receivers
6 Notice by a trustee–*cestui que trust*–co-trustees
7 Notice by co-lessors, coparceners or co-sharers
8 Notice by lessor assigns–landlord's transferees
9 Notice by guardian *ad litem*–curator
10 Notice by manager of the Hindu undivided family
11 Notice by the Government
12 Notice by the Arbitrators–umpire in arbitration proceedings
13 Notice by expectant heir–by reversionary
14 Notice by the chief officer of a club or other body corporate
15 Notice by an individual having a trade-name
16 Notice by a Registered Firm
17 Notice by persons incompetent to contract–(minors, mentally ill person and under legal disabilities)

1 Competency to issue a notice

It is the settled law that any person who has no qualification to make a contract is not competent to give any notice. When any notice is to be served by a person who is incompetent to make any contract, such notice may be served by the legal curator of such person.[1]

Person unqualified to make contract

PERSON OF UNSOUND MIND Section 12 of the Contract Act provides that a person is said to be of sound mind for the purpose of making a contract, if, at the time when he makes it, he is capable of understanding it and of forming a rational judgment as to its effect upon his interests.

A person who is usually of unsound mind, but occasionally of sound mind, may make a contract when he is of sound mind.

1 Section 103 of the Transfer of Property Act.

A person who is usually of sound mind, but occasionally of unsound mind, may not make a contract when he is of unsound mind.

Minor A person is competent to make any contract if he has attained the age of majority according to law.[2] Section 3 of the Indian Majority Act prescribes that a person who is domiciled in India shall be deemed to have attained the age of majority when he shall have completed his age of 18 years and not before.[3]

2 Notice by a party direct

It is but natural that a notice shall be issued by a party personally. Section 106 of the Transfer of Property Act 1882, expressly provides that a notice to quit contemplated thereunder may be signed either by the person who gives it or by some other person on his behalf. Instances are not rare when a notice has really been signed by the party and is eventually proved to be a good notice.

A layman may not be expected to know intricacies of law and for the matter of that, requirements of law with which the notice must comply. In these days of specialisation, the authority of a party to issue a notice got gradually transferred to the party's lawyer who claimed to have special knowledge. This has proved convenient too. It is no wonder that notices are generally issued by the party's authorised counsel. Nevertheless, the prime authority remains with the party as before. In the event of termination of service, notice has to be issued to the party direct.[4]

3 Notice by court

Under Or. XL, r. 3 of the Supreme Court Rules 1966 the court may either dismiss the review petition or direct notice to the opposite party. In case notice is issued, the review petition will be listed for hearing, after notice is served.[5]

4 Notice by agent, constituted attorney, lawyer or solicitor

A notice may be signed and issued by a party personally or by his authorised agent.[6] What law requires is authorisation, such authority need not be in writing. Proper execution of an *Ammoktarnama* giving authority to sue in ejectment confers also power to issue a notice. But it is not necessary, as pointed out, that the authority should be in writing.[7] If a notice is signed by the landlord's *ammoktar* (constituted attorney) and the defendant admitted

2 Section 11 of the Indian Contract Act.
3 *R. Sudhakar Reddy* v *J. Govinda Reddy* 2015(2) ALD 531.
4 *Indra Kumar Chopra* v *Pradeshik Cooperative Dairy Federation Ltd.* (1992)4 SCC 17; AIR 1992 SC 2093.
5 *Delhi Administration* v *Gurdip Singh Uban* (2000)7 SCC 296; AIR 1999 SC 3822.
6 *Gobinda Chandra Saha* v *Dwarka Nath Patita* AIR 1915 Cal 313; AIR 1964 Ker 176.
7 *Bodardoza* v *Azimuddi* AIR 1929 Cal 651.

that the notice-giver was really the *ammoktar* of the landlord—the notice was held valid though the power of attorney was not produced in the court.[8] Section 106 of the Transfer of Property Act is also governed by the general law of agency. Hence a notice to quit under s. 106 of the TP Act can be given by an agent.[9] Conversely, where an unauthorised person gives a notice to quit on behalf of another the notice will be invalid. It cannot even be ratified by the person on whose behalf it purports to have been given. Mookerjee, J. disallowed a notice given by one of joint-receivers on behalf of both, though subsequently ratified by the other.[10]

Under the provisions of s. 96 of the Negotiable Instruments Act, a notice of dishonour of a cheque, promissory note or bill of exchange may be issued by an agent when the instrument is deposited with the agent for presentment.

When a notice is sent by a lawyer, the presumption normally is that the notice was issued on the basis of the instructions of his client. Hence in a notice issued by the lawyer, the notice invariably contains an averments as "*Under instructions from my client etc.*" Where in reply to a notice issued by the creditors claiming the amounts due under a pronote the Advocate of the debtor sends a notice acknowledging the liability, it has to be presumed, in the absence of any plea, that the advocate had no independent authority to send the notice and that the advocate issued the notice on the basis of the instructions given by the debtor.[11] Notice given by a pleader on behalf of his client is sufficient for s. 80, CPC.[12]

Notice to quit conveyed through phonogram by the Advocate of the landlord is not a valid notice under s. 106, Transfer of Property Act.[13]

When a notice under s. 106 of the Transfer of Property Act 1882, is given by an agent, i.e. an advocate, it can be in his name if he has a general authority, but if the agent acts under a special authority, the notice must be in the name of the principal or expressly on his behalf.[14]

Notice by husband for and on behalf of his wife is valid.[15]

Usual Form

(*a*) When issued by a solicitor or a lawyer—"Under instructions from my client Sri/Mr./Mrs. (name, address, description of the party on whose behalf notice is issued) I do hereby give you this notice as follows:

8 26 IC 962.
9 *Tulsiram Shaw* v *R.C. Pal Ltd.* AIR 1953 Cal 160; AIR 1935 Cal 577.
10 34 IC 221.
11 AIR 1964 Ker 175.
12 AIR 1928 Bom 338.
13 *Shyam Narayan* v *Raghunath Prasad* AIR 1977 Pat 155.
14 *Ranumal* v *Municipal Council* AIR 1972 Raj 55.
15 *Kankarathanammal* v *V.S. Loganatha Mudliar* AIR 1965 SC 271; *Parbati Sham Achary* v *Manashi* AIR 1977 Ori 139.

Or,

Being instructed by my client Sri A.B., son of Sri C.D. residing at .... P.S. ......Dist. ...... to give you a notice I hereby write to you as follows:

Or,

"I am instructed by my client M/s. ...., a firm registered under the Indian Partnership Act with its principal place of business at .... P.S. .... Dist. .... to issue a notice which I hereby do on the facts and circumstances appearing below:

Or,

"Please take notice that my client Sri .... etc.

(*b*) When issued by an agent/constituted attorney:

"As agent and constituted attorney of Sri A.B., son of Sri C.D. residing at .... P.S. .... Dist. .... I do hereby write to you .... etc.

Or,

"I being an agent of Sri A.B., son of late C.D. of .... P.S. .... Dist. .... address you as follows:

Or,

"I am an agent of Sri A.B., son of Sri C.D. residing at ...... P.S. .... Dist. .... As desired by my said principal I write to you as follows:

5 Notice by a receiver—by joint-receivers

Under Or. 40, r. 1 of the Code of Civil Procedure, the court can appoint receiver in respect of property in suit. A receiver appointed by the court can, if so authorised by the order of appointment, issue a notice to quit against a tenant of the property of which he has been appointed a receiver.[16] Receiver, in the capacity of *custodia legis,* can issue notice to the tenants, to vacate the premises.[17]

A notice to quit given by one of the two joint-receivers is not valid. The reason is that the object of the court in appointing joint-receivers is that the estate may have the benefit of opinion of both as regards its management. Hence, one of the receivers cannot delegate his duties to the other. What is more, such a notice by one receiver on behalf of both without the authority of the other is not valid and cannot be rendered valid by subsequent ratification by the other. "When two persons are appointed joint-receivers of an estate, they should, in the absence of a direction or indication to the contrary, meet and discuss together questions which come before them in the course of the management of the estate, and in all matters which require the exercise of judgment and are not purely ministerial, the action taken

16 ILR 18 Cal 477.
17 *Usha Harshadkumar Dalal* v *O.R.G. Systems* (2000)1 SCC 742; AIR 2000 SC 2719.

should be the result of their united deliberation......It is plain that tenancy held under them, if terminable, must be determined by a notice to quit given by them jointly".[18]

6 Notice by a trustee—cestui que trust—co-trustees

A trustee of a religious society is competent to deal with the property of the society. Therefore, it is proper that the trustee of a religious society can give notice to quit to a tenant of property belonging to the society.[19]

The legal position of a *cestui que trust* is a bit different. A *cestui que trust* is not the agent of the trustee. A *cestui que trust* cannot give a notice to quit. It is only the trustee or his agent who can give a notice.

When there are joint-trustees or co-trustees, one of them alone is not competent to issue a notice. A notice to quit by one of the two Urlans of a Malabar Devaswom is invalid.[20] But when under legal arrangement between co-trustees of a 'Chhatram' they were in management of separate properties—notice by one with regard to property under his separate arrangement is valid.[21]

7 Notice by co-lessors, coparceners or co-sharers

Be it a notice to quit or otherwise the law is that all the co-lessors should unite to give a notice. Earlier on the strength of English cases,[22] (containing reference to such English cases where it was held that any one of the co-lessors could issue a notice), it was held by courts in our country as well that any one of the co-lessors could legally issue a notice to quit and the notice would be sufficient. Yet another illustration is provided in *Sri Raja Simhadri Appa Rao* v *Prattipati Ramayya*[23] where it was held by Subrahmania Ayyer, Offg. CJ: "A tenant-in-common may have ejectment to the extent of his interest on proper notice to quit" and Sankharan Nair, J. held: "Any one of the joint-tenants may determine the entire tenancy on behalf of all, even though not authorised by the rest, and the lessee has accordingly to surrender possession not only of the share of the joint-tenant who gives the notice but of the entire property. The reason is stated to be 'that the tenant holds the share of each so long as he and each shall please, but that he holds the whole of all so long as he and all shall please. If the tenant is compelled to surrender only a portion, it might be a hardship on him as he might not be willing to continue to hold the rest; and if, therefore, he is to have the right of treating the tenancy as the whole estate determined on such notice, the same right must be recognised to subsist in the other joint-tenants'."

18 *Cassim Ahmed Molla* v *Eusuf Haji Ajam Pepardi* 34 IC 221 (*per* Mookerjee, J.).
19 8 CWN 918.
20 AIR 1924 Mad 771.
21 18 IC 77.
22 *Cassim Ahmed Molla* v *Eusuf Haji Ajam Pepardi* 34 IC 221.
23 ILR 29 Mad 28.

Subsequent reported decisions, however, appear not to favour the above views. Conformably to general view in different High Courts in India, a lease cannot be determined by a notice by one or by some of the co-sharers alone. In *Thakur Ram* v *Shakroo Mian*, Mr. Justice Chatterjee, quoting *Gopal Ram Mohuri* v *Dhakeswar Pershad Narayan*[1] held: Where the relation of joint-landlords continues, it would seem the tenancy of the lessee cannot be put to an end to except by all the lessors acting together.[2] This view is based on the reasoning that the relationship created by contract with several joint-landlords continues, until there exists a new and complete volition to change it. In a Calcutta case R.C. Mitter, J. held that when two tenancies were created in favour of the defendants, one in respect of property belonging to the plaintiff alone and another in respect of property of which the plaintiff was one of the co-owners and the plaintiff's agent served a notice to quit requiring the defendants to vacate both the premises, held that the notice was invalid in so far as the joint property was concerned as the relation created by the contract with joint-landlords continues till all of them determine it.[3]

Extending the principle further, it was held that one co-lessor cannot give a notice to quit even as to his own share in the property.[4]

But the position would be obviously different if such co-owner acts on behalf of other co-sharers. This is based on the principle of 'agency'. In *Devji Arjan Dalvadi* v *Bhoja Vaija Kachar*,[5] where one of the co-sharer landlords sent a notice to terminate the lease on behalf of himself and others and said others admitted that he was acting for them by joining in the suit—*held*, the notice was valid and binding.

Where a notice determining a lease was issued on behalf of some of the owners, it is a sufficient compliance with the requirements of s. 106 of the Transfer of Property Act, if the other co-owners are proved to have assented to it by their conduct.[6] A notice to quit by the coparceners to whom the property in possession of the tenant is allotted on partition of a Hindu joint family property is a valid one.[7] Notice (under s. 106, Transfer of Property Act) sent on behalf of both the landlords, although signed by only one of them, was held to be given on behalf of both. Such notice is not defective.[8]

Co-owner landlord is an 'owner' and the suit by such landlord on the ground of reasonable requirement of members of the family is maintainable.[9]

1 7 CLJ 383.
2 5 IC 277.
3 AIR 1933 Cal 577.
4 ILR 31 Cal 786; 8 CWN 325 and AIR 1930 Cal 513 may also be seen.
5 AIR 1935 Bom 219.
6 34 IC 56 (*per* Sharafuddin and Chapman, JJ.).
7 AIR 1965 MP 1.
8 *Jamuna Devi* v *Paras Ram Trivedi* AIR 1980 NOC 98 (All); 1971 All LJ 752 relied on.
9 *Sri Ram Pasricha* v *Jagannath* AIR 1976 SC 2335.

One of the co-owners is competent to maintain a suit in pursuance of a notice given by him for terminating the tenancy. If one of the co-owners who used to collect rent for and on behalf of all other co-owners and when he was functioning for all other co-owners as landlord, a notice given by him for termination of tenancy is a valid one.[10] Notice of ejectment issued by one of the co-owners held valid.[11] But where one of the notice-givers is not entitled to give the notice, the notice is infirm and such defect is fatal to the suit.[12] If there is sufficient identity between karta of HUF and the person filing a suit, the cause of action accrued at the time of giving the notice, as if the karta is giving the notice in the capacity of karta and on behalf of other coparceners.[13]

Calcutta Thika Tenancy Act 1949, s. 5

Where the notice to quit under s. 4 mentions that the same is from and on behalf of all the co-owners including minors and the notice is signed amongst others by the guardian of minor, the omission by the guardian to mention that he was signing on behalf of the minor would not invalidate the notice. Even assuring that notice was not given on behalf of one of the co-owner landlords, yet the notice would be good and valid.[14] Notice to quit by joint-lessors but mentioning "We give you notice, etc."—Notice held was on behalf of all lessors.[15]

Where one co-sharer has been acting as the manager on behalf of all the co-sharers, he can give a valid notice to quit on behalf of all.[16] In the case of notice determining the lease to be given by all co-owners, it is not necessary that it should be signed by all of them. It is sufficient if it is given by someone acting as agent on behalf of the co-owners. The agent may be one of the co-owners himself or he may be a third person. Such an agency may be express or implied. But such authority must exist at the date when notice is given: subsequent ratification of the notice would not be sufficient.[17]

However, the Calcutta Thika Tenancy Act 1949 was repealed by s. 21 of the Calcutta Thika and Other Tenancies and Lands (Acquisition and Regulation) Act 1981 (West Bengal Act XXXVII of 1981). By the said Act, the lands comprised in, or apartment to tenancies have vested in the State free from all incumbrances. Now the owners have no right, title and interest in thika land so as to issue any notice of ejectment of the thika tenant. However,

10 *Giriraj* v *Trilokinath* AIR 1988 All 305.
11 *Kanta Goel* v *B.P. Pattak* AIR 1977 SC 1599.
12 *Ratanlal* v *Kishorilal* 1993(1) CLJ 193.
13 *Beohar Rajendra Sinha* v *State of MP* (1969)1 SCC 796; AIR 1969 SC 1256.
14 *Subhendu Prosad Roy Choudhury* v *Kamala Bala Roy Choudhury* AIR 1978 SC 835; *Sri Ram Pasricha* v *Jagannath* AIR 1976 SC 2335 relied on.
15 *Madhusudan Parshad Agarwal* v *Sushmabala Dasi* AIR 1979 Pat 6.
16 *Indu Bhusan Bose Choudhary* v *Hari Bhajan Singh* AIR 1976 Pat 282.
17 *Nanalal Girdharlal* v *Gulamnabi Jamalbhai Motorwala* AIR 1973 Guj 131.

the thika tenant may proceed to evict the *bharatias* in accordance with the West Bengal Premises Tenancy Act wherein the procedure of eviction has to be preceded by service of notice.

Again, the Act of 1981 came to be repealed (vide s. 27) of the West Bengal Thika Tenancy (Acquisition and Regulation) Act 2001 (West Bengal Act No. 32 of 2001). However, the Act of 2001 has retained the same procedure as in the Act of 1981 by laying down that the tenancies of *bharatias* would be governed by the West Bengal Premises Tenancy Act of 1997. This means that the eviction of any *bharatia* has to be preceded by service of notice in accordance with the provisions of the West Bengal Premises Tenancy Act.

8 Notice by lessor assigns—landlord's transferees

Where the lessor has assigned his interest in the property to others, the latter can give notice to quit, even though a notice of assignment has not been given to the lessee.[18] Again, when under the terms of assignment, the landlord has undertaken to recover possession from the tenant and hand over the property to the transferee, a notice to quit by the assignor even after the assignment will be valid and effective. "If there was an arrangement between the Government and the plaintiffs that the Government's right to recover possession was to continue and that they should get possession from the tenant and hand it over to *pattadars*, the right to possession for that limited purpose will still remain with the Government, though *pattas* may have been granted. If this is so, I do not see why the Government is not a proper authority to issue the notice to quit".[19]

A joint notice to quit by a landlord's transferees, owning distinct portions of property—single tenant: notice is not bad. The combined result of the common notice is that the defendant has been served with a notice terminating his tenancy in respect of each portion by a person who was competent to serve that notice with regard to that portion. The defendant did not misunderstand the meaning and effect of the notice and knew that the three plaintiffs acting together had terminated his tenancy.[20]

9 Notice by guardian ad litem—curator

When under provisions of Chapter IV of the Transfer of Property Act 1882 a notice is desired to be served on or by any person incompetent to contract, a notice may be served on or by the legal curator of the property of such incompetent person. A legal curator is a person appointed under any provision of law to protect the property of any person. So, where a curator has been appointed, it is he who is to serve the notice and it is he on whom the notice may be served to bind the incompetent person.

18 53 IC 865.
19 AIR 1924 Mad 904 (*per* Krishnan, J.).
20 *Shambhoo Dayal* v *Chandra Kali Devi* AIR 1964 All 350.

The Code of Civil Procedure 1908, contemplates appointment of guardian *ad litem* for minors and persons of unsound mind for the purpose of proceedings taken against them in a court of law. A guardian *ad litem* is to be appointed only where no legal curator has been appointed (vide Or. 32, r. 3 and r. 15 of CPC).

The above may be read with s. 69 and s. 103 of the Transfer of Property Act. Section 103 enjoins that notice, under the provisions of Chapter IV of the Act, has to be served on the legal curator of the property and in his absence to the guardian *ad litem* with prior prayer to the court. Section 103 further enjoins that in such a case provisions under Or. 32 of CPC shall apply. Section 69(2)(*a*) speaks of notice prior to sale of mortgaged property by the mortgagee. Notice in such cases may be served on the guardian *ad litem* after appointment.[21]

10 Notice by manager of the Hindu undivided family

In the case of a property belonging to Hindu joint family, a notice to quit by the manager of that family is enough.[1] So much the better if the manager is the '*Karta*' of Hindu joint family. The house belonged to Dewan Hari Singh. It was leased out by Bansilal, one of his sons, on his behalf. Sometime after a notice to quit was sent on the defendant by the said Bansilal. Hari Singh's another son, Gopal Lal, joined his brother Bansilal. A suit for ejectment was first brought by Bansilal and Gopal Lal. Afterwards their sons also were added as plaintiffs. Even if it can be said that the sons of Bansilal and Gopal Lal were coparceners with their father, still Bansilal and Gopal Lal would be competent, as the leading members of the family, to give the notice of ejectment, specially as the sons were, with the exception of one, all minors.[1]

11 Notice by the Government

It is a fact that s. 106 of the Transfer of Property Act does not apply to leases of land obtained by the Government. Section 2 of the Crown Grants Act (Act XV) of 1895 (now re-titled the Government Grants Act) enjoins that the provisions of the Transfer of Property Act 1882, does not apply to transfer of land or interests in land by or on behalf of the Crown (now Government).

Nevertheless, relying on principles of justice, equity and good conscience, the English Common law rule has been applied to such cases. In *Secretary of State* v *Babu Rajendra Prasad*,[2] it was held that a lease by the Government for building purpose fixing no terms must be presumed to be a yearly tenancy determinable by a proper notice expiring with a year of tenancy. Inasmuch as no such notice was served on them, they were not liable to be ejected

21 AIR 1959 Pat 457.
1 51 IC 121.
2 AIR 1937 Pat 391.

without such notice. The Government as the lessee has to serve a notice to quit. In such an eventuality, a notice to quit given on behalf of the Government need not be signed by the Secretary of State for himself. A notice signed by the Collector of the district will be enough.[3]

A settlee, in whose favour land vesting in the Government by virtue of the West Bengal Estates Acquisition Act 1954, has been settled at a certain rental, gets a tenancy of some description once the Government accepts rent from him. It does not mean that the settlement was a licence. The settlement being in the nature of a tenancy, it can be terminated only by a valid notice to quit given by a person authorised to do so. A Junior Land Reforms Officer (now BLLRO) not being authorised to issue the notice, the notice given by him asking the settlee to vacate and quit the land is invalid. Public officers cannot be allowed to issue notices which they are not authorised in law to issue on behalf of the Government.[4] Notice issued by the State Government under s. 7(3) of the Sikh Gurdwara Act 1925 is a valid notice.[5] Notice issued by the Central Board of Direct Taxes with regard to amount of Income Tax pursuant to Indo-Mauritius Double Taxation Avoidance Convention 1983 is *intra vires* and valid.[6]

12 Notice by the Arbitrators—umpire in arbitration proceedings

Arbitrators or Umpire, as the case may be, or both, may have to serve notices on the parties to an arbitration agreement intimating dates of sitting as also subsequently of making and signing the award under s. 14(1) of the Arbitration Act 1940 (corresponds to ss. 24(2) and 31 of the Arbitration & Conciliation Act 1996). Their agents may also issue such notices.

13 Notice by expectant heir—by reversionary

The rule of English law that the person entitled to the immediate reversion of the demised premises is the proper person to give notice to quit is applicable to India.[7] In a suit for recovery of rent and ejectment from the house, it appeared that the defendants were monthly tenants of house belonging to one 'H'. On 1st October 1917, 'H' leased the house to the plaintiff who on 10th February 1918, gave the defendants a notice to vacate the house, Martineau, J. held in *Parbhu Ram* v *Tekchand*: "As to the right of the plaintiff to give the defendants notice to quit, this appears to be clear from s. 109 of the Transfer of Property Act. The transferee ...... in the absence of a contract to the contrary, shall possess all the rights of the lessor and to the property transferred .... I hold, therefore, that the plaintiff was entitled to serve the defendants with a notice to quit the house".[8]

3 8 CLJ 34.
4 *Abdul Haque* v *State of West Bengal* AIR 1964 Cal 183.
5 *Dalip Singh* v *Sikh Gurdwara Prabhandak* (2003)1 SCW 5736.
6 *Union of India* v *Azadi Bachao Andolan* 2002(125) Taxman 826.
7 43 IC 210 (*per* Spencer and Krishnan, JJ.).
8 53 IC 865.

14 Notice by the chief officer of a club or other body corporate

For an association, the secretary is the agent for all the members. He may be a paid or an honorary incumbent. A notice sent by him is a notice for the association. When a dispute between the members of an association is referred to arbitration in terms of its rules and bye-laws, a notice sent by the secretary of the association is a notice from a party for purposes of s. 9 of the Arbitration Act 1940 as the secretary is the agent of all members.[9] But there is no such provision in the Arbitration and Conciliation Act 1996 as in s. 9 of the Arbitration Act 1940.

Order 29 of the Code of Civil Procedure speaks of provisions how a pleading has to be signed and verified on behalf of a corporation and on whom a process has to be served in a suit against a corporation. When a corporation is a statutory body the secretary, or any director or other principal officer of the corporation is the man who is to issue a notice, when necessary. But an unregistered company or an unincorporated body of persons, or an unregistered club or a society does not enjoy the same privilege. Even then it ignores all common sense if it be desired that a notice has to be signed by all the members of such a body. A notice may have to be served, if necessary on all the members but the chief officer, as agent of other members of the association, is perfectly competent to issue a notice binding the addressee.

Usual Form

When a notice is issued by a Principal Officer—"I, being the Secretary of (Name of the Association with address) do hereby give you this notice on the facts and circumstances appearing hereinunder:

Or

"As the Chairman of ...., a body Corporate with its Office at .... P.S. .... Dist. .... I do hereby give you a notice as follows:"

15 Notice by an individual having a trade-name

When an individual carries on business in some name and style will he issue the notice in his own name or in the trade-name? The issue went up to the Supreme Court where it was held that the notice should be in the name of the individual. The particular case is very illustrative. A notice was issued by S.N. Dutt & Co. of Krishnanagar and in the plaint, the description of the plaintiff was Surendra Nath Dutt, sole proprietor of a business carried on under the name and style of S.N. Dutt & Co. of Krishnanagar, P.S. Krishnanagar, Nadia—Wanchoo, J. observed: "The question, therefore, that arises is whether S.N. Dutt who filed the suit was the person who gave the notice and the answer is obvious that it is not so. It may be that S.N. Dutt

9 AIR 1951 All 359.

is the sole proprietor of S.N. Dutt & Co. and is carrying on business in that name and style; but that does not mean that these notices were by S.N. Dutt. Any one reading these notices would not necessarily come to the conclusion that S.N. Dutt & Co. was rarely the name and style in which an individual was carrying on business. The *prima facie* impression from reading the notices would be that S.N. Dutt & Co. was some kind of partnership firm and notices were being given in the name of that partnership firm". Obviously the notice was defective as it was issued in the trade-name.[10]

Usual Form

"I Sri Suresh Chandra Poddar, proprietor of .... and carrying on business under the trade-name of M/s. Poddar & Co. at .... etc."

Or,

"Under instructions from my client Sri .... son of ....carrying on business in the trade name of 'Basanti Vastralaya' at .... etc."

16 Notice by a Registered Firm

Order 30 of the Code of Civil Procedure enjoins that a firm may sue or be sued in the name of the firm and any one of the persons constituting the firm is authorised to sign, verify or certify plaint etc. It does not speak on our present subject. We are, therefore, led to refer to provisions of the Indian Partnership Act. One partner is the agent of another partner. Therefore, it stands to reason that any partner may issue a notice on behalf of the firm. If again, the partnership deed contains delegation of authority, the partner authorised therein should, in the fitness of things, issue the notice.

A registered firm is competent to issue a notice in the firm's name. A dissolved firm is also competent to do so.[11]

Usual Form

"Under instructions from my clients M/s. Jormal Harakchand, a firm registered under the Indian Partnership Act with registered office at .... etc." Or,

"Please take notice etc.

Yours faithfully,

....

Partner for

Jormal Harakchand, Cooch Behar"

10 AIR 1961 SC 1449. This view was overruled by the Supreme Court in *Ghanshyam Dass* v *Dominion of India* (1984)3 SCC 46; AIR 1984 SC 1004 and affirming *Raghu Nath Das* v *Union of India* AIR 1969 SC 674; *State of Madras* v *C.P. Agencies* AIR 1960 SC 1309; *Amar Nath Dogra* v *Union of India* AIR 1963 SC 424.

11 AIR 1963 MP 37.

17 Notice by persons incompetent to contract—(minors, mentally ill person and under legal disabilities)

A minor is incompetent to enter into worldly transactions and so also is a mentally ill person while some are under legal disabilities to act for themselves. They are represented lawfully by their guardians and/or next friends. It is the guardian or the next friend who is competent to issue a notice on their behalf.

Usual Form

"I, Smt. .... widow of .... being a certificated guardian/mother and natural guardian of Sri .... son of late .... a minor, residing at .... P.S. .... District .... hereby give you this notice on the following lines:"

Or,

"I, as the next friend of .... son of .... of .... P.S. .... District .... do issue this notice on behalf of the said Sri ...., a minor/a mentally ill person on the following grounds:"

CHAPTER 6

Persons Competent to Accept Notice

SYNOPSIS

1 Notice to party
2 Notice to agent is notice to principal
3 Notice to party's lawyer, solicitor, attorney, etc.
4 Notice to manager of a firm
5 Notice to members of a Hindu undivided family
6 Notice to the principal officer of an association of persons
7 Notice to unregistered society, club
8 Notice to a Body Corporate, Registered Society, Corporation, etc.
9 Notice to a group of persons having a trade-name or carrying on business in names other than their own
10 Notice to others—miscellaneous cases

1 Notice to party

The first and foremost right to receive a notice is of the party concerned. It is a general principle of law that a notice should be served on such person who is intended to be bound by it. This proposition has its own merits: (*i*) it is natural and judicious; and (*ii*) it is convenient.

2 Notice to agent is notice to principal

Section 229 of the Indian Contract Act reads: "Any notice given to or information obtained by the agent, provided it be given or obtained in the course of the business transacted by him for the principal, shall, as between the principal and third parties, have the same legal consequences as if it had been given to or obtained by the principal." Under the general law, a notice served on an agent, who is duly authorised to receive it, will bind the principal, although such notices may not actually reach or be brought to the knowledge of the principal.[1] Along with this may be read the provisions of s. 229 of the Indian Contract Act quoted above. In accordance with the spirit therein, service of a notice on the agent shall have the same legal consequences as if the notice had been given to the principal.

1 *Harihar Banerji* v *Ramsashi Roy* AIR 1918 PC 102.

A partner is deemed to be an agent of its principal, the firm. Notice on a partner is notice to the firm.[2] The provision applies also to notice to quit under s. 106, Transfer of Property Act.[3] A notice was delivered by the postal peon to an assessee's son who was living with his father and when on previous occasions notices had to be served on the assessee those were taken delivery by his son. Mukherji and Benett, JJ. *held*: "In proper circumstances, a minor son may be an agent of his father. We hold, in the circumstances, that the delivery of the postal article, namely, the notice, was a good delivery. It would follow, therefore, and we hold accordingly that the service of the notice in the circumstances of this case was a good service."[4]

A notice to an agent is thus a notice to the principal,[5] and fixes him with knowledge whether it is communicated to him or not, except where there has been a fraud on the part of the agent.[6] But any knowledge on the part of an agent prior to his employment as such agent would not amount to information of the fact obtained by the agent in the course of the business transacted by him as an agent so as to operate as a notice to the principal.[7] It is not merely a constructive notice or inference of fact. It is a rule of law of universal application which imputes the knowledge of the agent to the principal.[8]

The agent is the *alter ego*, i.e. alternate or second-self of the principal. Necessarily, actual or constructive whatever may be the nature, a notice is imputed to the principal. An agent stands in the place of his principal: so his acts and knowledge are the acts and knowledge of his principal for the purpose of a business.[9] Had it not been so, a notice could be avoided by employing agents.

Where a notice of determination of tenancy, the purpose of which is to make the persons concerned aware of the purport of the contents of such notice, is received by a person who is a constituted attorney of the tenant in respect of leased premises at the material time, such service on the attorney, though made in personal capacity, would amount to a valid notice on the tenant also.[10]

There is one condition which must be remembered to make the principle effective. A notice, whether express or constructive, should be during the

2 AIR 1931 Lah 227.
3 *Haroon Haji Hamid* v *Meher Ali Din Mahomed* AIR 1927 Sind 24.
4 *Fazihzzman* v *Anwar Husain* AIR 1932 All 374.
5 *Somanchol Mahapatra* v *Budhiran Padhi* AIR 1976 Ori 113.
6 *Rasila* v *Haveli* 119 IC 754; AIR 1929 Lah 500.
7 *Gunabai* v *Motilal* 89 IC 625; AIR 1925 Nag 398; *Chabildas* v *Dayal* 34 IA 179; *Wells* v *Smith* [1914]3 KB 722.
8 6 CWN 849.
9 7 CWN 441.
10 *J. Mc. Gaffin* v *L.I.C. of India* AIR 1978 Cal 123.

subsistence of the agency, in his capacity as agent, in the course of the business and in a matter material thereto.[11] Those are the requirements of s. 229 of the Indian Contract Act.

There may be circumstances when the rule of imputed notice is of no avail. Where the agent acts fraudulently with his principal, this rule of imputed notice suffers defeat. An agent may, in extreme conceivable cases, conceal facts to defraud his principal.[12] How the principal can be bound by a notice served on an insincere agent? But the exception does not apply where the fraud is not against the principal but against a third party.

Before we go on to the next subject, we would do well to remember that this rule of imputed notice is so strong that the court will be reluctant to go into an allegation that the agent was negligent to communicate the notice to his principal.

Usual Form

To

Sri ....

Son of Late ....

17 Hitendra Narayan Road

P.O. .... District ....

Agent of M/s. ....

of 12 Rupchand Street, Kolkata 700 007

(*For form of a notice to an agent binding the principal–See infra*).

3 Notice to party's lawyer, solicitor, attorney, etc.

The service of a notice to a lawyer of a party will ordinarily be not valid; for a lawyer gets authority only after he has been authorised by a party by execution of a *vakalatnama*. Accordingly, service of a notice to quit on a party's pleader or solicitor will not be valid under s. 106 of the Transfer of Property Act unless such pleader or solicitor is authorised as an agent to receive such a notice. In *Haroon Haji Hamid* v *Meher Ali Din Mahomed*,[13] it was urged that the notice was not valid as it was not served on the defendant personally or on a member of his family as contemplated in s. 106 of the Transfer of Property Act. Relying on the case of *Bhojhabai Allarakhia* v *Hayem Samuel*,[14] Rupchand Bilaram, A.J.C. held: "According to the English law, a notice to quit need not be served personally upon the tenant. It may be served upon his agent and, when so served, it is not necessary to prove

11 11 CWN 1109.
12 *Texas & Co.* v *Bombay Banking Co.* 46 IA 250.
13 AIR 1927 Sind 24.
14 ILR (1898)22 Bom 754.

that it actually came to his knowledge. It is sufficient if the fact of the agency is established".[15] Apart from the provisions of s. 106 of the Transfer of Property Act, the same considerations would apply here. Both under s. 229 of the Indian Contract Act and s. 3 of the Transfer of Property Act, a notice to the agent in the course of the business transacted by him on behalf of his principal has, as between the principal and third parties, the same effect as if it has been given to or obtained by the principal.[16] Again, a notice given to a *mukhtyar* binds his client. When a notice is sent to a pleader and he in turn sends it to the party, this would amount to personal service, though it is just an indirect mode of service.[17] The sole question is whether the party's lawyer acted as agent and had the authority. If he had such authority, service on him was good.

Notice to quit under s. 106, Transfer of Property Act is not invalid merely because it is addressed to a lawyer when the copy of such notice has also been forwarded to the tenant.[18]

4 Notice to manager of a firm

In the case of a firm, a notice has to be served either on the manager or on a member of the firm. The definition of 'person' in the General Clauses Act includes 'any company or association or body of individuals, whether incorporated or not.' A firm is, therefore, a 'person'. Where, therefore, a notice is addressed to the firm itself, instead of its manager or a partner, it is quite in order and a presumption of service under s. 27 of the General Clauses Act will arise.

Such a presumption, however, is rebuttable and the affected party may raise the plea that the person receiving the notice was not authorised to receive it.

Usual Form

To

(*i*) Sri ....
Manager of M/s ....
with officer at ....

Or,

(*ii*) The Manager ....
Committee ....
P.O. ....
District ....

15 Halsbury's *Laws of England*, 4th Ed., vol. 18, para 20 may be seen.
16 *Haroon Haji Hamid* v *Meher Ali Din Mahomed* AIR 1927 Sind 24; 25 All 1.
17 97 IA 577.
18 *Sohansingh Bharatsingh* v *Narhar Naraya Godbole* AIR 1972 Bom 67.

Or,

(*iii*) The Manager of the joint Hindu family business under the name and style of ....

....

P.O. ....

District ....

5 Notice to members of a Hindu undivided family

A question may arise whether any notice meant for members of a Hindu undivided family has to be served on all the individual members constituting the family or one notice to the head of the family will do. The answer is twofold: in some cases it may be, while in some it may not be so. The main point for consideration is whether such person or persons on whom the notice is served is or are competent to represent all the members of the family on whom the notice was not served. Section 63 of the Income-tax Act provides an exception but within limitations.[19]

Mr. Justice Mookerji and Mr. Justice Carnduff *held*: A notice to some of the transferees who are members of a joint Mitakshara family is not a sufficient notice to others unless it is provided that those on whom the notices were given were entitled to represent the others.[20] Justice Sir Asutosh Mukherjee and Mr. Justice Chotzner *held* in *Kedarnath Sadhu Khan* v *Madhu Sudan Das*[21]: "Where there was a tender or delivery of the notice of ejectment to the head member of the family, there is sufficient service notwithstanding that there is no proof of prior tender or delivery to each of the joint-tenants personally."

Usual Form

(*i*) To

Sri .... son of .... the Karta of the joint Hindu family business running a business under the name and style of .... at .... P.O. .... District ....

Or,

(*ii*) To

Messrs (*i*) ....

(*ii*) ....

(*iii*) ....

Constituting a Hindu undivided family residing at ...... etc.

6 Notice to the principal officer of an association of persons

Order 29, CPC speaks of provisions relating to framing of a suit by or against a corporation. We confess, we have no specific law or reported case

19 AIR 1966 Guj 106.
20 13 IC 637.
21 75 IC 105.

to show us the way as to whom a notice has to be served when the notice is meant to be sent to an association of persons.

The trend of opinion is, however, in favour of addressing a notice to the principal officer of the association—say, the secretary, or the chief executive officer or the president, or the director or the chairman. But why not to all the members of the executive committee or the managing committee? The matter assumes importance when the question of service of a mandatory notice arises, for example, a notice under s. 106, Transfer of Property Act when the tenancy is in the name of an association.

Order 1, r. 8(2) of the Code of Civil Procedure mandates that the court in all cases where a permission or direction is given, to allow one more person to sue or be sued or may defend any suit, on behalf of or for the benefit of all persons so interested, to give notice of institution of the suit to all persons so interested either by personal service or by public advertisement. If notices were served to 3 or 4 persons out of 75-80 persons of an Association, it is valid and the suit is maintainable accordingly.[22]

A parcel of Nazul land was allotted in favour of a society. A notice regarding cancellation of such allotment was served on office bearers of the society. It shall be presumed that the society has got notice in this regard though it was not served through President.[23]

7 Notice to unregistered society, club

In the case of an association, if a notice is required to be served, it has to be served on the principal officer of the association. In the case of registered society, the notice may be addressed to the society at its registered address. But when a group of persons constitute an unregistered body, a statutory notice be better served on all the members lest anybody should seek shelter behind the plea of non-service of a notice. Service of a notice on a corporation may be effected by a service on one of its officers (Vide Or. XXIX, r. 2, CPC).

8 Notice to a Body Corporate, Registered Society, Corporation, etc.

According to the general principles of law, a notice has to be served upon such person as is intended to be bound by the same. Service of a notice on the body corporate or a registered society or corporation etc. may be effected by service on its principal officer. Such notice may be addressed to the society at its registered address.

A body registered under a statute is a body corporate by the name under which it is registered with perpetual succession and a common seal with power to enter into contracts, to institute and defend suit or other legal proceedings, to acquire, hold and dispose of property and to do all such

22 *Subhash Market Association* v *Municipal Corporation of Delhi* AIR 2005 Del 209.
23 *Scheduled Castes Co-op. Society* v *State of Punjab* AIR 2005 P&H 100; (2005)1 Punj LR 665.

things as are necessary to be done under the objects of the society. Every such registered society has an address registered in accordance with the requirements laid down by the concerned statute to which all such notices may be sent. In other words, the notice has to be sent to the registered office of such body or society in accordance with the provisions of the controlling statute or rules and regulations made thereunder. Where a society changes its address, it is obligatory to send a notice in writing to the appropriate authority who is a creature of the said governing statute.

As the society acquires legal personality after registration, a notice can be addressed to the society in its registered name and can be sent by registered post at its registered office.

In a suit against a Corporation, the notice was addressed to the Commissioner but not the Corporation. Requirement as to notice to Corporation is mandatory. So dismissal of the suit for non-compliance of the mandatory requirement is not illegal.[24]

9 Notice to a group of persons having a trade-name or carrying on business in names other than their own

Order 30, r. 10, CPC enjoins:

> "Any person carrying on business in a name or style other than his own name, or a Hindu undivided family carrying on business under any name, may be sued in such name or style as if it were a firm name, and, in so far as the nature of such case permits, all rules under this Order shall apply accordingly."

Though as a notice-giver, such person has to issue a notice in his own name it may be served addressed to the name and style in which he is carrying business. It will not be bad if a notice is served on 'X', the owner of 'Y' (name and style of the business). This rule applies not only to a single individual carrying on a business under a firm name or an assumed name but it also applies to a number of individuals carrying on business that way when those individuals do not constitute a partnership in law.[1] When names of all the individuals are not known to the notice-giver, it is definitely safe to send the notice to the firm name or the assumed name for trade.

10 Notice to others—miscellaneous cases

(i) *Notice to one partner in a firm*

Under s. 18 of the Indian Partnership Act each partner is deemed to be an agent of the firm. Since each partner is an agent of the firm, a notice to one partner of the firm is a notice to the firm. This is more so when the partner receiving such notice is an acting partner of the firm.

24 *Jal Praday Karmachari Kalyan Sangh* v *Ayukt Nagar Nigam, Jabalpur* AIR 2005 MP 222; (2005)3 MPLJ 145.

1 *Jamunadhar Poddar* v *Jamunarain* AIR 1944 Cal 138.

Notice under s. 106, Transfer of Property Act was issued to a partner of a firm to terminate the tenancy. If the firm be the tenant, notice to rest of the partners is not necessary.[2]

Usual Form

To

Sri ....

Acting Partner of M/s. Ashkaran Subhkaran

22 Kalakar Street, Kolkata 700 013.

(ii) *Notice to one of the directors of a company*

Where a notice is addressed to a company and served on one of the directors, it will not be presumed to be a notice to the Company unless it is shown that the Director had authority to act for the Company in the particular matter in which the notice was given. Where one person is an officer of two companies, his personal knowledge is not necessarily the knowledge of both the companies. The knowledge which he has acquired as officer of one Company will not be imputed to the other Company unless he has some duty imposed on him to communicate his knowledge to the Company sought to be affected by the notice, and some duty imposed on him by that Company to receive the notice.[3]

(iii) *Notice on the principal*

As long as the principal does not surrender his right of receiving his notice, a notice to the principal will be quite a valid notice. Thus, where a clause in a lease deed executed by the Government of India provided that any notice to be given to them shall be considered as duly given if sent by the landlord through post addressed to the Lands, Hirings and Disposal Service, but the notice was sent to the Government of India. Held, that it was an enabling provision for the landlord and the notice sent to the Government of India was not invalid.[4]

(iv) *Notice on the counsel of the party*

As s. 43 of the Arbitration Act 1940 (since repealed and replaced by the Arbitration and Conciliation Act 1996) makes the provisions of the Code of Civil Procedure applicable to all the proceedings before the court under the Arbitration Act 1940, in view of Or. 3, r. 5 of CPC the provision relating to the service of notice to the parties, sub-sec. (2) of s. 14 of the Arbitration Act 1940 is complied with when a notice is served upon a counsel of a party.[5]

2 *Jai Narain Dass* v *Smt. Zubeda Khatoon* AIR 1972 All 494.
3 *T.R. Pran Ltd.* v *E.D. Sassoon* AIR 1936 Bom 62.
4 AIR 1957 J&K 27.
5 *Ram Bharosey* v *Peary Lal* AIR 1957 All 265.

Section 42 of the Arbitration Act 1940 deals with service of notice by party or arbitrator. Any notice can be served (*a*) by delivering it to the person on whom it is to be served, or (*b*) by sending it by post in a letter addressed to that person at his usual or last known place of abode or business in India and registered under Chapter VI of Indian Post Office Act 1898.

Incidentally we are led to the discussion of the provisions of Or. 3, r. 5 of CPC. It reads:

> "Any process served on the pleader who has been duly appointed to act in court for any party or left at the office or ordinary residence of such pleader, and whether the same is for the personal appearance of the party or not, shall be presumed to be duly communicated and made known to the party whom the pleader represents, and, unless the court otherwise directs, shall be as effectual for all purposes as if the same had been given to or served on the party in person."

Obviously the provision relates to service of process generally and, that again, when a suit is pending in a court of law. It does not apply to service of notice on a party when no suit is pending. Besides, Or. 3, r. 5, CPC applies only when the court orders that process be served on the pleader.[6] Similar to a process, a notice meant for the party in a suit may be served on his pleader under Or. 3, r. 5, CPC. Even the pleader is allowed to waive the formalities in effecting service.[7]

(v) *Notice to a firm*

When the firm is the addressee the notice is required to be served on the firm. It is not necessary that the notice should be served on the manager or a member of the firm. If the notice is addressed to the firm itself and is received by a person authorised to receive it, the notice is sufficient and the service is effective. Where a notice was sent to an Assessee-firm by registered post properly addressed and postage prepaid and received by an employee of the firm, that would raise a presumption of due service under s. 27 of the General Clauses Act which presumption, however, is rebuttable; and it is open to the assessee to prove that the notice was not received by him.[8] The notice on the partnership firm in firm's name determining the tenancy which was in the name of the firm is valid.[9]

(vi) *Notice to minors and persons of unsound mind*

According to English Law, a person under 21 years of age is an "infant." Instead of using the word 'infant,' the word "minor" is used in India.

6 63 IC 47.
7 AIR 1927 Pat 135.
8 *M.K. De Naronha & Sons* v *Commissioner of Income-tax, U.P.* AIR 1952 All 137.
9 *Shew Karan Agarwala* v *Satyanarain Mansinka* AIR 1978 Cal 495.

According to the Indian Majority Act, any person under 18 years is a minor. But where a guardian is appointed to such minor under the Guardians and Wards Act or where he is a ward of the Court of Wards, the period for majority is extended to 21 years.

A minor is represented by his guardian and therefore, notices which must be served in order to affect the minor's property, as for instance, notice of foreclosure, should be served on the guardian of the minor's estate.[10] "If there be no legal guardian, it is generally best to effect service upon the minor and also upon the person in whose custody he is." (cf. E.T. Trevelyan's *Law Relating to Minors*).

Notice relating to guardianship of a minor must be given to the person having custody of the minor. If such notice is not given, the order appointing a guardian will be set aside.[11]

When a person of unsound mind is meant to be bound by a notice the same has to be served on his guardian.

Order XXXII, rr. 1 and 3 contain the provision, which prescribes procedure to be adopted when a suit is filed by or against a minor. In case where the minor is plaintiff he shall sue through his next friend while in the second case, where the minor is defendant, i.e. suit is filed against a minor, the Court shall appoint a proper person to be the guardian for conducting the suit and to safeguard the interest of such minor. Same provision has been prescribed under Or. XXXII, r. 15 for person adjudged to be of unsound mind and to persons who though not so adjudged are found by the Court on inquiry, by reason of unsoundness of mind or mental infirmity, to be incapable of protecting his interest when such person is plaintiff or defendant.

Thus, as a matter of principle and logic, a minor is represented by his guardian and, therefore, notices which must be served in order to affect minor's interest or his property, should be served on the guardian of minor's estate and natural guardian. Where there is no legal guardian, in both cases it is best to effect service, logically and legally, on the natural guardian or on the next friend.

The first part of s. 12 of the Indian Contract Act, says "A person is said to be of sound mind for the purpose of making a contract, if, at the time when he makes it, he is capable of understanding it and of forming a rational judgment as to its effect upon his interests". Law always presumes sanity till the contrary is shown.[12] A person pleading unsoundness of mind shall have to prove it. Mere weakness of mind is not sufficient to prove unsoundness.

10 4 MIA 392.
11 *Jhandeshur* v *Baij Nath* 27 IC 121; 18 OC 66.
12 *Indar Singh* v *Parmesdhari Singh* AIR 1957 Pat 491.

Although it is not necessary to prove utter mental darkness, it must at least be shown that the person is incapable of understanding business and of forming a rational judgment, as held in *Mahomed* v *Abdul*.[13] Temporary forgetfulness is insufficient to show defective mental capacity.

Usual Form

To

Sri ....

Through his guardian/next friend

(State here name, address and description)

NOTICE TO GOVERNMENT

The object of notice to Government is to inform Government or the public officers concerned, generally of the nature of the suit which is supposed to be filed against them. It is well-settled that such notices must not be too strictly or too narrowly construed. The notice must be considered sufficient if it substantially fulfils its object in informing the parties concerned generally of the nature of the suit intended to be filed.[14]

A suit for recovery of bill amount regarding supply for material was filed. Notice regarding this was filed on Secretary to Urban Development Department of Government which is not essential when it was served on the Collector of the District.[15]

(vii) *Notice to a receiver*

No notice under s. 80, CPC is necessary when the suit is not in respect of any acts or omission done by the receiver in his personal capacity.[16]

For meaning of the word 'act' in s. 80, CPC—See *Amalgamated Electricity Co.* v *Municipal Committee*.[17]

(viii) *Notice to illiterate person*

When any notice is served on an illiterate person who is unable to put his signature on it, such notice cannot be said to have been served on that person personally.[18]

13 AIR 1932 Pat 127.

14 *Jahangir M. Cussedji* v *Secretary of State for India in Council* ILR 27 Bom 189.

15 *State of Orissa* v *Pratibha Prakash Bhawan* AIR 2005 Ori 58.

16 *S.V. Sreekanthayya* v *Lakshmi Hardware Stores* AIR 1978 Kant 100.

17 (1969)1 SCR 430.

18 *Orissa Industrial Infrastructure Development Corporation* v *Supai Munda* AIR 2004 SC 390; (2004)12 SCC 306.

(ix) *Notice on tenants in common*

In case of tenants in common the notice may be served on one of the tenants in common but it should be addressed to all.[19] But the question would be otherwise if the tenants are joint tenants. On the death of the tenant his heirs inherit the lease-hold interest of which they are joint tenants. So, notice on one of them is sufficient.[20]

19 *Budh Sen* v *Sheela Chandra Agarwal* 1977 All WC 553.
20 *Ramubai* v *Jiwaram* AIR 1964 Bom 96; *Shambu Dayal* v *Suleman* 1978 MPLJ 541; *Sumilita* v *Nila* (1989)2 Cal LJ 351.

CHAPTER 7

Effects of Notice of Joint-interest Holders

SYNOPSIS

1 Notice on co-lessees—joint tenants
2 Notice on co-heirs
3 Notice on lessee's co-assignees
4 Service of notice on karta of HUF
5 Notice on benamdars
6 Notice on sub-tenants (sub-lessees)

1 Notice on co-lessees—joint tenants

A notice to quit is to be served on the lessee by a lessor or by a person authorised on his behalf. Law permits a notice to be sent to the person in whom the leasehold interest vests.

Where the leasehold interest vests in persons more than one or, in other words, where there are several lessees, are notices on all of them necessary? Discretion and prudence dictate that notices should be served on each of them. Where the leasehold interest is not vested in a single person but in joint tenants, the notice to quit has to be served on all the joint tenants.[1] In *Bijoy Chand Mahatab* v *Kali Prasanna Seal*,[2] Suhrawardy and Cunning, JJ. *held*: "Reading the section (s. 106, Transfer of Property Act is meant) as it stands without any help of the comments upon it by decided cases, it is manifest that it was the intention of the legislature that the notice must be served on the person who is intended to be bound by it. The notice must be addressed to and served on the person intended to be bound by it in any one of the modes suggested by the section. The section does not make any exception or lay down any special or peculiar procedure in the case of joint tenants."

However, a notice addressed to all the joint tenants but served on one of them has been held sufficient. In *Harihar Banerji* v *Ramshashi Roy*,[3] it was

1 *Harihar Banerji* v *Ramshashi Roy* AIR 1918 PC 102.
2 AIR 1925 Cal 75.
3 AIR 1918 PC 102.

held that in the case of joint tenants service of a notice to quit under s. 106, Transfer of Property Act, upon one was *prima facie* evidence that it reached the other also.[4] Personal service may also be effected on a duly authorised agent. It is no plea that the agent had not communicated the service to his principal.[5]

When a notice to quit addressed to all the joint tenants was handed over to one of them who signed an acknowledgment of it the service is held to be good service.[6] The Supreme Court also has held that if a notice is addressed to both the joint tenants but served on one, the service is valid.[7] When the original tenant has died, a notice addressed to all the heirs but served on one of them is also held to be a valid service.[8] When one tenant holds a power of attorney for all the co-tenants service upon such power of attorney holder is held to be service to all.[9]

When one of the joint tenants was tendered the notice to quit addressed to all and he refused to accept the tender, such refusal amounts to service of notice on all joint tenants.[10] The earlier view of the Supreme Court reflected in *Kanji Manji* v *Trustees of the Port of Bombay* (supra) was that service on a joint tenant was good service no doubt, but the notice was to be addressed to all the joint tenants.[11] This view has been modified by the Supreme Court in *H.C. Pandey* v *G.C. Paul*,[12] wherein it is held that when a tenant dies, his tenancy devolves upon the heirs as joint tenants and not tenants-in-common and even if the notice under s. 106 of the Transfer of Property Act is issued and served upon one of the heirs of the deceased tenant is a valid service of notice even if the notice was neither addressed to nor served upon the others. The Calcutta High Court has followed the Supreme Court decision in *Kamala Devi* v *Arun.*[13] *H.C. Pandey's* case (supra) has been reiterated by the Supreme Court in *K.K. Manjerintha* v *V.M.T. Kalliani.*[14] However, a Division Bench of the Calcutta High Court in *Amal Aditya* v *Ganesh Das*[15] followed an earlier judgment of the Supreme Court by a three-judge Bench in *Boddu Venkatakrishna Rao* v *Boddu Satyavathi*[16] and without placing

4 AIR 1918 PC 102.
5 AIR 1918 PC 102.
6 *Ajit Kumar Ray* v *Satya Bala* AIR 1973 Cal 339.
7 *Kanji* v *Trustees of the Port of Bombay* AIR 1963 SC 468.
8 *A.M. Abdul Samad* v *Gulam Ahmed* AIR 1975 Guj 1; *Raman Bhai* v *Jivaram Sharma* AIR 1964 Bom 96.
9 *Abdul Sattar* v *Rameshwar* AIR 1992 SC 2065.
10 *Roshan* v *Purshottam Lal* AIR 1965 All 287.
11 AIR 1963 SC 468.
12 AIR 1989 SC 1470; (1989)3 SCC 77.
13 (1993)2 CHN 74.
14 1995 Supp (3) SCC 403.
15 (1998)1 CHN 521.
16 AIR 1968 SC 751.

any reliance on *H.C. Pandey's* case[17] held that the heirs of a tenant hold as tenants-in-common and not as joint tenants.

Where in a case of joint lease a notice is addressed to all the joint lessees, but is served only on one of them there is sufficient compliance.[18]

This raises a question whether a single copy of notice (with the mention of all the names of joint tenants) will do or whether there should be one copy for each of the joint tenants. Where such joint tenants constitute members of a joint family living together in the same house, service on one of them at their residence of a notice addressed to all of them is enough. In such a case, it is not necessary that separate copies must be served.[19]

Yet there is another circumstance when a lease is granted to one member of a Hindu joint family; for example, the oldest male member or a brother in a joint family but the demised premises are in occupation of all the members constituting the family. In such a case, the lease can be determined by a notice to quit issued to such member alone and it is not necessary to serve notice on all the members of the family.

The principle that a notice to quit addressed to all the tenants but served on one of them is sufficient, applies not only to the case of joint tenants but also to the case of tenants-in-common.[20]

Many tenants, certain tenant receiving notice in the capacity of General Power of Attorney holder on behalf of all tenants—There is service of notice on all tenants.[1]

2 Notice on co-heirs

A monthly tenancy is heritable and on the tenant's death his heirs inherit the property demised as 'tenants-in-common' and not as 'joint tenants' except in the case of coparceners in a joint Hindu family. In the case of co-tenants a notice addressed to one and served upon him is sufficient if the intention to terminate tenancy as a whole is clear.[2] Section 106 of the Transfer of Property Act does not require that the notice should be addressed to all the co-tenants or to everyone of them.

17 AIR 1989 SC 1470.

18 1956 All LJ 650; AIR 1964 All 52. Also see *Roshan* v *Purshottam Lal* AIR 1965 All 287; *Raman Bhai* v *Jivaram Sharma* AIR 1964 Bom 96; *Bhusan Chandra Paul* v *Bengal Coal Co. Ltd.* AIR 1966 Cal 63. Also see *Radhey Lal Mannia Lal* v *Bimal Kumar Jain* AIR 1980 All 84; *Budh Sen* v *Sheel Chandra Agarwal* AIR 1978 All 88; *Zakir* v *Md. Hussain Khan* AIR 1977 All 476.

19 4 CWN 572.

20 *Vatiyaveettil Konnappan* v *Mangot Vetia Kunniyil* AIR 1968 Ker 229; *Ajit Kumar Roy* v *Satyabala Dutta* AIR 1973 Cal 339 contra: *Ramesh Chand Bose* v *Gopeswar Pd. Sharma* AIR 1977 All 38.

1 *Abdul Sattar* v *Rameshwar* AIR 1992 SC 2065.

2 *Smt. Vishnuwati* v *Bhagwat Vithu Chowdhury* AIR 1970 All 389.

It may so happen that a lessee died leaving many heirs on whom devolved the leasehold interest of the deceased. To whom the notice is to be served? To any of them or to all? The answer is: to all. In *Anwarali Bepari* v *Jamini Lal Roy Chowdhury*, Nasim Ali, J. *held*: where a lessee dies leaving a number of heirs, all the heirs must be served with a notice to quit if the lease is to be determined. Further, where there are several co-lessees, one of whom dies, a notice to quit to the survivors alone is not enough. The notice to quit must be served on the heirs of the deceased also. Otherwise, the notice will not be sufficient to determine the lease.[3]

This principle applies equally to the cases where a sole tenant dies leaving several heirs. Separate notices to quit served on all of them are enough to determine the lease.

Again, where the lands of a tenure originally held by one person are sub-divided amongst his representatives in the title who continues to pay separately their portions of the rent, whether aliquot or otherwise, in the name of the original tenant, the landlord addressed separate notices to the present holder to quit the lands in their possession—*Held*, the notices to suit were good and valid.[4]

Where the lessee died leaving behind a widow and three sons and there was nothing to show that they were living in common society; a notice served on the widow alone is not sufficient despite the fact that the names of the sons were also mentioned in it.[5] The heirs of the lessee are co-tenants and not joint tenants. This is the position in view of s. 19(*b*) of the Hindu Succession Act 1956. The principle of joint tenancy is restricted in Hindu Law to the relations between the coparceners. It has no application outside the coparcenery. It does not apply to the relation between the coparceners and their landlord. Courts strongly lean against joint tenants.[6]

Co-tenancy and joint tenancy—distinguished in *Ram Awalamb* v *Jata Sankar*.[7]

3 Notice on lessee's co-assignees

The assignee of a lessee is entitled to a notice to quit under s. 106 of the Transfer of Property Act 1882; for an assignee stands in the shoes of the assignor, i.e. original lessee and there is privity between such assignee and the lessor.[8] It stands to reason, therefore, that if there be joint or co-assignees, each of them is entitled to a notice to quit.

3 AIR 1940 Cal 89. Dissented in *Tata Iron & Steel Co.* v *Abdul Ahad* AIR 1970 Pat 338.
4 6 CWN 134 (*per* Rampini and Gupta, JJ.).
5 *Ganga Pershad* v *Smt. Tribeni Devi* AIR 1976 Del 145.
6 *Ganga Pershad* v *Smt. Tribeni Devi* AIR 1976 Del 145 at p. 146.
7 AIR 1969 All 526.
8 5 CLJ 205.

4 Service of notice on karta of HUF

When the tenancy was taken by a joint Hindu family, whether the tenancy is joint tenancy or tenancy in common, service of notice upon the *karta* is a valid service.[9]

5 Notice on benamdars

A *benamdar* is not entitled to receive a notice whether it be a notice to quit or otherwise.

Where a tenancy is purchased by one person in *benami* in the name of another, a notice to the real purchaser will serve the purpose of law. A notice to *benamdar* is not necessary; for, neither he is interested nor he has any business save lending his name. In *Gopal Chandra Das* v *Satya Bhanu Ghosal*, Newbould, J. *held*: the defendant No. 8 was the *benamdar* of his father, the defendant No. 7. It could not be urged that any notice on the defendant's son was necessary.[10]

If *benamdars* are more than one, the position remains the same.

6 Notice on sub-tenants (sub-lessees)

A sub-lessee, for obvious reason, is not entitled to any notice to quit from the landlord or the lessor before he can be ejected by the superior lessor; the reason being that there is no privity between the two.[11] The same provision applies to the case where there are several sub-lessees. The determination of a lease by a valid notice by the lessor will automatically put an end to any sub-lease granted by the lessee.[12]

Where during the pendency of an ejectment suit by the landlord against the tenant and the sub-tenant, the latter is declared a direct tenant under s. 16(3) of the West Bengal Premises Tenancy Act 1956 (corresponding to s. 26(3) of the West Bengal Premises Tenancy Act 1997), the upgraded sub-tenant is neither entitled to a notice under s. 106 of the Transfer of Property Act nor one under sub-sec. (6) of s. 13 of the West Bengal Premises Tenancy Act 1956 (corresponds to s. 6(4) of the West Bengal Premises Tenancy Act 1997). Such a tenancy is not a lease and the landlord is not required to determine it by a notice under s. 106 of the Transfer of Property Act.[13]

9 *Jayanta* v *Sarama* ILR (1968)1 Cal 385.
10 AIR 1926 Cal 634.
11 5 CLJ 205.
12 *Shambhu* v *Kanai* AIR 1936 Cal 581.
13 *V.R. Verma* v *Mohan Kumar Mukherjee* AIR 1962 Cal 563.

CHAPTER 8

Waiver of Notice

SYNOPSIS

1 Waiver of a notice—meaning of the expression
2 Waiver of a notice under the Transfer of Property Act
3 Waiver of notice under the West Bengal Premises Tenancy Act
4 Waiver of a notice under s. 80 of the Code of Civil Procedure
5 Waiver of a notice under s. 106 of the Railways Act 1989
6 Waiver of a notice under the Municipal Acts
7 Waiver of a notice under the Revenue law
8 Waiver of a notice under other Acts
9 Right to plead waiver—third party not entitled
10 Waiver—what amounts to

1 Waiver of a notice—meaning of the expression

Waiver of notice means the loss of a right to make a claim or argument because it was not raised at the right time or because its maker otherwise did not follow necessary rules.[1] To waive is to forbear to insist on a right or to forbear to exercise a right and 'waiver' is explicit waiving a right. A waiver is an intentional relinquishment of a known right. There can be no waiver unless the person against whom the waiver is claimed had further knowledge of his rights and of facts enabling him to take effective action for the enforcement of such rights.[2] In most litigious situations the expression 'waiver' is used to describe a voluntary, informed and unequivocal election by a party not to claim a right or raise an objection which it is open to that party to claim or raise.[3] It is in this sense that the term 'waiver' has been used in legal texts. The principle of waiver connotes issuance of notice and non-response thereto. Everyone has a right to waive an advantage or protection which law seeks to give him/her undoubtedly. If a notice is issued and no representation is made by the concerned person, it would amount to waive the opportunity and such person cannot be permitted to turn around.[4]

1 *Black's Law Dictionary*, 10th Edition.
2 *Associated Hotels of India Ltd.* v *SB Sardar Ranjit Singh* AIR 1968 SC 933.
3 *Millor* v *Dickson* [2002]3 All ER 1041 (PC).
4 *Jaswantsingh Mathurasingh* v *Ahmedabad Municipal Corporation* 1992 Supp (1) SCC 5; AIR 1991 SC 2130.

But there may be circumstances when law permits waiver of a notice. To take an example, a man had issued a notice, he could bring an action. Instead, he accepts rent from the tenant in respect of the demised premises, for the period subsequent to notice. The notice to quit is waived. When the Defendant Union of India in a Railway claim case or in any other suit or the State Government does not raise in the written statement or even during trial any objection as to the notice under s. 80, CPC, the notice should be deemed to have been waived.

It is entirely wrong to say that a statutory notice cannot be waived; for "there is no inconsistency between the propositions that the provisions in the section are mandatory and must be enforced by the court and that they may be waived by the authority for whose benefit they are provided."[5]

The fact of waiver can be ascertained from the express words of the authority concerned or from their conduct[6] and the mandatory nature of a notice is not a bar to its waiver.[7] When an employee in a government service opts for voluntary retirement from service by giving three months' notice in writing, and also requests for *waiver of notice* period, if any proceeding is not pending against such employee, the retirement shall come into force automatically if the appointing authority does not refuse the permission during the notice period.[8]

2 Waiver of a notice under the Transfer of Property Act

Section 111 of the Transfer of Property Act deals with determination of lease by issue of a notice. It reads:

> "111. A lease of immovable property determines—
>
> * * *
>
> "(*h*) on the expiration of a notice to determine the lease, or to quit, or of intention to quit, the property leased, duly given by one party to the other."[9]

Again, s. 113 of the Transfer of Property Act reads:

> "113. A notice given under section 111, clause (*h*), is waived, with the express or implied consent of the person to whom it is given, by any act on the part of the person giving it showing an intention to treat the lease as subsisting."

Illustrations, appended to s. 113 of the Act, give instances of what constitutes a waiver.

> *Illustration: (a) A*, the lessor, gives *B*, the lessee, notice to quit the property leased. The notice expires. *B* tenders and *A* accepts, rent which has become due in respect of the property since the expiration of the notice. The notice is waived.

5 *Vellayyaram Chettiar* v *Government of the Province of Madras* AIR 1947 PC 197.
6 *Ramcharan Mahato* v *Custodian of Evacuee Property* AIR 1964 Pat 275.
7 *Vellayyaram Chettiar* v *Government of the Province of Madras* AIR 1947 PC 197; *State of Bihar* v *Kamaksha Prasad* AIR 1962 Pat 303.
8 *State of Haryana* v *S.K. Singhal* (1999)4 SCC 293; AIR 1999 SC 1829.
9 *Palani Ammal* v *Viswanatha Chettiar* (1998)3 SCC 654; AIR 1998 SC 1309.

Illustration: (b) A, the lessor, gives *B*, the lessee, notice to quit the property leased. The notice expires, and *B* remains in possession. *A* gives to *B* as lessee a second notice to quit. The first notice is waived.

Acceptance of rent accrued due subsequent to the notice is a waiver of the notice.[10] If after the notice to quit, the tenant tendered rent for the post notice period by money order to the landlord and continued in possession and thereafter second notice was served on him, in such case it may be said that there was implied waiver of the first notice.[11] The landlord gave a notice to quit to the tenant, who gave a reply that the notice was not valid, and he continued in possession after the expiry of the notice period. Landlord, thereafter, treating the lease as subsisting gave a subsequent notice to quit. The first notice was impliedly waived.[12] But mere receipt of money for any period subsequent to the period of notice would not amount to waiver unless it could be shown that the said money was knowingly accepted by the landlord as rent and that too with the intention to treat the lease as subsisting.[13] Mere acceptance of the sum tendered by the tenant after service of notice is not sufficient to constitute waiver. Intention to continue the lease is necessary.[14]

The acceptance by mistake will not be a waiver.[15] The acceptance of rent must be by the lessor. The lessor cannot be bound by activities of a stranger. Receiving rent for 60 days period given to vacate the premises under notice cannot be treated as waiver to such notice.[16] Acceptance of rent by an unauthorised person will not be a waiver of notice.[17]

Where the suit for eviction was based on second notice but there was no pleading by the defendant lessee as to unilateral waiver of the first notice by the plaintiff nor there was evidence that the first notice was acted upon by the defendant, the contention that it could not be said that there was unilateral waiver of the first notice on the part of the plaintiff was rejected.[18] Issuance of the second notice amounts to waiver of its earlier one. So, if any suit is filed within 12 years from the date of second notice is in time.[1] Waiver

10 *Maniklal* v *Kadambini* AIR 1926 Cal 763; *Ram Dayal* v *Jawla Prasad* AIR 1966 All 623; *Tayabali Jaferbhai Tankiwala* v *M/s. Asha & Co.* AIR 1971 SC 102; (1970)1 SCC 46.

11 *Malina Mondal* v *Puspa Rani Dasi* AIR 1991 Cal 291.

12 *Sudhir Kumar Paul* v *Indu Prova Ghosh* AIR 1976 Cal 274.

13 *Satya Prakesh* v *5th A.D.J.* 1999 AIHC 1799 (All).

14 *New India Assurance Company Ltd.* v *Ghanshyam Das* AIR 1997 All 383.

15 *Commissioners of Hazaribagh Municipality* v *Fulchand Agarwalla* AIR 1966 Pat 434; *Post Master General, Lucknow* v *District Judge, Mathura* AIR 2006 All 1.

16 *Lachmi Lal* v *Ganesh Chamar* AIR 1932 Pat 259; *Hasmat Rai* v *Tarachand* AIR 1979 Bom 95.

17 *Ganga Narain* v *Bal Kishan* AIR 1964 Punj 356.

18 *Provash Chandra Chatterjee* v *Chand Mohon Basak* AIR 1978 Cal 224.

1 *B.S. Sadananda* v *K.S. Chinnappa* AIR 2006 Kant 57; 2006 AIHC 23 NOC.

of first notice by service of second notice—latter, in reply to tenant's communication on first notice, extending time to vacate only for the reason that the first notice had not been acted upon—*Held*, there is no waiver of first notice.[2]

Acceptance of rent for the period subsequent to notice under protest as where he stated that he accepted it as damages for use and occupation will not prevent it from operating as a waiver of the notice,[3] but acceptance of rent accrued due for a period anterior to the notice to quit is not a waiver of the notice to quit.[4] The acceptance of rent must be by the lessor. The lessor cannot be bound by activities of a stranger. In *Lachmi Lal* v *Ganesh Chamar*,[5] it was held: Acceptance of rent by an unauthorised person does not bind the landlord and will not constitute a waiver of the notice.

Reading s. 106 and s. 111(*h*) of the Transfer of Property Act together, it is evident that the monthly lease comes to an end on expiration of 30 days from the date of service of notice under s. 106, T.P. Act on the lessee. So, even after the issuance of notice under s. 106 of the T.P. Act by the lessor to the lessee, the tenancy continues for a period of 30 days from the date of service of such notice on the lessee and the lease stands determined on expiration of the said period of 30 days from the date of service of the said notice. Therefore, the lessee continues to be liable for rent for the said period of 30 days from the date of service of notice. So acceptance of rent for such period would not amount to waiver.[6]

Where a contractual tenancy is terminated by notice to quit, the tenant becomes a statutory tenant. The mere fact that the arrears of rent tendered by the legal representative of the tenant were accepted by the plaintiff does not make him his tenant. For mere acceptance of rent does not operate as a waiver of notice to quit served upon the tenant since deceased.[7] Again, "where a contractual tenancy to which the Rent Control legislation applies has expired by efflux of time or by determination by notice to quit and the tenant continues in possession of the premises, acceptance of rent from the tenant by the landlord after the expiration or determination of the contractual tenancy will not afford ground for holding that the landlord has assented to a new contractual tenancy.[8] This was followed in *Jamil-ud-din Khan* v *Niaz*

2 *Narang Overseas Pvt. Ltd.* v *Mehar Chand Kohli* AIR 1977 NOC 363 (Del).

3 *B.N. Rly. Co.* v *Bal Mukund* AIR 1923 Cal 663.

4 *Ratneswar* v *Sreekamal Deb* AIR 1921 Cal 126; 63 IC 191.

5 AIR 1932 Pat 259; *Hashmat Rai* v *Tarachand* AIR 1979 Bom 95 (for a period before the expiry of notice).

6 *Yashpal Lala Shiv Narain* v *Allatala Tala Malik Waqf Ajakhan Mus* AIR 2006 All 115; (2006)2 ALJ 204; *Sarup Singh Gupta* v *S. Jagdish Singh* AIR 2006 SC 1734; (2006)4 SCC 205.

7 *Ganga Narain* v *Balkishan* AIR 1964 Punj 356.

8 *Ganga Dutt Murarka* v *Kartick Chandra Das* AIR 1961 SC 1067.

Ahmad holding, *inter alia*, no fresh tenancy was created by the acceptance of rent nor there was a waiver.[9]

Coming to Illustration (b)

Section 113 of the Transfer of Property Act permits the waiver of notice by the express or implied consent of the person upon whom it is served. When the tenant on the receipt of the first notice continues to remain in possession of the disputed property, he thereby gives his implied consent to the waiver of the notice.[10] The giving of a second notice to quit is a waiver of the first notice so far as the person giving notice is concerned. Further, if the first notice is bad in law, it is hardly a notice which should call for any waiver.[11]

Illustration (*b*) of s. 113 of the Transfer of Property Act shows that if a tenant continues in possession after expiry of the period of notice given by the lessor and the lessor serves a second notice, there is waiver of the first notice. Once a notice to quit is served upon the tenant the tenancy comes to an end on expiry of the term of the notice and, unless consent of other party is obtained to continue the old tenancy, no second notice can be issued. The Supreme Court in *Calcutta Credit Corporation Ltd.* v *Happy Homes Pvt. Ltd.*[12] has expressed this view. But in *Tayabali* v *Asha & Co.*[13] the Supreme Court, in the light of Illustration (*b*) of s. 113, has held that when subsequently another notice is served upon the tenant, and the tenant did not act upon the first notice, issuance of second notice acts as the waiver of the first notice to quit.

3 Waiver of notice under the West Bengal Premises Tenancy Act

After service of first quit notice the tenant continues to be in possession even after expiry of notice period. Second quit notice is served. There is implied waiver of first notice. Suit on the basis of second notice is not bad.[14] Notice asking the tenant to execute fresh rent note, sent during routine administration of trust property—Earlier notice to quit not waived.[15]

A notice under s. 106 of the Transfer of Property Act, not being under the special Act, can be waived by a tenant.[16]

9 AIR 1964 All 393.
10 *Ram Dayal* v *Jawla Prasad* AIR 1966 All 623.
11 AIR 1961 Raj 136.
12 AIR 1968 SC 471; (1968)2 SCR 20.
13 AIR 1971 SC 102; see also *Chandra Kishore* v *Renuka* 84 CWN 314.
14 *Sm. Malina Mondal* v *Puspa Rani Dasi* AIR 1991 Cal 291; *Balmiki Das Gupta* v *Lt. Col. S.K. Mitra* 94 CWN 1129.
15 AIR 1963 Raj 113.
16 *K.N. Ramakrishnan* v *C. Keral Chand* AIR 1971 Mad 150.

4 Waiver of a notice under s. 80 of the Code of Civil Procedure

It is open to a defendant, for whose benefit a notice is prescribed by law, to waive it.[17] Thus where the plea of defect in or want of notice was not pressed in the trial court, nor was it raised in the memorandum of the first appeal and of the second appeal, the High Court, in the circumstances of the case, held that the right based on the ground of notice was waived.[18]

A mandatory provision can also be waived.[19] The notice required to be given under s. 80, CPC is for the protection of the authority concerned. If in a particular case he does not require that protection and says so, he can lawfully waive his right to the notice. In other words, there is no reason why the notice should not be waived if the authority concerned thinks fit to waive it.[20] Waiver of notice under s. 80, CPC is possible under law. Where plea regarding lack of valid notice was taken up in original written statement, it was not necessary that after amendment of plaint the plea should be taken up again in the amended written statement. Not taking up the plea in the amended written statement, did not, in fact, amount to waiver of the requirement of valid notice.[1]

If State has not raised an issue of non-service of notice under s. 80, CPC in the written statement or additional written statement filed in the suit, it is deemed to have waived the objection.[2] By mere filing of an application under s. 80(2), CPC, it cannot be presumed that the application is granted. If the application filed under s. 80(2) is ultimately granted, the objection with regard to non-issue of notice cannot be raised and in that event the suit would not fail on account of non-issuance of notice under s. 80(1), CPC.[3]

Where the cause of action against the provincial Government is the passing of an Act which deprives the plaintiff of his rights to property and the Government, knowing that a notice under s. 80, CPC required a period of two months, gives effect to the Act whereby the plaintiff is actually deprived of his rights to property within a month of the coming into operation of the Act, the Government must be held to have waived its right to the notice under the section.[4] Where a notice under s. 80 is given to the Secretary of

17 *State of Bihar* v *Kamaksha Prosad* AIR 1962 Pat 303.

18 *District Board, Banaras* v *Churhu Rai* AIR 1956 All 680. Also see *Paleti Sivaramakrishnaiah* v *Executive Engineer* AIR 1978 AP 389; *State* v *Bamadev* AIR 1971 Ori 227 and *Hirachand Himatlal* v *Kashinath Thakurji* AIR 1942 Bom 339.

19 *Dhirendra Nath Gorai* v *Sudhir Chandra Ghosh* AIR 1964 SC 1300.

20 *Vellayyaram Chettiyar* v *Govt. of the Province of Madras* AIR 1947 PC 197.

1 *Bishandayal & Sons* v *State of Orissa* (2001)1 SCC 555; AIR 2001 SC 544.

2 *State of AP* v *Pioneer Builders, AP* (2006)12 SCC 119.

3 *State of Kerala* v *Sudhir Kumar Sharma* (2013)10 SCC 178.

4 *Province of Bihar* v *Kamakshya Narain Singh* AIR 1950 Pat 366 contra: *State of Bihar* v *Jiwandas Arya* AIR 1971 Pat 141.

State for India in Council but not to the Public Officer and in the suit for damages for the wrongful act of the latter filed against both of them, no objection is taken at an early stage that the suit is bad for want of a notice to the Public Officer, the notice will be deemed to have been waived and the suit cannot be dismissed in its entirety because it has been dismissed against the Public Officer for want of notice.[5] The defendant filed a full and complete written statement on merits—raised objection of court-fees and joined issues with the plaintiffs on this point and fought up to High Court. After one year and nine months, the defendant filed an additional written statement in which he put forward a plea for the first time as to the want of notice under s. 80—*Held* that with the facts in the background, coupled with the delay, the defendant should be deemed to have waived his rights to a notice under s. 80, CPC.[6] Objection as to the notice raised in a written statement but not pressed at the trial and regarding which no issue was raised must be treated as waived.[7] Where the written statement that contained to objection that the suit was not the maintainable for want of notice, nor was any issue framed thereon and the defendant did not apply to amend the written statement for incorporating the plea, it must be held that the defendant waived objection.[8]

But there may be cases where mere delay did not amount to waiver.[9] Likewise, mere failure to raise the question of notice under s. 80, CPC cannot be *per se* a waiver of the notice. It was enough if the objection was raised before the trial commenced.[10] Mere negligence in not raising plea as to notice at early stage will not amount to waiver or estoppel unless there is duty of care.[11] Causing of serious and irreparable damages resulting from service of a notice under s. 80, CPC and waiting for a statutory interval of two months cannot be regarded as constituting waiver on the part of the Government.[12] Impossibility of compliance cannot attract the principle of waiver.[13] Any prejudice to the plaintiff caused by the delay would result in the defendant being deemed to have waived his right to notice, even though delay, however long, would not necessarily by itself be a ground for holding that he has waived it.[14]

5 *Secretary of State* v *Sheoramjee Hanumantrao* AIR 1952 Nag 213 (DB).
6 *Vasant* v *Khaddathar* AIR 1949 Nag 25.
7 *Purna Chandra Sarkar* v *Radharani Dasya* AIR 1931 Cal 175.
8 *Suraj Bhan* v *Executive Engineer* AIR 1973 All 269.
9 *Ramcharan Mahoto* v *Custodian of Evacuee Property* AIR 1964 Pat 275.
10 *Murarilal* v *E.V. David* AIR 1925 All 241.
11 *Vellayyaram Chettiyar* v *Govt. of the Province of Madras* AIR 1947 PC 197.
12 *State of Bihar* v *Kamaksha Prasad Sarma* AIR 1962 Pat 303; *Bhagchand Dagdusa Gujrati* v *Secretary of State for India* AIR 1927 PC 176; *Vellayyaram Chettiar* v *Government of the Province of Madras* (supra) relied on.
13 *State of Bihar* v *Jiwandas Arya* AIR 1971 Pat 141.
14 *Hirachand Himatlal* v *Kashinath* AIR 1942 Bom 339.

Who is competent to waive the notice is the next question. The object of a notice under s. 80, CPC is well established. In *Gaja* v *Dasa Koeri*, Gangeswar Prasad, J. held: "It is to acquaint the authorities mentioned in the section of the facts and circumstances which are said to necessitate the institution of the threatened suit and to afford them an opportunity to take stock of the situation and avoid litigation, if so advised, by settling the claim or making amends. The section is thus intended to grant to such authorities a special protection for their own benefit of which, if they so choose, they may avail. It is also well established, and on the basis of this accepted purpose of s. 80, that the objection to entertainability of a suit for want of notice may be waived by the authorities concerned."[15] It is permissible for a party, for whose advantage for provision of notice under s. 80 of the Code of Civil Procedure has been made, to waive it.[16] Want of notice cannot be pleaded by strangers.[17] In other words, it is open to the party protected by s. 80 to waive his rights to a notice and his waiver binds the rest of the parties. "A third party is not competent to raise the question of notice when the Secretary of State has waived it."[18] In *Hira Chand Himat Lal* v *Kashinath Thakarji*,[19] it was held: A party who has himself no right to notice cannot challenge a suit on the ground of want of notice.

Whether or not in the particular circumstances of a case there has been a waiver is a different matter. The court can take note of a waiver either from the express words of the authority concerned or from their conduct.[20] Hereinbelow is an example when waiver was inferred from conduct: "If the State Government could be said to have waived its objection by not taking a plea to that effect in a written statement filed by it, it can, in my opinion, be said with equal reason that the State Government waived it by filing no written statement at all".[1]

When an amendment of plaint introduced a new cause of action then a fresh notice is required. Right of such a notice can be waived by the party for whose benefit it has been provided.[2] The mandatory nature of s. 80, CPC is not a bar to waiver of a notice under the section.[3] Notice under s. 80, CPC or equivalent notices under s. 527 of the Bombay Municipal Corporation Act

15 *Gaja* v *Dasa Koeri* AIR 1964 All 471.
16 *Lakshmi Narain Gauri* v *Union of India* AIR 1958 Pat 489.
17 AIR 1965 SC 1938.
18 AIR 1933 Pat 49.
19 AIR 1942 Bom 339; *Gaja* v *Dasa Koeri* AIR 1964 All 471. Also see *The Commissioner of Taxes* v *Golak Nath Kakati* AIR 1979 Gau 10.
20 *Province of Bihar* v *Kamakshya Narain Singh* AIR 1950 Pat 366; *Gaja* v *Dasa Koeri* AIR 1964 All 471.
1 *Gaja* v *Dasa Koeri* (supra).
2 *Bishandayal* v *State of Orissa* AIR 2001 SC 544; (2001)1 SCC 555.
3 *Vellayyaram Chettiar* v *Govt. of the Province of Madras* AIR 1947 PC 197; *State of Bihar* v *Kamaksha Prosad* AIR 1962 Pat 303.

are for the benefit of the respondent and the same can be waived as they do not go to the root of jurisdiction.[4]

If a statute makes it imperative to do something which creates a protection or right in favour of the authority, the mere fact of there being tremendous difficulty in compliance with that requirement even going to the extent of impossibility would not attract the principle of waiver and cannot lead to the conclusion that in such a situation the authority will be deemed to have waived its right to get the notice.[5]

5 Waiver of a notice under s. 106 of the Railways Act 1989

Requirements of a notice under s. 106 (corresponds to s. 78B of the Indian Railways Act 1890) of the Railways Act may be waived[6] in proper circumstances though in another Calcutta case it was held by Bachawat, J. that there could not be any waiver.[7] On the face of it, the decision of the latter case is opposed to the first. The controversy was resolved by the Supreme Court in *Governor-General in Council* v *Musaddilal*[8] which is in conformity with Division Bench of the Calcutta High Court in *Gajanon Dhanuka* v *Union of India.*[9] Having regard to the "imperative language of the section", the courts have held that the service of notice is mandatory and not merely discretionary.

While the service of notice under s. 106 of the Act is mandatory, it would depend in certain circumstances whether the notice has waived such protection of law.

A notice of a claim on the Chief Commercial Manager does not amount to preferment of a claim to the Railway Administration. But where the Chief Commercial Superintendent in reply to the notice refused to entertain the claim on the ground that there was no negligence or misconduct on the part of the railway or its servants, but did not say that the claim could not be entertained for non-service of notice under s. 106 nor was the validity of the notice disputed, it amounted to waiver by the Chief Commercial Superintendent of the protection of s. 106, and as he was dealing with the claim as an agent of the Railway Administration which term included the

4 *Amar Nath Dogra* v *Union of India* AIR 1963 SC 424; *State of Punjab* v *Geeta Iron and Brass Works Ltd.* (1978)1 SCC 68; AIR 1978 SC 1608; *Ghanshyam Dass* v *Dominion of India* (1984)3 SCC 46; *Vasant Ambades Pondit* v *Bombay Municipal Corporation* AIR 1981 Bom 394; *Gangappa Gurupadappa Gugwad* v *Rachawwa* AIR 1971 SC 442; (1970)3 SCC 716; *Bishandayal & Sons* v *State of Orissa* (2001)1 SCC 555; AIR 2001 SC 544.

5 *State of Bihar* v *Kamaksha Prasad* AIR 1962 Pat 303; *State of Bihar* v *Jiwandas Arya* AIR 1971 Pat 141.

6 *Gajanan Dhanuka* v *Union of India* 56 CWN 83.

7 *Radhamadhab Kundu* v *Union of India* 61 CWN 433.

8 AIR 1961 SC 725.

9 AIR 1959 Cal 215; 63 CWN 581.

defendant, the Union of India, the waiver of the Chief Commercial Superintendent amounted in law to waiver by the Union of India.[10] Again, where the Claims Officer did entertain the claim made by plaintiffs and did not turn it down on the ground that proper notice under s. 106 of the Railways Act 1989 had not been served on the General Manager: *Held*, that service of notice under s. 106 of the Railways Act 1989, according to the procedure prescribed in s. 140 (new s. 192 of Railways Act 1989) was waived by the Railway Administration in this case, inasmuch as it allowed the Claims Officer to investigate the claim made by the plaintiffs even without service of notice according to the statute.[11] Where the Railway Administration contested the suit on the footing that it was a case of non-delivery and not of loss, and the defence failed, the Railway Administration cannot claim that the suit should be dismissed for want of notice under s. 77 of 1890 Act.[12] When a defective notice is addressed to a proper officer and such officer, instead of ignoring the defective notice, enters into correspondence and makes enquiries, the defect in the notice stands waived.[13]

6 Waiver of a notice under the Municipal Acts

The principle that a notice under s. 80, CPC is for the protection of the authority concerned and, if in a particular case, he does not require that notice, he can lawfully waive his right to the notice, applies to a notice under s. 48 of the CP and Berar Municipalities Act. When in a suit against the Municipal Committee no objection was raised in the written statement by any of the defendants about the notice under s. 48, it should be taken that they waived their right to such a notice.[14] Waiver of a notice depends upon the facts and circumstances of each case.[15]

It stands to reason that in like circumstances the principle of waiver will apply to Acts of other Municipalities as well which prescribe issue of notice prior to institution of a suit.

7 Waiver of a notice under the Revenue law

In taxation Acts, a notice is mandatory and, generally speaking, there can be no waiver of any notice under the provisions of such Acts. Revenue statutes are based on public policy. Revenue statutes protect the public on the one hand and confer power on the State on the other. If a notice under s. 7(2) of the Assam Taxation on Goods Carried by Road or on Inland Waterways Act 1961 was not issued, such non-issuances of notice could not be pleaded as waiver of right to assessment under this Act. Estoppel is not

10 *South Indian Co-operative Stores* v *Union of India* AIR 1957 Cal 17; 60 CWN 985.
11 *Gajanon Dhanuka* v *Union of India* AIR 1959 Cal 215.
12 *Mahadeo Lal* v *Union of India* AIR 1959 Pat 202; ILR 37 Pat 1034.
13 *State of West Bengal* v *Union of India* 1986(1) Cal HN 75; AIR 1987 Cal 226.
14 *Kishore* v *Municipal Committee, Piparia* AIR 1958 MP 393.
15 *Chandra Kant Khaire* v *Dr. Shanta Ram Kale* AIR 1988 SC 1665; (1988)4 SCC 577.

a cause of action but waiver is contractual and may constitute a cause of action. The reason is that waiver is an agreement to release or not to assert a right. There is no such thing as "estoppel by waiver". A procedural provision may be waived by conduct or agreement.[16]

The want of a notice affects the jurisdiction of the Income-tax Officer to proceed with the assessment. Assessee's filing of the 'Return' under protest or his failure to raise specifically the point in his application for revision under s. 27 could not constitute a waiver.[17]

8 Waiver of a notice under other Acts

Where time has not been made the essence of the contract or, by reason of waiver, the time fixed has ceased to be applicable, the employing party may by notice fix a reasonable time for the completion of the work and dismiss the employed party on a failure to complete by the date so fixed.[18] In the absence of notice (under s. 8(2) of the Arbitration Act 1940, now s. 11(4) of the Arbitration and Conciliation Act 1996) of the request by one of the parties to the other party to appoint an arbitrator, the court has no power to appoint an arbitrator.[19]

9 Right to plead waiver—third party not entitled

It is only the party entitled to a notice who can raise the question of maintainability of a suit on the ground of want of notice.[20] A third party is not competent.[21]

> "Objection as to non-service of notice can properly be taken not by third parties, but only by the person on whom the notice is not served".[22]

10 Waiver—what amounts to

It is explicitly waiving a right.

To sum up: "To be a waiver, there must be conscious relinquishment of one's right. To waive rights there must be not only the knowledge of these rights but unequivocal expression of intention to waive them".[23] Waiver may be inferred from conduct as well.[24]

16 *Supdt. of Taxes* v *Onkarmal Nathmal Trust* (1976)1 SCC 766.
17 AIR 1961 Assam 35.
18 *Hind Construction Contractors* v *State of Maharashtra* (1979)2 SCC 70; AIR 1979 SC 720.
19 *Poran Lal* v *Rupchand* AIR 1931 All 761.
20 *Gaja* v *Dasa Koeri* AIR 1964 All 471.
21 *Hira Chand Himat Lal* v *Kashinath Thakarji* AIR 1933 Pat 49; *Venkataswami* v *Mahalakshmi* AIR 1949 Mad 747; *Kenakku Karthiyani Pillai* v *Neelacanta Pillai* AIR 1969 Ker 280.
22 AIR 1965 SC 1938.
23 73 CWN 192 (*per* Sabyasachi Mukherjee, J.).
24 *Batto Mal* v *Rameshwar Nath* AIR 1971 Del 98.

CHAPTER 9

Savings of Limitation where Notice is Statutory

[Section 15(2) of the Limitation Act 1963]

SYNOPSIS

1 Computation of the period of limitation–exclusion of the period of notice of suit
2 Notice–not a notice of suit–exclusion of the period disallowed
3 Exclusion of period disallowed when no cause of action arises
4 Notice against one of several defendants–exclusion allowed
5 Adverse possession–notice of suit when obligatory–exclusion allowed
6 Effects of s. 15(2), Limitation Act–does not alter the period of limitation
7 Arbitration and Conciliation Act–application of the Limitation Act 1963
8 Miscellaneous cases where exclusion allowed or disallowed under s. 15(2) of the Limitation Act 1963

1 Computation of the period of limitation—exclusion of the period of notice of suit

There are cases when a notice of suit is a condition precedent to the institution of a suit. Unless the notice contemplated has been served on the proposed defendant, the plaintiff, in the event of a suit being brought, will be non-suited. To illustrate, a notice under s. 80, CPC in a suit against the Union or a State Government or a Public Officer of any of such Governments, a notice to quit under s. 106 of the Transfer of Property Act on the lessee, a notice under s. 89 under the Waqf Act 1995 on the Board, a notice under s. 50(1) of the Administration of Evacuee Property Act on the custodian, a notice under s. 52 of the Land Acquisition Act, a notice under s. 90 of the Right to Fair Compensation and Transparency in Land Acquisition, Rehabilitation and Resettlement Act 2013 and so on. The list is only illustrative and not comprehensive. In such cases where a notice has to be given in accordance with requirements of any enactment for the time being in force in computing the period of limitation, the period of such notice shall be excluded.

The relevant provision of the Limitation Act of 1963 is virtually the same as in the Limitation Act 1908, which reads:

Section 15(2). "In computing the period of limitation for any suit of which notice has been given, or for which the previous consent or sanction of the Government or any other authority is required, in accordance with the requirements of any law for the time being in force, the period of such notice or, as the case may be, the time required for obtaining such consent or sanction shall be excluded."

For application of benefits of s. 15(2) a notice must be given and, secondly, the notice must conform to the requirements of the existing law.

It, therefore, appears that the provision in sub-sec. (2) of s. 15 of the Limitation Act 1963 will apply only where the enactment requires that a notice should be given before a suit is commenced. Section 167 of the Bombay Municipal Act enjoins that no suit be commenced without one month's notice in writing, nor after six months from the date of the act complained of. Baker, J. *held* in *Chhagan Lal Sarkar Lal* v *The Municipality of Thana*[1]: "I hold therefore that s. 167, Bombay District Municipal Act is subject to s. 15(2) of the Limitation Act and, therefore, the plaintiff is entitled to exclude the period of one month of notice from the period of limitation for this suit. The plaintiff is entitled to include in the limitation period the two-month period required to serve a notice as required by s. 31 of the Bombay Court of Wards Act (Act 1 of 1905), on defendants who were Government wards at the time the cause of action arose, and the extension cannot be refused on the ground that they ceased to be wards before the suit came up for hearing.[2] It, therefore, stands to reason that subsequently even when a notice becomes unnecessary, the plaintiff is still entitled to exclusion if at the time of giving notice it was required to be given by law. The law was fully discussed in *Oudh Behari Lal* v *Collector of Etah* where it was *held*: The defendant is Ward of Court and under the local Court of Wards Act a notice of two months is necessary to the Court of Wards before a suit can be instituted. The plaintiff was, therefore, entitled to bring a suit within 12 years and 2 months.[3]

Where a plaintiff is required to give notice to the Government under s. 80, Code of Civil Procedure he is entitled under s., 15(2) of the Act to exclude the period of notice, i.e. two months in computing the period of limitation prescribed for the suit.[4] Section 80, CPC only prescribes a condition precedent for the institution of the suit and has nothing to do with the period of limitation for a suit except that under s. 15(2) of the Limitation Act

1 AIR 1932 Bom 259.
2 *B & N.W. Rly.* v *Ram Sarup Khanderao* v *Chanmallappa* AIR 1924 Bom 364 (365).
3 *Oudh Behari Lal* v *Collector of Etah* AIR 1928 All 625.
4 *N.W. Roy* v *Ramdhan* 38 IC 600; AIR 1923 Mad 665; *State of Rajasthan* v *Rao Dhir Singh* AIR 1972 Raj 241; *Amar Chand Inani* v *Union of India* AIR 1973 SC 313; (1972)2 SCWR 805; (1973)1 SCC 115; *Laxmichand* v *Dominion of India* AIR 1955 Nag 265; *I.S.P. Trading Co.* v *Union of India* AIR 1973 Cal 74.

1963 and the period of notice can be deducted in calculating the period of limitation.[5]

In *Jai Singh* v *Mansha Ram*[6] the above principle was followed: "What the section provides is that in computing the period of limitation prescribed for any suit the period of notice given in accordance with the requirement of any enactment for the time being in force shall be excluded". In computing the period of limitation prescribed under s. 320(2) of the Assam Municipal Act, the plaintiff is entitled to exclude the period of one month's notice prescribed in that section by reason of s. 29(2) of the 1963 Act.[7] Where a plaintiff brings a suit against a State Railway, he is entitled to deduct the period of two months' notice given to the Secretary of State.[8]

When a notice is served upon the Railway authority under s. 80, CPC and the suit is filed before expiry of two months and application for dispensing with necessity of notice was also filed and when the court does not return the plaint as required under s. 80(2), CPC but granted permission, in such a case the plaintiff cannot be deprived of the statutory benefit of extension of limitation of two months as provided in s. 15(2) of the Limitation Act.[9] The two months period of notice would commence from the date of expiry of the period of limitation.[10] If in a single suit against several defendants jointly, the plaintiff is required to give notice under s. 80, Code of Civil Procedure to one of the defendants, he is entitled to a deduction of time against all the defendants.[11]

The plaintiff is entitled to exclude the period of two months' notice required to be served under s. 31 of the Bombay Court of Wards Act on defendants who were Government Wards and the time when the cause of action arose; and the extension cannot be refused on the ground that they ceased to be wards before the suit came up for hearing.[12]

In a suit against Government a statutory notice under s. 80, CPC is issued few days before the expiry of three years of limitation. If suit is filed immediately on reopening of court after expiry of the statutory notice period such suit cannot be held to be barred by limitation.[13]

5 *Amar Chand Inani* v *Union of India* (1973)1 SCC 115; AIR 1973 SC 313.
6 *Jai Singh* v *Mansha Ram* AIR 1963 HP 37; *Union of India* v *Jutharam* AIR 1968 Pat 35.
7 *Tinsukri Municipal Board* v *Bankem* AIR 1950 Assam 101.
8 *B & N.W. Rly.* v *Ram Sarup* AIR 1922 Pat 549.
9 *Union of India* v *Kerala State Small Industries Development and Employment Corporation Ltd.* AIR 2003 NOC 489 (Ker); (2002)3 Ker LT 660.
10 *Disha Constructions* v *State of Goa* AIR 2012 SC 1769; (2012)1 SCC 690.
11 *Mohammed Sharif* v *Nasir Ali* AIR 1930 All 742; *B & N.W. Rly.* v *Ram Sarup Khanderao* v *Chanmallappa* AIR 1924 Bom 364; *E.I. Rly.* v *Rahimullah* AIR 1928 Lah 349; *Laxmichand* v *Dominion of India* AIR 1955 Nag 265; *Jai Singh* v *Mansa Ram* AIR 1964 HP 17; *B & N.W. Rly.* v *Ram Sarup* AIR 1922 Pat 549.
12 *Khanderao* v *Chanmallappa (supra)*; *B.L. Chopra* v *State of Punjab* AIR 1961 Punj 150.
13 *Vijoy Construction Company* v *State of Gujarat* AIR 2016 Guj 167; (2016)4 Guj LR 3314.

2 Notice—not a notice of suit—exclusion of the period disallowed

The provision in sub-sec. (2) of s. 15 of the Limitation Act applies only to those cases where notice by some provision of law is obligatory before institution of the suit. It has, therefore, no application where such notice is not a notice of suit but has been given only as an information of particulars of the claim to the defendant. A notification of a claim under s. 17 of the U.P. Court of Wards Act being merely an information to the Collector of the particulars of claim, the period intervening between the date of notifying the claim and the date on which the claim was disallowed cannot be deducted.[14]

In a suit for damages against railways, the period of notice under s. 77 of the Indian Railways Act 1890 (s. 78B following Act 39 of 1961 and s. 106 following Railways Act 1989) cannot be excluded; for a notice under s. 77 is not a condition precedent for bringing a suit against the railways. In *Union of India* v *Kedarnath Babulal*,[15] it was *held*: "The notice given under s. 77 of the Indian Railways Act is not a condition precedent for bringing a suit against the carrier for compensation for loss or damage. Section 77, by its terms, does not impose a bar against the court entertaining a suit in the absence of a notice contemplated by it. It merely disentitles the plaintiff to the relief which he claims. Therefore, the period of 15 days allowed to the railway under s. 77, the Indian Railways Act, cannot be excluded in computing the period of limitation for a suit against the railway for damages for loss of or injury to goods." In the case of *Dominion of India* v *Hazari Lal*,[16] decided earlier, it was held that s. 77 did not provide that no suit should be brought in the absence of a notice but only provided that it could not be decreed and so the court had always the jurisdiction to entertain the suit and then to decide the necessity of a notice before granting a decree. This Full Bench decision of the Patna High Court fully clarifies the nature of a notice under s. 77 of the Indian Railways Act which is no better than a notice of claim. *Dominion of India* v *W.N. Sareen & Co.*[17] is in the same line where it was held that the plaintiff was not entitled to exclude the time granted under s. 106 of the Railways Act 1989 for the purpose of computing the limitation under s. 15(2) of the Limitation Act and that the claim under s. 106 of the Railways Act was not a notice of the suit but was only a notice of the claim .... In computing the period of limitation, the plaintiff was no doubt entitled to exclude the period of two months' notice under s. 80, CPC, but he was not entitled to exclude the period of correspondence with the Railway Administration in pursuing his claim under s. 106 of the Railways Act 1989.[17]

14 *Kaviraj Baroda Kanta* v *Court of Wards* AIR 1931 All 752.
15 AIR 1959 Pat 252.
16 AIR 1949 Pat 410.
17 *Dominion of India* v *W.N. Sareen Co.* AIR 1953 Nag 10.

Under s. 15(2), Limitation Act, the notice must be a notice of suit and the enactment requiring such notice to be given must prescribe the period of notice before the expiry of which the claimant cannot institute a suit. The claim under s. 77 (new s. 106) of the Indian Railways Act 1890 is not a notice of suit and no period is prescribed by the section.[18]

The fallacy arose from the reported decision in *B. & N.W. Railway Co.* v *Ram Sarup Lal Chowdhury*[19] where it was held that the consignee was entitled to deduct from that period of limitation the time given by him to the railway company to settle his claim made under s. 77 (now s. 106) of the Indian Railways Act 1890. But the reported cases of AIR 1959 Pat 252 and AIR 1953 Nag 10, referred to above overruled this decision.

But the position is otherwise with regard to a notice under s. 80 of CPC.

Limitation for inquiry regarding professional misconduct starts running from date of issuance of notice by Disciplinary Committee but not from the date of receipt of complaint.[20]

Two months period of notice under s. 80, Code of Civil Procedure shall be excluded from period of Limitation in view of s. 15(2), Limitation Act as such a notice is condition precedent for institution of the suit against Railway for short delivery of goods.[21] When the notice is the requirement of any law for the time being in force, the period spent on a notice is to be excluded.[1] So if the notice is not issued as per requirement of the law, the period of notice cannot be excluded in computing the limitation.[2] For a suit brought against a civil surgeon for damages for the death of patient due to his negligent act in operating the patient. The suit was filed within one year of the death excluding the period of two months for the notice under s. 80, CPC is held to be within time.[3] Even in filing a suit under Or. 21, r. 63, CPC the period of notice under s. 80, CPC can be excluded under s. 15(2) of the Limitation Act.[4]

3 Exclusion of period disallowed when no cause of action arises

Section 15(2) of the Limitation Act lays down that where notice has to be given with requirements of any enactment for the time being in force, such period of notice shall be excluded. Where there is no cause of action against a party, no suit shall lie. Necessarily, there is no obligation to issue a notice

18 *Prem Lata Agarwal* v *Lakshman Prasad Gupta* AIR 1970 SC 1525; (1971)2 SCJ 55.
19 *B & N.W. Rly.* v *Ram Sarup* AIR 1922 Pat 594.
20 *C. Dinakar* v *Karnataka State Bar Council* AIR 2006 Kant 252.
21 *Union of India* v *Tata Engineering* AIR 1989 Pat 272; *Amar Chand Inani* v *Union of India* AIR 1973 SC 313 foll.
1 *Union of India* v *West Coast Paper Mills Ltd.* AIR 2004 SC 3079; (2004)3 SCC 458.
2 *Punjab and Sind Bank* v *Managing Committee, Guru Nanak College* (2017)188 PLR 538.
3 *Ram Behari* v *Dr. T.N. Srivastava* AIR 1985 MP 150.
4 *Sawai Singhai Nirmal Chand* v *Union of India* AIR 1966 SC 1068; (1966)1 SCR 986.

against such party. Even if, pursuant to an erroneous belief or otherwise, notice is served will the plaintiff be allowed extension of time? Our answer would be in the negative.

Section 80, CPC, provides *inter alia* that in a notice under s. 80, CPC the cause of action shall be stated. Harnarain Singh, J. *held*: "Where the plaintiff has no cause of action against the Union of India in computing the period of limitation prescribed for the suit, the period of notice given to the Union of India cannot be excluded."[5]

Sub-section (2) expressly provides for the exclusion of the period required for obtaining the previous consent or sanction of the Government or any other authority in computing limitation.[6]

Extreme case

A suit against Union of India and Marine Products Exports Development Authority filed after two months from notice under s. 80, CPC though s. 80 is not applicable to the said authority, was not barred by limitation in view of s. 15(2) of Limitation Act.[7] The period of notice given in accordance with the requirement of any enactment for the time being in force shall be excluded.[8]

4 Notice against one of several defendants—exclusion allowed

There is a conflict of judicial opinion on the point whether the period of notice under s. 80, CPC, served on a defendant, to whom such a notice was necessary, can be excluded against a co-defendant as well, to whom such a notice was not necessary.

In a single suit brought against several defendants, if the plaintiff is entitled to deduct a certain period from the period of limitation in respect of one defendant, he is also entitled to the same period of limitation in case of the other defendants.[9] Relying on the decision of the Madras High Court[10] and the Supreme Court,[11] it was *held* in Himachal Pradesh: "If a plaintiff *prima facie* had cause of action against the defendant to whom notice was necessary and had been given, the period of notice should be excluded against all the defendants in computing the period of limitation.[12]

The principle underlying may be illustrated thus: In a case there may be different classes of defendants including the Government to sue whom a notice may be necessary. If it is necessary or even permissible for a plaintiff

5 *State* v *Jamna Das* AIR 1955 Punj 117.
6 Vide ss. 86 and 87, Civil Procedure Code.
7 *T.P.K. Nair* v *Union of India* AIR 1991 Ker 80.
8 *P.N. Roy* v *K.L. Saha* AIR 1967 Cal 802.
9 *E.I. Rly.* v *Rahimullah* AIR 1928 Lah 349 (*per* Tek Chand, J.).
10 AIR 1951 Mad 969.
11 *Sir Chunilal* v *Mehta and Sons Ltd.* v *Century Spinning and Manufacturing Co. Ltd.* AIR 1962 SC 1314.
12 *Jai Singh* v *Bali Bhadar* AIR 1964 HP 17.

to bring a suit claiming relief against all the defendants jointly, and if a notice under s. 80, CPC, was necessary against one of the defendants and was in fact given, the period of notice is to be excluded in computing the period of limitation for the suit and not merely so far as the defendant to whom notice was given is concerned.[13] But where the plaintiff by indulging in misjoinder of parties, whether knowingly or through error, impleads a party to sue whom a notice shall be necessary, though there was no cause of action against such party and, therefore, an unnecessary party, the plaintiff is not entitled to the exclusion of the period of notice. It was *held* in *Ladli Prasad* v *Nizamuddin*, by Stuart, JC: "The plaintiff is not entitled to claim deduction of time as against private individuals by impleading the Secretary of State or a Public Officer unnecessarily and giving him notice though he might have done so under a mistake of law of fact, for the law nowhere says to a plaintiff that he is under no disability but erroneously imagines himself to be under a disability, he will obtain any relaxation of the ordinary law of limitation."[14]

5 Adverse possession—notice of suit when obligatory—exclusion allowed

When the defendant is a Ward of Court and the law provides that a notice of suit will be necessary before institution of a suit, the principle under s. 15(2) of the Limitation Act applies. In *Oudh Behari Lal* v *Collector of Etah* Dalal, J. *held*: The right to sue accrued to the plaintiffs on the death of certain female on 10th February, 1911. They instituted the suit on 9th April, 1925. The lower Appellate Court pointed out that as 12 years had elapsed the plaintiff's remedy was barred, presumably under the provisions of s. 28, Limitation Act .... The defendant is a Ward of Court and under the local Court of Wards Act a notice of two months is necessary to the Court of Wards before a suit can be instituted. The plaintiffs were, therefore, entitled to bring a suit within 12 years and 2 months. Section 15(2) of the Limitation Act was held applicable.[15]

6 Effects of s. 15(2), Limitation Act—does not alter the period of limitation

A question may naturally arise as to whether the provision of s. 15(2) of the Limitation Act has the scope to alter the statutory period of limitation. The answer, for obvious reasons, is in the negative. Section 15(2) does not prescribe any new period of limitation but only gives a date from which the period of limitation is to run. Baker, J. *held*: The effect is not to alter the period of limitation but to alter the date from which limitation is to be calculated.[16]

13 *Mohammed Sharif* v *Nasir Ali* AIR 1930 All 742; *Udharam Vassanmal* v *Garhams Trading Co. Ltd.* AIR 1937 Sind 281; *Laxmichand* v *Dominion of India* AIR 1955 Nag 265; *Jai Singh* v *Mansha Ram* AIR 1963 HP 37.

14 54 IC 535.

15 AIR 1928 All 625.

16 *Chhagan Lal Sarkar Lal* v *Municipality of Thana* AIR 1932 Bom 261.

7 Arbitration and Conciliation Act—application of the Limitation Act 1963

Section 43 of the Arbitration and Conciliation Act 1996 provides that the Limitation Act 1963 shall apply to arbitration as it applies to proceedings in court. Thus all the provisions of the Limitation Act 1963 are equally applicable to arbitrations as they apply to proceedings in court. For the purposes of s. 43 of the Arbitration and Conciliation Act and Limitation Act 1963 an arbitration shall be deemed to have commenced on the date referred to in s. 21 of the Act.

Where an arbitration agreement provides provision for written communications to be made in a specific manner, all the parties to the agreement shall follow the terms and conditions of the agreement with respect to written communications. The deeming provision under s. 3 of the Arbitration and Conciliation Act 1996 applies if the parties have not agreed otherwise. The circumstances under which this section applies is similar to the old s. 42 of the earlier Arbitration and Conciliation Act. Notices made by an arbitrator or a permanent arbitral institution on behalf the arbitral tribunal may be considered as a notice by the arbitrator or an arbitral tribal. Parties may, however, agree to communication being addressed by or on behalf of the arbitral tribunal by a particular arbitrator specifically nominated for this purpose.

The communication made under this section is deemed to have been received on the day it is "so delivered". Section 27 of the General Clauses Act may come as a legal fiction about the interpretation of this section in the sense whether the date of receipt of the communication would mean that the communication has been delivered when so sent.

However, it is not mandatory that unless and until a notice under s. 3 is given no proceeding under s. 9 of the Arbitration and Conciliation Act 1996 could be invoked. Now, the doubts stand clear and set at rest and it is not necessary that arbitral proceedings must be pending or at least a notice invoking arbitration clause must have been issued before an application under s. 9 is filed.[17]

Under s. 31(3) of the 1996 Act the arbitral tribunal shall state reasons upon which award is based unless the parties have agreed that no reasons are to be given or that the award is an arbitral award on agreed terms under s. 30 of the 1996 Act. Mere perusal, therefore, would by itself indicate that it is not fundamental policy of law that in arbitral proceedings the award must contain reasons. Parties by agreement can exclude giving of reasons. Nevertheless, if clause in the agreement between the parties which contemplates that if any of the parties does not give notice to the tribunal, then the tribunal is not bound to give reasons. Even if s. 31 of the 1996 Act

17 *Sundaram Finance Ltd.* v *M/s. NEPC India Ltd.* AIR 1999 SC 565; 1999(1) Arb LR 305.

is considered, the award would be within requirement of law giving of reasons, therefore, cannot be said to be a fundamental policy of Indian law insofar as arbitral proceedings are concerned, as by statute the requirement to give reasons is not mandatory insofar as domestic award is concerned. The statute itself dispenses with the requirement to give reasons if parties agree that reasons need not be given.[18]

In the event of an additional award under s. 33(4) of the 1996 Act, it is upon receipt of the arbitral award within thirty days it is necessary to issue notice to the other party for claiming any additional award.[19]

For correction, interpretation, or claim for additional award, it is mandatory under s. 33 of the 1996 Act to give notice to the other party in the proceeding for any rectification of the award.

In the event of improper or inappropriate issue of notice of appointment of an arbitrator or an arbitral tribunal, an arbitral award may be set aside by a court under s. 34(2)(*a*)(*iii*) of the Act.

If the arbitration proceeding is to be administered by permanent arbitral institution no time limit is prescribed by the Act. The significance of the date of commencement is now lost especially with conjoint reading of ss. 21 and 43 of the 1996 Act. The notice issued by the arbitral tribunal is well covered under the provisions of s. 3 of the 1996 Act. UNCITRAL arbitration rules, however, envisage notice of arbitration on the other party either with or without the statement of claim.

In order to enforce a foreign award it is mandatory under s. 48(1)(*b*) that the party against whom the Award is invoked should be given proper notice of appointment of arbitrator or of the arbitral proceedings. In the absence of such a notice the enforcement of the foreign award may be refused if the party against whom such an award would be enforced upon furnishing to the court the proof of non-service of proper notice of the appointment of the arbitrator or of the arbitral proceedings. Accordingly, rules and principles of natural justice are embodied in the aforesaid provisions and, therefore, when a party applies seeking for enforcement of an award notice has to go to the other party at least to the extent of intimating him that such an application has been filed in the court seeking for enforcement of the award. On service of notice the court shall proceed to hear the parties in order to determine and record its satisfaction and at that stage the court would examine existence or otherwise of the two conditions as found in s. 48(2) of the 1996 Act as also the objection if filed by the party under s. 48(1) of the Act is disposed of by recording satisfaction as envisaged under s. 49 of the 1996 Act. Any contrary argument and decision to the effect that no notice is required to be given to the parties at that stage is fallacious and without merit. Once the award is held to be enforceable by the court then

18 *Force Shipping Limited* v *Ashapura Minechem Limited* 2003(52) Arb LR 432 (Bom).
19 *Union of India* v *Nav Bharat Nirman Company* 2003(52) Arb LR 309 (Del).

the same becomes binding on all the parties connected with the said award and thus the said award becomes a deemed decree in accordance with the provisions of the Act, which would be and could be executed through the process of the court.[20] Article 5(*b*) of Convention on the Recognition and Enforcement of Foreign Arbitral Awards also recognised the principles of enforcement of foreign award upon notice. Section 62 of the 1996 Act provides for commencement of conciliation proceedings upon written invitation by one of the parties to the others. Such an invitation in common parlance may be construed as a form of notice.

The provision of s. 2(4) of the Act (corresponding to s. 46 of the Arbitration Act 1940) lays down that the Limitation Act will not be applicable to statutory arbitration. Where an arbitrator in a statutory arbitration did not apply the law of limitation to a claim made by a society, the Bombay High Court held that failure to do so could not be an objection to the legality of the award.[1]

8 Miscellaneous cases where exclusion allowed or disallowed under s. 15(2) of the Limitation Act 1963

When a notice to the Government is compulsory under s. 80 of Code of Civil Procedure, the period of two months should be excluded in computing the period of limitation for the suit against the Government.[2] When the Government is a proper party, s. 15(2) of the Limitation Act applies.[3] Section 80 of the Code of Civil Procedure, which extends the period of limitation by two months under s. 15(2), Limitation Act, applies whether an officer acts in good faith or bad faith.[4]

A notice determining tenancy under the provisions of the Transfer of Property Act or under the West Bengal Premises Tenancy Act 1997—whether is a mere notice of determination of tenancy or is a notice of suit? In a decision of the Calcutta High Court, it was *held*: "An under-raiyat's liability to ejectment begins as soon as his tenancy has been terminated by the ejectment notice required by the law, that is as soon as the notice expires......Neither s. 15(2), Limitation Act, nor anything contained in s. 185, Bengal Tenancy Act would appear to operate so as to exclude from the benefit of the proviso to s. 48C of the Act any period covered by the ejectment notice.[5]

A suit to recover water-cess paid under protest—notice under s. 80 of Code of Civil Procedure served. *Held*, exclusion of the period of notice under

20 *Fuerst Day Lawson Ltd.* v *Jindal Export Ltd.* 1999(1) Arb LR 571 (Del).
1 *Savitra Khandu Beradi* v *Nagar A.S.P. Cooperative Society* AIR 1951 Bom 178.
2 *N.W. Ry.* v *Ramdhan* 38 IC 600.
3 *Commissioners of Port of Calcutta* v *General Trading Corporation Ltd.* AIR 1964 Cal 290.
4 *Udharam Vassanmal* v *Garhams Trading Co. Ltd.* AIR 1937 Sind 281.
5 *Krishna Kanta* v *Rajeshwar* AIR 1937 Cal 656.

s. 80, Code of Civil Procedure allowed under s. 15(2), Limitation Act.[6] The provision applies in computing the special limitation as well as with regard to the West Bengal Municipal Act.[7] In a word, if there be notice of suit, the provisions of s. 15(2) would apply.[8]

Necessarily, the position would be otherwise if the notice is not a notice of suit but is a notice of claim, as discussed in Note 2 *ante*. Illustrations are not rare when notice acts merely as information. In an Allahabad case it was *held*: "The notification of the claim under s. 17, Court of Wards Act, is merely an information to the Collector of the particulars of the claim. It is not necessarily a notice of a civil suit on the basis of that claim. Section 15(2) of the Limitation Act would, therefore, not apply to the notifying of the claim under s. 17, Court of Wards Act".[9]

The notice of award under s. 37(2) of the Right to Fair Compensation and Transparency in Land Acquisition, Rehabilitation and Resettlement Act 2013 mandates that the Collector shall give immediate notice of his awards to such of the persons interested who are not present personally or through their representatives when the awards are made. No particular form of notice has been prescribed. Non-mention of all the details of the award including the manner of determination of compensation does not render the notice invalid. Limitation for filing application for reference begins to run from the moment the notice under s. 37(2) is received or as envisaged by s. 64(2) of the Right to Fair Compensation and Transparency in Land Acquisition, Rehabilitation and Resettlement Act 2013. Statutory operation of limitation does not depend on the ministerial act of communication of notice in any particular form when the Act or Rules has not prescribed any form.[10]

Section 87 of the Bombay Port Trust Act insists on notice of one month. This period may legitimately be tacked on to the six-month period mentioned in the section vide s. 15(2), Limitation Act 1963. The starting point of limitation is the accrual of the cause of action.[11]

6 AIR 1923 Mad 652.
7 *Commissioner Patna Municipality* v *N.S.D. Basak* AIR 1942 Cal 544.
8 Also see AIR 1967 Mad 194.
9 *Kaviraj Baroda Kanta* v *Court of Wards* AIR 1931 All 752.
10 *State of Punjab* v *Satinder Bir Singh* (1995)3 SCC 330.
11 *Trustees of Port of Bombay* v *Premier Automobiles Ltd.* (1974)4 SCC 710; AIR 1974 SC 923.

CHAPTER 10

Miscellaneous Facts about Notices

SYNOPSIS

1 Registration of a notice–delivery and non-delivery of a registered notice–sender's receipt–acknowledgment due (A/D) receipt–(s. 28 of the Indian Post Office Act 1898, and provisions of Post Office Guide Part-I, cls. 161-162)
2 A/D receipts without signature of addressee–through mistake or omission
3 Notice sent under Certificate of Posting–presumption
4 Period in a notice–statutory and reasonable periods–computation or calculation of periods–application of s. 10 of the General Clauses Act
5 Date of letter/notice–date of posting
6 Stamp and court-fees on notice–if required?
7 Construction and interpretation of a notice
8 Mistakes and defects in a notice–waiver thereof
9 Contents of a refused notice–knowledge thereof
10 Onus probandi
11 Non-service of notice–who is competent to raise objection
12 Estoppel
13 Mode of pleading a notice

1 Registration of a notice—delivery and non-delivery of a registered notice—sender's receipt—acknowledgment due (A/D) receipt—(s. 28 of the Indian Post Office Act 1898, and provisions of Post Office Guide Part-I, cls. 161-162)

When a letter is delivered to an accepting or receiving post office in normal course, it is expected to be delivered to the addressee.[1]

Section 27 of the General Clauses Act 1897, speaks of despatch of a notice under registered post only. 'Notice by Registered Post', wherever the expression occurs, means registered under provisions of the Indian Post Office Act 1898.[2]

Clause 156 of the Post Office Guide (Part I, June 1960) enjoins that letters, etc., may be registered at any post office for transmission by post to any other post office. Section 28 of the Indian Post Office Act 1898, reads: "The sender of a postal article may, subject to the other provisions of this

1 *Vide* s. 3(*c*) of the Post Office Act 1898—discussed in *Gangaram* v *Smt. Fulwati* AIR 1970 All 446.

2 Act of 1866 changed to Act of 1898.

Act, have the article registered at the post office at which it is posted, and require a receipt (sender's receipt) thereof; and the Central Government may, by notification in the Official Gazette, direct that in addition to any postage chargeable under this Act, such further fee as may be fixed by notification shall be paid on account of the registration of postal articles." To sum up, a letter, etc., may be registered at the despatching post office with notified additional fees. Postage should be prepaid is the direction in s. 27 of the General Clauses Act. Clause 157 of the Post Office Guide (Part I) enjoins: "The prepayment of the postage and registration fee is compulsory in the case of all registered articles."

Section 29 of the Indian Post Office Act provides for powers to the Central Government to make rules as to the registration of postal articles. As a matter of fact, various rules have been framed, as may be seen in the Post Office Guide referred to herein above. In Chapter 4, i.e. 'Service of a Notice' *ante* we have noticed that wherever service of notice by post has been directed, the additional direction is that it should be sent by 'registered post with postage prepaid'. Clause 155 of the Post Office Guide (Part I) enjoins: "Registration makes the transmission of an article more secure, as it passes through the hands of postal officers, under special precautions." Because a postal article, when sent by registered post, carries with it a special care, a notice should, it is submitted, be sent by registered post. A notice-giver may reasonably expect that when the notice is so sent it would reach the addressee. And, because of the assurance of special care the presumption under s. 114 of the Evidence Act would not be unreasonable.

The delivery of a postal article at the house or office of the addressee or to the addressee or his servant or agent or other person considered to be authorised to receive the article according to the usual manners of delivering postal articles to the addressee is deemed to be delivered to the addressee under the Indian Post Office Act. But delivery of registered articles stands on a different footing. Clause 35 of the Post Office Guide (Part I) enjoins: "No registered article will be delivered to the addressee unless and until he or his agent authorised in writing has signed a receipt for it, in the prescribed form which will be presented to him for signature by the postman who delivers the registered article."

Clause 36 of the said Guide speaks with regard to non-delivery of a registered article: "If the addressee, while refusing to take delivery on presentation of the registered article to him, makes an application in writing to the post office of delivery for the detention of the article, or if the addressee is not found at the address given on the article, the article shall be detained in the post office for a period not exceeding seven days from the date of its presentation to the addressee or from the date it is sent out for delivery as the case may be. If the addressee fails to take delivery of the article from the post office within the said period of seven days, the article will be returned to the office of posting for delivery to the sender."

In case of non-delivery for refusal by or non-availability of the addressee, the registered letter is returned to the sender unopened and without delay with noting of refusal by or non-availability of the addressee as the case may be. Clause 161 of the Post Office Guide (Part I) enjoins: "If the sender of a registered article pays at the time of posting the article the prescribed fee in addition to the postage and registration fee, will be sent to him on the delivery of the article a formal acknowledgment signed in ink by the addressee or his authorised agent.

NOTE: The receipt granted to the sender of a registered article in respect of which a fee for special acknowledgment has been paid will have the letters 'A.D.' written across it.

This A.D. receipt is of special importance in a court of law which proves service of the notice, on the addressee, sent by registered post. There may be occasion when the original A.D. receipt is lost or does not come back to the sender of the registered article, but the notice-giver requires it. Surely, he cannot have the original A.D. receipt hence, there is a provision for supply by the post office of an attested copy of the receipt. Clause 162 of the Post Office Guide lays down: "The sender of a registered article may obtain an attested copy of the original receipt signed by the addressee on payment of the prescribed special fee provided that he makes his application for it within six months of the date on which the addressee signed the original receipt."

A.D. receipt signed by someone at other end, comes back to the notice-giver. This would raise a presumption that the notice was received on behalf of the addressee. Such presumption can, however, be rebutted.[3]

A problem remains to be considered and that is with regard to refusal of a notice sent by registered post. Not unoften registered letters are refused by their addressees. Refusal is service; for the sender could do nothing more. To prove refusal, a statement to that effect is necessary before the court and the Post Office Guide makes a provision for that. Clause 161 of the Post Office Guide enjoins: "If either the addressee or the agent refuses to sign, the acknowledgment of delivery will bear a statement to that effect." In some cases, a note is entered in the body of the registered cover by the concerned postman to that effect. To prove refusal, such entry is generally proved by summoning the postman to the witness box. We have seen above that in case of non-delivery the registered article will be sent back to the office of posting for delivery to the sender. It shall be returned to him unopened and without delay; for Note to cl. 158 of the Post Office Guide enjoins: "The sender of a postal article of the letter mail is recommended to write his name and address on the cover in the lower left hand corner, so that the postal article in case of non-delivery may be returned to him unopened and without delay."

3 *Commissioner of Hazaribagh Municipality* v *Fulchand Agarwala* AIR 1966 Pat 434.

In case the letter contained in the registered cover is returned unopened, the court has the opportunity to open the envelope and satisfy itself if the refused article was really a notice as claimed by the sender thereof.

2 AD receipts without signature of addressee—through mistake or omission

An AD receipt may come back without signature of the addressee. It does not mean that the addressee did not receive the notice. To quote Lord Atkinson in *Harihar Banerji* v *Ramshashi Roy*[4] "It is an entire mistake to suppose that the addressee must sign the receipt for a registered letter." Presumption of due delivery would arise if the letter is sent per registered post, postage prepaid and correctly addressed.[5]

3 Notice sent under Certificate of Posting—presumption

We have seen in Chapter 4— 'Service of a Notice' *ante* that notices can as well be served by post under 'certificate of posting' and that a notice so sent raises a presumption under s. 114 of the Evidence Act[6] that the notice in question reached the addressee unless something is proved to the contrary. It is entirely wrong for the court to work on the presumption that the certificate of posting is a forgery.[7] However, the Supreme Court has taken judicial notice that certificates of posting are notoriously easily available. What was seen as a possible but rare occurrence is now in 1981 seen as common.[8] The Supreme Court in *Shiv Kumar* v *State of Haryana*[9] said:

> "We have not felt safe to decide the controversy at hand on the basis of the certificates produced before us, it is not difficult to get such postal seal at any point of time."

Does the Certificate carry any special sanctity? For the answer let us refer to cl. 31 of the Post Office Guide (Part I) framed by the Government of India under the Indian Post Office Act. It lays down: "The object in granting 'certificate of posting' is to afford the public an assurance that letters and other articles entrusted to servants or messengers for posting have actually been posted. The grant of a certificate will not, however, mean that the letters and articles in respect of which the certificate is issued were fully prepaid with posting stamps, nor will it guarantee in any way the despatch of the articles entered in the certificate on the same day, unless they are handed over well in time to catch the last despatch of mails for the

4 AIR 1918 PC 102; 23 CWN 77.

5 Also see 71 CWN 302.

6 *Sukumar Guha* v *Naresh Chandra Ghosh* AIR 1968 Cal 49; *Chhaya Debia* v *Lahoriram* 67 CWN 819; *Mrs. Achamma Thomas* v *E.R. Fairman* AIR 1970 Mys 77; *Kanaklata Ghosh (Smt.)* v *Amal Kumar Ghosh* AIR 1970 Cal 328.

7 *Hemangiri* v *Sarnalatiko* AIR 1940 Cal 227.

8 *M.S. Madhusoodhanan* v *Kerala Kaumudi Pvt. Ltd.* 2003(117) Comp Cas 19 (SC); *Ummu Saleema, L.M.S.* v *B.B. Gujaral* (1981)3 SCC 317.

9 (1994)4 SCC 445.

day the particular destination concerned. It must be clearly understood that the articles in respect of which such certificates are issued are not registered and that they are treated in exactly the same manner as if they had been posted in a letter box. In the event of loss, damage or delay, the certificates will confer no claim for compensation; nor do they furnish any proof of the nature of contents."

It, therefore, transpires that a certificate of posting does not attach any special guarantee that the letter would receive special care or even that it would reach the addressee at all. The only guarantee the certificate confers is that the letter in question was actually posted. There is no denying the fact that the certificate of posting raises a presumption but the presumption is a weak one and is decidedly weaker than the presumption attendant on a notice sent by registered post. Hence, wherever any enactment prescribes postal service of a notice it invariably speaks of service by registered post. Besides, a certificate of posting does not furnish any proof of nature of contents of articles sent under a certificate of posting. It is submitted that notices, when required to be served by post, should not be sent under certificate of posting.

The Supreme Court in *Ummu Saleema's* case[10] said that a certificate of posting might lead to a presumption if the letter was duly addressed and was posted, that it in due course, reached the addressee. "But, that is only a permissible and not an inevitable presumption. Neither s. 16 nor s. 114 of the Evidence Act compels the court to draw a presumption. The presumption may or may not be drawn. On the facts and circumstances of case, the court may refuse to draw the presumption. On the other hand, presumption may be drawn initially but on a consideration of the evidence the court may hold a presumption rebutted and may arrive at the conclusion that no letter was received by the addressee or that no letter was ever despatched as claimed."

4 Period in a notice—statutory and reasonable periods—computation or calculation of periods—application of s. 10 of the General Clauses Act

By the term 'period' in relation to a notice, we mean the time allowed in a notice by the notice-giver for compliance with the instructions made therein or to meet the demands made or to grant reliefs sought for therein.

The period allowed in a notice is never arbitrary. In some cases, the period is fixed by an enactment, while in other cases, while law is silent, the period is a reasonable period depending on facts and circumstances of each case.

Under s. 50B of the West Bengal Municipal Act 1993 for the first meeting of the Board of Councillors after notification of the persons elected, the District Magistrate shall give seven days notice. Under s. 209 of the West

10 *Ummu Saleema, L.M.S.* v *B.B. Gujaral* (1981)3 SCC 317; AIR 1981 SC 1191.

Bengal Municipal Act 1993, not less than seven days before any person commences to erect or re-erect a building the owner of the building shall send to the Chairman a written notice specifying the date on which he proposes the commencement of the work. It means exclusive of day of service and exclusive of day on which meeting[11] is held.

Section 392 of the West Bengal Municipal Act 1993 provides for the issuance and service of public notices and advertisements. Such notices are to be in writing and under the signature of the Chairman or any duly authorised officer of the Municipality. The notice shall be widely made known in the locality to be affected by affixing copies thereof in conspicuous public places or by advertisement in local newspaper or by publishing the same otherwise as Chairman-in-Council may think fit. If no date is mentioned such notices are to fix reasonable time under s. 394 of the Act.[12]

In a claim for compensation for delay in execution of contract, the committee of Arbitrators direct to pay award amount. But the terms of contract require the contractor to give notice to the employer within a stipulated time. If such notice is not given within that stipulated time, plea can be taken that the notice was not given.[13]

Giving of notice—when directory.[14]

'Giving'—"Giving of anything as ordinarily understood in the English language is not complete unless it has reached the hands of the person to whom it has to be given. In the eye of law, however, 'giving' is complete in many matters where it has been offered to a person but not accepted by him. Tendering of a notice is in law, therefore, giving of notice even though the person to whom it is tendered refuses to accept it. Thus as soon as the person with a legal duty to give the notice despatches the notice to the address of the person to whom it has to be given, the giving is not complete."[15]

"Shall" give.[16]

There are cases when a notice is statutory and is, therefore, mandatory in nature and is made a condition precedent for institution of a suit. For example, a notice under s. 80, Code of Civil Procedure, against the Central or a State Government or against a Public Officer of any of such Governments, a notice of suit under s. 98 of the Right to Fair Compensation and Transparency in Land Acquisition, Rehabilitation and Resettlement Act 2013 corresponds to s. 52 of the Land Acquisition Act 1894, a notice of suit under s. 50(1) of the Administration of Evacuee Property Act 1950, a notice

11 See Shackleton on *Meetings*, 5th Ed.
12 *Jnanendra Nath Pramanick* v *District Magistrate, Nadia* AIR 1978 Cal 324.
13 *State of Orissa* v *Larsen & Toubro Ltd.* AIR 2005 Ori 183.
14 *Montreal Street Railway Co.* v *Normandin* [1917] AC 170; AIR 1917 PC 142.
15 *K. Narasimhiah* v *H.C. Sengri* AIR 1966 SC 330.
16 *State of UP* v *Manbodhanlal Srivastava* AIR 1957 SC 912 (917).

of proceedings under s. 198 of the Sea Customs Act 1878, a notice of suit under s. 56 of the Wakf Act 1954 (now s. 89 of the Waqf Act 1995) and so on. In cases like these, where notice is statutory, the law also specifies the period which the notice should allow. To wit, s. 80, Code of Civil Procedure prescribes a period of two months, s. 98 of the Right to Fair Compensation and Transparency in Land Acquisition, Rehabilitation and Resettlement Act 2013 (corresponds to s. 52 of the Land Acquisition Act 1894) provides a period of one month, s. 89 of the Waqf Act 1995 (corresponds to s. 52 of the Wakf Act 1954) prescribes a period of two months, a notice under s. 106 of the Transfer of Property Act allows a period of six months or one month and/ or 15 days as the case may be.

In cases of statutory notices, the intention of the legislature to allow a particular period of time is to afford a scope to the defendant to look to the claims of the notice-giver and to meet the claim amicably outside the court. With respect to provisions of s. 80, Code of Civil Procedure it was held that the section is intended to afford a defendant an opportunity to reconsider the position and make amends or settle claims, if so advised, without recourse to the trouble and cost of litigation.[17] The object of a notice under s. 80 of the Civil Procedure Code is to give intimation to the Government of the grievance that the subject has and to give to the Government an opportunity to redress that grievance before it is brought to court.[18]

Next, with regard to notices which are statutory but the enactment does not prescribe any particular period, the notice has to allow a reasonable period. To wit, a notice (under s. 50(1) of the Administration of Evacuee Property Act 1950) of suit to the Custodian of Evacuee Property; a notice under s. 10 of the Carriers Act 1865. Relevant provisions enjoin that a notice must precede a suit and that is all. In such cases the notice should be a notice for a reasonable period.

Yet another class of notice is the optional notice which, from equitable considerations, allows reasonable period for compliance.

The question of period assumes special importance when the notice is statutory and the enactment itself provides the time-limit. Hair-splitting calculation is not rare: for, during the currency of notice, i.e. before the expiry of the period in a notice a suit, if brought, will be premature and, therefore, will fail. Section 80, Code of Civil Procedure is express, explicit and mandatory and admits of no implications or exceptions. A suit against the Secretary of State instituted during the currency of notice under s. 80 is not maintainable and must be dismissed *in limine*.[19] A suit cannot, therefore, be brought before expiry of two months of notice under s. 80, Code

17 *Braham Dutt* v *East Punjab* AIR 1958 Punj 351; AIR 1956 Pat 478.
18 AIR 1951 Bom 72.
19 AIR 1941 Pat 517.

of Civil Procedure.[20] What has been held with regard to notice under s. 80, Code of Civil Procedure that applies to cases where there are like statutory provisions prescribing some period.

Where the notice is voluntary, the notice-giver is expected to honour the terms he dictated in his notice. It is expected that he would allow the period which he mentioned in his notice before he brought any suit actually. But where no notice is required at all, yet a notice was given, the suit will not fail even if the suit was brought earlier than the period allowed.

Whether s. 10 of the General Clauses Act 1897 applies to calculation of the period in a notice is no more a controversy. Section 10 of the General Clauses Act is an enabling section permitting one to do on the opening day which one could have done on a holiday. The object of s. 10, in other words, is to enable a person to do what he could have done on a holiday.[21] Since s. 80 does not direct that any act or proceeding should be done or taken in any court or office on a certain day or within a prescribed period, s. 10 of the General Clauses Act does not apply to computation of time of a notice under s. 80, Code of Civil Procedure.

The day of delivery of a notice under s. 80, Code of Civil Procedure must be excluded from two months provided by s. 80, Code of Civil Procedure.[22] The period of two months, as laid down in s. 80, Code of Civil Procedure should be taken as exclusive of the day on which notice is served.[23] Two British calendar months are meant. The date of delivery of the notice under the section and fraction of a day cannot be counted.[1] In calculating the 15 days' notice mentioned in s. 106, Transfer of Property Act, the day on which the notice is served is excluded, but the day on which it expires is taken into account.[2]

"Notice of not less than 3 months" means notice of at least 3 months [vide Railway Establishment Code V. 2, R 2046(*h*).] 'Notice of 2 months' (80, CPC) does not mean 60 days. The calculation of the period must be made monthwise.[3] "After expiry of two months" (in a Notice under s. 80, CPC), Notice served on 17th July 1963: suit filed on 18th September 1963. Suit held filed after expiry of 2 months and could not be said to be premature.[4]

"Shall give not less than 15 clear days' notice of meeting"—It means exclusive of day of service and exclusive of day on which meeting is held.[5]

20 *Chandulal Vadilal* v *Govt. of the Province of Bombay* AIR 1943 Bom 138.
21 *Harinder Singh* v *S. Karnail Singh* AIR 1957 SC 271; *Kaushalendra Prasad Narayan Singh* v *R.P. Singh* AIR 1958 Pat 196.
22 AIR 1941 Mad 446; *Province of Madras* v *Vikrama Deo* AIR 1943 Mad 284.
23 AIR 1945 Cal 341.
1 *Madurai K. Rengiah Chettiar* v *Union of India* AIR 1971 Mad 34.
2 26 IC 962.
3 *Lakshmi Narain Ramnarain* v *State of Bihar* AIR 1977 Pat 73.
4 *Baijnath Prosad* v *Union of India* AIR 1980 NOC 96 (All); AIR 1967 SC 1634 followed.
5 *Jnanendra Nath Pramanick* v *District Magistrate, Nadia* AIR 1978 Cal 324.

"Notice of 10 clear days" [vide Rule 10B of the Bihar High Schools (Constitution, Powers and Functions of Managing Committee) Rules 1964]—same view.[6]

Tenancy month expiring on 9th of calendar month, Notice determining tenancy with effect from the 10th of a month is valid.[7]

[8]This statutory period cannot be varied. When in a notice demand is for payment within 30 days but the suit is actually filed after the statutory period of two months, the notice is not invalidated.[9] Since Limitation Act does not apply in case of election petitions, the time for computation of limitation under s. 81(1) of the Representation of the People Act 1951 would follow s. 10 of the General Clauses Act.[10]

5 Date of letter/notice—date of posting

The date of posting of a letter containing notice is an important factor for obvious reasons. The date in a notice or letter is not necessarily the date of posting; for a letter may be posted subsequent to a date when it was dated and signed.[11]

6 Stamp and court-fees on notice—if required?

A notice may be written or typed on a plain paper. It does not require any stamp or court-fees.

7 Construction and interpretation of a notice

Generally speaking, a notice does not require a particular form. Only the thing required of a notice is its clarity. The addressee must know on perusal of the notice the facts with certainty. The notice should be informative: but the information must not be vague but rather it should be definite and unambiguous.

A notice should be sufficient if it satisfies the maxim '*Id certum est quod certum reddi potest*'.........The maxim means: "that is certain which can be made certain." The test is whether that amount of certainty is available in a notice which the notice could make certain. In *Harihar Banerji* v *Ramshashi Roy* it was *held*: "Notice to quit though not strictly accurate or consistent in the statements embodied in them may still be good and effective in law. The

6 *Harish Chandra Singh* v *State of Bihar* AIR 1971 Pat 406.
7 *Dr. Jagdish Lal Chawla* v *Ratan Chand* AIR 1979 MP 186.
8 "When a period is fixed before the expiration of which an act may not be done, the person for whose benefit the delay is prescribed has the benefit of the entire period, and accordingly in computing it the day from which it runs as well as the day on which it expires must be excluded and the act cannot be done before midnight of that day"—Halsbury's *Laws of England,* 3rd Ed., vol. 37, para 166.
9 AIR 1955 Cal 360; AIR 1952 Assam 141.
10 *Manohar Joshi* v *Nitin Bhaurao Patil* (1996)1 SCC 169 (399).
11 26 IC 962.

test of their sufficiency is not what they would mean to a stranger ignorant of all the facts and circumstances touching the holding to which they purport to refer, but what they would mean to the tenants presumably conversant with all those facts and circumstances. Further, notices to quit are to be construed not with a desire to find faults with them which would render them defective but to be construed '*ut res magis valeat quam pereat*', i.e. an act may prevail rather than perish.[12] The Privy Council case was discussed by the Gujarat High Court[13] and was relied on. The same reasoning prevailed with Venkatasubba Rao, J. in *A.S. Gnanaprakasam Pillai* v *F.S. Vaz*[14] where it was held that a notice to quit should be given a rational interpretation and ought not to be construed to find fault with it but with a view to its validity. In a Calcutta case, when it was held that a notice of ejectment under s. 106 of the Transfer of Property Act must be construed very strictly, it meant that the terms of lease whether were strictly reflected in the notice and not that wordings suffered from inaccuracy.[15] There may be mistakes but a notice, on a rational interpretation, may be found valid. In another Calcutta case, a notice to quit was held good notwithstanding the fact that the addressee was described therein as a trespasser and not as a tenant and more time was given therein than prescribed.[16]

This principle of rational interpretation applies to a notice under s. 70 of the Bombay Co-operative Societies Act[17] and under s. 80 of the Code of Civil Procedure as well. Although strict compliance with the terms of s. 80, Code of Civil Procedure is necessary, it is not necessary to scrutinize a notice under s. 80, Code of Civil Procedure in pedantic manner or in a manner devoid of common sense.[18] The notice under s. 80, Code of Civil Procedure should not be construed as if it were a pleading. It need not set out all the details and facts of the case. On the other hand, it is necessary to import a little commonsense into notices of this kind.[19] Tek Chand, J. in *Sodhi Shamser Singh* v *Pepsu State held*: "The provisions of s. 80 ought not to be construed hypercritically with an eye for a flaw or an omission, however inconsequential, with a view to depriving the subject of his remedy, but rather liberally with due regard to commonsense and bearing in view of the object of the legislature in enacting the law."[20] The principle explained in AIR 1965 SC 11 may also be looked into.[21]

12 *Harihar Banerji* v *Ramshashi Roy* AIR 1918 PC 102; 23 CWN 77.
13 AIR 1962 Guj 229.
14 AIR 1931 Mad 352.
15 AIR 1936 Cal 581.
16 AIR 1933 Cal 260.
17 AIR 1962 Mys 48.
18 AIR 1958 SC 270; AIR 1951 SC 253; *Bhagwan Lal* v *Union of India* AIR 1961 Pat 200; AIR 1960 SC 1309.
19 *Samrathmal* v *Union of India* AIR 1959 MP 305.
20 AIR 1961 Punj 358; AIR 1962 Punj 262.
21 *State of Andhra Pradesh* v *Gundugola Venkata Suryanarayana Garu* AIR 1965 SC 11; (1964)4 SCR 945.

To sum up: Interpretation of a notice requires commonsense and not a pedantic view.[22] A notice has to be interpreted not pedantically but in the light of commonsense without being hypercritical about the language.[23]

8 Mistakes and defects in a notice—waiver thereof

To err is human. It is no wonder that a notice may contain errors. There may be inaccuracies as well. Law excuses *bona fide* mistakes and/or venial defects, i.e. mistakes honestly but inadvertently made. It was held in *Harihar Banerji* v *Ramashashi Roy*[1] that notices to quit are to be construed not with a desire to find faults in them which would render them defective but to be construed '*ut res magis valeat quam pereat*' (that an act may prevail rather than perish). Applying this principle, it may be stated that notices containing errors or defects, *bona fide* in nature, are to be construed relying on the maxim and such defects may be ignored. But the principle would be entirely inapplicable to inaccuracies deliberately inserted for fraudulent purpose.

Any defect which relates to minor particulars in a notice under s. 77 of Indian Railways Act 1890 (which came to be renumbered by the Amending Act of 1961 and finally replaced by s. 106 of the Railways Act 1989) would not vitiate the notice. Only in cases where the defect is a major one, which might prejudice the Railway Administration or the Government in failing to locate the particulars of the claim, the notice might be vitiated. The notice is not invalidated merely because the plaintiff mentions a wrong place of destination when the plaintiff had mentioned all other particulars correctly, namely, the number of railway receipt, the place of despatch and there is nothing which would prevent the defendant railway from making inquiries about the location of the consignment. It may be that under certain circumstances, the notice might be vitiated due to a wrong mention of the place of despatch which might prevent the Railway Administration from making enquiry or from taking any further action in regard to the notice of a claim made by a plaintiff. But it is not that in every case a notice would be vitiated. Such cases might be exceptional ones; but, then, each case would have to be decided upon its own facts. But mention of a wrong place of destination where all other particulars were correctly given, does not invalidate the notice.[2] Failure to state correctly the name of railway station from which the consignment is booked in the notice under s. 106 of the Railways Act 1989 and s. 80, Code of Civil Procedure is not merely a mistake but a fatal defect, because it affects the cause of action.[3]

22 *Amar Nath Dogra* v *Union of India* AIR 1963 SC 424.
23 Also see 59 CWN 405 at 415.
1 *Harihar Banerji* v *Ramshashi Roy* AIR 1918 PC 102; 23 CWN 77 reaffirmed in AIR 1965 MP 140 at 142.
2 AIR 1961 MP 220.
3 AIR 1961 Pat 334; rel. on *Surjit Singh Atwal* v *Union of India* AIR 1959 MP 232; AIR 1959 MP 305; *State of Madras* v *C.A. Agencies* AIR 1954 Nag 342 followed. See also *Union of India* v *Nageshwar Prasad* AIR 1964 Pat 373.

The date of the railway receipt in notice, in a suit based on it, is as important as its number.[4] In a suit, therefore, based on a railway receipt, a notice reciting the wrong number of receipts is invalid,[5] and cannot be excused as a *bona fide* mistake. But this view is no longer tenable. A notice has to be interpreted keeping in view other facts alleged. Mentioning of incorrect number of a railway receipt does not invalidate a notice.[6]

Minor omissions are excusable. In a suit against the Railway Administration for damages where the notice mentions the name and residence of the plaintiff, merely because the parentage of the plaintiff was not given or that the amount subsequently claimed in the suit is different—is not sufficient to invalidate the notice.[7]

Coming to a notice under s. 80 of the Code of Civil Procedure, we may note that the same principle of equity has been adhered to. Despite rigours of a notice under s. 80, Code of Civil Procedure a notice would be valid if requirements under the section have been substantially complied with. In a notice under s. 80, Code of Civil Procedure in connection with a suit for the loss of goods despatched through the railway, a *bona fide* error with reference to the date of the railway receipt, the number of the railway receipt being quite accurate—*held*, the mistake did not change the character of the cause of action and, therefore, did not vitiate the notice.[8] Where the claim in the notice under s. 80, Code of Civil Procedure was one in respect of compensation for non-delivery and after service of notice the respondents were able to trace the consignment and effect delivery (though late and in a deteriorated condition) and the plaintiff eventually reduced its claim for non-delivery to one for the delivery and deterioration of goods—it does not follow that notice became ineffective or invalid.[9]

Variations in the notice and plaint which are not material or are mere superfluous matters stated in a notice but not incorporated in the plaint will not invalidate a notice under s. 80, Code of Civil Procedure.

Superfluous matters mentioned in a notice under s. 80, Code of Civil Procedure but omitted from the plaint does not render the notice invalid. What s. 80 requires is that the notice should contain the cause of action, etc. and the relief claimed. If the fact that the particular rule was *ultra vires* is mentioned in the notice and omitted from the plaint, the notice does not

4 AIR 1956 Ajmere 49.
5 1950 All LJ 595.
6 *Harish Chand* v *Union of India* AIR 1962 All 307; *Deokishan Srigopal (Firm)* v *Union of India* AIR 1966 All 16.
7 AIR 1949 Pat 268.
8 AIR 1949 Pat 93; also see *Deokishan Srigopal (Firm)* v *Union of India* AIR 1966 All 16.
9 AIR 1959 MP 305.

become invalid on that ground.[10] However clumsy and curious the notice might be, if it fulfils the requirements, the notice was valid.[11]

Complete variance between the claim made in a notice under s. 80, Code of Civil Procedure and the claim in the plaint is a fatal defect.[12]

Where variations between the two descriptions—one in the notice under s. 80, Code of Civil Procedure and the other given in the plaint in respect of the plaintiff's name etc.—did not make material difference, the notice was valid.[13] Even if a notice under s. 80 fails to mention the defendant, whom the plaintiff wishes to sue correctly or does not mention him at all except in general manner, then his suit cannot be dismissed on the ground that he has not complied with the requirements of s. 80 so long as he states the cause of action and gives his own name, description and address and states the relief which he claims, and so long as the party whom he subsequently sues is the party from whom he is entitled to that relief.[14]

Misdescription of the defendant in the notice is not fatal.[15]

The expression '*hereby*' used in a notice means 'through this notice' and "not from today".[16]

An unsigned notice is not always a defective notice.

9 Contents of a refused notice—knowledge thereof

Refusal to accept a notice, broadly speaking, tantamounts to service of notice. Relying on this broad principle, a school of thought will not hesitate to penalise the maker of refusal as having knowledge of the contents of the refused notice. It was held by Pigot and Rampini, JJ. in *Jogendra Chunder Ghose* v *Dwarkanath Karmokar* that when a notice was served through registered post, a tenant refusing to receive the notice cannot plead ignorance of its contents.[17] After a couple of decades, the above view finds support in *Srinath* v *Saraswati Devi Jaiswal*[18] where it was *held*: "Where a closed envelope is tendered to a person and he refused to accept delivery of the same, he, of course, has no knowledge of the contents of that envelope, but when he does not care to accept delivery of the envelope, the law should impute knowledge of the contents thereof to him, and it is on that basis that refusal to accept delivery of a registered or unregistered notice is regarded as sufficient notice of the contents of the envelope to the addressee. And if,

10 AIR 1934 Pat 701.
11 AIR 1961 Cal 626.
12 *Amar Nath Dogra* v *Union of India* AIR 1963 SC 424.
13 AIR 1959 MP 232.
14 AIR 1964 Raj 41.
15 AIR 1961 Punj 358.
16 *Mohammad Hazi* v *Umanand Kamath* AIR 1976 Ker 26.
17 ILR 15 Cal 681.
18 AIR 1964 All 52.

in the case of a joint lease, service of the notice is to be deemed sufficient on the tenant other than the one to whom it was actually tendered (provided he was also one of the addressees) even he may be presumed to have constructive knowledge of the contents of the sealed or closed envelope."

The opposite view has come from Beaumont, CJ. in *Vaman Vithal Kulkarni* v *Khanderao Ram Rao Sholapukar*:[19] "Even if the refusal had been proved, I should not be prepared to hold that a registered letter tendered to the addressee and returned and brought back unopened was well served. There are, I know, some authorities in this court to the contrary, but it seems to me impossible to say that a letter has been served so as to bring the contents to the notice of the person to whom the letter is addressed if the agent for service states that in fact the notice was not served, although the reason may have been that the addressee declined to accept it. One cannot assume that because an addressee declines to accept a particular sealed envelope he has guessed correctly as to its contents."

But it would be too hard to saddle every refusal with knowledge of the refused notice. But when one makes a deliberate refusal, he cannot be allowed in a court to say: "I do not know what the notice meant".[20]

10 Onus probandi

Order VI, r. 11 of the Code of Civil Procedure reads: "Wherever it is material to allege notice to any person of any fact, matter or thing, it shall be sufficient to allege such notice as a fact, unless the form or the precise terms of such notice, or the circumstances from which such notice is to be inferred, are material."

Where service of notice is statutory, the plaint should contain an averment that the notice has been served. Mere statement that a notice was given will not be helpful.[1]

The burden of proof (or, the *onus probandi*) of service of notice is upon the person claiming to have served the notice. But there may be circumstances when the burden shifts. A notice, duly sent conforming to requirements as in s. 27 of the General Clauses Act, carries with it presumption of service and the burden is on the addressee to rebut the presumption. On the question of burden no hard and fast rule can be risked. It would depend on facts and circumstances of each case.

When a notice-giver claims that he had sent the notice per registered post and complied with the requirements as provided for in s. 27 of the General Clauses Act, he can reasonably claim a discharge from the obligation of proving the service of notice, though, where practicable, he, in his interest

19 AIR 1935 Bom 247.
20 Decision in AIR 1935 Bom 247—discussed and dissented from in AIR 1965 All 287 at 288.
1 *Amar Nath Dogra* v *Union of India* AIR 1963 SC 424.

should take all possible measures to prove the effective service thereof, relying on the principle of s. 27 of the General Clauses Act. It has been laid down in *Salilgram Rai Chunilal Bahadur* v *Abdul Gani*[2] that there is no obligation upon a lessor to prove service of a notice upon the lessee if he sends a notice by registered post properly addressed. In *Durganath* v *Rajendra Nath*[3] and *Girish Chaira* v *Kishore Mohan*[4] it has been held by Calcutta High Court that the production of postal endorsement would be sufficient proof.

11 Non-service of notice—who is competent to raise objection

Only the person who has a right to receive the notice can raise objection as to non-service of notice: Objection as to non-service of notice can properly be taken not by third parties but only by the person on whom the notice is not served.[5] In a suit against the Government and others, when the Government does not appear and contest the suit or appears but does not challenge service of notice, it is not open to others to raise objection as to the non-service of notice. Notice under s. 80, Code of Civil Procedure or such other statutory notices are creatures of law conferring a right on the intended addressee. Others cannot assume the right of raising objection.

12 Estoppel

Failure to raise all pleas and to raise issue may lead a plaintiff to be under the impression that the defendant has waived his right and is not relying on that point. A rule requiring notice of termination of tenancy before the landlord can ask for eviction of a tenant not being under a special Act (viz., Rent Control Act). But under the Transfer of Property Act, a tenant can waive his right to such notice.[6]

Tenant's failure to plead want of notice will attract estoppel by representation under s. 115 of the Evidence Act. In absence of the plea parties cannot raise the plea in revision.[7]

13 Mode of pleading a notice

Order VI, r. 11 of CPC provides that wherever it is material to allege notice to any person of any fact, matter or thing, it shall be sufficient to allege such notice as a fact, unless, the form or the precise terms of such notice, or the circumstances from which such notice is to be inferred, are material. Order VI, r. 11 merely prescribes the form which the pleading should take in such cases as it is material to allege notice.[8]

2 AIR 1953 Assam 206.
3 17 CWN 1073.
4 AIR 1920 Cal 287.
5 AIR 1965 SC 1838.
6 AIR 1947 PC 197; *Maganlal Chhotabhai* v *Chandrakant Motilal* AIR 1969 SC 37; *K.N. Ramakrishnan* v *C. Keral Chand* AIR 1971 Mad 150.
7 *K.N. Ramakrishnan* v *C. Keral Chand* AIR 1971 Mad 150.
8 *Krishna* v *Adya* AIR 1944 Pat 77.

CHAPTER 11

Notices under the Code of Civil Procedure 1908

SYNOPSIS

1 Notice under s. 80, CPC—object of the notice
2 Form and contents of a notice under s. 80, CPC
3 Name, description and place of residence of the plaintiff—mention thereof in a notice under s. 80, CPC
4 Name, description and address of the proposed defendant in a notice under s. 80, CPC
5 'Cause of action'—mention thereof in a notice under s. 80, CPC
6 Reliefs sought for—mention thereof in a notice under s. 80, CPC
7 Notice—a condition precedent to a suit against (*a*) Government, (*b*) Public Officer
8 Exceptions
9 Notice—where Government or Public Officer is a mere pro forma defendant or a co-defendant
10 Amendments in s. 80, CPC—notice where not necessary
11 Suit against Government or Public Officer for injunction
12 Interpretation and construction of a notice under s. 80, CPC—inartistic and careless drafting of notice
13 Defects in a notice under s. 80, CPC—how far excusable
14 Waiver of a notice under s. 80, CPC
15 Service of a notice under s. 80, CPC—when service is effected
16 Period of notice under s. 80, CPC—computation of the period—application of s. 10 of the General Clauses Act 1897
17 Savings of limitation—application of s. 15(2) of the Limitation Act 1963
18 Suit before expiry of two months—suit during currency of notice
19 Identity of notice—giver with the plaintiff
20 Withdrawal of a suit—whether fresh notice necessary? Question of *res judicata*
21 Amendment of plaint—fresh notice if required
22 Variation in a notice and in the plaint
23 *State* v *State*—notice if required
24 Mentioning of service of notice in the plaint

1 Notice under s. 80, CPC—object of the notice

Before a suit is to be instituted against the Central Government or against a State Government or against a Public Officer of any of such Governments in respect of any act purporting to be done by such Public Officer in his official capacity, a notice is to be served on the proposed defendant under s. 80 of CPC.

Section 80(1), CPC reads:

> "Save as otherwise provided in sub-sec. (2), no suit shall be instituted against the Government (including the Government of the State of Jammu and Kashmir) or against a public officer in respect of any act purporting to be done by such public officer in his official capacity, until the expiration of two months next after notice in writing has been delivered to, or left at the office of—
>
> (*a*) in the case of a suit against the Central Government, except where it relates to a railway, a Secretary to that Government;
>
> (*b*) in the case of a suit against the Central Government, where it relates to a railway, the General Manager of that railway;
>
> (*bb*) in the case of a suit against the Government of the State of Jammu and Kashmir, the Chief Secretary to that Government or any other officer authorized by that Government in this behalf;
>
> (*c*) in the case of a suit against any other State Government, a Secretary to that Government or the Collector of the district;
>
> and, in the case of a public officer, delivered to him or left at his office, stating the cause of action, the name, description and place of residence of the plaintiff and the relief which he claims; and the plaint shall contain a statement that such notice has been so delivered or left."

What for is this notice? This question leads to a discussion of the object of a notice under s. 80, CPC. In *State of Madras* v *C.P. Agencies*,[1] the Supreme Court held that the object of the notice under s. 80, Code of Civil Procedure is manifestly to give the Government or the Public Officer sufficient notice of the case which is proposed to be brought against it or him so that it or he may consider the position and decide for itself or himself whether the claim of the plaintiff should be accepted or resisted. Relying on the aforesaid Supreme Court decision Calcutta High Court in *Sudhir Ranjan Halder* v *State of West Bengal*[2] and Punjab High Court in *Union of India* v *L.E. & Foundry Works*[3] held that notice under s. 80, CPC.

"...... intends to afford the defendant an opportunity to reconsider his position with regard to the claim made, and to make amends and settle the claim, if so advised, without recourse to the trouble and cost of litigation." The same view has been taken by the Patna High Court in *Bhagwan Lal* v *Union of India*.[4]

The Supreme Court in a later decision in the *State of Andhra Pradesh* v *Gundugola Venkata Suryanarayana Garu*[5] reiterated that the object of the

1 AIR 1960 SC 1309.
2 AIR 1961 Cal 626.
3 AIR 1962 Punj 262.
4 AIR 1961 Pat 200.
5 AIR 1965 SC 11; *Harbanssingh Ajitsingh* v *Union of India* AIR 1973 Bom 363; (1973)75 Bom LR 559.

notice under s. 80, CPC is to give to the Government or the public servant concerned an opportunity to reconsider its or his legal position and if that course is justified to make amends or settle the claim out of court.

Requirements of the section have been inserted by the legislature in such a way that the proposed defendant may be sure to form an idea as to who raised the claim and for what as also to judge whether meeting the claim would be prudent and resistance futile.

The object of a notice contemplated by s. 80 of the Code was to give to the concerned Governments and public officers opportunity to reconsider the legal position and to make amends and settle the claim, if so advised without litigation.[6] The legislative intention behind that section is that public money and time should not be wasted on unnecessary litigation and the Government and the public officers should be given a reasonable opportunity to examine the claim made against them lest they should be drawn into avoidable litigations. The purpose of law is advancement of justice.[7]

The whole object of serving notice under s. 80 is to give the Government sufficient warning of the case which is going to be instituted against it that the Government, if it so wished, settled the claim without litigation or afford restitution without recourse to a court of law.[8]

Notice under s. 80, CPC is requirement of law and not a mere formality. Public authorities must take it in all seriousness.[9]

The provisions in s. 80 are not intended to be used as booby traps against ignorant and illiterate persons.[10]

The requirement of the service of notice under s. 80 is mandatory. To test the proposition, it may be useful to examine the object of the provisions of the section. It is plain that the section is intended to afford the defendant an opportunity to reconsider the position and make amends or settle the claim without recourse to litigation. This can be done only if sufficient time for the purpose is granted, and the element of time, therefore, must be held to be important. The defendant must also be held to be entitled to avail of the entire period mentioned in the section while considering the matter and taking a decision. The duration of the period, therefore, appears to be of vital importance.[11]

In all suits against the Government of India notice under s. 80, CPC is not necessary. Under s. 55 of the Union Territories Act (1963) all suits and proceedings in connection with the administration of a Union Territory are

6 *Bihari Chowdhary* v *State of Bihar* AIR 1984 SC 1043; (1984)2 SCC 627.
7 *Raghu Nath Das* v *Union of India* AIR 1969 SC 674.
8 *Ghanshyam Dass* v *Dominion of India* (1984)3 SCC 46; AIR 1984 SC 1004.
9 *New India Assurance Co. Ltd.* v *Delhi Development Authority* AIR 1991 Del 298.
10 *State of MP* v *Sardarmal* AIR 1987 MP 156.
11 *Lakshmi Narain Ram Narain* v *State of Bihar* AIR 1977 Pat 73.

to be instituted by or against the Government of India. The term 'Government of India' is not defined in any statute. The definition of 'Central Government' in s. 3(8) of the General Clauses Act 1897 cannot lead to the conclusion that the Central Government and the Government of India mean one and the same legal entity. Hence s. 80 of the Code of Civil Procedure which speaks of suits against Central Government and State Governments only and not against the Government of India, does not apply to suit against the Government of India and in a suit which is to be filed against the Government of India under s. 55 of the Union Territories Act a notice to the Secretary of the Central Government is not necessary.[12]

2 Form and contents of a notice under s. 80, CPC

Section 80, CPC does not prescribe any particular form of a notice under this section.

A notice under s. 80, CPC need not be in any particular or technical form.[13] It need not set out all details and facts of the case.[14]

A notice does not have to state section under which it is made so long as the ingredients of s. 80(3), CPC are met. A suit was filed against partial termination of Government contract after rejection of writ petition and before preferring a writ appeal. Notice sent to State Government was only under s. 80, CPC in the event writ appeal failed and a suit would have to be filed. Such notice is in proper compliance with s. 80, CPC.[15]

There may not be any form but essentials of a valid notice under s. 80, CPC must be there. It is no doubt true that a notice under s. 80, CPC is not a pleading and need not be a copy of the plaint and that no particular or technical form is prescribed for such a notice, still having regard to the object for which s. 80 has been enacted, the details which it contains should be sufficient to inform the party on whom it is served of the nature and basis of the claim and the relief sought.[16] The Supreme Court in *State of Andhra Pradesh* v *Gundugola Venkata Suryanarayana Garu*[17] mentions the essentials which any notice under s. 80, CPC should contain.

Despite the opinion that s. 80, CPC notice need not have any specific form, contents of a valid notice should be specified therein; for, there is no scope for speculation. "It may be that on reading of the notice it might be possible to spell out as to what relief the intending plaintiff wanted to claim. The wordings of s. 80 do not show that the court should embark upon a

12 *Kanhaiya Lal Oswal* v *Govt. of India* AIR 1975 Gau 37.
13 *Raj Kishan Jain* v *Tulsi Dass* AIR 1958 Raj 23; *Kashinath* v *Nawalo* AIR 1934 Pat 346.
14 AIR 1955 Bom 98; AIR 1959 AP 192.
15 *Y. Savarimuthu* v *State of Tamil Nadu* (2019)13 SCC 142.
16 *Amar Nath Dogra* v *Union of India* AIR 1963 SC 424.
17 AIR 1965 SC 11; (1964)4 SCR 945.

speculation as to what relief the plaintiff wanted to claim. It is the duty of the plaintiff to say in the notice as to what relief he wants to seek."[18] When it was not clear the notice was invalid.

As there is no specific form a notice-giver may indulge in incorporating in the notice superfluous matters. But superfluous matters mentioned in the notice but omitted from the plaint do not render the notice invalid.[19]

It may be mentioned that s. 80, CPC enacts only the rule of procedure for getting relief in respect of a cause of action.[20] Ingredients of a valid notice under s. 80 are only name, description and place of residence of the plaintiff and relief which he claims—mere fact that an incorrect statement of fact has inadvertently been made in the body of the notice relating to matter which would make no difference to real issue involved in controversy cannot render the notice invalid.[21] If requirements of the section are complied with, the form and language are of lesser significance.

Whatever may have been stated above a notice under s. 80, CPC will be valid if in such notice—

(*a*) the name, description and the residence of the plaintiff had been so given as to enable the appropriate authority or the public officer to identify the person serving the notice and such notice had been delivered or left at the office of the appropriate authority specified in sub-sec. (1), and

(*b*) the cause of action and the relief claimed by the plaintiff had been substantially indicated.

3 Name, description and place of residence of the plaintiff—mention thereof in a notice under s. 80, CPC

A notice under s. 80, CPC should state names, descriptions and places of residence of all plaintiffs,[22] so that the defendant may learn the identity of the person or persons who intends or intend to sue. It is, therefore, desired that the name and description of the plaintiff should be given in the plaint exactly as in the notice. Notice issued by a person in his own name will not be sufficient for a suit instituted by him as manager of the Hindu Joint Family.[23]

18 *Raj Kishan Jain* v *Tulsi Dass* AIR 1958 Raj 23.
19 *Sourendra Mohan* v *Secy. of State* AIR 1934 Pat 701.
20 *State of Seraikella* v *Union of India* AIR 1951 SC 253.
21 AIR 1967 P&H 497.
22 *Secretary of State* v *Chimanlal Jamnadas* AIR 1942 Bom 161; ILR 40 Cal 503; *Bihari Chowdhary* v *State of Bihar* (1984)2 SCC 627; AIR 1984 SC 1043; *Ghanshyam Dass* v *Dominion of India* (1984)3 SCC 46; AIR 1984 SC 1004.
23 *Ramachandra Naidu* v *Kandaswamy Mudaliar* AIR 1949 Mad 416.

What sort of description is required? It is not stated in s. 80 what kind of description of the plaintiffs ought to be given who desire to file a suit. "It would be sufficient if the plaintiffs are described in such a manner that they could be easily identified, and if the fathers' names of all the plaintiffs are given and their places of residence are given, the failure to give their surnames, caste or occupation does not make the notice defective".[24] Let us refer to a few illustrations: (*i*) Notice issued in the name of the family firm cannot be converted as notice by managing member of the family firm.[25] (*ii*) Notice given by a private firm is bad in a suit brought by the proprietor in his individual capacity.[1] (*iii*) Notice stating plaintiff is a partnership firm is not invalid because it omits to state that it is a registered partnership.[2] (*iv*) Notice by an unregistered firm does not become invalid for want of description that it is a registered firm.[3]

On the subject of identity of the notice-giver and the actual plaintiff in the plaint, we should remember that law enjoins strict identity. Section 80 requires the notice to state the name of the plaintiff—the names of all, when there are more than one, must be given. When the notice under s. 80 has been given by only one of the two plaintiffs who have instituted a suit against the Government it is not a compliance with s. 80.[4] Code of Civil Procedure (5 of 1908) s. 80 (as it stood before the Amendment of 1976)—suit against Government by several plaintiffs some of whom had not given the notice under s. 80 is not maintainable.[5] But this was the position before the Amendment of 1976. It is no longer good law.[6] The position becomes different with regard to a representative suit against the Government under Or. 1, r. 8, CPC. In a case where notice was served by two persons but the suit was instituted by only one of them with permission of the court to institute such a representative action, the fact that the other person did not join in the suit would not render the plaint and proceedings in the suit defective.[7] Notice in the name of the firm but the suit filed by all the partners constituting the firm—notice not bad.[8]

24 AIR 1942 Bom 161.
25 AIR 1957 Mys 94.
1 *Surajmal Jain* v *Union of India* AIR 1956 Pat 478.
2 *State of Madras* v *C.P. Agencies* AIR 1954 Nag 342.
3 *State of Madras* v *C.P. Agencies* AIR 1954 Nag 342 at 345.
4 *Government of Madras* v *Vellayan Chettiar* AIR 1944 Mad 544.
5 *Dagdusa Gujarathi* v *Secy. of State for India* AIR 1927 PC 176; *Vaiya Puri* v *Sinnaih* AIR 1931 Mad 175; *Chalid Kaishman* v *Rama Malan* AIR 1935 Mad 289; *Government of Madras Province* v *Vellayan Chettiar* AIR 1944 Mad 544; AIR 1947 PC 197 foll. ILR (1901)24 Mad 279.
6 *Shama Rao Hanumantharao Kulkarni* v *State of Karnataka* AIR 1981 Kant 135.
7 *Vegetable Products Ltd.* v *Their Workmen* AIR 1965 SC 11.
8 AIR 1958 MP 314.

4 Name, description and address of the proposed defendant in a notice under s. 80, CPC

It is not the function of the court to prick holes in the notice in order to invalidate it.[9] Therefore, failure to mention the exact style under which the defendant is to be impleaded is immaterial when the notice makes it clear against whom the suit is to be filed.[10] A misdescription of the proposed defendant should not invalidate the notice provided it is made clear that it is the Government against whom the plaintiff is seeking relief.[11]

In a notice under s. 80, CPC, the name of the proposed defendant need not be stated although, of course, it is expected that the person against whom the relief is sought would be particularised.[12] To quote Pandalai, J. in *Ramaswami* v *Secretary of State*: "We are not bound to abandon all commonsense but on the contrary, we must look at the document and understand it in a fair and reasonable sense in the way in which the writer meant and the addressee understood it".[13]

It is a fact that s. 80 does not require that the notice has to state the specific style under which the defendant has to be addressed and later to be sued. Omission to mention in the notice may not be fatal if from reading the notice as a whole it may be understood against whom the plaintiff seeks relief. But when the name of the defendant has been mentioned wrongly, such defect cannot be excused as a mere misdescription. And consequences will follow. Something of the kind was expressed by Reuben, J. in *Governor-General in Council* v *Amirlal*: "It is not necessary that the notice should mention the exact style under which the defendant is to be impleaded. It is sufficient if it is clear against whom the suit is to be filed and, in the case of a suit against the Central Government, this notice is to be delivered to or left at the office of the Secretary to that Government. The actual style under which the defendant is to be described is necessarily determined by the provisions of s. 79".[14] In another case, the plaintiff did not state specifically whom he would sue. The fact that it was not so mentioned would not invalidate the notice. "Any person who reads this notice can have no doubt that it is a suit proposed to be filed against the Crown or the Government. There is no reason to think that the suit was to be against the Secretary as a Public Officer concerned. Obviously he has had nothing to do with any of these transactions in question, and the only reasonable way of understanding the notice is that it is given as indicated in s. 80 to the Secretary of the Railway Department, because it is a suit which is intended to be filed against the

9 AIR 1963 Bom 13.
10 *Madho Prasad Salig Ram* v *Vindhya Pradesh State* AIR 1955 VP 1.
11 AIR 1958 Cal 183 (*per* Renupada Mookerjee, J.).
12 AIR 1953 Mad 838.
13 AIR 1953 Mad 105.
14 AIR 1947 Pat 81.

Government.[15] The latest view is of course that in the decision of the Rajasthan High Court[16] which confirms broadly the principle quoted above.

In a suit against Central Government relating to railway, the notice was left at the office of General Manager in the hands of a responsible senior official. Notice left at the office, held, duly complied with the statutory requirement under s. 80. Personal notice is not a condition precedent to the institution of the suit.[17]

Section 80, CPC contemplates institution of a suit against the Central Government even though it relates to a railway. A suit against the Central Government in terms of s. 79, CPC will necessarily have to be brought against the Union of India.[18]

Section 80 does not prescribe the particular person to whom it should be addressed.[19]

5 'Cause of action'—mention thereof in a notice under s. 80, CPC

Notice under s. 80 should state the cause of action and reliefs claimed.[20]

To state a cause of action, it may be sufficient to give a legal description by which a particular cause of action is known.[1] The phrase 'cause of action' in s. 80, CPC need not be narrowly construed so as to render a notice, which informs the defendant substantially of the ground of complaint, insufficient.[2] In a decision of the Bombay High Court[3] Chagla, CJ *held*: "The section is not intended to be an instrument of oppression against the subject." Where, therefore, there is no substantial variation between a notice and a plaint or, to put otherwise, the cause of action stated in the notice is substantially the same as in the plaint, maintainability of the suit will not be affected.

The object of the requirement of a notice under s. 80 of the Code of Civil Procedure is to afford the defendant an opportunity to consider his position with regard to the claim, and this object is sufficiently satisfied if the notice informs the defendant generally of the nature of the suit intended to be filed and the relief sought to be claimed. Hence the mere fact that the notice does not give any details of claim does not render it invalid.[4] Where the plaintiff has stated in his notice that he is entitled to the possession of lands in dispute in his capacity as a tenant thereof, he can sue for a declaration of

15 AIR 1951 Mad 416—AIR 1946 Mad 366 shaken.
16 AIR 1964 Raj 41.
17 *Union of India* v *Tamil Nadu Small Industries Corporation Ltd.* AIR 1981 Mad 316.
18 *State of Kerala* v *G.M., Southern Railway* AIR 1976 SC 2538; (1976)4 SCC 265.
19 *Harbansingh Ajitsingh* v *Union of India* AIR 1973 Bom 363; 75 Bom LR 559.
20 AIR 1966 All 333.
1 AIR 1938 Pat 556.
2 AIR 1954 Nag 342.
3 AIR 1951 Bom 72.
4 AIR 1961 Punj 329.

his title as also for possession without being under necessity to inform the Government in his notice under s. 80, CPC that he claimed a like declaration. The object of s. 80, CPC is fulfilled if the notice states the bundle of facts which gave rise to a right to sue. The various reliefs which can be claimed on the basis of the facts alleged in the notice is a matter governed by the substantive law and the Government cannot be heard to say that it had no notice of such claims as might under the law be founded on the facts alleged in the notice.[5] To take another illustration, a case reported in AIR 1958 SC 905, the plaintiff by his notice claimed reliefs that he was entitled to reinstatement and also demanded damages, pay etc., as if he was not discharged, but in the plaint the main relief claimed was a declaration that the order of discharge was illegal. Apparently, there was no substantial variation of the cause of action and relief claimed in the suit from the notice. The notice was held valid.

If a pleading was amended but no fresh cause of action was introduced, no fresh notice is required.[6] If an entirely new cause of action is being introduced by amendment of plaint a fresh notice under s. 80 of CPC would be required to be given. The same not having been given, the suit on this new cause of action is not maintainable.[7]

Plaintiff undertaking construction work for defendant. Defendant cancelled the contract. Subsequently, plaintiff again continued the work on the basis of revised estimates. Defendant finally terminated the contract. Plaintiff gave a notice under s. 80 with reference to earlier termination of a contract but the cause of action was based on subsequent termination of contract. *Held*, suit cannot be entertained in absence of fresh notice.[8]

A notice under s. 80 does not form cause of action. The place of sending notice does not give jurisdiction to the court of that place to entertain a suit.[9] But where a case set up in the plaint is different from the case stated in the notice, the suit is not maintainable.[10]

A notice under s. 80 of the Code is not to be construed in a pedantic manner and the court should not be hyper-technical in interpreting it. The 'cause of action' means the reason which impels a plaintiff to seek his remedy against the defendant to a suit, or, in other words, that which, according to the plaintiff, gives him a right to sue a defendant.

The facts on which the claim of the plaintiff was founded in the suit were not at all mentioned in the notice. The only other thing that was mentioned

5 AIR 1961 MP 339.
6 *Sheo Prasad Santhelia* v *State of Bihar* AIR 1975 Pat 321.
7 *Bishandayal* v *State of Orissa* AIR 2001 SC 544; (2001)1 SCC 555.
8 *R. Kamalam* v *State of Tamil Nadu* AIR 1980 Mad 86.
9 *Surya Vijay Singh* v *State of Bihar* AIR 1970 Pat 213.
10 AIR 1956 HP 9; AIR 1928 PC 176; *Vellayyaram Chettiar* v *Govt. of the Province of Madras* AIR 1947 PC 197 foll.

was that the cause of action arose to the plaintiff on the date when the order of the dismissal was passed, as also on the date when the order of dismissal was served on him and on the date on which the appeal filed by him was rejected. It was submitted that the particular act which gave the plaintiff his cause of complaint was the order of dismissal itself and this was pointed out in the notice.

It was *held*, that the reason which gave the plaintiff the right to sue was no doubt the order of dismissal. But that by itself was not sufficient to be stated. The facts on the basis of which it was stated that the order was illegal and invalid should have been stated in the notice. The notice in the instant case did not comply with the requirements of s. 80 and therefore, the suit was bad for want of a proper and valid notice.[11]

When a notice substantially informs the defendant of the nature of the suit and the grounds of complaint, the legal requirement would stand satisfied. An order for reversion to earlier order was passed. The plaintiff, therefore served a notice. Subsequent order was a mere repetition of the earlier one. The relief sought for by the plaintiff in the notice and the relief claimed by him in the plaint were substantially the same. The first notice would meet the requirement of law.[12]

6 Reliefs sought for—mention thereof in a notice under s. 80, CPC

A notice under s. 80, CPC is to state the relief which the intending plaintiff claims.

The question of relief in a notice has been viewed generally in Note 6 of Chapter 3 and with regard to relief under s. 80, CPC in particular in present notes of this Chapter.

Herein we would discuss about the splitting up of reliefs, addition of reliefs, change of reliefs, and about ancillary reliefs. As a general proposition, it may be worthwhile to quote the reported case in AIR 1963 SC 424: "It is no doubt true that a notice under s. 80 is not a pleading and need not be a copy of the plaint and that no particular or technical form is prescribed for such a notice, still having regard to the object for which s. 80 has been enacted, the details which it contains should be sufficient to inform the party, on whom it is served, of the nature and basis of the claim and the relief sought.[13]

Now, relief may be split up in circumstances as are: a joint notice given by all the plaintiffs of different suits mentioning the total amount payable by the Secretary of State is proper when the sum total demanded in the separate suits does not exceed the amount mentioned in the notice. There

11 *Qamaruddin* v *Union of India* AIR 1982 All 169.
12 *Pratap Narain Sinha* v *State of Bihar* AIR 1984 Pat 212.
13 *Amar Nath Dogra* v *Union of India* AIR 1963 SC 424.

is no particular form of notice prescribed anywhere and so long as the notice served satisfies the condition provided in s. 80, the mere splitting up of the notified claim into different suits does not render the suits non-maintainable for want of notice.[14]

Addition in the plaint of a relief,[15] which was not covered by the notice will not entail dismissal of the entire suit if the plaintiffs amend their plaint and proceed with the suit without that releif.[16]

Change of relief by way of reduction is permissible. The fact that in the suit the claim made is reduced to a smaller amount than in the notice does not change cause of action for the suit or make the notice invalid.[17]

All forms of relief need not be given in detail.[18] Reliefs which are ancillary to the main relief claimed may be admitted.

Where the notice under s. 80 precisely stated that the plaintiff, amongst others, would claim the relief of damages on the unpaid price of the goods for the period the price was withheld, the trial judge would not be justified in rejecting the claim of the plaintiff in this respect on the ground that the rate of interest to be claimed or the actual quantum of damages by way of interest had not been specified in the notice.[19]

Amendment of plaint seeking changed reliefs. If no new cause of action, may be allowed.[20]

After amendment in s. 80 by the CPC (Amendment) Act 1976 rigours with regard to 'relief' in a notice have been slackened. The amendment cl. (*b*) of sub-sec. (3) enjoins that the notice would be a valid notice if the cause of action and the relief claimed by the plaintiff have been substantially indicated therein.

Technical defect or a venial defect cannot be allowed to make the notice invalid.

7 Notice—a condition precedent to a suit against (*a*) Government, (*b*) Public Officer

(a) *Against Government*

Broadly speaking, a notice under s. 80, CPC, must be given in all classes of suits against a Government.[1] In respect of suits to which s. 80 applies compliance with it is mandatory. Therefore, a suit which does not satisfy its

14 AIR 1934 Pat 346.
15 *State of Rajasthan* v *Associated Stone Industries Kota Ltd.* AIR 1971 Raj 128; 1971 Raj LW 334.
16 *Braham Dutt* v *East Punjab* AIR 1958 Punj 351.
17 AIR 1958 Punj 351.
18 *Sourendra Mohan* v *Secy. of State* AIR 1934 Pat 701.
19 *State of West Bengal* v *Ajit Kumar Mukherjee* AIR 1977 Cal 273; 81 CWN 36.
20 *Sheo Prasad Santhelia* v *State of Bihar* AIR 1975 Pat 321.
1 AIR 1947 Cal 26.

terms is liable to be dismissed.[2] If the plaintiff's cause of action is against a Government and the plaint does not show that notice under s. 80, of the Code of Civil Procedure claiming relief was served in terms of the said section, it would be the duty of the court to reject the plaint recording an order to the effect with reasons for that order. In such a case the court should not embark upon a trial of all the issues involved and such rejection would not preclude the plaintiff from presenting a fresh plaint in respect of the same cause of action.[3] It must now be regarded as the settled law that a suit against the Government or a public officer, to which the requirement of a prior notice under s. 80, CPC is attracted cannot be validly instituted until the expiration of the period of two months next after the notice in writing has been delivered to the authorities concerned in the manner prescribed for in the section and, if filed before the expiry of the said period, the suit has to be dismissed as not maintainable.[4] Non-compliance with it takes away the jurisdiction of the court to entertain a suit. Thus, when the section has not been complied with, the court has no jurisdiction to try the suit against a Government.[5] If any suit is filed against the Government without notice under s. 80, CPC, plaint must be rejected under Or. 7, r. 11(*d*).[6]

For suits against the Government of India—notice is not necessary.[7]

The suit, for non-compliance with s. 80, can be dismissed. However, as the dismissal of the suit visits the plaintiff with more disadvantages than the rejection of the plaint, it is to the advantage of the plaintiff to have the plaint rejected since in that case a further suit on the same cause of action is not barred.[8]

A permission to file a suit without service of any notice as required under s. 80, CPC against State Government was granted on the day of institution of the suit such suit is valid and cannot be interfered with.[9]

Once the court is seized of an application under s. 80(2) it ought to have disposed of that application first either by granting leave or refusing it. But if the applicant's suit was already registered by court and an *ex parte* interim

2 *Amar Nath Dogra* v *Union of India* AIR 1963 SC 424.

3 *Gangappa Gurupadappa Gugwad Gulbarga* v *Rachawwa* (1970)3 SCC 716; AIR 1971 SC 442.

4 *Bihari Chowdhary* v *State of Bihar* AIR 1984 SC 1043; (1984)2 SCC 627 rel. on in *Premier Enterprises* v *State of Meghalaya* AIR 1992 Gau 98.

5 *Government of Madras Province* v *Vellayan Chettiar* AIR 1944 Mad 544; AIR 1956 HP 9.

6 *B.L. Chopra* v *Punjab State* AIR 1961 Punj 150; *Lakshmi Narain* v *Union of India* AIR 1962 Pat 64; *Ebrahimbhai* v *State of Maharashtra* AIR 1975 Bom 13; 75 Bom LR 769; *M/s. Premier Enterprises* v *State of Meghalaya* AIR 1992 Gau 98.

7 See *Kanhaiya Lal Oswal* v *Government of India* AIR 1975 Gau 37.

8 *R.T.O.* v *N.V. Motor Service, Kozhikode* AIR 1973 Ker 219; 1973 Ker LJ 608.

9 *State of UP* v *Jaman Singh* AIR 2007 Uttar 10.

order was passed, it could be presumed that the court had impliedly granted leave to institute the suit or that notice stood waived in the facts and circumstances of the case. Therefore, such a suit cannot be dismissed for want of notice.[10]

(b) *Against Public Officer*[11]

There are two parts of the section. One, in regard to the institution of the suit against the Government and the other against a public officer. The inhibition contained in the section as to the institution of suit against the Government is unqualified. No suit can be instituted against the Government or, for that matter, against the State or the Union until the expiration of two months next after notice in writing has been given to the proper authority. It matters little whether the suit relates to the past action of the Government or is in relation to the threatened action or injury and the suit is in the nature of a bill *quia timet*. But if the suit is to be filed against a public officer, notice is mandatory only when it is in respect of any act purporting to be done by such public officer in his official capacity. If the act is not one purporting to be done by the officer in his official capacity, no notice is necessary.[12]

In short, the law on the subject is settled. There must be nexus between the right or the official capacity of the authority passing the order and the act complained against. In the absence of any such nexus or connection, a person who may be a public officer otherwise shall not be protected by the provisions under s. 80 of the Code. A public officer is entitled to such a notice if the act complained of is done by him in his official capacity.[13]

In the case of Public Officer notice is necessary only where the suit is in respect of any act purporting to be done by such public officer in his official

10 *Smt. Yashod Kumari* v *Municipal Corporation of Delhi* AIR 2004 Del 225; (2004)111 DLT 33.

11 (1) The Public Officer—The definition of public officer in s. 2(17)(*h*) of Code of Civil Procedure and that of Public servant in s. 21(9) of the Indian Penal Code is quite identical and includes 'every officer in the services or pay of the Government or remunerated by fees or commission for the performance of any public duty'.

(2) 'In respect of any act purporting to be done'—covers not only past but also future acts (*Union of India* v *Baijnath Sarda* AIR 1971 Cal 56).

(3) Suit against State Government in respect of acts done by public official (Tehsildar).

Notice—copy of notice, addressed to State Government, was sent to Tehsildar. *Held,* not sufficient. Independent notice has to be delivered to Tehsildar. The suit is liable to be dismissed for want of proper notice (*B.S. Yadava* v *Prabhudayal* AIR 1992 MP 203).

12 *State of Bihar* v *Jiwan Das Arya* AIR 1971 Pat 141.

13 *Bidhu Bhusan* v *S.A. Aziz* AIR 1985 Pat 165; *Bihari Chowdhary* v *State of Bihar* (1984)2 SCC 627; AIR 1984 SC 1043; *Ghanshyam Dass* v *Dominion of India* (1984)2 SCC 46; *State of Maharashtra* v *Shri Chander Kant* (1977)1 SCC 257.

capacity.[14] Where the defendant, a public officer, had purported to act in the discharge of his public duty though in fact it was not so, the provisions of s. 80, CPC are attracted.[15] A Minister of State is a Public Officer and accordingly notice under s. 80, CPC would be required.[16] If official act is done even with *mala fide* intention, but in official discharge of duty or under the colour of office, it will still be an official act so as to attract the provision of s. 80, CPC. In such a case, without notice a suit is not maintainable and no interim injunction can be granted.[1] Suit for malicious prosecution against police officers—Notice under s. 80 is essential irrespective of whether they acted *mala fide* or *bona fide*, for maintainability of suit.[2]

But there may be circumstances when a public officer may be sued without a prior notice, i.e. cases where he does not act as a public officer. Public Officer has been defined in s. 2(17) of the Code of Civil Procedure. To be brief, it means every officer in the service or pay of the Government as renumerated by fees or commission in s. 2(17)(*h*) of the Code. For the question whether a notice under s. 80, CPC is required or not, the points to be determined are (*i*) whether the officer intended to be sued is a Public Officer; and (*ii*) whether the act sought to be challenged in the suit was done by such officer in his official capacity.

If the first condition is fulfilled, the notice is required generally. But there may be exceptions. Where the suit is not in respect of the act done by a public officer, no notice is necessary though he is impleaded as a defendant in a suit.[3] For suit in respect of a property of a company in custody of the Official Liquidator—no notice under s. 80 of the CPC is necessary. Though the Official Liquidator is a Public Officer, the suit is not in respect of any act done by the Official Liquidator. Even after the liquidation proceedings the company exists in a separate and independent character. Therefore, a suit in respect of property of such a company, which must necessarily be through the Official Liquidator, cannot be described to be a suit against the Official Liquidator in respect of an act done in his official capacity. So in essence the cause of action is against the company and not against any act done by the Official Liquidator as such.[4] Where at the time of the institution of the suit the defendant has ceased to be a public officer, s. 80, CPC has no application.[5] An act was done by a public officer when he was in service.

14 AIR 1941 Cal 643.
15 52 CWN 494.
16 *Shiv Bahadur* v *State of Vindhya Pradesh* AIR 1953 SC 394; *Bakshi Ghulam Md.* v *G.M. Sadiq* AIR 1968 J&K 98.
1 *U.R. Agarwal* v *Brahm Singh* AIR 1976 All 243.
2 *B.L. Shukla* v *Fatmabai Ismail* AIR 1976 Guj 29.
3 54 CWN 960; AIR 1943 Bom 138.
4 *United Bank of India* v *Tatanagar Foundry Co. Ltd.* AIR 1974 Cal 213.
5 AIR 1942 Mad 288.

After retirement of that officer a suit was filed against him. It follows logically that no notice was necessary.

Again s. 80, CPC does not apply where no relief is sought against a Public Officer personally.[6]

It will not cover acts of the Public Officer which are outside the sphere of his duties. The section is meant to cover acts done by such Public Officer in his official capacity.[7]

Where a Public Officer holds a lent-service or over office in private body (e.g. Receiver, Trustee, Administrator of a Municipality) which is not his office, for any act done by him, not being an act "purporting to be done by such Public Officer in his official capacity"—notice is not required.[8] This does not militate against the decision of Calcutta High Court[9] where the Commissioner of Calcutta Corporation was held to be a Public Officer within the meaning of s. 2(17) of the Code of Civil Procedure, and an officer in the service of the Government.

In any suit against the Commissioner, a notice under s. 80, CPC was necessary to maintain the suit. Special notice under s. 586(1) of the Calcutta Municipal Act 1951 (now the Kolkata Municipal Corporation Act 1980) cannot be suitable for that.[10] Reliance was placed in the judgment of G.K. Mitter, J. in Suit No. 3662 of 1953 decided on 18th April 1958—unreported, Calcutta—but see *Gowardhandas Rathi* v *Calcutta Municipality*[11] and *Metro General Traders* v *Commissioners, Corporation of Calcutta*.[12] The Commissioner of the Corporation of Calcutta was, *held*, not a Government servant. Notice under s. 80 of the Code was not necessary. In both the Bench decisions, the aforesaid single Bench decision in *Central Glass Industries Ltd.* v *Commissioners, Corporation of Calcutta*[13] and *Shivadhar* v *Corporation of Calcutta*[14] have been dissented from [Followed in *Municipal Commissioners of Howrah* v *Hindusthan Mfg. Co.*].[15]

6 *State of Madras* v *C.P. Agencies* AIR 1960 SC 1309; AIR 1962 Cal 625; AIR 1934 PC 96; *Chandrakant Govind Deshmukh* v *State of Maharashtra through Collector Amravati* AIR 1970 Bom 301; AIR 1950 Pat 427; AIR 1942 Cal 394; *Bhuban Mohini Debi* v *Biraj Mohan Ghosh* AIR 1940 Cal 1.

7 52 CWN 494.

8 44 CWN 74; 41 CWN 322.

9 *Shivadhar* v *Calcutta Corporation* 64 CWN 60.

10 *Raja Jagdish Chandra* v *Debendra Prasad* 35 CWN 161; *Central Glass Industries* v *Commissioner, Corporation of Calcutta* ILR (1957)1 Cal 432; *Shivadhar* v *Corporation of Calcutta* 64 CWN 60.

11 AIR 1970 Cal 539.

12 69 CWN 584.

13 AIR 1957 Cal 432.

14 64 CWN 60.

15 (1979)2 CLJ 140.

But what about Public Officers holding post in unofficial bodies? There may be cases when some Public Officers are taken in a body corporate as official members (*ex-officio*), e.g. in the managing committee of a school or a college or a like institution or in a body of trustees, as Government nominee. In such cases two situations may occur: if the body is a registered body provision of Or. XXIX, CPC will apply. If the suit be against the registered body no notice under s. 80, CPC will be required. But if the body be an unregistered body and each individual composing the body has to be impleaded in the suit, a notice under s. 80, CPC may be required before the institution of the suit to avoid a technical defect.

It is submitted that this view may not be correct. Only where such member discharges his functions as a Public Officer notice will be required.

Suit against Government in respect of acts done by public officer (Tehsildar) and a copy of notice under s. 80, CPC, addressed to State Government, was sent to Tehsildar. *Held,* notice was not sufficient. Independent notice has to be delivered to Tehsildar. The suit is liable to be dismissed for want of proper notice.[16]

Coal Mines Provident Commissioner is a public officer—suit against such officer without notice under s. 80 is not maintainable.[17]

8 Exceptions

(i) *Application under ss. 92A, 110A of the M.V. Act 1939 (now under s. 140/166 of the M.V. Act 1988)*

Under the Motor Vehicles Act no provision is made regarding any procedure to be followed before presentation of the claim before the Claims Tribunal. The only antecedent procedure prescribed is that the application should be filed within a specified period. What procedure is to be followed by the Claims Tribunal is left to its discretion subject to rules framed by the State in that behalf. No rules have been made so as to apply s. 80 of the Code of Civil Procedure to the proceedings before the Claims Tribunal if a claim is made against the Government. The provisions of the Code of Civil Procedure have been made applicable only to the extent of taking evidence on oath, enforcing the attendance of witnesses and compelling of discovery and production of documents etc. It cannot, therefore, be said that s. 80 of the Code becomes automatically applicable to the proceedings before the Claims Tribunal. Hence, notice under s. 80, Code of Civil Procedure is not necessary for an application for compensation when filed under s. 110A (now s. 166) of the M.V. Act against the Government before a Claims Tribunal constituted

16 *B.S. Yadava* v *Prabhudayal* AIR 1992 MP 203; 1992 MPLJ 304.

17 *Coal Mines Provident Fund Commissioner* v *Ramesh Chander Jha* AIR 1990 SC 648; (1990)1 SCC 589.

under the Act.[18] When a public officer is made Respondent before the Tribunal notice under s. 80, Code of Civil Procedure is not necessary.[19]

(ii) *Suit in respect of property of a Company in custody of an Official Liquidator*

Though the Official Liquidator is a public officer the suit is not in respect of any act done by the Official Liquidator. Even after the liquidation proceedings the company exists in a separate and independent character. Therefore, a suit in respect of property of such company, which must necessarily be through the Official Liquidator, cannot be described to be a suit against the Official Liquidator in respect of an act done in his official capacity. So in essence the cause of action is against the company and not against any act done by the Official Liquidator as such.[20]

(iii) *Suit against a Receiver*

Receiver appointed by court is a public officer and is entitled to notice under s. 80 of the Code of Civil Procedure if the suit against him is in respect of any act done in his official capacity.[1] No notice under s. 80, CPC is necessary when the suit is not for any act or omission done by the Receiver in his personal capacity.[2]

Notice is necessary only when complaint is made of some act done by the Reciver in his official capacity, but not so when he is impleaded as receiver in possession of property.[3] Failure to pay a claim by Receiver cannot be said to be an act done in official capacity.[4]

(iv) *Suits under special statutes—notice under s. 80, CPC is not necessary*

It is not disputed that the Code of Civil Procedure is applicable to suits coming within its province and it would not be applicable to suits or proceedings under special statutes unless the said statute adopts the Code and makes it applicable thereto and to the extent it is so adopted.

The legislature under s. 204 of the Panchayat Act had adopted the CPC only for the purpose of trial of Election petitions. Rule 75 has not adopted the whole CPC but only such of the provisions thereof as are applicable at the stage of trial of suits. The legislature had not adopted s. 80, CPC and had not made it applicable to Election petitions under s. 204. In other words, s. 80 is not applicable to election petitions.[5] No notice is necessary if a suit is filed against municipality.[6]

18 *Mangilal Ganpat* v *Union of India* AIR 1974 MP 159; 1973 ACJ 352.
19 *State of Assam* v *Urmilla Dutta* 1974 ACJ 414.
20 *United Bank of India* v *Tatanagar Foundry Co. Ltd.* AIR 1974 Cal 213.
1 *Surendra* v *Jagat Narain* AIR 1946 Pat 31.
2 *S.V. Sreekanthayya* v *Lakshmi Hardware Stores* AIR 1978 Kant 100.
3 *Haridas* v *Manmatha* 41 CWN 322.
4 *Surendra* v *Jagat Narain* AIR 1946 Pat 31.
5 *Anil Pahar* v *Subhas Mahato* AIR 1985 Cal 169.
6 *City Municipal Council Bhalki* v *Gurappa* AIR 2015 SC 3826; (2016)2 SCC 200.

9 Notice—where Government or Public Officer is a mere pro forma defendant or a co-defendant

Issue of a notice and service thereof is obligatory in any suit against the Government and Public Officer. Where Government or a public officer is a mere pro forma defendant, notice is necessary.[7] Where the Government or the public officer is one of the several defendants still notice is necessary.[8]

But in a case where the Government has been made a party and the cause of action against the Government can be separated from the cause of action against other defendants, the suit can be allowed to proceed[9] after amendment. The above reported case in AIR 1953 Bhopal 28 *holds*: "Where a suit is instituted against several defendants one of whom is the Government and a valid notice under s. 80 has not been given, the whole suit is not bad but is so only with reference to the Government if the causes of action against the Government or other defendants are separable. Where the causes of action against the defendants are not separable, the whole suit is bad".[10]

A filed a suit for declaration of title and possession. The State Government was impleaded as a pro forma defendant, but did not put in appearance. The suit of *A* was decreed. Notice under s. 80, CPC was not served by 'A'. Subsequently, one of the defendants raised a plea as to want of notice under s. 80 of CPC. *Held*, it could not be raised as the State Government by non-appearance must be deemed to have waived the plea.[11]

The Official Assignee or the Receiver in insolvency is a public officer and, therefore, no suit can be instituted against him in respect of any act done by him in his capacity as such public officer without previous notice prescribed under s. 80, CPC.[12] Section 80 applies to non-feasance as well as misfeasance.[12]

10 Amendments in s. 80, CPC—notice where not necessary

A question arises as to whether a notice under s. 80, CPC is absolutely necessary in a suit against a Government Officer, a Railway Administration, a public officer or a Government in respect of any act purporting to be done by such public officer in his official capacity. The answer is in the negative.

The original s. 80 has been amended by the CPC (Amendment) Act 1976 by re-numbering s. 80 as sub-sec. (1) by re-casting its contents and by insertion of sub-secs. (2) and (3).

7 *Province of Madras* v *Maharaja of Jeypore* AIR 1943 Mad 284; AIR 1953 Bhopal 28.
8 AIR 1938 Pat 127; AIR 1939 Pat 32.
9 AIR 1964 Pat 275; AIR 1970 MP 5.
10 Also see AIR 1936 Pat 339.
11 *Ishtiyaq Hussain Abbas Hussain* v *Zafrul Islam Afzal Hussain* AIR 1969 All 161.
12 *Prasaddas* v *K.S. Banerjee* ILR (1930)57 Cal 1127.

Contents of sub-sec. (2) have been reproduced herein under Notes 11. A plaintiff is entitled to bring a suit against any Government—Central or State or any Public Officer of any Government and against the Union of India owning and representing Railway Administrations without serving a notice under s. 80(1) of CPC provided the plaintiff can satisfy the court that by the intended suit he intends to obtain an urgent or immediate relief against the Government, the Railway Administration or any public officer in respect of any act purporting to be done by such public officer in his official capacity. But for any such suit the plaintiff has to obtain leave of the court.

The court, however, shall not grant relief in the suit, whether interim or otherwise except after giving to the Government or public officer, as the case may be, a reasonable opportunity of showing cause in respect of the relief prayed for in the suit.

Therefore, it is not absolutely necessary to serve a notice under s. 80(1), CPC in all cases. To wit, cases of urgency are excepted.

However, from a conjoint reading of sub-secs. (1) and (2) of s. 80, the legislative intent is clear, namely, service of notice under sub-sec. (1) is imperative except where urgent and immediate relief is to be granted by the court, in which case a suit against the Government or public officer may be instituted, but with the leave of the court and in such case leave of the court is a condition precedent. Such leave must precede the institution of a suit without serving notice. Even though s. 80(2) does not specify how the leave is to be sought for or given, the order granting leave must indicate the ground(s) pleaded and application of mind thereon. A restriction on the exercise of power by the court has been imposed, namely, the court cannot grant relief, whether interim or otherwise, except after giving the Government or a public officer a reasonable opportunity of showing cause in respect of relief prayed for in the suit.[13]

In case the plaintiff fails to satisfy the court as to urgent necessity of the relief the plaintiff is put to start anew. For, his plaint is returned and he has to comply with provisions of s. 80(1) of the Code before re-filing of the plaint.

The amendment is welcome; but one has mixed feelings about the amendment, Provisions of s. 80(1) and s. 80(2) and Or. 39, r. 2(2), Proviso, cl. (*f*).

Clause (*f*) of the proviso to Or. 39, r. 2(2) aforementioned provides that no temporary injunction shall be granted to restrain any auction intended to be made or, the effect of any auction made, by the Government.

Where temporary injunction was sought against Government restraining them from holding of any auction or giving effect to the same, in such a case as in view of proviso to Or. 39, r. 2(2) no temporary injunction could be

13 *State of AP* v *Pioneer Builders, AP* AIR 2007 SC 113.

granted the service of notice under s. 80(1) could not be dispensed with by leave of the trial court.[14]

11 Suit against Government or Public Officer for injunction

Section 80, CPC is applicable to all forms of action including those in which the whole or part of relief claimed is an injunction. For many years there has been a marked difference of opinion between the High Court of Bombay, on the one hand, and all the other High Courts in India on the other hand as to the true application of s. 80 of the Code of Civil Procedure 1908 ...... when part or the whole of the relief claimed is a perpetual injunction. After some differences of opinion among their subordinate courts, the High Courts of Calcutta, Madras and Allahabad have now agreed in deciding that these sections are to be strictly complied with and are applicable to all forms of action and all kinds of relief ...... In Bombay, on the other hand ...... it has been held that if the immediate result of the act would be to inflict irremediable harm, s. 80 does not compel the plaintiff to wait for two months before bringing his suit, though if nothing is to he apprehended beyond what payment of damages would compensate, the rule is otherwise and section applies ...... It is certainly undesirable that a difference of opinion such as this is, should be left unresolved ...... Section 80 is express, explicit and mandatory, and it admits of no implications or exception. A suit in which *inter alia* an injunction is prayed is still a 'suit' within the words of the section, and to read any qualification into it is an encroachment on the function of legislation. The view that a suit can be brought when part or the whole of the relief claimed is an injunction without a notice is not valid.[15] Notice under s. 80, CPC not given. Suit not maintainable and no interim injunction can be granted.[16]

Where a suit has been filed against the State impleading the concerned public authority as State's agency, notice under s. 80, CPC issued by the plaintiff to the State cannot be challenged in the suit on ground of failure to issue notice to such authority.[17]

In 1927, the Madras High Court *held*: A suit merely for injunction restraining future acts, and not based on any past act of a Public Officer is not within the scope of s. 80, CPC and no notice is necessary in such a case. Ramesam, J. observed: "In respect of acts of public servants done in their official capacity, the section applies only in the case of past acts completed or begun but incomplete and not to threatened acts." Another judge of the

14 *Islamia Jr. H. School* v *State of UP* AIR 1986 All 92.

15 *Bhagchand Dagdusa* v *Secretary of State* AIR 1927 PC 176; *Sawai Singh Rai Nirmal Chand* v *Union of India* AIR 1966 SC 1068; AIR 1971 All 209; *Union of India* v *Baijnath Sarda* AIR 1971 Cal 56; *Vellayan Chettiar* v *Government of Province of Madras* AIR 1947 PC 197; AIR 1969 SC 674 distinguished.

16 *U.R. Agarwal* v *Brahm Singh* AIR 1976 All 243.

17 *Ghulam Rasool* v *State of J&K* (1983)4 SCC 623; AIR 1983 SC 1188.

some Bench, Relly, J. observed: "The words 'in respect of any act purporting to be done' cover only a past act and do not include a future act."[18]

Since then many years have passed and the question came up in different courts. Reliance has generally been placed on the case of the Privy Council. It has been held that s. 80 applies to any kind of suit, whatever the relief sought including a suit for injunction and that it applies to suits which relate to mandatory injunctions in respect of acts which have already been performed as well as a suit in which prohibitory injunctions in respect of threatened acts are asked for.[19] Again, reasoning in support of service of a notice in a suit for injunction, coming from the Andhra Pradesh High Court, appears to be interesting and at the same time convincing. Threatened injury, sought to be restrained, initiated from past acts of a Public Officer. Therefore, a notice is all the more necessary even in respect of future acts. It was *held*: "In the case of a threatened injury which is sought to be restrained by an injunction, it is difficult to imagine a plaint which does not contain allegations on which the fear of the threat complained of could be justified."[1]

If, therefore, the allegations in the plaint relate to acts purporting to be done by such public officer, whatever the relief may be that was prayed, the section is attracted and the notice is mandatory.[2]

In brief, s. 80 applies to any kind of suit, whatever relief sought, including a suit or injucntion.[3] It is doubtful if the case in 35 Bom 362 can be of any help. But in a suit for perpetual injunction against the Corporation of Calcutta coming within s. 54 of the Special Relief Act, no prior notice is required.[4]

After amendment in s. 80 of CPC by the CPC (Amendment) Act 1976, the position has changed.

The provision in s. 80, CPC has been quoted under Note 1 of this Chapter. The language of s. 80, CPC has been re-cast. Original s. 80 has been re-numbered as sub-sec. (1) and sub-secs. (2) and (3) have been inserted by the Amendment Act 1976.

Sub-section (2) enjoins:

A suit to obtain an urgent or immediate relief against the Government (including the Government of the State of Jammu and Kashmir) or any

18 AIR 1928 Mad 166.

19 AIR 1955 MB 55.

1 AIR 1957 AP 675.

2 *Sawai Singhai Nirmal Chand* v *Union of India* AIR 1966 SC 1068; (1966)1 SCR 986; *Union of India* v *R.K. Binodo Singh* AIR 1970 Manipur 90; *Union of India* v *Baijnath Sarda* AIR 1971 Cal 56; *State of Bihar* v *Jiwandas Arya* AIR 1971 Pat 141; *Certificate Officer* v *Kasturichand Malu* AIR 1970 Ori 239 case reported in AIR 1960 Pat 530 is of no avail.

3 AIR 1946 Lah 247.

4 70 CWN 969.

public officer in respect of any act purporting to be done by such public officer in his official capacity, may be instituted, with the leave of the court, without serving any notice as required by sub-sec. (1); but the court shall not grant relief in the suit, whether interim or otherwise, except after giving to the Government or public officer, as the case may be, a reasonable opportunity of showing cause in respect of the relief prayed for in the suit. Section 80(2) is in the nature of an exception to s. 80(1).

A perusal of sub-sec. (2) of s. 80, CPC reveals clearly that the grant of leave is left to the judicial discretion of the trial court. The proviso to sub-sec. (2) clearly states that the court shall, if it is satisfied, after hearing the parties, that no urgent or immediate relief need be granted in the suit, return the plaint for presentation to it after complying with the requirements of sub-sec. (1). In the matter of grant of leave dispensing with the service of notice under s. 80(1), CPC, therefore, the trial court is competent to consider whether on the ultimate analysis there is or is not in existence urgency or likelihood of immediate relief being granted to the plaintiff. Where the court considers that there is no such urgency existing or immediate relief cannot be granted, it is within its powers to decline to grant the leave.[5]

When the relief is needed urgently, but the suit would be frustrated if compliance with s. 80(1) was to be made than the court may grant liberty to file suit without serving notice.[6] Leave granted for dispensing with provisions of s. 80(1). Finding of Written Statement and taking of all steps and orders passed in presence of counsel for State—formal notice thereafter under s. 80(1) not mandatory.[7]

Section 80(2)

Application by plaintiff for leave to institute suit without serving s. 80(1) notice. Court must pass specific order on the application on considering nature of the case and reaching conclusion whether or not immediate relief is required to be afforded. No express or formal order of the court granting leave is required. Such leave can be presumed from the facts of the case, e.g. where the plaintiff has made necessary application for leave and the court directs the registration of the case.[8] Under s. 80(2) for obtaining urgent relief, suit can be filed with the leave of the court without serving notice under s. 80(1), but no *ex parte* injunction or interim relief can be granted without affording reasonable opportunity to the Government. Section 80 is mandatory.[8]

5 *Islamia Junior High School* v *State of UP* AIR 1986 All 92.
6 *Harish Chandra* v *Corporation Bank* AIR 1992 Del 279.
7 *Shri Kailash Chandra Jain* v *State of Madhya Pradesh* AIR 1992 MP 242.
8 *Janak Raj Devi* v *Chandrabati Devi* AIR 2002 Cal 11.

Return of plaint—s. 80(2) proviso

Return is permissible only if the court is satisfied that no urgent or immediate relief need be granted.[9] The court coming to conclusion that it cannot grant relief claimed by plaintiff under s. 80(2). It must return plaint with direction that it should be presented after serving notice.[10]

The provision is not without mixed results. On the one hand, it removes the obstacle of filing the suit without serving a notice and waiting for two months to watch the reaction; on the other hand, it takes away court's jurisdiction to pass an *ex parte* order even if there were urgency.

They only benefit granted by the amendment lies in removal of time-lag which may save a plaintiff from an impending wrong. Main condition of the enabling provision is the necessity for an urgent or immediate relief which cannot brook delay of two months required in a notice under s. 80(1), CPC.

The prerequisite is 'leave of the court'. Prayer for leave may be oral or in writing. The court has to be satisfied that the plaintiff has a *prima facie* case and the suit is proper to be filed without complying with sub-sec. (1) of s. 80 with an eye to urgency of the relief.

Therefore, it cannot be said now that suit against Government without a notice under s. 80, CPC should be dismissed *in limine* in all cases.

12 Interpretation and construction of a notice under s. 80, CPC—inartistic and careless drafting of notice

Several decisions of the Supreme Court will indicate as to how a notice under s. 80, CPC should be interpreted and construed. Although strict compliance with the terms of section is necessary, it is not necessary to scrutinize the notice in a pedantic manner devoid of commonsense.[11] Notices must be read in a rational and sensible manner. It is not the function of the court to prick holes in the notice in order to invalidate it.[12] What is more, the provision is not intended to set up booby traps against ignorant and illiterate persons.[13] Section 80, CPC should be construed with some regard to commonsense bearing in mind the object for which it stands.[14] Section 80 of the Code is but a part of the Code of Civil Procedure enacted to provide the regulation and machinery, by means of which the courts may do justice between the parties. It is, therefore, merely a part of the adjective law and deals with procedure alone and must be interpretated in a manner so as to

9 *K.K. Sharma* v *State of Punjab* AIR 1989 P&H 7.
10 AIR 1985 P&H 32.
11 *Dhian Singh Sobha Singh* v *Union of India* AIR 1958 SC 274; *State* v *C.P. Agencies* AIR 1960 SC 1309; *Amar Nath Dogra* v *Union of India* AIR 1963 SC 424; (1963)1 SCR 657.
12 AIR 1963 Bom 13.
13 *Raghu Nath Das* v *Union of India* AIR 1969 SC 674; (1969)1 SCR 450.
14 *Union of India* v *Mangilal Janakiprasad* AIR 1979 Gau 17.

subserve and advance the cause of justice rather than to defeat it. In *Sangram Singh* v *Election Tribunal, Kotah*,[15] Vivian Bose, J. in his illuminating language dealing with the Code of Civil Procedure said:

> "It is *Procedure*, something designed to facilitate justice and further its ends: not a penal enactment for punishment and penalties: not a thing designed to trip people up. Too technical a construction of sections that leaves no room for reasonable elasticity of interpretation should, therefore, be guarded against (provided always that—justice is done to both sides) lest the very means designed for the furtherance of justice be used to frustrate it."

Our laws of procedure are based on the principle that "as far as possible, no proceeding in a court of law should be allowed to be defeated on mere technicalities."[16]

The Supreme Court in *State of Andhra Pradesh* v *Gundugola Venkata Suryanarayana Garu* has observed: Every venial error or defect cannot be permitted to be treated as a peg to hang a defence to defeat a just claim. In each case, in considering whether imperative provisions of the statute are complied with, the court must face the following questions:

(*a*) whether the name, description and residence of the plaintiff are given so as to enable the authorities to identify the person serving the notice;

(*b*) whether the cause of action and the relief which the plaintiff claims are set out with sufficient particularity;

(*c*) whether the notice in writing has been delivered to or left at the office of the appropriate authority mentioned in the section; and

(*d*) whether the suit is instituted after the expiration of two months next after notice has been served, and the plaint contains a statement that such a notice has been so delivered or left.

In construing the notice the court cannot ignore the object of the legislature to give to the Government or the public servant concerned an opportunity to reconcile its or his legal position. If, on a reasonable reading but not to make undue assumptions, the plaintiff is shown to have given the information which the statute requires him to give, any incidental defects or errors may be ignored.[17] Little commonsense should be imported.[18] Where the notice contained all the particulars required by s. 80, CPC the mere fact that it was

15 (1955)2 SCR 1; AIR 1955 SC 425.

16 *Ghanashyam Das* v *Dominion of India* AIR 1984 SC 1004.

17 *State of Andhra Pradesh* v *Gundugola Venkata Suryanarayana Garu* AIR 1965 SC 11; (1964)4 SCR 945.

18 59 CWN 405.

signed by some person other than the plaintiff under the authority of the plaintiff and on his behalf, the notice would not be invalid.[19]

The mere fact that a notice under s. 80 is inartistically and carelessly drafted, that by itself should not defeat the plaintiff's claim against Government when all the necessary information is contained in the notice and there is no vital difference between the notice and the plaint.[20] Where a notice under s. 80, even though not an exact copy of the plaint, mentions all material ingredients of the plaint, it is legal, valid and sufficient.[21]

13 Defects in a notice under s. 80, CPC—how far excusable

When the Government is neither a necessary party nor a proper party to an action, any defect in the notice under s. 80, CPC issued to the Government would not affect the suit so far as the defendants were concerned.[22] The section admits of no exceptions or implications. Therefore, a notice which does not state the intention to file a suit will not constitute a valid notice under this section. Thus, a notice is not valid where it simply states that the plaintiff 'reserves his right to claim the damages', a right which he might or might not exercise.[23] Defect of misdescription of the proposed defendant does not make the notice improper.[1]

If a notice under s. 80 be defective, the same would not *per se* render the suit bad in the eye of law, the suit requiring issuance of such a notice as a precondition for instituting the same; as such a defect if minor in nature can be waived. The protection provided by s. 80 is a protection given to the person concerned and if in any particular case that person does not require that protection he can lawfully waive his right. A distinction is to be made where the benefit conferred is to serve "an important purpose", in which case there would not be waiver.[2]

Wrong number of a railway receipt in a notice under s. 80, CPC in connection with railway claim case does not necessarily invalidate a notice.[3]

Section 80, CPC has been amended by the CPC (Amendment) Act 1976. Sub-sections (2) and (3) have been inserted. In particular sub-sec. (3) refers to trifling defects in a notice under s. 80 which may not invalidate a notice otherwise valid.

19 *Sahdul Man Md. Mian* v *Union of India* AIR 1968 Pat 188.
20 *Sohaja Bomma Divera* v *State of Andhra Pradesh* AIR 1972 AP 130.
21 *Surendra Nath Mondal* v *State of West Bengal* AIR 1985 Cal 53.
22 AIR 1963 Mad 362.
23 AIR 1958 Punj 351.
1 AIR 1953 Mad 838.
2 *Krishan Lal* v *State of J&K* (1994)4 SCC 422. See also *Vellayan Chettiar* v *Government of Province of Madras* AIR 1947 PC 197; 74 IA 223; *Bhagchand Dagadussa* v *Secretary of State* 54 IA 338.
3 AIR 1966 All 16.

Sub-section (3) enjoins that no suit shall be dismissed merely by reason of any error or defect in the notice if in such notices—

(*i*) name, residence and description of the plaintiff have been so given as to enable the defendant to identify the person serving the notice;

(*ii*) such notice had been delivered or left at the office of the appropriate authority specified in sub-sec. (1);

(*iii*) the cause of action and relief claimed have been substantially indicated.

14 Waiver of a notice under s. 80, CPC

Mere impossibility of compliance with the requirements of a notice under s. 80, CPC cannot attract the principle of waiver.[4]

The provision under s. 80, CPC is mandatory but the right can be waived by the party for whose benefit it has been provided.[5]

Where the written statement that contained no objection that the suit was not maintainable for want of notice, nor was any issue framed thereon and the defendant did not apply to amend the written statement for incorporating the plea, it must be held that the defendant waived the objection.[6]

Government files written statement after long delay but raising plea of want of notice under s. 80. No waiver.[7] But notice should be deemed to have been waived, if objection is raised at a late stage (delay of two years).[8]

If a notice has been given to the concerned necessary party in the proper way, the requirement of service of notice upon the other parties may be waived.[9]

15 Service of a notice under s. 80, CPC—when service is effected

Delivery of a notice or to leave a notice at the office will constitute sufficient service of a notice under s. 80, CPC. The delivery of a notice or the act of leaving a notice may be in person as well as by post.

The section does not specify whom the notice has to be addressed to. Normally, a notice is delivered to or left at the office of a person who is addressed therein. Depending on this normal course of affairs, it may be held that there is no harm,

4 *State of Bihar* v *Jiwandas Arya* AIR 1971 Pat 141.

5 *Dayanand* v *State* AIR 2001 Raj 257; *Municipality* v *Gas Authority of India Ltd.* AIR 2006 MP 17.

6 *Suraj Bhan* v *Executive Engineer* AIR 1973 All 269; *Paleti Sivaramakrishnaiah* v *Executive Engineer* AIR 1978 AP 389.

7 *Ebrahimbhai* v *State of Maharashtra* AIR 1975 Bom 13.

8 *Union* v *Tejnarain* AIR 1957 MB 108.

9 *Manindra Ch. Paul* v *State of Tripura* AIR 2007 Gau 103; (2008)1 Civ CC 771.

(*i*) if in a suit against the Central Government (except where it relates to a railway) the notice is addressed to the Secretary to that Government;

(*ii*) if in a suit against the Central Government where it relates to a railway the notice is addressed to the General Manager of that railway;

(*iii*) if in a suit against a State Government the notice is addressed either to a Secretary to that Government or to the Collector of the district; and

(*iv*) if in a suit against a Public Officer, the notice is addressed to such Public Officer.

And, as a matter of fact, this is usually done; and no court found the practice erroneous. We may refer to two Patna High Court decisions where it has been *held*: When a notice has to be delivered or left at the office of a Secretary to the Government, it must obviously mean that the notice has also to be addressed in such a case to the Secretary to that Government.[10]

Mere despatch of a notice under s. 80, CPC to the address of person is not sufficient. It must be actually either delivered or tendered to the persons to whom they are required to be given.[11]

Service of notice under s. 80, CPC by the father of the plaintiff prior to filing the suit for recovery of damages is not sufficient. Plaintiff being an aggrieved party himself ought to have served notice. Such a suit is not maintainable.[12]

If the notice, per chance, is not rightly addressed does it matter much? No.

A few reported cases, as herein below, would explain the position on this issue. Those are:

(*i*) Suit against the Union of India—notice sent to Collector. *Held*, valid.[13]

(*ii*) Section 80 shows that the notice is not required to be addressed to the Government and the fact that the notice is not addressed to the Government but to the Secretary to the Government does not make it invalid.[14]

(*iii*) Where the letter addressed to and received by the Director of Consumer Goods contains an endorsement that a copy was sent

10 *Governor-General in Council* v *Amirlal* AIR 1947 Pat 81; AIR 1949 Pat 416.

11 *State of Karnataka* v *M. Muniraju* AIR 2002 Kant 287; (2002)1 Mad LJ 186; (2002)1 Mad LW 57.

12 *Manoj Kumar Shrivastava* v *Arvind Kumar Choubey* AIR 2002 MP 152; (2002)1 MPLJ 172.

13 AIR 1963 HP 37.

14 *State of Bombay* v *N.T. Advani* AIR 1963 Bom 13.

to the Secretary, Civil Supplies Department, in view of this fact, even the slightest evidence that has been produced to show the posting of a copy of the letter which had in fact been sent to the Secretary, Civil Supplies Department—the fact that the original letter had been addressed to the Director of Consumer Goods does not take away the legal effect of the letter.[15]

(*iv*) Notice of a suit against the State of Madras addressed to the Secretary to the Commissioner of Civil Supplies, Government of Madras who was also the Secretary, Civil Supplies Food Department, Madras and received by the latter. *Held*, the notice was sufficient.[16]

(*v*) *Section 80(3) (as amended by Amendment Act 1976), Coal Mines (Notification Act 1973)—s. 20—notice under.*

Notice can be delivered to or left at the address of Secretary to Government or Collector of the district. In a suit for refund of excess payment of royalty under the Coal Mines (Notification) Act 1973 the notice was sent to the District Mining Officer, authorised agent of the State to realise royalty. *Held*, the State was not prejudiced. The notice was not invalid on grounds that it was not addressed to the Secretary of the State.[17]

(*vi*) In a suit questioning the order of vesting, notice under s. 80 should be issued to the Government and the Government should be impleaded as a party.[18]

16 Period of notice under s. 80, CPC—computation of the period—application of s. 10 of the General Clauses Act 1897

Section 80 enjoins: "No suit shall be instituted .... until the expiration of two months next after notice in writing has been delivered to or left at ...." meaning thereby that the period of notice is for two months.

The day of delivery of notice must be excluded from two months provided by the section. The period of two months as laid down in s. 80 should be taken as exclusive of the day on which the notice is served.[19] A suit, therefore, brought on 11th January 1939, when the notice was served on 11th November 1938, should be regarded as premature and unsustainable *in limine*.[20] Notice served on the 17th July 1963, suit filed on the 18th

15 *S.N. Banik* v *State of West Bengal* AIR 1963 Cal 79 (*per* A.K. Mookerji, J).
16 *State of Madras* v *C.P. Agencies* AIR 1954 Nag 342. Also see AIR 1953 Mad 838; AIR 1958 Cal 183.
17 *State of Bihar* v *Bera Colliery Co.* AIR 1991 Pat 178.
18 *Smt. Sooraj* v *S.D.O., Rehli* AIR 1995 SC 872.
19 *Madurai K. Chettiar & Co.* v *Union of India* AIR 1971 Mad 34.
20 AIR 1945 Cal 431.

September 1963. Suit held filed after expiry of two months and could not be said to be premature.[1] The day on which a notice was actually served should be excluded in calculating the period of two months.[2] A notice under s. 80, CPC should be of two months exclusive of the day on which the notice was served.[3]

There is no warrant for the proposition that the period of two months should mean 60 days. The calculation of the period must be made monthwise.[4]

Where s. 10 of the General Clauses Act 1897, applies to calculation of the period in a notice under s. 80, CPC is no longer a controversy. Section 10 of the General Clauses Act is an enabling section permitting one to do on the opening day which he could have done on a holiday. Since s. 80 does not direct that any act or proceeding should be done or taken in any court or office in a certain day or within a prescribed period s. 10 of the General Clauses Act does not apply to computation of time of a notice under s. 80, CPC.

17 Savings of limitation—application of s. 15(2) of the Limitation Act 1963

Where a suit is, under a statute, to be followed by a notice, the period of such notice shall be excluded in computing the period of limitation as provided in s. 15(2) of the Limitation Act 1963.

Section 80, CPC only prescribes a condition precedent for institution of the suit and has nothing to do with the period of limitation for a suit except that under s. 15(2) of the Limitation Act, the period of notice can be deducted in calculating the period of limitation.[5]

18 Suit before expiry of two months—suit during currency of notice

A suit against the Government and the Public Officer has to be filed after the expiry of two months after service of notice. A suit cannot be lawfully instituted before the expiry of two months and if filed before expiry of said period, the suit has to be dismissed as not maintainable.[6] A suit against the Government instituted during the currency of notice must be dismissed *in limine*.[7] Where a suit is instituted against the Government before the expiry of the statutory period under s. 80, CPC the suit must be deemed not to have been instituted at all.[8] The plaint should be rejected under Or. 7, r. 11, CPC.

1 *Baijnath Prasad* v *Union of India* AIR 1980 NOC 96 (All).
2 AIR 1943 Mad 284.
3 *B.L. Chopra* v *State of Punjab* AIR 1961 Punj 150; *Madurai K. Rangiah Chettiar & Co.* v *Union of India* AIR 1971 Mad 34.
4 *Lakshmi Narain Ram Narain* v *State of Bihar* AIR 1977 Pat 73.
5 *Amar Chand Inani* v *Union of India* (1973)1 SCC 115; AIR 1973 SC 313.
6 *Bihari Chowdhary* v *State of Bihar* (1984)2 SCC 627; AIR 1984 SC 1043.
7 *Bhagchand Dagdusa* v *Secretary of State* 54 IA 338; AIR 1927 PC 176.
8 *D. Bala Krishna Murty* v *Municipal Commissioner* AIR 1961 AP 488; *Union of India* v *Devangere Cotton Mills Ltd.* AIR 1976 Mad 20.

"The plain and literal meaning of this provision (s. 80, CPC is meant) is to my mind obvious that the entire period of two months is allowed to the Government or the officer concerned ...... 'if clear two months' period was not intended by the language of the section, the words 'next after' would not have been used after the words 'notice in writing has been delivered to or left at the office of—' and these words make it obvious that two entire and clear months have been given by the statute."[9] A notice under s. 80, CPC should be of two months exclusive of the day on which notice was served. Notice served on 18th September 1953, suit filed on 18th November 1953—is premature by a day and should be dismissed (*ibid*). Service of notice on 12th June 1968, presentation of plaint on 12th August 1968. The suit is hit by s. 80.[10]

Two months' does not mean 60 days. There is no warrant for the proposition that the period of two months should mean 60 days. The calculation of the period must be made monthwise.[11] Notice was issued on 7th August 1963 and was received by the Chief Commercial Manager. Southern Railway on 8th August 1963 and the plaint was presented on 8th October 1963. The court held that after the service of notice on 8th August 1963, two months period had not expired by 8th October 1963 when the suit was instituted and therefore, the suit was hit by s. 80.[12]

Though we should be reluctant to institute a suit before the expiry of the statutory period of two months, if inadvertently a plaint is filed we may profit by the decision in *Nani Amma Nannini Amma* v *State of Kerala* where His Lordship M. Madhavan Nair, J. held: "The object of s. 80 (observed by the Supreme Court in *State of Madras* v *C.P. Agencies*)[13] is manifestly to give the Government or the public officer sufficient notice of the case which is proposed to be brought against it or him so that it or he may consider the position and decide for itself or himself whether the claim of the plaintiff should be accepted or resisted. It then follows that s. 80, CPC is not a provision of public policy but one for the benefit of particular parties who are competent to waive or disregard it. The indication is thus clear that the requirements of a notice and the expiry of a particular period thereafter are not jurisdictional facts, for jurisdiction cannot be dependent on the consent or waiver of a party ...... There is nothing in s. 80 expressly affecting the jurisdiction of the court to try suits instituted before the expiry of the period prescribed therein. The section only makes suits instituted before the expiry of two months after service of notice premature and therefore dismissible *in*

9 *B.L. Chopra* v *State of Punjab* AIR 1961 Punj 150 (*per* Mehar Singh, J.).

10 *Union of India* v *Devangere Cotton Mills Ltd.* AIR 1976 Mad 20.

11 *Lakshmi Narain* v *Union of India* AIR 1962 Pat 64; *Lakshmi Narain Ram Narain* v *State of Bihar* AIR 1977 Pat 73.

12 *Madurai K. Rengiah Chettiar* v *Union of India* AIR 1971 Mad 34.

13 AIR 1960 SC 1309.

limine. But if it has not been so dismissed and the Government or the Public Officer does not show to have been prejudiced by the premature institution of the suit, it need not necessarily be dismissed long after the expiry of the period of its prematurity."[14]

A suit filed during the currency of notice may be withdrawn with condition of refiling. The latter suit may be on the basis of the earlier notice.[15] Contra: The fact that the plaint was returned and was subsequently re-presented will have no effect whatever on the plea that by the time the plaint was re-presented the two months period contemplated by s. 80, Code of Civil Procedure had expired. The reason is that a suit is instituted when the plaint is presented for the first time.[16]

19 Identity of notice-giver with the plaintiff

One who serves a notice under s. 80, CPC and one who brings the suit must be identical. There is non-compliance with s. 80 when such identity is not established.[17] The legal representative of the intending plaintiff cannot institute the suit on a notice given by the deceased who died in the meantime. He has to serve a fresh notice for the simple reason that the identity is lost. So, when the plaintiff's father served notice but his son brought a suit on the same cause of action as the plaintiff, the notice was insufficient.[18] Again, notice given by the father—father died prior to filing of suit. The notice cannot be availed of by the plaintiff.[19] Where a composite notice under s. 80, CPC and s. 77, the Indian Railways Act 1890 (since repealed) was issued by K. Mills, of which Kuthari Trading Co., were the proprietors but the suit was filed by M/s. Kuthari Trading Co., who were the owners of K. Mills—*held* there was identity of the person who had issued the notice with the person who brought the suit and, as such, the notice fulfilled the requirements of s. 80 of CPC.[20] Provision of cl. (*a*) of sub-sec. (3) of the amended s. 80 of CPC may be seen in this connection.

Where the registered firm 'Balbagas Hullas Chand' besides its principal place of business in Calcutta carried on business also at its branch in Cuttack in the name of 'Bharadia Brothers' which was not shown as partners of the firm or the firm-name, a suit by Bharadia Brothers against the Railway for damages, cannot be treated as on behalf of the firm and would be barred under s. 69(2) of the Partnership Act and the notice issued under s. 80, Code of Civil Procedure by Bharadia Brothers cannot be treated as notice by the firm.[1]

14 *Nani Amma Nannini Amma* v *State of Kerala* AIR 1963 Ker 114.
15 AIR 1935 Bom 21.
16 *Union of India* v *Devangere Cotton Mills Ltd.* AIR 1976 Mad 20.
17 *Ramji Lal* v *Union of India* AIR 1974 Raj 18.
18 *Mahadev* v *Secretary of State* AIR 1930 Bom 367.
19 AIR 1950 Ori 257.
20 *Union of India* v *Kuthari Trading Co. Ltd.* AIR 1969 A&N 84.
1 *Bharadia Bros.* v *Union of India* AIR 1973 Ori 28.

Where the notice was issued on behalf of 'M/s. Ramjilal Giraj Prasad' and the suit was filed by Ramjilal, manager of the joint family business carried on under the name and style of 'Ramjilal Giraj Prasad' but it was not mentioned in the notice that Ramjilal was the proprietor of the business, it could not be said that the person sending the notice is the same as the person suing. Thus, there being non-compliance with s. 80, the suit was liable to be dismissed.[2] But the matter is different where the notice under s. 80 was sent by 'Kozhikode Lime Centre' and the suit was filed by 'Kozhikode Lime Centre' by Proprietor P.P. Abubacker, it was held that the difference in name caused no confusion in the defendant regarding the identity of the party and was not fatal.[3] When a notice was given by the firm but the suit was filed by the proprietor, such notice is invalid.[4]

But where a notice under s. 80, CPC was given by *karta* of a joint family and the partition was effected subsequent to notice. Notice held sufficient to sustain a suit by coparceners.[5]

But the above is to be distinguished from:

(*i*) *Bachu Singh* v *Secretary of State*[6]—A notice given by a person is not available to a successor-in-interest;

(*ii*) *Mahadev* v *Secretary of State*[7]—The benefit under the notice issued under s. 80, CPC cannot be taken advantage of by another;

(*iii*) *Venkatarangiah* v *Secretary of State*[8]—There should be identity of the person who issued the notice with the person that brings the suit.[9] A suit brought by a legal representative of a deceased person and a suit brought by a transferee would offend against s. 80, CPC if the notice required by that section was given by the deceased man or the transferor.[10]

2 *Ramji Lal* v *Union of India* AIR 1974 Raj 18.

3 *P.P. Abubacker* v *Union of India* AIR 1972 Ker 103; *Raghu Nath Das* v *Union of India* AIR 1969 SC 674; *Beohar Rajendra Sinha* v *State of Madhya Pradesh* AIR 1969 SC 1256 relied on.

4 *S.N. Dutt* v *Union of India* AIR 1961 SC 1449; (1962)1 SCR 560; *Naseema Textiles* v *Union of India* AIR 1971 Ker 192; *Union of India* v *Shankar Store* AIR 1974 Ori 85.

5 *Beohar Rajendra Sinha* v *State of Madhya Pradesh* AIR 1969 SC 1256; (1969)1 SCC 796.

6 ILR (1903)25 All 187.

7 AIR 1930 Bom 356.

8 AIR 1931 Mad 175.

9 On identity of the notice-giver and the plaintiff following cases may also be seen (*State of Andhra Pradesh* v *Suryanarayana* AIR 1965 SC 11; *B.R. Sinha* v *State of MP* AIR 1969 SC 1256; *Vellayan Chettiar* v *Government of the Province of Madras* AIR 1947 PC 197; *Govt. of the Province of Bombay* v *Pestonji Ardeshir Wadia* AIR 1949 PC 143; *B. Tiruvallor Pillai* v *Seshadri Iyer* AIR 1974 Mad 282).

10 *Venkatarangiah* v *Secretary of State* AIR 1935 Mad 389 followed in *Secretary of State* v *Hargondas* AIR 1935 Bom 229 (confirmed by D.B.).

Contra:

(*iv*) *Zamindar of Sivaganga* v *Muthayya Chettiyar*[11]—Legal representatives and assignees of the predecessor who issued the notice under s. 80 are entitled to maintain the suit on the basis of the said notice.

20 Withdrawal of a suit—whether fresh notice necessary? Question of res judicata

Withdrawal of a suit with liberty to bring fresh suit does not necessarily require service of a fresh notice under s. 80, CPC before refiling of the suit. What s. 80, CPC requires is that a notice should precede the institution of the second suit. If the plaint which is being considered by the court has been preceded by a notice which satisfies the requirements of s. 80, then the fact that before the plaint then under consideration, there had been another plaint which had been filed and withdrawn, it cannot, on any principle, be held to have exhausted or extinguished the vitality of the notice issued.[12]

Where the suit was defective for non-compliance of the mandatory provisions of s. 80, was not rejected under Or. 7, r. 11 but was tried on merits and dismissed for such non-compliance, a fresh suit for the same relief would not be barred by principles of *res judicata*. The first suit itself was not maintainable and the court which tried it, in view of s. 80, CPC, had no jurisdiction to entertain it. Since the plaint ought to have been rejected, there was no issue at all for determination between the parties. Further, for the principles of *res judicata* to apply, the court which tried the first suit should have had jurisdiction to try it.[13]

21 Amendment of plaint—fresh notice if required

Amendment of a plaint may be of various nature. In some cases reliefs prayed are amended. Since in a notice under s. 80, CPC reliefs sought for have to be mentioned, amendment in reliefs in a plaint requires fresh notice. In other words, where amendment of the plaint introduces a new cause of action or a new set of reliefs, not specified in the original notice, further notice was necessary.[14] Conversely, an amendment of a plaint which does not alter reliefs asked for in the notice and the suit, no further notice prior to amendment is necessary.[15] Again, where the amendment of the plaint gives further grounds in support of the contentions and allegations which constitute the plaintiff's cause of action, a further notice under s. 80 is not

11 AIR 1936 Mad 583.
12 AIR 1963 SC 420.
13 *Shantipada Ganguli* v *Union of India* AIR 1976 Pat 74; *N.M. Siddique* v *Union of India* (1978)2 SCC 349; AIR 1978 SC 386.
14 *Province of Madras* v *Poddar Firm* AIR 1949 Mad 214.
15 *Bishandayal and Sons* v *State of Orissa* AIR 2001 SC 544; (2001)1 SCC 555; AIR 1956 MB 98.

necessary.[16] The same principle would apply to plaintiff's additional written statement necessitated by the amendments introduced by the defendant.[17]

It, therefore, stands to reason that every amendment of a plaint would not require prior notice under s. 80, CPC. It is only when a new relief is sought or when the amendment introduces a new cause of action not mentioned in the original notice that a further notice under s. 80 is necessary. Every formal amendment of a plaint or an amendment which merely seeks to clarify what is already stated and claimed in the plaint does not require a further notice under s. 80, CPC.[18] In appropriate cases the court can grant relief not claimed in the notice.[19]

22 Variation in a notice and in the plaint

Amendment of plaint introducing discordance between facts alleged in the notice under s. 80, CPC and those pleaded in the plaint—although reliefs may be the same—plaint has to be rejected under Or. 7, r. 11.[20] Amendment introducing discord shall not be allowed.[21]

Notice under s. 80, CPC is not a pleading and need not be a verbatim copy of the plaint, but it must contain such details of facts as are sufficient to inform the parties regarding the nature and basis of the claim and the relief sought. Where there is substantial variance between notice and plaint—notice is not valid.[22]

23 State v State—notice if required

In any suit instituted in any State against any other State, a notice under s. 80, CPC must be served prior to institution of a suit (State of J&K was sued in West Bengal).[23]

24 Mentioning of service of notice in the plaint

The concluding sentence in s. 80(1) reads: "and the plaint shall contain a statement that such notice has been so delivered or left". Therefore, plaints not mentioning that such notice was served on the defendants it must be held that they were not served with any notice under s. 80 of Code of Civil Procedure.[24]

16 *Dinbai* v *Dominion of India* AIR 1951 Bom 72 (*per* Chagla, C.J.); *Bishandayal and Sons* v *State of Orissa* AIR 2001 SC 544; (2001)1 SCC 555.
17 *Lalchand* v *Union of India* AIR 1960 Cal 270.
18 *Ghulam Mohiuddin* v *State of J&K* AIR 1961 J&K 6.
19 *State of Rajasthan* v *Associated Store Industries Kota Ltd.* AIR 1971 Raj 128 contra: *New Churulia Coal Co.* v *Union of India* AIR 1959 Cal 585.
20 *Union of India* v *Abdul Manaf* AIR 1970 Manipur 44.
21 *Union of India* v *Wahengbam Lalmani Singh* AIR 1970 Manipur 54.
22 *Union of India* v *Shanker Store* AIR 1974 Ori 85.
23 72 CWN 795.
24 *Bakshi Ghulam Mohammad* v *G.M. Sadeq* AIR 1968 J&K 98.

FORMS

Form 1

Notice under s. 80, CPC

Dated .... 20 ....

To

The Secretary
.... Department
Government of ....

Dear Sir,

Notice is hereby given under s. 80, CPC stating the following particulars:

(1) *Name and description of the plaintiff:* Sri .... son of .... by caste .... by occupation .... residing at ....

(2) *Cause of action:* Non-payment of Bills dated .... for construction of a metalled road at .... from 1st July 2019 to 16th November 2019 under a contract dated .... between the plaintiff and the Governor of the State of..............

(3) *Relief claimed:* ₹ .... being the amount due under the aforesaid Bills.

In default of payment within two months the plaintiff shall bring a suit for recovery of the said sum and costs of suit.

Yours faithfully,

....

Form 2

Notice of suit under s. 80 of the CPC against the Central Government

Regd. with A/D
Dated .... 20 ....

To

The Secretary to the Government of India
.... Department
Central Secretariat
New Delhi

Notice under s. 80 of the Code of Civil Procedure

Dear Sir,

Under instructions from my client .... an employee in section .... of the Department of ...., Central Secretariat, New Delhi, I hereby give you notice under s. 80 of the CPC and state that my aforesaid client intends to sue the Union of India owning and representing the Department of .... Central Secretariat, New Delhi after the expiry of two months after the service of this notice unless reliefs claimed hereinbelow are granted to my said client within the said period of two months. The particulars of the nature of the claim, cause of action and reliefs claimed are as given below:

(1) Name and description of the plaintiff:

Sri .... son of .... by occupation .... residing at ....

(2) Cause of action:

(*a*) Sri .... was an employee in .... section of the Department of ...., Government of India, Central Secretariat, New Delhi. He has been dismissed from service illegally with effect from ....

(*b*) Sri .... was charged falsely for an alleged theft in the office on .... and was charge sheeted and ultimately dismissed from service with effect from ....

(*c*) Cause of action for the suit arose on .... the date of dismissal.

(3) Reliefs sought for:

(*a*) Reinstatement of Sri ....

(*b*) Recovery of salary for the period of .... to ....

Yours faithfully,

....

Advocate

Form 3

Notice under s. 80 of the Code of Civil Procedure 1908

Notice is hereby given by me, A.B. (or for and behalf of C.D.) fully described below pursuant to s. 80 of the Code of Civil Procedure 1908 calling upon the Central Government/State Government to (state the act required to be done or not done) within a period of two months next after this notice has been delivered.

The information required by the Government under s. 80, aforesaid is hereunder given:

1. Name and description of the prospective plaintiff (Give the full name).
2. Description and place of residence (Give the description and residence).
3. Cause of action (state, with dates, the cause of action on which the suit will be based).
4. Relief claimed by the plaintiff—as given above also state that in default the plaintiff would claim damages in the sum of ₹ .... together with all costs.

Yours faithfully

A.B.

(or C.D. advocate for A.B.)

Signature

Form 4

Notice under s. 80, CPC to the Central Government

Registered Acknowledgement Due

To,
The Secretary to Government,
Government of India,
Ministry of Finance,
Department of Accounts, New Delhi

Subject: Notice under s. 80, CPC on behalf of Mr................................
....

Dear Sir,

Under instructions from my client, above named, I give you this notice under s. 80, CPC with the facts and circumstances, as given below:

1. That ....
2. That ....
3. That ....
4. That ....
5. That ....
6. That the cause of action arose on ....
7. That the relief claimed by my client is ....

Please, therefore take this notice under s. 80 of the Code of Civil Procedure and note that if you do not settle the claim of my client as stated above, my client shall be compelled to take shelter under appropriate forum against the Union of India and in that case you shall be responsible for the cost of suit and other damages.

Please bear the cost of this notice, which is ₹ .... only.

Yours faithfully,
Advocate

Form 5

Notice to Railway under s. 80, CPC

Registered Acknowledgement Due

From:
....
........................, Advocate

Kolkata ....
....

To,
The General Manager,
.... Railway,
....

Subject: Notice under s. 80, CPC and under s. 106 of the Railways Act.

Dear Sir,

Under instructions from my client Messers Book Publishing Co., 20, C.R. Avenue, Kolkata 700 012 and for and on his behalf I give you this notice under s. 80, CPC and under s. 106 of the Railways Act on the facts and circumstances given hereunder:

1. That on 20.02.2020 a consignment of law books, containing six bundles was delivered to you for booking to New Delhi by goods train and R/R No. .... was obtained. The reasonable time to reach the goods to its destination is not more than a fortnight.
2. The consignor of the consignment is M/s. Book Publishing Co. and goods were booked self. The R/R has been endorsed in favour of the consignee Messers Eastern Law House (P) Ltd., New Delhi.
3. The consignment was 180 Kg. containing six bundles.
4. That more than three months have passed and your New Delhi station has finally told the consignee that the consignment is not traceable,

   or

   That the consignment was found to be in damaged condition and short by one bundle.
5. That your New Delhi station has given open delivery of the goods, and the goods has been compared with the Bill No. .... dated ....
6. That out of six bundles .... books have been damaged and are not in saleable condition.
7. That the goods of the sixth bundle, which was missing at the time of taking delivery, has also been worked out with the help of the Bill, the goods of which were despatched.
8. That a shortage and damages goods certificate has been obtained from the New Delhi Station Authorities, on .... at the time of taking of delivery, which is attached herewith.
9. That the delivery was taken before two witnesses, both are respectable Advocates; panchnama was prepared and was signed by the railway authorities, consignee and the witnesses, which is attached herewith.
10. That a claim of damages has been filed with the Chief Commercial Superintendent of Claims, who has registered the claim under file No. .... and has issued a receipt of the same. Photocopy of the receipt is enclosed.
11. That the cause of action arose on ....
12. That my client claims following reliefs:
    1. ....
    2. ....
    3. ....

I, therefore, give you this notice for and on behalf of my client, above named, and advise you to pay the sum of ...., the detail of which is given in ground No. .... within two months from the date of receipt of this notice failing which my client will file a civil suit in the court of competent jurisdiction against Union of India through Railways and against your Railway Administration and in that case you shall be responsible for interest at the rate of 18% from the date, the cause of action arisen and also costs of the suit.

Please bear the cost of this notice which ₹ ....

Yours very truly,

Advocate

Form 6

Notice to produce documents under Order 11, rule 16 of CPC

Before the Court .... Civil Judge (Junior Division) ....

Title Suit No. .... of .... (District ....)

Sri .... s/o .... r/o .... Plaintiff

Versus

Sri .... s/o .... r/o .... Defendant

Dear Sir,

I .... Advocate, Counsel for the plaintiff/defendant do hereby give you the following notice on behalf of and under instructions from my client.

That the plaintiff/defendant asks you to produce for his inspection the following documents mentioned in your plaint/written statement/affidavit dated ....

(1) ....

(2) ....

(3) ....

(4) .... (description of documents)

Dated .... Yours faithfully

Place ....

Sd/-

Counsel for the plaintiff/defendant

To

Sri ...., Advocate
Counsel for the plaintiff/defendant

NOTES: 1. Order 11, r. 16 enjoins that the notice shall be in Form No. 7, Appendix C of the Code of Civil Procedure.

2. It is not necessary to use the exact words of the Form—AIR 1922 All 235.

3. Application for production of document should be supported by Affidavit, when court requires. In default the prayer for production of document may be rejected—*National Rice* v *Suraj Singh* AIR 1975 HP 12.

Form 7

Notice to inspect documents under Order 11, rule 17, CPC

Before the Court .... Civil Judge (Senior Division) ....

Other Suit No. .... of 20......... (District ....)

Sri .... s/o .... r/o .... Plaintiff

Versus

Sri .... s/o .... r/o .... Defendant

Sir,

On behalf of and under instruction of my client I ...... Advocate, Counsel for the plaintiff/ defendant, do hereby give you the following notice.

That you can inspect the documents described in your notice dated ...... at ...... (describes the place of inspection) on ...... (date & day) between ...... hours (describe the term for inspection).

Dated ....

Place ....

Yours faithfully

....

Sd/-

Counsel for the plaintiff/defendant

To

Sir ...., Advocate

Counsel for the plaintiff/defendant.

Form 8

Notice to admit documents

(Or. 12, r. 3)

To

Take notice that the plaintiff (or defendant) in this suit proposes to adduce in evidence the several documents hereunder specified, and that the same may be inspected by the defendant (or plaintiff), his pleader or agent, at .... on .... between the hours of.........; and the defendant (or plaintiff), is hereby required, within 48 hours from the last-mentioned hour, to admit that such of the said documents as are specified to be originals were respectively written, signed or executed, as they purport respectively to have been; that such as are specified as copies are true copies; and such documents as are stated to have been served, sent or delivered were so served, sent or delivered, respectively, saving all just exceptions to the admissibility of all such documents as evidence in this suit.

G.H., pleader (or agent) for plaintiff (or defendant)

To E.F., pleader (or agent) for defendant (or plaintiff)

(Here describe the documents and specify as to each document whether it is original or a copy).

NOTES: 1. See Form No. 9 of Appendix C of Code of Civil Procedure with such variations as circumstances may require.

2. Order XII, r. 2–Either party may call upon the other party to admit within 7 days from the date of service of the notice any document saving all just exceptions ....

Form 9

Notice to admit facts

(Or. 12, r. 5)

To,

Take notice that the plaintiff (or defendant) in this suit requires the defendant (or plaintiff) to admit, for the purposes of this suit only, the several facts respectively hereunder specified;

and the defendant (or plaintiff) is hereby required, within six days from the service of the notice, to admit the said several facts, saving all just exceptions to the admissibility of such facts as evidence in this suit.

G.H., pleader (or agent) for plaintiff or defendant

To E.F., pleader (or agent) for plaintiff (or defendant).

The facts, the admission of which is required are—

1. That M. died on the 1st of January 1952.
2. That he died intestate.
3. That N. was his only lawful son.
4. That O. died on the 1st of April 1896.
5. That O. was never married.

NOTE: See Form No. 10 of Appendix C of Code of Civil Procedure.

Form 10

Notice to produce (General Form)

(Or. 12, r. 8)

Take notice that you are hereby required to produce and show to the Court at the first hearing of this suit all books, papers, letters, copies of letters and other writings and documents in your custody, possession or power, containing any entry, memorandum or minute relating to the matters in question in this suit and particularly:—(name papers/documents required to be produced).

G.H., Pleader Advocate (or agent) for plaintiff (or defendant)

To E.F., Pleader Advocate (or agent) for defendant (or plaintiff)

NOTES: 1. See Form No. 12 of Appendix C of Code of Civil Procedure.

2. No adverse presumption can be drawn against a party for its failure to produce documents in its possession, if the opposite party has not called upon it to produce the same (AIR 1954 Cal 480).

3. Order 12, r. 8 refers to a notice to produce documents 'at the time of hearing' so that if they are not produced, the party calling for them may give secondary evidence of the same (AIR 1962 AP 249).

Form 11

Notice to state objections to draft of document

(Or. 21, r. 34)

(Title)

To

Take notice that on the ...... day of .... 20 ...., the decree-holder in the above suit presented an application to this Court that the Court may execute on your behalf a deed of ......, whereof a draft is hereunto annexed of the immovable property specified hereunder, and that the ...... day of ...... 20 ......, is appointed for the hearing of the said application, and that you are at liberty to appear on the said day and to state in writing any objections to the said draft.

Description of Property

Given under my hand and the seal of the Court, this .... day of .... 20 ......

Judge

NOTES: 1. Order 21, r. 34(1)—The decree-holder may prepare a draft and deliver the same to the court.

Rule 34(2)—The court shall then serve copy of draft on the judgment-debtor and solicit objections.

2. Order 21, r. 34(2) is mandatory. Non-compliance with that provision vitiates the order (AIR 1959 AP 666).

Form 12

Notice to person in possession of movable property sold in execution

(Or. 21, r. 79)

(Title)

To

Whereas .... has become the purchaser at a public sale in execution of the decree in the above suit of .... now in your possession, you are hereby prohibited from delivering possession of the said ...... to any person except the said ....

Given under my hand and the seal of the Court, this .... day of .... 20 ......

Judge

NOTES: 1. See Or. 21, r. 79 of the C.P. Code 1908.

2. See Form No. 32 of Appendix E of Code of Civil Procedure.

Form 13

Notice of payment into Court

(Or. 24, r. 2)

(Title)

Take notice that the defendant has paid into Court ₹ .... and says that the sum is sufficient to satisfy the plaintiff's claim in full.

X.Y., Pleader for the defendant

To

Z, Pleader for the plaintiff.

NOTES: 1. See Form No. 3 of Appendix H of C.P. Code.

2. Order 24, r. 2. Notice of the deposit shall be given through the Court by the Defendant to the Plaintiff, and the amount of deposit shall (unless the Court otherwise directs) be paid to the Plaintiff on his application.

(For West Bengal as Prescribed by the Civil Rules and Orders Vol. II, Published by the Calcutta High Court).

Form 14

Notice to minor defendant of an application for appointment of the guardian to be guardian for the suit

(Or. 32, r. 3, C.P. Code)

District ....

In the Court of .... at

Suit No. .... of 20 ....

.... Plaintiff

versus

.... Defendant

To

....

(Defendant)

Whereas an application has been presented on the part of the plaintiff in the above suit for the appointment of Mr.* .... as guardian for the suit to the minor defendant, you the said minor are hereby required to take notice that unless within ...... days from the service upon him of a similar notice he gives his consent to be appointed to act as guardian, the Court will proceed, subject to the decision of any objection that may be raised on your behalf within .... days from the service of this notice upon you, to appoint some other person or an officer of the court to act as guardian to you the minor for the suit.

Given under my hand and the seal of this Court, this .... day of .... 20 ......

Judge.

* Here insert name of guardian.

NOTES: 1. Order should not be made unless necessary notices are given to the persons referred to in the rule (AIR 1952 Ori 111).

2. Omission to send the notices required by this rule is only an irregularity which will not vitiate the proceedings unless it is proved that the minor has been prejudiced thereby in his defence or there is fraud or collusion on the part of the guardian (AIR 1938 All 437).

Form 15

Notice to guardian of application for appointment of the guardian to be guardian for the suit

(Or. 32, r. 3, C.P. Code)

District ....

In the Court of .... at

Suit No. .... of 20 ....

.... Plaintiff

versus

.... Defendant

To

Guardian (appointed by authority or natural, or the person in .... whose care the minor is, as the case may be).

Whereas an application has been presented on the part of the plaintiff in the above suit for the appointment of you* .... as guardian for the suit to the minor defendant, you* are hereby required in the above suit for the appointment of you* .... as guardian for the suit to the minor defendant, you* are hereby required to take notice that unless within .... days from the service upon you of this notice you* give your consent to be appointed to act as guardian the court will proceed, subject to the decision of any objection that may be raised on your behalf or on behalf of the said minor defendant within .... days from the service of a similar notice upon him, to appoint some other person or an officer of the Court to act as guardian to the minor of the suit.

Given under my hand and the seal of this Court, this .... day of .... 20 ......

Judge.

* Here insert name of guardian.

NOTES: 1. See Form No. 11 of Appendix H of C.P. Code.

2. See Or. 32, r. 3(4) of C.P. Code—No order shall be made on any application except upon notice to the minor and to any guardian of the minor appointed or declared by an authority competent in that behalf. Or, where there is no such guardian, upon notice to the father or where there is no father to the mother or where there is no father or mother, to other natural guardian of the minor, or where there is no father, mother or other natural guardian to the person in whose care the minor is, and after hearing any objection, which may be urged on behalf of any person served with notice under this sub-rule.

3. A defect in following the rules is not necessarily fatal to the proceedings (38 Ind App 182 PC).

Form 16

Notice to minor defendant of application for appointment of another person to be guardian for the suit

(Or. 32, r. 3, C.P. Code)

District ....

In the Court of .... at

Suit No. .... of......... 20 ....

.... Plaintiff

versus

.... Defendant

.... minor Defendant

To

Whereas an application has been presented on the part of the plaintiff in the above suit for the appointment of *......... as guardian for the suit to the minor defendant, you are hereby required to take notice that unless within ...... days from the service upon him (your guardian) of a similar notice, your guardian ** ...... makes an application for the appointment of himself or of some friend of you the minor to act as guardian, the Court will proceed, subject to the decision of any objection that may be raised on your behalf within .... days of the service of this notice upon you, to appoint * .... or an officer of the Court to act as guardian to you the minor for the said suit.

Given under my hand and the seal of this Court, this .... day of .... 20 ......

Judge.

* Here insert name and description of the proposed guardian.

** Here insert name of guardian upon whom the notice is to be served.

Form 17

Notice to guardian of application for appointment of another person to be guardian for the suit

(Or. 32, r. 3, C.P. Code)

District ....

In the Court of .... at

Suit No. .... of......... 20 ....

.... Plaintiff

versus

.... Defendant

To

(Address) ....

Guardian (appointed by authority or natural, or the person in whose care the minor is).

Whereas an application has been presented on the part of the plaintiff in the above suit for the appointment of * ...... as guardian for the suit to the minor defendant .... you** are hereby required to take notice that unless within ...... days from the service upon you of this notice, you make an application for the appointment of yourself or of some friend of the minor to act to as guardian, the court will proceed, subject to the decision of any objection that may be raised on behalf of the said minor defendant within ...... days from the service of a similar notice upon him, to appoint or an officer of the court to act as guardian to the minor for the said suit.

Given under my hand and the seal of this Court, this .... day of .... 20 ......

Judge.

* Here insert name and description of the proposed guardian.

** Here insert name of guardian upon whom the notice is to be served.

Form 18

Notice to opposite party of day fixed for hearing evidence of applicant's being an indigent person

(Or. 33, r. 6, C.P. Code)

District ....

In the Court of .... at ......

Suit No. .... of......... 20 ....

.... Applicant

versus

.... Opposite party

To

Whereas .... has applied to this Court for permission to institute a suit against .... in *forma pauperis* under Order XXXIII of the Code of Civil Procedure 1908; and whereas the Court sees no reason to reject the application; and whereas the .... day of .... 20 ......, has been fixed for receiving such evidence as the applicant may adduce in proof of his indigency and for hearing any evidence which may be adduced in disproof thereof:

Notice is hereby given to you under r. 6 of Order XXXIII that in case you may wish to offer any evidence to disprove the indigency of the applicant you may do so on appearing in this Court on the said ...... day of ...... 20 ......

Given under my hand and the seal of this Court, this .... day of .... 20 ......

Judge.

NOTES: 1. See Form No. 12 of Appendix H of C.P. Code.

2. The provision directing notice is imperative (AIR 1927 Cal 454); therefore, an order made without notice to the Government pleader or to the opposite party is without jurisdiction—AIR 1927 Cal 464; AIR 1951 Kutch 96.

3. Notice under this rule must be served on the whole body of the opposite party if there be more than one (AIR 1941 Pat 594).

Form 19

Notice to Respondent of the day fixed for the hearing of the appeal

(Or. 41, r. 14, C.P. Code)

District ....

In the Court of .... at ......

Title Appeal No. .... of......... 20 ....

.... Appellant

versus

.... Respondent

Appeal from the .... of the Court of .... dated the ....day of ...... 20 ......

To

Take notice that an appeal from the decree of .... in this case has been presented by .... and registered in this Court and that the .... day of ...... 20 .... has been fixed by this court for the hearing of this appeal.

If no appearance is made on your behalf by yourself, your pleader, or by some one by law authorised to act for you in this appeal, it will be heard and decided in your absence.

Given under my hand and the seal of this Court, this .... day of .... 20 ......

Judge.

NOTES: 1. An appeal cannot be heard and decided without fixing a date for such hearing or without giving the respondent due notice of such date. But failure to give notice to an unnecessary respondent does not vitiate the appeal (AIR 1923 Cal 221).

2. See High Court amendments (in any standard book on Civil Procedure Code) in Rule 14 of Or. 41, C.P. Code.

Form 20

Notice to a party to a suit not made a party to the appeal but joined by the court as a respondent

(Or. 41, r. 20, C.P. Code)

District ....

In the Court of .... at ......

Title Appeal No. .... of......... 20 ....

.... Appellant

versus

.... Respondent

To

Whereas you were a party in suit No. .... of 20 .... in the court of .... and whereas the .... has preferred an appeal to this Court from the decree passed against him in the said suit and it appears to this Court that you are interested in the result of the said appeal:

This is to give you notice that this Court has directed you to be made a respondent in the said appeal and has adjourned the hearing thereof till the ...... day of ......20 ...... at ...... a.m. If no appearance is made on your behalf on the said day and at the said hour the appeal will be heard and decided in your absence.

Given under my hand and the seal of this Court, this .... day of .... 20 ......

Judge.

Form 21

Notice of appeal as an indigent person

(Or. 44, r. 1, C.P. Code)

District ....

In the Court of .... at ......

Suit No. .... of......... 20 ....

.... Applicant

versus

.... Opposite party

Whereas the above-named ...... has applied to be allowed to appeal as an indigent person from the decree in the above suit No. ...... dated the ...... day of ...... 20 .... and whereas the ...... day of ...... 20 ... has been fixed for hearing the application, notice is hereby given to you that if you desire to show cause why the applicant should not be allowed to appeal as an indigent person, an opportunity will be given to you ...... of doing so on the aforementioned date.

Given under my hand and the seal of this Court, this .... day of .... 20 ......

Judge.

Notes: 1. See Form No. 11 of Appendix G of C.P. Code.
2. Notice is necessary because court cannot decide question of the applicant's indigency in his favour without giving opposite party, an opportunity to be heard on the question (AIR 1948 All 323).

Form 22

Notice to show cause why a review should not be granted

(Or. 47, r. 4, C.P. Code)

District ....

In the Court of .... at ....

.... Plaintiff

versus

.... Defendant

To

Take notice that ...... has applied to this court for a review of its decree passed on the ...... day of ...... 20 ...... in the above case. The ...... day of ...... 20 ...... is fixed for you to show cause why the court should not grant a review of its decree in this case.

Given under my hand and the seal of this Court, this .... day of .... 20 ......

Judge.

NOTE: A notice of an application by the plaintiff for review of an order passed in a suit must be served on all the defendants and not merely on the opposing defendants who had appeared when the decree or order sought to be reviewed was passed (AIR 1949 Pat 117).

Form 23

Notice under s. 82 of C.P. Code for execution of decree/orders/award against

(*i*) the Union of India,

(*ii*) a State,

(*iii*) a Public Officer.

By registered post with AD

....

Date ....

To

1. The Secretary to the Government of India,
   Deptt. of ....
   New Delhi.
2. The Collector of the district of ......
   for the State Government of West Bengal.
3. The ....
   ....

Sir,

A decree was passed on ...... by the ...... (*name of the court*) in Money Suit No. ...... of the year against the Union of India/State Government of ....../the .... (*when a Public Officer, state the official designation with address*) ...... a public officer of the State of ....../ Union of India and two months' time was specified in the decree for satisfaction of the decretal amount (or, no time was specified in the said decree for satisfaction of the decretal dues, as the case may be).

That the judgment-debtor did not satisfy the dues of the decree-holder within the specified time, (or, the decretal dues have not been paid even after expiry of three months' time after the decree).

Take notice that the decree-holder shall apply for execution of the said decree unless decretal dues are paid within 15 days hereof.

Yours faithfully,

....

(Decree-holder)

NOTES: 1. The object of the section is to allow time and opportunity to the Government or Public Officer to satisfy the decree amicably before execution proceedings are started against them (AIR 1942 Cal 569).

2. Under the amended section (effective from 1.2.1977) no decree can be exempted against Union Government, State Government or Public Officer unless three months expire from the date of the decree.

3. Limitation for execution of decree commences from the date after expiry of three months from the date of decree—AIR 1970 Ori 137.

Form 24

Notice of deposit with the court of decretal amount

(Or. 21, r. 1(2), C.P. Code)

In the Court of .... at ......

To

....

Take notice that ...... the plaintiff/defendant etc. (as the case may be), in ...... No. ...... of ...... 20 ......, has on the ...... day of ...... 20 ...... deposited into court the sum of ₹ .... (in words ....) as detailed below as the amount payable to you under the decree/order dated ...... in suit/case No. ...... of ...... 20 ......, and you are informed that you may withdraw the amount in person or get it transmitted to you by money order on your making a request under Rule 162 of Ch. 10, Part I, Civil Rules and Orders, Volume I.

Amount ....

Interest ....

Costs ....

Total ....

Dated .... 20 ....

Judge.

NOTES: 1. Sub-rule (2) casts no special duty on the court to issue notice on its own initiative. It is the duty of the judgment-debtor to give notice of the deposit to the decree-holder through Court or otherwise (AIR 1957 Trav-Co 241).

2. Notice of payment must be in writing and be served on the decree-holder (AIR 1925 Nag 52).

Form 25

Notice to show cause why a payment or adjustment should not be recorded as certified

(Or. 21, r. 2, C.P. Code)

District ....

In the Court of .... at ......

Suit No. ...... of ...... 20......

.... Plaintiff

versus

.... Defendant

To

Whereas in execution of the decree in the above-numbered suit .... the decree-holder has applied to this court that the sum of ₹........ recoverable under the decree has been paid/adjusted and should be recorded as certified, this is to give you notice that you are to appear before this Court on the .... day of .... 20 ...., to show cause why the payment/adjustment aforesaid should not be recorded as certified.

Given under my hand and the seal of this Court, this .... day of .... 20 ......

Judge.

NOTES: 1. See Form No. 1 of Appendix E of C.P. Code.

2. When the judgment-debtor applies under sub-rule (2) the court is bound to issue a notice to the decree-holder to show cause why the payment or adjustment should not be recorded as certified (AIR 1923 Nag 20).

3. Order allowing a certification without notice to the decree-holder is bad in law (AIR 1930 Lah 113; AIR 1944 Nag 231).

Form 26

Notice of application for execution of a decree transferred by assignment

(Or. 21, r. 16, C.P. Code)

District ....

In the Court of .... at ......

Suit No. ...... of ...... 20......

.... of .... Plaintiff

versus

...... of .... Defendant

To

Whereas ...... has made application to this court for execution of a decree in suit No. .... of 20 ...... on the allegation that the same has been transferred to ...... by assignment namely, by* ...... this is to give you notice that you are to appear before this Court on the .... day of .... 20 ......, either in person, or by a pleader of this Court, or agent duly authorised and instructed to show cause, if any, why execution should not be granted.

* Here enter particulars of assignment.

Given under my hand and the seal of the Court, this .... day of .... 20 ....

Judge.

NOTES: 1. See Form No. 7 of Appendix E of C.P. Code.

2. The notice that is to be given under this rule is of the application for execution and not of the assignment (1954 Ker LT 434).
3. The provisions of this rule as to notice are imperative (AIR 1949 Bom 63; AIR 1946 Bom 27).
4. A combined notice under this rule and Rule 22 (see Model Form No. 23 of Notice under the Code of Civil Procedure) will be sufficient (AIR 1942 Bom 134).

Form 27

Notice to show cause why execution should not issue

(Or. 21, r. 22, C.P. Code)

District ....

In the Court of .... at ......

.... of .... Plaintiff

versus

...... of .... Defendant

To

Whereas ...... has made application to this Court for execution of decree in Suit No. .... of 20 ......

*(1) which was passed against you more than one year previous to the said application/ *(2) on the allegation that you are the legal representative of the judgment-debtor or ...... this is to give you notice that you are to appear before this court on the ...... day of ...... 20 ...., either in person, or by a pleader of this Court or agent duly authorised and instructed to show cause why execution should not be granted.

Given under my hand and the seal of the Court, this ... day of ... 20 ......

Judge.

* Strike out (1) or (2) as the case may be.

NOTES: 1. The provisions of this rule are mandatory (AIR 1917 Cal 728). The issue of notice is condition precedent to the validity of the execution proceedings.

2. Failure to issue notice will render the proceedings null and void (AIR 1950 Mad 801).

Form 28

Notice to show cause why warrant of arrest should not be issued

(Or. 21, r. 37, C.P. Code)

District ....

In the Court of .... at ......

Suit No. ...... of ...... 20......

.... of .... Plaintiff

versus

...... of .... Defendant

To

Whereas ...... has made application to this Court for execution of a decree in Suit No. .... of 20 ...... by arrest and imprisonment of your person, you are hereby required to appear before this Court on the .... day of .... 20 .... to show cause why you should not be committed to the civil prison in execution of the said decree.

Given under my hand and the seal of the Court, this .... day of .... 20 ......

Judge.

NOTES: 1. See Form No. 12 of Appendix E of the Code of Civil Procedure.

2. The court is bound under this rule to issue, in the first instance, a notice to the judgment-debtor to appear and show cause. The court cannot issue a notice and a warrant of arrest at the same time with directions for arrest (AIR 1932 Pat 315: AIR 1932 All 692).

Form 29

Notice of attachment of a decree to the Court which passed it

[Or. 21, r. 53, C.P. Code]

District ....

In the Court of .... at ......

Suit No. ...... of ...... 20......

.... of ....

versus

.... of ....

To ....

THE JUDGE OF THE COURT OF

Sir,

I have the honour to inform you that the decree obtained in your Court on the ...... day of ...... 20 ...... by ...... in Suit No. ...... of ......, in which he was ...... and ...... was .... has been attached by this Court on the application of ......, the ...... in the suit specified above. You are therefore requested to stay the execution of the decree of your Court until you receive an intimation from this Court that the present notice has been cancelled, or until execution of the said decree is applied for by the holder of the decree now sought to be executed or by his judgment-debtor.

Dated the .... day of .... 20 — I have the honour, etc.

Judge.

NOTE: See Form No. 22 of Appendix E of the Code of Civil Procedure.

Form 30

Notice of attachment of a decree to the holder of the decree, or to the judgment-debtor

[Or. 21, r. 53(4) and (6), C.P. Code]

District ....

In the Court of .... at ......

Suit No. ...... of ...... 20......

.... of ....

versus

.... of ....

To

Whereas an application has been made in this court by the decree-holder in the above suit for the attachment of a decree obtained by/against you on the ...... day of ...... 20 ......, in the .... court of .... was/were .... and .... was/were .... it is ordered that you the said .... be, and you are hereby, prohibited and restrained until the further order of this court, from .... transferring or charging/making payment or adjustment of .... the same in any way.

Given under my hand the seal of the Court, this .... day of 20 ....

Judge.

NOTE: See Form No. 23 of Appendix E of the Code of Civil Procedure.

Form 31

Prohibitory order, where the property consists of immovable property

(Or. 21, r. 54, C.P. Code)

District ....

In the Court of .... at ......

defendant

To

Whereas you have failed to satisfy a decree passed against you on the ...... day of ...... 20 ......, in .... Suit No. .... of 20...... in favour of .... for ₹...... it is ordered that you, the said .... be, and you are hereby, prohibited and restrained, until the further order of this Court, from transferring or charging the property specified in the schedule hereunto annexed, by sale, gift, or otherwise, and that all persons be and that they are hereby, prohibited from receiving the same by purchase, gift, or otherwise.

Given under my hand and the seal of the Court, this .... day of .... 20 ......

Judge.

NOTE: Form No. 24 of Appendix E of the Code of Civil Procedure.

Form 32

Notice to attaching creditor

(Or. 21, r. 66, C.P. Code)

District ....

In the Court of .... at ......

Suit No. ...... of ...... 20......

.... of ....

versus

.... of ....

To

Whereas .... has made application to this court for the removal of attachment on .... placed at your instance in execution of the decree in Suit No. ...... of 20 .... this is to give you notice to appear before this Court on .... the ...... day of ...... 20...... either in person, or by a pleader of the Court duly instructed to support your claim as attaching creditor.

Given under my hand and the seal of the Court, this .... day of .... 20 ......

Judge.

NOTE: See Form No. 26 of Appendix E of Code of Civil Procedure.

Form 33

Notice of the day fixed for settling a sale-proclamation

(Or. 21, r. 66, C.P. Code)

District ....

In the Court of .... at ......

Civil/Rent Suit No. ...... of ...... 20......

.... Plaintiff (decree-holder)

versus

.... Defendant (judgment-debtor)

To

Whereas in the above-named suit ...... the decree-holder has applied for the sale of .... You are hereby informed .... that the .... day of .... 20...... has been fixed for settling the terms of the proclamation of sale........

Given under my hand and the seal of the Court, this .... day of .... 20 ......

Judge.

NOTE: See Form No. 28 of Appendix E of C.P. Code.

Form 34

Notice to show cause why sale should not be set aside

(Or. 21, rr. 90, 92, C.P. Code)

District ....

In the Court of .... at ......

Suit No. ...... of ...... 20......

.... of .... Plaintiff

versus

...... of .... Defendant

To

Whereas in the under-mentioned property was sold on the .... day of ...... 20......, in execution of the decree passed in the above-named suit, and whereas the decree-holder (or judgment-debtor or purchaser) has applied to this court to set aside the sale of the said property on the ground .... of a material irregularity (or fraud) in publishing (or conducting) the sale; .... that the judgment-debtor had no saleable interest therein; ....

Take notice that if you have any cause to show why the said application should not be granted, you should appear with your, in this Court on the .... 20......, when the said application will be heard and determined.

Given under my hand and the seal of the Court, this .... day of .... 20 ......

(description of property)

Judge.

NOTE: See Form No. 36 of Appendix E of C.P. Code.

Form 35

Notice of application for the transfer of suit to another court for trial

(Section 24, C.P. Code)

In the Court of the District Judge of ....

No. ...... of ...... 20......

Whereas an application, dated the .... day of ...... 20...... has been made to this Court by ...... the ...... in Suit No. ...... 20...... now pending in the court of the .... at ...... in which ...... is plaintiff and ...... is defendant .... for transfer of the suit for trial to the court of the ...... at ......

You are hereby informed that the ...... day of ...... 20 ...... has been fixed for the hearing of the application, when you will be heard if you desire to offer any objection to it.

Given under my hand and the seal of the Court, this .... day of .... 20 ......

Judge.

NOTES: 1. If a party applies for transfer, notice is imperative (AIR 1945 Mad 69; AIR 1958 Pat 9). But where court acts under the section *suo motu* no notice need be given (AIR 1936 Mad 55).

2. Notice may be waived by the party entitled to it.

3. Transfer on application without notice is bad for illegality or material irregularity (AIR 1933 All 178; AIR 1916 Cal 859).

Form 36

Notice to surety of his liability under a decree

(Section 145, C.P. Code)

District ....

In the Court of .... at ......

Suit No. ...... of ...... 20 ......

.... Plaintiff

versus

.... Defendant

To

.... (*Name & address of surety*)

Whereas you .... did on .... become liable as surety for the performance of any decree which might be passed against the said .... defendant in the above suit; and whereas a decree was passed on the ...... day of ...... 20 ...... against the said defendant for the payment of .... and whereas application has been made for execution of the said decree against you.

Take notice that you are hereby required on or before the .... day of .... 20 .... to show cause why the said decree should not be executed against you and if no sufficient cause shall be, within the time specified, shown to the satisfaction of the Court, an order for its execution will be forthwith issued in the terms of the said application.

Given under my hand and the seal of the Court, this .... day of .... 20 ......

Judge.

NOTE: Form No. 13 of Appendix H of C.P. Code.

Form 37

Notice to show cause (general form)

District ....

In the Court of .... at ......

Suit/Case No. ...... of ...... 20 ......

.... Plaintiff

versus

.... Opposite party

To

Whereas the above-named .... has made application to this Court that ....

You are hereby warned to appear in this Court in person or by a pleader Advocate duly instructed on the .... day of .... 20 .... at 10 o'clock in the forenoon, to show cause against the application, failing wherein, the said application will be heard and determined *ex parte*.

Given under my hand and the seal of the Court, this .... day of .... 20 ......

Judge.

NOTE: See Form No. 4 of Appendix H of the Code of Civil Procedure.

Form 38

Notice to defendant

(Or. 9, r. 6, C.P. Code)

District ....

In the Court of .... at ......

Suit No. ...... of ...... 20 ......

.... Plaintiff

versus

.... Defendant

To

(*Name, description and place of residence*)

Whereas this day was fixed for the hearing of the above suit and a summons was issued to you and the plaintiff has appeared in this Court and you did not so appear, but from the return of the Nazir it has been proved to the satisfaction of the court that the said summons was served on you but not in sufficient time to enable you to appear and answer on the day fixed in the said summons.

Notice is hereby given to you that the hearing of the suit is adjourned this day and that the .... day of ...... 20 ...... is not fixed for the hearing of the same; in default of your appearance on the day last mentioned the suit will be heard and determined in your absence.

Given under my hand and the seal of the Court, this .... day of .... 20 ......

Judge.

NOTE: See Form No. 12 of Appendix B of the Code of Civil Procedure.

Form 39

Notice to take objections to draft of document

(Under Or. 21, r. 34, C.P. Code)

In the Court of the......... Judge Junior Division/Asst. District Judge at ......

O.C. Suit No. ...... of ...... 20 ...

Sri .... s/o ....

(of State the address etc.)

.... Plaintiff

versus

Sri .... s/o ....

of (State the address etc.)

.... Defendant

To

Sri .... s/o .... (as above)

Take notice that on the ...... day of...... 20 ...... the decree-holder in the abovenoted suit has presented to this Court (a draft of the document) that the Court may execute on your behalf a deed of ......, whereof a draft is hereunto annexed of the immovable property specified hereunder, and that the day of ...... 20 ...... is fixed for .... and that you are required to appear on the said date either personally or through a Counsel and to state in writing any objections to the said draft.

Description of the property.

....

....

Given under the hand and the seal of this Court, this the .... day of .... 20 ......

Judge Junior Division

NOTE: See Or. 21, r. 34, C.P. Code.

On receipt of the draft the Court shall cause the draft to be served upon the judgment-debtor together with a notice requiring his objection (if any) to be made within such time as the Court fixes in this behalf (Or. 21, r. 34(2), C.P. Code).

CHAPTER 12

Notices under the Railways Act 1989

SYNOPSIS

1 Notification of claims to refunds of overcharges and to compensation for losses (s. 106)–foreign railway
2 Object of a notice under s. 106 of the Railways Act 1989
3 Form and contents of a notice under s. 106
4 Can the notice under s. 106 be dispensed with?
5 Notice in case of non-delivery/short delivery
6 Waiver of a notice under s. 106
7 A combined notice under s. 106, Railways Act and under s. 80 of the Code of Civil Procedure
8 Whether the notice under s. 80, CPC is necessary in view of introduction of the Railway Claims Tribunal Act 1987?
9 Mistakes or defects in a notice under s. 106–how far excusable
10 Interpretation and construing a notice under s. 106
11 Limitation and period of notice under s. 106
12 Application of s. 15(2) of the Limitation Act to a notice under s. 106 of the Railways Act
13 To whom a notice under s. 106 is to be sent?
14 Is each Railway involved in transit entitled to a notice?
15 When through traffic–one notice under s. 106 held sufficient
16 Distinction between short delivery and non-delivery–cases when a notice of claim under s. 106 required
17 Case of paying double charge distinguished from over-charge–notice under s. 106, if required?
18 Case of tortious liabilities–if notice under s. 106 is required
19 Service of notice to railway administration (s. 192)
20 Notice under s. 106–when consignment despatched through out-agency and common carriers-cum-railway
21 Service of notice by the railway administration (s. 193)
22 Presumption where a notice under the Railways Act is served by post (s. 194)
23 Notice under the Railway Establishment Code–period of notice–insufficient notice
24 Notice for public auction of unclaimed consignment
25 Other cases

1 Notification of claims to refunds of overcharges and to compensation for losses (s. 106)—foreign railway[1]

Notice must be given to safeguard the position of the railway when it seeks to sell the goods as 'not claimed'. In other cases, failure to issue notice does

1 Not affected any way by the Railway Claims Tribunal Act 1987 (Assent 23.12.87) except with regard to notice of suit under s. 80, CPC.

not entail any liability as the railway is not under any obligation to give notice.[2] Section 77 of the Indian Railways Act 1890 (now s. 106 of the Railways Act 1989) provided that in order to entitle a person to claim compensation for the loss, amongst others, or goods delivered to be carried by the railway, a claim to compensation was to be made in writing to the Railway Administration within six months of the date of delivery of goods to consigning railway for carriage.[3]

Section 78B of the Act of 1890 has been recasted and instead s. 106 has been incorporated in the Act of 1989. Section 106 of the new Act repeats virtually s. 78B of the Act of 1890 but adds to it specifically to whom such claim has to be made and further, what would constitute really a claim to refund or to compensation as the case may be. Even a cursory glance would show that the new section has enlarged the hitherto restricted sphere of the old section. A particular notice which could not be considered as a valid notice under s. 78B of the Act of 1890 may now be deemed a valid notice under s. 106 of the Act.

Section 78B of the Indian Railways Act 1890 (corresponds to s. 106 of the Railways Act 1989) contemplates a notice of claim in writing to be served. The effect of s. 78B and s. 140 (both of the Act of 1890) is to bar plaintiff's claims unless he can show that he has complied with the requirements of law as regards notice of claim.[4] The object of service of notice is obviously to enable the Railway Administration to make an enquiry and investigate as to whether the loss, destruction or deterioration or non-delivery was due to consignor's laches or due to wilful neglect of the Railway Administration or its servants or due to the theft or robbery committed by the servants of the railway.[5]

The further object is to prevent stale and possibly dishonest claims being made when owing to delay it may be practicably impossible to trace the transaction or to check the allegation of the consignor. Bearing in mind the object of the section it has been held by several High Courts that a notice under s. 77 of the Act of 1890 which is corresponds to s. 106 of the Act of 1989, should be liberally construed. The purpose of the legislature must have been to afford a protection to the Railway Administration against fraud and not to provide a reason for depriving the consignors of their legitimate claim.[6]

The notice must satisfy the requirements of s. 78B of the Act of 1890 (corresponds to s. 106 of the Act of 1989). In *Salem Dayalbagh Stores Ltd.*

2 *Panna Lal* v *E.I. Railway* AIR 1952 All 880.
3 *Governor-General in Council* v *Gouri Shankar Mills Ltd.* AIR 1949 Pat 347; 28 Pat 178 (FB).
4 *Mahadeva* v *S.I. Railway Co.* 45 Mad 135.
5 *Jethmull Bhojraj* v *Darjeeling Himalayan Railway Co. Ltd.* AIR 1962 SC 1879.
6 *Union of India* v *Bihar Food & Civil Suppl. Corpn.* (1991)1 TAC 718.

v *Governor-General in Council* Madras High Court held that a mere letter by a consignee to the railway company that the goods had not arrived and asking that enquiries might be made cannot be regarded as a notice satisfying the requirements of s. 77 of the Act of 1890 which was supplemented by s. 78B of the Act of 1890 when no claim for compensation was made in that letter.[7] In *Martab Ali* v *Union of India*, Bombay High Court held that word 'loss' in s. 77 of the 1890 Act is applicable to the case of non-delivery as well as to cases of negligence and wrongful detention or conversion on the part of the Railway Administration.[8] The Supreme Court, however, held in a later case that a letter stating that a part of a consignment had not reached the destination and requesting the General Manager to make a search for the goods is a sufficient notice.[9] Patna High Court held the filing of a claim within time as sufficient compliance. When a complainant avails of statutory procedure of the Act within six months then it is a sufficient compliance of s. 78B of the Act of 1890 (now s. 106 of the Railways Act 1989).[10]

To appreciate what would and what would not be a valid notice we may refer to s. 106 of the Railways Act 1989 which reads as under:

> (1) A person shall not be entitled to claim compensation against a railway administration for the loss, destruction, damage, deterioration or non-delivery of goods carried by railway, unless a notice thereof is served by him or on his behalf,—
>
> (*a*) to the railway administration to which the goods are entrusted for carriage; or
>
> (*b*) to the railway administration on whose railway the destination station lies, or the loss, destruction, damage or deterioration occurs,
>
> within a period of six months from the date of entrustment of the goods.
>
> (2) Any information demanded or enquiry made in writing from, or any complaint made in writing to, any of the railway administrations mentioned in sub-sec. (1) by or on behalf of the person within the said period of six months regarding the non-delivery or delayed delivery of the goods with particulars sufficient to identify the goods shall, for the purpose of this section, be deemed to be a notice of claim for compensation.
>
> (3) A person shall not be entitled to a refund of an overcharge in respect of goods carried by railway unless a notice therefor has been served by him or on his behalf to the railway administration to which the overcharge has been paid within six months from the date of such payment or the date of delivery of such goods at the destination station, whichever is later.[11]

7 *Salem Dayalbagh Stores Ltd.* v *Governor-General in Council* AIR 1947 Mad 362.
8 *Martab Ali* v *Union of India* AIR 1954 Bom 297.
9 *Jemull Bhojraj* v *Darjeeling Himalayan Railway Co. Ltd.* AIR 1962 SC 1879.
10 *Union of India* v *Bihar Food & Civil Suppl. Corpn.* (1991)1 TAC 718.
11 Section 78B was inserted by Act 39 of 1961 in place of old s. 77 and now substituted by s. 106 of Act 24 of 1989.

Therefore, s. 78B (now s. 106) provides a pre-condition that no claim for compensation and refund of overcharge can be made against a Railway Administration without serving a notice in writing by the claimant within six months from the date of entrustment of the goods. In other words, notice is a condition precedent to the maintainability of a claim for compensation for goods lost, destroyed or deteriorated while in the custody of the Railway Administration.[12] Non-service of notice is fatal to the claim.[13] A notice under s. 77 of the Act of 1890 (corresponds to s. 106 of the Act of 1989) is mandatory and such notice is necessary in all cases whether it is a case of deterioration, loss or non-delivery.[14] For non-delivery of a part of consignment notice is necessary.[15] A suit will be barred for want of a notice under s. 77 (now s. 106).[16]

The position would be otherwise when the matter relates to a foreign railway. "The expression 'Railway Administration' or 'Railway' can only refer to the railway system carrying on business within the Indian Union and not to any foreign Railway Administration or foreign railway. Where the goods were consigned and delivered for carriage to a railway situate in Pakistan to be delivered to a station in Indian Union—*Held*: there was no delivery of goods in an Indian Railway for carriage as contemplated in s. 77 (now s. 106). Hence a notice under s. 77 (now s. 106) was not necessary.[17]

2 Object of a notice under s. 106 of the Railways Act 1989

The principal object of a notice under s. 106 (old s. 77) is to bring to the notice of the railway concerned a person's claim at an early date and thereby to see that the Railway Administration is not harassed by a stale claim. Framers of law did not intend that a *bona fide* claim should be resisted, but at the same time they intended that there should not be unnecessary litigations. In *Martab Ali* v *Union of India,* Bombay High Court held: "Though not intended to deprive the customers of the railway their just dues, it is at the same time intended as a weapon of defence against fraud to protect railways against litigation."[18]

The section was enacted "with a view to enabling the Railway Administration, to make inquires and, if possible, to recover the goods and to deliver them to the consignee and to prevent stale claims.[19] Its purpose

12 *Governor-General in Council* v *Musaddi Lal* AIR 1961 SC 725; AIR 1967 Cal 47 at p. 48.
13 *Niranjan Lall* v *Union of India* AIR 1962 Cal 42.
14 AIR 1962 MP 374.
15 *Union of India* v *Abdulla Akbarali & Co.* AIR 1964 Pat 392.
16 *Lakshmi Narain Ram Narain* v *Union of India* AIR 1966 Pat 19; *Union of India* v *Banarashi Lal Agarwalla* AIR 1975 Cal 417; *State of West Bengal* v *Union of India* AIR 1987 Cal 226.
17 *Union of India* v *Madan Mohan Gour* AIR 1961 Cal 542.
18 *Martab Ali* v *Union of India* AIR 1954 Bom 297.
19 *Governor-General in Council* v *Musadilal* AIR 1961 SC 725; (1961)3 SCR 647.

is to enable the railway to have an opportunity of settling the claim by making an inquiry into the matter in time with a view to preventing dishonest claims being put up all of a sudden by unscrupulous persons after a long time taking advantage of the fact that the railway records have been weeded out.[20]

A prompt inquiry is desirable both for the customer and the Railway Administration. The object of a notice under s. 78B (now s. 106) is to enable the Railway Administration to make a prompt inquiry into a claim,[21] and not to provide a means for depriving the consignors of their legitimate claims for compensation for the loss of or damage caused to the consignments during the course of transit on the railway.[1] Yet another reported case tells us plainly the object of the s. 78B (now s. 106 of the Act of 1989) thus: "It is to prevent stale and possibly dishonest claims for loss when due to delay it might be impossible to trace the transaction or check the allegations made and when the evidence necessary to rebut a dishonest claim might no longer be available. It is intended as a weapon of defence against fraud, not as a means to enable the railway authorities to deprive their customers of their just dues."[2]

In *Governor-General in Council* v *Musaddilal*[3] the Supreme Court held that notice under s. 77 of 1890 Act (corresponds to s. 106 of the Act of 1989) is necessary in case of non-delivery or short delivery whether it is due to loss, destruction or deterioration or it is due to negligence or even wrongful act of the railway administration. But because the Limitation Act 1963 provides different points of time for which the period of limitation is to run, it is not possible to infer that the claim covered by any Article is not for compensation for loss, destruction or deterioration of the goods. The position has been reaffirmed by the Supreme Court in *Union of India* v *Mahadeo Lal Prabhudayal*.[4]

3 Form and contents of a notice under s. 106

Section 106 does not prescribe any particular form or words which should regulate either the structure or the wordings of a notice under this section.

A notice under s. 78B (now s. 106) would be sufficient if it indicates clearly the intention of the notice-giver to inform the railway administration of his claim. All that it requires is that a claim for compensation shall be preferred to the Railway Administration in writing within six months.[5]

20 *Oudh & Tirhut Railway* v *Mrs. Karam Chand Paras Chand* AIR 1958 All 234; *Union of India* v *Kalinga Textiles* AIR 1969 Bom 401.
21 *Governor-General in Council* v *Gouri Shankar Mills Ltd.* AIR 1949 Pat 347.
1 *Jetmull Bhojraj* v *D.H. Railway Co. Ltd.* AIR 1962 SC 1879.
2 AIR 1930 Cal 332.
3 AIR 1961 SC 725; (1961)3 SCR 647.
4 AIR 1965 SC 1755; (1965)3 SCR 145.
5 *Samrathmal* v *Union of India* AIR 1959 MP 305.

One thing should be borne in mind that information demanded, inquiry made or complaint lodged must be in writing within the specified time (i.e. six months) and should contain particulars sufficient to identify the consignment. The above three acts will be deemed preferment of a proper claim though none of those may contain any claim or demand for specified money. Money value of the claim need not be stated.[6] Where within six months of booking of the consignment the consignor brought to the notice of the Railway Administration by a letter that part of the consignment had not reached the destination and requested the General Manager of the railway to make a search for the goods without delay the Supreme Court *held*, per majority (A.K. Sarkar, J. contra), the letter amounts to sufficient notice for the purposes of s. 77 (now s. 106). The Supreme Court observed: "It is true that a claim for compensation has not been made by the consignor in the notice. However, such claim must be deemed to be implied in the notice.[7] But with the introduction of s. 106, it is doubtless, there would not have been perhaps any contrary finding.

As the section does not require any particular form, a letter asking for open delivery could as well be treated as a notice.[8] A letter for open delivery of the goods based on suspicion of shortage or damage can be regarded as preferment of a claim under s. 77 (now s. 106).[9]

Contrary situations

(*i*) A letter by a consignee to the Railway Administration asking to make inquiries about goods not received but making no claim for compensation—notice not valid.[10]

(*ii*) A notification of claim under s. 77 (now s. 106), must, of necessity, contain a demand for compensation. The exact amount claimed need not be mentioned even so, the letter must contain a demand for compensation.[11]

(*iii*) Requests for early delivery of the goods which could not be traced cannot be taken as a notice of a claim for compensation.[12]

(*iv*) Letter informing non-receipt of consignment and requesting early delivery but there was no claim for compensation or no indication that goods had been lost or destroyed, such a letter is no notice.[13]

Since after 1961 when s. 77 was substituted by s. 78B, and now substituted by s. 106 all conflicting views should have little or no scope for keeping the

6 *Firm of Sheonath Joinarain* v *G.I.P. Railway Co.* AIR 1926 Nag 405.
7 *Jetmull Bhojraj* v *Darjeeling Himalayan Rly. Co.* AIR 1962 SC 1879.
8 *Murugasam* v *M.J. Gnana* AIR 1917 PC 6.
9 *Amarchand* v *Union of India* AIR 1955 Assam 221.
10 *Salem Dayalbagh Stores Ltd.* v *Governor-General in Council* AIR 1947 Mad 362.
11 *Martab Ali* v *Union of India* AIR 1954 Bom 297.
12 *D.H. Rly. Co.* v *Jetmull Bhojraj* AIR 1956 Cal 390; 60 CWN 683.
13 AIR 1961 Manipur 45.

question open. It cannot be said in view of the proviso to s. 78B (which is now s. 106(2) of the Act of 1989) that a notice under s. 78B should invariably contain a claim for compensation or a claim to refund. If the consignee or the consignor wants an information as to the fate of the consignment or makes an inquiry into the fate of the consignment or simply submits a complaint in writing and within the prescribed period of six months, that would be a sufficient notice.

It is not necessary that the claimant should notify that he intends to bring an action.[14]

4 Can the notice under s. 106 be dispensed with?

Generally speaking, our answer would be in the negative. But there may be exceptional circumstances when a notice under s. 106 can be dispensed with. The argument, in its support, can be traced in a case reported in AIR 1958 Nag 17 where it was *held*: "Section 77 is only intended to give an opportunity to the Railway company to make satisfactory investigation. Where, therefore, the railway company has admitted that loss of goods belonging to the plaintiff had occurred in transit, that admission itself dispenses with the inquiry into the validity or invalidity of the notice of the claim made by the plaintiff.[15] When the plaintiff laid a claim to one railway but the claim rested with another railway and the former railway entered into correspondence with the latter railway long before the expiry of six months required for the notice: *Held*, the latter railway had notice and s. 77 (now s. 106) was sufficiently complied with.[16] An admission of short delivery by the Railway Administration does not dispense with an inquiry into the validity or invalidity of the notice under s. 77.

The notice under s. 77 (now s. 106) of the Indian Railways Act 1890 is a condition precedent to any claim covered by the section and it cannot be dispensed with because its object is considered to have been otherwise served.[17] It is submitted that it would not be wise to assume that the Railway Administration had sufficient notice or that it had proper knowledge.

Notice under s. 77 (now s. 106) is necessary and so in the absence of such notice the suit is not maintainable.[18] The service of notice is a *sine qua non* for instituting a suit against carrier.[19]

14 *Amarchand* v *Union of India* AIR 1955 Assam 221.
15 AIR 1958 Nag 17.
16 AIR 1952 Mad 795.
17 AIR 1959 MP 276.
18 *G.-G. in Council* v *Musaddi Lal* AIR 1961 SC 725; *Union of India* v *Bararashi Lal Agarwala* AIR 1975 Cal 417.
19 *The Jullundur Ex-Servicemen Motor Transport Co-operative Society Ltd.* v *The General Assurance Society Ltd.* (1978)80 Punj LR 415.

In view of s. 78B of the old Act when delivery of goods is made to one railway for transhipment and the goods are transhipped through the line of that railway and another, and while in transit through the latter the goods are lost, it is open to sue either of the railways for damages. But under s. 77 of the old Act, it was not enough if the notice of claim is given to that railway to which goods were delivered and such notice must be given to that railway to which goods were delivered, and such notice must be given within the prescribed time to the railway when the plaintiff wishes to hold it liable. It was incumbent on the plaintiff to serve notice on all railways.[20]

5 Notice in case of non-delivery/short delivery

In case of non-delivery, the cause of action is the same as in loss. Notice under s. 78B is mandatory.[21] The controversy was settled by the decision of the Supreme Court in *G.-G. in Council* v *Musaddi Lal*.[1]

Where non-delivery is due to "loss, destruction or deterioration" of the goods, then a notice under s. 77 of the Indian Railways Act 1890 (corresponds to s. 106 of the present Act) is required, but where non-delivery is due to any other cause, such as conversion, detention, misconduct, misdelivery, wrongful delivery, capricious acts, then a notice is not necessary.[2]

6 Waiver of a notice under s. 106

Requirements of notice under s. 77 (now s. 106) may be waived.[3] The principles will apply to s. 78B (now s. 106) for obvious reasons.

Section 77 of the 1890 Act requires service of notice in the manner laid down in s. 140 of the old Act. But the protection can be waived.[4]

In *S.I. Co-operative Stores* v *Union of India*, the notice under s. 77 was sent to the Chief Commercial Manager who by his letter repudiated the claim of the plaintiff. The court observed that a notice of claim on the Chief Commercial Manager does not amount to the preferment of a claim to the Railway Administration. But where the Chief Commercial Superintendent in reply to the notice refused to entertain the claim on the ground that there was no negligence or misconduct on the part of the railway or its servants but he did not say that no claim be entertained until and unless notice as required under s. 77 (now s. 106) has been served: *Held*, it amounted to waiver of notice.[5]

20 *Jetmull Bhojraj* v *D.H. Railway* AIR 1962 SC 1879; *State of West Bengal* v *Union of India* (1986)1 CHN 75.

21 *Union of India* v *Mahadeolal* AIR 1965 SC 1755; *Bhola Ram & Sons* v *Union of India* 1977 All WC 106.

1 AIR 1961 SC 725 reaffirmed by the Supreme Court in AIR 1965 SC 1755.

2 *Musaddi Lal* v *Governor-General in Council* AIR 1952 All 897; *Governor-General in Council* v *Mahabir Ram* AIR 1952 All 891; *Ram Narian* v *Dominion of India* AIR 1953 All 460.

3 *Radhamadhav Kundu* v *Union of India* 61 CWN 433.

4 *South Indian Co-op. Stores* v *Union of India* 60 CWN 985; AIR 1957 Cal 17.

5 *South Indian Co-op. Stores* v *Union of India* AIR 1957 Cal 17; 60 CWN 985.

In *Gajanan Dhanuka* v *Union of India*,[6] it was held that where the Claims Officer did entertain the claim and did not turn it down on the ground that proper notice under s. 77 of Act of 1890 was not served, the service of notice under the section was waived by the Railway Administration.

Where the Railway Administration contested the suit on the footing that it was a case of non-delivery and not of loss and the defence failed, the Railway Administration cannot claim that the suit should be dismissed, for want of notice under s. 77 of the 1890 Act (now s. 106 of the Railways Act 1989).[7] When a defective notice is addressed to a proper officer and when such officer instead of ignoring the defective notice enters into correspondence, makes enquiries, the defect in the notice stands waived.[8]

7 A combined notice under s. 106, Railways Act and under s. 80 of the Code of Civil Procedure

One notice containing in it all the elements of a notice under s. 106 of the Railways Act and those of a notice under s. 80 of the Code of Civil Procedure 1908 is popularly known as a combined notice for the above purpose. Here two notices are combined in one. Necessarily, a combined notice must fulfil the requirements of both the sections.

A combined notice under the above sections must be served within six months in writing from the delivery of the goods to the railway for carriage as is required under s. 78B (now s. 106) of the Indian Railways Act 1890, and the suit is to be filed after the expiry of the statutory period of two months as is required under s. 80, CPC. A notice under s. 78B may be served on the Chief Commercial Superintendent as well but a combined notice must have to be served on the General Manager.[9] A notice under s. 80, CPC may be construed as a combined notice under both s. 77 (now s. 106) of the Indian Railways Act and under s. 80 of the Code of Civil Procedure.[10]

Again, while a notice under s. 78B (now s. 106) may be served either on the General Manager of the railway in whose administration the booking station lies or on the General Manager of the railway in whose administration the destination station lies, a combined notice has to be served not only on the General Manager of such railway but also on the General Manager of all the railways who are impleaded as co-defendants.

A combined notice under s. 78B (now s. 106) and s. 80, CPC in itself does not vitiate the law of notice.[11] Where a notice specifically states that it is a

6 AIR 1959 Cal 215; *State of West Bengal* v *Union of India* (1986)1 CHN 75.
7 *Mahadeo Lal* v *Union of India* AIR 1959 Pat 202.
8 *State of West Bengal* v *Union of India* (1986)1 CHN 75.
9 *Mooljibhai Maneklal* v *Dominion of India* AIR 1952 Nag 22; *Dharamsi Liladhar* v *Union of India* AIR 1952 Cal 439.
10 *Dasa K. Lakshmia* v *Union Government* AIR 1969 AP 386.
11 *Chaturbhai Bhaitabhai Patel* v *Union of India* AIR 1961 Pat 334; *Union of India* v *Lakshmi Narain* AIR 1954 Pat 424.

notice both under s. 77 (now s. 106) of the Indian Railways Act and s. 80, CPC and complies with all the requirements of both these provisions, such a notice is perfectly valid as both these notices have now to go to the same person or authority, namely, the General Manager of the railway concerned.[12]

A very lenient view was adopted by the Rajasthan High Court in the last-mentioned reported case: If the plaintiff gives a notice under s. 80, which is invalid, this is not enough to non-suit the plaintiff if the second notice given under s. 77 (now s. 106) of the Indian Railways Act 1890 can be accepted as good notice both for the purposes of s. 77 (now s. 106) of the Indian Railways Act 1890 and s. 80, CPC. It was *held*: "If notice in its substance, in the hard core of it, fulfils all the requirements of s. 77 (now s. 106) of the Indian Railways Act 1890 as well as s. 80, CPC and was given to the Manager of the railway concerned who knows his business reasonably well, the notice should not be thrown out as invalid on the ground that it was stated to have been given under s. 77 of the Indian Railways Act 1890 only, when its terms could deceive no reasonable person that it could serve equally well as a notice under s. 80, CPC, understood in its totality.[13]

After the amendment in s. 80 of CPC by the CPC (Amendment) Act 1976, a suit against the Union of India owning and representing Railway Administration may be filed without serving a notice under s. 80 of CPC on the strength of the provision in sub-sec. (2) of s. 80 of CPC.

Under s. 3(6) of the Indian Railways Act 1890 manager of the railway includes Government.[14]

8 Whether the notice under s. 80, CPC is necessary in view of introduction of the Railway Claims Tribunal Act 1987?

The position of law earlier was different and that position of law must prevail till the date of enforcement of the Railway Claims Tribunal Act. A suit for any claim against railway being essentially a suit against the Union Government, notice under s. 80 was mandatory. In suits against State-owned railways, a previous notice of suit was required to be given to the General Manager of the railway concerned containing the particulars specified in s. 80 of the Code of Civil Procedure. A notice under s. 77 of the Indian Railways Act 1890 did not dispense with the necessity of a notice under s. 80, Code of Civil Procedure.[15]

12 *Mooljibhai Maneklal* v *Dominion of India* AIR 1952 Nag 22; *Dharamsi Liladhar* v *Union of India* AIR 1952 Cal 439; *Union of India* v *Lakshmi Narain* AIR 1954 Pat 424; *Nannah* v *Union of India* AIR 1964 Raj 41.

13 *Nannah* v *Union of India* AIR 1964 Raj 41.

14 *State of Kerala* v *The General Manager, Southern Railway, Madras* (1976)4 SCC 265.

15 *Shaik Elahi* v *E.I. Railway* AIR 1931 Pat 326; *Secretary of State* v *Fazaluddin* AIR 1933 All 53; *Vellayyaram Chettiar* v *Government of the Province of Madras* AIR 1947 PC 197.

A notice under s. 80(1)(*b*) of CPC is a must for any suit against the Railways, unless leave under s. 80(2), CPC [inserted by CPC (Amendment) Act 1976] is obtained from the court for obtaining an urgent or immediate relief.

In view of introduction of the Railway Claims Tribunal Act 1987 it is now competent for an aggrieved person to file an application under (s. 80 of the Indian Railways Act corresponds to s. 107 of the Railways Act 1989) before the Claims Tribunal for compensation for loss of the life of, or personal injury to a passenger or for loss, destruction, damage, deterioration or non-delivery of animals, goods, etc.

This is in terms of s. 16 read with s. 13(1) of the Railway Claims Tribunal Act.[16]

Application, not being a suit, need not follow a notice under s. 80 of CPC.

Further, under s. 18 of the Railway Claims Tribunal Act 1987, Railway Claims Tribunal shall not be bound by the procedure laid down by the Code of Civil Procedure 1908.........[17]

9 Mistakes or defects in a notice under s. 106—how far excusable

Mistakes or errors in a notice under s. 106 may not be unusual as to err is human.

A court of law has little or no hesitation to excuse a *bona fide* but excusable mistake in a notice. In the railway claim cases too, mistakes or errors in a notice have been ignored in fit cases. In *M/s. Bishan Chand Lal Chand* v *Union of India*,[18] P.K. Tare, J., *held*: "As to the requirements of notices under s. 77 (now s. 106) of the Indian Railways Act and s. 80 of the Code of Civil Procedure, there have been a series of decisions of this court. The *ratio decidendi* of those discussions is that any defect which relates to minor particulars in a notice would not vitiate the notice. If the defect be a major one, which might prejudice the Railway Administration of the Government in finding to locate the particulars of the claim, in those cases only the notice might be vitiated".[19]

Here are some illustrations where mistakes have been condoned and where not:

(a) *Mistakes condoned*

(*i*) *Farooq* v *G.-G. in Council*[20]—Mistake as to date of Railway Receipt.

16 By s. 33 of the Railway Claims Tribunal Act 1987, s. 80 of the Railways Act has been amended and substituted by new s. 80, 'Application for Compensation'.

17 By s. 32 of the Railway Claims Tribunal Act 1987 in s. 78A of the Railways Act, for the word 'suit' the words "application before the Claims Tribunal" have been substituted.

18 AIR 1961 MP 220.

19 *M/s. Bishan Chand Lal Chand* v *Union of India* AIR 1961 MP 220.

20 AIR 1949 Pat 93.

(*ii*) *Begraj* v *E.I. Rly.*[21]—Sufficiency of notice to be determined on facts of each case.

(*iii*) *G.-G. in Council* v *Kasiram Marwari*[1]—Variance between amount in notice and amount claimed in suit.

(*iv*) *M/s. Bishan Chand Lal Chand* v *Union of India*[2]—Plaintiff mentions a wrong place of destination.[3]

(b) *Mistakes held fatal*

(*i*) Failure to state correctly the name of the railway station, from which the consignment is booked in the notice under s. 77 (now s. 106) is not merely a mistake but a fatal defect because it affects the cause of action.[4]

(*ii*) A wrong number of receipt on which the claim is based is not a mistake but a defect and renders the notice invalid.[5] But this had been dissented from AIR 1962 All 307 where a notice under s. 80, CPC contained a wrong number of R/R. Wrong number of R/R was given in the Short Certificate issued at the time of delivery. While the number of packages in the consignment, nature of the goods booked, the date of booking and the station of delivery were correctly given. *Held*, notice is not bad.[6]

(*iii*) A time-barred notice is of no avail.[7]

(*iv*) Notice under s. 78B (of Act of 1890) sent more than six months after the date on which goods were delivered for carriage. Notice was bad. Decree passed in such suit is illegal. Starting point of limitation could not be from the date the goods were delivered to the consignee.[8]

10 Interpretation and construing a notice under s. 106

Though a notice of claim to compensation under s. 77 (now s. 106) read with s. 140 (now s. 192) is not to be construed with extreme strictness, there must be substantial compliance with the provisions of those sections.[9] Even then

21 *Begraj Gadhuram* v *E.I. Rly. Co.* AIR 1928 Cal 697.
1 AIR 1949 Pat 268.
2 AIR 1961 MP 220.
3 *Begraj Gadhuram* v *E.I. Rly. Co.* AIR 1928 Cal 697.
4 *Chaturbhai Bhailalbhai Patil* v *Union of India* AIR 1961 Pat 334; AIR 1943 Pat 93; *Union of India* v *Nagashwar Prasad* AIR 1964 Pat 373.
5 1950 All LJ 595.
6 AIR 1966 All 16.
7 *Tahsil Co-op. Agri. Assocn. Ltd.* v *Union of India* AIR 1968 MP 185.
8 *Union of India* v *M/s. K.T. Rizvi* AIR 1985 Bom 84. Also see *Union of India* v *Firm Ramdas* AIR 1965 Raj 127; *Union of India* v *Nirmal Kumar* AIR 1964 Pat 392; *G.-G. in Council* v *Musaddi Lal* AIR 1961 SC 725.
9 *Shamji Bhanji & Co.* v *North Western Rly. Co.* AIR 1947 Bom 169.

it cannot be said that a notice under s. 77 (now s. 106) should be considered too lightly. Equity cannot be prayed in aid in construing a like notice.[10] But it should be construed liberally. We would remember in this connexion observations of the Supreme Court in *Jetmull Bhojraj* v *Darjeeling Himalayan Railway Co. Ltd.*[11]—"A notice under s. 77 should be liberally construed. In our opinion, that would be the proper way of construing a notice under that section. In enacting the section, the intention of the legislature must have been to afford only a protection to the Railway Administration against fraud and not to provide a means for depriving the consignors of their legitimate claims for compensation for the loss of or damage caused to their consignments during the course of transit on the railways".

11 Limitation and period of notice under s. 106

A claim to refund or compensation has to be preferred in writing to the Railway Administration—

"Within a period of six months from the date of entrustment of the goods."

This portion of s. 78B (now s. 106) is rather vague giving rise to a controversy as to from when the period of six months is to be calculated. Practically speaking, there are two schools of opinion on this issue. The first school,—numerically champions of this school happen to be stronger—advocates that the notice under s. 78B has to be preferred within six months from the date when the goods were delivered to the railway "for carriage by railway".[12] The other school holds that the period of six months should be counted from the day when the goods were to be delivered to the consignee or his agent representative at the destination station.

The controversy came up in *Amar Chand* v *Union of India*,[13] before Assam High Court when Chief Justice Sarjoo Prosad held thus:

"I have my own doubt as to whether this period of six months should be calculated from the date on which the goods were delivered to the consignee or his representative or from the date on which the goods were originally consigned to the railway. The words 'for carriage by railway' may be read as qualifying the term 'goods' only, and not the date of delivery of the goods. It seems to me more reasonable to hold that the period of limitation should be counted from the day when the goods were to be delivered or delivered to the consignee or his representative, and not from the date when the goods were originally consigned.

"There are some decisions in support of this viewpoint. It was, for instance, held in *Bala Prasad* v *B.N.W. Rly. Co.*[14] by a Division Bench that in a suit

10 *G.G.-in Council* v *Sarbeswar Das* AIR 1949 Cal 420.
11 *Jetmull Bhojraj* v *Darjeeling Himalayan Co. Ltd.* AIR 1962 SC 1879.
12 AIR 1925 All 144.
13 AIR 1955 Assam 221.
14 AIR 1927 Oudh 478.

for non-delivery of goods, time begins to run when the goods ought to be delivered, i.e. when the consignee is entitled to open delivery. It is held, on the contrary, that if the limitation period should run from the date when the goods were first consigned or delivered for carriage to the railway, we are then reduced to the anomalous position that, in certain cases the claim under s. 77 will have to be preferred even before the goods are delivered or even before the consignee is aware whether any loss or damage has been caused. Cases are not unknown where goods are actually delivered long after six months from the date of consignment and it is only when delivery is taken that the consignee is made aware of any shortage in or damage to the goods.

"I am conscious of the fact that there are several decisions of the courts in India which prefer to adopt this latter view, in spite of the difficulties which, at any rate, are apparent to me. The legislature, in my opinion, should consider whether s. 77, the Indian Railways Act, should be appropriately recast."[15]

The aforesaid Assam case has been dissented from in *O. & T. Railways* v *M/s. Karamchand;*[16] *Union of India* v *M. Pullappa;*[17] *Union of India* v *Shah Vastimull,*[18] *Union of India* v *K.T. Rijvi.*[19]

Incidentally, the legislature has indeed recast s. 77; and s. 78B (now s. 106) is the result. But we stand exactly where we were as because this controversial portion of the section was not amended. The reported cases, however, make it clear that a notice has to be served within six months from the date of delivery of the goods to the booking railway.[20]

In *Governor-General in Council* v *Sarbeswar Das*, it was *held*: "Equity cannot be prayed in aid in construing a section such as s. 77. The period of six months is six months of the goods being delivered to the railway for carriage and not from the date of the delivery of goods to the consignee.[21] The notice contemplated under s. 77 should be given within six months from the date of delivery of the goods for carriage by railways and not within six months from the date of the delivery to the consignee, for there may not be any delivery at all; the goods might have been lost in transit.[22]

15 *Amarchand Pannalal* v *Union of India* AIR 1955 Assam 221.
16 AIR 1955 All 234.
17 AIR 1958 AP 475.
18 AIR 1959 Mys 13.
19 AIR 1985 Bom 84.
20 *Darjeeling Himalayan Co. Ltd.* v *Jetmull Bhojraj* AIR 1956 Cal 390; *Union of India* v *Asharafi Devi* AIR 1957 MP 114.
21 AIR 1949 Cal 420 (*per* Harries, CJ.).
22 *Union of India* v *Mitayagiri* AIR 1958 AP 475. Also see *Governor-General in Council* v *Sarbeswar Das* AIR 1949 Cal 420; *Union of India* v *Maghraj* AIR 1958 Cal 434; *Union of India* v *Sha Vestimull Harakchand* AIR 1959 Mys 13; AIR 1959 MP 276; *Union of India* v *Ramdas Amritlal Pali* AIR 1965 Raj 127; *Union of India* v *Haji Jiwakhan* AIR 1962 MP 374; *Union of India* v *M/s. Lakshmi Textiles* AIR 1968 Ker 23.

It then logically follows that a suit filed against railways for a claim for which the notice was issued beyond the prescribed period of six months is not maintainable.[23] A time-barred notice is of no avail.[24] But the bar of limitation prescribed under s. 106(3) of the Railways Act 1989 is not applicable where the freight was realised illegally.[25]

The words "carriage by railway" qualify the word "delivery" and not the word "goods". The period of six months should be counted from the date of consignment of the goods to the railway for carriage.[1] Section 78B of the Act of 1890 does not speak about the knowledge of the person. A consignor has to claim delivery within six months of the date of consignment and if delivery within six months is not given, he would be entitled to claim compensation for non-delivery of goods and will be under the obligation to give notice. He cannot wait indefinitely. The time begins to run from the date of delivering of the goods for carriage by railway and the consignor or the consignee has to give notice within six months of the date of delivery. If he does not give such a notice, the claim will be time barred.[2]

The next important question comes whether posting of a letter within six months will be a sufficient compliance or the letter containing the notice must reach the addressee within six months' time. Allahabad High Court has held in *Secretary of State* v *Firm Imperial Metal Works*:[3] "The law requires that the notice should not merely be preferred, but preferred to the Railway Administration within six months ...... If the notice was so posted that in the ordinary course of post it should have been delivered to the railway company within six months, this would have been a sufficient compliance with the law." A different view, however, was taken by Patna High Court in *Ram Gopal* v *B. & N.W. Rly*. In case the letter had been posted within six months, but too late to reach the addressee within six months. It was *held*: "The question is whether this posting complies with the terms of s. 77 (*now s. 106*)* that is to say, whether the posting of the letter containing the notice was a proper service of notice as contemplated by s. 77 (*now s. 106*)* .... Reading, however, s. 140(*c*) [*now s. 192*(*c*)] it would seem quite plain that the preferment of the claim has to be made by forwarding the letter by post, that is to say, by posting a registered letter. It seems clear also that when the letter was posted the claim was preferred as contemplated in s. 77. The section only means that the claim should be preferred within the period and not that it should also reach the Railway Administration before its expiry".[4]

23 *Governor-General in Council* v *Musaddilal* AIR 1961 SC 725; AIR 1962 MP 301.
24 *Tahsil Co-op. Agri. Marketing Assocn.* v *Union of India* AIR 1968 MP 185.
25 *Hindustan Petroleum Corporation Ltd.* v *Union of India* AIR 2018 SC 444.
1 *Union of India* v *Lakshmi Textiles* AIR 1968 Ker 23.
2 *Bhola Ram* v *Union of India* 1977 All WC 106.
3 *Secretary of State* v *Firm Imperial Metal Works* AIR 1926 All 214.
* Added by the Reviser.
4 *Ram Gopal Marwari* v *Bengal and N.W. Railway* AIR 1927 Pat 241; AIR 1957 MP 114.

Mere posting of notice on the last day of limitation is not sufficient. It must be so posted as to reach the addressee within six months in normal course.[5] The notice has not only to be posted within six months but it must also reach the hands of the Railways Administration within the said period.[6]

12 Application of s. 15(2) of the Limitation Act to a notice under s. 106 of the Railways Act

A notice under s. 77 (now s. 106) of the Indian Railways Act is not a notice of suit. No period is prescribed by that section (and also by the new s. 106) before the expiry of which a claimant cannot institute a suit. Section 15(2) of the Limitation Act applies only where a notice of suit should precede a suit under the provision of a statute. Therefore, "the period taken in correspondence between the claimant and the railway in disposing a claim under s. 77 (now s. 106) cannot be excluded under s. 15(2) of the Limitation Act, from the period of limitation for a suit for compensation".[7]

Demand by claimants for taking open delivery of goods after preparation of statutory report by railway authorities within statutory period regarding claim of compensation was not barred by limitation.[8] Where the claim of excess freight charges was denied on the ground of limitation, the plea of the claimant that it should be granted to him as limitation starts running from the date of discovery of such mistake by operation of s. 17(1)(*c*) of the Limitation Act have no application to the Railway Tribunal.[9]

13 To whom a notice under s. 106 is to be sent?

Section 106 requires that a notice under this section has to be preferred in writing to the 'Railway Administration'. Now, what is a Railway Administration?

'Railway Administration' has been defined in s. 2(32) of the Railways Act 1989. Railway Administration in relation to a Government railway, means the General Manager of a Zonal Railway and in relation to a non-Government railway, means the person who is the owner or lessee of the railway or the person working the railway under an agreement. Therefore, a notice to be served on a Railway Administration may be served, in the case of a railway administered by Government, on the General Manager of a Zonal Railway and in the case of a railway company on the agent in India of such railway company. In other words, the notice is to be sent to the Railway Administration, addressed either to the General Manager of a Zonal Railway or to the agent, as the case may be.

5 *Union of India* v *Firm Banshidhar Premsukh Dass* AIR 1976 All 491.
6 *Union of India* v *M/s. Amin Chand Pyarelal* AIR 1974 Punj 190.
7 *Union of India* v *Asharfi Devi* AIR 1957 MP 114.
8 *Union of India* v *India Cements Ltd.* 1996 AIHC 3047 (Ker).
9 *Birla Cement Works* v *G.M., Western Rly.* AIR 1955 SC 1111.

Coming to the question of 'Managers', one is likely to be in a fix when there are so many managers (namely, Commercial Manager, Traffic Manager, General Manager) who in particular should be addressed, more so, when there is no post as manager *simpliciter.* We may refer to conditions printed at the back of a railway receipt. The railway receipt, granted to a consignor, in respect of articles booked, enjoins upon the consignee to file his claim for compensation to the Chief Commercial Manager or Traffic Manager. It, therefore, may be held that a notice under s. 78B (now s. 106) may be given to any officer of the railway competent to deal with the claim. In *Governor-General in Council* v *Gauri Shankar Mills Ltd.,* Manohar Lall, Meredith and Mahabir Prasad, JJ. *held*: "The requirements of s. 77 (now s. 106) read with s. 140 (now s. 192) are satisfied by serving a notice within the prescribed period on the Chief Commercial Manager or any other subordinate officer of a railway company owned by the Government provided it is established as a fact that the railway company by its course of business or the terms of the contract between the parties has held out a particular official as competent to deal with the claims on receipt of notice to him."[10] Notice under s. 77 (now s. 106) (prior to amendment in 1961) for a claim for loss of goods in transit on Eastern Railway when served on the Chief Commercial Superintendent of that Railway is valid. That officer being specially engaged in the enquiry into claims and being of such status as can look into truth or falsity of the claim is the proper authority to receive notice of claim under s. 77.[11]

In *Niranjan Lall Agarwalla*[12] the notice under s. 77 of the old Act was served on the Chief Commercial Manager (Claims & Refunds) of the erstwhile Bengal and Assam Railway which did not have any officer of the designation of a Manager. It was found that Chief Commercial Manager (Claims & Refunds) was of equal status to the Manager. On these facts the Supreme Court found that the service of notice on Chief Commercial Manager (Claims & Refunds) is a sufficient compliance with s. 140 read with s. 3(6) of the old Railways Act.

It, therefore, follows that while s. 80, CPC specifies that a notice under s. 80, CPC in a suit against the railway has to be served on the General Manager of the railway, a notice under s. 78B (now s. 106) may be served on other competent officials as well. Notice under s. 77 (now s. 106) in respect of a claim for non-delivery of goods consigned, served on the Chief Commercial Manager of the railway who is the officer responsible for investigating claims instead of on the General Manager, is a good notice to

10 *Governor-General in Council* v *Gauri Shankar Mills Ltd.* AIR 1949 Pat 347 (FB). Also see AIR 1922 Mad 362; AIR 1933 Pat 45.

11 *Radhamadhab Kundu* v *Union of India* 61 CWN 433; *Niranjan Lall Agarwalla* v *Union of India* AIR 1969 SC 23; *Indian Iron & Steel Co. Ltd.* v *Union of India* AIR 1978 Cal 46. Also see *Jetmull Bhojraj* v *Union of India* AIR 1962 SC 1879; AIR 1967 Cal 47; *Nagarmal More* v *Union of India* AIR 1971 Assam 41.

12 AIR 1969 SC 23; (1968)3 SCR 415.

the Railway Administration because if it had been served on the General Manager he would merely have forwarded it to the Chief Commercial Manager.[13] In the case of loss of goods on a railway owned by the Government, a notice of claim to compensation given to the Railway Administration or its General Traffic Manager or General Manager is sufficient compliance with s. 77 (now s. 106) read with s. 140 (now s. 192).[14] Notice to an officer authorised to receive notice is sufficient.[15]

Again, when it is found that the Railway Administration had otherwise sufficient notice of the claim, it would be of little importance that a notice was served on the General Manager or other officer. The object of a notice under s. 78B (now s. 106) is to prevent stale and dishonest claims. It is not the intention of the Railway Administration to resist a just claim of the aggrieved party. Necessarily, some courts have a tendency to relax the rigidity of the rule in favour of the claimant when, particularly, it is found that the railways had sufficient notice of the claim. In *Union of India* v *Imperial Tobacco Co. of India Ltd.*,[16] it was *held*: "The notice under s. 77 (*now s. 106*) was addressed to the Managers of both the railways and a copy was sent to the Superintendent of Claims of G.I.P. Railway, Bombay. Though the plaintiff did not file the acknowledgments addressed to the manager of the two railways, there was a postal acknowledgment signed by the Chief Traffic Manager on record. The Superintendent of Claims, G.I.P. Railway, Bombay, who was the officer deputed by the General Manager to deal with such claims, actually received a copy of the notice. *Held*, the notice was a valid notice."

The following cases on this point may be borne in mind:

(*i*) Notice served on the Chief Transportation Manager held not sufficient.[17] Notice to Traffic Superintendent does not amount to proper notice.[18]

(*ii*) Same view in another Calcutta case.[19]

(*iii*) Notice served on the Chief Commercial Manager held not sufficient.[20]

Notice served on the Chief Commercial Superintendent, Gorakhpur although both the Railways, i.e. the Railways of booking and Railways of

13 AIR 1945 Cal 412; AIR 1955 Cal 448.
14 *Shamji Bhanji & Co.* v *North Western Rly. Co.* AIR 1947 Bom 169.
15 *Bharat Kumar* v *Union of India* AIR 2005 Raj 124; *Brook Bond India Ltd.* v *Union of India* AIR 1969 Cal 39.
16 *Union of India* v *Imperial Tobacco Co. of India Ltd.* AIR 1959 MP 232.
17 *Surendra Nath* v *Governor-General in Council* AIR 1952 Cal 340.
18 *State of West Bengal* v *Union of India* 91 CWN 376; (1986)2 CHN 75; AIR 1987 Cal 226.
19 *Union of India* v *Indumati Saha w/o Upendra Nath* AIR 1951 Cal 512.
20 *Union of India* v *Durgadutt Poddar* AIR 1957 Cal 202; 59 CWN 1064.

destination had General Managers, who were superior in rank to Chief Commercial Superintendent. The Allahabad decision[21] was rendered for a cause of action that arose prior to the amendment of s. 140 of the old Railways Act by the Indian Railways (Amendment) Act 1961 with effect from 1st January 1962. Change of law has neutralised the ratio of the decision in *Rampadarath*[22] Orissa High Court held that after the change in law service upon Chief Commercial Superintendent is valid.[23] As a matter of fact, the said amending Act provides that notice may be served upon the Chief Commercial Superintendent also. A notice to an officer authorised by the Ministry of Railways to receive the notice satisfies the requirements of the statute.[24] Notice must be served if the plaintiff wants to succeed. If he does not serve the notice his claim will fail.[25]

(*iv*) AIR 1962 Cal 42; 69 CWN 614 and 69 CWN 692—Same view. Contra: AIR 1955 Cal 448; AIR 1945 Cal 412; AIR 1952 Cal 35 (FB); 56 CWN 83; *Union of India* v *The Steel Stock Holders' Syndicate, Poona* (1976)3 SCC 108.

14 Is each Railway involved in transit entitled to a notice?

It is a controversial issue as to whether, where more than one railway is concerned in the transit, each of the Railway Administrations is entitled to separate and independent notice under s. 78B (now s. 106) or not. Section 78B (now s. 106) enjoins that a notice has to be given (*i*) to the Railway Administration on which booked articles were delivered to be carried by the railway; or (*ii*) to the Railway Administration on whose railway the destination station lies; or, (*iii*) to the Railway Administration on whose railway the loss, destruction, deterioration or damage occurs. Thus, three alternative courses are made open to the claimant notice-giver. A claimant can elect to serve notice on the Railway Administration of the booking station or on that of the destination station. But with regard to the third alternative, the position seems a bit otherwise.

For, it may not be possible for the claimant to know precisely and with certainty when a consignment passed through several railways, as to where the loss, destruction, damage or deterioration occurred, i.e. which Railway Administration was responsible for the harm. In such a case, where a consignment passes through more than one railway, it is always safe to serve separate and independent notices on each of the railways concerned in the transit and necessarily involved in the claim. In *Union of India* v *Durga Dutt* it was *held*, several State railways involved—one notice against

21 *Union of India* v *Durgadutt Poddar* AIR 1957 Cal 202; 59 CWN 1064.
22 *Rampadarath* v *Union of India* AIR 1974 All 465.
23 *Union of India* v *Khetwat Oil Mills* AIR 1988 Ori 233.
24 *Brooke Bond India (Pvt.) Ltd.* v *Union of India* AIR 1960 Cal 34.
25 *Surendra Nath* v *Governor-General in Council* AIR 1952 Cal 340.

the Union of India as representing all the railways would not be sufficient.[26] A few other recently reported cases are a pointer to this view.

(*i*) A notice under s. 77 (now s. 106) must be separately given to each Railway Administration impleaded as a defendant. This is because each Railway Administration is to be treated as a separate entity with separate existence and personality for the purpose of a suit under s. 80, CPC.[1]

(*ii*) Goods booked by the Western Railway for delivery at a station on the North-Eastern Railway. A notice under s. 77 (now s. 106) was issued to latter railway. There were no proof that loss or damage took place within jurisdiction of North-Eastern Railway. The decree for damages cannot be granted against the Union of India as owner of that railway.[2]

(*iii*) Section 77 (now s. 106) read with s. 80, CPC of the Indian Railways Act 1890 makes it clear that s. 77 treats each of the Railway Administrations as a separate entity though they happen to be now owned by the Central Government—Hence, any Railway Administration against whom relief is sought must be served with notice under s. 77 of the Indian Railways Act.[3]

(*iv*) Each Railway Administration is a separate entity and a different legal person capable of suing and being sued independently. Notice against one Railway Administration of the claim of the plaintiff is not, therefore, sufficient compliance of the provision of s. 77 to constitute a notice against the other Railway Administration.[4]

(*v*) Notice on one Railway Administration would not be a notice on all the railways.[5]

For opposite view the following cases may be seen:

(*a*) *G.-G. in Council* v *Ajitbhai Jayantilal.*[6]

(*b*) *P.R. Narayanswami Iyer* v *Union of India.*[7]

(*c*) *Union of India* v *Landra Engineering & Foundry Works.*[8]

26 AIR 1957 Cal 202; AIR 1953 All 234.

1 *Kondappalli Virraju* v *General Manager, South Eastern Railway* AIR 1959 AP 594; AIR 1959 AP 276.

2 *Union of India* v *Nawab Pandey* AIR 1964 Pat 383.

3 *Kondappalli Virraju* v *General Manager, South Eastern Railway* AIR 1959 AP 594; *Union of India* v *Bhagat Ram* AIR 1972 All 288.

4 AIR 1956 Ori 29; AIR 1931 Cal 585.

5 *Union of India* v *Eastern Match Co.* AIR 1964 AP 172; *Managing Agents* v *Deokinandan* AIR 1959 MP 276; *Jethmall Bhojraj* v *D. Himalayan Railway Co. Ltd.* AIR 1962 SC 1879; *Union of India* v *Firm Munnalal Pasari* AIR 1971 MP 131; *Md. Jaffar Haji Ebrahim* v *Union of India* AIR 1972 Ori 101.

6 AIR 1952 Mad 795.

7 AIR 1960 Mad 58.

8 AIR 1962 Punj 262.

(*d*) Consigned goods passing over different railways in transit and the consignor is unable to locate loss on particular railway. Notice to one of the railways meets requirement of s. 77. *Held*, notice to one railway amounts to giving notice to other railways also.[9]

Option to serve notice on any of the Railway Administrations is ultimately negated. It is, however, always wise that a notice under s. 78B (now s. 106) should be sent to all the Railway Administrations over which the consignment passed. In this connection we would do well to remember the observations of the Hon'ble Supreme Court—notice under s. 77 must be given to every railway against whom suit is eventually filed.[10]

To sum up: notice under s. 78B of the Indian Railways Act 1890 (now s. 106) may be served on any of the Railway Administrations but notice under s. 80, CPC must have to be served on all the Railway Administrations who are impleaded in the suit (discussed in AIR 1966 Cal 540 at 544). Section 80, CPC notice served on the General Manager of the booking Railway Administration with copies of such notice to the General Managers of other Railway Administrations—such copies could be treated as individual notices to them, and was sufficient compliance with the provision under s. 80 of CPC.[11]

15 When through traffic—one notice under s. 106 held sufficient

Ordinarily each railway involved in transit is entitled to have a notice under s. 106. But in a case of 'through traffic' the position may be different.

In a case of through traffic a notice to the General Manager of one of the Railway Administrations is sufficient. An earlier, but important, decision on this issue *Narayanswami Iyer* v *Union of India*[12] held that one notice under s. 77 (now s. 106) to a General Manager of any Government railway concerned in the route over which through traffic passed will be sufficient because all the railways over which the traffic passed, are owned by the Central Government. In the absence of any specific enactment either in s. 77 (now s. 106) or in s. 140 (now s. 192) indicating the particular General Manager to whom notice ought to be given in a case of through traffic carried over more than one zonal unit of the Government railways, notice to any one of such General Managers is sufficient compliance with these provisions. In case of through traffic notice to one railway and a copy to the other—notice claiming compensation against both railways is sufficient. The notice is valid even to the other railway to which a copy alone was sent.[13]

9 AIR 1966 All 16.
10 *Jethmull Bhojraj* v *D.H. Railway Co. Ltd.* AIR 1962 SC 1879.
11 *G.G. in Council* v *Sakarappa* AIR 1953 Mad 838; *Jethmull Bhojraj* v *D.H. Railway Co. Ltd.* AIR 1962 SC 1879; *Dasa K. Lakshmiah* v *Union Government* AIR 1969 AP 386.
12 AIR 1960 Mad 58; *Shivchand Aggarwal* v *Union of India* AIR 1963 Punj 224.
13 AIR 1963 Ori 56.

16 Distinction between short delivery and non-delivery—cases when notice of claim under s. 106 required

In case of short delivery there is delivery of goods but delivery is partial, while in case of non-delivery there is no delivery at all.

There was a conflict of decisions on the point as to whether in case of non-delivery of goods notice under s. 77 (now s. 106) of the Indian Railways Act 1890 is necessary. The Supreme Court in *Union of India* v *Mahadeolal*[14] has held that in case of non-delivery the cause of action is the same as in loss and notice under s. 78B (then s. 77 and now s. 106) was mandatory. Section 78B of the old Act has inserted the word 'non-delivery'. So there is no speck of doubt that in case of non-delivery too, notice under s. 78B of the old Act (corresponding to s. 106 of the new Act) is mandatory.[15]

Short delivery may be due to loss of goods or for some other reason, namely, conversion, detention, misconduct, misdelivery, wrongful sale of goods, capricious acts etc. If short delivery is due to loss of the goods, a notice is required under s. 77 (now s. 106).[16] Notice was held necessary where short delivery was due to loss of goods by rain and flood.[17] But if the reason for short delivery is not due to loss but be otherwise, namely, detention, conversion, etc., notice is not required.[18] Goods detained by railways—no loss alleged or proved—s. 77 (now s. 106) is not attracted.[19] Wrongful refusal to give delivery of goods—suit for compensation—*held,* notice under s. 77 is not necessary.[1]

Non-delivery of the consignment may be due to various causes. It may be due to loss. It may be due to detention, conversion, etc., as enumerated above. The principle whether a notice in cases of non-delivery has to be given or not is exactly the same as in the case of short delivery. When non-delivery is due to loss, notice is obligatory, but when non-delivery is due to some other reason, notice is not required.

A suit for compensation to be within the mischief of s. 78B (now s. 106) must be for loss of goods by the railway.

In *Mutsaddilal* v *Governor-General in Council*[2] it has been held by the Full Bench of the Allahabad High Court that where non-delivery is due to loss, destruction or deterioration of the goods, then a notice under s. 77 of the

14 (1965)3 SCR 145; AIR 1965 SC 1755.
15 *Bhola Ram* v *Union of India* 1977 All WC 106.
16 AIR 1925 Cal 725; AIR 1949 Cal 420.
17 AIR 1959 MP 276.
18 AIR 1951 Punj 383; *Governor-General in Council* v *Mahabir Ram* AIR 1952 All 891; AIR 1953 Punj 184; AIR 1961 Manipur 45; AIR 1960 All 131.
19 AIR 1960 Cal 571.
1 AIR 1960 Mys 283; *Makhanlal Harnarain* v *Union of India* AIR 1960 Pat 150; AIR 1960 Pat 419.
2 AIR 1952 All 897.

Indian Railways Act 1890 (now s. 106 of the Railways Act 1989) is required but where non-delivery is due to any other cause, e.g. conversion, detention, misconduct, misdelivery, wrongful delivery, capricious acts etc., then a notice under s. 77 is not necessary. A similar view has been taken in the undernoted cases.[3] But a contrary view has been taken by Bombay and Patna High Courts. In *Martab Ali* v *Union of India*,[4] Bombay High Court held that the word "loss" in s. 77 of the 1890 Act is applicable to the case of non-delivery as well as to cases of negligence and wrongful detention or conversion on the part of the Railway Administration. In a Full Bench decision of the Patna High Court where the plaintiff's case in the plaint is that the goods have been lost due to the negligence on the part of the servants of the defendant company, the case must be treated as one of loss even though the plaintiff may have framed the suit as for non-delivery.[5]

The controversy has been resolved by the decision of the Supreme Court in *Governor-General in Council* v *Musaddilal.*[6] The Supreme Court held that notice under s. 77 (of 1890 Act) is necessary in case of non-delivery or short delivery whether it is due to "loss, destruction or deterioration" or it is due to negligence or even wrongful act of the Railway Administration. The position has been reaffirmed by the Supreme Court in *Union of India* v *Mahadeolal Prabhudayal.*[7]

Thus non-delivery may be due to loss as well as for other reasons. Where in a suit for damages against a railway administration for non-delivery of a part of the consignment, the plaintiff established that the non-delivery was due to misconduct on the part of the Railway Administration and there is no finding that it was due to loss, destruction, or deterioration, the suit cannot fail for want of notice under s. 77 of the Indian Railways Act 1890 (corresponds to s. 106 of the Railways Act 1989).[8]

'Loss' in s. 77 (now s. 106) necessarily includes non-delivery but non-delivery would not necessarily include loss. Section 77 (now s. 106) is applicable to a case where the non-delivery on the part of the Railway Administration is due to loss by theft.[9] The word 'loss' in s. 77 (now s. 106)

3 *Governor-General in Council* v *Mahabir Ram* AIR 1952 All 891 (FB); *Ram Narain* v *Dominion of India* AIR 1953 All 460; *Haridas Banmalidass* v *M & S.M. Railway* 41 Mad 871; *Shamsul Huq* v *Secretary of State* AIR 1930 Cal 312; *E.I. Railway* v *Jogpat Singh* AIR 1924 Cal 725; 28 CWN 1001; 51 Cal 615; *Gobinda Chandra* v *Union of India* AIR 1960 Cal 571; *Makhanlal Harnarain* v *Union of India* AIR 1960 Pat 150.

4 AIR 1954 Bom 297; 56 Bom LR 150.

5 *Dominion of India* v *Hazarilal* AIR 1949 Pat 410 (FB).

6 AIR 1961 SC 725; (1961)3 SCR 647; (1961)1 SCJ 597.

7 AIR 1965 SC 1755; (1965)3 SCR 145.

8 *Ram Narain* v *Dominion of India* AIR 1953 All 460.

9 AIR 1952 Cal 341. Also see *Governor-General in Council* v *Mahabir Ram* AIR 1952 All 891 (FB); AIR 1953 Punj 184; *Ram Narain* v *Dominion of India* AIR 1953 All 460; AIR 1958 Pat 536; AIR 1958 Pat 489; *Union of India* v *Genddal Nathuram* AIR 1958 MP 314; 1958 MPLJ 500.

has a wider connotation and includes cases where the goods are not forthcoming and hence service of notice in such cases is equally obligatory.[10]

17 Case of paying double charge distinguished from over-charge—notice under s. 106, if required?

An overcharge is simply a charge in excess of that which is due according to law.[11] A claim for refund of excess amount paid towards freight is a claim for overcharge.[12] It cannot include any money which has been paid through mistake or realised when nothing was really due. The decision in *Kaluram* v *B.N. Rly.*[13] may be seen. The consignee not knowing that the consignor pre-paid the freight at the time of booking had to pay over again the freight owing to the non-receipt of R/R. Such double payment is illegal being unauthorised collection and was not a case of overcharge. Hence no notice under s. 78B of the Act of 1890 (now s. 106 of the Act of 1989) was required. Claim that charges were collected illegally, arbitrarily and unreasonably—claim is not one of 'overcharges' attracting provisions of s. 78B.[14]

It is submitted, however, that the applicability of the Gujarat High Court decision of 1975 is not free from doubt. After all, 'overcharge' occurring in s. 106(3) of the Railways Act 1989 according to its plain natural sense means any charge in excess of that prescribed or permitted by law. Double payment is, in our opinion, necessarily partakes of the same character as overcharge. As observed in another Gujarat case,[15] overcharge is simply a charge in excess of what is due according to law. On this view, a notice under s. 106 is mandatory for claiming refund of the excess amount.

18 Case of tortious liabilities—if notice under s. 106 is required

There may be cases where a wrong is both a breach of contract as well as a tortious liability. For example, when a person travels by a train and suffers injury owing to negligence of the Railway Administration, the wrong is both a breach of contract as well as a tort. For tortious liabilities, his remedy is damages as in cases of other tortious liabilities. Wordings of s. 78B (now s. 106) of the Indian Railways Act 1890 indicate that when a railway commits torts it is not entitled to a notice as envisaged in s. 78B. In *Sundarji Sivaji* v *Secretary of State*, Courtney-Terrell, J. *held*: "Section 77 (now s. 106) refers only to a claim to a refund of an over-charge or compensation for loss, destruction or deterioration of goods, delivered to be so carried, that is to say, it refers to a suit against the carrier in his capacity

10 AIR 1965 Raj 127.
11 *Union of India* v *West Coast Paper Mills Ltd.* (2004)3 SCC 458.
12 *Malhar Cement* v *Union of India* AIR 2012 MP 104; *Union of India* v *Rashtriya Ispat Nigam Ltd.* AIR 2005 AP 184.
13 *Kaluram* v *B.N. Railway Co.* 13 Cut LT 60.
14 *Union of India* v *Mansukhlal Jethalal* AIR 1975 Guj 116.
15 *Shah Raichand Amulakh* v *Union of India* 12 Guj LR 93.

as a carrier for the loss, destruction or deterioration of goods. The section, therefore, refers to the special liability of the carrier as such; it has no application to the broad liability of the railway company in this case as tortfeasors quite apart from their position of railway carriers".[16] And, therefore, no notice is necessary before bringing such a suit. Again Bennet, J. in the *Secretary of State* v *Simla Footwear Company held*: "Section 77 (now s. 106 of the Act of 1989) comes in Chapter VII of the Indian Railways Act, which is headed "Responsibility of Railway Administration as Carriers".[17] That Chapter VII begins with s. 72 which lays down the responsibility of the Railway Administration for the loss, destruction or deterioration of animals or goods, and it is stated that the responsibility is that of a bailee under ss. 151, 152 or 162, Contract Act. Those sections do not refer to the action of a bailee in selling the goods as in the present case, nor is a bailee entitled to do so. The right of a railway company as distinct from an ordinary bailee to sell goods depends on the statutory provisions in ss. 56, 56A, Chapter VI of the Indian Railways Act 1890. Any claim which would arise from a railway company failing to act under those sections although it purported to act under them, would not come under Chapter VII. Accordingly, the notice provided by s. 77, Chapter VII, clearly does not apply to the present case.[18] [In this case the railway administration sold the goods of the plaintiff from the Railway Lost Property Office and offered the plaintiff sale-proceeds thereof].

19 Service of notice to railway administration (s. 192)

We have seen that a notice meant for the Railway Administration has to be served on the Manager when such railway is owned by a railway company. Section 192 of the Railways Act 1989 reads:

> "Any notice or other documents required or authorised by this Act to be served on a railway administration may be served, in the case of a Zonal Railway, on the General Manager or any of the railway servant authorised by the General Manager, and in the case of any other railway, on the owner or lessee of the railway or the person working the railway under an agreement—
>
> (*a*) by delivering it to him; or
>
> (*b*) by leaving at his office; or
>
> (*c*) by registered post to his office address."

A claim under s. 78B (now s. 106), when forwarded by post, has to be in accordance with cl. (*c*) of s. 140 of the old Act and when so forwarded the presumption under s. 142 (now s. 194) is attracted.[19]

16 AIR 1934 Pat 507.
17 Now Chapter XI of the Railways Act 1989.
18 AIR 1935 All 601.
19 *Union of India* v *M/s. Lakshmi Textiles* AIR 1968 Ker 23.

Section 192 of the Railways Act provides the mode of service of notices and other documents on the Railway Administrations. Clauses (*a*) and (*b*) relate to service of a notice or other document through a messenger of the sender of such notice or document. A notice or a document would be deemed to be served if it was sent by post under registered cover and properly addressed. Denial of service by the addressee may shift the burden and the plaintiff is to prove service by some other evidence.[20] But if a notice is issued under certificate of posting and when it is not properly addressed, the presumption of proper service does not arise.[21]

A pertinent question arises if notice must have to be served on the Manager of a State railway (and on the agent of a company administered railway) or it may as well be served on the railway administration through some official of the railway concerned. There has been sharp difference in opinion on this simple issue among different judges in different courts. When a notice is sent to the General Manager of the railway concerned it is well and good. But when a notice is sent to some other official, what happens? Does it comply with the provisions of s. 140 (now s. 192)?

"The requirements of s. 77 (now s. 106) read with s. 140 (now s. 192), the Indian Railways Act, are satisfied by serving a notice within prescribed period on the Chief Commercial Manager,[22] or any other subordinate officer of a railway company owned by the Government provided it is established as a fact that the railway company by its course of business or the terms of the contract between the parties has held out a particular official as competent to deal with the claims on receipt of notice to him.[23] Again, there is nothing in the Act that prevents the railway administration or its agent or manager from deputing an officer to receive the notice required by ss. 77 and 140 (now ss. 106 and 192) on its behalf .... It is unlikely that the agent or manager would attend personally to losses and in the ordinary course of business he would depute the Traffic Manager or the District Traffic Superintendent to investigate the matter and report.[24] There will be no harm if the notice be sent to that official to whom the notice will pass on ultimately, had it been sent to the manager or agent.

The above view, as outlined at the beginning, did not find approbation from all quarters till recently. It was once a view that a notice to a subordinate of the agent or of the manager is not a notice.[25] Notice of a claim under s. 77 (now s. 106) served upon the Chief Commercial Manager is not a sufficient compliance with the section.[1] But the recent decisions speak

20 *Puwada Venkatasewara Rao* v *C.V. Raman* AIR 1976 SC 869; (1976)2 SCC 409.
21 *Union of India* v *Punjab State Co-op. Supply* AIR 1984 P&H 41.
22 *Nagarmal More* v *Union of India* AIR 1971 Assam 41.
23 AIR 1943 Pat 347.
24 AIR 1922 Mad 362.
25 AIR 1923 Lah 84.
1 AIR 1957 Cal 202.

otherwise. Even if initially a notice is not served on the proper authority according to law but if it ultimately reaches the proper authority within due time, it is good and valid notice according to law.[2] Requirements of s. 77 (now s. 106) are satisfied if the claim is preferred in writing to any person authorised by the Manager to receive the claim on his behalf.[3]

In brief, s. 140 of the Act of 1890 names the railway official to whom a notice under the Indian Railways Act 1890 is to be sent. The expression 'may be served' indicates that the notice-giver has had the option to choose any of the three modes prescribed in the section. If a notice is not served in any of those three modes, it must be held that there is no notice at all.[4]

Requirements of s. 140 (now s. 192) will be satisfied if the notice is ultimately served on the Manager or the Chief Commercial Superintendent or the agent, either by leaving the notice at his office or by forwarding it to him by registered post. It is not the law that the Manager or the Chief Commercial Superintendent or the agent has to receive the notice by himself, for any of them may depute a subordinate officer to receive a notice on his behalf. An inference of such delegation of authority by the Manager or the Chief Commercial Superintendent or the agent will be presumed by direct evidence or by the ordinary course of conduct.[5]

In *Niranjan Lall* v *Union of India*[6] Supreme Court observed: In the light of s. 3(6) there would be sufficient compliance with s. 77 (now s. 106) if the notice was served on the Manager of the State-owned railway, s. 140 (now s. 192) only provides for manner of service. In this case notice served on the Chief Commercial Superintendent was held valid.

When a notice under s. 77 (now s. 106) was sent to one railway with a copy of the notice sent to the other railway, it may be in proper circumstances a valid notice to the railway. What are the circumstances? When a notice of claim is given under s. 77 to one railway administration while a copy of that notice is sent to the agent of other railway administration 'for information' and compensation is demanded from the latter, there is no valid notice to the latter railway under s. 77 (now s. 106).[7] But when the copy of the notice is sent to the latter railway 'for favour of necessary action,' there was a valid notice to the latter railway. For obvious reasons the latter case is distinguishable from the Calcutta case reported above. The words 'for favour of necessary action' would ordinarily mean that a claim was made against the other railway also".[8] In *Laxminarayan Govindaram* v *Union of India*,

2 AIR 1955 Pep 51.
3 61 CWN 433; *Amer Chand Pannalal* v *Union of India* AIR 1955 Assam 221; AIR 1953 Mys 16.
4 AIR 1925 Oudh 419.
5 AIR 1924 Nag 288; Dist. AIR 1926 Pat 413.
6 AIR 1969 SC 23; (1968)3 SCR 415.
7 AIR 1931 Cal 585.
8 AIR 1963 Ori 54.

the above view was confirmed relying on the decision in AIR 1962 SC 1879 that a copy of the notice to the other railway was sufficient when the contents of the notice brought clearly a claim against both the railway administrations.[9] Under the present law, even though there is no delegation by the General Manager or the Chief Commercial Superintendent of their right to receive notice authorisation by the Ministry of Railways to any other officer is sufficient. A notice to an officer so authorised satisfies the requirements of the statute.[10]

In order to take back possession of the premises which was given to its Employee by railway administration it is a condition precedent that the railway administration sought to have proved that the premises belonged to it before invoking notice in writing under s. 138 of the Railways Act for evicting. The railway administration may be owner, mortgagee, lessee or licensee.[11]

20 Notice under s. 106—when consignment despatched through out-agency and common carriers-cum-railway

"An out-agency is an office opened in places situated away from a railway station in order to facilitate the booking of traffic directly to or from such place" (cf. Para 1702, p. 103 of the Indian Railway Code—Commercial). "Out-agencies may be worked departmentally or through contractors, the latter executing an agreement before the out-agency is opened, containing terms and conditions under which the out-agency will be worked" (cf. Para 1704 *ibid*).

Again, from the specimen form of out-agency agreement in Appendix XII of the said Railway Code, it transpires that contractors shall be deemed to be agents of the railway administration. As such, when claim for loss etc. of a consignment despatched through the out-agency of a railway is to be made, a notice under s. 78B (now s. 106) on the railway administration would be sufficient. No separate notice on the out-agency (agent of the railway) will be required.

21 Service of notice by the railway administration (s. 193)

The Indian Railways Act provides three modes of service of notice, required under the Act to be served on any person. Those are personal service, service at residence and service by post.

Section 193 reads:

> "Unless otherwise provided in this Act or the rules framed thereunder, any notice or other document required or authorized by this Act to be served on any person by a railway administration may be served—

9 AIR 1963 Ori 56.
10 *Brooke Bond India (Pvt.) Ltd.* v *Union of India* AIR 1960 Cal 39.
11 *S.K. Sarma* v *Mahesh Kumar Verma* (2002)7 SCC 505; *Union of India* v *B.N. Prasad* (1978)2 SCC 462.

(*a*) by delivering it to the person; or

(*b*) by leaving it at the usual or last known place of abode of the person; or

(*c*) by registered post addressed to the person at his usual or last known place of abode."

By address, the usual address is meant. In a case where the defendant resided at Loharchaul, Bombay and, occasionally used to attend his brother's place of business at Fanaswadu, it was held that the latter address was not the defendant's "last known address or place of abode."[12]

22 Presumption where a notice under the Railways Act is served by post (s. 194)

Section 194 of the Railways Act 1989 speaks of presumption of service of a notice when it is served by post duly stamped, pre-paid, properly addressed and registered. The section reads as follows:

> "Where a notice or other document is served by post, it shall be deemed to have been served at the time when the letter containing it would be delivered in the ordinary course of post, and in proving such service, it shall be sufficient to prove that the letter containing the notice or other document was properly addressed and registered."

In addition to the presumption under s. 194 of the Act, the absence of any specific denial by the railway concerned 'must lead to the inference that the notice under s. 77 (now s. 106) was duly served by registered post and duly received'.[13]

When notice is issued under certificate of posting and that too is not properly addressed the presumption of the old Act does not arise.[14] The Supreme Court in interpreting s. 27, General Clauses Act read with s. 114(*e*), Evidence Act has laid down denial of service by the addressee may shift the burden and then the plaintiff is to prove service by some other evidence.[15] The ratio of this decision may not be applicable to a notice under s. 194 of the Railways Act 1989 in view of the words "shall be deemed" occurring in s. 194 of the Act.

23 Notice under the Railway Establishment Code—period of notice—insufficient notice

A 'notice of not less than three months' in Rule No. 2046(*h*) of Vol. II of the Code means a notice of at least three months. A notice which is insufficient is prejudicial and invalid, such a notice taking effect from the date of service and not from the date of issue.[16]

12 ILR 5 Bom 223.
13 AIR 1963 Ori 54 (*per* Narashimham, C.J.).
14 *Union of India* v *Punjab State Coop. Supply* AIR 1984 P&H 41.
15 *Puwada Venkataswara Rao* v *C.V. Raman* AIR 1976 SC 869; (1976)2 SCC 409.
16 *Poonamchand Joshi* v *Union of India* AIR 1971 Raj 12.

24 Notice for public auction of unclaimed consignment

A notice for public auction of unclaimed consignment must be given to safeguard the position of the railway. But failure to issue notice does not entail any liability as the railway is not under any obligation to give notice.[17] For a sale under s. 84 of the Railways Act 1989, a notice of 14 days is sufficient.[18]

The object of a public notice of auction under s. 83 of the Railways Act 1989 and the provision that the notice is to be inserted in the local newspapers is an indication that it was the intention of the legislature that the local public shall be informed of a particular auction in order that persons may be attracted to bid at the auction. In order to attract bidders to the auction, the notice should contain adequate materials so that possible bidders may be informed of the class of the goods and the time and the place of auction. A notice that does not state when the sale would take place or the nature of the goods or the places at which they would be sold or the condition of the goods or indeed any particulars which would be calculated to attract purchasers to the sale is not 'notice of the intended sale' as prescribed by s. 55 of the Indian Railways Act 1890 which corresponds to s. 83 of the Railways Act 1989.[19]

25 Other cases

Section 78B (now s. 106) of the Railways Act provides that any refund on account of overcharge or excess payment in respect of goods or animals carried by Railways must be made by notice in writing within six months from the date of delivery by Railways. Since the notice of claim made by the petitioner to Railways on account of overcharge beyond six months the claim becomes barred by limitation.[20]

In the event no notice under s. 78B (now s. 106) is served on the railways within the stipulated time, but the railway administration admits of short-delivery, then the amount on short-delivery becomes payable.[21] Award of interest to seller on amount of price not paid by buyer within a reasonable time cannot be denied merely because in the notice served under s. 80, CPC, the seller has not claimed interest.

Notice given under s. 78B (now s. 106) to Railway Administration alleging gross negligence and misconduct on its part for carelessness in handling the goods, it was held that since the instant case falls under s. 77(2) of the Indian Railways Act 1890 (corresponds to s. 106 of the Railways Act 1989) which itself provides for the limited period of liability as a bailee, the claims cannot be made under ss. 72 and 76 of the Act of 1890.[22]

17 *Panna Lal* v *E.I. Railway* AIR 1952 All 880; (1952) ALJ 657.
18 *Secretary of State* v *Simla Footwear* AIR 1935 All 601; 57 All 843.
19 *Sunderji* v *Secretary of State* AIR 1934 Pat 507; 151 IC 995.
20 *Birla Cement Works* v *G.M., Western Railways* (1995)2 SCC 493.
21 *Marwar Tent Factory* v *Union of India* (1990)1 SCC 71.
22 *St. Joseph Textiles* v *Union of India* 1993 Supp (3) SCC 469.

FORMS

Form 1

Notice to the General Manager of a railway administration claiming compensation for short-delivery of goods consigned under s. 106 of the Railways Act 1989

Notice by party (simple form)

Registered with AD

Dated the .... 20 ......

Notice under s. 106 of the Railways Act 1989 (Preferring claim)

To

The General Manager .... Railway,

(*Name the railway with address*)

Details of Consignment

Ex. .... in .... Rly. .... to .... in .... Rly. .... Invoice No. .... P.W.B./R.R. No. .... dated .... Sender/Consignor .... Consignee .... (*Where there is endorsement*) endorsed to (State name and address of endorsee) .... for valuable consideration.

Contents .... bags/bale/tins etc. of .... each bag/bale/tin weighing/ containing ....

Date of delivery at the destination .... Condition in which delivered (state here shortage, loss, deterioration etc.).

Short (*or damage*) Certificate No. .... issued by .... on ....

Sir,

I call upon you to pay to me within 30 days from the date of receipt of this notice a sum of Rs. .... as compensation on account of shortage (or loss/deterioration) of .... in the consignment. Particulars of which are furnished hereinabove.

Yours faithfully,

NOTES:
1. The notice must be given and given within six months from the date of delivery of the goods to railway, i.e. from the date in P.W.B./R.R. (see s. 106).
2. General Manager of all the railways through which goods are conveyed, need not be given notice. One notice to one of the railways (either the consigning or the destination) will do.
3. In addition, proportionate railway freight may be claimed but whether the same will be allowed or not depends upon circumstances detailed in AIR 1965 Pat 316.
4. Requirements in a notice under s. 106 (see AIR 1967 Cal 47).
5. Notice need not be addressed to the Union of India. It is sufficient if the notice is addressed to the General Manager of the Railway concerned (AIR 1957 Mys 94; AIR 1952 Ass 88; (1969)71 Bom LR 214).

Form 2

Notice to the General Manager, Railway claiming compensation for non-delivery/short-delivery/deterioration etc.

(By party's lawyer)

Registered with AD

Dated the .... 20 ....

To

The General Manager .... Rly. ....

....

....

Notice under s. 106 of the Railways Act 1989

Dear Sir,

Under instructions from my client Sri .... son of .... of (or M/s. .... a firm registered under the Indian Partnership Act with its registered office at) .... P.S. .... Distt. .... I hereby give you this notice claiming a sum of Rs. .... as compensation for loss (in case of non-delivery/shortage (*in case of short-delivery/* destruction/deterioration (*as the case is*) in the consignment stated below:

That a consignment of .... bags/packet/tins, etc. of .... each bag etc. weighing .... kg., of .... was/were despatched from .... in .... Rly. under P.W.B./B.R. No....... dated .... to .... a station in the .... Rly., the consignor/sender being Sri/M/s. .... and the consignee being .... (or self), endorsed to my said client for valuable consideration.

That on the occasion of taking delivery of the consignment on .... it was found that (*state here the condition in which the consignment is received*) and there was shortage of .... in the said consignment. A Short Certificate was issued by the .... railway station on .... certifying above shortage/deterioration etc.

(or, the said consignment has not reached the destination as yet and consequently not delivered to my aforesaid client in spite of repeated requests and demands).

I am instructed by my aforesaid client to call upon you to pay to me or to my said client, within 30 days from the date of receipt of this notice, the said sum of Rs. .... as per account in the Schedule of claim appended below:

Schedule of claim

(Give here details of claim)

1. For shortage of ....
   at Rs. .... per qtl.
   (As per Bijuk/market rate) — Rs. ....
2. For proportionate railway freight (in case of partial delivery) paid — Rs. ....
3. Other costs (packing cost etc.) — Rs. ....
4. Costs of statutory notices etc. — Rs. ....

Total Rs.

Yours faithfully,

NOTES: 1. Footnotes under Notice No. 1 may be seen.

2. Regarding tenability of claim for proportionate railway freight in case of partial delivery (see AIR 1965 Pat 316).

3. A notice under s. 106 is a notice of claim and not a notice of suit. It need not state that suit would follow unless claim is met.

Form 3

Notice to the General Manager of a railway claiming refund of overcharges—(by party's lawyer)

Dated the .... 20 ....

To

The General Manager .... Railway, (address)

Notice under s. 106 of the Indian Railways Act, 1989

Dear Sir,

Under instructions from my client .... (*name, description and address*) I hereby give you a notice calling upon you to refund to my said client, within 30 days from the date of receipt of this notice, a sum of Rs. .... which you have carelessly and illegally charged, in excess of actual and really payable railway freight, and which my client has paid by Money Receipt No. .... dated ...... to .... Railway, for consignment despatched Ex. ......, a station in the .... Railway to .... a station in the .... Railway, under R/ R/PWB No. .... dated .... the consignor being (*name and address*) and the consignee being (*name and address*) endorsed to my client for valuable consideration.

2. Please note that a true copy of this notice is kept in my office for future use, if necessary.

Yours faithfully,

Advocate

NOTE: See provisions of s. 106 of the Act.

Form 4

Notice to a railway claiming damages for tortious liabilities of a railway administration. (Case of bodily injury)

(Notice by lawyer)

Registered with AD

Dated the ...... 20 ......

To

The General Manager, ... Railway

.... (address)

Dear Sir,

As per instructions of my client (*state here name, description and address*) I hereby give you a notice claiming damages of Rs. .... for the reasons appearing herein below:

That my said client had on (date) .... purchased a 2nd Class ticket at .... railway station in the .... Railway for a journey from .... to .... by .... (205 UP Assam

Express, etc. *name the train*) and availed himself of a seat in a 2nd Class compartment of the train. On .... at about .... hours the train met with an accident after it collided with another train waiting in .... station of the .... railway. As a result of the accident my client has lost both of his arms and he has been permanently disabled and unfit for carrying on his livelihood as a mill labour.

That it transpires that the accident was due to gross negligence of the employees of the aforesaid .... railway administration.

That my client is entitled to recover from the Union of India (owning the aforesaid .... railway), the said sum of Rs. ...... as per account below.

Please take notice that you are requested to pay to my client the said sum of Rs. ...., within 30 days from the date of receipt of this notice. In default of payment I have instructions to take legal proceedings against the Union of India after service of the statutory notice under section 80 of the Code of Civil Procedure.

Schedule of claim

(*a*) Medical expenses for treatment Rs. ....
(*b*) Physical and mental agony caused by injury Rs. ....
(*c*) Value of loss of two arms Rs. ....

Yours faithfully,

NOTES: 1. Notice of claim for damages is optional in case of tortious liability.

2. No suit can be brought after this notice. In addition, a notice under s. 80, CPC must have to be served.

3. Limitation one year. Notice should be sent in time keeping the period of limitation in mind.

4. Reasonable value in the Schedule of claim should be put—basis of valuation may be average income he used to derive as a mill labour during the last 12 months immediately preceding the accident.

Form 5

A combined notice under s. 106 of the Railways Act and under s. 80 of the Code of Civil Procedure

Registered with AD

Dated the .... 20 ......

Notice under s. 106 of the Indian Railways Act and under s. 80 of the CPC

To

(1) The General Manager .... Railway,
(address)

(2) The General Manager .... Railway,
(address)

Dear Sir,

Please take notice that my client (*name, description*) ...... of .... (*address*) intends to bring a suit against the Union of India, owning and representing the aforesaid Railway

Administrations in a competent court of law after expiry of two months after service of this notice of claim-cum-notice of suit under s. 106 of the Indian Railways Act and s. 80 of the Code of Civil Procedure unless relief claimed hereinbelow be granted to my client within the said period of two months.

Facts giving rise to claim and constituting the cause of action, and reliefs sought for appear hereinbelow:–

That a consignment of .... bags of .... each bag weighing .... kg. of ...... was despatched from ...., a station .... Rly. to .... a station in the .... Rly. under P.W.B. No. .... dated ....; consignor being M/s. .... of .... and the consignee being self, endorsed to my client for valuable consideration. The said consignment did not reach the destination as yet and was not delivered to my client in spite of demands.

That loss consequent on non-delivery of the consignment is due to wilful misconduct, carelessness and gross negligence of the aforesaid railway administrations, their agents and/ or employees concerned.

That my client hereby claims a sum of Rs. .... as per account in the Schedule of claim below and is entitled to recover from the Union of India the said sum with incidental costs.

That the cause of action for the intended suit arose for causing loss to my client for non-delivery of the consignment without just and sufficient reason.

SCHEDULE OF CLAIM

(*Give here details of claim*)

Yours faithfully,

Advocate

NOTES: 1. A combined notice must now be sent to the General Manager of a railway.

2. It must be served within six months (AIR 1952 Nag 22) from the date of booking.

3. It must contain essentials of notice provided for under both the sections (AIR 1954 Pat 424; 55 CWN 665).

Form 6

Notice of suit to the General Manager of different Railways under section 80, CPC claiming compensation for short-delivery

Registered with A/D

Cooch Behar

The ...... 20 ......

To

(1) The General Manager, ... Railway,

....

(2) The General Manager, ... Railway,

....

(3) The General Manager, ... Railway,

....

Notice under section 80 of the Code of Civil Procedure

Dear Sir,

Please take notice that my client (*state here name, description and address*) intends to sue the Union of India, owning and representing the aforesaid Railway administrations, in a competent court of law after expiry of two months after service of this notice unless satisfactory amends are made within the said period of two months. Facts constituting the cause of action and reliefs to be claimed are as follows:—

1. That a consignment of .... bags of .... each bag containing weighing .... was despatched from ...., a station in the .... railway under Invoice No. .... R.R./P.W.B. No. ...... dated ...... to ......, a station in the .... railway, the sender/consignor being .... and the consignee being .... endorsed to ...... for valuable consideration. Out of the said consignment .... bags were found and received short (or ...... bags were received badly torn etc. resulting in shortage of .... in the consignment) at the time of taking delivery on ....

2. A short Certificate No. ...... dated .... for shortage was issued by the Station Master .... on .... to above effect. This shortage of .... in the aforesaid consignment caused a loss to my said client, and my client is entitled to recover compensation therefore, to the extent of Rs. .... as per account shown in the Schedule below. Such shortage of .... is due to gross negligence, misconduct and carelessness of aforesaid Railway Administrations, their agents and/or employees concerned.

3. My client (*name the client*) .... has served upon you a notice dated ...... through his lawyer, per registered post with A/D, under s. 106 of the Indian Railways Act calling upon you to pay to my client the said sum of Rs. ...... within 30 days from the date of receipt of the said notice. You have received the notice but failed to pay the money.

4. The cause of action for the intended suit arose first on ......, the date when there was short-delivery of the consignment and thereafter on the expiry of 30 days' period mentioned in the notice under s. 106 of the Indian Railways Act.

5. A true copy of this notice is being kept in my office for future use, if necessary.

SCHEDULE OF CLAIM

Yours faithfully,

Advocate

NOTES: 1. Notice must be addressed to the General Manager of a railway (see s. 80, CPC).

2. Notice must be sent to each of the railways concerned.

Form 7

Notice of suit under s. 80, CPC to the General Manager of a railway claiming dues

Registered with AD

Dated the .... 20 ......

To

The General Manager, ... Railway

....

Notice under s. 80, CPC

Dear Sir,

Please take notice that my client .... (*state here name, description and address*) intends to bring a suit against the Union of India owning and representing N.F. Rly. administration, in a competent court of law after expiry of two months after the service of this notice, unless reliefs claimed hereinbelow are granted to my client within the said period of two months.

The cause of action arose in the circumstances appearing below and reliefs sought for are as follows:–

1. That my client was a permanent hand under the N.F. Rly., and he retired as a goods clerk at .... railway station in the N.F. Rly. on .... That on the occasion of retirement my client was entitled to a sum of Rs. .... as a special contribution to Provident Fund, a sum of Rs. .... as bonus and a sum of Rs. .... as gratuity.

2. That towards the end of 1969 my client was paid an amount of Rs. .... as gratuity and another sum of Rs. .... as bonus and special Contribution to Provident Fund making a total of Rs. .... out of a total claim of Rs. .... i.e., leaving a balance of Rs. .... due to my client.

3. That of the said dues of Rs. .... a sum of Rs. .... is admittedly due to the Union Government on account of flood advance, demurrage charge, uniform debits and other admitted debits. After adjusting the admitted debits of Rs. ...... my client is entitled to recover from the Union Government a sum of Rs. ....

4. That it transpires that out of the granted bonus of Rs. .... a sum of Rs. ...... was ordered to be deducted. Of the said sum of Rs. .... my client admits dues of the Union Government a sum of Rs. ...... as stated in para 3 hereinabove. Deduction of Rs. ...... in excess has been illegal and unjust.

5. That of the sum of Rs. ......, granted as special contribution to Provident Fund, the entire of it together with balance of Rs. ...... from bonus head making a total of Rs. ...... has been withheld illegally for reasons best known to the authorities.

6. That my client understands that the finalisation of objected debits is still pending though a reasonable time has passed.

7. That my client is, therefore, entitled to recover from the Union Government the said sum of Rs. ...... together with all incidental costs.

8. That the cause of action for the intended suit arose for not paying to my client his just dues within reasonable time.

Yours faithfully,

Advocate

NOTES: 1. For recovery of dues from the Railway Administration, the Union of India has to be sued after service of a notice under s. 80, CPC to the General Manager of the railway concerned.

2. It is doubtful if a suit can be brought at all for gratuity.

CHAPTER 13

Notices under the Indian Partnership Act 1932

SYNOPSIS

1 Notice to an acting partner of the firm (s. 24)–effect
2 Public notice by a partner (once minor) after attainment of majority [s. 30(5)]
3 Notice for retirement of a partner in a partnership-at-will [s. 32(1)(c)]
4 Public notice by the retired partner–liabilities to third parties [s. 32(3)]
5 Dissolution of partnership-at-will by a notice [s. 43]
6 Is notice essential for dissolution?
7 Resolutions of partners did not amount to a notice contemplated in s. 43(1)
8 Date in the notice is the date of dissolution [s. 43(2)]
9 Notice to Registrar of Firms relating to changes in the constitution of a firm [s. 63(1)]–effects of non-compliance–mischief under [s. 69(2)]
10 Notice to one of the judgment debtor partners—effect
11 Modes of service of public notice under the Indian Partnership Act (s. 72)

1 Notice to an acting partner of the firm (s. 24)—effect

It is one of the well-known principles of law of agency that notice to an agent is a notice to the principal. In s. 24 of the Indian Partnership Act, the same principle is imported, that is, a notice given to an acting partner of any matter relating to the affairs of the business tentamounts to the notice to the firm. Following conditions are required to be fulfilled before this principle of agency will operate in relation to the partnership business:

(1) Notice should be given to a partner who habitually acts in the business of the firm;

(2) Notice should relate to a matter which is a part of the affairs of the firm;

(3) The partner on receiving such notice should not have kept it from the notice of the other partners of the firm either by his own fraud or in collusion with the person giving the notice.[1]

1 *Ashutosh* v *State of Rajasthan* AIR 2005 SC 3434; (2005)7 SCC 308.

Notice to any of the partners of a firm is not necessarily a notice to the firm. But there may be circumstances when a notice to a partner may operate as a notice to the firm. This is so when such partner is the acting partner of the firm.

Section 24 of the Indian Partnership Act lays down:

> "Notice to a partner, who habitually acts in the business of the firm of any matter relating to the affairs of the firm operates as notice to the firm, except in the case of a fraud on the firm committed by or with the consent of that partner."

Notice means actual notice and not constructive notice.

The condition to make a notice effective to the firm is that such a notice must be served on such a partner who "habitually acts in the business of the firm", i.e. on one who is an acting partner. In other words, he must be an active partner as opposed to a dormant or sleeping partner. A managing partner definitely occupies the position of a partner who habitually acts in the business. In *Kanhaiya Lal* v *Devi Das Jagan Nath*,[2] Aga Haidar, J. (agreed by Tek Chand, J.) *held*: "The notice sent to the firm of Kanhaiya Lal Piare Lal and received by Piare Lal, a member of the firm, is just as good a notice as if it were directly delivered to Kanhaiya Lal himself". Section 18 of the Partnership Act claims a partner to be the agent of the firm for the purpose of the business of the firm, of course, subject to limitations contained in s. 19 and s. 22 of the Act. Under s. 229 of the Indian Contract Act, as agent is deemed *alter ego* (second-self) of the principal and a notice to the agent is a notice to the principal. It is no wonder that a notice to a partner, an agent of the firm, is a notice to the firm. Section 24 of the Partnership Act is wholly based on the above principle of law. The notice, to be effective against it, must be a matter relating to the firm.

The exception given in s. 24 mentions circumstances when a notice to an acting partner shall not be a notice to the firm. When such a partner commits a fraud on the firm or when a fraud is committed on the firm with the consent of such partner, i.e. when he himself is a party to such fraud, a notice to such partner will not bind the firm.[3]

2 Public notice by a partner (once minor) after attainment of majority [s. 30(5)]

A minor may not be a partner in a firm, but with the consent of all the partners for the time being, such minor may be admitted to the benefits of partnership.

The position is otherwise after the minor becomes a major. After attainment of majority, the partner (once minor) may elect to become or not to become a partner in the firm, and he may give a public notice to that

2 AIR 1931 Lab 227 p. 229; 131 IC 289.

3 Also see *P. Sen (Engineering) P. Ltd.* v *Delite Builders (Pvt) Ltd.* AIR 1993 Cal 28.

effect. Under s. 30(5) the quondam minor at any time within six months of his attaining majority, or of its obtaining knowledge that he had been admitted to the benefits of partnership, whichever date is later, may give a public notice that he has elected to become or that he has elected not to become a partner in the firm and such notice shall determine his position as regards the firm. If he failed to give a notice, he would become a partner in the said firm after the expiry of the said period of six months. In the event a partnership firm stands dissolved before the minor became a major, the minor cannot elect to become a partner of the firm by virtue of issuance of the notice under s. 30(5) which ceased to exist. The entire scheme of s. 30 posits the existence of a firm and negatives any theory of its application to a stage when the firm ceased to exist. One cannot become or remain a partner of a firm that does not exist.[4]

Section 30(5) enjoins:

> "At any time within six months of his attaining majority, or of his obtaining knowledge that he had been admitted to the benefits of partnership, whichever date is later, such person may give public notice that he has elected to become or that he has elected not to become a partner in the firm, and such notice shall determine his position as regards the firm:
>
> Provided that, if he fails to give such notice, he shall become a partner in the firm on the expiry of the said six months."

The giving of the public notice is directory yet optional; for, the word used in s. 30(5) is 'may'. It is a choice given to him whether he should continue his partnership or sever his connection from the partnership. Six months' time is given to him for deliberations so that he can make up his mind. If he does not give the notice, law will not help him further. The proviso to s. 30(5) will apply on his failure. His silence will make him a partner in the firm, whether he likes it or not, on the expiry of the said six months. Before the expiry of six months, he cannot be saddled with the liabilities of the partnership firm. Where a suit for enforcing partnership liability had been instituted before the expiry of six months allowed to the minor, after his attainment of majority, to repudiate his connection with the partnership, it is a case in which he could not issue the public notice required by sub-sec. (5) of s. 30 and he cannot be considered a partner merely for the reason of failure to issue such public notice.[5]

Period of six months has to be calculated on the following basis:

(*a*) within six months of minor's attaining majority;

(*b*) within six months of minor's obtaining knowledge that he has been admitted to the benefits of partnership, whichever is later.

4 *Shivaguda Rajiv Patil* v *Chandrakant Neelkanth Sadalge* AIR 1965 SC 212; (1964)8 SCR 233.

5 *Kunchachumma* v *Chalapuram Bank* AIR 1958 Ker 318.

It is submitted: 'month' should be meant as defined in the General Clauses Act.

3 Notice for retirement of a partner in a partnership-at-will [s. 32(1)(*c*)]

Section 7 of the Indian Partnership Act 1932 has defined a 'partnership-at-will' as: "Where no provision is made by contract between the partners for the duration of their partnership, or for the determination of their partnership, the partnership is partnership-at-will." In a partnership-at-will, a partner may retire by issue of a notice to all the other partners. Section 32(1)(*c*) of the Act lays down the provision:

A partner may retire:

(*a*) ... ...

(*b*) ... ...

(*c*) Where the partnership is at will, by giving notice in writing to all the other partners of his intention to retire.

Retirement of a partner is not the same thing as dissolution of the partnership. This is because on retirement of a partner the firm continues to exist as such, which is not the case when a partnership is dissolved. So the retirement of a partner does not comprehend dissolution.[6]

Unless there was a notice as contemplated in s. 32(1)(*c*), there could be no valid and effective retirement. In the case of a partnership-at-will, a partner cannot retire without giving a notice in writing under s. 32(1)(*c*). Their Lordships observed: "In face of the provisions of s. 32, any contention against that was without force."[7] A retirement, to have effect, must be to the knowledge of other partners. In general, an unambiguous intention to retire should be communicated to other partners by a formal notice or some overt act signifying a clear intention to cease to be a member of the partnership. Any arrangement arrived at between some of the partners behind the back of the others cannot have the effect of dissolving the partnership as a whole.[8] To sum up: Retirement of a partner must be after notice to others. A partner can retire, but the retirement can only be by and upon a notice to the other side.[9] Section 32(1)(*c*) requires that there should be a notice in writing which involves the idea that the notice should reach the other partners.[10]

What is retirement of a partner? Does it mean dissolution of the firm? We would do well to remember that a partner retires when he ceases to be a member of the firm without prejudice to the subsisting relations between

6 *P.V.V. Reddy* v *C.C. Reddy* (2003)3 SCC 445.
7 *Banwari Lal* v *Roop Kishore* AIR 1945 All 332.
8 AIR 1933 All 226.
9 *Chunni Lal* v *Sheo Charan* AIR 1925 All 787.
10 *Badrivishal Pillie* v *J.V. Narsing Rao* AIR 1959 AP 116.

the other members or between the firm and third parties. The Special Committee in their notes on 'Objects and reasons' observed:

> "In this section, the word 'retire' is properly confined to cases where a partner withdraws from a firm and the remaining partners continue to carry on the business of the firm without dissolution of the partnership as between them." "It does not cover the case where a partner withdraws from a firm by dissolving it, which should properly be referred and considered as a 'dissolution', and not as a retirement."

The present provision of law contemplates issue of a notice of retirement when the firm is likely to continue. If the contract of partnership confers a right on a partner to retire from the partnership as envisaged under s. 32(1) of the Partnership Act, and when a specific clause in the deed of partnership mentions that such retirement is possible without dissolving the firm and continuing the ongoing business is incorporated as a term of the contract, the right of a partner to retire by one month's notice from partnership has to be ascertained as per the terms of the contract and there is no relevancy of the fact whether the partnership is at will or for a fixed duration. Even the notice of such retirement, need not to be strictly for a clear one month, as even a seven days shortfall would be considered as a valid notice for retirement without dissolving the business of the firm.[11]

4 Public notice by the retired partner—liabilities to third parties [s. 32(3)]

Until a public notice has been given of retirement, a retiring partner cannot escape his liability to third parties. Section 32(3) lays down: "Notwithstanding the retirement of a partner from a firm, he (the retiring partner) and the partners continue to be liable as partners to third parties for any act done by any of them which would have been an act of the firm if done before the retirement, until public notice is given of the retirement." Again, sub-sec. (4) enjoins: "Notices under sub-sec. (3) may be given by the retired partner or by any partner of the reconstituted firm." In this connection, we may remember the provisions of s. 264 of the Indian Contract Act 1872,[12] which of course stands repealed by the Indian Partnership Act 1932. Section 264 read: "Persons dealing with a firm will not be affected by a dissolution of which no public notice has been given, unless they themselves had notice of such dissolution."

Proviso to s. 32(3) of the Partnership Act enjoins: "Provided that a retired partner is not liable to any third party who deals with the firm without knowing that he was a partner."

Public notice here is directory. Unless a notice is given, a retiring partner will be held liable. And that is all. In *Bengal National Bank Ltd.* v *Jatindra*

11 *Vishnu Chandra* v *Chandrika Prosad Agarwal* (1983)1 SCC 22; AIR 1983 SC 523.
12 Sections 239-266 of the Indian Contract Act had been repealed by Act IX of 1932.

Nath Maxumdar,[13] it was held that acknowledgment by one of several partners in the absence of notice of dissolution by the resigning partner is binding on such a resigning partner. In *Jawaladutt R. Pillani* v *Bansilal Motilal,*[14] it was *held* that where on the dissolution of partnership, the public notice of dissolution is given but no notice is given to the old customers, the retiring partner is still liable to the old customers if he continues to give credit to the partnership.[14] In the case of dissolution of partnership of which no notice has been given, the liability of an ex-partner to an old customer for post-dissolution transactions with the supposed old firm does not depend on the customer knowing that such partner was a partner prior to dissolution.[15] In a case where public notice or individual notice to old customers was not given and one partner carrying on business in the old firm's name—pronote issued by him: *Held* that the retired partner could not escape liability in view of the provisions of s. 264 of the Contract Act. "Even though public notice by advertisement has been given, an additional personal notice is necessary in the case of old customers, while in the case of new customers a public notice would be quite sufficient."[16]

The authority to issue the public notice is given to the retiring partner as also to any partner of the reconstituted firm. Interest is the only concern. To safeguard the interest, a retiring partner should publicly sever his connection. Similarly, to escape being entangled by a retired partner's transactions, the reconstituted firm may issue the notice.

There is yet another aspect of a notice under s. 32(2) of the Partnership Act. Can there be a circumstance when a retired partner can escape liability without issuing a public notice? S. Ramachandra Iyer, CJ. in *Central United Bank Ltd., Rajapalayam* v *B.A. Venkatarama Naidu* observed: "Section 32(3) is not intended to create a liability where none existed before or to penalise a retired partner who failed to give public notice of his retirement. The true basis of the liability of a retiring partner is, as we have said, on the principle of holding out. There can be no holding out if the person who deals with the new firm is aware of the retirement of a particular partner. In *Ratnaji Bhagwanji and Co.* v *Prem Shanker*[17] Misra, J. recognised that a retiring partner could escape liability in respect of transactions entered into by the continuing partners after his retirement if the third party was aware that the former had ceased to be a partner of the firm.[18] In our opinion, the

13 AIR 1929 Cal 714 (*per* Lord Williams, J.).
14 AIR 1929 PC 132 (*per* Viscount Dunedin).
15 AIR 1933 Lah 417; AIR 1932 Cal 236.
16 AIR 1936 Lah 31 [AIR 1929 PC 132 rel. on. Also see *Juggilal Kamlapat* v *Sew Chand Bagri* AIR 1963 Cal 505—retired partner held liable by virtue of s. 45(1)—*per* Sinha, J.]. [Under the old Contract Act].
17 AIR 1938 All 619.
18 See *Vinayak Keshar Pananjape* v *Dena Bank* AIR 1998 Bom 356.

proviso to s. 32(3) and the corresponding provision in s. 45 with proviso indicate, beyond doubt, that only persons who were not aware of the retirement of a particular partner could take advantage of s. 32(3) or s. 45. The purpose of s. 32(3) is more to specify how notice should be given. Its main object is to avoid the necessity of giving actual or private notice to the various persons. In other words, it specifies the mode by which the retiring partner may be relieved of the responsibility of issuing notice to the various classes of persons who might enter into transactions with the surviving partners.

> "Public notice is intended only to serve a purpose, namely, to bring home to the persons concerned the fact of retirement. That purpose will undoubtedly be served in a better way by personal or actual notice."[19]

Section 72 of the Act defines the mode of giving a public notice (see Note 7 *infra*). That provision read with s. 32(3) requires that a notice of retirement should be given to the Registrar of Firms by publication in the Official Gazette and in at least one vernacular newspaper circulating in the district where the firm to which it relates has its place or principal place of business, as to the fact of retirement.

> "The rule that makes a retiring partner liable for acts done on behalf of the firm after retirement is one based on estoppel, because the persons deal with it in the belief that all the partners of the firm still continue; but in our view, when the third parties, in fact, knew that certain of the partners in fact retired from the partnership, there is no scope for the application of the rule of estoppel to make the partners who had already retired liable for the subsequent acts on behalf of the firm."[20]

5 Dissolution of partnership-at-will by a notice [s. 43]

The dissolution of partnership between all the partners of a firm is called the "dissolution of the firm", as defined in s. 39 of the Indian Partnership Act 1932. It is different from the severance of the connection of one partner with the firm. It is the "complete breakdown of the relations of partnership between all the partners".

Chapter VI of the Indian Partnership Act deals with the dissolution of a firm. Dissolution may be in one of different ways. Section 40 of the Act speaks of dissolution of a firm with the consent of all the partners, i.e. dissolution by agreement, while s. 41 refers to circumstances warranting compulsory dissolution. Again, s. 42 deals with the dissolution on the happening of certain specified contingencies. Section 43 refers to dissolution of partnership-at-will by notice in writing, while s. 44 is about a dissolution

19 *Central United Bank Ltd., Rajapalayam* v *B.A. Venkatarama Naidu* AIR 1963 Mad 302.

20 *Rama Rao* v *Venkateshwara Rao* AIR 1963 AP 154 (*per* Chandrasekhara, J.).

by the court. We are concerned here with the provisions of s. 43 providing dissolution of partnership-at-will by a notice in writing. Section 43 reads:

> Section 43. (1) Where the partnership is at will, the firm may be dissolved by any partner giving notice in writing to all the other partners of his intention to dissolve the firm.
>
> (2) The firm is dissolved as from the date mentioned in the notice as the date of dissolution or, if no date is so mentioned, as from the date of the communication of the notice.

It is clear from s. 32 of the Partnership Act, read with relevant sections in Chapter VI of the said Act, that by mere retirement of a partner a firm is not dissolved. The retiring partner must give notice of his intention to dissolve the firm in order to bring about its dissolution.[21]

On scrutiny, it appears that s. 43(1) demands that (*i*) there should be a notice; (*ii*) the notice must be in writing to all the other partners of the firm, and (*iii*) the notice should contain an expression of intention to dissolve the firm. Section 43 will not come into operation unless all these conditions are complied with.[22] The same view was expressed four years later in a Nagpur case where it was *held*: to operate as a notice for dissolution of partnership-at-will under s. 43 of the Partnership Act, the notice must fulfil the following conditions: (*a*) the notice must clearly state the intention of the partner giving notice to dissolve the firm; and (*b*) it must be given in writing to all the other partners of the firm. Such a notice must not be ambiguous or vague but must be factual, explicit and final.[23] Notice in this case only stated that the appellant should render accounts and not proceed with certain construction works and that failing it necessary action would be taken. The court said that this certainly was not a notice of dissolution.

A notice may not be essential. Dissolution of a firm-at-will could be inferred from circumstances such as filing a plaint in a suit for dissolution by one partner is enough of itself to put an end to partnership-at-will. It was held in *Tajammul Hussain* v *Sheikh Ahmad Ali* that in the case of dissolution of partnership-at-will by notice, if the assistance of the court is required by means of a decree for dissolution, the suit for dissolution must follow the notice (in the instant case the notice purportedly under s. 43 was given more than four months after the institution of the suit).[1] Where a partnership-at-will is formed apart from the circumstances in which the court may dissolve it, it can come to an end by a notice of dissolution or abandonment by one of the partners of the partnership.[2]

21 *Shohanlal Pachisia & Co.* v *Bilasray Khemani* AIR 1954 Cal 179 (*per* Bose, J.).
22 *Dhulia Amalner M.T.* v *Raychand Rupsi Dharamsi* AIR 1952 Bom 337.
23 *Chain Karan* v *Radha Krishan* AIR 1956 Nag 46; overruled on other points in *CIT* v *Seth Govind Sugar Mills Ltd.* AIR 1966 SC 24.
1 AIR 1937 Oudh 438.
2 AIR 1940 Bom 263 (*per* Kania, J.).

Where a letter was addressed by a partner to his own lawyer, appointing him as the arbitrator in the dispute between him and the other partners and also asking him to consider the matter of the dissolution of the firm, it was held that this was neither a notice of dissolution nor it had the effect of dissolving the firm.[3]

6 Is notice essential for dissolution?

It is clear from the reading of ss. 40 to 44 of the Indian Partnership Act that a partnership can be dissolved according to ways in the said sections; and s. 43 is just one of those. It cannot be said that s. 43 is the controlling section over all the modes of dissolution of a firm. It cannot, therefore, be argued that a notice is essential in all the cases.

Exactly in *Lilabati Rana* v *Lalit Mohan Dey*[4] R.P. Mookerjee, J. *held*: "On a reading of the sections themselves, there is no doubt that the provisions contained in s. 43 of the Act do not control the other provisions in this chapter (Chapter VI of the Act) and that it is possible to have the partnership of a firm dissolved even when no notice in writing has been given as required under s. 43."

Notice of dissolution should be served upon all the partners. The notice becomes inoperative if a single member is left uninformed.

7 Resolutions of partners did not amount to a notice contemplated in s. 43(1)

The notice contemplated in s. 43(1) of the Partnership Act is a statutory notice and nothing but a notice of the nature contemplated therein can be a lawful and sufficient substitute for the notice. In *Dhulia Amalner Motor Transport Ltd.* v *Raychand Rupsi Dharamsi*, the following was observed:

"A statutory notice as contemplated by s. 43 is a totally different thing from a resolution which is merely a record of the deliberations arrived at by a majority of votes at a particular meeting. A resolution passed at a meeting cannot amount to an explicit notice by one or more partners of the firm to dissolve the firm from a definite date".[5]

Again, the contention that the service of summons accompanied by a copy of the plaint amounts to giving notice in writing to the other partners of the intention of the plaintiff to dissolve the firm within the meaning of s. 43(1) and that the firm stands dissolved from the date of the service of summons is untenable.[6]

Such a plaint for dissolution of partnership cannot fall within the expression "notice" used in sub-sec. (2) of s. 43 of the Act.

3 *Tilakram Ghosh* v *Gitu Rani Sadhukha* AIR 1989 Cal 254.
4 AIR 1952 Cal 499.
5 *Dhulia Amalner Motor Transport Ltd.* v *Raychand Rupsi Dharamsi* AIR 1952 Bom 337.
6 *Krishnakumar Poddar* v *Ramkumar Agarwal* AIR 1978 NOC 25 (Pat).

8 Date in the notice is the date of dissolution [s. 43(2)]

Under Note 5 *ante*, we have seen the provisions of s. 43(2) of the Partnership Act as to what would be the date of dissolution of a partnership. Not the date of issue of a notice but the date which is mentioned in a notice under s. 43(1) when the partnership is to dissolve is the date from which the partnership stands dissolved. It is advisable that the notice should specify the date from which the partnership would stand dissolved. Per chance, if there be no date in the notice, the partnership stands dissolved, under provisions of s. 43(2), from the date of communication of the notice to other partner or partners. A unilateral notice by a partner in a partnership-at-will cannot effectuate the firm's dissolution as from an anterior date. Having regard to the scheme underlying partnership law as codified, and having particular concern for the nature and incidents of partnership-at-will, it is clear that the provision in s. 43(2) cannot be read as entitling a partner to undo a partnership with retrospective effect.

A partner-at-will can, under the section, undoubtedly mention a date as from which the firm would stand dissolved, but that date can, in no case, be prior to the date of issue of his notice. It would be proper to construe the provision only as entitling the partners to notify the dissolution *in futuro*.[7]

When instead of issuing notice a partner wants to go to the court for effecting the dissolution of the firm, he will be bound by the procedure laid down in Or. 20, r. 15 of CPC which is of general application to all the partnerships. The date of dissolution in such a case will be the date fixed in the preliminary decree passed under Or. 20, r. 15, CPC. "Even assuming", said Mudholkar, J. in *Banarsi Das* v *Kansi Ram*[8] "that the term 'notice' in the provision is wide enough to include within it a plaint filed in a suit for dissolution of partnership, the sub-section itself provides that the firm will be deemed to be dissolved as from the date of communication of the notice. It would follow, therefore, that a partnership would be deemed to be dissolved when the summons accompanied by a copy of the plaint is served on the defendant where there is only one defendant, and on all defendants where there are several defendants. Since a partnership will be deemed to be dissolved only from one date, the date of dissolution would have to be regarded to be the one on which the last summons was served".[8] The date of dissolution is the date of execution of the dissolution deed and not a future date mentioned in the deed.[9]

7 *V.V.P. Thangaraju* v *K.V. Perumal Chettiar* AIR 1980 Mad 7.
8 AIR 1963 SC 1165.
9 *Faral Bhai Dhala* v *Custodian-General, Evacuee Property* AIR 1961 SC 1397; (1962)1 SCR 456.

9 Notice to Registrar of Firms relating to changes in the constitution of a firm [s. 63(1)]—effects of non-compliance—mischief under [s. 69(2)]

A change in the constitution of a registered firm due to entry of a new partner or exit of a partner or death of a partner does not require fresh registration of the firm with the Registrar of Firms. But such change has to be intimated to the Registrar who would take note of such change in the relevant Register.

Section 63(1) of the Partnership Act lays down:

> "When a change occurs in the constitution of a registered firm any incoming, continuing or outgoing partner, and when a registered firm is dissolved any person who was a partner immediately before the dissolution, or the agent of any such partner or person specially authorised in this behalf, may give notice to the Registrar of such change or dissolution, specifying the date thereof, and the Registrar shall make a record of the notice in the entry relating to the firm in the Register of Firms, and shall file the notice along with the statement relating to the firm filed under section 59".

The notice contemplated in s. 63(1) is imperative. A reconstituted firm without such correction in the Register of Firms cannot sue because effects of non-registration, as detailed in s. 69(2), will follow. Where the son of a partner, on the latter's death, sues without getting the Register of Firms corrected as provided in s. 63(1), the suit is barred under s. 69(2), the s. 63(1) being mandatory.[10] J.N. Modi, J. *held* in *Kesrimal* v *Dali Chand*:[11] "The language of s. 63 is permissive as it uses the word 'may' and not 'shall'. It has, therefore been held and I respectfully agree with that view, that a change in the constitution of a registered firm owing to the coming in or going out of a partner or by the death of a partner does not occasion the necessity of any fresh registration, but all that is required is that the change, thus brought about, should be notified to the Registrar and it is then for the latter to make a note of it in the relevant Register. Where one of the partners of the plaintiff-firm having died, his son comes into partnership and he is one of the two persons who brought the suit, although his name admittedly was not registered in the Register of Firms at any time, until the suit was brought, the first condition in s. 69(2) stands fulfilled, but the second condition not. The suit must be held to be bad and unmaintainable".

It has been held in *Lakshmi Vilas Bank Ltd.* v *Sun Finance*,[12] that s. 63(1) does not make it imperative but merely permissive to the partner incoming, continuing or outgoing, when a change occurs to the constitution

10 AIR 1944 Mad 443.
11 AIR 1959 Raj 140.
12 1996 AIHC 3105 (Mad).

of a registered firm, to give notice to the Registrar of such change specifying the date thereof. Section 63(1) does not prescribe any limitation as to the period within which such notice should be filed. Notice should, however, be given within a reasonable time.

There is no time-limit when such a notice will have to be issued to the Registrar of Firms. Prudence suggests that intimation has to be sent at earliest convenience after a change in the constitution of the firm occurs. It was *held* by Blackwell, J. in *Pratap Chand Ram Chand & Co.* v *Jehangirji Bomanji Chinoy*:[13] "There is no time-limit fixed in any of the ss. 60 to 63 as to when notice[14] of alterations or changes should be given. The word 'when', with which each of these sections begins, does not involve an obligation upon the person proposing to give notice of the change to give it immediately upon the change occurring".

10 Notice to one of the judgment debtor partners—effect

In an execution case which was filed against a firm in which one of the judgment debtor partners has been impleaded, such notice to one of the judgment debtors cannot be treated as notice to other judgment debtors who happened to be the partners of the firm.[15]

11 Modes of service of public notice under the Indian Partnership Act (s. 72)

In Chapter II under notes 'Private and Public Notices', we have examined the relative merits of notices which are 'public' as also of those which, distinguished from public notices, may be termed 'private'.

A public notice carries with it the idea of the largest possible circulation, particularly if the subject-matter is of major importance affecting a good many persons.

Objects and reasons, mentioned in the Special Committee Report, are to the effect: "We have made an important change in this clause by requiring that all public notices shall be published in the *Gazette* and in a local vernacular newspaper. In addition, public notices relating to registered firms must also be communicated to the Registrar of Firms. In view of the wide area in which many firms in India operate and innumerable persons having transaction with the firm, it seems to us to be insufficient that public notices relating to registered firms should be made merely by intimation to a Registrar of Firms".

We shall now look to the provision of s. 72 of the Act. It reads:

"A public notice under this Act is given—

(*a*) where it relates to the retirement or expulsion of a partner from a registered firm, or to the dissolution of a registered

13 AIR 1940 Bom 257.
14 For Forms of Notice see Forms *infra*.
15 *Achamma George* v *Trio Packaging Co.* (1993)1 Ker LT 868.

firm, or to the election to become or not to become a partner in a registered firm by a person attaining majority, who was admitted as a minor to the benefits of partnership, by notice to the Registrar of Firms under section 63, and by publication in the Official Gazette and in at least one vernacular newspaper circulating in the district where the firm to which it relates has its place or principal place of business, and

(*b*) in any other case, by publication in the Official Gazette, and in at least one vernacular newspaper circulating in the district where the firm to which it relates has its place or principal place of business".

A public notice is necessary in the following cases:

(1) when a partner retires;

(2) when a firm is dissolved;

(3) where a minor has been admitted to the benefits of the firm and on attaining majority has to give public notice of his decision to become or not to become a partner.

Public notice has to be given by intimation to the Registrar of Firms under s. 63 and by publication in the Official Gazette and at least one vernacular newspaper circulating in the district where the firm to which it relates has its place or principal place of business. All the requirements of s. 72 have to be complied with.[16] Wherever a notice is required by law to be given, it ought to be given in such manner as the law deems sufficient. In other words, such notices are regulated by the Partnership Act.[17] (This section takes special care in publication of the notice in the widest possible ways).

Unless and until a public notice is given in the prescribed form it cannot be a valid notice.[18]

FORMS

Form 1

Notice of dissolution of a partnership

Notice is hereby given that the partnership under the firm-name of .... with its principal place of business (or with its registered office) at .... heretofore subsisting between the undersigned and Mr. A.B. of .... has been dissolved by mutual consent (or, by efflux of time or by death of A.B.) as from the .... 20 ....

16 *C. Assiamma* v *State Bank of Mysore* AIR 1990 Ker 157.
17 *Lakshmi Vilas Bank Ltd.* v *Sun Finance* 1995 AIHC 3105 (Mad).
18 *Lakshmi Vilas Bank Ltd.* v *Sun Finance* (supra).

All debts due to or by the said partnership shall be received and paid by the undersigned who would carry on the said business under the said firm-name as sole-proprietor thereof.

Date ....

....

(State here name and address of the notice-giver)

NOTES: 1. Under s. 43 of the Partnership Act where the Partnership at will, the firm may be dissolved by any partner by giving notice in writing to all the other partners of his intention to dissolve the firm. The firm is dissolved as from the date mentioned in the notice as the date of dissolution or, if no date is so mentioned, as from the date of the communication of the notice.

2. The right of a partner to dissolve the firm by service of a notice under s. 43 is an absolute legal right, which cannot possibly be denied to him by any court or judicial authority.

3. Right to dissolve a partnership at will is not an equitable right, but a legal right (AIR 1924 PC 2; 28 CWN 566).

4. In a partnership at will, it stands dissolved from the date of notice (AIR 1976 Gau 12). It is not open to the partners to dissolve the firm retrospectively (AIR 1961 SC 1397; AIR 1980 Mad 7).

5. Notice must be unambiguous—AIR 1956 Nag 46 (Also see AIR 1966 SC 24).

6. The notice must clearly show an intention to dissolve the firm and the intention must be final one (AIR 1952 Bom 337; AIR 1956 Nag 46).

7. The firm is dissolved as from the date mentioned in the notice as the date of dissolution or, if no date is so mentioned as from the date of the communication of the notice.

Form 2

Notice of election by the minor concerning partnership

Notice is hereby given that the undersigned A.B. who was a minor and was admitted to the benefits of partnership, subsisting between X and Y, carrying on the business of Textile goods under the firm-name of .... having attained majority on .... does hereby elect to become a partner in the said firm.

Date ....

....

(A.B.)

1. Section 30(1)—Law allows a minor to be admitted to the benefits of partnership provided all other partners give their consent.
2. "Benefits of partnership" include benefits which the minor would enjoy if he were a major—86 IC 944.
3. If the minor elects to become a partner (*a*) his rights and liabilities as a minor will continue up to the date on which becomes a partner, but he will also become personally liable to third parties for all acts of the firm done since he was admitted

to the benefits of the partnership; and (*b*) his share in the property and profits of the firm shall be the share to which he was entitled as a minor.

Form 3

Notice of dissolution of a partnership-at-will

Dated the .... 20 ...

Notice is hereby given that the partnership subsisting now between the partners 'X' and 'Y' under the name and style of M/s (*name of the firm*) and carrying on business at (*give here the address of the firm*) is dissolved with effect from .... (date) by mutual consent (or, by efflux of time, or under clause No. ...... of the partnership deed).

(The aforesaid business will henceforward be carried exclusively by 'X' alone on his sole responsibility under the old firm name–(*add if necessary*).

Signature of 'X'
Signature of 'Y'

NOTES: 1. After dissolution the partnership business may be carried on by the remaining partner on his sole responsibility in the old firm name.

2. Notice of dissolution of partnership to be published in local Gazette and in at least one vernacular newspaper circulating in the district where the firm to which it relates has its place or principal place of business.

3. Provisions of s. 43(1) of the Indian Partnership Act may be seen.

Form 4

Notice of dissolution of a partnership-at-will

By registered post with AD.

Dated the .... 20 ...

To

Sri A.B.

Sri C.D.

Partners of M/s. ....

....

P.O. .... Dt. ....

Dear Sirs,

1. Yourselves and myself constituted and were partners in the firm of M/s. ...... with its Registered Office at .... P.S. .... Dt. .... said partnership was a partnership-at-will.

2. I do hereby issue this notice under s. 43(1) of the Indian Partnership Act expressing my intention to dissolve the firm with effect from .... 20....

3. Accounts of the said partnership should be settled in the meantime.

Sd. E.F.
Partner of M/s. ....

NOTES: 1. See s. 43(1) of the Indian Partnership Act 1932.

2. Three things are required—(*i*) the giving of a notice; (*ii*) the notice must be in writing; (*iii*) the notice must express an intention to dissolve the firm (AIR 1952 Bom 337).
3. Under s. 43(2) the firm is dissolved as from the date mentioned in the notice or as the date of the communication of the notice.
4. For dissolution of a firm through intervention of a court of law see s. 44 of the Act.

Form 5

Notice by a partner to determine a partnership

To

Mr. A.B.
Partner of M/s. ......
....

Dear Sir,

In exercise of the power contained in the deed of partnership dated the ...... the day of .... 20... made between yourself, of the one part and myself, of the other part, I do hereby give you notice that it is my intention to dissolve the aforesaid partnership with effect from the 1st day of January, 20....

Yours faithfully,
Partner of M/s. ....
....

Form 6

Notice of expulsion of a partner

Dated the .... 20 ...

To

....
....
Partner of M/s. ......

(*Name and address of the partnership*)

Sir,

In exercise of the power and authority vested in us by virtue of Clause No. .... of the partnership deed dated .... we hereby determine the aforesaid partnership, subsisting up till now between you and ourselves, with effect from .... so far as it relates to you and your interest in the partnership and expel you therefrom for your misconduct (*state here the nature of misconduct*).

Yours faithfully,
(Signature of other partners)

NOTE: A partnership deed may contain penal provisions for misconduct. In that case refer to the clause of the instrument.

Form 7

Notice of retirement of partner in a partnership-at-will

Dated the .... 20 ...

To

1. ....
2. ....
3. ....

(*Name the partners with their respective addresses*)—Partners of .... name the partnership firm with registered address).

Gentlemen,

I hereby give you notice of my intention to retire from the partnership aforesaid, now subsisting between me and yourselves, on the expiration of one calendar month after service of this notice.

Yours faithfully,
(Signature of Retiring Partner)

NOTES: 1. In partnership-at-will, any partner may retire by giving notice in writing to all the other partners of his intention to retire.

2. Section 7 defines partnership-at-will and s. 32(1)(*c*) provides for issue of a notice, such notice must be in writing.

3. Unless there was a notice as contemplated in s. 32(1)(*c*), there could be no valid and effective retirement.

Form 8

Notice by a partner to determine a partnership under (s. 32 or s. 45 of the Indian Partnership Act) terms of partnership deed

Dated the .... 20 ...

To

(1) ....
(2) ....
Partner of M/s. ....
....
....

(*Name and address of the firm*)

Gentlemen,

In exercise of the power given in Cl. .... of the partnership deed dated ...... I do hereby, give you a notice of my intention to dissolve the partnership aforesaid on expiry of three (or, as provided in the deed) calendar months after service of this notice.

Yours faithfully,
Partner.

NOTES: 1. Provisions of s. 32 of the Partnership Act may be seen.

2. By mere retirement of a partner the partnership is not dissolved, the retiring partner must give a notice of his intention to dissolve the firm in order to bring about a dissolution (AIR 1954 Cal 179).

Form 9

Public notice of election by the minor concerning a partnership

Public notice of election to become a partner in the firm of

M/s. ...., Darjeeling.

I have been admitted to the benefits of the partnership in the firm between

(*i*) A.B. son of C.D.

(*ii*) E.F. son of G.H.

(*iii*) M.N. son of P.Q.

carrying on business of textile goods with its registered office and principal place of business at Darjeeling, District Darjeeling, with the consent of all the partners since ....

Notice is given hereby that I, Sri .... son of ...... having attained majority on .... do hereby elect to become a partner in the said partnership.

....
(Name of the partner
electing to become a partner)

NOTES: 1. See s. 30(5) of the Indian Partnership Act 1932.

2. Notice is directive but optional. If he fails to give such notice he shall become a partner of the firm on the expiry of six months, mentioned in s. 30(5) of the Act.

3. He has to give notice at any time within six months of his attaining majority, or of his obtaining knowledge that he had been admitted to the benefits of partnership, whichever date is later.

CHAPTER 14

Notices under the Sale of Goods Act 1930

SYNOPSIS

1 Doctrine of notice (ss. 27 to 30)
2 Buyer's notice to seller while rejecting goods (s. 43)
3 Notice of stoppage in transit by an unpaid seller—notice to principal (s. 52)
4 Notice to buyer by an unpaid seller of his intention to re-sell (s. 54)

1 Doctrine of notice (ss. 27 to 30)

A man should not and cannot be punished for what he does in good faith and does unawares. But if he has notice of a thing that his transaction relating to that is likely to be *mala fide* if it be such what should not have been after such notice. Law does not come to his rescue who acted *mala fide* and his unclean hands shut the door of equity. Provisions of ss. 27 to 30 of the Sale of Goods Act contain in them this equitable doctrine of notice in relation to transfer of title by sale.

Section 27 relates to sale of goods by a person who is not the owner thereof and who does not sell them under the authority or with the consent of the owner. In the event of such an unauthorised sale, the buyer gets no better title to the goods than the seller had. While a transfer of shares may be effective between the transferor and transferee from the date of transfer, but a transfer effective between the transferor and transferee is not effective as against the company and persons without notice of the transfer until the transfer is registered in the company's register.[1] The proviso to the section adds that if a buyer purchases from a mercantile agent, who with the consent of the owner is in possession of goods or of a document of title to the goods, the sale is valid "provided the buyer acts in good faith and has not at the time of the contract of sale notice that the seller has no authority to sell". To absolve himself from a liability for having purchased goods from a person

1 *Life Insurance Corpn. of India* v *Escorts Ltd.* (1986)1 SCC 264; AIR 1986 SC 1370.

who is not the owner thereof and to avail himself of the plea of purchase in good faith, the purchaser must bring his case within the proviso of s. 27.[2] The unpaid vendor can have no claim against the innocent third party.[3]

Section 28 of the Act is concerned with sale by one of several joint owners. "If one of several joint owners of goods has the sole possession of them by permission of the co-owners, the property in the goods is transferred to any person who buys them of such joint owner in good faith and has not at the time of the contract of sale notice that the seller has no authority to sell." Only honest purchase will not do. The purchaser must take care to know from whom he is purchasing, for an honest purchase made carelessly, without making proper inquiries, cannot be said to have been made in 'good faith' so as to convey good title.[4]

Section 29 of the Act deals with the sale by a person in possession under a voidable contract. When the seller has obtained possession over goods under a voidable contract, the purchase from him will not be affected if the buyer purchased in good faith and without notice of the seller's defect of title.

Section 30(1) of the Act relates to a sale by a seller who is in possession of goods sold by him and s. 30(2) relates to a sale by a buyer obtaining possession of goods with the consent of the seller, where the original sale was on credit. In both the cases the subsequent buyer is protected if he received the goods in good faith and without notice.[5]

2 Buyer's notice to seller while rejecting goods (s. 43)

When a buyer rejects the goods properly, i.e. under a lawful excuse, it is not his obligation to send the goods back to the seller. It will be enough for him to give a clear notice to the seller that those are not accepted. In that case, the goods are at the risk of the seller.[6]

Section 43 of the Sale of Goods Act enjoins: "Unless otherwise agreed, where goods are delivered to the buyer and he refuses to accept them, having the right so to do, he is not bound to return them to the seller, but it is sufficient if he intimates to the seller that he refuses to accept them."

Such intimation may be in the nature of a notice. As a matter of fact, experience tells us that notices are issued by the buyer in such cases. In *N. Buch & Co.* v *Gobardhandas Marj*, it was *held*: When the buyer does not accept goods, he is not bound to return them to the seller. It is sufficient for him to give a clear notice that goods are not accepted and those remain at

2 AIR 1936 Rang 283.
3 AIR 1933 Sind 401 at p. 402.
4 12 IC 809.
5 *The Morvi Mercantile Bank Ltd.* v *Union of India* AIR 1965 SC 1954.
6 *Sha Thilokchand Poosaji* v *Crystal & Co.* AIR 1955 Mad 481.

the seller's risk.[7] If a buyer retains the goods beyond reasonable time without rejecting them he is deemed to have accepted them. So if the buyer wants to reject the goods he must give a notice to the seller stating his intention to reject. But he is neither bound to do more nor to return the goods to the seller.[8]

3 Notice of stoppage in transit by an unpaid seller—notice to principal (s. 52)

Section 45 of the Act defines an unpaid seller. The seller of goods is an unpaid seller—

(*i*) when the whole of the price has not been paid or tendered;

(*ii*) when a bill of exchange or other negotiable instrument has been received as conditional payment, and the condition on which it was received has not been fulfilled by reason of the dishonour of the instrument or otherwise.

The unpaid seller has certain rights under the provisions of law. Section 46(1)(*b*) enumerates ...."the unpaid seller of goods has, by implication of law, in case of the insolvency of the buyer, a right of stopping the goods in transit after he has parted with the possession of them". This right of stoppage in transit has been explained again in s. 50 of the Sale of Goods Act which reads:

> "Subject to the provisions of this Act, when the buyer of goods becomes insolvent, the unpaid seller who has parted with the possession of the goods has the right of stopping them in transit, that is to say, he may resume possession of the goods as long as they are in the course of transit, and may retain them until payment or tender of the price."

This right of stoppage in transit is an equitable right arising from insolvency of the buyer alone.[9] But in a Calcutta case this right was deemed more than an equitable right. It was *held*: Right of stoppage in transit is both legal and statutory, and is a common law right from the law of the merchant.[10]

How stoppage in transit is effected? The simple answer is by issuing a notice to the carrier or other bailee in whose possession the goods then are. We refer to provisions of s. 52 of the Sale of Goods Act:

Section 52(1). "The unpaid seller may exercise his right of stoppage in transit either by taking actual possession of the goods, or by giving notice of his claim to the carrier or other bailee in whose possession the goods are. Such notice may be given either to the person in actual possession of the

7 *N. Buch & Co.* v *Gobardhandas Marj* AIR 1923 Bom 92 (*per* Mulla, J.); (1922)24 Bom LR 991.

8 *Union of India* v *Sitaram Jaiswal* (1976)4 SCC 505.

9 AIR 1936 Sind 106.

10 AIR 1923 Cal 182.

goods or to his principal......" A notice to the carrier defeats the buyer's rights to goods in transit.[11] Again, a telegram by an unpaid seller to the Railway company is sufficient notice to effect a stoppage in transit.[12]

It is an established principle that if the seller intends to exercise his right of stoppage in transit by issue of a notice, such notice may be given to the principal of the person who is in actual possession of the goods. The latter half of s. 52 reads:

"...... Such notice may be given either to the person in actual possession of the goods or to his principal. In the latter case the notice, to be effectual, shall be given at such time and in such circumstances that the principal, by the exercise of reasonable diligence, may communicate it to his servant or agent in time to prevent a delivery to the buyer." Learned authors Pollock and Mulla (Sale of Goods Act, pp. 264-265, 3rd Ed.) observed: "Where the transit is by sea that expression includes the shipowner, who is the person most likely to know where the ship and its master are to be found." Lord Blackburn observed in the House of Lords in 1882 commenting on a doubt on this point, expressed in the Court of Appeal.[13] "I had always myself understood that the law was that when you became aware that a man, to whom you had sold goods which had been shipped, had become insolvent, your best way, or at least a very good way of stopping them *in transitu* was to give notice to the shipowner in order that he might send it on. He knew where his master was likely to be and he might send it on; and I have always been under the belief that, although such a notice, if sent, cast upon the shipowner who received it an obligation to send it on with reasonable diligence yet if, though he used reasonable diligence, somehow or other the goods were delivered before it reached, he would not be responsible. I have always thought that a stoppage, if effected thus, was a sufficient stoppage *in transitu*. I have always thought that when the shipowner, having received such a notice, used reasonable diligence and sent the notice on, and it arrived before the goods were delivered, that was a perfect stoppage *in transitu*".

Section 52(1) contemplates exercise of reasonable diligence by the principal so that delivery may be prevented well in time. Therefore, a notice of stoppage in transit to be effectual must be given in such a way as to enable the principal to communicate it to his servant or agent in time. A notice addressed to the consignee and not to the carrier or other bailee in whose possession the goods are, not to their principal, is not a valid notice.

4 Notice to buyer by an unpaid seller of his intention to re-sell (s. 54)

In the foregoing pages we have noticed the right of an unpaid seller. Such an unpaid seller has further a right to resell the goods and appropriate

11 AIR 1923 Cal 182.
12 AIR 1914 Sind 145.
13 *Kemp* v *Falk* 7 App Cas 585.

profits by such resale under certain circumstances.[14] Where the Forest Authority served upon the firm a notice by the State Government to the effect that the forest products agreed to be purchased by the firm would be resold and the deficit if any, would be claimed from the firm. *Held*, that the amount claimed by the State was in the nature of damages recoverable under s. 54 and not as the balance of the price of the said goods.[15]

Section 54(2) of the Sale of Goods Act reads: "Where the goods are of a perishable nature, or where the unpaid seller who has exercised his right of lien or stoppage in transit gives notice to the buyer of his intention to re-sell, the unpaid seller may, if the buyer does not within a reasonable time pay or tender the price, re-sell the goods within a reasonable time and recover from the original buyer damages for any loss occasioned by his breach of contract, but the buyer shall not be entitled to any profit which may occur on the resale. If such notice is not given, the unpaid seller shall not be entitled to recover such damages and the buyer shall be entitled to the profit, if any, on the resale."

It, therefore, stands to reason that s. 54(2) applies when situations are:

(*i*) Property in goods sold should have passed on to the buyer;

(*ii*) the goods sold should be in actual possession of the unpaid seller; and

(*iii*) that the buyer should have failed to pay or tender the price within a reasonable time from being called upon to do so.

The Supreme Court in *PSNS Ambalavana Chettiar & Co. Ltd.* v *Express Newspapers Ltd.*[16] has held that the statutory power for resale under s. 54(2) arises if the property in the goods has passed to the buyer subject to the lien of the unpaid seller. Where the property in goods has not passed to the buyer, the seller has no right of resale.

The notice contemplated in s. 54(2) is mandatory inasmuch as the giving of notice is a condition precedent to the lawful exercise of power of resale by the vendor.[17] Under s. 54, the unpaid seller can resell after giving due notice.[18] Law does not permit an unpaid seller to exercise his right to resale without a notice.[19] Again, where the buyer refuses to take delivery the seller has a right to resell the goods. But those must be resold within a reasonable

14 *Shamji Bhanji & Co.* v *North Western Rly. Co.* AIR 1947 Bom 169; AIR 1948 Pat 36; AIR 1946 Cal 245; AIR 1963 Ker 13.
15 *State of Madhya Pradesh* v *Firms Gobardhan Dass Kailash Nath* (1973)1 SCC 668.
16 AIR 1968 SC 741.
17 AIR 1924 Nag 162.
18 AIR 1936 Oudh 308.
19 *Hirji Bharmal, Bombay* v *Bombay Cotton, Ltd., Bombay* AIR 1958 Bom 411; *Neney Kasi Vishwanathan* v *Gadigay Sanna Lingappa Dakappa* AIR 1952 Mad 185.

time after giving due notice to the buyer.[20] Section 54(2) cannot be invoked if notice of intention to resell is not served.[21]

We have said that provisions of this section as to notice are mandatory. "But trade-usage to the contrary can be pleaded. The onus of proof lies upon the party propounding the same and its incidents and details ought to be indicated clearly."[22]

Absence of notice before resale puts the unpaid seller to handicaps. Resale without notice to the vendee—vendee can recover earnest money,[1] while the vendor cannot claim the difference on resale.[2] Resale of goods without notice to buyer: seller cannot claim any damages from the buyer.[3] Resale without notice—unpaid seller is not entitled to recover damages whatever. The buyer is justified in asking for refund of advance.[4]

But resale with prior notice to buyer: profits on resale go to the seller and not to the buyer. The position is different when a notice is given and the buyer is then entitled to the profits of the resale and is not liable for damages.[5]

One word more: Notice is to be pleaded and proved by the plaintiff-vendor.[6]

FORMS

Form 1

Notice of resale of goods on buyer's default

By registered post with AD

....

Dated the .... 20......

To

....

....

Dear Sirs,

As per your indent dated .... we had supplied to you 10 Qts. of .... on credit, by M/s. Hindustan Road Transport (a common carrier) of (*the place*) under a Consignment Note No. .... dated .... The said consignment note together with Invoice was sent to the .... bank, Dinhata, for collection. It appears that you did not retrieve the consignment note on payment of the bill, though intimated by the said bank in time.

20 AIR 1952 All 242.
21 *Endupuni Narsimhan* v *Mahadevram Udimram* AIR 1974 Ori 98; *Kanhaiyalal* v *Kasturchand* AIR 1957 MB 168.
22 *Sital Prasad* v *Ranjit Singh* AIR 1931 All 583.
1 AIR 1925 Oudh 310.
2 AIR 1952 Mad 185.
3 *Kalka Prasad* v *Harish Chandra* AIR 1957 All 25.
4 AIR 1957 Mad 228.
5 *Dhanrajamal Gobindram* v *Shanji Kalidas* AIR 1961 SC 1285.
6 AIR 1924 Nag 162.

2. You are hereby called upon to pay to us a sum of ₹......... being the value of the said consignment within 10 days hereof. If you make default therein we shall be compelled to take delivery of the consignment and re-sell the goods in the open market and hold you liable for the loss, if any, on such resale.

3. Awaiting compliance.

Account of goods purchased.

Yours faithfully,

Partner

....

....

NOTES: 1. See s. 54(2) of the Sale of Goods Act.

2. Resale without notice–seller cannot claim damages, and resale with a notice enables the seller to appropriate profits on resale (AIR 1961 SC 1285).

Form 2

Buyer's notice to seller rejecting goods

By registered post with AD

....

Dated ....

To

M/s. ....

P.O. ....

Dt. ....

Gentlemen,

1. An indent was made to you as back as September, 20... for supply of fancy sarees, quality being mentioned in the said indent. You were instructed therein that the consignment should reach here at least 15 days ahead of the Pujas, held in October, 20.... Otherwise the same should not be accepted.

2. That the consignment reached here only in November 20... when I had no market for the said goods.

3. In the circumstances, I regret, I refuse to accept the consignment which remains at your risk.

4. Kindly arrange to lift the goods concerned.

Thanking you,
Yours faithfully,

NOTES: 1. See s. 43 of the Indian Sale of Goods Act, 1930.

2. If the buyer has a lawful excuse, it will suffice to intimate the seller of his refusal (AIR 1953 Mad 481).

3. When time is the essence of contract, failure to deliver goods in time gives right to the buyer to repudiate the contract and the seller cannot claim damages against the buyer (Sale of Goods Act–sec. 11–AIR 1971 Cal 395).

Form 3

Notice of stoppage in transit by an unpaid seller

By registered post with AD

Dated the ...... 20 ......

To

M/s. Everest Roadways,

P.O. ....

....

Dear Sirs,

A consignment of textile goods was despatched ex, Calcutta to Gauhati through your carrier service under Consignment Note No. ...... date ...... issued by your Calcutta office, consignee being Sri A.B. of .... (address).

2. Please take notice that you are hereby called upon not to deliver the said consignment to the aforesaid consignee till you hear from me.

Yours faithfully,

....

(Signature of the seller)

Copy to Sri A.B.

By registered post with AD

....

Dated the ...... 20 ......

....

The carrier has been instructed as above in exercise of our right of stoppage in transit.

....

(Signature of the seller)

NOTES: 1. See s. 50 of the Indian Sale of Goods Act, 1930.

2. To exercise the right (*i*) the seller has to be an unpaid seller, (*ii*) notice has to be issued to the bailee or the carrier in whose possession the goods are.

Form 4

Notice of acceptance of the offer

Registered with AD

Dear Sir,

Dated the .... 20 ......

You had expressed your willingness to supply to me ...., bags of cereals at a price of ₹ .... per bag as per your letter, dated ...... Please take notice that I do hereby accept the aforesaid offer. You are required to make the aforesaid supply on or before .... at .... my godown at .... when you will be paid for the aforesaid supply.

Yours faithfully,

Form 5

Buyer's notice to seller

By registered post with AD

Dated the .... 20 ....

From

Sri ....

s/o ....

r/o ....

To

M/s ....

.... (Seller)

Dear Sir,

Please take notice that I had made an indent for supply of .... stated in the indent to you .... On the occasion of indent you were instructed that the consignment must reach me on ..../or before .... failing which I shall not accept the same. It appears that you sent the consignment on .... which reached me only on .... against my instructions. The consignment will have no market for delayed delivery.

I, therefore, refuse to accept the aforesaid consignment. The aforesaid consignment has been rebooked to you at your expenses.

Yours faithfully,

Form 6

Notice of the revocation of the offer

By registered post with AD

Dated the .... 20 ....

Dear Sir,

Please take notice that by my letter dated .... I had communicated to you my offer for supplying .... bags of cereals/rice (as the case may be) at a price of ₹ .... per bag. Since then I have been compelled to close down my business making it impossible to make the supply.

As you have not yet signified your assent to my said offer, I hereby do revoke my offer.

Yours faithfully,

CHAPTER 15

Notices under the Arbitration & Conciliation Act 1996

SYNOPSIS

1 Notice by parties to arbitration
2 Whether a reference is necessary
3 Computation of the period of notice
4 Non-service of notice amounting to misconduct
5 Notice by Arbitrator of signing and making an award
6 Computation of the period of limitation
7 Service of notice under the Arbitration and Conciliation Act 1996
8 Appointment of Arbitrator through court
9 Arbitration agreement with Government—notice under s. 80, CPC

1 Notice by parties to arbitration

The procedure for appointment of arbitrations is contained in s. 11 of the Act of 1996. It is evident from sub-secs. (4) and (5) of s. 11 that except in the case of a request to appoint a third arbitrator, a request for appointment of an arbitrator made to the Chief Justice or his designate must be preceded by a request made by that party to the other party for appointment of or agreement on an arbitrator, received by the other party at least 30 days prior to the making of request to the Chief Justice or his designate. In the absence of notice of request by one of the parties to the other party to appoint an arbitrator, the court has no power to appoint an arbitrator.[1] In *Poran Lal's* case[1] it was decided that the rule as to notice is a rule of procedure and failure to comply with the same would not amount to want of jurisdiction. The act of the court would be illegal and there would be material irregularity in procedure attracting the proviso of s. 115, CPC.

In order to make the notice valid it must be served on the appropriate Ministry when the matter involves Government.[2] Notice is not required to be signed by the party giving the notice. It may be signed by its duly authorised attorney. According to Russell on *Arbitration,* the appointment of an arbitrator by a party is not complete without communication thereof to the other party.

1 *Poran Lal* v *Rupchand* AIR 1931 All 761.
2 *Ranjit Chandra Mittar* v *Union of India* AIR 1963 Cal 594.

On a perusal of s. 11(4)(*a*) it is clear that a party upon receipt of notice of request from the other party to appoint an arbitrator must nominate its arbitrator within 30 days and shall communicate the same within 30 days for the other party.

A party which had violated the agreed procedure for appointment of an arbitrator, e.g. by rejecting the entire panel of names for arbitrators instead of selecting one from the panel, is not entitled to approach under s. 11 for appointment of arbitrator.[3]

2 Whether a reference is necessary

The present Act (1996) has done away with the earlier procedure of arbitration through the intervention of the court. It has been held by the Supreme Court in *Konkan Rly. Construction Corpn. Ltd.* v *Mehul Construction Co.*[4] and *P. Anand Gajapathi Raju* v *P.V.G. Raju*[5] that there is no provision in the new Act for referring the matter to an arbitrator by the intervention of the court. Section 11 of the present Act does not empower the Chief Justice or his designate to make a reference of the disputes to the arbitrator appointed by him except while acting under sub-sec. (6) of s. 11 (as enacted vide the Amendment Act 33 of 2019, though the date of its enforcement is yet to be notified by the Central Government).

3 Computation of the period of notice

It was earlier held that the statutory period of 15 days (as the law stood then) should be calculated after the service of the written notice and not from the date of posting of the notice.[6]

In calculating 15 clear days under the Act of 1940, two terminal days must be excluded. The rule of law is that when words such as so many clear days or 'so many days at least' are used and not less than so many days are to intervene the two terminal days must be excluded from computation.[7]

Section 11(4) of the Arbitration & Conciliation Act requires 'thirty days' notice. The method of computation of thirty days will be the same as held earlier, namely, by excluding the two terminal days.

4 Non-service of notice amounting to misconduct

Section 34 of the Arbitration & Conciliation Act 1996 deals with the grounds for setting aside an arbitral award. If the party aggrieved was not given proper notice of the appointment of an arbitrator or of the arbitral proceedings or was otherwise unable to present his case—award may be set aside.

3 *D. Raja Reddy* v *Director General, National Institute* 1999(2) Arb LR 212 (AP).
4 AIR 2000 SC 2821; 2000 AIR SCW 2960.
5 (2000)4 SCC 539; also see *Tamil Nadu Electricity Board* v *Sumathi* AIR 2000 SC 1603.
6 AIR 1929 Sind 58.
7 *Satyanarayan Agarwal* v *Baidya Mandal* AIR 1972 Pat 29; *Rambharoselal Gahoe* v *State of MP* AIR 1955 Nag 35.

Any breach of duty causing miscarriage of justice is misconduct. Amongst others, hearing only one party in the absence of the other[8] and the arbitrator's is failure to give notice to both the parties are instances of misconduct. Notice may be oral[9] but to both the parties it is indispensable.[10]

5 Notice by Arbitrator of signing and making an award

Once an award is ready, an arbitrator is required to give notice in writing to the parties of the making and signing of the award and of the amount of fees and charges payable in respect of arbitration and award. Now the arbitral tribunal has to deliver a signed copy of the arbitral award to each party under the provisions of s. 31(5) of the 1996 Act. Under the present Act it will be on the receipt of signed copy of the award by a party that the period of limitation of three months for making of an application to set aside an award will start running under s. 34(4) of the present Act. In compliance with the request of any party to the arbitration agreement, the arbitrators or the umpire shall cause the award, or a signed copy of it, to be filed in court and the court shall thereupon give notice to the parties of the filing of award.

6 Computation of the period of limitation

It has been held in some decisions[11] that an application under s. 11 of the Arbitration and Conciliation Act 1996 is governed by three years' limitation under Art. 137 of the Limitation Act 1963. The starting point of limitation would be when one party served notice on the other party requiring the appointment of an arbitrator. In other words, the starting point of limitation would be the date when the appointing authority failed to act under the agreed appointment procedure giving right to apply to the other party.

7 Service of notice under the Arbitration and Conciliation Act 1996

Section 3(1) of the present Act lays down that a written communication shall be deemed to have been received if (*a*) it is delivered to the addressee personally or at his place of business, habitual residence or mailing address, and (*b*) if none of the places referred to in cl. (*a*) can be found after making a reasonable enquiry; a written communication is deemed to have been received if it is sent to the addressee's last known place of business, habitual residence or mailing address by registered letter or by any other means which provides a record of the attempt to deliver it.

8 AIR 1953 SC 21; AIR 1955 Nag 116.

9 AIR 1927 MP 1010; AIR 1954 Ori 134.

10 45 IC 763; 56 IC 325; *Ganga Prasad* v *Nagarmal* AIR 1951 Pat 321; *Pratap Singh* v *Kishan Prasad & Co. Ltd.* AIR 1932 Bom 68.

11 *M.V.V. Satyanarayana* v *Union of India* 1998(2) Arb LR 533 (AP); *Nyayneshvar Bhiku Dhargalkar* v *E.E. PWD, Goa* 1999 Arb WLJ 787 (Bom); *Pandit Munshiram and Associates (Pvt) Ltd.* v *DDA* AIR 2001 Del 82; *National Dairy Development Board* v *Suraj Singh* 2003 Arb WLJ 164 (MP); *Andhra Pradesh Beverage Corporation Ltd.* v *IBM Global Services India Ltd.* AIR 2011 AP 122; 2011(3) Arb LR 457 (AP).

Section 3(2) provides that the communication is deemed to have been received, on the day it is so delivered. Section 3 however, states that does not apply to written communications in respect of proceedings of any judicial authority.

The provision in s. 3 applies to notice required by the Arbitration & Conciliation Act to be served by a party, an arbitrator or an umpire.

8 Appointment of Arbitrator through court

See section 11, Arbitration and Conciliation Act 1996. Sub-sections (4) and (5) of section 11 that except in the case of a request to appoint a third arbitrator, a request for appointment of an arbitrator made to the Chief Justice or any person or institution designated by him be preceded by a request made by that party to other party for an appointment or an agreement on an arbitrator, received by the other party at least 30 days prior to the making of request to the Chief Justice or any person or institution designated by him.

9 Arbitration agreement with Government—notice under s. 80, CPC

No notice under s. 80, CPC is required to be given before making an application (now notice of request) for appointment of an arbitrator. This is so because proceedings pursuant to an application for appointment of an arbitrator are not a suit.[12] When there is an arbitration agreement with the Government and a petition is filed accordingly, it is held that such proceedings take the nature of suits. Nevertheless notice under s. 80, CPC is not necessary.[13]

FORMS

Form 1

Notice to the arbitrator to act alone

From

Sri .... s/o ....r/o ....

To

Sri .... s/o .... r/o .... the arbitrator.

Subject: Notice to the arbitrator to act alone*

12 *Union of India* v *Gorkah Mohan Das* AIR 1964 All 477.

13 *S.P. Consolidated Engineering Co. (P) Ltd.* v *Union of India* AIR 1966 Cal 259.

* Section 11(5) of the Arbitration and Conciliation Act 1996 provides that if there is no agreement on a procedure for appointment, in an arbitration with a sole arbitrator, if the parties fail to agree on the arbitrator within 30 days from receipt of a request by one party from the other party to so agree, the appointment shall be made, upon request of a party, by the Chief Justice or any person or institution designated by him.

Sir,

Please take notice

That the other party to the dispute referred to you, Sri ...... s/o .... r/o ......, has failed to appoint/reappoint an arbitrator despite the service of my notice to appoint arbitrator upon him and despite the lapse of ...... days time given by the said notice for the appointment/reappointment of the arbitrator by him.

I do hereby call upon you to act and perform as the sole arbitrator with regard to the dispute/disputes referred to you.

Dated ....

Place ....

Yours

....

Sd/-

Copy to

Sri ...... s/o ...... r/o ....

the other party to the dispute

Form 2

Notice by a party to another party to appoint an arbitrator

From

Sri .... s/o ....r/o ....

To

Sri .... s/o .... r/o ....

Subject: Notice to appoint an arbitrator

Sir,

I do hereby give you the following notice–

(1) That the following disputes/differences have arisen between us with regard to agreement dated ....

(*a*) ....

(*b*) ....

(*c*) ....

(2) That as per terms of the agreement dated ....

the disputes/differences are referable to arbitrators one to be appointed by each of us.

(3) That I have appointed Sri .... s/o .... r/o .... as my arbitrator and do hereby request you to appoint your arbitrator within .... days of the receipt of this notice.

Dated ....

Place ....

Yours

....

Sd/-

Copy to

Sri ...... s/o ...... r/o ....

(The arbitrator)

Form 3

Notices of hearing of the reference by the arbitrator

From

Sri .... s/o ....r/o .... (The Arbitrator)

To

Sri .... s/o .... r/o ....

Subject: Notice of the hearing of the reference

No. .... of 20 ...... between Sri ....

s/o .... r/o .... and Sri ....

s/o .... r/o ....

Sir,

Please take notice

(1) That the aforesaid reference shall be heard and decided by me on .... at ...... a.m./p.m. at .... (complete address of the location).

(2) That you are required to be present personally/through advocate on the date, time and place mentioned above along with all the relevant books, papers and other materials for the purpose of assisting me in the determination of the dispute/difference under reference.

(3) That in the event of your default, the aforesaid reference shall be heard and decided *ex parte* and in your absence.

Dated .... (Arbitrator)

Place ....

Sd/-

Form 4

Notice to arbitrator to commence proceedings

We, the parties to the arbitration agreement dated .... (a photocopy of the same is enclosed) request you to please start the arbitration proceeding at your earliest and send notices to the parties, so that the arbitration award may be given as contemplated by the agreement.

Sd/- .... 1st party

Sd/- .... 2nd party

Sd/- .... 3rd party

Form 5

Another form of notice to arbitrators

Please refer arbitration agreement dated .... under which you were appointed as arbitrator to settle the disputes which have arisen in the partnership business.

As per agreement under reference you are supposed to settle the disputes within 60 days from the date of agreement. It is because more than one month has passed and you have not started the proceeding, we request you to please start the same at your earliest so that the matter be finalised and our dispute settled.

Sd/- .... 1st party

Sd/- .... 2nd party

Sd/- .... 3rd party

Form 6

Notice by arbitrator to attend

Whereas I have been appointed as sole Arbitrator under arbitration agreement dated .... to settle the dispute which has arisen in partnership business, I hereby give you notice to attend my office situated at .... on ...... (dated) ...... at ...... p.m. or send duly authorised representative or counsel who can act on your behalf. Please note that if you or your authorised representative or counsel do not turn up on the said date at the fixed time and place, I shall start the proceeding *ex parte*.

Dated ....

Sd/- ....

Sole Arbitrator

Form 7

Notice of revocation of arbitration agreement

To

Sri ....

....

....

Dear Sir,

Please refer to arbitration agreement dated .... by which you were appointed arbitrator to settle the disputes arisen between us.

We have cancelled the arbitration agreement by mutual consent.

Therefore, please take notice that now you are no more an arbitrator to arbitrate the dispute.

Sd/- .... 1st party

Sd/- .... 2nd party

Form 8

Revocation notice (another form)

To

....

....

Dear Sir,

Please refer to the arbitration agreement dated .... under which you were appointed arbitrator by me to settle the disputes arisen between myself and Mr. ....

Please note that by an agreement dated .... a copy of which is enclosed for your reference, the said agreement has been terminated.

You are, therefore, requested to please return all papers, account books and other documents which were given to you in connection with the arbitration.

Dated ....

Sd/- ....

Form 9

Application for appointment of an arbitrator

In the High Court at Delhi

In the matter of Arbitration and Conciliation Act, 1996

And

In the matter of an application under section 11
of the said Act for appointment of an arbitrator

And

AB of .... Delhi .... Petitioner

Versus

XY of .... Delhi .... Respondents

The Hon'ble Mr. ... Chief Justice and His companion Justices of the said Hon'ble Court

The humble petition of AB the petitioner above named most respectfully sheweth:

1. On 4th ...... 20 ... the petitioner and the respondent entered into an agreement providing *inter alia* for referring disputes and differences arising between the parties in respect of the said agreement to the arbitrator to be appointed by the consent of the parties.
2. There have arisen differences and disputes between the parties in respect of the said agreement as provided in the arbitration clause. Such disputes and differences have arisen on 5th .... 20 .... The parties have not been able to appoint an arbitrator after the original arbitrator appointed by the parties had failed to enter upon the reference. The intention in the arbitration clause is not that the vacancy should not be supplied. The parties have failed to supply the vacancy.
3. The petitioner gave notice to the respondent on 5th ...... 20 ...... by registered post to concur in the appointment of Mr. .... as the sole arbitrator but the respondent has not concurred in such appointment within the stipulated 15 days after service of the said notice.
4. The subject-matter of reference is within the jurisdiction of this Hon'ble Court and as such this Hon'ble Court has the jurisdiction to entertain, try and determine the dispute.

Your petitioner therefore humbly prays

Your Lordships for the following orders:

(*a*) An arbitrator be appointed under the arbitration agreement of reference dated .... 20 ... hereinabove mentioned;

(*b*) Further orders be made as this Hon'ble Court may deem fit and proper.

And your petitioner as in duty bound shall ever pray.

Form 10

Application for setting aside award

In the High Court at Delhi

In the matter of Arbitration and Conciliation Act, 1996

And

In the matter of an application under section 34(2)
of the said Act for setting aside award dated .... 20 ...

And

DB of .... Delhi .... Petitioner

Versus

1. XY of .... Delhi

2. Mr. .... of ... Delhi .... Respondents

The Hon'ble Mr. ... Chief Justice and His companion Justices of the said Hon'ble Court

The humble petition of DB, the petitioner above-named most respectfully SHEWETH:

1. The parties entered into an agreement containing arbitration clause. Disputes and differences arose between the petitioner and first respondent and the same were referred to the arbitration of the second respondent.
2. The said arbitrator entered into the reference on 5th .... 20... and made the award on 6th .... 20 ... a copy whereof is annexed hereto.
3. The said award is invalid and should be set aside on the following among other.

GROUNDS

I. The learned arbitrator acted in fraud himself inasmuch as he took evidence after the close of arguments of the petitioner and without any notice to the petitioner.

II. The learned arbitrator took extraneous matters into consideration not being within the scope of the arbitration agreement.

III. The learned arbitrator gave the award which is beyond the scope of reference and not covered by issues framed.

4. Your petitioner received the notice on 2nd .... 20 ...
5. This Hon'ble Court has the jurisdiction over the subject-matter.
6. Your petitioner states that in the interest of justice the said award be set aside as void.

Your petitioner, therefore, humbly prays Your Lordships for the following order:

(*a*) The award dated 6th .... 20 ...... be set aside;

(*b*) Further orders be made as this Hon'ble Court may deem fit and proper.

And your petitioner as in duty bound shall ever pray.

Form 11

Application for appointment of Receiver and grant of injunction under s. 9 of the Arbitration and Conciliation Act 1996

In the High Court at Delhi

XY of .... Delhi .... Petitioner

Versus

KL of .... Delhi .... Respondent

The Hon'ble Mr. .... Chief Justice and His companion Justices of the said Hon'ble Court

The humble petition of XY, the petitioner above named most respectfully SHEWETH:

1. By and under an agreement dated .... 20 ... between the parties herein the petitioner supplied jute goods to the respondent for Rs. 2 lac.
2. The respondent accepted the said goods without protest and appropriated the same. The respondent also received the bill for the said goods without any protest.

3. After a lapse of three months the respondent has raised an alleged dispute as to quality of the goods.
4. Your petitioner in terms of the arbitration clause in the said agreement by a notice dated .... 20... requested the respondent to nominate the arbitrator which the respondent has failed and neglected to do.
5. Your petitioner has thereafter filed an application under section 11 of the Arbitration and Conciliation Act 1996.
6. Your petitioner has learned that a portion of the said goods is lying in a godown which is leaking in the rainy season and will be decomposed and become waste in a few days.
7. The respondent is wrongfully disposing of his assets with a view to defrauding the petitioner of the legitimate dues. The respondent has already removed some of his assets from the jurisdiction of this Hon'ble Court. Unless restrained by an order of injunction and unless a receiver is appointed by the time the decree is passed in the said suit nothing would be left to execute the decree.
8. In the premises your petitioner states that a receiver be appointed over the assets of the respondent and by an order of injunction the respondent be restrained from disposing of or dealing with his assets in any manner whatsoever without first paying the claims of the petitioner.
9. Unless orders are made as prayed for your petitioner will suffer irreparable loss and prejudice.
10. This application is made *bona fide* and in the interest of justice.

Your petitioner, therefore, humbly prays Your Lordships for the following orders:

(*a*) A Receiver be appointed over the assets and business of the respondent with direction to make inventory and submit a report to this Hon'ble Court;

(*b*) Injunction restraining the respondent from disposing of, encumbering, transferring, or dealing with his assets in any manner without first paying the claims of the petitioner;

(*c*) *Ad-interim* orders in terms of the prayers (*a*) and (*b*) above;

(*d*) Costs of this application be paid by the respondent;

(*e*) Further orders be made and directions be given as this Hon'ble Court may deem fit and proper to afford complete relief to the petitioner.

And your petitioner as in duty bound shall ever pray.

Form 12

Notice to appoint an Arbitrator for refusal or death of appointed Arbitrator

In the matter of Arbitration between *A* and *B* under instructions from my client *A*, I, hereby give you notice that Mr. *M* the arbitrator appointed by you in the above matter has refused to act (or incapable of acting or has died) my client requires you within seven clear days after receipt of this notice upon you, to appoint an arbitrator in place of the said *M* and in default of any appointment by you, he will appoint *S* the arbitrator appointed by him in the above matter to act as the sole arbitrator in the reference.

Dated the .... day of ....
Signed
Advocate for *A*

To

....

CHAPTER 16

Notices under the Indian Contract Act 1872

SYNOPSIS

1 Notice of revocation or renunciation of agency (s. 206)
2 Notice to agent—effects thereof (s. 229)
3 Notice of sale—requirements in a notice —determination of reasonableness (s. 176)

1 Notice of revocation or renunciation of agency (s. 206)

An agency is terminated by the principal revoking his authority; or by the agent renouncing the business of the agency; or by the business of the agency being completed; or by either the principal or agent dying or becoming of unsound mind; or by the principal being adjudicated an insolvent under the provisions of any Act for the time being in force for the relief of insolvent debtors: vide s. 201 of the Indian Contract Act.

Section 205 of the Indian Contract Act enjoins that the agency may be continued for any period of time as agreed upon between the principal and the agent either by express or implied contract. For any previous revocation or renunciation of the agency without sufficient cause, the principal must make compensation to the agent or the agent to the principal, as the case may be. But where there is no express or implied contract that the agency should continue for any fixed period, the authority given to the agent may be revoked by the principal or the agent may renounce the business of agency by issue of a reasonable notice in time. Section 206 of the Indian Contract Act reads:

> "Reasonable notice must be given of such revocation or renunciation; otherwise the damage thereby resulting to the principal or the agent, as the case may be, must be made good to the one by the other."

This means that when there is no stipulation as to the duration of agency, the agency can be terminated by issuing a reasonable notice.[1] Conversely,

1 AIR 1964 PC 6.

it is not correct that the agency cannot be revoked or renounced unless a prior notice was given. It can be revoked or renounced without a notice, but the absence of notice will penalise the defaulting party; and that is all. The effect of want of notice to the agent does not invalidate the revocation or termination of his authority, but makes the principal liable for any damage that results to the agent by reason of such want of notice.[2]

Section 206 has to be understood as being general in scope and not impinging only upon s. 205 because the word 'such' is used in s. 206. The revocation or renunciation of a contract of agency may take place in myriad ways: the rights and obligations flowing therefrom can only be after the party intending to snap the relationship puts the other party on reasonable notice.[3]

What is and is not a reasonable notice depends on particular circumstances of each case. The nature of employment, nature of work are important considerations in determining the reasonableness of a notice. To illustrate, we may refer to the reported case of *Sohrabji Dhunjibhoy* v *Oriental Government Security Life Assurance Co.*[4] wherein Chagla, J. *held*: "In determining the reasonableness of a notice, a very important element to be taken into consideration is the nature of employment. In the instant case, the plaintiffs were earning a net income of ₹ 4,000 a month from their Chief Agency business. It would be impossible for the plaintiffs to find any other job in the insurance business where they would get an income anything so large. The income was the result of the organisation that the plaintiffs built up by labour of years." Chagla, J. continued: "Taking everything into consideration, I think that this is a case of a very exceptional character, and I think I would be justified in holding that the reasonable notice in this case should have been a notice of two years". On appeal it was approved by Stone, CJ., and Kania, J.

But where the relationship between the parties, is of only buyer and seller it cannot be held that such a relationship is in the nature of agent and principal and to terminate the distributorship of sale of two wheelers, notice under s. 206 should have been given.[5]

2 Notice to agent—effects thereof (s. 229)

Section 182 of the Indian Contract Act defines 'Agent' and 'Principal'. An 'agent' is a person employed to do any act for another or to represent another in dealings with third persons. The person for whom such act is done, or who is so represented is called the 'principal'.

2 AIR 1962 Mad 515.
3 *J.K. Sayani* v *Bright Brothers* AIR 1980 Mad 162.
4 *Sohrabji Dhunjibhoy* v *Oriental Government Security Life Assurance Co.* AIR 1944 Bom 166.
5 *Vijay Traders* v *Bajaj Auto Ltd.* (1995)6 SCC 566.

Thus the definition of an 'agent' contains in it the idea of the agent becoming second-self of the principal. It has been aptly said that an agent is '*alter ego*' (the other self).

Section 229 of the Indian Contract Act reads:[6]

> "Any notice given to or information obtained by the agent, provided it be given or obtained in the course of the business transacted by him for the principal, shall, as between the principal and third parties, have the same legal consequences as if it had been given to or obtained by the principal".

Under s. 229 of the Indian Contract Act the knowledge of the agent can be imputed to the principal only when the agent acquires knowledge in the course of his employment or business to which that fact is material. Knowledge cannot be attributed to the plaintiff or appellant by invoking the doctrine of constructive notice.[7] Where the buyer had duly intimated to the selling agent his refusal to take delivery of a part of the goods supplied, *held* it was a proper intention of the rejection of goods to the principal.[8] Where the notice of retirement of a firm's partner was given to the secretary of a society with which the firm was having dealings, *held* the secretary being *de facto* and *de jure* agent as well of the society, the notice constituted a valid and binding intimation to the society.[9] Where a notice of revocation or termination was served on the other party's agent with the knowledge that the agent had no authority to receive it on behalf of his principal, *held,* it was not a valid notice and did not terminate the contract.[10]

3 Notice of sale—requirements in a notice—determination of reasonableness (s. 176)

Section 176 of the Indian Contract Act speaks of a pawnee's right where the pawnor makes default. The pawnee may bring a suit upon the debt or promise or "he may sell the thing pledged, on giving the pawnor reasonable notice of the sale".

Section 176 not only gives the pawnee the right to retain the goods pledged as collateral security but also entitles the pawnee to sell the pledged goods after giving the pawnor reasonable notice of the same.[11] If the proceeds of the sale are less than the amount due, the pawnor continues to be liable to pay the balance; on the other hand, if the proceeds realised on the sale being made are greater than the amount due the pawnee is under an obligation to pay over the surplus to the pawnor.

6 Readers are referred to Note 5 of Chapter 2 dealing with constructive notice as under Explanation III to s. 3 of the Transfer of Property Act.
7 71 CWN 31; AIR 1929 Cal 497.
8 AIR 1976 Ori 113.
9 *Jani Nautamlal Venishankar* v *Shri Vivekanand Co. Op. Housing Socy. Ltd.* AIR 1986 Guj 162.
10 *State of Orissa* v *Goenka I. & M. Industries Pvt. Ltd.* AIR 1983 Cal 438.
11 *Standard Chartered Bank* v *Custodian* (2000)6 SCC 427.

A pawnee who has given a reasonable notice of sale under s. 176, can sell at any time and is not bound to sell within a reasonable time after the expiry of the period mentioned in the notice. Section 176 talks of a reasonable notice of sale. This means that the pawnor is warned by notice that if he does not discharge the debts within a reasonable time, the pledged goods would be put to sale after expiry of a reasonable period from the date of the notice. However, it does not mean that after a reasonable period has expired from the date of notice, the pawnor is debarred from all time to redeem his pledged goods. Pawnor can redeem the pledged goods any time before the sale of such goods.[12]

Before exercising the power of sale the pawnee should give to the pledger reasonable notice of the sale. Notwithstanding anything to the contrary, a notice has to be given. At the time of entering into a contract of pledge the pawnor cannot agree to waive notice as it would be inconsistent with the provisions of s. 176.[13]

The notice contemplated herein is mandatory, for, where no notice under s. 176 is given, the sale is invalid and cannot be upheld.[14] Provisions of s. 176 relating to a reasonable notice of the sale are mandatory and supersede any contract to the contrary.[15] Therefore, a pledgee's power of sale under s. 176 is conditional on the notice being given to the pawnor. Notice is necessary only before the goods are sold.[16] Since the notice is mandatory, the provision supersedes any contract to the contrary.[17] Even if there is an agreement, the same is void.[18] Failure to issue a notice before sale not only makes the sale void *ab initio* but the seller is further saddled with serious difficulties. If the goods are sold by the pawnee without a notice, they will be deemed to have been converted and an action for conversion of the same would lie against the pawnee.[19] Such sale is not binding on the pawnor.[20]

No form of a notice under s. 176 has been prescribed. But it must refer to the debt for which the pledged goods are to be sold.[1] "A notice of the character contemplated by s. 176 cannot be implied"—*per* D.P. Uniyal, J. The notice should be reasonable so that the pawnor may get a preparation in time and money to secure release of the pledged article. Notice need not

12 *Vimal Chandra Grover* v *Bank of India with approval of* AIR 1956 Punj 155 (DB); *Bharat Bank Ltd.* v *Bodhraj* (2000)5 SCC 122.
13 AIR 1960 AP 273.
14 AIR 1950 PC 21; AIR 1955 Pat 288.
15 *Co.-operative H. Bank* v *Surendra* AIR 1932 Cal 524 relied on.
16 AIR 1933 Lab 536.
17 AIR 1958 Cal 644; AIR 1958 Pat 174.
18 *Prabhat Bank Ltd.* v *Babu Ram* AIR 1966 All 134.
19 AIR 1958 Punj 222.
20 *Prabhat Bank Ltd.* v *Babu Ram* AIR 1966 All 134.
1 *Strauss & Co.,* in re AIR 1937 Bom 16.

specify the date, time and place of the intended sale of article,[2] nor specify the amount.[3] But D.P. Uniyal, J. *held*: "Such notice has to be clear and specific in language indicating the intention of the pawnee to dispose of the security." A notice of the character contemplated by s. 176 cannot be implied.[4]

"The fact that the notice did not give the place, date and time of the sale does not make it necessarily unreasonable. A notice of sale may be sufficiently given without specifying the date, place and time of the sale"—*per* Bachawat, J. "It cannot be laid down as a general proposition of law that no mention of the date, time and place in the notice is necessary. It cannot also be equally laid down that the said three elements are absolutely necessary to bring a notice within the category of a reasonable notice within the meaning of s. 176. It depends upon the facts of each case and no standard or guide can be laid down to govern all the cases.[5]

Sale in s. 176 means the intended sale and not the sale that has been actually arranged by the pawnee. All that is necessary is that a notice should be given of the pawnee's intention to sell in default of payment by the pawner within a specified date. The reasonable notice of the sale under s. 176 does not require specification of the date, time and place of the sale.[6]

A notice, to be valid under s. 176, must be a reasonable notice and it must specify the amount for which the goods were pledged and for recovering which the pledged goods are to be sold. Otherwise it will not be a proper notice.[7]

FORMS

Form 1

Notice of sale of a pledge by a lawyer of the pledgee

By registered post with AD

Date ....

To

Sri ....

(Name and address of the pledgor)

Sir,

Under instructions from my client Sri ...... son of Sri .... residing at ...... P.S. ...... District ......I do hereby demand from you payment to my said client of a sum of ₹ .... together with interest @ ...... % per annum for the loan you took on ...... by pledging your ornaments, listed below, within 15 days from the date of receipt of this notice.

2 AIR 1958 Cal 644.
3 *Moti* v *Lakhmi* AIR 1943 Nag 162.
4 *Prabhat Bank Ltd.* v *Babu Ram* AIR 1966 All 134.
5 AIR 1963 Cal 132 *per* Laik, J.
6 AIR 1958 Cal 644; contra Tek Chand, J. AIR 1960 Punj 98.
7 38 Bom LR 982. See however (1990)1 Mad LW 86.

2. Please take notice that if you fail to pay the money within the time allowed hereinbefore, the articles, listed below and pledged by you as security against the above loan, shall be sold by public auction on ...... (*date of proposed sale*) at ...... (*time*).

3. That my client shall appropriate from the sale proceeds,–

(*i*) first, the actual expenses incurred for bringing the pledged articles to sale,

(*ii*) secondly, all interest as admissible up to the date of sale,

(*iii*) thirdly, the principal.

And, after such appropriation, the balance, if any, shall be paid to you.

4. That if there be any deficiency after the application of the sale proceeds as above, the balance will be recovered by way of suit.

5. You are requested to present yourself on the date and at the appointed hour of sale and place in your own interest.

List of pledged articles

1. One pair of gold bangles.	50 gram.
2. One pair of ear-rings.	8 gram.

Yours faithfully,

Advocate.

NOTES: 1. See s. 176 of the Indian Contract Act.

2. A pawnee or pledgee may sell things pledged on giving the pawnor or pledgor a reasonable notice of sale–notice is mandatory (AIR 1958 Cal 664).

3. For contents of a notice–non-mention of date, time and place of sale does not necessarily make the notice unreasonable (AIR 1963 Cal 132).

Form 2

Notice by a bailor to a bailee (gratuitous) to redeliver goods bailed

By registered post with AD

Dated the ...... day of...... 20 ......

To

Sri ....

(*Name and address*)

Sir,

Before my departure for the continent I left with you on ...... (*date of bailment*) one tape-recorder and a refrigerator of the description and make noted below which you agreed to keep in your custody as a gratuitous bailee and to return the same on demand on my return.

On my return I had requested you on .... to redeliver to me the said articles but you did not.

Please take notice that you are requested hereby to redeliver the said articles to me within seven days from the date of receipt of this notice, in default I shall be compelled to sue you for–

(*i*) recovery of the said articles,

(*ii*) in lieu, value thereof,

(*iii*) compensation for non-delivery.

Description of articles with value

Yours faithfully,

NOTES: 1. See ss. 159 and 160 of the Contract Act.

2. For bailee's responsibility when goods are not duly returned (see s. 161).

3. A gratuitous bailment is terminated by the death either of the bailor or of the bailee (s. 162). Liability for a wrong caused by the bailee in respect of goods bailed, thereby causing loss to the bailor, does not come to an end with the death of the bailee, where the bailment is gratuitous. On the death of the bailee his estate is liable for the loss—*Jawaladutt* v *Bansilal* 115 IC 707 (PC).

Form 3

Notice to an agent for money binding the principal

By registered post with AD

Dated the ... day of ......20 ...

To

Sri A.B. (*Name and address of the agent*)

Agent of Sri C.D. (*Name and address of the principal*)

Sir,

You are an accredited agent of said Sri C.D. and, as such, you purchased (*name the things purchased*) from my shop valued at ₹ ...... on ...... credit. Your said principal owes me a sum of ₹ ...... for aforesaid credit-purchase.

2. Please take notice for and on behalf of you or the said principal C.D. that the said C.D. is hereby requested to pay to me the said sum of ₹ ...... together with interest thereon at 8% per annum within 15 days hereof and if he fails therein a suit shall be filed against him for recovery of the said sum without further reference.

Yours faithfully,

....

Form 4

Public notice by the principal of revocation/termination of agency

Notice is hereby given that the agency of (*name, description and address of the agent*) under the undersigned has been terminated with effect from (*date of termination*).

Said (*name of agent*) has no authority as from the date of termination to act on behalf of the undersigned and any person dealing with him shall do at his/their risk.

Or,

Notice is hereby given that the power of attorney given by the undersigned to (*name and address of the constituted attorney*) has been revoked as from (*date of revocation*).

Said .... (*state here name of agent*) has no authority as from (*the date of termination*) to act on behalf of the undersigned and any person/persons dealing with him shall do at his/their risk.

Signature of the Principal
with date and address.

NOTES: 1. See s. 201 of the Indian Contract Act as qualified by ss. 202 to 210 of the Act.

2. Section 206 of the Contract Act provides 'Reasonable notice must be given of revocation or renunciation; otherwise the damage thereby resulting to the principal or the agent, as the case may be, must be made good to the one by the other'.

3. One month's notice may, in the absence of special stipulation, be regarded as sufficient—146 IC 122.

4. For express or implied revocation—See s. 207.

5. Publication through a daily in circulation in the field of agency is required.

Form 5

Notice to determine continuing guarantee

By registered post with AD

Cooch Behar, June 7, 20 ......

To

The Manger/Agent
Bank of India
Finance Corporation
(*State here name and address of the Creditor*)

Sir/Gentlemen,

I, Sri .... son of .... of Cooch Behar Town, P.S. Kotwali, District Cooch Behar give you notice that the guarantee I had executed in your favour, on .... for payment by Sri A.B., son of C.D., of Cooch Behar town of all moneys (or state the sum with interest thereon at the prescribed rate) which were due then or which might be due to you from said A.B., on the balance of the account, i.e. is hereby revoked.

2. Please take notice that if you make further advances to said A.B., or grant further loan to said A.B., I shall have no obligation for the same touching the said guarantee which I revoke hereby.

3. Copy of this notice is being sent to Sri A.B., by regd. post separately.

Yours faithfully,

c.c. to Sri A.B. for information.

NOTES: 1. See s. 130 of the Contract Act 1872.

2. A mere denial of his liability by a surety in a previous suit instituted against him by the creditor cannot operate as notice of revocation of suretyship—*Bhikabhai* v *Bhuri* 27 Bom 418 (424).

3. Unless there is a contract to the contrary, the death of a surety operates as a revocation of a continuing guarantee (s. 131). When express provision in the contract, death of surety would not operate as a revocation–*Durga* v *Durga* 55 Cal 154.

Form 6

Notice of termination of agency given to the agent

By registered post with AD

Date the .... day of .... 20....

From

Sri .... s/o ....

(*Name and address of the Principal*)

To

Sri .... s/o .... r/o ....

(Name and address of the Agent)

Sir,

This is to inform you that you were engaged by me as my agent for transacting my ...... business at ...... for and on my behalf. For your unsatisfactory nature of works (misconduct in the business of agency). I have terminated your agency with effect from ....

2. Please note that you shall not have any authority to transact any business, receive any money and to any work for or on my behalf and the general power of attorney which I had executed in your favour on .... has been revoked.

You are required to submit to me proper accounts of the aforesaid business on or before ....

Yours faithfully,

NOTES: 1. Reasonable notice must be given of such revocation or renunciation (s. 206 of the Contract Act). One month's notice may, in the absence of special stipulation, be regarded as sufficient—146 IC 122.

2. What is a reasonable notice is a question which varies with the circumstances of each case—29 IC 597. Two years, notice of termination of agency was deemed reasonable—AIR 1944 Bom 166.

3. An agent is entitled to get compensation on termination of agency without reasonable cause when the period of agency is not fixed—AIR 1980 Mad 162.

4. An agent is bound to render proper accounts to his principal on demand (s. 213 of the Contract Act).

CHAPTER 17

Notices under the Constitution of India, Law of Wrongful Dismissal and the Law of Torts

SYNOPSIS

1 Notice of suit—Art. 300 of the Constitution of India
2 Statutory show-cause notice—Art. 311 of the Constitution of India—nature of the notice—stages of show-cause notice
3 Theory of double opportunity—two notices—contents of notice—defective notice—a few illustrations
4 Belated notice
5 Cases where two notices not necessary
6 Show-cause notice—temporary incumbents—application of Art. 311 of the Constitution of India
7 Notice to private and non-Government employees—principles of natural justice—maxim *'audi alteram partem'*
8 Notice in contract services
9 Reasonable notice of termination of service
10 Forfeiture of right to notice—private servant—Government servant
11 Suit against the President or Governor of a State—Art. 361 (4) of the Constitution of India
12 Form of notice
13 Service of notice

1 Notice of suit—Art. 300 of the Constitution of India

The Government of India may sue or be sued by the name of the Union of India and the Government of a State may sue or be sued by the name of the State and may, subject to any provisions which may be made by Act of Parliament or of the legislature of such State enacted by virtue of powers conferred by this Constitution, sue or be sued in relation to their respective affairs in the like cases as the Dominion of India and the corresponding Provinces or the corresponding Indian States might have sued or been sued it this Constitution had not been enacted.[1]

A notice under s. 80 of the CPC is a prerequisite for suing the Union of India or a State Government.

1 *Chief Conservator of Forests, Govt. of A.P.* v *Collector* AIR 2003 SC 1805. Article 300(1) of the Constitution of India.

2 Statutory show-cause notice—Art. 311 of the Constitution of India—nature of the notice—stages of show-cause notice

Article 311 of the Constitution of India embodies what are known as principles of 'natural justice'. Natural justice is antithesis of arbitrariness.[2] The embargo on arbitrariness is embodied in Art. 14 of the Constitution.[3] In *Mukhtar Singh* v *State of Uttar Pradesh*,[4] Agarwalla, J. *held*: "The principles of natural justice are those rules which have been laid down by the courts as being the minimum protection of rights of the individual against the arbitrary procedure that may be adopted by a judicial or a quasi-judicial authority while making an order affecting those rights. These rules are intended to prevent such authority from doing injustice. These principles are now well settled and are four in number:

(*i*) that every person whose civil rights are affected must have a reasonable notice of the case he has to meet;

(*ii*) that he must have reasonable opportunity of being heard in his defence;

(*iii*) that the hearing must be by an impartial tribunal, i.e. a person who is neither directly or indirectly a party to the case;

(*iv*) that the authority must act in good faith, and not arbitrarily but reasonably".

The very first principle of 'natural justice' postulates issue of a notice to the affected party in respect of the case he has to meet. In other words, he should be served with a notice to show-cause against the charge and the proposed punishment. During these days of social legislation, the issue of a notice conforming to the above principles is a common feature.[5] Article 311(2) of the Constitution of India contemplates issue of a notice consistently to the first principle quoted above. Article 311 reads:

"311. (1) No person who is a member of a Civil Service of the Union or an All-India Service or a Civil Service of a State or holds a Civil Post under the Union or a State shall be dismissed or removed by an authority subordinate to that by which he was appointed.

(2) No such person as aforesaid shall be dismissed or removed or reduced in rank except after an inquiry in which he has been informed of the charges

---

2 *Basudeo Tewary* v *Sido Kanhu University* (1998)8 SCC 194.

3 *Dai-lahi Karkaria Ltd.* v *Union of India* (2000)4 SCC 57.

4 AIR 1957 All 297.

5 See (*a*) Part XII—Conduct and Discipline. Rule 55 of the Civil Service (Classification, Control and Appeal) Rules. (*b*) All India Services (Discipline and Appeal) Rules 1955. (*c*) Central Services (Temporary Service) Rules 1945. (*d*) Public Servants (Inquiries) Act 1856. (*e*) Industrial Employment (Standing Orders) Central Rules 1946—Rule 14(4). (*f*) Sastri Award—Desai Award for Banks etc.—June 1962. (*g*) For West Bengal—See West Bengal Services (Classification, Control and Appeal) Rules 1971 and Duties, Rights & Obligations of the Government Employees, Rules 1980.

against him and given a reasonable opportunity of being heard in respect of those charges:

Provided that where it is proposed after such inquiry, to impose upon him any such penalty, such penalty may be imposed on the basis of the evidence adduced during such inquiry and it shall not be necessary to give such person any opportunity of making representation on the penalty proposed:

Provided further that this clause shall not apply—

(*a*) where a person is dismissed or removed or reduced in rank on the ground of conduct which has led to his conviction on a criminal charge; or

(*b*) where the authority empowered to dismiss or remove a person or to reduce him in rank is satisfied that for some reason, to be recorded by that authority in writing, it is not reasonably practicable to hold such inquiry; or

(*c*) where the President or Governor, as the case may be, is satisfied that in the interest of the security of the State, it is not expedient to hold such inquiry.

(3) If, in respect of any such person as aforesaid, a question arises whether it is reasonably practicable to hold such inquiry as is referred to in clause (2), the decision thereon of the authority empowered to dismiss or remove such person or to reduce him in rank shall be final."

Article 311(2) of the Constitution of India contemplates issue of a show-cause notice to any Government employee (Civil)—Central or Provincial, temporary or permanent. Such a notice can legitimately be dispensed with if situations in provisos (*a*) to (*c*) above arise.

Article 311(1) uses the expressions—

(*a*) member of Civil Service of the Union;

(*b*) member of All India Service;

(*c*) member of Civil Service of a State;

(*d*) one who holds a Civil Post under the Union Government; and

(*e*) one who holds a Civil Post under a State Government.

Necessarily, incumbents of all the above categories of Government servants can claim the protection envisaged in Art. 311(2) of the Constitution. The expression does not make any difference between permanent and temporary hands, particularly after the decision in *Purushotam Lal Dhingra* v *Union of India*.[6]

The rule of common law or principles of natural justice follow the maxim "*audi alteram partem*" (hear the other side) or as differently put by continental jurists, "*audiatur et pars*" (also hear the other side). It presupposes issue of a notice asking the employee to show cause against the charges levelled

6 AIR 1958 SC 36.

against him and also against the punishment to be imposed in case charges were established. The principles in the above maxim and the statutory obligation under Art. 311(2) are not different. In other words, the notice embodies the principles laid down in the said two maxims. "The essence of the rule is notice, adequate opportunity to be heard, consideration and solemn judgment. It was pithily put by Sir Edward Coke: (*i*) vocate, (*ii*) interrogate and (*iii*) judicate, that is to say, call, question and adjudicate.[7]

Generally the maxim *audi alteram partem* includes two elements, i.e. (*i*) notice of the case to be met; and (*ii*) opportunity to explain.[8] Before any action is taken, the affected party must be given a notice to show cause against the action proposed to be taken and seek his explanation. It is a *sine qua non* of the right of fair hearing. An order passed without giving notice is against the principle of natural justice, and is void *ab initio.*[9]

It is a matter of general principle that a person should not be condemned on *ex parte* statements.[10] He should be given a reasonable opportunity to defend himself.

[For genesis, development and culmination of the rules of natural justice, readers are referred to AIR 1963 Punj 255 (pp. 268 to 273). What constitutes reasonable opportunity—refer to AIR 1963 Guj 244; AIR 1963 Tripura 20].

Both under the common law and under the statute or the Constitution, the essential ingredients of reasonable opportunity are three in number:

(*a*) that the employee proceeded against should be clearly and specifically informed of the charges standing against him;

(*b*) he should be given full and adequate opportunity to explain and establish his innocence; and

(*c*) in case charge is established, to show cause against the proposed punishment unless the later opportunity is restricted by rules in that behalf.

The opportunity must be a reasonable opportunity. The concept of reasonable opportunity is flexible and is not susceptible of easy and precise definition. What is reasonable under one set of circumstances is not reasonable under different circumstances.[11] The opportunity contemplated by Art. 311 of the Constitution is not afforded if the opportunity does not allow an adequate notice to the servant of what is alleged against him and he is further given a chance to meet the same. "Reasonable opportunity" means

7 AIR 1963 Punj 255 (*per* Tekchand, J.).

8 *Mahinder Singh Gill* v *Chief Election Commissioner* AIR 1978 SC 851; (1978)1 SCC 405.

9 *Municipal Board, Puskar* v *State Transport Authority* AIR 1965 SC 458; 1963 Supp (2) SCR 373.

10 AIR 1955 Pat 272.

11 *Mineral Development Ltd.* v *State of Bihar* AIR 1960 SC 468.

not only framing of charges and asking for explanation but much more. He must be apprised of the materials on which the charges were framed so that he could have a proper opportunity of testing or challenging the material so far as would be possible for him.[12] In *State of Bombay* v *Gajanan Mahadev*,[13] it was *held*: "The court has held that a reasonable opportunity is only afforded to the servant when he can show cause not only against the punishment but also against the grounds on which the State proposes to punish him. Therefore, it is not sufficient that the State should call upon the servant to show cause against the quantum of punishment intended to be inflicted upon him; the State must also call upon the servant to show cause against the decision arrived at by a departmental enquiry if that decision constitutes the ground on which the Government proposes to take action against the servant." The view expressed by Chagla, CJ. in *State of Bombay* v *Gajanan Mahadev* (ibid) was impliedly overruled by *State of Mysore* v *Shivabasappa Shivappa Makapur*.[14] Notice to answer charges merely does not amount to affording a reasonable opportunity to show cause against the action proposed within the meaning of Art. 311(2).[15]

Where the notice to show cause was against a lesser punishment but a greater punishment was imposed ultimately, there would be no compliance with the provisions of Art. 311(2);[16] but if it were otherwise, i.e. the notice to show cause was against a greater punishment but a lesser punishment was imposed, the opportunity given would be deemed to be sufficient in view of the maxim that 'the greater contains less'.[17]

3 Theory of double opportunity—two notices—contents of notice—defective notice—a few illustrations

The principle of reasonable opportunity is that nobody should be condemned unheard. Before, therefore, condemning a person he should be fully heard as to why he should be condemned. In other words, he must be told of the charges against him, and the action will follow if charges are established. Article 311 of the Constitution does not speak of double opportunity but cl. (2) enjoins that a reasonable opportunity has to be given with regard to penal measures mentioned in the said cl. (2).

For constituting reasonable opportunity the following conditions are required to be observed:

(*a*) Each party must have a notice of hearing.

12 AIR 1963 MP 76.
13 AIR 1954 Bom 351.
14 AIR 1963 SC 375; (1963)2 SCR 943.
15 AIR 1953 Ori 329.
16 AIR 1955 Ori 33.
17 AIR 1963 MP 115.

(*b*) Each party must have a reasonable opportunity to be present at the hearing along with his advisers and witnesses.

(*c*) Each party must have the opportunity to be present throughout the hearing.

(*d*) Each party must have a reasonable opportunity to present evidence and argument in support of his own case.

(*e*) Each party must have a reasonable opportunity to test his opponent's case by cross-examination of his witnesses, presenting rebutting evidence and addressing oral argument.

(*f*) The hearing must, unless the contrary is expressly agreed, be the occasion when the parties present the whole of their evidence and argument.[18]

The opportunity of hearing is not an empty formality. To afford an opportunity to a party in a proceeding to explain his stand is one of the vital parts of fair hearing.[19]

The theory of two notices or the theory of double opportunity had undergone a controversy since the 42nd Amendment (1976) which, however, came to be resolved in 1991.[20] Those who advocate the theory of two notices, claim that Government servants conforming to the description in Art. 311 are entitled to two opportunities.[21] The question directly came up in the last-mentioned reported case of *Gopy Kishore* v *State of Bihar*.[1] In *I.M. Lal's* case,[2] the Privy Council laid down that if the servant got two opportunities at two different stages that should not be grudged.[3]

Cases against the above view are not too little. In *Jyotinath* v *State of Assam*.[4] Their Lordships pointed out that Art. 311 of the Constitution did not contemplate two notices and in circumstances of that case one notice was held sufficient to meet the requirements of Art. 311(2). In *Jotindranath* v *R. Gupta*, Singha, J. *held*: "If there was a single charge and the proposed punishment, and the civil servant had the amplest opportunity at the enquiry stage to meet the whole case, a second opportunity may not be necessary."[5] This view was followed in *Balai Charan Basak* v *N. Roy Choudhury*.[6] For

18 *Sohan Lal Gupta (dead) through LRs.* v *Asha Devi Gupta* (2003)7 SCC 492.
19 B.C. Sarma, *Fair Hearing and Access to Justice*, Ed. 2012, p. 72.
20 *Union of India* v *Md. Ramzan Khan* AIR 1991 SC 471 (at Paragraph 18).
21 AIR 1955 Hyd 48; AIR 1953 Nag 175; AIR 1955 Pat 372; *Union of India* v *HC Goel* AIR 1964 SC 364 at p. 367.
1 AIR 1955 Pat 37.
2 AIR 1958 PC 121.
3 *Khem Chand* v *Union of India* AIR 1958 SC 300.
4 AIR 1955 Assam 171.
5 AIR 1954 Cal 383.
6 AIR 1954 Cal 495.

the extreme view we may refer to the reported case of *Haleem* v *The State*[7] where it was observed by Their Lordships: "We are not prepared to hold that under Art. 311(2), as it is worded, there is any statutory obligation to give two separate notices, one of the charges and the other of the punishment."

In an inquiry under Art. 311 of the Constitution, two notices would be necessary to be given, one for charges or allegations and other for the proposed punishment. By the Constitution (42nd Amendment) Act 1976 the provision regarding the second notice has been omitted.[8]

It is now well settled that a public officer against whom disciplinary proceedings are intended to be taken is entitled to have two opportunities before disciplinary action is finally taken against him. At the first stage of the proceedings, he is entitled to have an opportunity to defend himself. When the enquiry is over and the enquiring officer submits his report, the dismissing authority has to consider the report and decide whether it agrees with the conclusions of the report or not; if the findings in the report are against the public officer and the dismissing authority agrees with the said findings, a stage is reached for giving another opportunity to the public officer to show why disciplinary action should not be taken against him. In issuing the second notice, the dismissing authority naturally has to come to a tentative or provisional conclusion about the guilt of the public officer as well as about the punishment which would meet the requirement of justice in his case, and it is only after reaching conclusions in both these matters provisionally that the dismissing authority issues the second notice.[9] The true ambit of the second stage of the proceedings is only to show cause against the proposed punishment and not against the truth and validity of the charges on which conclusions have already been reached.[10]

What should be the contents of notices under Art. 311(2)? Contents of such notice should correspond to the stage of proceedings when notice is issued. The first notice contains charges and the delinquent is asked to show cause. It is followed by an enquiry into the charges. When the authority after enquiry has come to some conclusion, then we reach the second stage and the second notice is to be issued. This notice need not mention about the truth or validity of charges. The delinquent should be asked to show cause against the proposed punishment. Having based on decisions in *I.M. Lal's* case and in *Khem Chand* v *Union of India*[11] it was *held*: "An opportunity of showing cause against the proposed punishment can be given only after the action proposed has been tentatively decided upon. The stage for this decision

7 AIR 1955 Hyd 240.

8 *Union of India* v *Tulsiram Patel* AIR 1986 SC 1416; (1985)2 SCR 131.

9 *Union of India* v *Rajappa Menon* AIR 1970 SC 748; AIR 1963 SC 1612.

10 AIR 1966 Manipur 18. See also Samaraditya Pal, *India's Constitution: Origins & Evolution*, vol. 9, pp. 934ff.

11 AIR 1958 SC 300.

is reached only after the authority has considered the case against the officer charged on merits and has come to the tentative conclusion that the charges have been established and has also provisionally decided to inflict a particular punishment upon him. It is, therefore, obvious that the stage of show cause notice would only arrive when the authority is seized of the case and long after the trial of the Enquiry Officer has concluded the departmental proceedings and submitted his findings to the authority".[12]

A few illustrations would serve our purpose:

Second show cause notice (*a*) Civil servant is entitled to be heard on merits as well on quantum of punishment. If reply of civil servant is not considered on merits, order of his dismissal is void.[13]

(*b*) Where the notice to show cause contained six charges and specified the punishment proposed to be inflicted by the Government on that basis but after the completion of the enquiry he was found guilty of only one charge, the punishment inflicted on the basis of the notice first issued, without serving on him a fresh notice of proposed punishment on the basis of only one charge, cannot be sustained. "It may be", His Lordship *held*, "that if the appellant was guilty of one of the six articles of charge, the Government may have embodied in the notice a lesser form of punishment and punished him on that basis".[14]

(*c*) Where in the show cause notice the Government informed the delinquent officer that after consideration of the report of the Enquiry Officer it had found him guilty and also accepted recommendations of the Enquiry Officer that he should be dismissed from service, the notice is vitiated. "It is wrong on the part of the Government to accept at the time of the notice the recommendations of the Enquiry Officer regarding the nature of the punishment to be imposed upon the Government servant, namely, the plaintiff. It is true that in the notice itself the Government say that they give an opportunity to the plaintiff to show cause why he should not be dismissed forthwith. According to the Government, they had already decided to dismiss the plaintiff and the only question remained whether they should dismiss him forthwith or later on. That was the only point on which he was asked to show cause. The show cause notice is, therefore, vitiated.[15]

(*d*) If in the second show cause notice the dismissing authority does not indicate its concurrence with the conclusions of the Enquiry Officer, it cannot be said that the notice did not give reasonable opportunity as in Art. 311(2).[16]

12 AIR 1961 All 122.

13 *State of Bombay* v *Raojibhai Motibhai Patel* AIR 1961 Guj 130.

14 AIR 1963 Ker 151.

15 *State of Bombay* v *Amar Singh Raval* AIR 1963 Guj 244; *Khem Chand* v *Union of India* AIR 1958 SC 300 foll. (*per* V.R. Raju, J.).

16 AIR 1963 SC 1612.

(*e*) The show cause notice is not invalid because it does not specify the separate punishments intended to be given for the different charges.[17]

But the entire principles governing the Art. 311(2) went a radical change with *Tulsiram Patel* case.[18] By introducing Art. 311(2) by way of the 42nd Amendment (1976) a right to a second opportunity to show cause against the proposed punishment is taken away. Only right to make a representation on the proposed penalty is now allowed. In a sense, the Natural Justice principles are completely excluded from the purview of Art. 311(2). The phrase "this clause shall not apply" in Art. 311(2) is mandatory and not directory, leaving absolutely no scope for introducing into Art. 311(2) any kind of inquiry or opportunity by process of inference or implication: the maxim '*expressum facit cessare tacitum*' applies. The condition precedent of the application of Art. 311(2) requires that the conduct of the concerned Government servant is such that it justifies the penalties proposed under Art. 311(2). Once that conclusion is reached and the condition specified in Art. 311(2) is satisfied, the proviso become applicable and Government servant is not entitled to an inquiry. Though there is no prior opportunity to a Government servant to defend himself against the charges made against him, he has opportunity to show in an appeal filed by him that the charges made against him are not true—this, according to the Supreme Court, would be a sufficient compliance with the requirement of Natural Justice.[19]

4 Belated notice

A belated notice is not a sufficient notice.[20] Defective wording of show cause notice is not sufficient to render the entire notice void.[21]

5 Cases where two notices not necessary

In case of stoppage of increment by way of punishment, two notices are not called for or required, as in the case of dismissal, removal or reduction in rank.[22]

In the event two show cause notices of order of dismissal were passed in hot haste before the concerned person could reply to the said notices, the impugned order of dismissal flowing from such notices will be bad.[23]

17 AIR 1963 MP 115; *A.N. D'Silva* v *Union of India* AIR 1962 SC 1130; AIR 1959 SC 356 rel. on.
18 *Union of India* v *Tulsiram Patel* (1985)3 SCC 398.
19 *Union of India* v *Tulsiram Patel* (1985)3 SCC 398.
20 AIR 1956 All 393; *Lokmat Newspaper (P) Ltd.* v *Shankarprasad* (1999)6 SCC 275.
21 *Jagdish Pandey* v *Vice-Chancellor University of Bihar* AIR 1965 Pat 11.
22 70 CWN 44.
23 *Jaswant Singh* v *State of Punjab* (1991)1 SCC 362.

6 Show-cause notice—temporary incumbents—application of Art. 311 of the Constitution of India

Article 311 applies both to permanent and temporary employees with equal force. Where misconduct of a temporary servant is a mere motive for termination of his service by one month's notice, the order would be innocuous.[24] A few lines after, in the said reported case, it was held that if the termination was as a measure of punishment, the requirements of Art. 311 must be complied with.

But, "if the order of termination is a mere garb for camouflaging the real intention of the Government which was to punish the employee, and the order has a tendency to imperil the prospects of the employee, then it should be construed to be a measure of punishment, and the provisions of Art. 311 could be attracted".[1] Again, two Supreme Court decisions, as follow, indicate the same view. Where service of a temporary Government servant is liable to be terminated by one month's notice without assigning any reason, but as a matter of fact is not so terminated, and, on the contrary, an enquiry is held into his misconduct, the termination of service is by way of punishment. In such a case, he is entitled to protection of Art. 311(2) of the Constitution.[2] Discharge of the petitioner from service not as a result of reduction of establishment—order terminating his service by one month's notice was held liable to be quashed.[3]

7 Notice to private and non-Government employees—principles of natural justice—maxim 'audi alteram partem'

While Art. 311 governs cases of Government servants, the laws relating to master and servant govern domestic and personal servants.[4] Their cases are guided, for obvious reasons, by the rules of natural justice (for meaning of natural justice, refer to *Dipa Pal's* case in AIR 1954 Cal 594 and to *Province of Bombay* v *Madhukar* reported in AIR 1952 Bom 37) and the basic principles of law. It may be added here that the right of a person to be heard in defence is a right under the general law of the land,[5] whether such person be a Government employee or a private employee. But how often we come across cases when this basic right is denied under rigid interpretation of law?[6]

24 *Purshotam Lal Dhingra* v *Union of India* AIR 1958 SC 36.
1 AIR 1963 All 390.
2 AIR 1963 SC 531; *State of Bihar* v *Gopi Kishore* AIR 1960 SC 689 foll.
3 *Rajendra Sareen* v *State of Haryana* AIR 1970 Del 132.
4 *Union of India* v *Taj Narain Dar* AIR 1957 MB 108.
5 AIR 1952 Cal 879.
6 The Industrial Employment (Standing Orders) Central Rules, 1946—Rule 13 contemplates one month's notice in the case of monthly-rated workman and two weeks' notice in the case of other workmen. Rule 14(4) *ibid* enjoins: "No order of dismissal shall be made unless the workman concerned is informed in writing of the alleged misconduct and is given an opportunity to explain the circumstances alleged

The principles of natural justice are required to be complied with having regard to the fact situation obtaining therein. It cannot be put in a strait jacket formula. It cannot be applied in a vacuum without reference to the relevant facts and circumstances of the case.[7]

Articles of Association of a company empowered its Directors to appoint and remove any officer, clerk, agent or servant whether permanent, temporary or under special contract and did not provide for any notice before terminating the service. The discharge by a company of an employee by paying him six months' salary in lieu of notice was, therefore, not illegal.[8] Does it not go against the maxim *audi alteram partem* (hear the other side)? For, the rule of Common Law or principles of Natural Justice forbid *ex parte* condemnation.

Our country has adopted a socialistic pattern of society and of late there have been many social legislations. Barring domestic servants and servants or private individuals, all other private employees (under firms, corporations, companies, societies, institutions) are entitled to the protection from whims in certain cases of certain employers, as contemplated in the maxim *audi alteram partem*. In other words, they have a right to be told of the action proposed to be taken against them and a right to be heard in their defence. There are rules in Municipal bodies, in the Sastri Award for employees in banking institutions, in School Codes and like collections, provisions in the Industrial Disputes Act and other like legislations—all showing a tendency to accept the principle contained in the said maxim.

(For purport of natural justice—See AIR 1965 SC 1303; AIR 1965 J&K 23.)[9]

It, therefore, stands to reason that employees affected by these social legislations are bound to honour the principles of natural justice. Law does not and cannot compel a master to accept or retain in service an undesirable servant. Even then, the questions of justifiability of the grounds of dismissal and sufficiency of notice are questions which have drawn the attention of judges. In *Bhawani Sahay* v *Nequi Imam*[10] it was *held*: Even if Art. 311 did not apply to the petitioner, who was a copyist in the copying department of a civil court, was he entitled to any notice and an opportunity to be heard before discharge? It was held that the order of discharge was a quasi-judicial order, and that in passing the order of discharge without notice and without

against him ......" For bank employees, see provisios in rules of disciplinary proceedings at pp. 258-266 of Sastri Award, 1962 [National Industrial Tribunal (Bank Dispute) Award, June 1962] modified by Desai Award. See s. 15 of the West Bengal Shops and Establishment Act (Act XIII of 1953-notice of termination of service for persons employed in shops and establishments in the State of West Bengal.

7 *State of Punjab* v *Jagir Singh* (2004)8 SCC 129; *Karnataka SRTC* v *S.G. Kotturappa* (2005)3 SCC 409.

8 AIR 1957 Pat 10.

9 *State of UP* v *Pradhan Sangh Kshettra Samili* 1995 Supp (2) SCC 305; AIR 1995 SC 1512.

10 AIR 1956 Pat 257.

giving an opportunity to show cause, there has been a violation of the principles of natural justice expressed in the maxim *audi alteram partem* and, therefore, the order of dismissal was bad in law. Again, service of a professor of R.K. College (Madhubani in Bihar) was terminated without previous notice. *Held*, although s. 4 of the Bihar Act 13 of 1962 did not expressly say that notice must be given to the teacher who is to be affected prejudicially by the order of the Chancellor, it is well established as a matter of law that in such a case a notice is necessary. As a matter of necessary legal implication, the Chancellor was bound to act in accordance with natural justice before exercise of the statutory power conferred by s. 4 of the statute. Order of the Chancellor is liable to be set aside as it violated the principles of natural justice.[11]

8 Notice in contract services

In the context of notice for termination of service, a notice is an intention of the notice-giver to the other party, i.e. the addressee indicating termination of service with effect from a particular future date. It is a period of time which must elapse between the announced intention to terminate and the actual termination of the contract.

Service contract may be for an agreed specified time with right both to the employer and the employee to terminate the service by notice of an intention so to terminate. It may be as well that the contract does not specify any fixed period. Or, in other words, the contract is for an indefinite period. In the latter case also, terms of the contract may provide for termination of service by issuing a notice. In any case, notice is contractual and it must precede the actual termination.

It may, therefore, be said that contractual notices are obligatory and should abide by the terms of contract both as to time and period of the contemplated notice. Want of a contractual notice will amount to wrongful termination of service contract entitling the wronged employee to damages. A servant of the Life Insurance Corporation of India, under contract of service, was paid one month's notice-pay in terms of contract prior to termination of his service for unsatisfactory work. He had accepted the pay. It was not open to him to challenge the order of termination under Art. 226 of the Constitution.[12]

Offer of pay in lieu of notice, where the contract does not permit so, will make the dismissal wrongful.[13] The position is different with Government employees. Pay may be offered in lieu of notice (West Bengal Finance Department Circular).

11 AIR 1964 Pat 41.
12 AIR 1961 Cal 108.
13 AIR 1956 Mad 505.

Regulation 9(*b*) of the Delhi Transport Regulations authorising to issue the notice of termination of service by simply giving a month's time or pay in lieu thereof, without recording any reason in the order and without giving any hearing to the employee to controvert the allegation on the basis of which the purported order of termination of the service is made is void under s. 23 of the Contract Act as being opposed to public policy and is also *ultra vires* Art. 14 of the Constitution of India. In other words, reasons must exist for termination. Reasons must be there, reasons must be perceptible, reasons must be relevant and the reasons must be of authority independently, fairly and objectively arrived at.[14]

9 Reasonable notice of termination of service

Where the service is for a particular period and terms of the contract enjoin issue of a notice for a particular period, as discussed above, there is hardly any point for dispute. But where the contract does not specify any period and a notice has been issued, the notice must be a reasonable notice. What would or would not constitute a reasonable notice depends on the peculiar circumstances of each case. There cannot be any hard and fast rule with regard to that. In some cases, 15 days' notice may suffice, while in some other cases one month's notice may appear reasonable, and still in some other cases, a notice of less than three months may not be found reasonable.

There is, as submitted earlier, no fixed period which a court of law will insist on in any and every case. In order to find out whether a notice has been reasonable or not, we are to judge the particular intention behind the issue of the notice. In such cases, a notice is intended to enable the employee to find out a suitable employment elsewhere within the notice period so that the employee is not put to difficulties all on a sudden. The notice issued by the employee to his master has at its back a similar intention, viz. to enable the master to recruit a new hand within the notice period so that the master does not suffer. Therefore, whether a notice has been reasonable or not depends on the facts of a particular case. The propriety or otherwise of a notice has to be judged wholly on such circumstances.

On discussion of certain reported cases we would have an opportunity to notice that the courts of law have considered the following factors in finding whether the notice was reasonable or otherwise. Those are: How the employee was being paid his wages—monthly or fortnightly, etc.? What was the nature of the servant's employment? For how long did he serve? For how long he was to serve? And, notice for what period would be just in a particular case? The relative convenience of the parties was no less an important factor in determination of the reasonableness of the notice issued, for it would not be desirable to put the master into inconvenience at a time when leaving his

14 *Delhi Transport Corporation* v *D.T.C. Mazdoor Congress* 1991 (Supp) 1 SCC 600; AIR 1991 SC 101. See *Ridge* v *Baldwin* (1963)2 All ER 66.

service would be definitely injurious to his interest, or, when he cannot recruit a suitable hand forthwith. Similarly, it would be equally undesirable to put the servant into difficulties when service of a notice for termination would only inconvenience him. On these equitable considerations, the problem of notice in like cases has been tackled, e.g.: A Central Government servant putting in three years' service—given one month's pay in lieu of notice: *Held*, not illegal.[15]

The following illustrations will show how the question of reasonableness of a notice has been judged:

(*a*) When an employee is asked to explain the charges by giving him less than one day's time, it is not reasonable opportunity.[16] When only one hour's time was given for explanation, the time was not sufficient.[17] If 48 hours' time is given but the petitioner neither objects nor asks for more time, he cannot complain about it.[18]

(*b*) One day's notice was held reasonable in the case of a servant on daily pay.[19]

When a charge-sheet is sent to a worker at outstation and he is asked to show cause by the very next day of the despatch of the charge-sheet, then it is hardly a reasonable opportunity to show cause.[20]

(*c*) 15 days' notice was held required for servants on monthly pay. "The ordinary rule of law is that in the absence of an express agreement or established custom to the contrary, the contract of service is terminable by reasonable notice. Fifteen days' notice was held sufficient.[21] Person on monthly salary—month's notice given. *Held* valid.[22]

(*d*) One month's notice was insisted on in *David* v *Superintendent, St. Anthony's High School*[23]—it was *held* that there was no authority for holding that a servant paid by the month was entitled to a month's notice. 15 days' notice was held sufficient. There is no rule that a clerk is entitled to three months' notice. "All that the law requires that he should be given a reasonable notice". One

15 AIR 1961 Cal 454.
16 *Mr. Vicharey* v *State of MP* AIR 1952 Nag 288.
17 *Kanhaiya Lal* v *State* AIR 1958 Raj 1.
18 *Prafulla K. Sen* v *Calcutta State TPT* AIR 1963 Cal 116.
19 *Arjoon Vishnu* v *Hormusjee; contra Sheprafi Seervai* ILR 46 Bom 44.
20 *Sudhir Ranjan Haldar* v *State of West Bengal* AIR 1961 Cal 626.
21 *Sir Ganga Ram, Kt.* v *Duni Chand Bhandari* 78 IC 764.
22 *Secretary of State* v *Ramlal Kohli* 1936 Lab 663. Also see *Lala Lela Ram* v *Baijnath* 168 IC 697; *M.E. Moola* v *K.C. Bose* 33 IC 981.
23 6 IC 982.

month's notice was held sufficient.[1] A person engaged as a teacher by the month and there is nothing in the agreement, providing for notice to leave on either side, the contract would be terminated by a reasonable notice. One month's notice was held reasonable.[2]

(*e*) Three months' notice was held necessary in the following cases: In *Raja Kirtyanand Singh* v *Nirod Chandra Ray*[3]—the rule of one month's notice which is applicable to menials does not apply to the case of a schoolmaster. "In the case of a schoolmaster, especially when he was intending to leave his profession and join another, a notice of three months would be reasonable."

(*f*) A notice for the sake of notice cannot be treated as a reasonable notice, for "the giving of notice to show cause against charges of misconduct in a disciplinary proceeding is not merely a matter of form but of substance. The person accused of misconduct must not only be given an opportunity to show cause, but such opportunity must be a reasonable one. Thus, to give only one day's time to show cause to a person residing abroad is not really giving him a notice. It merely satisfied a formality."[4]

(*g*) An employer is entitled to satisfy itself as to the competence of a probationer to be confirmed in service and for this purpose satisfy itself fairly as to truth of any allegation that may have been made about the employee. If it is a question of inability to meet the requirement of the post, then the clauses 3 and 4 of the letter of appointment specifying the procedure of termination on notice will apply.[5]

10 Forfeiture of right to notice—private servant—Government servant

There may be cases when a private servant, because of his own conduct, forfeits his right to notice. Where the plaintiff left the work without leave, without sanction of the defendant employer and did not turn up for five or six days, the defendant was justified in dismissing the plaintiff without notice.[6] But overstay of a Government servant on the expire of leave even

1 *Detaram* v *Forbes* AIR 1930 Sind 17.
2 *Maung Thein Pe* v *J.P. D'Souza* AIR 1929 Rang 167.
3 80 IC 308 (*per* Mr. Justice Jwala Prasad and Mr. Justice Adame). Also see *Kamini Kumar Chandra* v *Rebatiraman Das* 33 CLJ 336; *Bhupendar Mohon* v *Jatindra Chandra Bose* 49 CLJ 191; *Wittenbaker* v *Galstaun* ILR 44 Cal 217; *Ramaswami Ayyangar* v *State of Madras* AIR 1962 Mad 887; *Municipality of Tata* v *Asarunal Chandoomal* AIR 1914 Sind 125.
4 *Sudhir Ranjan Halder* v *State of West Bengal* AIR 1961 Cal 626; *Khem Chand* v *Union of India* AIR 1958 SC 300 rel. on.
5 *Pavanendra Narayan Verma* v *Sanjay Gandhi PGI of Medical Sciences* (2002)1 SCC 520.
6 AIR 1925 All 610.

if regulations provide automatic termination stands on a different footing. Notice to show cause is still obligatory. Hence removal from service without giving opportunity to show cause is illegal.[7] Again, in another case the servant was found to have committed theft. The servant was liable to be discharged without notice.[8] In other words, in case of proved misconduct the servant is not entitled to any notice. Broadly speaking, immorality, drunkenness, insolence, grave insubordination, criminal conduct and conduct affecting the relationship of master and servant may in fit cases stand as a bar to notice.

Proviso to Art. 311(2) of the Constitution of India mentions three instances when a Government employee forfeits his right to reasonable opportunity and cannot claim a notice.

(*a*) A convict on a criminal charge;

(*b*) Where it is not reasonably practicable to give an opportunity of showing cause;

(*c*) Where the interest of the security of the State is a bar to allow opportunity.

The conduct leading to conviction on a criminal charge may not involve moral turpitude. Nevertheless, the provision will apply. A Government employee can be dismissed for drunkenness without observing the provisions of the Constitution.[9]

If a servant cannot perform his duty for which he is employed, whether on account of age or otherwise, he is not entitled to any notice for termination of his service.[10]

11 Suit against the President or Governor of a State—Art. 361(4) of the Constitution of India

Article 361(4) of the Constitution contemplates issue of a notice in writing of two months for a civil proceeding intended against the President or the Governor of State. The relevant provision reads as follows:

> "No civil proceedings in which relief is claimed against the President, or the Governor of a State, shall be instituted during his term of office in any court in respect of any act done or purporting to be done by him in his personal capacity, whether before or after he entered upon his office as President or as Governor of such State, until the expiration of two months next after notice in writing has been delivered to the President or the Governor, as the case may be, or left at his office

7 AIR 1966 SC 492.
8 AIR 1936 Lab 581.
9 AIR 1957 Punj 97.
10 AIR 1930 Sind 17.

stating the nature of the proceedings, the cause of action therefor, the name, description and place of residence of the party by whom such proceedings are to be instituted and the relief which he claims."

Article 361(4) of the Constitution of India which requires a notice to be delivered to the Governor before he is sued in respect of an act done by him, applies to all cases in which a Governor is sued in that way irrespective of the fact whether he was or was not the Ruler of the Former Indian State. The protection under Art. 361(4), Constitution of India is in addition to that afforded by s. 87B, CPC.[11]

There is no prescribed form of a like notice. Conditions of a valid notice under Art. 361(4) are:

It should contain:

(*i*) a statement as to nature of the proceedings;

(*ii*) cause of action;

(*iii*) name, description and place of residence of the plaintiff/petitioner;

(*iv*) reliefs sought for.

Such a notice must be in writing and for two calendar months. Writ proceedings cannot be brought against the President or the Governor of a State with reference to any act or omission in his official capacity.[12]

12 Form of notice

Although no form of notice has been prescribed, it can be said that a notice should contain all particulars which appear to be necessary to be given on the face of those provisions of the Constitution under which the notice is given. Thus, as already mentioned, a notice under Art. 361 of the Constitution shall contain the name, description and place of residence of the person who intends to start proceedings under that Article, the nature of the proceedings which he is intent upon starting, the cause of action and the relief demanded. Furthermore, two months' notice must be given in writing. A show-cause notice under Art. 310 and Art. 311 must state the charge and the punishment inflicted or proposed to be inflicted. It must entirely satisfy the requirements of the relevant Article. Again, before a suit is instituted under Art. 300 against the Government, a notice under s. 80 of the Code of Civil Procedure 1908 must be given. Such notice, obviously, must comply with the requirements of that section.

13 Service of notice

A notice is given by the party intending to claim relief. So far as Arts. 32, 226 and 227 are concerned, the party who wishes to file a writ petition shall

11 *H.V.R. Ather* v *Chief Secretary* AIR 1963 Mys 171.
12 AIR 1956 Pat 384.

give notice. In the same way, in regard to Arts. 300 and 361, notice is to be given by the party intending to institute suit or proceedings claiming relief. In the matter of Arts. 310 and 311, show-cause notice would be given by the authority competent to give such notice. Where permitted by the relevant law, a notice may be given by the party's Advocate. A notice given by an Advocate, for and on behalf of his client is deemed to be notice given by the said party. Thus, the relevant law is the guide. Thus, while a notice under Art. 361, may be given by an Advocate being the representative of his client, a show-cause notice under Arts. 310 and 311 cannot be given by an Advocate engaged by the competent authority.

FORMS

Form 1

Order of suspension (State Government)

Government of West Bengal

Office of the

(here state the name & address of office)

Dated .... 20 ...

In exercise of the power conferred by sub-rule (1)(*a*) of Rule 7 of the West Bengal Services (Classifications, Control and Appeal) Rules, 1971. Shri......... driver of vehicle No. .... under ....

(*name of incumbent*)

is hereby placed under suspension with

(name of office)

effect from the date of order.

During the period of suspension Shri .... will

(*name of incumbent*)

draw subsistence allowance equivalent to half of his grade pay (basic) plus other allowances as may be admissible under the Rules.

It is further ordered that recoveries on account of Government dues, such loans, advances, etc., if any, shall be made from the subsistence grant of Shri (name of incumbent) under rule 7(2) of W.B.S.R. Part–I

Sd/- ....

(Name and designation of the

officer with office address)

Memorandum No. .... Dated .... August 20...

Copy forwarded for information and necessary action to:–

1.

2.

3. Driver

(name of incumbent) (Office)

(address as required)

Sd/-

Officer,

with office address

See West Bengal Services (Classification Control & Appeal) Rules, 1971.

Form 2

Notice of suspension pending criminal proceedings in a court of law

To Dated .... 20 ....

Whereas a criminal case (G.R. No. ..../20 .... (*State if and when the number and year is known to the authority*) was started against you by the State for alleged offence of .... and the same is under trial/inquiry/investigation (*in the Court of C.J.M., Cooch Behar*).

Or, whereas you were arrested by the police for an alleged offence of .... on ...... and were in police custody without intimation to the authority in the establishment till ......

Now, in exercise of my powers under Cl. No. .... of the Standing Orders/Service Rules, I hereby place you under suspension with immediate effect.

(Employer/Manager)

Form 3

Order for revocation of order of suspension when the delinquent is acquitted of charge

To

Whereas you Sri .... were placed under suspension by an Order No. .... dated .... by the ....

And, whereas you have been exonerated of the charges levelled against you by the court of law.

Now, therefore, the undersigned, in exercise of powers conferred by Standing Orders/ Service Rules (Quote Cl. No./Rule No. .:........ as the case may be) the undersigned revokes the said order of suspension with immediate effect.

2. You would be entitled to full pay and allowances, for the period under suspension, as admissible.

Sd/ ....

(Designation of the authorized officer)

Form 4

State Government model form of charge-sheet

Government of West Bengal

Office of the .... Dist ....

Dated .... 20 ....

Charge-sheet in the matter of departmental proceedings drawn up against Shri .... (designation), now attached to ....

(State here office with address)

The undersigned proposes to hold an enquiry under Rule 10 of the West Bengal Services (Classification, Control and Appeal) Rules, 1971, against Shri ... (designation) now attached to ... office of ... The substance of imputations of misconduct in respect of which the enquiry is proposed to be held is set out in the Articles of Charges (Annexure-I).

2. A statement of the imputations of misconduct in support of each Article of Charge is enclosed (Annexure-II). A list of documents by which the Articles of Charge are proposed to be sustained is also enclosed (Annexure-III).

Shri......... (*designation*) is directed to submit within 15 (fifteen) days of the receipt of this Memorandum a written statement of his defence to the Enquiring Authority Officer,

....

(*here insert name, qualification, designation, office etc.*) appointed for this purpose and also to state whether he desires to be heard in person.

3. He is informed that an enquiry will be held only in respect of those Articles of Charges as are not admitted. He should, therefore, specifically admit or deny each Article of Charge.

4. He is further informed that if he does not submit his written statement of defence on or before the date specified in paragraph 2 above, or does not appear in person before the Enquiring Officer or otherwise fails or refuses to comply with the provisions of the rules/orders/directions issued in pursuance of rule of West Bengal Services (Classification, Control and Appeal) Rules, 1971, the Enquiring Officer may hold the enquiry against him *ex parte*.

5. Attention of Shri (*here insert name and designation of delinquent*) is invited to Rule 22 of West Bengal Government Servants' Conduct Rules, 1959, under which no Govt. servant shall bring or attempt to bring any political or outside influence to bear upon any superior authority to further his interests in respect of matters pertaining to his service under the Govt. If any representation received on his behalf from another person in respect of any matter dealt with in these proceedings, it will be presumed that Shri (name of delinquent) is aware of such representation and that it has been made at his instance and action will be taken against him for violation of Rule 8 of the West Bengal Services (Duties, Rights and Obligations of the Government Employees) Rules, 1980.

The receipt of this memorandum may be acknowledged.

Sd/- ....

(Designation of the Head of the Dept.

and Office, district etc.)

ANNEXURE I

Statement of Articles of Charge against Shri *(here insert the name of the delinquent and his designation with office attached and address thereof.)*

ARTICLE OF CHARGE I

That the said Shri (name of the delinquent) while functioning as (state duties performed) under the (state here where duties performed) were entrusted with depositing at the Hqrs. Store one used but almost new tube with one patch of the aforesaid vehicle after fitting a new tube into the vehicle on .... but instead of depositing the aforesaid tube he tried to deposit an old tube having 7/8 patches for personal gain, which was not accepted. The new tube in question, therefore, is presumed to have been misappropriated by him.

ARTICLE OF CHARGE II

That during the period of tour from .... to .... at various places by Shri (name of the delinquent) Technical Adviser .... in connection with Indo-Nepal boundary demarcation work the said Shri (name of the delinquent) driver while entrusted to drive the vehicle with the aforesaid officer for the tour from .... to .... morning he was given to pour in the vehicle 58 litres of petrol by which he covered 280 km., i.e. during the aforesaid period the vehicle was run approximately 5 km. per litre. On the other hand, for the tours from .... evening to .... he was given 196 litres of petrol by which he covered only 594 km. i.e. during the period the vehicle was run only 3.06 km. per litre. There is, therefore, sufficient reason to believe that for the journeys from .... evening to .... the aforesaid driver Shri .... misappropriated approximately 80 litres of petrol, for personal gain.

ARTICLE OF CHARGE III

That on a complaint lodged by Shri ....

(name, designation and office address)

for misappropriation of at least 20 litres of petrol by the aforesaid driver .... during his tour with the aforesaid vehicle on .... and ...... an order calling for explanation for misappropriation of the aforesaid quantity of petrol was issued on him by the undersigned as per Memo. No. ...... dated ......

Since he did not submit any reply to that effect, there is, therefore, reason to believe that he actually misappropriated the aforesaid quantity of petrol for personal gain for which he had no explanation to offer.

ARTICLE OF CHARGE IV

That by not submitting any reply to the aforesaid charge Shri .... driver had disobeyed the official order of the superior authority and thus violated the relevant Service Rules applicable to the Government Servants.

Sd/- ....

(Name, designation, office etc.)

ANNEXURE II

Statement of imputations of misconduct or misbehaviour in support of the Articles of Charge framed against Shri .... driver now attached to .... Office, Cooch Behar.

ARTICLE OF CHARGE I

That Shri .... driver while attached to Govt. vehicle No. .... under the .... Officer, Cooch Behar, was entrusted to deposit at the Hqrs. Store an almost new tube of the aforesaid vehicle with one patch after fitting a new tube on .... But, in place of the aforesaid tube he tried to deposit an old tube with 7/8 patches for some wrongful gain, which was not accepted. The new tube in question is, therefore, presumed to have been misappropriated by him.

ARTICLE OF CHARGE II

That the aforesaid driver Shri .... was entrusted with the duties of driving the aforesaid vehicle during the course of tour by Shri .... Technical Adviser, ... during the period from .... to .... in connection with Indo-Nepal Boundary demarcation work.

For the tours from .... to .... morning the aforesaid driver was given to pour in the aforesaid vehicle 58 litres of petrol by which he covered 280 km., i.e. approximately 5 km. per litre of petrol.

For the tours on .... evening he was given 30 litres of petrol and he covered only 10 km.

For the tours on .... and .... he was given 20 litres of petrol by which he covered 57 km. and 10 km. respectively during the days.

For the tours on .... he was given 48 litres of petrol by which he covered 111 km.

For the tours on .... he was given 25 litres of petrol by which he covered 90 km.

For the tours on .... and .... he was given 28 litres of petrol by which he covered 80 km. and 35 km. respectively during the days.

For the tours on .... he was give 45 litres of petrol by which he covered 201 km.

That is, for the tours from ...... evening to .... he was given altogether 196 litres of petrol by which he covered 594 km. only. Thereby, during the tours from ...... evening to ...... he ran the vehicle 3.06 km. per litre of petrol. Whereas during the tours from .... to .... morning he ran the said vehicle approximately 5 km. per litre of petrol. There is, therefore, reason to hold that during the aforesaid tours he misappropriated 80 litres of petrol approximately for some wrongful gain.

ARTICLE OF CHARGE III

That the aforesaid driver Shri .... was given 30 litres of petrol on .... evening making the tank full for the journey on .... to the .... Training Camp at .... With the above quantity of petrol on .... evening he covered only 7 km. and on ...., 33 km., i.e. altogether 40 km. For a further trip to elsewhere from .... on the ground of exhaustion of petrol he had to pour in further litres of petrol. When the average millage was 5 km. per litre of petrol at the time, by covering only the distance of 40 km. with petrol tank nearly full (40 litres approximately) for the journeys on .... evening and for the first trip on .... he misappropriated at least 20 litres of petrol during the aforesaid days for some wrongful gain.

ARTICLE OF CHARGE IV

For the above misappropriation of petrol an explanation was called for from the aforesaid driver Shri .... under .... Office Memo

No. ...... dtd. ...... with direction to submit reply to the above charges at Article of Charge III within 10 days of receipt of the order. The above order was received by him on .... But no reply or explanation thereof was given by him within the stipulated period and not even on any subsequent date. Thereby, he violated the official order of the superior authority which is in contravention to Service Conduct Rules.

ANNEXURE III

List of documents by which the Articles of Charge framed against Shri ...., driver are proposed to be sustained.

1. Complaint dated .... and synopsis of the report from Shri .... Officer, Cooch Behar.
2. Log Book for the material tours from .... to ....
3. Petrol coupons for the material tours.
4. Complaint dated .... by Shri .... Office and .... Officer, Cooch Behar.
5. Letters dated .... from Shri .... Officer and the then .... Officer .... Officer, addressed to Hqrs. .... Officer, Cooch Behar.
6. Statement dated ...... by Shri .... the then Cleaner addressed to the Hqrs. .... Officer, Cooch Behar.
7. Log Book for the period from .... to ....
8. The material petrol coupons for .... and ....
9. .... Officer's order bearing Memo. No. ...... dated ....
10. Acknowledgment receipt showing service of the above order .... on Shri .... driver.

Sd/- ....
(Name, designation and office
of the issuing officer)

Form 5

Notice for holding an enquiry against a delinquent employee

By registered post with AD
Dated ....

To

....

Sub:—Disciplinary proceedings.
Ref:—Your explanation dated ....

1. Your explanation dated .... in respect of charges levelled against you in the charge-sheet dated .... appears unsatisfactory.

2. The Management intends to hold an enquiry into the said allegations.

3. Shri (name with designation) has been appointed Enquiring Officer to hold and conduct the enquiry on the .... day of August 20..., at 1 p.m. at the premises of ....

4. Take notice that you are instructed to appear before the Enquiring Officer at the appointed date and time at .... with all documents and witnesses you may rely upon in your defence failing which the enquiry will be held *ex parte*.

Sd/- ....

(Manager/Secretary)

Copy to the .... with the request to hold the enquiry and submit his finding. All connected papers are annexed.

Form 6

Appointment of Enquiring Officer (State Government)

Government of West Bengal

Office of

ORDER

In exercise of the power conferred by sub-rule (4) of Rule 10 of the West Bengal Service (Classification, Control and Appeal) Rules, 1971, the undersigned hereby appoints Shri .... Officer, ... as Enquiring Authority (Officer) to enquire into the charges framed under this office Memo. No. .... dated .... against Shri ...., Driver now attached to .... Office ....

Sd/- ....

(Name, designation and office address of the issuing officer)

Memo. No. .... Dated ...... the .... 20....

Copy along with the Annexures I to III forwarded to:–

1. Shri .... Officer of .... and Enquiring Officer for information and guidance.
2. Shri .... Driver for information.

Sd/-

(Name and designation of the issuing officer)

Form 7

Notice to the delinquent by the Enquiring Officer

Dated ...., 20...

To

(Name)

(*address of the delinquent*)

Whereas I have been appointed as an Inquiring Officer by the .... to hold an enquiry into the charges made against you by the said .... by Order No. ...... dated ......, 20 ....

1. Take notice that the said enquiry will be held by me on .... at .... p.m., at the (premises). You are hereby instructed to present yourself at the enquiry.

2. If you intend to adduce any evidence oral and/or documentary you will bring the same and produce at the enquiry.

3. You are permitted to represent yourself through any of your fellow-workman/Secretary of the Union you belong to.

4. You would not be permitted to represent yourself through a lawyer.

5. You may inspect all connected papers and take pencil notes of the same in presence of my staff.

6. If you intend to rely on any document lying with the management and if you desire its production at the enquiry you would intimate the undersigned in writing 24/48 hours ahead of the sitting.

7. In the event of your failure to attend the enquiry, the enquiry will be held *ex parte*.

Sd/-

Enquiry Officer

Form 8

Notice of discharge to a temporary employee

To

.... Dated .... 20 ....

....

Sir,

Since you were appointed temporarily by this concern/Company against leave vacancy of .... your service will terminate with effect from forenoon of August 7, 20 .....

Yours faithfully,

Sd/-

(Manager/Director)

Form 9

Notice of discharge to a probationer

To

.... Dated .... 20 ....

....

Sir,

Please refer to your appointment in this establishment by Order No. ...... dated ...... 20 .... You were appointed to the post of .... on probation for six months. Your performance has not been satisfactory and the Company is not interested to retain you as staff on expiry of the period of probation.

Take notice that your service would terminate with effect from ...... 20 ....

Yours faithfully,

(Manager/Director/Employer)

NOTE: Termination of service of a probationer Salesman before expiry of the probationary period without assigning reason—in the facts of the case, was capricious, unreasonable and not justified (AIR 1973 SC 2634).

Form 10

Notice of Second Show Cause for discharge after an enquiry

To Order

.... Dated .... 20 ....

You were served with a charge-sheet dated .... alleging therein the charge of .... You replied to the charge-sheet on .... Since the reply was considered unsatisfactory, it was decided to hold an enquiry into the charges levelled against you. Accordingly, the enquiry was held on ....

We find from the proceedings of the enquiry that you were afforded fair opportunity of adequately representing your case by hearing the evidence in support of the charge and cross-examining the witnesses produced against you and also rebutting the evidence led against you by examining witnesses including yourself. Consequently, the enquiry was held with scrupulous regard for the rules of natural justice.

We have applied our mind and carefully gone through the records of the enquiry, the connected papers and documents including your reply to the charge-sheet and finding of the Enquiry Officer and concur with his findings that on the basis of the evidence recorded at the enquiry, the charge levelled against you has conclusively been established and proved beyond reasonable doubt.

The charge levelled and proved against you are major misdemeanours warranting dismissal from service.

It is, therefore, proposed to dismiss you from the service of the company. You are being furnished with a copy of the Enquiry proceedings along with Report of the Enquiry Officer and you are hereby asked to submit within 3 (three) days of the receipt hereof your representation against the proposed action.

Should you fail to submit your representation, as advised, it will be presumed that you have no representation to offer and the matter will be disposed of as per due process of law.

(Name and designation of
Competent Authority)

Form 11

Notice of dismissal after enquiry

Ref.: .... Dated .... 20 ....

Dear Sir,

You were served with a charge-sheet by a letter No. .... dated ...... and .... by .... alleging therein the charges of .... You submitted your reply on .... Since the reply was considered unsatisfactory, it was decided to hold an enquiry into the charges levelled against you. Accordingly, the enquiry was held on ....

It appears from proceedings of the enquiry that you were afforded fair and adequate opportunity of representing your cases by hearing the evidence in support of the charge and cross-examining the witnesses produced against you and also rebutting the evidence led against you by examining yourself. You did not produce any witness in spite of being asked to do so. Consequently, the enquiry was held with scrupulous regard for the rule of natural justice.

I have applied my mind and carefully gone through the records of the enquiry, the connected papers and documents including your reply to the charge-sheet and finding of the Enquiry Officer and concurred with his findings that on the basis of the evidence recorded at the enquiry, the charges levelled against you have been conclusively established and proved beyond reasonable doubt.

Since the charges levelled and proved against you were major misdemeanours, it was proposed to dismiss you from the service of the company. Accordingly, you were furnished with a report of the Enquiry Officer along with a second Show-Cause Notice No. .... dated .... whereby you were advised to submit your representation, if any, against the proposed punishment.

You submitted your representation by a letter dated .... You have contended that .... Your contentions do not have any basis whatsoever prompting revision or modification of the proposed punishment.

The established charges against you at the enquiry being grave and serious, the punishment warranted is that of dismissal from service which is commensurate with the nature of misconduct committed.

Your past record with us has been looked into with a view to finding if there are extenuating circumstances, but there are none.

Accordingly, you are hereby dismissed from the service of the Company with immediate effect.

The Accounts Department has been instructed to pay off your dues which you may collect on any working day during office hours.

Sd/-

(Manager/Employer)

c.c. Accounts Department with instructions to

Establishment Section for ....

Form 12

Notice claiming damages for wrongful dismissal

To Dated .... 20 ....

(State here the name and address of the Employer)

Dear Sir,

I was appointed in the post of ...... in your establishment/factory as per an appointment letter, dated ...... issued by ....

2. I joined the said post on ...... in the said establishment/factory, situated at .... and that I had been working in the said post diligently and to the best of my ability.

3. It is painful to note that in spite of my hard work in the said post to the satisfaction of my superior officer and despite there being no complaint against my work, you have terminated my services under your letter, dated .... Such termination of my service is absolutely arbitrary, illegal and wrongful.

I request by this notice to reinstate me in the post I held and to pay me my salary/wages till termination of service. I further request you to pay my salary/wages till termination and in case you do not reinstate me to pay compensation/damages to me, amounting to six months' salary for wrongful termination of my service within a week from the receipt of this notice.

In default, I shall be compelled to initiate legal proceedings against you for admissible reliefs, at your peril.

Yours faithfully,

Form 13

Notice on behalf of dismissed employee claiming damages for wrongful dismissal—notice by a lawyer

Dated .... the ...... 20 ......

Sir,

Under instructions from my client (*state here name, description and address*) to give you a notice, which I hereby do and state that my said client has been dismissed from the office of (*name here the post*) under you on ...... illegally and in breach of the terms of his appointment.

Or, that dismissal of my client from his office of (*name the post*) on .... has been illegal, arbitrary, wrongful and against principles of natural justice he having been denied any reasonable opportunity to defend himself against the alleged offences of (*state here substance of the charges*).

For such wrongful (or illegal) dismissal my client is entitled to recover from you damages, and further his withheld pay and allowances, provident fund deposits as per account detailed below.

Please take notice that you are hereby called upon to pay to my client a sum of ₹. .... as shown in the account below, within 15 days of the receipt of this notice. On your failure to comply with the request made herein, within the time aforesaid, my client shall be constrained to sue you for recovery of the same along with all incidental costs as would be admissible in law.

Particulars of claim:—

1. Withheld pay and allowances from .... to ...... 20 ...... ₹ ....
2. Provident fund deposits ₹ ....
3. Damages for wrongful dismissal 6 months' pay and allowances @ ₹ .... p.m. ₹ ....

₹ ....

Rupees .... (in words) .... only.

Yours faithfully,

NOTES: 1. Notice is optional.

2. Employees, other than Government servants, are not entitled to reinstatement. If dismissal is proved illegal or wrongful, their only remedy lies in damages. The quantum of damages depends upon merits of each particular case.

CHAPTER 18

Notices under the Negotiable Instruments Act 1881

SYNOPSIS

1 Notice of dishonour of a bill of exchange, cheque, etc.—by and to whom such notice is to be given (ss. 93, 95 to 97)
2 Object of a notice of dishonour
3 Mode in which a notice of dishonour may be given (s. 94)
4 Cases where notice of dishonour is not necessary (s. 98)
5 Notice of dishonour—reasonable time for giving a notice (ss. 105 to 107)
6 Dishonour of cheque for insufficiency, etc. of funds in the account (ss. 138 to 142)

1 Notice of dishonour of a bill of exchange, cheque, etc.—by and to whom such notice is to be given (ss. 93, 95 to 97)

A promissory note, bill of exchange or a cheque is said to be dishonoured by non-acceptance or non-payment when the maker of the note, acceptor of the bill or drawee of the cheque makes default in payment upon being duly required to pay the same. Section 93 of the Negotiable Instruments Act provides for notice of dishonour of the instrument by the holder thereof.

Section 93 of the Act reads: "When a promissory note, bill of exchange or cheque is dishonoured by non-acceptance or non-payment, the holder thereof, or some party thereto who remains liable thereon, must give notice that the instrument has been so dishonoured to all other parties, whom the holder seeks to make severally liable thereon, and to someone of several parties whom he seeks to make jointly liable thereon."

"Nothing in this section renders it necessary to give notice to the maker of the dishonoured promissory note, or the drawee or the acceptor of the dishonoured bill of exchange or cheque."

It would transpire that s. 93 of the Act enumerates classes of persons by and to whom notice is to be given.[1] The holder must give notice of dishonour

1 *Nanakchand* v *Lalchand* AIR 1958 Punj 222.

to persons other than the drawee or the acceptor whom he seeks to make liable on the bill, except in cases enumerated in s. 98 of the Act.[2]

Failure to give notice within a reasonable time is saddled with penalties. Neglect to give notice of dishonour within a reasonable time exonerates endorsees and others where they are likely to suffer damage thereby. In the absence of notice of dishonour, an endorsee of a promissory note is not liable unless a special contract to the contrary is proved.[3] When a cheque has been dishonoured, the endorsee has to serve the endorser with a notice of dishonour under s. 93, and, in the absence of such notice, he cannot sue on original consideration.[4]

The notice of dishonour contemplated in s. 93 must contain in it, amongst others, two main facts—(*i*) payment was demanded but was refused; and (*ii*) notice-giver makes the person notified liable on the instrument. In *Kanhyalal* v *Ramkumar*, Wanchoo, CJ., *held*: "The notice may be oral or written, but it is necessary that it must have been given within a reasonable time. The notice must also clearly intimate that payment was demanded from the drawee but refused and that the holder holds the person notified liable on the instrument. The importance of this requirement lies in the consideration that the giving of a notice of dishonour is a part of the plaintiff's cause of action and is a condition precedent for making the endorser liable and in the absence of such a notice his liability to endorsee must stand extinguished."[5]

Again, any party receiving notice of dishonour must, in order to render any prior party liable to himself, give notice of dishonour to such party within a reasonable time unless such party otherwise receives due notice as provided for in s. 93 of the Act. There may be occasions when the instrument in question is deposited with the agent for presentment. Section 96 of the Act lays down:

> "When the instrument is deposited with an agent for presentment, the agent is entitled to the same time to give notice to his principal as if he were the holder giving notice of dishonour, and the principal is entitled to a further like period to give notice of dishonour".

Thus the agent is entitled to time as holder.

It may as well be the position that the party to whom the notice of dishonour is given is dead. Section 97 of the Act contemplates a situation like that and enjoins:

> "When the party to whom notice of dishonour is despatched is dead, but the party despatching the notice is ignorant of his death, the notice is sufficient."

2 AIR 1920 Lah 80; *Abdul Majid* v *Ganesh Das Kalooram* AIR 1954 Ori 124.
3 *Kailasam Pillai* v *Chidambaram Pillai* AIR 1935 Mad 22.
4 *Mohammed Rafi* v *Quzi Mazhar* AIR 1936 Lah 796.
5 *Kanhyalal* v *Ramkumar* AIR 1956 Raj 129.

2 Object of a notice of dishonour

By a notice of dishonour no demand is made. The actual state of affairs is made known to the endorser and to warn him of his continued liability.

The object of a notice of dishonour to the endorser is not to demand payment but clearly to indicate to the party notified that the contract arising on the Negotiable Instrument has been broken by the principal debtor and that the former being a surety will now be liable for the payment.[6] This object was explained in a Punjab case:[7] "The object of giving notice of dishonour is not to demand payment for the party giving notice but to warn the party of his liability and in the case of the drawer to enable him to protect him as against the drawee or acceptor who has dishonoured the draft. Generally, where the drawer has no funds belonging to himself in the drawee's hands, neither the presentment of the cheque for payment nor notice of dishonour is necessary to charge the drawer.

The notice of dishonour is given as a matter of principle and this rule is in perfect accord with justice, equity and good conscience.[8]

In absence of notice under s. 98 of the Negotiable Instruments Act—burden of proving lies on surety—failure as to—*Held* suit could not be held bad for want of notice.[9]

3 Mode in which a notice of dishonour may be given (s. 94)

Section 94 of the Negotiable Instruments Act speaks of the circumstances under which and by whom a notice of dishonour may be given. It also enjoins the modes in which a notice may be served. The section reads:

> "Notice of dishonour may be given to a duly authorised agent of the person to whom it is required to be given, or, where he has died, to his legal representative, or, where he has been declared an insolvent, to his assignee; may be oral or written; may, if written, be sent by post; and may be in any form; but it must inform the party to whom it is given, either in express terms or by reasonable intendment, that the instrument has been dishonoured, and in what way, and that he will be held liable thereon; and it must be given within a reasonable time after dishonour, at the place of business or (in case such party has no place of business) at the residence of the party for whom it is intended.
>
> "If the notice is duly directed and sent by post and miscarries, such miscarriage does not render the notice invalid."

6 *Kanhyalal* v *Ramkumar* AIR 1956 Raj 129.
7 AIR 1962 Punj 188.
8 *Kanhyalal* v *Ramkumar* AIR 1956 Raj 129.
9 *State Bank of India* v *M/s. Kashmir Art Printing Press* AIR 1981 P&H 188.

On analysis, six features demand our attention as follows:

(*i*) Notice may be given to a duly authorised agent of the person, in case of his death to his legal representative and in case he is adjudged insolvent then to his assignee.

(*ii*) A notice of dishonour may be oral or written. If the notice is in writing, it may be sent by post duly directed.

(*iii*) Notice does not require any particular form. Nevertheless, the intention of the notice-giver must be clear from the notice. The notice-giver has to express or the notice must be such that it should have been understood that—

(*a*) the instrument has been dishonoured;

(*b*) how it has been dishonoured;

(*c*) that the addressee would be held liable thereon.

(*iv*) Whether oral or written, the notice has to be given within a reasonable time after the instrument has been dishonoured. A notice of dishonour given four years after the dishonour cannot be said to have been given within a reasonable time.[10]

(*v*) A notice of dishonour has to be sent at the place of business of the addressee. In case such party has no place of business then, it is to be sent at the residence of the party meant.

(*vi*) The notice, when in writing, has to be sent by post. If in course of transmission the notice is miscarried, it would not be invalid provided,

(*a*) it is duly directed (*i.e.*, properly addressed);

(*b*) it is duly sent by post (*i.e.*, postage pre-paid).

4 Cases where notice of dishonour is not necessary (s. 98)

Section 98 of the Negotiable Instruments Act specifies circumstances when a notice of dishonour is not necessary. Those are:

(*a*) when it is dispensed with by the party entitled thereto;

(*b*) in order to charge the drawer, when he has countermanded payment;

(*c*) when the party charged could not suffer damage for want of notice;

(*d*) when the party entitled to notice cannot after due search be found; or the party bound to give notice is, for any other reason, unable without any fault of his own to give it;

10 *Nenu Ram* v *Shivkishen* AIR 1950 Raj 55 *per* Bapna, J.

(*e*) to charge the drawers, when the acceptor is also a drawer;

(*f*) in the case of a promissory note which is not negotiable; and

(*g*) when the party entitled to notice, knowing the facts, promises unconditionally to pay the amount due on the instrument.

It, therefore, follows that there are exceptional circumstances when a notice may not be necessary, meaning thereby that notice can only be dispensed with under circumstances mentioned in s. 98 of the Act.[1] The section contains the exceptions to the general rule requiring the notice of dishonour.

One who pleads the exception has the onus to establish that one comes under one or the other of the exceptions. In AIR 1929 Lah 577 it was *held* that it was for the person relying upon any such exception to establish all the requirements thereof.[2]

(A) Where it is alleged that a notice of dishonour was not necessary as the party charged could not suffer damage for want of notice, it is upon that party (who wants to excuse himself for non-presentation) the onus lies to prove that the other party could not suffer damage.[3]

(B) Where the suit by the holder is not for compensation on account of dishonour of the cheque but, on the contrary, for the recovery of the balance of money due on the original transaction of having supplied paddy and in discharge of which the dishonoured cheque was given, no question of notice of dishonour can arise (principles of s. 98 of the Act discussed).[4]

(C) Where the reason for dishonour of the cheque was that the drawer's account had been closed, no question of any damage to the drawer or his representatives by reason of absence of notice of dishonour would arise. In such a case, a suit on the basis of the dishonoured cheque cannot fail for want of notice of dishonour.[5]

Illustrations in reported cases in (A), (B) and (C) speak of the exceptional circumstances as enjoined by s. 98.

5 Notice of dishonour—reasonable time for giving a notice (ss. 105 to 107)

In Note 3 *ante* it has been noticed that a notice of dishonour has to be sent within a reasonable time after dishonour of the instrument in question. Section 105 of the Negotiable Instruments Act, though it does not prescribe any fixed period, gives a basis for calculation of the intended 'reasonable time'. It lays down:

1 14 IC 51 (*per* Sir George Knox).
2 Also see AIR 1920 Lah 80; *Nenu Ram* v *Shivkishen* AIR 1950 Raj 55; AIR 1954 Ori 124. For contra: see *Punjab National Bank* v *Iqbal Singh* AIR 1962 Punj 158.
3 AIR 1932 Nag 55.
4 *Abdul Majid* v *Ganesh Das Kalooram* AIR 1954 Ori 124 (126).
5 AIR 1953 Ass 94.

> "In determining what is a reasonable time for presentment for acceptance or payment, for giving notice of dishonour and for noting, regard shall be had to the nature of the instrument and the usual course of dealing with respect to similar instruments; and, in calculating such time, public holidays shall be excluded."

The section itself is clear. The nature of the instrument has to be judged as also the usual course of dealing with respect to similar instruments has to be considered in order to come to a finding whether the instrument was presented for acceptance or payment and whether the notice of dishonour was given within a reasonable time. We are concerned here with the giving of a notice of dishonour. Though s. 105 of the N.I. Act does not make any distinction between the bill of exchange payable on demand and a promissory note payable on demand, the section gives discretion to courts to distinguish between commercial negotiable instruments and pronotes, particularly those as between parties who are not merchants. It was held by Mack, J. in *K.G. Krishnappa* v *Pachiappa Goundan*.[6] "Parties being non-commercial persons and mutually accommodating, delay of six or seven days in issuing notice of dishonour—not unreasonable time within the meaning of s. 74 read with s. 105 of the Act".

Section 106 of the Act is, however, more specific about the question of reasonableness of time. The section reads:

> "If the holder and the party to whom notice of dishonour is given carry on business or live (as the case may be) in different places, such notice is given within a reasonable time if it is despatched by the next post or on the next day after the day of dishonour.
>
> "If the said parties carry on business or live in the same place, such notice is given within a reasonable time if it is despatched in time to reach its destination on the day next after the day of dishonour."

Thus, two different scales have been suggested for measuring the reasonableness: (*i*) when the parties carry on business or live in the same place: and (*ii*) when they do not do so. Where the parties carry on the business at the same place and the *hundi* is dishonoured on 2nd September 1943, a notice of dishonour given on 1st October 1943, is much beyond reasonable time within the meaning of s. 106.[7]

Then again, there may be cases of transmission of a notice of dishonour. Let us look to provisions of s. 107 of the Act.

> "A party receiving notice of dishonour, who seeks to enforce his right against a prior party, transmits the notice within a reasonable time if he transmits it within the same time after its receipt as he would have had to give notice if he had been the holder."

6 AIR 1954 Mad 855.
7 *Nanakchand* v *Lalchand* AIR 1958 Punj 222.

Law allows him some more time and demands diligent onward transmission.

6 Dishonour of cheque for insufficiency, etc. of funds in the account (ss. 138 to 142)

The provisions contained in ss. 138 to 142 to have been inserted by the Banking, Public Financial Institutions and Negotiable Instruments Laws (Amendment) Act 1988 with effect from 1st April 1989.

According to s. 138, whenever any cheque for discharge of any legally enforceable debt or other liability is dishonoured by the bank for want of funds and the payment is not made by the drawer despite a legal notice of demand, it shall be deemed to be a criminal offence. The salient features are:

(*i*) The cheque in question should have been issued in discharge of whole or part of a debt or liability.

(*ii*) The cheque in question should be presented within three months or its specific validity period, whichever in earlier.

(*iii*) The payee or holder should give notice demanding payment within thirty days of his receiving information of dishonour, which should be for no other reason than for insufficiency of funds. The earlier period of 15 days has been enhanced to 30 days by the Negotiable Instruments (Amendment and Miscellaneous Provisions) Act 2002, with effect from 6.2.2003.

(*iv*) Drawer can make payment within 15 days of receipt of the notice and only if he fails to do so, he is liable to be prosecuted.

(*v*) Complaint can be made only by the payee or the holder in due course within one month of arising of the cause of action.

The requirement of giving notice under proviso (*b*) of s. 138 is mandatory. There is no mode prescribed under s. 138 for serving the notice. It is sufficient that the notice is served on the drawer. It is not the giving of notice but its receipt that gives rise to cause of action.[8] But notice must be in writing. If no demand has been made in terms of proviso (*c*) within the specified time from the date of dishonour of cheque in question, the complaint will not be sustainable. Intimation to the drawer regarding dishonour of cheque which is verbal cannot be treated as a demand within the meaning of proviso to s. 138, it being not in writing requiring the drawer to pay the amount of cheque within the specified time. A complaint is to be instituted within 30 days of the first notice but a complaint filed within 30 days of the second notice is not within the period of limitation.[9] But in *SL Constructions* v *Srinivasa Rao*[10] it was held that where second notice was sent to correct

8 *Dalmia Cement (Bharat) Ltd.* v *Galaxy Traders and Agencies Ltd.* AIR 2001 SC 676; 2001(1) KLT 528 (SC).

9 *Produt Kumar Mohanty* v *Dilip Singh* 2001 Cr LJ 2322 (Ori).

10 2006(3) Andh LT (Cri) 163.

address and it was proved that the notice was received by the drawer but no payment was made, such second notice is to be treated as notice for reckoning the cause of action to file a complaint. Notice cannot be construed in a narrow technical sense without examining the substance of the matter. Where the cheques had been issued by the company through its director, notice issued to the said director who had also signed the cheque was held to be a valid notice to the drawer.[11] A notice issued through an advocate, despatched without bearing the advocate's signature, is not invalid.[12]

Ordinarily in computing the time, the rule observed is to exclude the first day and to include the last. The period of one month for filing the complaint will be reckoned from the day immediately following the day on which the period of 15 days from the date of receipt of the notice by the drawer expires.[13] The notice envisaged in proviso (*b*) to s. 138 transmitted by fax, has been held as compliance with the legal requirement.[14] In a notice under proviso (*b*), demand has to be made for the cheque amount. If no such demand is made the notice would fall short of legal requirement. Where in addition to 'the said amount', there is also a claim by way of interest, cost. etc. whether the notice is bad would defend on the language of the notice. If, in the notice, an omnibus demand is made without specifying what was due under the dishonoured cheque, the notice would be bad. If in a notice any other sum is indicated in addition to the said amount, like interest, cost etc. the notice would not be invalid.[15] A notice demanding an amount higher than that mentioned in the dishonoured cheque is vague and not legal.[16] Non-mentioning of cheque number in the demand notice cannot be a ground to hold that there was no demand.[17] In the notice cheque amount has been clearly stated. In addition, the complainant had claimed incidental and notice charge. The two amounts are severable. In the notice it has been stated that on failure to comply with the demand, necessary legal steps will be taken. If the accused had paid the cheque amount, he would have been absolved from the criminal liability under s. 138. Regarding other claims, a civil suit would be necessary.[18] However, no particular form of notice is prescribed under proviso (*b*) to s. 138. It only stipulates that a notice is writing should be given to the drawer of the cheque within 30 days of the receipt of information in writing from the bank regarding the return of the cheque unpaid, demanding the payment.

11 *Rajneesh Agarwal* v *Amit J. Bhella* 104 Comp Cas 332 (SC); *Bilakchand Gyanchand Co.* v *A. Chinnaswami* AIR 1999 SC 2182.
12 *Ibid.*
13 *Saketh India Ltd.* v *India Securities Ltd.* AIR 1999 SC 1090; (1999)3 SCC 1.
14 *SIL Import USA* v *Exim Aides Silk Exporters* 1999 Cr LJ 2276 (SC).
15 *Suman Sethi* v *Ajay K. Churiwal* (2000)100 Comp Cas 444 (SC).
16 *Gopa Devi Ozha* v *Sujit Paul* 1995 Cr LJ 3412 (Cal).
17 *Kapila Dairy Private Ltd.* v *Rajendra Bala Saheb Kulkarni* (2007)1 Bom CR 914.
18 *Suman Sethi* v *Ajay K. Churiwal* (supra).

FORMS

Form 1

Notice by a payee to the drawer of a Bill of Exchange for dishonour

By registered post with AD.

....

Date ....

To

M/s. ....

....

(*Name and address of the drawer of the bill of exchange*)

Gentlemen,

Please take notice that a Bill of Exchange for Rs. .... drawn by you on .... (date) on M/s. .... (*name of drawee*) and payable at .... Kolkata was dishonoured by non-acceptance (or, non-payment).

You are held responsible for the said money in the bill (or the instrument).

Particulars

Drawer–

Drawn on–

Payee–

Bill of Exchange dated .... for Rs. ....

Yours faithfully,

Sd/- ....

(*Name of payee of the Bill*)

NOTES: 1. Section 93 of the N.I. Act.

2. By a notice of dishonour no demand is made–only fact of dishonour is made known to warn the noticee of the continued liability.

Form 2

Notice of dishonour of a cheque by payee/endorsee

Dated ....

To

Sri ....

(*Name and address of drawer*)

Dear Sir,

Please take notice that the cheque No. .... dated .... for a sum of Rs. .... drawn by you on .... (*name of bank on which drawn*) payable to the undersigned or order has been dishonoured on (date of dishonour) by non-payment and your liability for the said amount continues (*or, you would be held liable thereon*).

(In the case of endorsee—please take notice (*as above*) payable to Sri ...... (name and address of original payee) and endorsed by said (name of endorser) to the undersigned has been dishonoured etc.).

Yours faithfully,

(Signature of Payee/Endorsee with address)

NOTES: 1. A notice of dishonour of a cheque, etc., may be oral as well as written. If written, to be sent by post (see s. 94 of the Negotiable Instruments Act).

2. It must be given within a reasonable time after dishonour.

3. The notice has no prescribed form, but it must express three things—(*a*) fact of dishonour, (*b*) mode how dishonoured and (*c*) liability of the drawer therefor.

Form 3

Notice by an endorsee to endorser of dishonour of a bill of exchange/hundi

By registered post with AD

The ...... day of ......, 20...

To

M/s. ....

(*state here name and address of the endorser of the bill of exchange/hundi*)

Dear Sirs,

A bill of exchange/hundi dated .... for Rs. ...... was drawn by M/s. .... (*name of drawer*) of .... (*address*) on M/s. .... (*name of drawee*) of .... (*address*). The said bill was endorsed to me by M/s. .... (*name of endorser*) on .... The bill was presented on .... but was not accepted (*or was dishonoured by non-payment*).

Please take notice that you are held liable or, responsible for the money under the said instrument.

Yours faithfully,

....

(Name of Endorsee)

NOTES: 1. See footnotes under Form No. 2.

2. The object of a notice of dishonour to endorser is not to demand payment but clearly to indicate to the party notified that the contract arising on the Negotiable Instruments has been broken by the principal debtor and that the former being a surety will now be liable for payment.

Form 4

Notice of Dishonour of Cheque

(Notice by counsel)

My client, Sri ....

of ....

To

Sri .... S/o ....
residing at .... P.O. ....
Dist. ....

Dear Sir,

On behalf and under instruction of my aforesaid client Sri .... I do hereby give you the following notice:

1. That you took a loan of Rs. .... from my said client on .... promising to pay back along with an interest at the rate of 18% per annum on or before ....
2. That you had delivered to my said client a Cheque No. .... drawn on .... Bank ......, dated .... for a sum of Rs. .... being the principal amount of the loan and interest thereon.
3. That the aforesaid cheque was presented for payment before the .... Bank on .... by my client. But the said cheque was returned unpaid to my client by the aforesaid Bank on .... for want of sufficient funds in your account with endorsement 'Refer to Drawer'.

That while issuing the cheque you were fully aware that you had no sufficient fund to your credit in your account and thus you cheated my client in respect of the said sum of money.

By this notice you are called upon to pay to my said client the said sum of Rs. .... together with interest thereon till date of payment within 15 days of the receipt of this notice failing which my client shall be compelled to initiate legal proceedings against you for the recovery of the aforesaid sum holding you liable for costs.

Yours faithfully,

....

Advocate

Form 5

Short form of the notice of dishonour

Dear Sir,

I am constrained to return to you the Cheque No. ...... drawn on .... Bank .... dated ...... in my favour in consideration* as because the said cheque has been dishonoured by your Banker for want of sufficient funds in your account.

Kindly make me the payment of Rs. .... by cash within a fortnight hereof to avoid unpleasant consequences.

Yours faithfully,

....

NOTE: Notice to be sent within thirty days of the dishonour of the cheque.

* State here the circumstances under which the cheque was issued.

Form 6

Notice under s. 138(b) of the Negotiable Instruments Act, 1881

Dear Sir,

Under instructions from my client Sri .... son of .... residing at .... I give you this notice:

1. That my said client runs a business of textile goods at .... (place of business).
2. That you have been purchasing various items of textile goods from my said clients on credit for the last severals years. During the financial year ...... 20 ... you made payments towards your credit purchases from time to time. Giving credit to all your payments till .... 20 ... a sum of Rs. 75,000 stood payable to my said client.
3. That my client having demanded of you on ...... 20 ... said sum of Rs. 75,000 you issued on .... an account payee cheque of Rs. 75,000 towards payment of the outstanding dues vide cheque No. .... dated .... drawn on the Bank of India, at ....
4. That my client deposited the said cheque with his bankers M/s. .... Bank at .... for collection of the proceeds of the cheque but the cheque bounced for want of sufficient fund in the Bank in your account.
5. That my client immediately contacted you and informed you about the fate of the cheque.
6. That on account of the said cheque having been dishonoured you have committed an offence under s. 138 of the Negotiable Instruments Act, 1881.
7. That on the occasion of issuing the cheque to my said client on .... you were fully aware of the fact that there was no sufficient fund in your account with your said bankers and you knew full well that the cheque was going to be dishonoured for want of sufficient funds in your said account. This betrays your motive.
8. That the dishonoured Cheque No. .... dated .... for Rs. 75,000 is enclosed herewith.

Now you are hereby called upon to pay to my client a sum of Rs. 75,000 in cash in lieu of the dishonoured cheque within 15 days of the receipt of this notice failing which a complaint under the Negotiable Instruments Act shall be filed against you in a competent Criminal Court. This is, however, without prejudice to my client's other rights to recover the said money by appropriate legal steps.

Yours faithfully,
Advocate

Form 7

Notice of dishonour to endorser of bill

By Regd. Post with AD

Bankura
The........... July, 20...

From

Sri ....
Son of ....
of ....
(Name and address of the sender of the notice)

To

Sri ....
Son of ....
of ....
(Name and address of the person on whom notice is to be served)

Dear Sir,

Please take notice that a Bill of Exchange, dated .... drawn by Sri .... s/o .... r/o .... on .... for an amount of Rs. .... payable to me or my order ...... months after presentment. Your endorsement has been dishonoured by non-acceptance.

I, therefore, hold you responsible for making the payment of the entire amount to me, holding you responsible for the dishonour.

2. You are hereby required to make the aforesaid payment to me on or before .... failing which I shall be compelled to initiate appropriate legal proceedings against you at your cost.

Yours faithfully,
Advocate

Form 8

Notice under s. 138(b) of the N.I. Act for dishonour of cheque (Another Form)

(Lawyer's Notice)

To Date ....

....

Sir,

Under instructions of my client M/s. (name the firm & with address) I am to inform you through this notice that you had purchased (name the goods) from the aforesaid firm of my client on ...... (date of purchase) for a sum of Rs. 65,000. Instead of making the cash payment for the aforesaid purchase you wanted to make payment by a cheque and you accordingly handed over to my said client a cheque bearing No. .... for the said amount of Rs. 65,000 drawn on the .... Bank dated .... in my client's favour. On .... the said cheque was accepted by my client in good faith.

The cheque was presented for payment to the said Bank on .... by my client. The Bank dishonoured your cheque on .... and returned the same to my client on the ground that the amount of money standing to your account was not sufficient to honour the cheque.

Thus you have defrauded my client with intention to cause wrongful loss to him. I have been instructed by my client to say that on the occasion of issuing the cheque you were fully aware that you did not have sufficient fund to your credit in the said bank by which the cheque could be honoured.

Please take notice that your are requested to pay to my client said sum of Rs. 65,000 together with interest (at the admissible rate) till date of payment to my client within a fortnight from the date of receipt of this notice failing which my client shall proceed against you in Civil and Criminal forums of law without further reference.

Yours faithfully,
Advocate

Form 9

Notice for dishonour of cheque

Regd. with AD

To Date ....

....

Sir,

Under instructions from and on behalf of my client M/s. .... (Bank), a bank constituted and functioning under the Banking Companies (Acquisition and Transfer of Undertakings) Act 1970, having its Head Office at .... and business office, a Branch Office at .... we have to serve you with the following notice:

1. That you on .... (date) approached my client for the purpose of sanctioning of a term loan to the tune of Rs. .... and you requested for the same.
2. That on .... (date), while acting on your request, my client sanctioned you a term loan on certain conditions, one of which was that you had to issue post dated cheques for the repayment of the loan by way of instalments. For this purpose you issued cheques for the repayment of the loan by way of instalments. For this purpose you issued .... (No. of cheques) cheques.
3. That for the sake of repayment of loan my client presented on its due maturity one of the cheques for the first time which was dated .... bearing No. ...., drawn on ....(Bank) which was dishonoured for the reason of insufficiency of funds.
4. That the cheque got dishonoured on .... (date of which my client got the information on .... (date).
5. That the term loan was sanctioned on your request and on your promises and assurances that the cheques so issued by you would in no circumstances be dishonoured for any reason whatsoever and had my client known that on its presentation the cheques would be dishonoured, they would not have granted and disbursed the above said loan.
6. That the cheque which was issued by you in discharge of your liability/debt has been dishonoured for the reason of insufficiency of funds. That the cheque so issued was for the purpose of deceiving my above said clients so that the loan could be taken as the cheque was issued without sufficient funds in your account nor any arrangement has been made for the payment of the same.
7. That thereafter my client(s) have been running from pillar to post to contact you but you have been avoiding the same.

8. That having understood that you issued the cheques to my client(s) against the sanctioning and disbursement of loan for the amount which you never had in your account at the time of issue of cheques and, therefore, it can be inferred that you took the loan by deceiving my client(s) when you issued the cheques knowing fully well that you had insufficient funds in your account to honour the same or the amount of the cheque exceeded the arrangement that you had made with your banker.
9. That it is now clear that your intentions were not good when you issued the above stated cheque as you had issued the cheque for the amount which you did not have in your account nor any arrangement had been made for such amount with the result that the cheque stood dishonoured.
10. That as the cheque is dishonoured for the reason of "insufficiency of funds", you may be held liable, civilly as well as criminally, particularly under section 420 of the Indian Penal Code 1860, section 138 of the Negotiable Instruments Act 1881 as amended up-to-date as also under Order XXXVII of the Code of Civil Procedure 1908 and for this purpose this mandatory notice is served upon you.

I, therefore, hereby call upon you to pay the amount for which the cheque so dishonoured was issued, i.e. Rs. ...., together with interest calculated at the rate of 24% per annum which comes to Rs. .... and Rs. .... towards the cost of this notice, within a period of 15 days from the date of receipt of this legal notice, failing which I have definite instructions from my client(s) to take appropriate legal action, civil as well as criminal, particularly under section 138 of the Negotiable Instruments Act 1881 as amended up-to-date, section 420 of the Indian Penal Code 1860 and Order XXXVII of the Code of Civil Procedure 1908. You shall be held responsible for all the costs and consequences for which please take this notice.

Take further notice that in future also such type of dishonouring should not be repeated, which would make you liable to not only civil but also to the criminal legal consequences.

Yours faithfully,

....

Advocate

Form 10

Notice for wrongful dishonouring of cheque issued for the application of shares

Regd. with AD

To Date ....

....

....

Sir,

Under instructions and on behalf of my client M/s. .... (Name and address), who are the account holder in your bank, vide Account No. .... I have to serve you with the following notice:

1. That as said above, my client is having a Current Bank Account with cheque book facility with you.

2. That on .... (date), my client issued a cheque upon you for a sum of Rs. .... and the cheque was bearing No. .... The said cheque was drawn in favour of ABC & Co. .... (Payee).

3. That as the cheque was issued for a sum of Rs. ...., my client was having in his account more sum than the aforestated cheque issued for.

4. That, to the utter dismay of my client the payee on presentment of the cheque got the same dishonoured for the reason of "insufficiency of funds" and the said reason was stated in the returning memo issued by you. The cheque was issued in the name of the aforesaid company as the application money for the shares applied for in the preference category and the same were allotted to all the applicants fully at a rate of Rs. .... whose market value is Rs. .... It may further be noted that my client applied for .... shares (number of shares applied for).

5. That, therefore, you dishonoured the above stated cheque for the reason that amount standing to the credit of my client's account was insufficient to honour the cheque and it exceeded the arrangement made for by the drawer, whereas sufficient funds were lying to the credit of my client's account.

6. That such conduct of yours amounts to gross negligence on your part and also amounts to 'deficiency in service' on your part for the reason my client is a customer and consumer of your bank and you were bound to honour the said cheque in the absence of any justifiable reason for the dishonouring of the same.

7. That due to the wrongful dishonouring of the cheque for the reason of 'insufficiency of funds' my client could not get the allotment of the aforesaid shares which he would have definitely got allotted in his favour had the cheque so issued not been dishonoured wrongfully for the reason of insufficiency of funds in the account of my client.

8. That had my client got the allotment of the aforesaid shares, he must have earned a profit of Rs. .... which he failed to earn due to the gross negligence on your part in dishonouring the aforesaid cheque for no fault of my client.

9. That such conduct of yours in dishonouring the cheque for unjustifiable reason amounts to 'deficiency in services' rendered by you to your customers under the Consumer Protection Act 1986.

10. That for the deficiency in the services on your part towards my client you are liable to pay compensation under the Consumer Protection Act 1986.

I, therefore, hereby call upon you to pay Rs. .... on account of above said loss and Rs. .... for the mental pain and agony that my client has gone through, together with Rs. .... towards the cost of this notice, within a period of one month from the date of receipt of this legal notice, failing which I have definite instructions from my client(s) to take appropriate legal action, particularly under the Consumer Protection Act 1986. You shall be held responsible for all the costs and consequences for which please take notice.

Take further notice that in future also such type of dishonouring should not be repeated, which would make you liable to not only civil but also to the criminal legal consequences.

Yours faithfully,

....

Advocate

Form 11

Dishonour of cheque—Notice by an individual

Regd. with AD/UPC

From:

To

Dear Sir,

Sub: Notice under section 138(*b*) of the Negotiable Instruments Act; Dishonour of cheque No .... dated.......... for Rs. ....drawn on ....

By this notice I like to inform you that your cheque No. .... dated .... for Rs. .... (Rupees ....) drawn on .... issued by you in discharge of your liability to pay the aforesaid amount on account of goods having been supplied to you, *vide* Invoice No. .... dated .... has been returned by your bankers with the remarks "Refer to Drawer"/"Insufficiency of Funds" in your account and you having failed to arrange for its payment, this cheque has been returned to me by my bankers, ... , on ....

2. That you are hereby required to take notice of demand under section 138 of the Negotiable Instruments Act 1881 and to pay the whole amount of the dishonoured cheque, i.e., Rs. .... (Rupees ....) within a period of fifteen days from the receipt of this notice, failing which you shall become liable under the penal provisions of the Negotiable Instruments Act 1881.

3. You are further required to note that if you fail to make the payment, you shall do so at your own cost and responsibility and shall be liable for legal action both under the civil and the criminal law applicable as on date. You are further liable for the cost of this notice.

Place .... Yours faithfully,

Dated ....

Copy retained. Signature of the person giving notice

N.B.: Notice must be sent within 15 days [30 days as per the Negotiable Instruments (Amendment and Miscellaneous Provisions) Act 2002] of the return of cheque by the Bank.

Form 12

Dishonour of cheque—Notice by a partner of the firm

Regd. with AD/UPC

From

M/s. ....

Through its partner Sri ....

s/o ....

r/o ....

To

Sri ....

s/o ....

r/o ....

Dear Sir,

Sub: Notice under section 138(b) of the Negotiable Instruments Act; Dishonour of cheque No. .... dated .... for Rs. .... drawn on ....

I .... give you the following notice:

1. That I am a partner of the firm M/s. .... and duly authorised to give you this notice. The said firm is carrying on the business of the sale of ....

2. That you had purchased .... *vide* Invoice No. .... dated .... worth Rs. .... from the aforesaid firm on .... and had delivered an account payee cheque No. .... dated .... drawn on .... of the aforesaid amount of rupees ....

3. That the said firm had deposited the cheque in their account in the .... Bank during the period of its validity on .... which was returned to the firm by the .... Bank on .... with the remarks "Refer to Drawer"/"Insufficiency of Funds" in your account.

4. That you had issued the said cheque despite your knowledge that you had no funds in your account. You have cheated the said firm and it seems that you do not want to pay the amount of Rs. .... to the firm.

Through this notice you are called upon to pay the aforesaid firm an amount of Rs. .... (Rupees ....) in lieu of the dishonoured cheque within a period of fifteen days from the receipt of this notice, failing which the said firm shall be compelled to initiate recovery proceeding against you in a competent Court of law and shall also initiate proceedings under the Negotiable Instruments Act 1881 and then you shall also be liable to the costs of these proceedings.

Dated ....   Yours faithfully,

Place ....

Copy retained.   Signature of the person giving notice

N.B. Notice to be given within 15 days [30 days as per the Negotiable Instruments (Amendment and Miscellaneous Provisions) Act 2002] of the dishonour of the cheque.

Form 13

Dishonour of cheque—notice to sole proprietor/partner of a firm/director of a company

Regd. with AD/UPC

From

To

....

Dear Sir,

Sub: Notice under section 138(b) of the Negotiable Instruments Act; Dishonour of cheque No. .... dated .... for Rs. .... drawn on ....

I have to serve the following notice on you being the sole proprietor of the firm .... /the partner of the firm M/s. .... /the Managing Director of the ....,carrying on business at ....,under section 138 of the Negotiable Instruments Act 1881.

That against the goods supplied by us to you/on account of the loan advanced to you for the property purchased by you/in discharge of your debt and liability on account of the work done by us for you and /or for services rendered to you, you issued a cheque .... dated .... for Rs. .... (Rupees ....) drawn on ...., in our favour.

2. That the said cheque was sent by us for collection through our bankers, ... but I was surprised to find that the same has been returned unpaid by your bankers with the remarks "Refer to Drawer"/"Insufficiency of Funds" in your account and you having failed to arrange for its payment, the cheque has been returned to me by my bankers, ..., on ....

3. That you are hereby required to take notice of demand under section 138 of the Negotiable Instruments Act 1881 and to pay the whole amount of the dishonoured cheque, i.e., Rs. .... (Rupees ....) within a period of fifteen days from the receipt of this notice, failing which you shall become liable under the penal provisions of the Negotiable Instruments Act 1881.

4. You are further required to note that if you fail to make the payment, you shall do so at your own cost and responsibility and shall be liable for legal action both under the civil and the criminal law applicable as on date. You are further liable for the cost of this notice.

Place .... Yours faithfully,

Dated ....

Copy retained Signature of the person giving notice

N.B. Notice must be sent within 15 days [30 days as per the Negotiable Instruments (Amendment and Miscellaneous Provisions) Act 2002] of the return of cheque by the Bank.

Form 14

Dishonour of cheque—notice on behalf of an individual by an Advocate

Regd. with AD/UPC

From

................................., Advocate

To

....

Dear Sir,

Sub: Notice under section 138(b) of the Negotiable Instruments Act; Dishonour of cheque No. .... dated .... for Rs. .... drawn on ....

Under instructions and authority from my client Shri .... s/o Shri .... r/o .... I like to serve upon you the following notice:

1. That my aforesaid client is dealing in the sale of .... and you have been purchasing the goods on credit from my client from time to time.

2. That in pursuance of the goods received by you and with a view to clear your liabilities towards my client, you had issued a cheque No. .... dated .... for Rs. .... (Rupees ....) drawn on .... as full/part settlement of pending bill(s).

3. That the said cheque was deposited with the bank by my client for payment on However, it is regretted that the said cheque was returned unpaid by your bankers with the remarks "Refer to Drawer"/"Insufficiency of Funds" in your account and the intimation with regard to the dishonour of cheque has been received by my client on .... You were duly informed about the same by my client on ....

4. That you apologised to my client for the dishonour of the cheque and at the same time requested him to re-deposit the same in the banks for fresh clearance. In terms of your assurance and instructions, as also relying upon your words, the said cheque was re-deposited again by my client on .... However, it is a matter of great regret that the said cheque was dishonoured again on .... with the remarks "Refer to Drawer"/"Insufficiency of Funds" in your account.

5. That the above facts make it abundantly clear that you have mischievously and intentionally issued the aforesaid cheque with ulterior designs and further instructed my client to present the same for encashment again, knowing fully well that the said cheque would not be honoured on presentation on account of insufficiency of funds in your account.

6. That the dishonour of the said cheque all over again clearly proves your intention to commit and perpetuate fraud on my client and indulge in cheating and criminal misappropriation. Besides, you have committed an offence under the provisions of the Negotiable Instruments Act 1881.

Under the circumstances, our client hereby serves upon you notice under section 138 of the Negotiable Instruments Act 1881 and you are hereby called upon to make the payment of Rs. .... (Rupees ....) in lieu of the dishonoured cheque within a period of fifteen days from the date of receipt of this notice, failing which I have definite instructions from my client to take necessary action against you in the competent Court of law, and in that event, you shall be liable for all the costs and consequences resulting therefrom.

You are also liable to pay a sum of Rs. .... towards charges for the present notice.

Yours faithfully,

Sd./ ....

Advocate

Place ....

Date ....

Copy retained.

N.B. Notice must be sent within 15 days [30 days as per the Negotiable Instruments (Amendment and Miscellaneous Provisions) Act 2002] of the return of cheque by the Bank.

Form 15

Dishonour of Cheque—notice on behalf of an individual by an Advocate

Regd. with AD/UPC

From

................................, Advocate

To

....

Dear Sir,

Sub: Notice under section 138(b) of the Negotiable Instruments Act on behalf of Sri .... s/o ....r/o ....

Dishonour of cheque No. .... dated ...... for Rs. .... drawn on ....

On behalf and under instructions of my aforesaid client Sri ...., I do hereby give you the following notice:

I. That you have taken a loan of Rs. ....from my client on payable alongwith interest at the rate of Rs. .... percent per annum on or before ....

2. That you failed to pay the aforesaid loan and the interest thereon on or before the aforesaid date.

3. That after the expiry of the aforesaid date my client approached you and demanded the repayment of the said loan and interest thereon.

4. That upon the said demand you delivered the cheque No. .... dated .... for Rs. .... (Rupees ....) drawn on .... which sum included the principal amount of the loan and interest thereon upto date to my client.

5. That the aforesaid cheque was presented for payment in the .... Bank on .... by my client. But the said cheque was returned unpaid to my client by the aforesaid Bank on .... with the remarks "Refer to Drawer"/"Insufficiency of Funds" in your account.

6. That you have dishonestly cheated my client and have caused him dishonestly wrongful loss of Rs. .... by not repaying the loan amount (abovenoted) and interest thereon as upto date.

Through this notice you are called upon to pay to my client a sum of Rs. .... (Rupees ....) in lieu of the dishonoured cheque within a period of fifteen days from the receipt of this notice, failing which my client shall be compelled to initiate legal proceedings against you for the recovery of the aforesaid amount and in that case you shall also be liable to pay the costs of the proceedings.

Yours faithfully,

Sd./ ....

Advocate

Dated ....

Place ....

Copy retained.

N.B. Notice must be sent within 15 days [30 days as per the Negotiable Instruments (Amendment and Miscellaneous Provisions) Act 2002] of the return of cheque by the Bank.

Form 16

Dishonour of cheque—notice by the Advocate on behalf of the Banker to the customer whose cheque has been dishonoured

Regd. with AD/UPC

From

..........................., Advocate

To

....

Dear Sir,

Sub: Notice under section 138(b) of the Negotiable Instruments Act for Dishonour of cheque No. .... dated .... for Rs. .... drawn on ....

Under instructions and authority from our client, ... Bank, we like to serve upon you the following notice:

1. That you, being a customer of our client, ... Bank, maintain a Savings Bank Account No. .... at .... with them. Our client has also issued and made available to you a Visa Card No. ....on the basis of which you can make purchases on credit worth Rs. .... (Rupees ....).

2. That you issued a cheque No. .... dated .... for Rs. .... (Rupees ....) drawn on .... to clear the outstanding dues (liability)/to clear part of your dues (liability). However, when the said cheque was presented for collection, our client was surprised to learn that the same had been returned unpaid with the remarks "Refer to Drawer"/"Insufficiency of Funds" in your account.

3. That our client informed you by a registered letter dated .... that the cheque issued by you had been returned with the aforesaid remarks. Our client also brought to your knowledge about the total outstanding amount in your account.

4. That subsequently, you requested our client on .... to present the cheque again for encashment and also assured that the said cheque would be duly honoured on presentation and that you have made necessary arrangements for the same. On your assurance, the said cheque was re-deposited by our client for encashment. It is a matter of great regret that the said cheque was again dishonoured by your bankers with the remarks "Refer to Drawer"/"Insufficiency of Funds" in your account and the intimation with regard to the dishonour has been received by our client on ....

5. That the dishonour of the said cheque all over again clearly proves your intention to commit and perpetrate fraud on our client and indulge in cheating and criminal misappropriation. Besides, you have committed an offence under the provisions of the Negotiable Instruments Act 1881.

Under these circumstances, our client hereby serves upon you notice under section 138 of the Negotiable Instruments Act 1881 and you are hereby called upon to make the payment of Rs. .... (Rupees ....) in lieu of the dishonoured cheque within a period of fifteen days from the receipt of this notice, failing which we have definite instructions from our client to take necessary action against you in the competent Court of law, and in that event, you shall be liable for all the costs and consequences resulting therefrom.

You are also liable to pay a sum of Rs. .... towards charges of the present notice.

Place .... Yours faithfully,

Dated .... Sd/ ....

Copy retained Advocate

N.B. Notice must be sent within 15 days [30 days as per the Negotiable Instruments (Amendment and Miscellaneous Provisions) Act 2002] of the return of cheque by the Bank.

CHAPTER 19

Notices Relating to Tenancy

SYNOPSIS

1 Effect of Amendment of s. 106 of the Transfer of Property Act
2 Notice—actual and constructive—provisions of s. 3, T.P. Act
3 Notice to quit under s. 106, T.P. Act—general principles—object
4 Service of notice—not amount to termination
5 Suit for ejectment—notice to quit under s. 106, T.P. Act—notice to be pleaded
6 Suit for ejectment—combined notice under s. 106, T.P. Act and under provisions of State Rent Control Acts—change in outlook
7 Change in position
8 Notice to quit under s. 106, T.P. Act—cases where there is a "contract to the contrary"—general observations
9 Notice to quit under s. 106, T.P. Act
10 Notice to quit where there is a "law to the contrary"
11 Notice to quit where there is a "usage to the contrary"
12 Transfer of leasehold premises—date of commencement of tenancy—notice of termination
13 Form and contents of a notice to quit (s. 106, T.P. Act)
14 Object and interpretation of a notice to quit—principles of the maxim "ut res magis valeat quam pereat"
15 Notice terminating tenancy—tenant's undertaking to vacate—fresh notice not necessary
16 Defects in a notice to quit—when excusable and when not
17 Other illustrations of valid and invalid notices
18 Period in a notice to quit under s. 106, T.P. Act
19 Notice in case of minor landlord
20 Period in a notice—modes how month and year counted
21 Who can give a notice to quit under s. 106, T.P. Act—lessor—lessee—co-lessors—co-assigns—receivers—trustees—agents—lawyers, etc.
22 To whom a notice to quit under s. 106, T.P. Act has to be given
23 Notice on the 'Karta' under s. 106, T.P. Act
24 Death of original tenant—when fresh notice necessary
25 Death of one of co-landlords—if fresh notice is necessary
26 Issue of second notice—if waiver of the first
27 Service of a notice to quit—various modes of service
28 Notice sent through electronic form
29 Notice sent through telegram
30 Effect of service of notice under s. 106, T.P. Act
31 Refusal of notice amounts to service by implication—distinction between "Refused" and "Left"
32 Lease by the Government—notice to quit
33 Lease by a municipality—notice to quit
34 A notice to quit under other circumstances
35 Notice of repairs of leasehold property—lessor's liability
36 Notice under s. 39 of the Transfer of Property Act 1882
37 Waiver of a notice to quit under s. 106, T.P. Act
38 Withdrawal of a notice to quit

SYNOPSIS—*continued*

39 Notice by lessee to the lessor regarding encroachment on and interference with lessor's rights concerning the leasehold property
40 Right of lessor's transferee—principles of attornment—provisions of s. 109, T.P. Act—notice of attornment
41 Notice intending to determine a lease—provisions of s. 111(*g*) of the Transfer of Property Act—waiver of notice
42 Forfeiture—provisions of s. 111(*g*)—whether notice by the Government is necessary
43 Notice to determine lease—provisions of s. 111(*h*), T.P. Act
44 Licence—termination of
45 Waiver of a notice to quit—provisions of s. 113, T.P. Act—acts amounting to and acts not amounting to waiver
46 Notice of suit in a lease determined by 'forfeiture' [s. 111(*g*), T.P. Act]—Relief against forfeiture (s. 114A, T.P. Act)—combined notice under s. 114A—mandatory provisions
47 Object and contents of a notice under s. 114A of the Transfer of Property Act
48 Notice of transfer of an actionable claim (s. 131, T.P. Act)—defective notice—waiver of a notice
49 Surrender of lease [s. 111(e), T.P. Act 1882]

1 Effect of Amendment of s. 106 of the Transfer of Property Act

Section 106 of the Transfer of Property Act has been amended by the Transfer of Property (Amendment) Act 2002 w.e.f. 1st January 2003.

Statement of Objects and Reasons

Objects and reasons for amendment of s. 106 are stated in the Bill. They are as follows: "Section 106 of the Transfer of Property Act 1882, *inter alia*, provides that the lease of immovable property for agricultural or manufacturing purposes shall be deemed to be a lease from year to year, which may be terminated either by the lessor or the lessee by six months' notice expiring with the end of the year of the tenancy; and a lease of the immovable property for any other purpose shall be deemed to be a lease from month to month, which may be the end of the month of the tenancy. The legal position, which has also been reiterated by the Supreme Court in *Mangilal* v *Sugan Chand*,[1] is that while computing the period of notice the day on which the notice is served is required to be excluded. The Law Commission of India in its 181st Report on Amendment to s. 106 of the Transfer of Property Act 1882 has examined the working of this section and found that a number of suits have been filed in ignorance of this legal position and these suits have been dismissed on this lone technicality. Such a position leads to serving of a fresh notice and filing of a fresh suit which amounts not only to serious injustice but also to multiplicity of litigation despite the fact that the defendant had more time available to him than the prescribed period of notice by the date which the suit is filed to evict him or even by the date of judgment dismissing the suit.

1 AIR 1965 SC 101 (104).

Hence, it is proposed that the period of notice shall commence from the date of its receipt and the amendment shall apply to the pending suits or proceedings and notices issued before the commencement of the proposed amendment.

The Bill seeks to achieve the aforesaid object."

The amended section is as under:

> 106. *Duration of certain leases in absence of written contract or local usage.* (1) In the absence of a contract or local law or usage to the contrary, a lease of immovable property for agricultural or manufacturing purposes shall be deemed to be a lease from year to year, terminable, on the part of either lessor or lessee, by six months' notice; and a lease of immovable property for any other purpose shall be deemed to be a lease from month to month, terminable, on the part of either lessor or lessee, by fifteen days' notice.
>
> (2) Notwithstanding anything contained in any other law for the time being in force, the period mentioned in sub-section (1) shall commence from the date of receipt of notice.
>
> (3) A notice under sub-section (1) shall not be deemed to be invalid merely because the period mentioned therein falls short of the period specified under that sub-section, where a suit or proceeding is filed after the expiry of the period mentioned in that sub-section.
>
> (4) Every notice under sub-section (1) must be in writing, signed by or on behalf of the person giving it, and either be sent by post to the party who is intended to be bound by it or be tendered or delivered personally to such party, or to one of his family or servants at his residence, or (if such tender or delivery is not practicable) affixed to a conspicuous part of the property.

Before amendment s. 106 stood as under:

> "106. *Duration of certain leases in absence of written contract or local usage.* In the absence of a contract or local law or usage to the contrary, a lease of immovable property for agricultural or manufacturing purposes shall be deemed to be a lease from year to year, terminable, on the part of either lessor or lessee, by six months' notice expiring with the end of a year of the tenancy; and a lease of immovable property for any other purpose shall be deemed to be a lease from month to month, terminable, on the part of either lessor or lessee, by fifteen days' notice expiring with the end of a month of the tenancy.
>
> Every notice under this section must be in writing, signed by or on behalf of the person giving it, and either be sent by post to the party who is intended to be bound by it or be tendered or delivered personally to such party, or to one of his family or servants at his residence, or (if such tender or delivery is not practicable) affixed to a conspicuous part of the property."

A comparison of the provisions of s. 106 as they stood before amendment and the provisions as adopted by amendment may be made.

For the old s. 106 a new section has been substituted. The present section has four sub-sections. Sub-section (1) corresponds to paragraph 1 of the old section. The only change that has been brought about in paragrapg 1 is the deletion of the words "expiring with the end of a year of tenancy" and "expiring with the end of a month of tenancy".

Sub-section (2) is altogether new and the law contained in this sub-section shall be effective 'notwithstanding anything contained in any other law for the time being in force'.

Like sub-sec. (2), sub-sec. (3) is new in every respect. This sub-section has been introduced to do substantial justice. It provides that a notice under sub-sec. (1) shall not be deemed to be invalid merely because the period mentioned therein falls short of the period specified under that sub-section, where a suit or proceeding is filed after the expiry of the period mentioned in that sub-section.

Sub-section (4) is the verbatim reproduction of paragraph 2 of the old sub-section.

Sub-section (1) of the amended s. 106

The question is what is the effect of deletion of the words 'expiring with the end of a year of tenancy' and 'expiring with the end of a month of tenancy'. Sub-section (1), like paragraph 1 of s. 106 before amendment, enacts a rule for the duration of leases in cases not governed by local law, contract or usage. It raises a fiction and indicates a deeming provision in respect of leases which do not fall within the ambit of paragraph 1 of s. 107. The presumption under this section is that the lease is from year to year or month to month, according to the nature of the property. On the question of termination of lease, the law as it stood prior to amendment provided that a lease from year to year could be terminated by six months' notice expiring with the end of year of the tenancy, whereas a lease from month to month could be terminated by fifteen days notice expiring with the end of a month of the tenancy. The requirement of the notice period expiring with the end of year or month, as the case may be, has since been omitted. This means that the tenancy can be validly terminated from any date. Many of the notices which were held to be invalid on this count would now be valid in view of sub-sec. (1) of s. 106.

Transitory provisions. The provisions of section 106 of the principal Act, as amended, shall apply to:

(*a*) all notices in pursuance of which any suit or proceeding is pending at the commencement of this Act; and

(*b*) all notices which have been issued before the commencement of this Act but where no suit or proceeding has been filed before such commencement.

These transitory provisions are retrospective in operation. They make it clear that not only in pending suits but even in those cases where notices had already been issued in terms of the old law, the provisions of the new s. 106 shall apply.

Sub-section (2)

Computation of period. Sub-section (2) provides how computation is to be made, that is, from which date the period of six months or fifteen days, as the case may be, is to be computed. Sub-section (2), *inter alia*, provides that the period shall commence 'from the date of receipt of notice'. Section 12(1) of the Limitation Act 1963 provides that in computing the period of limitation for any suit, appeal or application, the day from which such period is to be reckoned, shall be excluded. Similar provision of law is to be found in s. 9 of the General Clauses Act 1897 which runs as follows:

> "In any Central Act or Regulation made after the commencement of this Act, it shall be sufficient for the purpose of excluding the first in a series of days or any other time, to use the word 'from' and for the purpose of including the last in a series of days or any other period of time, to use the word 'to'."

But sub-sec. (2) of s. 106 begins with a *non-obstante* clause: "Notwithstanding anything contained in any other law for the time being in force". Because of this *non-obstante* clause the words "shall commence from the date of receipt of notice" get overriding effect. As such, in computing the period of six months or fifteen days, as the case may be, date of receipt of the notice shall have to be included.

Sub-section (3)

Validation of defective notice. The cumulative effect of sub-secs. (1) and (2) is that unless there is any contract or local law or usage to the contrary an agricultural or manufacturing lease is terminable by six months' notice and all other leases by fifteen days' notice and such period shall have to be computed from the date of receipt of notice. Sub-section (3) validates those notices where the periods mentioned above fall short, provided the suit or proceeding is filed after expiry of the periods specified in sub-sec. (1). The notice shall not be invalid if the suit is filed after the expiry of six months or fifteen days, as the case may be, from the date of receipt of the said notice. The use of the word 'shall' makes it abundantly clear that in applying sub-sec. (3), no discretion is left with the court. But if in the above circumstance the suit is filed before the expiry of six months from the date of receipt of the notice, sub-sec. (3) cannot be pressed into service for validating the notice.

Sub-section (4)

Mode of service of notice. Sub-section (4) is the verbatim reproduction of the second paragraph of s. 106 as existed prior to amendment by Act of 2002. This sub-section has two parts. The first part provides the requirements of notice. It says that (*i*) the notice must be in writing, and (*ii*) signed by or on behalf of the person giving it. As such, oral notice does not fulfil the requirements of sub-sec. (4). The word 'signed', in view of s. 3(52) of the General Clauses Act, includes putting 'mark'. If a person other than the lessor signs the notice purporting to be the agent of the lessor, it is to be proved that such signatory acted as the agent of the lessor.

The second part of sub-sec. (4) prescribes the mode of service of notice. The notice can be served in any of the following ways:

(*i*) by post;

(*ii*) tender or delivery personally to lessee;

(*iii*) personal delivery to one of lessee's family or servants at his residence;

(*iv*) when tender or delivery in the above ways is not practicable, the notice may be affixed to a conspicuous part of the property.

For various reasons service by post invites unnecessary complications. Other two modes of service, that is, tender or delivery of notice to the lessee, who is intended to be bound by the notice, or to his family member or servant is undoubtedly better when there is written acknowledgement for such service. Service by affixation can be resorted to only when personal service either to the lessee or to his family member or servant is not practicable. But service of notice in any of the modes provided in sub-sec. (4) is a must. Unless the lessor is able to prove service of notice, he will be at once non-suited only on that ground.

2 Notice—actual and constructive—provisions of s. 3, T.P. Act

Actual notice A notice may be either an actual notice or a constructive notice. Actual notice is a notice whereby a person acquires actual knowledge of fact. It must be definite information given in the course of negotiations by a person interested in the property, for a person is not bound to attend to vague rumours.[2] A person is said to have actual notice when the information conveyed is express and it brings home knowledge directly to the party.[3] Actual notice embraces all degrees and grades of evidence from the most direct and positive proof to the slightest evidence, from which a court would be warranted in inferring notice.[4]

Constructive notice Constructive notice, on the other hand, is knowledge which the courts impute to a party upon a presumption so strong that it cannot be allowed to be rebutted, that the knowledge must have been communicated.[5]

A person has knowledge of a transaction by way of paper publication effected in daily newspaper which is a constructive notice contemplated

2 *N. Kashinath* v *Arun R. Rawell* 2008(67) AIC 7.
3 *Dr. Govinddas* v *Shantibai (Smt.)* AIR 1972 SC 1520.
4 *Ibid.*
5 *Ibid*; *Ashiq Hussain* v *Chaturbhuj* AIR 1928 All 159.

under s. 3 of the TP Act.[6] Actual possession of suit lands with prior purchaser operates as constructive notice of the original agreement to the subsequent purchaser.[7] Constructive notice in equity treats a man who ought to have known a fact as if he actually knows it. Generally speaking, constructive notice may not be enforced unless some specific circumstances can be shown as a starting point of enquiry which, if pursued, would have led to the discovery of the fact.[8]

In Municipal areas the properties are subject to municipal tax and the taxes are first charge on the property. So failure to make enquiries as to the amount of the tax due amounts to wilful neglect or gross negligence and notice must be imputed to him.[9] A transfer by an executor is valid unless it is established that transferee had the notice that the executor was acting in breach of trust. In such a case mere failure to scrutinize the will does not amount to constructive notice of the transferee that money paid by him was not required for the administration of the estate of the testator.[10]

But when the register of the registered deed contains a reference to a prior agreement which created a charge on a particular land, but the agent of the mortgagee omitted to look at the entries, the mortgagees would be deemed to have constructive notice of the charge.[11] But a *bona fide* purchaser for value cannot be deemed to have notice of a prior agreement for sale when the person on the basis of the agreement is in possession of a small portion of the property.[12]

3 Notice to quit under s. 106, T.P. Act—general principles—object

A tenancy, except where it is at will, may be terminated only on the expiry of the notice of a specified duration under the contract, custom or statute governing the premises in question.[13] Service of formal notice to quit is not necessary for termination of a tenancy-at-will. A demand for possession or anything which amounts to demand for possession is sufficient.[14]

About contractual and customary durations, we have discussed hereinbelow under appropriate headings. About statutory duration we are here concerned with provisions of s.106, T.P. Act. A notice under s. 106 of the T.P. Act is intended to give a reasonably sufficient time to the defendant before his lease is determined. Another purpose of such a notice is to make

6 *Mohideen Sahib* v *A. Amena Bi* AIR 2007 Mad 133.
7 *Murlidhar Bapuji Valve* v *Yallappa Lalu Chaugule* AIR 1994 Bom 358.
8 *Mohd Norul Hoda* v *Bibi Raifunnisa* (1996)7 SCC 767.
9 *Lala Nawal Kishore* v *Municipal Board* AIR 1943 All 11 (FB).
10 *Geetarani* v *Narendra Krishna* 60 Cal 394.
11 *Renukabai* v *Bheosan Hafsaji* AIR 1939 Nag 132.
12 *Md. Mustafa* v *Haji Mohd.* AIR 1987 Pat 5; *Parthasarathy* v *Subbarayya* AIR 1924 Mad 67.
13 *Pandit Kishan Lal* v *Ganpat Ram Khosla* AIR 1961 SC 1554.
14 *Sudhir Kumar* v *Dhirendra Nath* AIR 1957 Cal 625.

him aware of the intention of the lessor to terminate the lease.[15] A notice to quit must be clear and unambiguous intimation to the lessor or the lessee, as the case may be, of the intention of the party giving the notice that the lease is to terminate at a certain time. No particular form is necessary.[1] A notice is to be construed liberally. Courts should give such construction as would not work hardship on the tenant and would not strain the language too much against the landlord.[2]

Court cannot read it in a hypercritical spirit so as to find faults in it on every conceivable ground.[3] A notice to quit should be liberally construed. The essential point to be decided is whether the tenant was asked to vacate in accordance with law.

By issuance of notice to quit the right created thereunder, namely, cessation of the lease, does not become effective automatically till the period prescribed in the notice or under s. 106 expires. On expiry thereof the lease becomes inoperative and the lessor acquires the right to have the tenant ejected. When the lessee fails to deliver vacant possession, the lessor would be entitled to have the tenant ejected and to take possession in due process of law. On the expiry of the notice period the right, title and interest in the property stood transferred by operation of law.[4]

4 Service of notice—not amount to termination

Mere breach of lease deed would not *ipso facto* mean that the tenancy stands terminated merely by serving a notice and possession reverts back to the lessor. If the lessor feels that the lessee has rendered himself liable for ejectment, he is required to approach the civil courts for ejectment of the lessee.[5]

5 Suit for ejectment—notice to quit under s. 106, T.P. Act—notice to be pleaded

A trespasser can be ejected without any previous notice[6] but a tenant can be ejected only after service of a notice under s. 106, T.P. Act, together with a notice if required under any special Act, provided the tenancy was governed by the provisions of the Transfer of Property Act 1882, and it did not come within the exemptions given in s. 106 (e.g. contract to the contrary, etc.). A decree in an ejectment suit cannot be passed unless it is established that the tenancy has been lawfully determined, i.e. where a notice is required, by issue of a notice.

15 *Gurdit Singh* v *Tata Iron and Steel Co. Ltd.* AIR 1965 Pat 311.
1 7 All 899.
2 *Rocheldas* v *Ratanchand Baghmal* AIR 1954 Nag 292; *Welfare Assocn. A.R.P., Maharashtra* v *Ranjit P. Gohil* AIR 2003 SC 1266.
3 *Kunj Behari* v *Acharyya Hard* AIR 1975 Raj 138.
4 *Vasant Kumar Radhakisan Vora (dead) by his LR* v *Board of Trustees of the Port of Bombay* (1991)1 SCC 761.
5 *Guramardeep Singh* v *Ved Vyas* AIR 2018 P&H 42.
6 AIR 1934 Cal 134.

In a suit for ejectment, notice under s. 106, T.P. Act has to be pleaded since it is one of the causes of action.[7] The plea of want of notice or want of valid notice has to be specifically pleaded in the written statement.[8] The failure of the tenant to take the plea of the invalidity of the notice in the written statement amounts to waiver.[9] The service of notice terminating the tenancy has been specifically pleaded in the plaint by the plaintiff landlord. But in the written statement the defendant only stated that notice referred to in the plaint was not according to law. He did not specifically deny the service of notice. In view of the above position, the Supreme Court has held that in the absence of specific or implied denial all allegations of service of notice as made by the plaintiff must be taken to have been admitted.[10]

Where a tenancy is established, the onus of proving in a suit for ejectment that the tenancy has been determined by a notice to quit or otherwise is on the plaintiff.[11] Where the defendant admits receipt of the notice but challenges its validity—onus is on the plaintiff to show that the notice was valid.[12] In a suit for ejectment it would not be open for the tenant to raise a dispute regarding the permitted increases in rent.[13]

A suit for ejectment must be preceded by two notices—one for determination of tenancy and to quit and the other—a notice of suit where the tenancy is governed not only by the T.P. Act but also by a State Rent Control and Eviction Act. In such cases, service of both the notices or a combined or composite notice fulfilling requirements of both the provisions of law is necessary prior to ejectment.[14] But the Supreme Court in *V. Dhanpal Chettiar* v *Yesodai Ammal,*[15] has held that for filing a suit for eviction of tenant under any State Rent Control Act there is no necessity to serve a notice under s. 106 of the Transfer of Property Act for determination of the tenancy. It has since been followed by Calcutta High Court.[16]

Notes in the following paragraphs deal with a Composite Notice.

6 Suit for ejectment—combined notice under s. 106, T.P. Act and under provisions of State Rent Control Acts—change in outlook

Before a suit for ejectment is instituted, two notices are required to be served—one is a notice for termination of tenancy under s. 106 of the T.P. Act and the other is a notice of suit as is provided in provincial Rent Control

7 *Batoomal* v *Rameshwar Nath* AIR 1971 Del 98.
8 *Munnilal* v *Nandlal* AIR 1971 Del 300.
9 *Balbir Singh* v *Kalawati* AIR 1976 All 434.
10 *Lohia Properties (P) Ltd.* v *Atma Ram Kumar* (1993)4 SCC 6.
11 *Mozam Shaikh* v *Ananda Prasad Bhadra* AIR 1942 Cal 341.
12 AIR 1928 Cal 436.
13 *Laxman Jiwaba Baherwade* v *Bapurao* (2002)7 SCC 618.
14 *Surya Property* v *Bimalendu* AIR 1964 Cal 1; 67 CWN 977 (SB).
15 AIR 1979 SC 1745; (1979)4 SCC 214.
16 *Shantilal Mukherjee* v *Mukund Lal* AIR 1980 Cal 381; see also *Ratan Gupta* v *Vandesh Chander* AIR 1976 SC 588.

Act, e.g. s. 13(6) of the West Bengal Premises Tenancy Act 1956. (Now s. 6(4) of the West Bengal Premises Tenancy Act 1997). The two notices may be combined into one with this condition that requirements of both the notices must be there.

We may refer to some of the State Acts:

(i) *West Bengal Premises Tenancy Act 1997—notice under s. 6(4) of the Act*

A notice contemplated under s. 6(4) of the West Bengal Premises Tenancy Act 1997, is a notice of suit.

Notice is valid even if there is no mention of the word 'suit' or 'proceeding' so long as it carries with it the necessary implication of the landlord's intention to file an ejectment suit in case of non-compliance on the tenant's part with the notice.[1] Notice containing words 'till evicted in due course of law' was a valid notice.[2] A notice setting out any of the grounds in s. 13 of the W.B. Premises Tenancy Act 1956 (now s. 6 of the West Bengal Premises Tenancy Act 1997) and particularly when written by a lawyer on behalf of the landlord is a sufficient compliance with s. 13(6) [now s. 6(4)] although there is no express statement that a suit will be filed in default of compliance with the notice.[3]

Service of a notice under s. 13(6) of the West Bengal Premises Tenancy Act 1956, (now s. 6(4) of the West Bengal Premises Tenancy Act 1997) does not require personal service. Service by post would be sufficient.[4]

Grounds of ejectment need not be stated in a notice under s. 13(6) of the West Bengal Premises Tenancy Act 1956[5] (or under s. 6(4) of the 1997 Act) but the landlord may set out such grounds although the notice will not be treated as a notice of such grounds. In other words, in the course of the proceedings he may rely on other grounds which are open to him.[6] The opposite view in 73 CWN 709 is that a valid notice of suit must contain, amongst others, the grounds of eviction. A pure and simple notice to quit even if given by a lawyer is not sufficient.

Where in the notice the ground of default only was taken but the suit was filed on the ground of *bona fide* requirement—*held*, omission in notice casts a great reflection.[7]

1 73 CWN 61; 68 CWN 296; *Surya Properties* v *Bimalendu* AIR 1964 Cal 1; 67 CWN 977; 68 CWN 184.

2 69 CWN 232.

3 73 CWN 61 (72).

4 *Surya Properties* v *Bimalendu* AIR 1964 Cal 1; 67 CWN 977; *Santosh* v *Smt. Chinmayee* AIR 1966 Cal 615.

5 *Surya Properties* v *Bimalendu* AIR 1964 Cal 1; AIR 1968 Cal 186; AIR 1968 Cal 554; *Mahananda Das Karmakar* v *Biswanath Dey* AIR 1976 Cal 185.

6 *Surya Properties* v *Bimalendu* 67 CWN 977.

7 ILR (1963)2 Punj 215.

(ii) *Bombay Rent Control Act*

Notices preceding suit for eviction and rent suit not maintainable unless two notices—one under s. 106 of the T.P. Act for determination of tenancy and another under s. 12(2) of the Bombay Rents, Hotel and Lodging House Rate Control Act are issued.[8]

(iii) *Maharashtra Housing and Area Development Act 1976*

It is held by the Supreme Court that service of notice upon the tenant of the Development Board Premises under the Maharashtra Housing and Area Development Act 1976 is the *sine qua non* for initiating proceedings for eviction. If no notice of termination of tenancy was issued the eviction proceeding is not maintainable.[9]

(iv) *M.P. Accommodation Control Act 1955*

Before a tenant can be evicted by the landlord, he must comply both with the provisions of s. 106, T.P. Act and those of s. 4 of the M.P. Accommodation Control Act.[10]

(v) *Mysore Rent Control Act*

A combined notice will do. It does not make any difference that those two notices were issued simultaneously or by one and the same document.[11]

(vi) *U.P. (Temporary) Control of Rent and Eviction Act 1947*

A composite notice or combined notice under s. 3(1)(*a*) of the U.P. (Temporary) Control of Rent and Eviction Act and s. 106 of the T.P. Act is a valid and legal notice. It is implicit, therefore, that the two periods contemplated by the two provisions can be synchronised by one notice. It is not required that both the periods (period of 30 days as provided in s. 106, T.P. Act as amended in U.P.) and the period of one month as provided in s. 3(1)(*a*) of the U.P. (Temporary) Control of Rent and Eviction Act should expire one after the other, before a suit for ejectment and rent can be filed.[12]

(vii) *Delhi Rent Control Act 1958*

Determination of contractual tenancy is essential before an ejectment application can be filed by a landlord against a tenant according to Rent Control legislation.[13]

8 AIR 1963 SC 120; AIR 1967 SC 405.
9 *Dattaram* v *Thukaram* (1999)6 SCC 764.
10 *Mangilal* v *Suganchand* AIR 1965 SC 101.
11 AIR 1965 Mys 65.
12 AIR 1965 All 291.
13 AIR 1964 SC 1341; *Mangilal* v *Suganchand* AIR 1965 SC 101; AIR 1969 Punj 110. Also see AIR 1971 Del 98 for observations of Deshpande, J. in *Baboo Mal* v *Rameshwar Nath*.

(viii) *Karnataka Rent Control Act (22 of 1961)*

Tenant holding over—tenancy held contractual: notice to quit is necessary.[14]

7 Change in position

There has been a change in outlook since about 1979. For ejectment of a tenant under a State Rent Act a notice under s. 106 of the T.P. Act has been held unnecessary.

It is pertinent to mention here the lucid observations of the Supreme Court in *V. Dhanpal Chettiar* v *Yesodai Ammal*[15] where Mr. Justice Untwalia has observed as follows:

> "To get a decree or order for eviction against a tenant under any State Rent Control Act it is not necessary to give notice under s. 106, T.P. Act. Determination of lease in accordance with the Transfer of Property Act is unnecessary and a mere surplusage because the landlord cannot get eviction of the tenant even after such determination. The tenant continues to be so even thereafter. That being so, making out a case under the Rent Act for eviction of the tenant by itself is sufficient and it is not obligatory to found the proceeding on the basis of determination of lease by issue of notice in accordance with s. 106 of the T.P. Act. It is not correct to say that s. 106 of the T.P. Act, merely providing for determination of a lease either by a lessor or the lessee by giving the requisite notice is an extra protection for eviction. The purpose of the provision is merely to terminate the contract which the overriding Rent Acts do not permit to be terminated. The tenant becomes liable to be evicted and forfeiture comes into play only if he has incurred the liability to be evicted under the State Rent Act, not otherwise".

This observation of the Supreme Court has been followed in the later cases reported in AIR 1980 SC 1756 and AIR 1982 SC 783(1). It is also relevant to mention in this connection that even if the notice mentioned in s. 106 of the T.P. Act, which according to the above observation of the Supreme Court is surplusage, has not been given the notice cannot be regarded as a bad notice as the notice specifically mentioned that it was a notice given under s. 13(6) of the West Bengal Premises Tenancy Act 1956 [s. 6(4) of the 1997 Act].

Even if the notice is taken as it is, still the notice cannot be held to be legally invalid or insufficient. It has been held that a notice is to be viewed not with the purpose of giving it a meaning which will invalidate it but with the purpose of seeing that the notice be properly interpreted as valid. Reference may be made in this connection to the observation of the Supreme

14 *P. Kannaswamy* v *B.L. Sankaranarayana Shetty* AIR 1977 Kant 72; *Ganga Dutt* v *Kartick Chanda Das* AIR 1961 SC 1067.

15 AIR 1979 SC 1745; (1981)2 SCC 535.

Court in AIR 1977 SC 1120 at p. 1122, where Bhagawati, J., in the case of *Bhagwandas Agarwalla* v *Bhagwandas Kanu* has said:

> "Now it is settled law that a notice to quit must be construed not with a desire to find faults in it, which would render it defective, but it must be construed *ut res magis valeat quam pereat*."[16]

8 Notice to quit under s. 106, T.P. Act—cases where there is a "contract to the contrary"—general observations

Where a lease is expressly made determinable by the lessor without any previous notice or where a lease is expressed to be determinable by notice but the notice is not of the kind required by this section, there is a 'contract to the contrary' within the meaning of s. 106. Where the contract is for a notice of one month for a monthly tenancy, or a Kabuliyat providing for two months' notice, contract for two months' notice in lease of homestead land, contractual notice not expiring with the month of the tenancy or any stipulation modifying the period of notice enjoined in s. 106 are illustrations of a 'contract to the contrary'. In the matter of a monthly tenancy where there is a contract governing the question of notice to terminate tenancy, the intention of the parties has to be ascertained from the contract.[17] Section 106 does not apply to it.[18] And, in such cases, s. 106 shall not apply.[19] But the contract must be a lawful contract. If it is no lawful contract the provisions of s. 106 will apply and regulate the duration of a lease.[20] When the tenancy is created by way of unregistered document three months' prior notice for termination of tenancy is not necessary.[21]

Contract to the contrary—term in original lease-deed that no notice under s. 106 would be necessary. This term will also hold good in the case of a new contract of lease formed by the tenant's holding over.[1] The Supreme Court observed in *Samir Mukherjee* v *Davinder K. Bajaj,* s. 106 lays down a rule of construction which is to apply when the parties have not specifically agreed upon as to whether the lease is yearly or monthly. On a plain reading of this section it is clear that the legislature has classified leases in two categories according to the purposes and this section would be attracted to construe the duration of valid lease in the absence of a

16 Quoted in *Bal Kissen Shaw* v *Kanupada Bhowmick* AIR 1985 Cal 129.

17 *Samir Mukherjee* v *Davinder K. Bojaj* (2001)5 SCC 259; AIR 2001 SC 1696.

18 *Aruanchala Naicker* v *Ghulam Md. Saheb* AIR 1951 Mad 408; *K. Nashir Basa* v *Turukkan Chatran* AIR 1976 Mad 120.

19 (1995)5 SCC 314.

20 *Ram Kumar Das* v *Jagadish Chandra Deo* AIR 1952 SC 23.

21 *Lakshmi Narayan Gupta* v *Secretary, Khadi Gramodyog Vikas Mandal, Buddhanpur* AIR 1914 Utr 14.

1 *Dayal Chand* v *Union of India* AIR 1971 Punj 23; *Chiranjit Lal* v *Narain Singh* AIR 1972 P&H 432.

contract or local usage to the contrary. Where the parties by a contract have indicated the duration of a lease, this section would not apply. What the section does is to prescribe the duration of the period of different kinds of leases by legal fiction—leases for agricultural or manufacturing purposes shall be deemed to be lease from year to year and all other leases shall be deemed to be from month to month. Existence of a valid lease is a prerequisite to invoke the rule of construction embodied in s. 106 of the Transfer of Property Act.[2]

9 Notice to quit under s. 106, T.P. Act

There are generally five types of cases of lease which contemplate a "contract to the contrary" as envisaged in s. 106 of T.P. Act.

Those are:

(*i*) lease for a term certain;

(*ii*) lease for life;

(*iii*) perpetual lease;

(*iv*) tenancy-at-will; and

(*v*) lease for an indefinite period.

(i) *Lease for a term certain*

A lease for a term certain is a lease in which there is a contract to the contrary within the meaning of s. 106. Thus, where a "contract period" is fixed as the "term of lease", there would be a contract to the contrary within the meaning of the aforesaid section and s. 106 will not apply in such cases.[3] In such a case the lease will automatically come to an end by efflux of time limited thereby. A notice under s. 106 will not be necessary.[4] Where a period of lease and the length of notice have been fixed by the parties, there being a contract to the contrary, s. 106 will not apply.[5] Recent decisions also lend support to earlier views as noticed above.[6]

A lease was granted for residential use for one year. Rent was accepted for period beyond that. *Held*, a fresh lease from month to month was created. Suit to eject without a notice to quit is invalid.[7]

2 *Samir Mukherjee* v *Davinder K. Bajaj* AIR 2001 SC 1696; (2001)5 SCC 259.

3 *Kundan Lal* v *Deepchand* AIR 1933 All 756.

4 78 IC 446; 44 IC 212; 90 IC 43; *Modern Hotel, Gudur* v *K. Radhakrishnaiah* AIR 1989 SC 1510.

5 AIR 1955 All 679.

6 *Shanti Devi* v *Amal Kumar Banerjee* AIR 1981 SC 157; *M. Vijayalakshmi* v *G. Goverdhan Reddy* (1997)11 SCC 358.

7 *Promode Das* v *Dharmadutta Sarma* AIR 1978 Gau 95.

Even though there was a provision for renewal on request of the tenant, even after the expiry of lease no renewal was made, but the tenant was paying rent and the landlord was accepting it. The tenancy which was governed by the Transfer of Property Act was held to be a tenancy from month to month terminable with notice of 30 days as provided in s. 106 of the Transfer of Property Act as amended by U.P. State Amendment enhancing the period of notice from 15 days to 30 days. As it was not tenancy either for manufacturing purposes or for agricultural purposes, six months' notice is not necessary to be given.[8]

Lease of building for business for three months. The lessee was required to surrender possession after expiry of the period on demand by the lessor. Lessee was to pay certain amount of rent if he continued in possession. The lessor is entitled to recover possession during such continuance without quit notice under s. 106 (a case of "contract to the contrary", "tenancy-at-will").[9]

STATUTORY TENANT

No notice is required under s. 106 of the Transfer of Property Act to determine the statutory tenancy.[10]

In contractual tenancy lease expired by efflux of time—payment and acceptance of contractual rent or statutory rent—status of tenant holding over not acquired—notice under s. 106 not necessary.[11] When a term of tenancy expires by efflux of time no question of statutory notice under s. 106 of T.P. Act would arise.[12] Payment and acceptance of rent from statutory tenant governed by State Rent Control Act after determination of tenancy by notice to quit does not amount to waiver of notice to quit.[13]

A clause in the lease providing for liability to surrender and right to evict in the event of default in rent is a contract to the contrary and gets incorporated even in the tenancy by holding over and exempts the landlord from issuing a notice to quit.[14]

Similarly, such a lease for a term certain cannot be determined before the end of the term fixed by a notice to quit.[15]

8 *Central Bank of India* v *Monohar Lal* AIR 1998 All 235.
9 *Devaki* v *Alavi* AIR 1979 Ker 108.
10 *V. Dhanpal Chettiar* v *Yesodai Ammal* AIR 1979 SC 1745; *Babubhai* v *Shah Bharatkumar Ratilal* AIR 1980 Guj 89.
11 *Ganga Dutt Murarka* v *Kartick Chandra Das* AIR 1961 SC 1067.
12 AIR 1964 SC 451; AIR 1962 Raj 100; AIR 1963 Raj 113. Contra *Punjalal* v *Bhagwat Prasad* AIR 1963 SC 120; *Mangilal* v *Sugan Chand Rathi* AIR 1965 SC 101; *Manujendra Dutta* v *Purnendu Prasad Roy* AIR 1967 SC 1419; *Parshotanlal* v *Kalayan Singh* AIR 1971 J&K 20.
13 *Ganga Dutt Murarka* v *Kartick Chandra Das* AIR 1961 SC 1067; *Mangilal* v *Sugan Chand Rathi* AIR 1965 SC 101; *Bhawarji* v *Himatlal* AIR 1972 SC 819.
14 *Jacob Philip* v *S.B. of Travancore* AIR 1973 Ker 51.
15 53 IC 109.

(ii) *Lease for life*

A lease for life is a lease granted to the lessee to subsist during the latter's lifetime. It determines on his death.

A lease for lifetime of the tenant is a lease where there is a 'contract to the contrary'. Naturally, a lease of this type cannot be determined by a mere notice to quit under this section. Moreover, such a notice will not be necessary for bringing a suit for ejectment against the tenant's representative, where the lease had terminated on the death of the tenant.[16]

(iii) *Perpetual lease*

Section 106 of the T.P. Act 1882, enjoins that a lease of immovable property may be made for a "certain time" or "in perpetuity". That is, it provides, amongst others, perpetual lease. Clear and unambiguous language would be required to infer such a lease. If the language is ambiguous the court would opt for the interpretation of the plea of the perpetual lease.[17]

A perpetual lease is not determinable by a notice under this section (s. 106),[18] inasmuch as there is a contract to the contrary in a perpetual lease within the meaning of this section. As a result, s. 106 does not apply.

(iv) *Tenancy-at-will*

Where in a lease the agreement between the parties is that the tenancy may be determined by either party and at any time the tenancy in such a case is tenancy-at-will. In such a case there is clearly a contract to the contrary.

Section 106 of the T.P. Act has no application at all to a case of tenancy-at-will.[19] Where the tenants undertake to give vacant possession of the premises whenever the landlords may desire them do so, the tenancy so created is a tenancy-at-will. In a case like that, no notice within the meaning of s. 106 is at all necessary to terminate the tenancy.[1] Though a notice under s. 106 will not be necessary,[2] nevertheless a tenancy-at-will can be determined by a notice to quit.[3] When a tenancy is terminable at the will of the tenant it must be held to be terminable at the will of the landlord also. It is not necessary to give the tenants a notice to quit in order to become entitled to

16 ILR 18 Bom 256; 7 CLJ 90; (1995)1 SCC 560.

17 *State of UP* v *Lalji Tandon (dead)* 2003(1) SCW 5559; *Laxmidas Bapudas Darbar* v *Rudravva (Smt)* (2001)7 SCC 409; AIR 2001 SC 3738.

18 ILR 9 Mad 307; 13 IA 32.

19 AIR 1959 J&K 87; *Uda Ram* v *Taj Karan* AIR 1975 Raj 147.

1 AIR 1964 Raj 79.

2 *Ram Rachhya Singh* v *Kumar Kamakhya* AIR 1925 Pat 256; *Sudhir Kumar* v *Dhirendra Nath* AIR 1957 Cal 625; AIR 1952 Kutch 13; AIR 1933 Pat 561; *Bansidhar* v *Ram Charan* AIR 1940 Oudh 401; *Sudhirkumar* v *Dhirendranath* 61 CWN 23.

3 AIR 1928 Cal 279.

obtain a decree of ejectment and damages for occupation.[4] Notice in such a type of lease is optional. Even where a notice is given, it need not comply with the requirement of s. 106 of the T.P. Act. Such a notice need not be for the period as provided in s. 106 of the Transfer of Property Act. A reasonable notice will be quite sufficient to determine the tenancy.[5] Five months' notice was held reasonable.[6]

A tenancy-at-will is ordinarily determined by the death of the tenant or the landlord.[7] A verbal demand for possession is sufficient.[8]

Tenancy of premises is terminable at will of landlord on mere demand for possession. Notice under s. 106 is not necessary because it is a contract in terms contrary to the operative part of s. 106 of the T.P. Act.[9] A stipulation in the lease deed that the tenant shall surrender on demand is a stipulation to show that the tenancy was at will and no notice under s. 106 is needed.[10]

It should be borne in mind that where Provincial Rent Control Acts enjoin issue of a notice, the provision is mandatory and must have to be followed even if a notice under s. 106 of the T.P. Act is not required.

Contract to the contrary cannot be read in an oral lease of house with a term requiring the tenant to 'vacate without protest whenever the landlord asks him to do so'. Therefore, notice under s. 106 is necessary for eviction in such a case.[11]

(v) *Lease for an indefinite period*

A lease in which no definite term is fixed may be termed as a lease for an indefinite period. Such a lease may contain a term how the lease is to be determined without specifying the period. That is, the lease is likely to continue as long as either of the parties desired. This uncertainty about the period of lease makes the lease a lease for an indefinite period.

A lease in which no definite term was fixed and which contained a clause enabling the parties to determine it by 15 days' notice cannot be said to be a lease for a definite period.[12] In a lease for an indefinite period the lessor may serve a notice to quit but the lessee refuses—the lessor then brings a suit for ejectment. *Held*, the lessee had lease for life and the lessor was not entitled to eject him that way.[13]

4 *Indu Bhusan Bose* v *Choudhary* v *Hari Bhajan Singh* AIR 1976 Pat 282. Also see *Narain Kumar* v *Onkar Nath Agrawal* AIR 1973 All 257.
5 AIR 1918 Cal 355.
6 *Ramanlal* v *Bhagwandas* AIR 1950 All 583.
7 AIR 1938 Nag 650; *Anwarali* v *Jamm Lall Roy* AIR 1940 Cal 89; AIR 1925 Pat 256.
8 *Janki* v *Kanhaiyalal* AIR 1936 Oudh 102; AIR 1957 Cal 625.
9 *Maharaj Singh* v *Prem Narain* AIR 1980 MP 117.
10 *Devaki* v *Alavi* AIR 1979 Ker 108 (FB); *V. Sidharthan* v *Pattiori* AIR 1984 Ker 181.
11 *Fakir Charan Das* v *Satchidananda Rajguru* AIR 1972 Ori 26.
12 AIR 1961 AP 1.
13 AIR 1926 Cal 379; (1978)4 SCC 1.

10 Notice to quit where there is a "law to the contrary"

Where determination of a lease is governed by provisions other than those of the Transfer of Property Act or, in other words, where the provisions of a statute militate against the provisions of s. 106 of the T.P. Act, s. 106 will not apply or where the right of a landlord to eject his tenant after determining his tenancy under the general law is interrupted by temporary enactments, there is a 'law to the contrary' within the meaning of s. 106 of the T.P. Act. It has nowhere been held that by virtue of the provisions of the Rent Act, the contract of term lease is completely obliterated in all respects. The effect of the Rent Act on tenancy under contract has been considered only to a limited extent, confirming it to the necessity of giving notice under s. 106 of the T.P. Act: *Laxmidas Bapudao Darbar* v *Rudrawa (Smt.)*.[14] A few illustrations would explain:

(*i*) When an order has been made under s. 6(2) or 6(3) of the Bengal Suppression of Immoral Traffic Act 1933, [now repealed by the Immoral Traffic (Prevention) Act 1956] the landlord becomes entitled to determine the tenancy immediately notwithstanding s. 106 of the T.P. Act as such power is given to the landlord under sub-sec. (8) which operates notwithstanding anything contained in any other law for the time being in force.[15]

(*ii*) The Bihar Buildings (Lease, Rent and Eviction) Control Act 1947 is a complete Act in itself. This Act and the T.P. Act are distinct and their provisions should be applied independently and a tenancy governed by the Act has to be dealt with under the provisions of the said Provincial Act.[16]

11 Notice to quit where there is a "usage to the contrary"

Where there is a usage to the contrary, the provisions of s. 106 of the T.P. Act do not apply.

The general principle has been observed in a reported case of *Prosanno Coomaree Debya* v *Sheikh Rutton Bepary*.[17] The presumption as to the duration of a tenancy and its mode of determinability under this section will not apply to cases where there is a usage to the contrary. Where local custom requires a monthly tenancy to be determined by a month's notice, it need not be served in the manner prescribed by s. 106 of the T.P. Act.[18] According to a local custom in Bombay, one month's notice to quit, instead of 15 days'

14 (2001)3 SCC 409.
15 ILR 1 Cal 404.
16 AIR 1956 Pat 305.
17 ILR 3 Cal 696.
18 AIR 1927 Sind 24.

notice required by s. 106 of the T.P. Act, will probably be necessary to determine a tenancy of buildings in the city of Bombay.[19]

12 Transfer of leasehold premises—date of commencement of tenancy—notice of termination

The true date of the commencement of the tenancy-month after transfer of leased premises is the date of tenancy which was in force between the tenant and the previous owner, in the absence of any evidence to suggest that the date was altered.[20]

Calcutta view

Where the rented premises are transferred by the landlord to another and the purchaser accepts the monthly rent from the tenant, a new tenancy is established between the tenant and the new landlord from the date of the transfer of premises for the purpose of s. 106.

Thus, where the date of transfer was 20th September 1965, the month of tenancy is from 20th of each month to 19th of the following month. Notice expiring on the 31st of the following month will not terminate the tenancy.[21]

A quit notice is issued by one of the transferees of a lessor *vis-a-vis* his portion only. It is not invalid since a lease always becomes severed *pro tanto* on transfer of part of the property.[22]

13 Form and contents of a notice to quit (s. 106, T.P. Act)

Section 106 of the T.P. Act does not enjoin any particular form or language. It may be said that no hard and fast rule or technical formula can be laid down about the language of a notice under s. 106. The precise words are immaterial provided the notice terminates the tenancy, i.e. it expresses a clear and unequivocal intention to terminate it.[1] All the surrounding circumstances will be considered including any previous correspondences between the parties.[2]

A notice under s. 106 should be a signed notice. It may be signed by a party personally or by his authorised agent.[3] Section 106(1) enjoins: "Every notice .... must be in writing, signed by or on behalf of the person giving it........." An unsigned notice merely bearing the typed name of the landlord will not do.[4] A notice bearing facsimile signature will not be valid. A notice

19 *Mahomedally Ebrahimji Leheri* v *Abdul Kazim* AIR 1925 Bom 167 (*per* Marten, J.); (1988)3 SCC 44; (1977)2 SCC 646.
20 *P. Ratnam Yeshwantraj* v *Vimal Chandra Shiv Data Grover* AIR 1973 Bom 111; *Mohan Lal* v *Vijay Narain* AIR 1961 Raj 136 rel. on.
21 *Bimalendu Bhusan Dass* v *Firm Mitra & Ghosh* AIR 1973 Cal 515.
22 *Subhash Chandra* v *Radhavallabh Saligram* AIR 1972 MP 206.
1 *Sushila* v *Manohar* AIR 1955 All 323.
2 *Sundar Lal* v *Ramkrishnan* AIR 1960 All 544.
3 AIR 1915 Cal 313; *Bhagwana* v *Shib Sametri* AIR 1925 All 199.
4 AIR 1951 All 483.

should be signed either by the person who gives the notice or by a person who signed on behalf of the person giving the notice. Where the landlords are two brothers, a notice of ejectment signed by the son of one of the brothers on behalf of the father and uncle is a valid notice.[5]

Coming to the contents of a notice, a notice should state only the intention to terminate the lease. It need not specify the grounds on which the landlord wants to determine the lease.[6] Section 13(6) of the West Bengal Premises Tenancy Act 1956 [now s. 6(4) of the 1997 Act] speaks of the necessity of issuing a month's notice, expiring with a month of the tenancy, but it does not suggest what should be the contents of the notice contemplated therein.

To be brief, by the notice under s. 106 of the T.P. Act the landlord must manifest his intention to the tenant that from a certain date the relationship of the landlord and the tenant should come to an end. Whether this was the intention or not by the giving of a particular notice will, by and large, depend on the tenor of the notice.[7]

Where a notice to quit the premises gave a date which according to the landlord was the date of expiry of the monthly tenancy and when it also gave an alternative date which was either earlier or later, it could not be said that the notice was vague or indefinite or incapable of being understood. The question whether a notice was vague would depend on whether upon its fair and reasonable construction the tenant was left by its terms in any doubt as to its intended effect.[8]

14 Object and interpretation of a notice to quit—principles of the maxim "ut res magis valeat quam pereat"

A notice to quit must be a clear and unambiguous intimation to the lessor or lessee, as the case may be, of the intention of the party giving the notice that the lease will terminate from a certain date. Though, as submitted above, no particular form is necessary, there must be no uncertainty or ambiguity in the notice on the point of the party's intention.[9] Expression of the intention of the lessor to terminate is the principal element.[10]

A notice has to be construed as a whole and not by reading one word in isolation.[11]

5 1952 Raj LW 400.
6 *Amarendra Nath* v *Bhibu Bhushan* AIR 1952 Cal 773.
7 *Hiranand* v *Umaid Raj* AIR 1973 Raj 120.
8 *Chotelal Barnual* v *Bhuneswar Prasad* AIR 1972 Pat 359.
9 7 All 899 (FB).
10 AIR 1965 Pat 311.
11 *Bipat* v *First Additional District Judge, Gonda* AIR 1980 All 142. Also see *Abdul Jalil* v *Haji Adbul Jalil* AIR 1974 All 402.

A notice to quit should not be construed with a view to finding fault with it but with a view to its validity.[12] The validity of a notice to quit ought not to turn on the splitting of a straw.[13] A notice to quit must not be interpreted too technically or in a spirit of hair-splitting.[14] Perhaps the reported case of *Harihar Banerjee* v *Ram Sashi Roy*[15] opened the door of liberal interpretation: "Notices to quit, though not strictly accurate or consistent in the statements embodied in them, may still be good and effective in law. The test of their sufficiency is not what they would mean to a stranger ignorant of all the facts and circumstances touching the holding to which they purport to refer, but what they would mean to tenants presumably conversant with all those facts and circumstances. Further, notices to quit are to be construed not with a desire to find faults in them which would render them defective but to be construed *ut res magis valeat quam pereat* (that an act may prevail rather than perish)". Yet another illustration is provided in a case reported in AIR 1963 All 54: "The object of the notice under s. 106 is to give the tenant sufficient time to vacate the premises and such a notice should be liberally construed." If the notice is not vague and the tenant understands the implication, it is sufficient.[16]

When there are inaccuracies in the notice the validity of the notice is to be determined not by what they would convey to a stranger ignorant of all the relevant facts and circumstances concerning the disputed tenancy but what they would mean to the tenant who is presumably conversant with all the facts and circumstances of the case.[17] Even if the notice does not strictly comply with the requirement of s. 106, such notice cannot be challenged if the tenant accepts it and acts upon it.[18] Even if the notice be defective, if it has been accepted and acted upon, the party receiving the notice will be estopped from denying its validity.[19]

When the language used in a notice is open to doubt, it is necessary to look at the intention of the landlord and the rule of construction is to make it sensible and not insensible.[20] When an intention to terminate the tenancy

12 AIR 1943 Bom 306; AIR 1931 Mad 352; AIR 1933 Cal 260; AIR 1959 MP 293; AIR 1956 Ass 96; AIR 1952 Nag 104; AIR 1953 Cal 352; *Raja Ram Soni* v *Krishna Prasad Singh* AIR 1973 Gau 17; *Nagrajmal Baid* v *Ram Rati Devi* AIR 1980 NOC 33 (Pat); *Harihar Banerjee* v *Ramsashi Roy* 45 Ind App 222; *Mangilal* v *Suganchand* AIR 1965 SC 101; *Kamalaksha* v *Kesham* AIR 1972 Ker 110.

13 *Sidebotham* v *Holland* [1895]1 QB 378—Quoted in 68 Cal LJ 411; AIR 1931 Mad 352; AIR 1954 Ajmer 62.

14 AIR 1952 Punj 422; (1977)2 SCC 646.

15 *Harihar* v *Ramshashi* AIR 1918 PC 102; (1988)3 SCC 44.

16 AIR 1965 Pat 311.

17 *Bhagabandas Agarwalla* v *Bhagwandas Kanu* AIR 1977 SC 1120; (1977)3 SCR 75; (1977)2 SCJ 43.

18 *Jaggoo* v *Gurmukh Singh* AIR 1974 All 250.

19 *Calcutta Credit Corporation* v *Happy Homes* AIR 1968 SC 471. But cf. *Maduri Satyanarayana* v *S. Veerabhadraswamy* AIR 1990 AP 169.

20 *Tulsiram Shaw* v *RC Pal Ltd.* AIR 1953 Cal 160.

is made out, it is sufficient.[21] The court would give such construction as would not work hardship on the tenant and would not strain the language too much against the landlord.[22] That is, the court interprets prejudicially to none of the parties. Where the language of the notice is such that it is difficult to come to the conclusion that the tenant must necessarily have understood the notice to mean that he was required to hand over possession of the properties upon the expiry of a full and clear year, the landlord cannot ask for interpretation of the notice upon a liberal construction. Benefits of slipshod language cannot be given to the landlord.[23]

(i) *Notice to determine a lease and notice to quit*

The distinction between a notice to determine the lease and a notice to quit is that in the former the notice-giver purports to determine the lease on the expiry of the requisite period and after the expiry of that period the lessee would be bound to quit and, if he does not, he would stay only as a trespasser and in the case of a notice to quit the lessee is required to vacate after the expiry of the requisite period and on the expiry of that period the lease would determine by operation of law under s. 111(*h*) even though the notice does not expressly state about such determination.

(ii) *Contents and form*

Contents of a notice did not specifically terminate the tenancy. The tenant, however, was informed to vacate premises within a month and deliver possession. *Held*, the notice clearly determinates the tenancy and is, therefore, valid.[24]

It is indisputable that under s. 106 of the T.P. Act the notice to quit must expire with the end of the month of the tenancy, or in other words, it must terminate the tenancy with effect from the expiration of the month of the tenancy. If it terminates the tenancy with effect from an earlier date it would be clearly invalid.[1]

The notice to terminate the tenancy must expire with the end of the month of the tenancy. If it terminates the tenancy with effect from an earlier date it would be clearly invalid under s. 106. The notice stated that the tenancy in favour of the tenant was "hereby" terminated and requested the tenant to vacate by the end of the month by which date the tenancy expired failing which appropriate steps for eviction of the tenant would be taken in a court of law. A fair reading of the notice clearly mentions that the plaintiff intended that the lease stood determined by the issue of the notice itself and

21 *Budh Sen* v *Smt. Rahiman* AIR 1978 All 549.
22 AIR 1954 Nag 292.
23 AIR 1956 Bom 113.
24 *Vedpal Singh* v *Harbansh Singh* AIR 1991 All 320 following AIR 1964 All 260.
1 *Bhagabandas* v *Bagwandas* AIR 1977 SC 1120.

thus the plaintiff used words "hereby terminated". Therefore, on a fair construction of the notice it can be concluded that the notice which determines the lease is not according to law and on the other hand, it is in contravention of the provisions of s. 106 read with s. 111(*h*).[2]

The plaintiff claiming to be the owner of an open piece of land claimed that the defendant was his tenant. A notice under s. 106 of the Transfer of Property Act was served whereupon the suit was filed for his eviction. The suit was resisted by the tenant on several grounds, but the main ground was that the defendant was continuing as tenant from the time of the plaintiff's father. It was also contended that since all the heirs had not joined in serving the notice, the plaintiff alone had no right to file the suit or to terminate the tenancy.

Held, that the plaintiff was collecting rent from the tenant. He functioned for all practical purposes as the landlord and notice served by him alone terminating the tenancy was valid.[3]

A notice requiring the lessee to vacate the premises on the expiry of 30 days from the date of receipt of the notice is invalid as it simply contains a demand for possession and does not purport to terminate the tenancy.[4]

At this stage, it is worthwhile to refer to the observations of Dharam, J., in *Ram Swarup* v *Brij Nandan Prasad*:[5] "The nature and purpose of the notice must be gathered by reading the document as a whole and not from any words read out of the context or from any omission to use the formal language of a solicitor. Where the landlord warns the tenant that if he fails to clear the arrears of rent within a month of the receipt of the notice he will be liable to ejectment and in that event he must treat the notice as a 'legal notice' and vacate the accommodation within a month, it is clear that the demand that the tenant should vacate the accommodation signifies the termination of the tenancy and the words 'legal notice' could only refer to a notice under s. 106 of the T.P. Act. I think the notice in this case was effective under s. 106 of the T.P. Act."

A notice under s. 106 of the T.P. Act 1882, must be liberally construed; but no constrained or unnatural meaning must be attributed to the language in order to make an otherwise invalid notice a valid notice.[6]

2 *Yerrabhothula Krishna Murthy* v *Addeplli Subba Rao* AIR 1988 AP 193.
3 *Girraj Kishore* v *Dr. Trilokinath Vimal* AIR 1988 All 305 following *Rangnath* v *State of UP* 1984 All Rent Case 642; *Sri Ram Pasricha* v *Jagannath* AIR 1976 SC 2335; *Kanta Goel* v *B.P. Pathak* AIR 1977 SC 1590.
4 *Abdul Jalil Haji* v *Abdul Jalil* AIR 1974 All 402.
5 AIR 1963 All 366.
6 *Baijnath Pandit* v *Smt. Narmada Devi Kejriwal* AIR 1973 Pat 286.

15 Notice terminating tenancy—tenant's undertaking to vacate—fresh notice not necessary

The landlord by giving one month's notice terminated the tenancy. The tenant accepted the position, but at his request the landlord allowed the tenant to stay in the premises for one more year on the tenant's executing an undertaking that if he failed to vacate within one year he would be treated as a trespasser and liable for eviction without notice. *Held* that the contention of the tenant that it was an agreement creating a new tenancy could not be upheld. The tenancy had already been terminated by the first notice. The second notice was not necessary before filing of the suit. Therefore, the contention that the second notice is invalid does not arise.[7]

A notice is necessary in the case of tenancy from year to year or from month to month; or where the lessee is holding over.[8] But no notice is necessary in case of a tenancy for a fixed period, which determines by efflux of time;[9] or where the tenancy is at will. Notice is not necessary where the lease is for a period of eleven months;[10] or where the lease is a permanent lease;[11] or where the lease sets up a disclaimer;[12] or where the lease is for a fixed period, which had expired but the lessee was in possession, but there was no assertion of holding over.[13]

16 Defects in a notice to quit—when excusable and when not

There may be defects in a notice to quit which may be in fit circumstances excused: for, every defect is not likely to invalidate a notice. Hereinbelow are a few cases:

(i) *Technical defects and clerical errors*

(1) Technical defects in a notice cannot make it invalid when there is substantial compliance with s. 106 of the T.P. Act.[14]

(2) A lease for one year commenced on Kartick Sudi 2005 S.Y. corresponding to 2.11.48 and, according to the English calendar month of the tenancy, expired on the 1st of the month. The notice to quit expired on 30th April 1950. Strictly speaking, the notice should have expired on the 1st of May. It was held that a clerical error as regards the date which did not mislead would not invalidate the notice.[15]

7 *Dinesh Chandra Chakravorti* v *Mahesh Chandra Roy* AIR 1972 Gau 95.
8 *Abdul Hameed* v *Balakrishna* AIR 1970 Ker 40; *Khadiru* v *Mythean Kunju* AIR 1972 Ker 63.
9 *Pooran Chand* v *Motilal* AIR 1964 SC 461; *Kishan Lal* v *Shivcharan Sharma* AIR 2017 NOC 349 (All).
10 *Harnamjit Singh* v *Hans Raj* 70 Punj LR 467.
11 *Thackerakavil* v *Noor Mohd.* AIR 1922 Mad 349.
12 *Ratneswar* v *Mongoli Chutiani* AIR 1951 Assam 70.
13 *Shanti Devi* v *Amal Kumar Banerjee* AIR 1981 SC 1550; *H. Vijayalakshmi* v *G. Goverdhan Reddy* (1997)11 SCC 358.
14 *Kodali Bapayya* v *Yadavalli Venkataratnam* AIR 1953 Mad 884.
15 6 Sau LR 450; AIR 1938 All 649; AIR 1952 All 141.

(3) When the tenancy is according to the Bengali calendar month and the correct Bengali date is given along with the corresponding date of the English calendar month, but wrongly, such wrong date will not invalidate the notice.

(4) The tenancy commenced from the 22nd of a month and, except the evidence of payment of rent, there was no evidence to prove or establish that the tenancy was at any time thereafter converted from the 1st day of the month. Mere payment of rent according to the Bengali calendar month may be the mode of payment and such payment, without further evidence, in the circumstances of the case, cannot lead the court to hold that the monthly tenancy was according to the Bengali calendar month. Notice according to the Bengali calendar month, *held*, invalid.[16]

(5) Monthly tenancy terminating on the 20th day of the month—notice requiring the tenant to give possession by the end of 21st day of the month is not valid.[17]

(6) Notice terminating the tenancy in question from the midnight of 31st August 1962, or on such date as the tenant thinks the tenancy expires—Notice is valid.[1]

(7) A notice calling upon the tenant to pay arrears of rent within two months and stating that a suit will be filed thereafter is a valid notice both for the purposes of s. 106 of the T.P. Act 1882, and s. 14(1) of the Delhi Rent Control Act 1958 since repealed and replaced by the Delhi Rent Control Act 1995.[2]

(8) Monthly tenancy after holding over to commence on the 2nd day of a month to the 1st day of the following month. Notice calling upon a tenant to deliver possession on the expiry of the month of November 1963 or at the end of a month of his tenancy which would expire next after one month from the receipt of the notice—*Held* notice to quit is good and valid.[3]

(9) Tenancy commencing from the 7th day of every month—Notice to quit expiring not with the expiry of tenancy that is the 6th day of a month but by the 7th—strict view as to the notice to quit has got to be taken—Notice held was bad and there was no determination of tenancy.[4]

(10) Where the landlord after stating that the tenant had failed to pay the rent and the house was being required by the landlord for his personal use, asked the tenant in the notice to quit, to vacate the house, the notice

16 75 CWN 478.
17 *Manjubala Das* v *Pradosh Ranjan Das* AIR 1971 Ass 97.
1 *Madanlal* v *Manak Chand* AIR 1971 Raj 55.
2 *Mangi Lal* v *Sugan Chand Rathi* AIR 1955 SC 101; *Raj Krishen Jain* v *Master Hosiar Singh* AIR 1971 Del 213.
3 *Mahasukrai Ramrichpal* v *Kishori Charan Law* AIR 1977 Cal 122.
4 *K.S. Rangaiah Setty* v *L.S. Vasudeva Murthy* AIR 1977 Kant 50; *Dattonpant Gopalvarao* v *Vithalrao Marutorao* AIR 1975 SC 1111.

would not be invalid merely because it was not specifically stated therein that the tenancy was terminated.[5]

(11) Notice in the alternative asking the tenant to vacate by the end of the month of the tenancy was a good notice.[6] A notice to quit directed the tenant to deliver up possession on the expiry of the 1st day of Kartick, 1376 or alternatively, at the end of the month which would expire next from the date of service of notice. *Held*, the notice was valid.[7]

(12) Lease expiring at midnight of the last day of month. Notice asking to vacate the premises on the morning of the next date is not invalid.[8]

(13) Expression "Expiring with the end of a month of tenancy": Tenancy month expiring on 9th of calendar month. Notice determining tenancy with effect from 10th of a month is valid.[9]

(14) Monthly tenancy: Notice requiring tenant to vacate on or before the last day of the month—notice is valid.[10]

(15) Notice sent on behalf of both landlords, although signed by only one of them. Plaint allegation also shows that it was given on behalf of both. Notice *held*, not defective.[11]

(ii) *Defects of minor omissions*

(16) A notice to quit does not become invalid merely because the particulars as regards the tenancy are not accurately set out in the notice.[12]

(17) A notice terminating the tenancy may include a demand for possession but notice only demanding possession cannot be interpreted as a notice terminating the tenancy.[13]

(18) Repeated notices demanding payment of rent with threat to terminate tenancy but there was no intention to terminate tenancy, such notice not valid.[14]

(19) Date of commencement of tenancy not mentioned in the notice—not invalid.[15]

5 *Mohammad Indris Mian* v *Doman Sah* AIR 1978 Pat 82.
6 *Mahasukrai Ramrichpal* v *Kishori Charan Law* AIR 1977 Cal 122.
7 *Baidyanath Dutta* v *Radheyshyam Dutta* AIR 1979 Cal 97.
8 *Madhusudan Prasad Agarwal* v *Smt. Sushmabala Dasi* AIR 1979 Pat 6.
9 *Dr. Jagdish Lal Chawala* v *Ratan Chand* AIR 1979 MP 186.
10 *Peter Paul* v *Smt. Constance D'Souza* AIR 1980 Kant 28.
11 *Smt. Jamuna Devi* v *Parasham Trivedi* AIR 1980 NOC 98 (All).
12 AIR 1955 Mad 206.
13 AIR 1963 All 581.
14 AIR 1950 All 544.
15 AIR 1955 Cal 615.

(iii) *Defects in signature*

(20) An unsigned notice merely bearing the typed name of the landlord at the end is invalid.[16]

(21) A notice not signed by the lessor or his agent is of no value.[17]

(iv) *Defects in address*

(22) Where the notice to quit, though not properly addressed, was accepted by the defendant and he even replied to it, the notice could not be held to be invalid on the mere ground that it was not properly addressed as the defendant was not prejudiced thereby.[18]

(23) Where instead of addressing the quit notice to a limited company which was the tenant it was addressed to a person who was the Managing Director himself and the name of the company was written after the name of the managing director with a 'limited' appended after the name and the notice was treated by the addressee and the company as a notice to the company itself—the notice was held valid.[19]

(v) *Defects of misdescription of leasehold property*

(24) A tenancy can be determined only as a whole or not at all. It cannot be determined piecemeal.[20]

(25) A notice to quit with reference to a portion of the holding is bad.[1]

(26) Under s. 111(*h*) of the T.P. Act, a notice must be in respect of the 'property leased'. Splitting up of tenancy is not permissible by the unilateral act of the landlord. Tenancy can be terminated only in its entirety and not partially. Unless the notice under s. 106 of the Act intends and purports to terminate the entire tenancy, it cannot be a valid notice and the tenant cannot be asked to vacate the premises leased.[2]

(27) Where the tenant was occupying Flats Nos. 3 and 3A—notice to quit mentioning, Flat No. 3 only—Receipts and correspondences showing that both parties understood that tenant was vacating entire premises—*Held*, in spite of the fact that there was slight misdescription, the notice was sufficient and legal.[3]

(28) Where there were two leases of the same property but one was invalid and the plaintiff gave a notice to quit in respect of the invalid lease, it was held that the defendant was not misled and prejudiced. The notice,

16 AIR 1951 All 483.
17 AIR 1951 Ori 262.
18 AIR 1956 All 187.
19 AIR 1953 Cal 160.
20 33 Cal LJ 518; 86 Cal LJ 198.
1 AIR 1939 Cal 291.
2 *Ghasi Ram* v *Jagat Narain* AIR 1976 All 221.
3 AIR 1953 Cal 585.

therefore, could be considered a proper notice terminating the only lease that bound the parties in jural relationship.[4]

(vi) *Notice to quit with fresh terms and conditions*

(29) A notice to quit is not bad merely because it provides that if the tenant fails to vacate the property by the date fixed in the notice, he will be liable for damages at a certain rate.[5]

(30) Where a notice clearly expresses an intention to terminate a lease by a certain date, the mere fact that it is coupled with an intimation that if the lessee continued in possession after such date he would be liable for enhanced rent does not make the notice bad.[6] Again, where a notice to quit clearly conveys the intention to terminate the lease by a certain date, the mere fact that the notice provides for its abandonment in case the other party agrees to an enhancement or reduction of the rent does not affect the validity of the notice.[7]

(vii) *Contra*

(31) A notice giving the lessee an option either to vacate the property by a certain date or to pay enhanced rent from such date will be bad.[8] A notice which merely informs the lessee that if he wants to keep the premises after a certain date, he has to pay enhanced rent at a certain rate is bad.[9] "The notice terminating the tenancy must be unconditional, unequivocal and clear, that is to say, a tenant whose tenancy is intended to be terminated and who is asked to quit has no power left to arrest the effect of it and a tenancy must stand terminated on the expiry of the notice period. But in a case where before the expiry of the notice period and before the tenancy actually comes to an end the tenant is offered some alternative or some condition on the compliance of which the existing tenancy continues even though on modified terms—such a notice would not be unequivocal, unambiguous and a clear notice to quit."[10]

(32) A notice under s. 106 of the T.P. Act, to a person through whom the tenant is inducted, is not a notice to a tenant.[11]

17 Other illustrations of valid and invalid notices

(1) A notice under s. 106 stating that the landlord was no longer willing to continue tenancy and that the tenant should vacate the premises on expiry

4 *V. Kamalaksha Pai* v *Keshava Bhatta* AIR 1972 Ker 110.
5 12 CWN 1059; AIR 1925 All 199.
6 AIR 1921 Pat 334.
7 AIR 1935 Bom 247; 2 IC 548.
8 ILR 11 Cal 533.
9 16 CLJ 561.
10 AIR 1965 All 323.
11 *Parshotam Lal* v *Kalayan Singh* AIR 1971 J&K 20.

of 30 days failing which a suit for ejectment would be filed the notice conveys intention to terminate the tenancy. It is a valid notice.

Even assuming that the notice was invalid, since it was accepted and acted upon by the party to whom it was given, the tenancy would be determined.[12]

(2) Where the landlord after requiring the tenant to pay arrears of rent within one month from date of service of notice proceeds to add in the notice 'failing which suit for ejectment will be filed'—*Held*, that the recitals clearly indicate the intentions of the landlord to terminate the tenancy of the tenant and such notice is valid.[13]

(3) A notice purporting to terminate the monthly tenancy on and from the last date of the month and requiring delivery of possession on or before the last date entitles the tenant to vacate the premises by the midnight of the last day of the month is a good and valid notice.[14]

(4) A notice calling upon the tenant to vacate the premises within one month of its service will be a notice within the provisions of s. 106.[15]

(5) A composite notice demanding arrears of rent and terminating the tenancy is not bad.[16]

(6) If it is only for vacation of the premises and not for termination of the tenancy—it is invalid.[17]

(7) Section 106 does not obviate the necessity of terminating the tenancy either in express or implied terms. A mere mention of s. 106 in the notice without there being a recital express or implied terminating the tenancy of the person to whom the notice is addressed, is not sufficient in law to bring about the termination of tenancy.[18]

18 Period in a notice to quit under s. 106, T.P. Act (As stood prior to the amendment—see note 1)

Section 106 of the Transfer of Property Act mentions three kinds of leases—(*a*) lease of immovable property for agricultural purposes; (*b*) lease of immovable property for manufacturing purposes—where the period of notice is six months expiring with the end of a year of the tenancy and (*c*) a lease of immovable property for any other purpose, the period of notice is 15 days expiring with the end of the month of tenancy.

12 *Smt. Jagoo* v *Sardar Gurmuk Singh* AIR 1974 All 250.
13 *Syed Mohd. Ibne Ali* v *Smt. Janab Begum* AIR 1974 All 195.
14 *Baijnath Pandit* v *Smt. Narvada Devi Kejariwal* AIR 1973 Pat 286.
15 *Suraj Prasad* v *Smt. Krisunlata Singh* AIR 1973 All 198.
16 *Suraj Prasad* v *Smt. Krisunlata Singh* AIR 1973 All 198.
17 *Kamta Prasad* v *Smt. Om Wati* AIR 1972 All 155.
18 *Sundar Lal* v *Yaqoob Ali* AIR 1979 NOC 38 (All).

The notice is statutory in character. The period of a notice to quit under s. 106 may be for a longer period than six months or 15 days as the case may be—no harm.[19] But the period of notice if shorter than required, such a notice will not be sufficient to terminate the lease,[20] and it is not curable.[1]

The notice must be of clear six months or 15 days as the case may be.[2] The day on which the notice is served must be excluded but not the day on which the tenancy is purported to be terminated.[3]

The day on which the notice is received by the tenant has to be excluded in counting 30 days—s. 106 of the T.P. Act 1882, has to be interpreted independently of ss. 9 and 10 of the General Clauses Act 1897.[4]

Another point is to be borne in mind: the notice under s. 106 must expire with the end of a year or a month of tenancy as the case may be. A notice, therefore, which does not expire with the end of a year or with the month of a tenancy will be invalid under s. 106 of the T.P. Act.[5] A notice under s. 106 terminating a lease dated 31st March 1951 is invalid as it did not expire with 31st March 1955,[6] but see illustration (3) in Note 16 above. Again, a notice terminating a lease not by midnight of the last day but at some time in the evening of the last day—bad in law.[7] Where a notice to quit does not expire with the end of a year or a month of tenancy, the mere fact that the notice is for a longer period than is required under this section will not invalidate the notice.[8]

19 Notice in case of minor landlord

It is settled law that a minor has no legal competency to enter into a contract or authorise another to do so on his behalf. A guardian has to step into and supplement the minor's defective capacity. Such a guardian can function within the doctrine of legal necessity or benefit and the validity of the transaction is judged with reference to the scope of his power to enter into a contract on behalf of the minor.[9]

A tenancy may commence from any day of a particular month or year.[10] It need not necessarily begin with the first day of the month or the year. The

19 AIR 1932 PC 279; AIR 1961 MP 232; AIR 1960 MP 134; AIR 1953 Cal 349.
20 AIR 1929 Nag 274.
1 AIR 1949 PC 90.
2 AIR 1960 MP 134.
3 AIR 1915 Cal 313; AIR 1951 Amjer 52.
4 *Shiv Narain* v *Chandrika Prasad* AIR 1973 All 155.
5 AIR 1944 Cal 84; AIR 1958 All 879.
6 AIR 1957 Cal 357.
7 AIR 1945 Pat 463.
8 AIR 1944 Cal 84; AIR 1923 Cal 524; contra AIR 1966 MP 206.
9 *Rajiv Nath Agarwal* v *Ankur Agarwal* 2005(1) Rent LR 459; 2004 All LJ 4194; 2005(1) RCR (Rent) 166; 2005 AIHC 684.
10 AIR 1950 Cal 19; AIR 1955 Raj 167.

month or year of tenancy has to be calculated with reference to the date of commencement of the tenancy in question.[11] It may be according to the English or Bengali or Samvat calendar month, and so on, according to terms of a particular tenancy.

Contra: See *Fakiragonda S. Patil* v *Smt. Parvatibai.*[12] Month to month tenancy notice given by the landlord to vacate by the end of December 1972 and before the beginning of January 1973, *held* invalid as the tenant was not given the full day of 31st December and hence did not end with the month of tenancy.[13]

20 Period in a notice—modes how month and year counted (As stood prior to the amendment—see note 1)

A few illustrations from reported cases would help us appreciate the modes of counting the period. Those are:

(*i*) A notice under s. 106 asking the tenant to vacate "within 30 days." It was contended that the notice was not a clear one month's notice. Dharam, J., *held*: "There is no difference between a notice asking a tenant to vacate, because in both cases, the time allowed expired on the midnight of the 30th day but not beyond it." The notice was valid.[14]

(*ii*) If there is a monthly tenancy it should end "with the end of the month of the tenancy" which would expire at midnight of the last day. "If there is a monthly tenancy and it commences from the 1st of July of the English calendar month, there can be no dispute that the end of the month of the tenancy be the 31st of July for the purpose of notice under s. 106. Consequently, when the landlord asked the tenant to vacate the suit premises on the 31st of July 1960, their intention was to give the tenant time till the midnight of 31st July 1960 to vacate the premises. It could not, therefore, be said that it was an invalid notice which did not expire with the end of a month of the tenancy as required by s. 106."—Notices expiring on the last day and those expiring on the next day—both valid, thus leaving out of account the fraction of day.[15]

(*iii*) A notice to quit on the tenant asking him to vacate the premises "within 30 days" of the service of notice—*Held* that the words used in the notice asking the tenant to vacate the premises within 30 days from the date of service of the notice only fixed the outer limit by which the tenant must vacate. The limit fixed was the last

11 AIR 1944 Cal 84; AIR 1953 Ass 202.
12 AIR 1977 Kant 112.
13 *Dattonpat Gopalvarao Devkate* v *Vithalrao Marutirao* AIR 1975 SC 1111 followed.
14 AIR 1964 All 416.
15 AIR 1965 MP 140.

moment of the 30th day of the notice and the notice so construed was strictly according to the letter and spirit of the law and was valid.[16]

(*iv*) The expression 'month' for the purpose of s. 106 of the T.P. Act means the calendar month [vide s. 3(35) of the General Clauses Act]. As in the instant case, the tenancy was a monthly tenancy commencing from the 30th of a particular month, the last day of the monthly tenancy would be 29th of the next month. Hence, the contention was that the notice should have expired on the 29th February 1935. But as the year 1955 was not a leap year and there was no date as 29th February in that year, the notice purported to expire by the midnight of the 28th February 1955 was held a valid notice to quit.[17]

Where a tenant, who enters into the premises in the middle of a quarter by agreement, pays a proportionate rent for the broken quarter and afterwards on the regular quarter days the tenancy is deemed to commence on the first day of such quarter days which follows his entry and a notice to quit must be given accordingly.

In the instant case, the tenant entered into the tenancy on 14th February, paid rent for the broken period and thereafter the rent was paid according to English calendar month. *Held*, the tenancy commenced on the 1st day of the calendar month and a notice to quit terminating the tenancy on the last day of September was valid.[18] The mention of English calendar month in notice instead of Bangla calendar month cannot disentitle the lessor for a decree of evictions, if otherwise entitled to it.[19] A suit which was filed before delivery of possession by the tenant is maintainable.[20]

(*v*) Notice determining tenancy from the 1st day of the month in respect of a tenancy commencing on the 2nd day of the month is valid.[1]

(*vi*) Tenancy for residential purposes commencing on 18th of a month—notice to quit on the 18th of the following month instead of 17th is not invalid.[2]

(*vii*) A notice to vacate premises on or before 1st October 1950 given on 12th September 1950 is invalid.[3]

16 AIR 1964 All 260; (2002)6 SCC 331.
17 AIR 1962 Ori 140.
18 *Lalbhai Ramjibhai* v *A.V. Seth* AIR 1974 Cal 362.
19 *Ganga Sen* v *Biswanath Gupta* AIR 1981 Pat 180.
20 *Sheela Jawarlal Nagori* v *Kantilal Nathmal Baldota* AIR 2014 SC (Supp) 1689.
1 AIR 1961 MP 138; AIR 1954 Nag 292; (1997)5 SCC 329; (2000)1 SCC 10.
2 AIR 1958 All 729; AIR 1956 Nag 125 and AIR 1954 Amjer 62.
3 AIR 1952 Pat 69.

(*viii*) Notice to quit on the next day after the last day of the month is valid.[4]

(*ix*) A notice to quit by the last day of a year of a month of the tenancy is valid.[5]—"On the last day of the English calendar month"—Notice valid.[6]

(*x*) A notice requiring the tenant to vacate immediately on the expiry of a month was held good.[7]

(*xi*) Notice requiring the tenant to give vacant possession by the end of June 1950, held good. The landlord's intention was that the tenant should quit by 30th June and not that the tenant was to quit before midnight of 30th June.[8]

(*xii*) Notice dated 9th November 1951 asking to vacate on expiry of one month from receipt of notice or on expiry of the month according to the defendant's own belief is valid.[9]

The tenant was asked to quit within one month of service of notice under s. 106 of the T.P. Act. One month means a month reckoned according to British calendar. When notice is given month can mean less than 30 days notice in the instant case asking the tenant to quit within one month, i.e. within less than 30 days held not bad.[10]

(*xiii*) A notice asking the tenant to vacate by the expiry of the last day of the tenancy for the month of October—*held*, notice valid.[11] A notice asking the tenant to quit and deliver possession by the end of the month is a valid notice.[12]

21 Who can give a notice to quit under s. 106, T.P. Act—lessor—lessee—co-lessors—co-assigns—receivers—trustees—agents—lawyers, etc.

It is not necessary that a notice has to be served by the landlord personally. His agent,[13] and advocate[14] are competent to issue a notice. Where there are several landlords all must join.[15] Notice by some of the co-owners is not valid.[16] Section 106 provides, *inter alia*, that every notice under the section must be in writing, signed by or on behalf of the person giving it. The test

4 68 CLJ 411.
5 AIR 1937 Nag 139.
6 AIR 1965 Pat 311.
7 AIR 1945 Pat 363.
8 AIR 1965 Ass 96; AIR 1918 PC 102 foll.
9 6 Sau LR 422 (445).
10 *Smt. Ram Kali* v *Sita Ram* AIR 1978 All 546.
11 70 CWN 967.
12 *Natho* v *Sital Prasad Sahu* AIR 1969 Pat 310.
13 65 CWN 1119; (1991)1 SCC 761.
14 1961 ALJ 258; (2000)6 SCC 427.
15 94 CLJ 263.
16 *Mahboobullah* v *Jwala Prasad* AIR 1974 All 413.

to determine the authority for giving notice is whether the notice is such that the tenant may act upon it with safety or, in other words, that it is a notice which is binding on the landlord. In the facts and circumstances proved in the case, it was clear that the actual management of the house was done by the plaintiff's husband. The defendant must be taken to be aware of the fact that the husband of the plaintiff was duly authorised to serve the notice and that the defendant had accepted the authority of the plaintiff's husband.[17]

Notice to quit by joint-lessors: Notice signed by one lessor but mentioning "We give you notice, etc."—Notice held was on behalf of all lessors.[18]

Where the plaintiff claiming himself to be the 'karta' of joint Hindu family and on behalf of joint family issued notice terminating tenancy of defendant when there was no joint family in existence: *Held*, the tenancy could not be determined by one co-owner alone, the notice was invalid.[19]

Where there are two or more co-lessors the tenancy can be put an end to only by the joint action of all co-lessors and the notice to quit must, therefore, be given by or on behalf of all co-lessors.[20]

Notice to quit must be on behalf of all lessors.[1] Property owned by co-sharers. One of them leased out the property. Notice under s. 106 by him alone and a suit for eviction by him alone is maintainable.[2]

Notice served by the landlord enures to the benefit of his successors and binds not only the tenant but also his successors-in-interest.[3] Notice served by a landlord who died after issue of the notice, his successor can bring a suit on the basis of the said notice.

22 To whom a notice to quit under s. 106, T.P. Act has to be given

Tenants-in-common—one notice will do.[4] Joint tenants—one notice addressed to all will do.[5] One notice is sufficient.[6] Contra: See *Ganga Parshad* v

17 *Parvaty Sham Aachary* v *Smt. Manasi Devi* AIR 1977 Ori 139; *Kanakarathanammal* v *V.S. Logonatha Munahire* AIR 1965 SC 271 rel. on.
18 *Madhusudan Prasad Agarwal* v *Smt. Sushma Bala Dasi* AIR 1979 Pat 6.
19 *Brijmohan Das Goyal* v *Smt. Nidhi Bai* AIR 1978 NOC 2 (All).
20 *Abdul Sami* v *Mohammad Ashfaq* AIR 1978 NOC 3 (All).
1 *Jamir Ahmad* v *Madhawnand* AIR 1979 All 104; *Arun Chandra Dowerah* v *Panchu Modak* AIR 1957 Ass 70
2 *Ram Charan Mowar* v *Ved Prakash* AIR 1980 All 27.
3 65 CWN 1009.
4 *Smt. Vishnawati* v *Bhagwat Vithu Chowdhury* AIR 1970 All 389.
5 *Kanji* v *Trustees of Port of Bombay* AIR 1963 SC 268; *Pt. Liladhar Pandey* v *L. Ramji Das* 1956 All LJ 650; *Sai Nath* v *Smt. Saraswati Devi* AIR 1964 All 52; *Roshan* v *Purshattam* AIR 1965 All 287; *Banubai* v *Jairam Sharma* AIR 1964 Bom 96; *Bhisan Chandra Pal* v *Bengal Coal Co. Ltd.* AIR 1966 Cal 63; *Sambhudayal* v *Suteman* AIR 1978 NOC 266 MP; (2003)7 SCC 336; (2002)6 SCC 678; (2002)9 SCC 108.
6 *Abdulahid Moulvi* v *Aulamahmad* AIR 1975 Guj 1; *Ajit Kumar Roy* v *Smt. Satyabala Dutt* AIR 1973 Cal 339; (1995)1 SCC 537; (2001)5 SCC 1; (2000)1 SCC 10.

Smt. Tribeni Devi,[7] a case of co-tenants—separate notice to each is necessary. Where there is evidence that one of the joint tenants paid rent on behalf of all and accepted notice also on behalf of all, the notice on him would be valid.[8] Semble that, where there is no such evidence, the notice must be served on all the heirs of the deceased lessee.[9]

In case of joint-tenancy, notice addressed to one of joint-tenants is valid.[10] When the original tenant dies, his legal heirs inherit the tenancy as joint tenants and occupation of one of the tenants is occupation of all the joint tenants. It is not necessary for the landlord to implead all the legal heirs of the deceased tenant, whether they are occupying the property or not. So, service of eviction notice on one of the legal heirs of the deceased tenant is sufficient service in case of joint tenancy.[11] Whether the lessors be joint tenants or tenants-in-common, notice be given by them all;[12] unless one of them has been acting for all and collecting rent on behalf of all.[13] In other words, if a co-lessor has been collecting rent and for all practical purposes has been functioning as lessor, the notice served by him alone terminating the tenancy would be valid.[14]

Where a notice of determination of tenancy, the purpose of which is to make the persons concerned aware of the purport of the contents of such notice is received by a person who is a constituted attorney of the tenant in respect of leased premises at the material time, such service on the attorney, though made in personal capacity, would amount to a valid notice on the tenant also.[15]

Notice under s. 106 to a partnership firm: The notice on the partnership firm in firm's name determining the tenancy which was in the name of the firm is valid.[16]

23 Notice on the 'Karta' under s. 106, T.P. Act

T.P. Act, s. 106—notice could be served on the *karta* on behalf of all the members—refused by *karta* should be treated as refusal on behalf of all of them. [M.P. Accommodation Control Act (41 of 1961)].[17]

7 *Ganga Prasad* v *Tribeni Devi* AIR 1976 Del 145; (1995)1 SCC 537; 1995 (Supp) 3 SCC 403.
8 *M.C. Pandey* v *G.C. Paul* AIR 1989 SC 1470 overruling *Ramesh Chand Bose* v *Gopeshwar Prasad Sharma* AIR 1977 All 38.
9 *Ganga Prasad* v *Tribeni Devi* AIR 1976 Del 145; *Prayivandas* v *Labhshankar Horgovinddas Bhatt* AIR 1982 Guj 152.
10 *Budh Sen* v *Sheel Chandra Agarwal* AIR 1978 All 88; *Kanji Manji* v *Trustee of the Port of Bombay* AIR 1963 SC 468; *Redhey Lal* v *Bimal Kumar Jain* AIR 1980 All 84.
11 *Suresh Kumar Kohli* v *Rakesh Jain* AIR 2018 SC 2708.
12 *Gopal Ram* v *Dhakeshwar Pershad* ILR 35 Cal 807; *Vagha* v *Manilal* AIR 1935 Bom 262; *Subhash Kumar Lata* v *R.C. Chhiba* AIR 1989 SC 458.
13 *Indu Bhusan Bose* v *Haribhajan Singh* AIR 1976 Pat 282.
14 *Girraj Kishore* v *Triloknath* AIR 1988 All 305.
15 *J. Mc. Gaffin* v *L.I.C. of India* AIR 1978 Cal 123.
16 *Shew Karan Agarwalla* v *Satyanarain Mansinka* AIR 1978 Cal 495.
17 *Budha* v *Bedariya* AIR 1981 MP 76.

24 Death of original tenant—when fresh notice necessary

Where the suit for ejectment against the original tenant has been dismissed by the court, the notice under s. 106 of the T.P. Act, ceases to have effect. The original tenant is then restored to the position of a contractual tenant and is liable to be ejected only after the termination of his tenancy by a fresh notice. That position will enure to the benefits of his heirs as well. They could not be treated as trespassers, and their ejectment could not be sought for without terminating their tenancy by a valid notice.[18]

25 Death of one of co-landlords—if fresh notice is necessary

Where all co-landlords gave notice and one of them died before the expiry of the notice period, the tenants cannot ask for a fresh notice from legal heirs of the deceased.[19]

26 Issue of second notice—if waiver of the first

In *Calcutta Credit Corporation* v *Happy Homes (P) Ltd.*[20] the Supreme Court held that once a notice is served upon the tenant, the tenancy comes to an end on the expiry of the term of the notice and unless consent of the other party is proved to treat the tenancy as subsisting there can be no second notice to quit. Such mutual consent may be express or implied. It is provided that a notice under cl. (*h*) of s. 111 of the Transfer of Property Act is waived, with the express or implied consent of the person to whom it is given by any act on the party of the person giving it showing an intention to treat the lease as subsisting.

Illustration (*b*) of s. 113 of the Act states:

> "*A*, the lessor, gives *B*, the lessee, notice to quit the property leased. The notice expires and *B* remains in possession. *A* gives to *B* as lessee a second notice to quit. The first notice is waived."

The Supreme Court too has held that when a first notice to quit is served on the tenant but he does not act upon such notice and the landlord issues a second notice it amounts to waiver of the first notice and eviction suit can be filed on the basis of the second notice.[21]

27 Service of a notice to quit—various modes of service

A notice under s. 106 of the Transfer of Property Act may be served in one or other of the four modes prescribed by the section itself.

18 *Makhanlal* v *Mrs. Chandrawati* AIR 1976 All 321; (1995)1 SCC 537.
19 *Royal Stationary* v *Azizul Haque* AIR 1973 Cal 363.
20 AIR 1968 SC 471.
21 *Tayeb Ali* v *Asan & Co.* AIR 1971 SC 102; *Mohena Mandal* v *Pusparani* Cal LT 1991(1) HC 380; *Probhes* v *Chanmani* 81 CWN 814; *Chandra Kishori* v *Renuka* 84 CWN 324.

Second paragraph of s. 106 provides that every notice under this section must be in writing signed by or on behalf of the person giving it and either be sent by post to the party who is intended to be bound by it or be tendered or delivered personally to such party or to one of his family or servants at his residence or (if such tender of delivery is not practicable) affixed to a conspicuous part of the property.

Those modes of service are:

(*i*) By delivery or tender to the addressee personally;

(*ii*) By delivery or tender to one of his family or servants at his residence;

(*iii*) By post; and

(*iv*) By affixing the notice to a conspicuous part of the demised property.

Out of the aforesaid four modes, the last mode of 'affixation' is to be resorted to only when other modes are not practicable.[22] The sender of the notice is free to adopt any of the first three modes of service as he may think fit.[1] The proposition that service by hanging up would not be valid until there is a failure of service by registered post even though personal service tender by the party was refused is not correct.[2] Service of notice by affixation is permissible only if tender or delivery of such notice personally to the tenant or to one of his family or servants at his residence is not practicable.[3] When the defendant has failed to prove that notice was not duly served upon him and he has not denied the service of notice either in pleadings or in evidence, service of notice is valid.[4] Service by affixation has to be made at the residence of the tenant. Vicarious tender or delivery not having been made at the residence of the tenant, when the tender to his employee was made at his business place and not at the residence of the tenant, the tender followed by affixation was held to be invalid.[5] Section 106 of the Transfer of Property Act does not provide that a notice of termination of the tenancy, should be sent by registered post, that such notice can also be sent by ordinary post and that where such notice is sent under a certificate of posting a presumption arises under s. 114, Evidence Act that there has been due service of such notice.[6]

Where a copy of notice to quit was tendered to the tenant personally, and he refused to accept the same, the service of notice to quit was complete. In such a case, simply because after refusal of notice by tenant, the same was

22 AIR 1939 PC 11.
1 AIR 1923 Cal 682.
2 65 CWN 1119 contra *Chhedilal* v *Munnu Sardar* AIR 1983 All 274.
3 *Chhedilal* v *Munnu Sardar* AIR 1983 All 274.
4 *Biswanath* v *Ramkrishna* AIR 2017 NOC 888 (Cal).
5 *Md. Shahariyar* v *R.P. Bhal* (1986)2 CHN 19 (DB).
6 *A. Govindraj Goud* v *Vikranthi & Co.* AIR 2004 AP 395.

affixed on the front door of premises, it could not be said that notice was illegal as when the landlord was not satisfied about the service by tender to the tenant he should have resorted to the third mode of service of notice under s. 106, viz. delivery to one of the tenant's family or servants before effecting service by affixation. Delivery of the notice after refusal by tenant to one of the tenant's family or servants was totally unnecessary and redundant and so also the service by affixation. Simply because an unnecessary step was taken by a layman, the legal effect of service, by delivery of notice to the tenant, cannot be said to have been destroyed. It was more so when, the service was in time.[7]

Modes as in (*i*) and (*ii*) above are commonly known as personal service. Where a notice to quit is not sent by post, the delivery or tender of the notice must be made to the addressee personally.[8] When such delivery or tender is made at the residence of the addressee, it may be made to one of the inmates of the family of the addressee or to one of his servants. This is known as vicarious service. A vicarious service can only be at the residence of the addressee.[9] The sender of the notice can get the notice served by delivery or tender to a member of the addressee's family or to one of his servants at his residence though service of the notice personally on the addressee is not impracticable.[10] Where the registered notice was first tendered to the tenant at his residence and at his behest was carried by the postman to the tenant's son at his shop and was accepted by him, the service of notice was held to be good.[11] When a notice is sent to a party's lawyer or solicitor who in turn sends the notice to the party, that would tantamount to a personal service on the party.[12]

Personal service may be effected on a duly authorised agent. It is no plea that the agent had not communicated the service to the principal.[13] A notice can be served on the agent of the tenant and it constitutes a valid service if it is tendered to his agent.[14] If the personal tender or service is possible at his place of residence, the same may be resorted to at his place of business.[15] When one tenant holds a power of attorney for all the co-tenants service upon such power of attorney holder is held to be service on all.[16]

7 *Thakur Chandra Nandi* v *Arun Kumar Roy Chowdhury* AIR 1986 Cal 249.
8 AIR 1923 Cal 682.
9 *Harihar Banerjee* v *Ramsashi Roy* AIR 1918 PC 102.
10 4 CWN 572; 70 CWN 262; *Sukumar Guha* v *Naresh Chandra Ghosh* AIR 1968 Cal 49; distinguished in *Thakur Chandra Nandi* v *Arun Kumar Roy Chowdhury* AIR 1986 Cal 249.
11 *Permanand* v *Smt. Anandi Bai* AIR 1974 Raj 65.
12 AIR 1927 Sind 24.
13 *Harihar Banerjee* v *Ramsashi Roy* AIR 1918 PC 102.
14 *Achhama Thanas* v *E.R. Fairman* AIR 1970 Mys 77.
15 *Ibid.*
16 *Abdul Sattar* v *Rameswar* 1993 (Supp)1 SCC 59; AIR 1992 SC 2065.

Service of notice through post has been judicially accepted and it is this position that has been restated by amending s. 106 of the T.P. Act in 1929. But it cannot be said that by this amendment, the legislature has done away with the tender or delivery of notice in case notice has been sent by post.[17]

Next, we come to the service of a notice to quit by post. The service by post may take three different forms—service by ordinary post, service through post under certificate of posting and the most generally accepted form, the service through registered post. (About service through ordinary post and through post under a certificate of posting—Notice under certificate of posting is sufficient.[18] Section 106 does not provide that notice must be sent by registered post. Such notice can also be sent by ordinary post and when such notice is sent under a certificate of posting, a presumption arises under s. 114 of the Evidence Act that there has been due service of such notice.[1]

The Supreme Court has also held that notice sent by under certificate of posting raises a presumption of service under s. 114(*f*) of the Evidence Act, but whether the court will draw such presumption will depend on facts and circumstances disclosed in each case.[2]

Ordinarily when a notice is meant to be given, it is sent per registered post with AD receipt affixed, intending return of AD receipt containing signature of the addressee. For service of a notice through registered post, the essentials are: (*i*) postage should be pre-paid, (*ii*) it should be correctly addressed (vide s. 27 of the General Clauses Act).

Normally when the notice is admittedly sent by registered post in correct address and pre-paid, the statutory presumption under s. 27 of the General Clauses Act arises and the notice is presumed to have been received by the addressee.[2]

Service of a notice to quit has been effected by registered post—AD receipt returned with signature purporting to be that of the defendant. Plaintiff is entitled to presumption arising from the fact of service of notice by registered post and the notice must be held to have been duly served on the defendant.[3] The postage has to be paid on the occasion of despatch of the letter containing the notice. There may arise a presumption under s. 114, Evidence Act, when a notice is sent by post irrespective of whether it is sent by ordinary post or under certificate of posting.[4] Service of notice by speed post is no less than a notice sent by registered post.[5]

17 *Sharad* v *Vishnu* AIR 1978 Bom 187.
18 *Jitendranath Das* v *Bijay Lal Dass* AIR 1976 Cal 478.
1 *Fitter Peera Shaheb* v *K. Balachandra Rao* AIR 1972 Mys 14; *Mrs. Achamma Thomas* v *E.R. Fairman* AIR 1970 Mys 77 rel. on.
2 *Ummu Salema* v *B.B. Gujral* AIR 1981 SC 1191; (1981)3 SCC 317; (1981)3 SCR 647.
3 AIR 1957 Cal 479.
4 *Sukumar Guha* v *Naresh Chandra Ghosh* AIR 1968 Cal 49.
5 *Smt. Jaswant Kaur* v *Additional District Judge Court No. 1, Faizabad* AIR 2018 NOC 92 (All).

The second essential is that the notice should be properly addressed. The presumption of due service applies only in cases in which it is shown that the notice was properly addressed.[6] Again, the express provision that the notice may be sent by post only contemplates the sending by post to the correct address.[7] An established home where a person's wife and children live is undoubtedly his residence for the purpose of s. 106, T.P. Act even though he may be employed elseshere.[8] This cannot be correct in all the circumstances conceivable. The tenant and his wife together with his children may live separately, by arrangement, in the ancestral house, while the husband lives away elsewhere permanently in a rented house.

Words requiring the delivery or tender of a notice to the lessee "personally or to one of his family or servants" did not apply to a notice sent by post.[9] In a case where the AD receipt was received back with the endorsement of acceptance purporting to be over the signature of the husband of the tenant-defendant—the presumption would be that the addressee received the notice.[10] Sending a notice by registered post duly addressed and postage prepaid carries with it a presumption of due service. A notice posted and properly directed raises presumption. Even if the signature in AD Receipt of the registered notice had been subscribed on behalf of the addressee by somebody who was not proved to have had any authority from the addressee to receive the notice, it would be no evidence that the notice did not reach the addressee.[11] Proof of service by calling the postal peon is not necessary. When a notice is returned as having been refused by the addressee—this will be sufficient service for the purpose of this section.[12]

Referring to the Allahabad decision in *Shiv Dutt Singh* v *Ram Dass*[13] and the Delhi decision in *Jagat Ram Khullar* v *Battu Mal*,[14] the Supreme Court held that in both the aforesaid decisions the question considered was as to the statement on oath by the tenant denying the tender and refusal to accept delivery. It was held in the said decisions that the bare statement of the tenant was sufficient to rebut the presumption of service. In the opinion of the Supreme Court, there could be no hard and fast rule on that aspect. Unchallenged testimony of a tenant in certain cases may be sufficient to rebut the presumption but if testimony of the tenant itself is inherently unreliable, the position may be different. It is always a question of fact in

6 7 CLJ 251.
7 *Prahladrai Choorewala* v *Commissioners for the Port of Calcutta* AIR 1939 PC 11.
8 AIR 1960 MP 167.
9 AIR 1958 All 369.
10 65 CWN 690.
11 *Seuli* v *Madhya* 74 CWN 647.
12 AIR 1920 All 104; AIR 1954 Ajmer 65.
13 AIR 1980 All 280.
14 AIR 1976 Del 111.

each case whether there was sufficient evidence from the tenant to discharge the initial burden.[15]

There cannot be any irrebuttable presumption in favour of proper service of notice simply because the notice has been sent as required by s. 27 of the General Clauses Act.[16] The presumption is not an irrebuttable presumption. The concerned party can lead evidence to rebut the presumption.[17]

When is a service by post deemed to have been complete? The answer is: when it is tendered or delivered. Requirements with regard to the service of a notice (under s. 106 of the T.P. Act) is fulfilled if it was sent by post to the person concerned and it was tendered or delivered personally to him. Section 106 (of the T.P. Act) does not say that the service is not complete unless the tenant accepts it, but merely that it should be tendered or delivered. Thus the section provides for a case where the tenant refuses the notice when it is tendered......if the joint-tenants are permitted to take shelter behind the refusal of one of them to accept it, it would be impossible for the landlord to serve a valid notice terminating a joint-tenancy; because one of the tenants would keep refusing the notice while the others keep out of its way.

A notice addressed to all the joint-tenants but served on one is a service on all the joint-tenants. It was argued in a case that "notice terminating the tenancy was invalid as the envelope was addressed to one of the joint-tenants. It was conceded that the notice itself was addressed to both, the address on the envelope is no part of the notice but only a direction to the post office to deliver the letter to a particular person. I am doubtful whether the post office would accept a registered letter addressed simultaneously to two different persons as this may create trouble for them if the two addressees become rival claimants for the letter. But even if the post offices do accept an envelope for delivery, the address on it is only a direction to them. The real notice is inside the envelope. I would, therefore, hold that a notice calling upon two joint-tenants to quit but sent to the address of one of them is in law a notice addressed to both".[18]

When a notice to quit addressed to all the joint tenants was handed over to one of them who signed an acknowledgment of it the service is held to be good service.[19] Supreme Court has also held that if a notice is addressed to both the joint tenants but served on one, the service is valid.[1] When the original tenant has died, a notice addressed to all the heirs but served on one of them is also held to be a valid service.[2]

15 *Anil Kumar* v *Nanakchandra Verma* (1990)3 SCC 603; AIR 1990 SC 1215.
16 *Sharad* v *Vishnu* AIR 1978 Bom 187.
17 *Matadin Sharma* v *Upendra Sharma* AIR 1972 Pat 292.
18 *Roshan* v *Purshottam Lal* AIR 1965 All 287; 69 CWN 234; AIR 1964 SC 468; 23 CWN 77.
19 *Ajit Kumar Ray* v *Satya Bala* AIR 1973 Cal 339.
1 *Kanji* v *Trustees for Port of Bombay* AIR 1963 SC 468.
2 *A.M. Abdul Samad* v *Gulam Ahmed* AIR 1975 Guj 1; *Raman Bhai* v *Jivaram Sharma* AIR 1964 Bom 96.

When a tenant dies his tenancy devolves upon the heirs as joint tenants and not tenants-in-common and even if the notice under s. 106 of the Transfer of Property Act is issued and served upon one of the heirs of the deceased tenant it is a valid service of notice even if the notice was neither addressed to nor served upon others.[3]

The residuary mode of service, i.e. service by affixation of the notice to a conspicuous part of the demised property, is open only when tender or delivery is not practicable. In the absence of such delivery or tender, mere affixing the notice to the wall of the house will not be enough.[4] Again, where a notice to quit is personally tendered to the addressee and it is refused that by itself would be good service. Even if it be otherwise, the residuary mode of service by hanging up the notice on the premises prescribed by s. 106, T.P. Act, would at once be attracted and become available.[5]

Where the statute does not specify any such additional or alternative mode of service, there can be no warrant for importing into the statute a method of service on the lines of the provisions of the CPC. Court would, therefore, not like to hold that a "substituted" service as the one effected by the landlord is a necessary or permissible requirement of the statute.[6]

Service of notice by affixation is permissible only if tender or delivery of such notice personally to the tenant or to one of her family or servants at his residence not practicable.[7] A personal service may also be effected on one of the family members or servants of the tenant but at the residence of the tenant. Thus once it is proved that a notice to quit has been served on one of the members of family of the tenant or his servant, it is valid service and the tenant cannot take the plea that he did not receive it.[8]

28 Notice sent through electronic form

After enactment of the Information Technology Act 2000, an electronic record got legal recognition and a notice may be sent through an electronic form.

Nowadays electronic mail (e-mail) is very much common for communicating messages. It is a way of sending messages and data to other people by means of computers connected together in a network.[9] E-mail means a mail and may include attachments or enclosures. E-mail generation is the same as the traditional postal mail which includes composing, posting

3 *H.C. Pandey* v *G.C. Paul* AIR 1989 SC 1470; *Kamala Devi* v *Arun* (1993)1 CHN 74; *K.K. Manjarantha* v *V.M.T. Kalliani* 1995 (Supp) 3 SCC 403.
4 AIR 1919 Cal 400.
5 *Radharani* v *Angurbala* 65 CWN 1119 (1123-1129) (DB).
6 *Madan & Co.* v *Wazir Jaivir Chand* (1989)1 SCC 264.
7 *Chhedi Lal* v *Munnu Sardar* AIR 1983 All 274.
8 *Manzoor Ali* v *Lal Devi* AIR 1951 All 396; *Ghulam Mohammad* v *Lakshmibux* AIR 1951 Raj 68.
9 *Oxford Advanced Learner's Dictionary*, 9th Ed.

to the mail server and thereafter delivering it to the recipient and *vice versa*. The mail servers of the sender and the receiver are the electronic post offices. The e-mail messages are traceable using IP address from which these originated.[10]

29 Notice sent through telegram

When a notice to quit is sent through telegram, it is not a valid notice as it does not contain the signature of the sender which is essentially required under s. 106 of the Transfer of Property Act.[11] Of course, the system has since been done away within India.

30 Effect of service of notice under s. 106, T.P. Act

The effect of service of a notice under s. 106 on the tenant is an expression of a desire to terminate the tenancy of the tenant after expiration of the period of notice. This does not mean that after service of notice under s. 106 though the tenancy is determined the tenant can be evicted and/or removed from the land under his occupation by the lessor forcibly. The lessor must take recourse to due process of law for ejectment of the tenant.[12]

31 Refusal of notice amounts to service by implication—distinction between "Refused" and "Left"

The tender and refusal of a notice is as good as delivery of the notice for the purpose of this section even where the refusal is not by the addressee himself but by one of his family or servants at his residence.[13]

Where a tenant knows that he is in arrears and he receives a registered letter from the landlord but refuses to accept it, presumption of receipt of notice by the tenant may be successfully raised.[14] Refusal would make the service complete.[15]

When a notice is sent per registered post and the addressee is not available and/or he is not found, the notice is returned with endorsement 'not found'. In such a case, it cannot be said that the notice has been duly served.

In case where the endorsement is 'not found'—sufficiency of service is relative. Where the notice sent by the landlord to the tenant at the correct address is returned with the endorsement 'not found' such service will be presumed to be good enough only when supported by evidence to infer that the tenant had evaded the service.[16]

10 V.R. Dinkar, *Scientific Expert Evidence*, 2nd Ed., pp. 323-324.
11 *Maduri Satyanarayana* v *Singamsetti Veerabhadraswamy* AIR 1990 AP 169.
12 AIR 1924 PC 144; AIR 1961 SC 1570 and AIR 1968 SC 620, foll. *M/s. Dutta & Associates* v *State* AIR 1982 Cal 225; 1995 (Supp) 2 SCC 667; (1981)2 SCC 535.
13 14 CWN 372; 16 IC 213.
14 AIR 1963 All 250.
15 AIR 1965 All 287.
16 *A.E.K. Kaliansa Nadar* v *S.V.K.R. Amirthavala etc.* AIR 1973 Mad 255.

The refusal of notice to quit by the tenant would mean in law his knowledge of the contents of the notice. In *Har Charan* v *Shiv Rani*[1] the apex court has observed that the presumption under s. 27 of the General Clauses Act as well as under s. 114(*e*) of the Evidence Act is one of proper or effective service which must mean service of having been conversant with the content in the notice and that the presumption under this Act is rebutable but in absence of proof to the contrary the presumption of proper or effective service would arise when the envelope containing the notice had been returned with endorsement 'refused'.

The notice may reach the addressee but he refuses to take delivery of the notice and the same is returned back to the sender with an endorsement "refused". In such cases refusal would make the service complete as we have held hereinabove.[2] But where the postman went to the tenant's house with a registered notice but he was informed by the brother of the tenant that he was out of station and on the request of the postman,[3] he refused to supply the address of the tenant, and the endorsement of refusal was made by the postal department on the basis of the report given by the postman,[4] the endorsement is wholly illegal as there was no offer by the postman to the tenant and in the absence of any offer, it was illegal to hold that the notice was refused by the tenant. There was, therefore, no service of notice on the tenant under s. 106.[5]

Where a notice terminating the tenancy, sent by registered post, by the landlord to the tenant confined in jail, on jail address is returned with postal endorsement 'refused', the presumption is that the endorsement as well as its initial is that of the postman. It is not necessary to examine the postman to prove the same. So also a notice directed to such tenant and acknowledged by the jail superintendent can be presumed to have been received by the tenant.[6]

Where a notice is sent per registered post and the same is returned to the sender with an endorsement "Left"—does it mean satisfactory service of the notice in question? Ordinarily, the presumption in favour of due service arises.[7] Is it the final say in the matter? No. The matter came up before their

1 AIR 1981 SC 1284; (1981)2 SCC 535.
2 *Ganga Ram* v *Smt. Fulwati* AIR 1970 All 446; *Mahammadoo Khan* v *Ghulam Rasul* AIR 1972 All 441; (1986)1 SCC 133.
3 See Note 22.
4 See Note 23.
5 *Shamim Ahmad Alvi* v *Azizul Rahman Khan* AIR 1974 All 354; (2002)2 SCC 383; (1995)6 SCC 491.
6 *Saeed Ahmed* v *S.Q Ali* AIR 1973 All 24; see *Jagat Ram Khullar* v *Battu Mal* AIR 1976 Del 111; *P.V. Rao* v *C.V. Ramana* AIR 1976 SC 869; *Shiv Dutt Singh* v *Ram Dass* AIR 1980 All 280.
7 51 CWN 650; AIR 1952 Cal 221.

Lordships in *H.K. Das* v *Hahnemann Pub. Co.*[8] where P.N. Mookherjee, J. *held*: "This *prima facie* means that the postal peon could not contact the defendant. Accordingly, it shall be taken that no tender of the notice was made to the defendant, particularly when there is no definite or specific evidence to that effect. The presumption which would have otherwise arisen under the law (vide s. 27 of the General Clauses Act and s. 28 of the Bengal General Clauses Act) in favour of the plaintiff and such presumption is on the face of it a rebuttable presumption, would be rebutted." It is submitted that *H.K. Das* v *Hahnemann Pub. Co.*[9] is no longer good law in view of *M/s. Surajmull Ghanashyamdas* v *Samadarshan Sur.*[10]

The *ratio decidendi* is: the question is one of fact depending on the facts and circumstances of each particular case. In proper circumstances the endorsement 'left' would mean satisfactory service and in other cases it may not mean that way.

Next, we come to the endorsement 'not claimed'—In proper circumstances it may mean service.[11]

This decision has been followed by the Calcutta High Court in *Kamal* v *Durga Charan.*[12] In *Deo Karan's* case the endorsement "not met" was held to be a good service when there is evidence that the original defendant was ailing at the time when the postal peon went to serve the registered cover and was residing there. But the presumption was duly rebutted by the fact that the date on which the notice was allegedly "not claimed" by the defendant was a Sunday and it is not expected that the postal peon would tender such a notice to the defendant on a Sunday and as such without examination of the postal peon no presumption of service could be drawn.[13]

32 Lease by the Government—notice to quit

Provisions of s. 106 of the T.P. Act applies to a lease by the Government and before termination of a lease a notice has to issue. Where the Government of India is the lessor, a notice to quit given on behalf of the Government need not be signed by the Secretary of State for India himself.[1] A notice signed by the Collector will be enough.[2]

Incidentally we may refer to provisions in the second proviso to s. 1(3) of the West Bengal Premises Tenancy Act 1956 (since repealed and replaced by the West Bengal Premises Tenancy Act 1997, w.e.f. 9.7.2001), which

8 70 CWN 262.
9 Ibid.
10 AIR 1969 Cal 109.
11 *Ganesh* v *J.N. Chatterjee* 70 CWN 676 (*per* P.N. Mookherjee, J.).
12 77 CWN 870; *Sachindra* v *Sudam* 81 CWN 739; *Deo Karan* v *Renuka* 82 CWN 306.
13 *Shib Nath Bhadra* v *S. Mrinalini Ghosh* 90 CWN 413.
1 (1988)3 SCC 44.
2 8 CLJ 34.

exclude, following the examples of Bombay and Delhi, from the operation of this Act the premises belonging to or taken on lease or requisitioned by the State Government or any local authority. In such case, i.e. where the lessor or the lessee is the Central or the Provincial Government or any local authority, the notice to quit should follow the provisions of s. 106 of the T.P. Act. Then, prior to the institution of a suit, a notice under s. 80, CPC, if the party sued is a Government, of a notice under the Municipal Act or any other Act, if there be a provision to that effect, if the party sued is a local authority will be required.

West Bengal Premises Tenancy Act 1956 has been repealed by the West Bengal Premises Tenancy Act 1997 which came into force on 10th July 2001. Section 3 of the 1997 Act *inter alia* provides that the said Act shall not apply to (*a*) any premises owned by (*i*) Central Government, or (*ii*) any State Government, or (*iii*) a Government undertaking or enterprise, or (*iv*) a statutory body which is not a local authority, (*v*) a Cantonment Board constituted under the Cantonments Act 1924, or (*vi*) a local authority, (*b*) any tenancy created by the Central Government or any State Government in respect of the premises tenancy on lease or requisitioned by the Government, (*c*) any tenancy where the lease with due consent of the tenant has been registered under the Registration Act 1908 after commencement of the 1997 Act, (*d*) any premises rented to a foreign mission or international agency.

Therefore, where the Government, Central or State, is a tenant in the premises belonging to any individual, the provisions of the West Bengal Premises Tenancy Act shall apply subject to the limitations prescribed in s. 3 of 1997 Act.

To evict, therefore, the Government—tenant of an individual in West Bengal, one has to issue two notices to wit, a notice under s. 80 of the CPC and a notice of suit under s. 13(6) of the West Bengal Premises Tenancy Act 1956 (Now s. 6(4) of the 1997 Act).

Notice terminating tenancy of the State with effect from a future date and claiming arrears of rent—Notice stated that in case of non-compliance a suit would be filed and that the notice was under s. 80. The notice was not complied with. Suit was filed two months after the service thereof. *Held*, there was proper service of notice.[3]

33 Lease by a municipality—notice to quit

A municipality is not beyond the purview of the provisions of the Transfer of Property Act relating to lease and termination thereof. When a municipality grants a lease or takes a lease—a notice under s. 106, T.P. Act has to issue before termination of the lease.[4] "A lease by a municipality cannot, in the

3 *Smt. Rava Bai* v *State of Maharashtra* AIR 1973 Bom 59.
4 AIR 1954 Mys 89; (1998)3 SCC 654; (1981)2 SCC 199.

absence of a contract to the contrary, be determined by a mere resolution passed by the Municipal Council and without any notice being served on the lessee in accordance with the provisions of this section."[5]

34 A notice to quit under other circumstances

(i) *Where tenancy and/or title of the landlord is denied*

If the tenants set up a different tenancy than the one alleged in the plaint and fail to prove it, is the plaintiff obliged to give a notice to quit and determine the particular tenancy pleaded by him in the plaint? The question has been answered in *Mayankanakath Muthamodkutty Haji* v *Edassevi Moodeenkutty* as: "In this case the defendant has not denied the landlord's title. He has only set up the contention that he was holding the property and the building under a tenancy, the terms of which were different from that set up in the plaint. In such a case, I think, if the landlord wants to recover possession of the property, he must have given the requisite notice to quit and determine the tenancy set up by him notwithstanding the contention of the defendant that he was in possession under a different tenancy."[6] But where there is a complete disclaimer of title by the lessee that will make the lessee liable to ejectment without notice.[7] Views are opposite, however, as to whether notice would be required—denial of title in the suit itself is enough.[8] When the defendant in his written statement denied the landlord's title, he was not entitled to a notice to quit.[9] Such denial is not sufficient.[10] This issue has subsequently been discussed threadbare in a case reported in AIR 1967 Pat 35 (at p. 40) relying on ILR 17 Mad 218.

If denial of title is read to denote the denial of the right of the landlord to maintain the petition for eviction—notice under s. 106 is necessary.[11] Here, the tenant never denied that the respondent was not the landlord but questioned *bona fides* of the claim of the respondent for demolition and reconstruction.

But the case is otherwise where the landlords treat the addressee as a trespasser. In the instant case, it was made clear in the notice that the landlords intended to terminate the tenancy on the expiry of 30 days in case the addressee regarded himself as a tenant of the premises. According to the addressee, the premises was in his tenancy and no forcible possession was taken thereon. Notice cannot be treated as invalid.[12]

5 AIR 1928 All 95.
6 AIR 1965 Ker 174.
7 AIR 1919 PC 1.
8 17 Bom 631; *Ratneswar Goswami* v *Mongoti* AIR 1951 Ass 70.
9 18 Bom 256.
10 17 Mad 218; 31 Mad 261.
11 *U. Nagalingam* v *T.K. Ramaswami Chettiar* AIR 1976 Mad 149.
12 *Balbir Singh* v *Smt. Kalawati* AIR 1976 All 434.

Again, where the title of the landlord is denied, the tenant would not be entitled to a notice to quit.[13]

Contra opinion in *Rambaran Paswan* v *Smt. Kalo Dei.*[14]

(ii) *Cases of sub-letting*

Determination of the main lease is sufficient to determine the unauthorised sub-leases. This is so because law presumes that a notice to quit served on the main lessee has been impliedly served on the sub-tenant.[15] The determination of a lease by a valid notice by the lessor will automatically put an end to any sub-lease granted by the lessee.[16]

(iii) *Cases of holding over*

Both s. 116 and s. 111(*a*) of the T.P. Act should be read together. It is for the lessee to prove that (1) the lessee remained in possession after determination of the lease and (2) the lessor or his legal representatives accepted rent from them or otherwise assented to their continuance in possession. Mere continuing in possession after determination of the term of lease does not indicate tenancy by holding over.[17]

In a case where after the determination of contractual tenancy on the expiration of the covenanted period, the tenant continued in possession on the same terms and the landlord went on accepting rent, the tenant must be deemed to have been holding over within the meaning under s. 116 of the T.P. Act and a notice under s. 106 would be necessary.[18]

Lease for a specified time—tenant holding over. The premises was leased for a period of ten years. In the deed there was a stipulation that the landlord could demand the premises by giving the tenant notice of six months at any time after a period of five years from the commencement of the lease. He did exercise the option. Even after the expiry of the lease, the tenant was allowed to remain in possession as a tenant holding over subject to condition that he should pay an enhanced rent. Some years afterwards, the landlord issued a notice to the tenant to quit the premises under the term of the lease. *Held,*

13 *Ratneswar Goswami* v *Mongoti* AIR 1951 Ass 70; *Namdeo* v *Narainadabai* AIR 1953 SC 228; *Bhura* v *Bahadur Singh* AIR 1976 Raj 249.

14 *Rambaran Paswan* v *Smt. Kalo Dei* AIR 1974 Pat 333; *Banarasi Lal* v *Jatadhari Das* AIR 1971 Pat 110 rel. on.

15 AIR 1932 Cal 241; (2003)6 SCC 423; (1996)5 SCC 423.

16 21 Bom 311; (1990)2 SCC 288; (1988)1 SCC 70.

17 *Bhawanji Lakhamshi* v *Himattal Jamnadas* AIR 1972 SC 819; *Md. Ahmed Amotia* v *Nirmal Chandra Roy* AIR 1978 Cal 312; (1980)1 SCC 321; (1977)4 SCC 402.

18 *Punjalal* v *Bhagwat Prasad* AIR 1963 SC 120; *Mahgilal* v *Sugan Chand Rathi* AIR 1965 SC 101; *Manujendra Dutta* v *Purnesh Prasad Roy Chowdhury* AIR 1967 SC 1419 and *Parshotam Lal* v *Kalayan Singh* AIR 1961 J&K 20.

that the notice was invalid. The stipulation as to the notice in the lease-deed would not continue to be a term of holding over.[1]

Monthly tenancy according to the English calendar stipulating one year period from 1st January till the end of the calendar year. Tenant is holding over. Notice to quit with expiry of December held valid.[2]

Tenant holding over after the expiry of lease—Notice under s. 106 is necessary for determining lease.[3]

Term in original lease deed that no notice under s. 106 would be necessary—term will also hold good in the case of new contract of lease formed by the tenant's holding over.[4]

Where the lease determines by efflux of time and the tenant continues in possession under the protection of the Rent Restriction Act, he acquires a status of irremovability unless there is something to show that he is a tenant holding over, mere payment of rent without necessary animus not being sufficient. Such a tenant for the sake of convenience is described as a statutory tenant. It would not be open to such a tenant to urge by way of defence, in a suit for ejectment brought against him under the provisions of the Rent Restriction Act, that by acceptance of rent a fresh tenancy was created which had to be determined by a fresh notice to quit.[5]

Tenant-holding over (on payment of rent) after expiry of fixed period of lease—tenancy month ending on the last day of calendar month—notice to quit by landlord terminating monthly tenancy by last day of a calendar month—it is valid—provision regarding exclusion of date of commencement under s. 110 not attracted to monthly tenancy by holding over.[6]

Lease of 30 years with renewal clause—tenant continuing in possession even after expiry of 30 years—possession will be under renewal clause though option was not expressly exercised—it is not a case of holding over under s. 116.[7]

(iv) *Cases where notice is issued though not required*

There may be cases where a notice under s. 106 of the Transfer of Property Act is not at all necessary for determination of a tenancy or, more clearly speaking, no notice to quit is necessary. Even when in such a case a notice

1 *Dasarathi Kumar* v *Sarat Chandra Ghosh* AIR 1934 Cal 135; *Bapayya* v *Venkataratnam* AIR 1953 Mad 884 rel. on *E. Keshavayya* v *R. Narasimha Prabhu* AIR 1976 Kant 41.
2 *Shambhunath Pal* v *Indian Iron & Steel Co. Ltd.* AIR 1975 Cal 194.
3 *Khadim Meera* v *Mythee Kunju* AIR 1972 Ker 63.
4 *Chiranjit Lal* v *Narian Singh* AIR 1972 P&H 432.
5 *Firm Sardari Lal* v *Pritam Singh* AIR 1978 SC 1518.
6 *Potluri Subbareddi* v *Kalabai Rathi* AIR 1982 AP 186.
7 AIR 1965 Cal 55, foll. *M/s. Dutta & Associates* v *State of West Bengal* AIR 1982 Cal 225.

to quit is given by the landlord, no tenancy is created merely by reason of such notice.[8]

(v) *Cases not governed by provisions of s. 106 of the T.P. Act—issue of a reasonable notice*

Requirements of s. 106 of the Transfer of Property Act as to the validity of a notice will not apply to leases not governed by this section. Broadly speaking, two types of cases may be conceived: (*i*) where the lease commenced before the T.P. Act came into force, (*ii*) where the Transfer of Property Act 1882 does not apply at all. In both the cases the lease is determinable by issue of a reasonable notice to the lessee.

In cases in which a lease is not governed by this section, it will be regarded, in the absence of a contract, local law or usage to the contrary, as determinable by a sufficient notice given by either party to the other. The lease will not be determinable without such notice.[9] Where the Transfer of Property Act is not in force, its equitable principles would apply. But it should not be meant that a notice issued should be examined in the light of s. 106 of the T.P. Act and may be rejected if it did not stand the test of s. 106. Reasonable notice is enough. Some illustrations would serve our purpose:

(*i*) Lease when T.P. Act was not in force—Notice under s. 106 not necessary.[10]

(*ii*) T.P. Act came into force on 1.7.1882—tenancy commencing prior to that date—"technical rule of s. 106 requiring the notice to expire with the end of month of tenancy cannot be invoked".[11]

(*iii*) A lease executed before the Transfer of Property Act came into force will be governed not by the provisions of that Act but by the local law.[12]

(*iv*) Notice to quit served on tenant—technical defects in notice cannot make it invalid when there is substantial compliance with s. 106.[13]

What is or is not a reasonable notice depends on facts and circumstances of each case. The question of the sufficiency of notice in the case of leases not governed by this section will have to be determined according to the principles of justice, equity and good conscience. It will have to be seen in each case whether the notice given is a reasonable one with regard both to the length of such notice and the time at which it is to expire.[14] In cases in which a lease

8 ILR 30 Cal 889.
9 AIR 1933 Mad 165; AIR 1957 MB 151; (1976)2 SCC 103.
10 ILR 9 Raj 97 (Gwalior State).
11 AIR 1957 MB 151.
12 AIR 1953 Sau 113.
13 AIR 1952 Mad 884.
14 ILR 15 Bom 415; AIR 1956 Ori 95.

is not governed by this section, local custom will have to be given due consideration in determining the reasonableness of a notice. The notice need not necessarily expire within a year of tenancy as is enjoined by s. 106, T.P. Act.[15] Nonetheless, a tenant cannot be asked to quit in mid-season which will be opposed to equity. Provisions of s. 106 may be kept in view as a guide to what may be a reasonable notice in a lease not governed by s. 106 of the T.P. Act.[16] A notice to quit does not become invalid merely because the particulars as regards the tenancy are not accurately set out in the notice.[17]

35 Notice of repairs of leasehold property—lessor's liability

Section 108 of the Transfer of Property Act speaks of rights and liability of the lessor and the lessee.

Clause (*f*) of s. 108 enjoins: "If the lessor neglects to make within a reasonable time after notice any repairs which he is bound to make to the property, the lessee may make the same himself, and deduct the expense of such repairs with interest from the rent or otherwise recover from the lessor."

A lessor under the law is not under any obligation to keep the demised premises in good repairs though in equity he has to keep the premises habitable. The above provision of law applies to cases where the lessor is bound to make repairs, i.e. when under the terms of the lease the lessor takes upon himself the obligation of effecting repairs to the property. If the lessor fails, the provision may not apply. If he fails due to his negligence, after expiry of the period, which must be a reasonable period, the remedy, as in the provision, is open to the lessee.

The lessee has to give the lessor a reasonable time to effect repairs. What should be or should not be reasonable time depends on circumstances of each particular case.

Incidentally, we may refer to ss. 35 and 36 of the West Bengal Premises Tenancy Act 1997 which correspond almost verbatim to ss. 34 and 35 of the old Act of 1956. Section 4(3) of the Act of 1997 lays down unambiguously that every landlord shall be bound to take measures for due maintenance of essential supply or service comprised in the tenancy, Firstly under the new Act, the landlord has the statutory obligation to make tenantable repairs of the premises or take measures for due maintenance of essential supply or service comprising the tenancy and if the landlord neglects or fails to perform his said statutory obligations, Rent Controller shall, on the application to him by the tenant in possession of the premises cause a notice to be served in the prescribed manner on the landlord requiring him to make such repair or take such measures for due maintenance therein of the essential supply

15 AIR 1925 Mad 346; AIR 1921 Cal 126.
16 17 CWN 1073.
17 AIR 1955 Mad 206.

or service. If after service of such notice the landlord fails to adopt proper course or neglects to make such repair or to take within reasonable time, such measures, as the case may be, the tenant may be permitted by the Controller to make such repair or to take such measures at such cost as may be specified by the Controller.

The provisions in ss. 3, 5 and 36 of the West Bengal Premises Tenancy Act 1997 are an improvement upon s. 108(1) of the T.P. Act allowing a lessee statutory right to repairs of the premises.

36 Notice under s. 39 of the Transfer of Property Act 1882

The expression 'notice' used under s. 39 of the Transfer of Property Act 1882 has to be read along with the definition clause as contained in s. 3 thereof, which could only lead to a conclusion that where a person is fully aware of the existing rights of the parties and more so where such transferee is a member of the family, it cannot be said that he is not aware of the rights of the other members or persons forming the party. No notice to them for charge towards maintenance is necessary.[18]

37 Waiver of a notice to quit under s. 106, T.P. Act

A tenant may waive his right to a notice under s. 106 of the T.P. Act.[19]

Where the suit for eviction was based on second notice but there was no pleading by the defendant lessee as to unilateral waiver of the first notice by the plaintiff nor there was evidence that the first notice was acted upon by the defendant, it could not be said that there was unilateral waiver of the first notice on the part of the plaintiff.[20]

38 Withdrawal of a notice to quit

Notice once served cannot be withdrawn without the consent of the other party. Once a notice is served determining the tenancy or showing an intention to quit on the expiry of the period of the notice, the tenancy is at an end unless with the consent of the other party to whom the notice is given the tenancy is agreed to be treated as subsisting. Whether the notice is given by the landlord or the tenant, the party to whom it is given is entitled to insist upon it, and it cannot be withdrawn without the consent of both.[1]

39 Notice by lessee to the lessor regarding encroachment on and interference with lessor's rights concerning the leasehold property

It is a bounden duty—both moral and legal—of the lessee to protect his lessor's property from encroachment by strangers, from unlawful eviction by any proceeding and also to inform his lessor about any interference with the

18 *C. Vemuna* v *V.P. Manohara* AIR 2004 AP 317.
19 *K.N. Ramakrishnan* v *C. Keral Chand* AIR 1971 Mad 150.
20 *Provash Chandra Chatterjee* v *Chand Mohon Basak* AIR 1978 Cal 224.
1 *Calcutta Credit Corporation* v *Happy Homes (P) Ltd.* AIR 1968 SC 471.

lessor's rights concerning the leasehold property. Section 108, cl. (*n*) of the T.P. Act reads:

Section 108(*n*) "If the lessee becomes aware of any proceeding to recover the property or any part thereof, or of any encroachment made upon, or any interference with, the lessor's rights concerning such property, he is bound to give, with reasonable diligence, notice thereof to the lessor".

Apparently this clause is for the benefit of both the lessor and lessee.

This clause throws a duty upon the lessee to give notice to the lessor. If the interference be such as prevents the lessee to pay rent to the lessor, the lessee is obliged to give the notice. The lessor does not owe a duty to the lessee to protect him from legal proceedings which would interfere with his possession. "This clause really throws a duty upon the lessee in order that the lessor may, if he chooses, protect his own interest and may be safeguarded against the results of a collusive eviction submitted to by the lessee".[2]

40 Right of lessor's transferee—principles of attornment—provisions of s. 109, T.P. Act—notice of attornment

It is not incumbent either on the transferor or on the transferee to give the lessee a transfer notice or a notice of assignment. To avoid any dispute in payment of rent by the lessee such a notice of attornment may be desirable. A notice to attorn is recommendatory in character. The only effect of absence of any attornment would be that, if any rent had been paid in the meantime to the old landlords, for the said rent, the defendant would have no further liability to the plaintiff as the new landlord".[3]

The section provides no penalty for want of such notice except the loss of rent which might have been paid by the lessee to the original lessor in ignorance of the transfer.[4] "We shall remember that no attornment is necessary under the Transfer of Property Act".[5]

Under s. 109 of the Transfer of Property Act, the title of the assignee is complete on the execution of the deed of assignment and is not postponed till the notice of assignment. It is true that under the Indian law, a letter of attornment is not necessary to complete the title of assignee, but nevertheless under the proviso to s. 109 the lessee is under no obligation to pay rent to the assignee if he has paid it to the assignor without having reason to believe that there was an assignment.[6]

2 *Indu Bhusan Chowdhury* v *Moazem Ali Biswas* AIR 1929 Cal 272 (*per* Rankin, C.J. and Mukherji, J.).
3 71 CWN 174 (*per* P.N. Mookerjee, J.).
4 *Bholanath* v *Supper* AIR 1923 Lah 389.
5 AIR 1939 Lah 49 (*per* Coldstream, J.).
6 *Pyarilal* v *Madhoji Jivan* 19 IC 865; 17 CLJ 372.

It is not of much importance from whom the lessee receives such notice—the lessor or his assignee. The matter of importance is that the fact of transfer is brought to the notice of the lessee. And that is all.

Right of lessor's transferee to terminate tenancy

A transferee of a part of a leased property acquires 'all the rights' of the lessor in respect of that part as if it alone had comprised the lease and a new relationship is created between the transferee and the lessee. The section creates a statutory attornment subsisting, but retaining the same effect of the contractual attornment. Title of the assignee is complete on execution of the deed of assignment and is not postponed till the notice of the assignment.

In view of such substitution made by the section it cannot be contended that since the lessor had no right to terminate the tenancy by a notice to quit a part of the demised premises he could not transfer such a right to the transferee.

"The right of ejectment is inherent in ownership. Therefore, by virtue of the section such transferee is entitled to evict the tenant from that part transferred to him not only when the lease had been determined before the transfer but also if it is determined after the transfer in any of the circumstances mentioned in s. 111. Thus he can terminate by a notice to quit the lease in respect of the property transferred to him".[7]

Originally as between lessor and lessee there can be no splitting of the tenancy and the court cannot by its decree otherwise direct splitting up the tenancy. However s. 109 is an exception to this principle. Therefore, when a partition is effected then it amounts to a splitting up of respective part of property within the meaning of s. 109 and this brings about splitting up of the tenancy which entitles the co-owner to eject the tenant from the property allotted to him in partition. For purposes of s. 109 partition has been held to be a transfer.[8] In view of the provisions of s. 109 of the Act, the Supreme Court held that when all the co-owners agree among themselves and split by partition the demised premises by metes and bounds and come to have a definite portion and identifiable shares in that property, they become separate and individual owners of each severed portion and can deal with that portion as also with the tenant thereof and can bring an eviction suit against that portion from the tenant separately.[9]

41 Notice intending to determine a lease—provisions of s. 111(*g*) of the Transfer of Property Act—waiver of notice

A lease of immovable property determines under the circumstances enumerated in cls. (*a*) to (*h*) of s. 111 of the Transfer of Property Act. We are concerned here with cl. (*g*) of s. 111, i.e. the principle of 'Forfeiture'.

7 *B.P. Pathak* v *Dr. Rayazuddin* AIR 1976 MP 55.
8 *Mohar Singh* v *Debi Charan* AIR 1988 SC 1365; (1988)3 SCC 63.
9 *Sk. Sattar Sk. Mohd Choudhuri* v *G.A. Bukate* (1996)6 SCC 373.

The particular clause reads:

"Section 111. A lease of immovable property determines—

* * *

(*g*) by forfeiture, that is to say, (1) in case the lessee breaks an express condition which provides that, on breach thereof, the lessor may re-enter; or (2) in case the lessee renounces his character as such by setting up a title in a third person or by claiming title in himself; or (3) the lessee is adjudicated an insolvent and the lease provides that the lessor may re-enter on the happening of such event; and in any of these cases the lessor or his transferee gives notice in writing to the lessee of his intention to determine the lease."

For determination of lease on the basis of forfeiture in any of the three circumstances shown above, the lessor or his transferee has to give a notice in writing to the lessee of his intention to determine the lease.[10]

Therefore, where a lease provides that on the breach of condition the lessee should be given notice according to law before ejectment, the tenant cannot be ejected unless a notice according to the contract is given.[11] The statutory requirement of notice specified in s. 111(*g*) of the Transfer of Property Act cannot be waived by contract and must prevail.[12]

The Indian law does not make any distinction between a condition and a covenant.[13] Under the Indian law, not only a breach of covenant but also a breach of condition entitles the lessor to re-entry if there is express provision in the lease deed for a right of re-entry on such breach of condition. The distinction between covenant and condition of the English law is absent in Indian law, and the right of entry can be expressly claimed both for breach of covenant or breach of condition.[14]

A transfer by the lessee in contravention of the terms of lease renders the lease voidable. The lessor may not exercise the option. So, if after the breach of covenant of alienation the landlord accepts rent from the transferee, then the transferee shall be entitled to remain in possession and the right is waived by the lessor.[15]

In order to constitute a disclaimer of title for purposes of s. 111(*g*) there must be a direct repudiation of the relationship of landlord and tenant and the denial must be by clear and unambiguous words and to the knowledge of the landlord. [In reply to the notice by landlord the tenant denied to treat the plaintiff as owner and/or entitled to realise rent]. There cannot be a more

10 AIR 1940 Oudh 92; AIR 1953 SC 228; AIR 1960 Cal 43; AIR 1954 All 649.
11 34 IC 516.
12 AIR 1960 Cal 40 (*per* S.K. Sen, J.).
13 *Peter Alan Basil* v *East India Pharmaceuticals Works Ltd.* AIR 1976 Cal 182.
14 *Tharumal* v *Masjid* (1994)3 SCC 575.
15 *Jamkhep* v *Kuer Majihi* AIR 1949 Ass 61.

unequivocal and defiant disclaimer of title of the landlord. Tenants had incurred forfeiture of tenancy and s. 111(*g*) was attracted.[1]

If the lessee renounces his character, it is known as disclaimer. The disclosure or renunciation must be in clear and unequivocal terms whether the same be in pleadings or in other document.[2]

The Supreme Court has held that there must exist jural relationship of lessor or lessee and an unequivocal and clear renouncement by lessee of his character as such prior to the notice issued by the landlord determining the lease on the ground of disclaimer. Non-acceptance of the landlord-tenant relationship by lessees by setting up title in themselves as owners on acquisition of title and continuance in possession by operation of law or taking plea of adverse possession would not constitute forfeiture under cl. (*g*)(2). It is made clear by the Supreme Court that non-acceptance of the relationship of landlord and tenant does not amount to disclaimer of title and since the very existence of jural relationship of a landlord and tenant is a pre-condition the landlord has to first establish such relationship and such relationship so established, if denied, would be a case of forfeiture.[3] Similarly mere statement of the tenant that he was not aware as to who was the landlord is not denial of the title of the landlord.[4] Since the consequence of applying the rule regarding disclaimer is serious, the denial has to be clear and in unequivocal terms.[5]

Where a lessee sold the leased house to a third person describing himself as owner of the house and thereby tried to set up a title to the suit house to himself and renounced character as lessee of the said house under the landlord whereby the lessee was exposed to the risk of forfeiting his lease as per s. 111(*g*) of the Act, this fact and the notice to quit by the lessor would amount to a forfeiture, as the two factors required under s. 111(*g*) were fulfilled. Therefore, even if the notice to quit is not found to be a valid notice under s. 106 the lessee would come within the mischief of s. 111(*g*) and the institution of suit for eviction on that score could not be questioned.[6] In other words, if a lessee describes himself as owner of the demised property, he sets up a disclaimer.

Where a tenant breaks an express condition in the lease by making a pucca construction on the premises and also falls in arrears of rent for more than four months, the plaintiff-landlord can sue the tenant for possession by terminating the tenancy by a simple notice to quit under s. 106, T.P. Act for

1 *Chanda Devi* v *Dr. Taroquad Sinha* AIR 1980 All 270; *Ram Chandra* v *Maha Devi* AIR 1946 Mad 57.
2 *Raja Mahomed Amir Ahmed Khan* v *Municipal Board of Setapur* AIR 1965 SC 1923.
3 *Guru Amarjit Singh* v *Rattan Chand* (1993)4 SCC 349; AIR 1994 SC 227.
4 *Munisanni Naidu* v *C. Raganathan* AIR 1991 SC 492; (1992)2 SCC 139.
5 *Kundan Mall* v *Gurudutt* (1989)1 SCC 522.
6 *Batakala Budhia Patra* v *Durgasi Dandasi Patro* AIR 1978 Ori 103.

non-payment of rent and it is not necessary to serve a notice of determination of tenancy under s. 111(*g*) for breach of the condition not to make pucca construction.[7] Prior notice terminating tenancy is sufficient. Second notice expressly mentioning a ground of forfeiture is not necessary.[8]

42 Forfeiture—provisions of s. 111(g)—whether notice by the Government is necessary

We should profit to refer to learned observations in the reported case in AIR 1964 AP 450 at p. 453 which gives an answer to the oft-raised question—is a notice by the Government necessary before re-entry or resumption?

"It is profitable to refer to the Government Grant Act (Act XV of 1895) in this connection. Section 2 of the Act categorically states that nothing in the Transfer of Property Act contained shall apply or be deemed ever to have applied to any grant or transfer of land or of interest therein and made by or on behalf of the Government to or in favour of any person whatsoever, but every grant and transfer shall be construed and take effect as if the said Act had not been passed. Section 3 enjoins that all provisions, restrictions, conditions and limitations ever contained in any such grant or transfer as aforesaid shall be valid and/or enactment of the legislature to the contrary notwithstanding...... It is not only the Transfer of Property Act that is affected by discretion of the Crown to impose such conditions and limitations at it thinks fit, no matter what the general law of the land is. The effect of s. 3, therefore, is that when a grant has been made by the Crown is not, with reference to that grant, bound by any of the sections of either the Tenancy Act or the Transfer of Property Act or any other law for the time being in force. It, therefore, follows that any grant made has to be construed in accordance with the tenor of the grant, and the grant will certainly be regulated is accordance with such tennor.[9] When no notice is contemplated under the tenor of the grant—the notice is not necessary.[10]

In *Namdeo Lakman* v *Narmadabai*, the principal question which arose for decision was whether notice under s. 111(*g*), as contemplated, was necessary for determination of a lease for non-payment of rent even where such lease was executed before the T.P. Act came into force. Discussing elaborately the law and authorities, Their Lordships came to the conclusion that no such notice was necessary and the defaulting lessee cannot claim the benefit of a notice in writing to complete the forfeiture he has incurred, and the lessor has to simply express an intention that he is going to avail of the forfeiture and that can be done by the filing of the suit, as in English law, in all cases not governed by the 'Transfer of Property Act."[11]

7 *Abrar Husain* v *Abdul Rahim* AIR 1979 NOC 83 (All).
8 AIR 1980 All 270 (supra).
9 AIR 1921 Mad 409; AIR 1938 Cal 211; AIR 1957 SC 286 and AIR 1960 Pat 486.
10 AIR 1954 AP 450.
11 AIR 1953 SC 228; see *Banarashilal Laroiya* v *Jatadhari Das* AIR 1971 Pat 110; *Kedar Das Mohta* v *Nand Lal Poddar* AIR 1971 Pat 253.

Forfeiture plus notice determines a lease. Forfeiture does not include a notice. The determination of a lease includes both and takes place upon the existence of both.[12]

A notice under s. 111(*g*) of the T.P. Act must precede a notice under s. 114A of the Act.[13]

Under cl. (*g*) read with s. 114 only one notice to quit is necessary and not two, but when the breach is capable of remedies, the lessor should give the lessee reasonable time to do so. While it is not capable of being remedied the lessor has to give a notice simply conveying his intention to determine the lease. No particular form of notice in the latter case is necessary, but in case the breach is capable of being remedied a notice to forthwith quit and vacate on the ground of forfeiture is bad.[14] A separate notice under s. 114A and s. 111(*g*) may be issued but a combined notice combining the element of both under s. 111(*g*) and under s. 114A is also valid.[15]

When the breach is assignment of the lease which is forbidden and re-entry is provided in breach thereof, a notice determining tenancy under s. 111(*g*) is sufficient and there is no necessity to issue a notice under s. 114A because the breach is not capable of being remedied.[16]

But it is open to the plaintiff to give up his right under s. 108(*q*) of the Act and accepting for purposes of the suit the tenant's denial of contract of tenancy in his reply to plaintiff's notice under s. 106 terminating tenancy, to claim ejectment of defendant on the ground of trespass by paying necessary court fees as in a suit based on title. In such a case, the plaintiff can succeed simply by proving his title, provided the defendant fails to prove any right to hold property. The suit not being based on right to re-enter by reason of forfeiture of lease, is not bad because notice under s. 111(*g*) has not been given.[17]

43 Notice to determine lease—provisions of s. 111(h), T.P. Act

We have seen before the mode of determination of lease under cl. (*g*) of s. 111. The present notes are devoted to provisions in cl. (*h*) of the said section. It reads:

> Section 111. A lease of immovable property determines—
>
> * * *
>
> (*h*) on the expiration of a notice to determine the lease, or to quit, or of intention to quit, the property leased, duly given by one party to the other.

12 74 CWN 531.
13 74 CWN 531.
14 *Provat* v *Bengal Central Bank* AIR 1938 Cal 589.
15 *Kshiroda Sundari* v *Bhupendra Mohan* AIR 1961 Ass 70.
16 *Chandra Nath* v *Chulai Pashi* AIR 1960 Cal 40.
17 *Bansraj Kahar* v *Kaushal Kishore Saren Singh* AIR 1973 All 99.

This, in brief, means: in the case of a lease from year to year or from month to month, it is, in the absence of a contract or local law or usage to the contrary, terminable by a notice to quit under s. 106 of the T.P. Act.[1] Where in the case of such leases there is a contract or local law or usage to the contrary and in case of a lease where the contract of tenancy provides for notice before determination of lease, the lease is terminable by a notice to determine the lease, as contemplated by the contract or local law or usage.[2] The landlord before succeeding in a suit for ejectment must prove that there was an overt act on his part to determine the lease.[3]

A notice to quit or to determine the lease is necessary only where the tenancy is valid and admitted to exist between the parties. Where there is no tenancy at all,[4] or where the tenancy is denied,[5] or where a lease is cancelled on the ground of fraud,[6] no such notice is necessary before suing for ejectment. Again, a lease, whether governed by the Transfer of Property Act or not, if not determined in any of the modes provided by cls. (*a*) to (*g*) of s. 111 of the T.P. Act, can be determined only by a proper notice to quit or to determine the lease.[7] But a tenancy not governed by the T.P. Act and not determined on any of the grounds referred to in cls. (*a*) to (*g*) of s. 111 can only be determined by a reasonable notice to quit. In an ejectment suit notice s. 111(*h*) of the T.P. Act—the tenant is unambiguously required to vacate the house and give possession on expiry of 30 days after receipt thereof—the notice is valid.[8]

An invalid notice does not determine the lease or render the possession of the tenant wrongful.[9] But where an invalid notice is accepted by the landlord and he has acted upon the notice and the defect is waived, the lease will be terminated.[10]

44 Licence—termination of

Section 105 of the T.P. Act does not indicate that for termination of licence, otherwise than provided in the agreement itself, notice is required. 'Licence' does not create interest in the property, it only permits one to occupy property of some other which otherwise that is, without permission or without licence, would be unlawful. Therefore, no notice to terminate licence is necessary.[11]

1 AIR 1920 Nag 62.
2 AIR 1958 All 729.
3 AIR 1941 Cal 506.
4 AIR 1932 Cal 221; AIR 1939 Pat 167.
5 AIR 1927 Cal 561.
6 AIR 1933 Mad 67.
7 AIR 1936 Cal 351; AIR 1937 Pat 391.
8 *Sita Ram* v *Moti Lal* AIR 1976 All 70.
9 AIR 1928 All 95.
10 86 IC 512.
11 *Upendra Mondal* v *Bhajahari Mondal* AIR 1991 NOC 107 (Gau).

45 Waiver of a notice to quit—provisions of s. 113, T.P. Act—acts amounting to and acts not amounting to waiver

A notice under s. 106, T.P. Act can be waived by a tenant.[12]

Section 113 of the Transfer of Property Act enjoins: "A notice given under s. 111(*h*) is waived, with the express or implied consent of the person to whom it is given, by any act on the part of the person giving it showing an intention to treat the lease as subsisting."

This section applies to leases that are to be determined by a notice to quit. Whether there has been a waiver or not, the intention of the parties is to be judged; for waiver is a matter of intention of parties.[13] The notice of ejectment can be waived under s. 113 by mutual consent of the lessor and the lessee. The consent of the lessee can be given expressly or, by implication; it can be inferred and the intention on the part of the lessor to continue to treat the lease as subsisting can be shown by any act of the lessor.[14] In other words, under s. 113 the notice is deemed to be waived only if the landlord by express words or by implication or by his conduct intends to treat the lease as subsisitng.[15]

The Supreme Court has pointed out under s. 113 a notice to quit is waived by an act showing the person giving the notice an intention to treat the lease as subsisting in spite of such notice, subject to this that there is express or implied consent of the person to whom it is given. Thus, where both the lessor and the lessee contend that by acceptance of rent under the old tenancy, the landlord indicated that the old tenancy was continuing, then there was waiver of notice to quit and the old tenancy was continuing.[16] Whenever there is acceptance by the landlord of any sum tendered by the tenant as rent, the court is obliged to look to such acceptance in the light of the requirement of s. 113 as to whether the acceptance has shown an intention on the part of the landlord to treat the lease as subsisting.[17] According to the principle enacted in s. 113, a notice by a landlord to a tenant would stand waived by a second and similar notice, provided that the tenant has consented, at least impliedly, to such waiver. So where the landlord is deemed to have waived the earlier notice, if any, he can succeed on proof of service of the later notice only.[18] The Supreme Court has held that the consent of the lessee to treat the old tenancy as subsisting is a new agreement.[19] It may

12 *K.N. Ramakrishnan* v *C. Keval Chand* AIR 1971 Mad 150; *Taeyabati Jaferbhai Tankiwala* v *Ashan & Co.* AIR 1971 SC 102; *Dahyalbhai Limjibhai* v *Amar Chand Jagjiwan* 1971 Guj 73.

13 AIR 1954 Cal 404.

14 AIR 1962 Ass 148.

15 AIR 1965 Ass 55.

16 *Ranjit* v *Mohitosh* AIR 1969 SC 1187.

17 *New India Assurance Co. Ltd.* v *Ghanshyam Das* AIR 1997 All 383.

18 *Mono Ranjan Dasgupta* v *Suchitra Ganguly* AIR 1989 Cal 14 (DB).

19 *Calcutta Credit Corporation* v *Happy Homes* AIR 1968 SC 471.

be mentioned that payment and acceptance of rent from statutory tenant governed by the State Rent Control Act after determination of the tenancy by notice to quit does not amount to waiver of notice to quit.[20]

Two illustrations of waiver have been appended to s. 113 of the Act which are:

(*a*) *A*, the lessor, gives *B*, the lessee, notice to quit the property leased. The notice expires. *B* tenders, and *A* accepts rent which has become due in respect of the property since the expiration of the notice. The notice is waived.

Acceptance of rent which has become due since the expiration of the notice to quit will be a waiver.[1] "The acceptance of rent after the expiry of the notice by itself may not necessarily constitute a waiver. But it is an act on the part of the lessor which will go to show the intention on his part to treat the lease as subsisting. Past conduct of the landlord in giving notice earlier for ejectment and thereafter not bringing any suit and accepting rent for three successive months will go to show that when the landlord accepted the rent after giving notice he intended to continue the tenancy and waive the notice.[2] Where the landlord filed a suit for ejectment and received rent, sent by money order by the tenant, after institution of the suit—suit was not withdrawn: action on the part of the landlord did not amount to a waiver.[3] The landlord withdrew rent deposited in court under the Rent Control Act—did not amount to waiver.[4]

The plain language of s. 113 is that the act of the lessor must be such as to constitute a clear evidence of his intention to treat the lease as subsisting and illustration (*a*) must be understood and applied in consonance with the principle underlying the section with due reference to the intention of the lessor.[5]

Coming to the second illustration, it reads:

(*b*) *A*, the lessor, gives *B*, the lessee, notice to quit the property leased. The notice expires, and *B* remains in possession. *A* gives to *B* as lessee a second notice to quit. The first notice is waived.

Legality of the second notice when the first notice not acted upon by both parties: Once a notice of termination is given it cannot be unilaterally retracted by the landlord and when determination of tenancy is accepted by

20 *Ganga Dutt* v *Kartick* AIR 1961 SC 1067; *Mangilal* v *Sugar* AIR 1965 SC 101; *Bhawarji* v *Himatlal* AIR 1972 SC 819.
1 AIR 1926 Cal 763.
2 AIR 1962 Ass 148; *Taiyabali Jaferbhai* v *M/s. Ahsan & Co.* AIR 1971 SC 102.
3 AIR 1962 J&K 2.
4 AIR 1965 Ass 55.
5 *Purohit Lakshman Chandji* v *Vekha Venkata Shree Ram Chandra Murthi* AIR 1976 AP 428.

both the parties the tenant cannot continue the tenancy again without the approval or consent of the landlord. But when the tenant does not accept the determination of that tenancy and the landlord also does not act upon that notice, the question of consent of the tenant for giving a second notice does not arise.

When even after the notice of determination of tenancy, the tenant asserts himself as a tenant and the landlord treats him as such, the first notice is waived. In such a case there is no illegality in the second notice given by the landlord.[6]

Again, where a tenant disputes the validity of a quit notice issued by the landlord and the landlord thereafter issues a second notice treating the lease as subsisting after the first notice—that implies waiver of the first notice.[7]

In *Tayeb Ali* v *Asan & Co.* Supreme Court in the light of illustration (*b*) of s. 113 has held that when subsequently another notice is served upon the tenant and the tenant did not act upon the first notice, issuance of second notice acts as the waiver of the first notice to quit.[8] Calcutta High Court has held that when the landlord issues a second notice treating the lease as subsisting even after service of first notice to quit and the tenant did not act upon the first notice, there is waiver of the first notice to quit.[9]

Giving of the second notice to the lessee is a waiver of the first notice.

Acts amounting to waiver of a notice to quit

(1) Acceptance of rent due subsequent to the notice to quit, even after the institution of a suit for ejectment, will operate as a waiver of notice.[10] Whether prior or subsequent to the institution of a suit, acceptance amounts to a waiver.[11]

(2) The fact that the lessor accepts the rent after service of notice under protest as where he states that he accepts it as damages for use and occupation will not prevent it from operating as a waiver of the notice.[12] But the acceptance of an amount as damages for use and occupation though tendered as rent will not amount to a waiver.[13] Decree for ejectment of tenant—acceptance of rent by

6 *K. Vasudeva Rao* v *Jadu Nandan Trivedi* AIR 1977 Cal 142.
7 *Sudhir Kumar Paul* v *Indu Prabha Ghosh* AIR 1976 Cal 274.
8 AIR 1971 SC 102.
9 *Chandra Kishore* v *Renuka* 84 CWN 314.
10 AIR 1926 Cal 763 contra AIR 1959 AP 346; AIR 1959 Bom 292; AIR 1954 Cal 460; AIR 1956 All 175 and AIR 1962 J&K 2.
11 *Ramdayal* v *Jawla Prasad* AIR 1966 All 623. See further 58 CWN 438; AIR 1947 Cal 627; 70 CWN 37 (41); *Om Prakash Saxena* v *Raja Bahu Saxena* AIR 1974 All 428.
12 AIR 1923 Cal 663; 80 IC 200.
13 AIR 1952 Cal 455.

plaintiff while appeal against decree pending—rent receipt clearly showing that rent was accepted under protest—*Held*, that the acceptance of rent did not give rise to inference of intention on the plaintiff's part to treat the lease as subsisting.[14]

(3) Lessor giving another notice to quit after expiry of the first notice—constitutes a waiver of the first notice.[15]

(4) Landlord giving first notice to quit on grounds of arrears of rent but tenant did not vacate. Second notice after about a year and demanded rent for period between first and second notice—In suit for ejectment the landlord claiming damages for use and occupation for a period subsequent to the second notice showing that the landlord was aware of the distinction between rent and compensation for use and occupation—*held*, first notice was waived and that the landlord had treated the tenancy as subsistng.[16]

(5) After giving a notice under s. 106, the landlord filed an ejectment application. The application was got dismissed by him. Thereafter he waited for more than a year and then filed another ejectment application. *Held*, that the landlord waived the notice and the application was liable to be dismissed.[17]

(6) Plea of want of notice—plea was raised four years after parties had proceeded to trial and led evidence on the basis that no notice was required—notice must be deemed to have been waived.[18]

(7) Where pending a second appeal against dismissal of the ejectment suit the landlord writes to the tenant that he would withdraw the appeal and that the tenant should pay him rent due till then within 30 days, failing which he would be liable to ejectment—the only inference possible is that the landlord waived the first notice of termination and created a fresh tenancy in favour of the defendant.[1]

Acts which did not amount to a waiver of a notice to quit

(1) The acceptance of rent accrued due before the date of the notice to quit is not waiver of the notice to quit.[2]

(2) A mere acceptance of amounts equivalent to rent by a landlord from tenant in possession after a lease had been determined by a notice to quit does not create new tenancy.[3]

14 *Ram Lal* v *Sardari Lal* AIR 1968 J&K 22.
15 AIR 1935 Bom 247.
16 *Taiyab Ali Jaferbhai* v *Ahsan Co.* AIR 1971 SC 102.
17 *Chuni Lal Om Prakash* v *Inder Singh* AIR 1973 P&H 353.
18 *Ram Pratap* v *Birla Cotton Spinning* AIR 1973 Del 124.
1 *Padam Chand Garg* v *Atar Singh Rickshawala* AIR 1972 All 217.
2 AIR 1952 All 862; 63 IC 191.
3 *Mohan Lal Goela* v *Siri Krishan* AIR 1978 Del 92.

(3) Some amount paid towards part-satisfaction of rent. There cannot be any waiver of a notice simply because the tenant had paid the rent for a period before the expiry of tenancy.[4]

(4) Acceptance of rent after institution of suit for ejectment by itself does not amount to waiver of notice. What is necessary under s. 113 on the part of recipient of the notice an intention or a consent to have the notice given to him waived and on the part of the person issuing the notice an intention to waive the notice and treat the lease as subsisitng.[5]

(5) Acceptance of rent for the period before the expiry of notice is not waiver.[6]

(6) Acceptance of rent by the lessor under a mistake will not amount to a waiver.[7]

(7) A mere demand for the rent accrued due subsequent to the notice, not followed by a promise by the tenant to pay, cannot operate as a waiver of the notice for want of the tenant's consent.[8]

(8) A claim in a suit for ejectment for the arrears of rent due is not a waiver of the notice.[9]

(9) Section 24 of the West Bengal Premises Tenancy Act 1956 (now s. 25 of the Act of 1997) speaks of a waiver of default and not of a waiver of a notice to quit. Acceptance of rent for the period subsequent to notice when suit is pending will not be a waiver of a notice vide s. 24 of the Act of 1997.

(10) Withdrawal of the amount by the landlord deposited in court under the Rent Control Act does not constitute a waiver in the absence of any evidence to show that the landlord intended to keep the lease subsisting.[10]

(11) Mere abortive negotiations between the parties with regard to the payment of rent subsequent to the notice do not constitute a waiver.[11]

(12) The mere fact that the tenant is allowed to remain in possession out of favour after expiry of the notice to quit or the fact that no suit is filed for ejectment immediately on the expiry of the notice does not operate as a waiver.[12]

4 *Hashmatrai* v *Tarachand* AIR 1979 Bom 95.
5 *Ramjilal* v *Gulabrao* AIR 1979 Bom 44.
6 AIR 1921 Cal 126.
7 (1946)2 All ER 779.
8 13 CB 178.
9 1 IC 753; 6 IC 477 and 42 IC 655.
10 AIR 1965 Ass 55.
11 AIR 1927 Rang 276.
12 AIR 1923 Nag 129.

(13) The acceptance of rent by an unauthorised person does not bind the landlord and will not constitute a waiver.[13] Acceptance of rent by the agent of the landlord after notice to quit by the principal contrary to the express intention of the principal to the knowledge of the tenant does not amount to a waiver of a notice.[14]

(14) In the case of co-sharers, acceptance of rent by one of them will operate as a wavier only in so far as he is concerned. The others will not be affected thereby.[15] A waiver to be binding must be made by the entire body of joint owners. It is not open to one of the joint-owners to waive a notice.[16]

(15) Acceptance of rent by the plaintiff while appeal against the decree is pending. Rent receipt clearly shows that rent was accepted under protest. Acceptance of rent did not give rise to the inference of intention on the plaintiff's part to treat the lease as subsisting.[17] It was held in the last-mentioned case that after the decree was passed the defendant became a trespasser and acceptance of rent must be presumed to be acceptance of rent as compensation for use and occupation.

(16) In order to create a fresh tenancy the acts of the parties must be voluntary and with the definite intention of creating a fresh tenancy and where after issue of notice terminating the tenancy the tenant remitted amounts as rent by M.O. and the landlord accepted the sums sent as rent but 'under protest' as compensation, the conduct of the landlord shows that he had no intention to waive the notice terminating the tenancy and therefore, no fresh tenancy is created.[18]

(17) Acceptance of rent after notice would not *ipso facto* constitute a waiver,[19] during pendency of the suit for ejectment. It does not amount to waiver. The tenant has to prove that the landlord by accepting the rent for the period subsequent to the termination of tenancy had an intention to treat the lease as subsisting.[20]

(18) Waiver of first notice by service of second notice—Letters, in reply to tenant's communication on first notice, extending time to vacate only for the reason that the first notice had not been acted upon—*Held*, there is no waiver of first notice.[1]

13 AIR 1932 Pat 259.
14 1954 All LJ 58.
15 AIR 1932 Pat 259.
16 AIR 1956 All 175.
17 AIR 1956 Cal 106; AIR 1954 Cal 404; AIR 1949 FC 124; AIR 1960 J&K 22.
18 *Pohumal T. Mardani* v *Tusharkanti Pal Chowdhury* AIR 1977 Gau 17.
19 *Deep Chand* v *Babu Ram* AIR 1976 All 478.
20 *Smt. Sharda Sharma* v *Smt. Gulab Devi* AIR 1972 All 435.
1 *Narang Overseas* v *Meher Chand Kohli* AIR 1977 NOC 363 (Del).

46 Notice of suit in a lease determined by 'forfeiture' [s. 111(g), T.P. Act]—Relief against forfeiture (s. 114A, T.P. Act)—combined notice under s. 114A—mandatory provisions

Under s. 111(*g*) of the T.P. Act it is necessary for determination of a lease for breach of a condition that the lessor should give a notice in writing to the lessee of his intention to determine the lease. Again s. 114A provides that after such determination under s. 111(*g*) it is necessary for the lessor, before he institutes a suit for ejectment, to serve on the lessor a notice in writing—

(*a*) specifying the particular breach complained of; and

(*b*) if the breach is capable of remedy, requiring the lessee to remedy the breach within a reasonable time of the service of notice.

However, non-compliance of s. 114A due to failure to mention by the lessor that the lessee should remedy the breach within a reasonable period is not a severe defect to invalidate the notice. Section 114A merely bars a suit for ejectment on the ground of the conditions laid down in s. 114A not being fulfilled.[2]

It is, therefore, obvious that in cases of breaches of conditions referred to in this section, two notices are necessary before the lessor can maintain a suit. He has to give first a notice of his intention to determine the lease and after determination he has next to serve another notice as required under s. 114A.

Prior to the institution of a suit the lessor after the service of notice has to wait for a 'reasonable period' from the date of service of notice for his anticipated compliance, i.e. for remedy of the breach, if the breach is capable of remedy. What should be the reasonable time depends upon particular circumstances of the case.

Three broad facts to be remembered in connection with a notice under s. 114A of the T.P. Act are:

(*a*) There is no bar under the Transfer of Property Act to issue a combined notice under s. 111(*g*) and s. 114A.[3]

(*b*) Notices both under s. 111(*g*) and s. 114A of the Act are required to be given to the tenant and no notice is to be given to an assignee of a part of the lessee's interest.[4]

(*c*) The notice is mandatory.[5] The right to institute a suit for ejectment accrues only after the requirements of s. 114A have been complied with. The section requires that the plaintiff should allege in the

2 *Basent Lal* v *State of UP* AIR 1981 SC 170; (1980)4 SCC 430.
3 AIR 1961 Ass 70.
4 AIR 1961 Ass 79.
5 AIR 1957 Ori 35.

plaint that the requirements of the section have been complied with. Where there is no evidence to show that the lease had been validly terminated by notice as required by s. 114A, the suit cannot be dismissed.[6] Even in a case where the contract of lease provides for the right of re-entry by the lessor upon the lessee's breach of an express condition as to payment of rent, the latter is entitled to a notice as envisaged by s. 114A.[7]

47 Object and contents of a notice under s. 114A of the Transfer of Property Act

The object of the notice under s. 114A of the T.P. Act is to give the lessee precise information of what is alleged against him and further what he is to do.[8] The section demands that the notice (*i*) should specify the particular breach complained of, and (*ii*) if the breach is capable of remedy, requiring the lessee to remedy the breach. However, once the notice is given and the provisions are substantially complied with and the breach is not remedied, mere technical defects in the notice would not stand in the way of landlord getting eviction on the ground of forfeiture.[9]

The notice has to be given in order to give an opportunity to the lessee to avoid forfeiture in cases where a breach of condition is capable of remedy and such a notice is required even in a case of alienation.[10]

But where the lessee has sublet the leasehold land or portions thereof such breach cannot be remedied by the lessee simply on his own volition because remedying the breach by the lessee may very well be frustrated by the sub-lessee who has some rights under the lease granted to him by the lessee. It is for this reason no distinction has been made in the proviso to s. 114A of the Act as to any sub-lease given to the entirety of the leasehold interest or a sub-lease given in respect of a part of the premises. Therefore, a lessee who has sublet part of the premises would not be entitled to any notice under s. 114A.[11]

A notice under s. 114A of the Transfer of Property Act need not be given if the ground on which the ejectment is prayed for is under s. 13(1)(*b*) of the West Bengal Premises Tenancy Act 1956 (now s. 6(1)(*f*) of the Act of 1997) that is, if a tenant or a person residing in the premises has done any act contrary to the provisions of cls. (*m*), (*o*), (*p*) of the Transfer of Property Act 1882.[12]

6 AIR 1954 All 649.
7 AIR 1967 All 209.
8 AIR 1953 Mad 313.
9 *Ibid.*
10 AIR 1960 Cal 40.
11 *Tarakpada Kirti* v *Ruplekha Chatterjee* AIR 1978 Cal 189.
12 *Bhagaban Biswas* v *Bejoy Singh Nahar* AIR 1980 Cal 70.

In case of forfeiture only one notice is required and not one under s. 111(*g*) and another under s. 114A. But the argument that no notice of ejectment is necessary at all in cases relating to forfeiture for non-payment of rent is not correct.[13]

48 Notice of transfer of an actionable claim (s. 131, T.P. Act)—defective notice—waiver of a notice

Section 3 of the Transfer of Property Act defines actionable claim. An actionable claim can be transferred. Section 130 of the T.P. Act provides for the right of transfer to sue the debtor for the same in his own name without obtaining the transferor's consent to such suit or proceedings without making him a party thereto.

Section 131 of the T.P. Act provides for a notice to debtor of the transfer of an actionable claim. It reads:

> "Every notice of transfer of an actionable claim shall be in writing, signed by the transferor or his agent duly authorised in this behalf, or, in case the transferor refuses to sign, by the transferee or his agent, and shall state the name and address of the transferee."

The primary duty to issue the notice is on the transferor. The transferee or his agent can sign the notice only when the transferor refuses to sign it.[14] The fact of such refusal need not be mentioned in the notice. The transferee need not set out the circumstances under which he gives notice. Again, if the transferor gives an invalid notice, the transferee is entitled to give a legal notice so as to prevent the original debtor from defeating the assignment.[15] The notice of transfer is to be given by the transferor and if given by the transferee, it should be alleged or shown that the transferor had refused to sign the notice, although that circumstance need not be mentioned in the notice.[16]

A notice under s. 131 must state the name and address of the transferee.[17] Where a notice states only the name and address of the transferee, the provisions of s. 131 are not complied with and the notice is not effective to bring the exception mentioned in the proviso to sub-sec. (1) of s. 130 into operation.[18] A notice under this section with a condition or qualification will not be bad provided the other requirements of the section are complied with.[19]

13 AIR 1955 Tripura 26; AIR 1958 Cal 589 rel on.
14 4 IC 420.
15 *Ibid.*
16 AIR 1951 Raj 74.
17 *Ibid.*
18 *Sadasook Ram Pradip* v *Hove Muller & Co.* AIR 1923 Cal 719.
19 4 IC 420 (*per* Abdul Rahim, J.).

Where the notice does not strictly comply with the provisions of this section and is defective in form, a question arises whether the debtor can waive the defects in the notice. In *Sadasook* v *Hoare Millar & Co.*, Mukherji, J., observed: "The answer to the question whether it is permissible to waive a particular provision depends upon its true nature. If the object of the legislature is to protect or benefit any individual litigant, it is open to him to waive the positive provisions of the statute. On the other hand, if the provision has been enacted for reasons of public policy, he cannot be permitted to waive it. The provisions of s. 131 fall, in any judgment, within the latter category, but I am not prepared to maintain as an abstract proposition of law that under no conceivable circumstance can the provision of s. 131 be waived by the debtor."[20]

Where a vendor had sold his premises and also transferred to the vendee the right to collect arrears of rent from the tenants on the premises, and both the sale deed and the document giving to the vendee the right to recover rent which is an actionable claim are registered documents, no notice under s. 131 by the vendee to the tenants is necessary to enable the vendee to recover arrears or rent.[1]

49 Surrender of lease [s. 111(*e*), T.P. Act 1882]

Lessee inducted in 1951. Lessee accepting registered lease for 15 years in 1955. Original lease ought to be held to have been surrendered.[2]

A month to month tenant intimated by a letter to his landlord that the tenant would surrender his lease three years after the date of his letter. The tenant did not surrender, but continued his possession after the expiry of the period. The landlord thereupon gave a notice to the tenant to quit by the end of the next month—the surrender was not accepted or acted upon in view of the notice allowing the lease to continue after three years and the original tenancy subsisted.[3]

In order to come within the ambit of cl. (*e*) of s. 111 it is necessary that the lessee should yield up his interest pursuant to an agreement with the lessor. The surrender must be to the lessor, that is, to the person in whom the reversion vests. There can be no surrender, if the lessor has either sold his reversion[4] or mortgaged the property.[5] There can be no surrender if the lease is for a fixed term and forbids surrender.[6] Surrender of demised estate means the yielding up of the estate to the landlord so that the lease-hold

20 AIR 1923 Cal 719.
1 *Prem Chand* v *Onkar Dutt Sharma* AIR 1972 All 415.
2 *Tarakpada Kirti* v *Ruplekha Chaterjee* AIR 1978 Cal 189.
3 *Gosto Behari Roy* v *Ramesh Chandra Das* AIR 1978 Cal 235.
4 *Ram Chandra* v *Sheikh Hussn* 3 Bom LR 679.
5 *Havu* v *Ganpati* AIR 1939 Bom 329.
6 *Jotindra Mohan* v *Eman Ali* (1909)2 Ind Case 633.

interest becomes extinct by mutual agreement between the parties or by operation of law.[7] The Supreme Court has held that unless the term is vested in the lessor, there can be no surrender, and it must be to a person in whom immediate reversion expectant on the term is vested. However, there must be taking of possession, but not necessarily physical possession, but something amounting to virtual taking of possession. Therefore, whether there has been a surrender or not is always a question of fact.[8]

In case of express surrender all the parties must agree. It cannot be unilateral.[9] Partial surrender does not put an end to the old tenancy and no new tenancy is created.[10]

FORMS

Form 1

Notice of assignment of a debt on behalf of the Assignor (Transfer of an actionable Claim) (by the Lawyer)

Dated the .... 20...

To

....

....

(Name and Address etc. of the debtor)

Sir,

Under instructions from my client .... *(name and address of client-creditor)* I hereby give you this notice of assignment as follows:

That by executing a registered instrument, dated .... my said client has sold and assigned to .... *(name and address of the assignee)* for valuable consideration the bond *(or, name the deed)* executed by you on .... under which you were bound to my client in the sum of Rs. .... together with interest (mention the rate of interest) thereon.

Please take notice that you are required by this notice to pay henceforward to said *(name of assignee)* the said sums as would be admissible.

Yours faithfully,

....

NOTES: 1. Section 131 of T.P. Act may be seen. For definition of actionable claim see s. 3 of the T.P. Act.

2. Notice should be sent per registered post.

3. Assignment in part is not permissible. [AIR 1925 Mad 753 (756) contra—AIR 1940 Pat 170].

7 *Mubaran Hossain* v *Custodian General* AIR 1957 Punj 197.

8 *Shah Mathuradas* v *Nagappa* AIR 1976 SC 1565; *Kamlabai* v *Mangilal* (1987)4 SCC 585.

9 *Sudhir* v *Phanendra* 62 CWN 176.

10 *Krishna Kur Khanna* v *Grindlays Bank* (1990)3 SCC 669; AIR 1991 SC 899.

4. Rate of interest and particulars of terms, if necessary, should be clearly stated.
5. Notice must be an express notice, not merely constructive.
6. The notice of transfer is to be given by the transferor. If notice is given by the transferee it should be alleged or shown that the transferor had refused to sign the notice, although it is not necessary to mention that fact in the notice—AIR 1951 Raj 74.
7. A notice is to contain the name and address of the transferee. There may be a valid transfer of debt between the transferor and the transferee. The person bound to pay the debt is not bound by the transfer unless he receives on express notice in writing conforming to provisions of s. 131, T.P. Act from the transferor, or if he refuses to sign, from the transferee, stating the name and address of transferee.

Form 2

Notice of assignment (by the assignor)

To

AB Dated .... 20.....

....

....

(*State here name, address etc. of the debtor*)

Dear Sir,

By an instrument in writing dated 5.7.20... and made between myself and one Sri CD of .... I have transferred and assigned unto said Sri C.D, for valuable consideration the Bond dated .... executed by you whereby you became bound to me in the sum of Rs. 10,00,000 (Rupees ten lakh) only.

I hereby give you notice to pay the said sum of Rs. 10,00,000 (Rupees ten lakh) only to said Sri C.D., his heirs, executors, administrators or assigns.

Yours faithfully,

PQ

Copy to

Sri CD

.... for favour of information

(P.Q.)

NOTES:
1. A transfer of an actionable claim takes effect from the date of transfer and not from the date of notice which the transferor or the transferee may or may not give to the debtor—AIR 1951 Raj 74; AIR 1945 Bom 11.
2. Where the notice given by the transferor does not contain the name and address of the transferee, the notice is insufficient—9 Bom LR 838.
3. The vesting of right to recover the arrears of rent does not depend upon the sending of a notice under s. 131—AIR 1972 All 415.
4. Savings s. 137 of the T.P. Act enjoins that s. 130 of the T.P. Act does not apply to assignments of negotiable instruments. Such instruments can be assigned according to the provisions of the Negotiable Instruments Act—*Venkatadri* v *Lakshinarasinha* 21 MLJ 80; 8 IC 33.

Form 3

Notice of assignment of a debt on behalf of the Assignee

Dated, the .... 20 ...

To

....

....

(*Name and Address of the debtor*)

Sir,

Under instructions from my client (*name and address of assignee*) I hereby give you this notice of assignment as follows:

That by executing a registered instrument, (*name the deed*) dated .... you became bound to .... (*name and address of the creditor-assignor*) in the sum of Rs. .... together with interest thereon at the rate ......, said (name of the creditor-assignor) by an instrument in writing dated ...... has in consideration of Rs. ...... assigned the said debt to my aforesaid client.

That the said .... (*name the assignor*) has refused to give you notice of assignment.

Please take notice that you are required to pay to my said client the said sum of Rs. .... together with all interest up to date, as admissible, from the date of assignment and that any payment made in respect of the said debt to said (*name creditor-assignor*) after receipt of this notice will be at your risk.

Yours faithfully,
Advocate

NOTES:
1. The word 'registered' may be dropped if unregistered.
2. Notes 16 of Chapter 21 may be seen (see 4 IC 420; *Kanraj* v *Vijoy Singh* AIR 1951 Raj 74).
3. A notice must comply with requirement of s. 131 of the T.P. Act—*Sadasook* v *Hoare Miller & Co.* AIR 1923 Cal 719.

Form 4

Notice of assignment of a Lease

To

Mr. ....

....

(Lessor)

Dear Sir,

I do hereby give you a notice to the effect that by a Deed of Assignment bearing the date .... made between Mr. A.B., son of Late C.D. of (*address*) ...., of the one part and myself, of the other part, the leasehold interest in the premises, described in the Schedule below, has been assigned by the said Mr. A.B. in my favour for the residue of 3 years as provided in the lease dated ...... subject to my performance of the terms and conditions of the lease.

2. Receipt of this notice may please be acknowledged.

Schedule

Yours faithfully,

Sd/- ....

NOTES: 1. A non-agricultural tenancy created after the passing of T.P. Act is transferable unless any custom or contract is established to the contrary—*Kishore Lal* v *Kanine* 37 Cal 377 (383).

2. A tenancy from month to month is assignable—*Rambarai Singh* v *Tirthapada* AIR 1957 Cal 173.

Form 5

Notice by the assignee of transfer of mortgage with demand for dues under the mortgage

By Registered Post with AD
Dated the .... 20......

To

Sri ....

(*State here name and address of the mortgagor*)

Sir,

Please take notice that all that principal sum of Rs. .... together with interest at 8% per annum owing from you to Sri .... son of .... of .... (*name and address of the mortgagee*) secured by a registered deed of mortgage dated .... executed by you in favour of said .... (*name and address of the mortgagee*) has been assigned to me by said Sri .... (*name of the mortgagee*) absolutely on .... by a registered deed of assignment for consideration.

You are hereby called upon to pay to me, and not to said Sri .... (*name of mortgagee*), all sums payable as principal and interest under the said mortgage.

Yours faithfully,
(Sd/- ....)
(*Name of assignee of the mortgagee*)

NOTES: 1. Right to sue for mortgage money—See s. 68 of the T.P. Act.

2. Sale of mortgaged property by the mortgagee—Notice in writing shall have to be served three months' notice before sale—see s. 69 of the T.P. Act—*Babamiya* v *Jehangir* AIR 1941 Bom 339.

3. For mortgaged debt—see s. 134 of the T.P. Act.

4. A transfer of an actionable claim (e.g., debt) can be made not only by way of absolute sale, but also by way of mortgage—21 IC 316.

5. Assignment of rights under policy of insurance against fire—see s. 135 of the T.P. Act. (But assignment of rights under Policy of Marine Insurance has been repealed with effect from 1.8.63 by s. 92, Marine Insurance Act 1963).

Form 6

Notice of deposit

(Section 83 of the Transfer of Property Act 1882)

In the Court of .... at ....

Mortgage Suit No. .... of 20 ....

.... plaintiff

versus

.................................defendant

To

....

Take notice that A.B. has deposited in this Court to your account the sum of Rs. .... said to be the sum remaining due on a mortgage executed on the .... day of ...... 20 ...... between .... and ....

Given under my hand and the seal of the Court, this .... day of ......, 20 ....

Judge.

Form 7

Notice by the lessor to a tenant to attorn

Dated the ....20...

To

Sri ....

(*Name and Address of the tenant*)

Sir,

I do hereby inform you that the premises described in the Schedule below and which you so long held under me as a (monthly) tenant has been sold by me to Sri .... (*name and address of the transferee*) on (*date of transfer*).

Please take notice that you are requested to attorn to and become a tenant of said (*name of transferee*) in respect of the said premises and are hereby authorised and instructed to pay all rents which became due since transfer and will become due hereafter in respect of the said premises to said Sri .... (*name of transferee*).

SCHEDULE OF THE PREMISES

(*Give particulars of the premises rented out*)

Yours faithfully,

....

NOTES:

1. Section 109 of T.P. Act may be seen. A notice of this type is recommendatory in character.
2. The essential requirement of the notice is that the fact of transfer should be brought to the notice of the tenant (19 IC 865).
3. Lessor's transferee may also issue notice claiming rent since transfer.

4. If the lessor transfers also his claim of rent for the period prior to transfer of the premises, that would come under s. 131 of T.P. Act. Notice, in such cases, should be suitably amended.

Form 8

Notice by tenant for renewal of lease

To

(Name and Address of the Landlord)

Sub: Renewal of lease of the premises No. ....

Dated .... 20 ....

Dear Sir,

I, the undersigned (name), your tenant of premises No. .... of ...., hereby give you notice that, in pursuance of the agreement for renewal contained in the deed of lease dated the .... day of .... 20 .... and made between yourself of the one part, and myself of the other part, I hereby give notice of my intention to have a renewed lease of the premises comprised in the said deed of lease for a further term of .... years. I do hereby request you to grant me a renewed lease on the terms and conditions specified in the said deed of lease.

Yours faithfully,

(Tenant)

Form 9

Notice by a tenant for renewal of lease (Another form)

Reg. Premises at ....
....

To

Sri A.B.

....

....

(Landlord)

Dear Sir,

I have been holding the premises, described at the foot of this notice, as a monthly tenant under you on the strength of an Agreement of Tenancy dated the ...... day of .... 20 ..., made between yourself of the one part and myself of the other part.

2. The said Agreement of Tenancy contains a provision for renewal of the tenancy. Pursuant to said clause of renewal, I hereby give you notice of my intention for renewal of my tenancy in respect of the said premises for a further term of 5 (five) years.

3. You are hereby requested to accord renewal of tenancy for a further term of 5 years on expiry of the present term.

Particulars of the premises

Yours faithfully,

....

(Tenant)

Form 10

Notice of determination of a tenancy-at-will on behalf of the landlord

(Under s. 106 of T.P. Act 1882)

Dated the 20

To

The ....

....

Dear Sir,

Under instructions from my client .... (*name, description and address*) I call upon you to deliver up possession of the premises, detailed below, within 30 days hereof which you now hold of my client as a tenant.

2. In default of your compliance your occupation of the premises, after the period allowed hereinabove, will be wrongful and an act of trespass and you will be liable to pay damages to my client at the rate of Rs. .... per day of your wrongful occupation of the same till you are ejected therefrom and that my client will sue you for your eviction and for recovery of damages.

3. A copy of this notice is being kept in my office for future use, if necessary.

Schedule of premises

Yours faithfully,

....

Advocate

NOTES: 1. Notice is optional. Section 106 of T.P. Act has no application to a tenancy-at-will.

2. A verbal demand for possession is sufficient—AIR 1957 Cal 625.

Form 11

Notice by a tenant/lessee seeking renewal of lease when agreement provides option of renewal

By Registered Post with AD

....

The ....day of .... 20...

To

Sri ....

....

(*Name and address of the lessor/landlord*)

Dear Sir,

I have been occupying the premises, more fully described in the Schedule appended below, under you for a term of five years to expire with the month of April, 20..., pursuant to an agreement of tenancy/lease executed by myself of the one part and yourself of the other part on. ...

Clause No. .... of the said agreement provides option of renewal of the said tenancy lease under existing terms. In terms of the said clause of the agreement, I do hereby give you this notice intimating to you my intention to have the tenancy/lease of the said property in the Schedule below renewed for a further term of five years on expiry of the current term, on the terms and conditions contained in the said agreement.

Please take notice that you are hereby requested to grant me a renewed tenancy/lease of the said premises in the Schedule below, as sought for.

SCHEDULE

(*State here description of the premises*)

Yours faithfully,

....

(Tenant/Lessee)

Form 12

Notice by the ex-landlord demanding possession after expiry of lease

By Registered Post with AD

.... 20 ....

To

....

....

Sir,

As the owner and ex-landlord of the premises described in the Schedule below, I do hereby give you a notice to the effect that the lease/tenancy dated ...... made between you and myself covering the said property in the Schedule below expired on .... by efflux of time.

2. You did not seek for renewal of the lease/tenancy nor I agreed to renewal thereof.

3. Take notice that I demand delivery of possession of the said premises in the Schedule on or before .... 20 .... If you fail therein you would be treated a trespasser therein and I would be constrained to agitate the matter before a court of law for admissible reliefs. Or, if you fail and/or neglect to comply with this notice I shall institute legal proceedings against you making you liable for *mesne profits*, damages and costs.

SCHEDULE

(*State here particulars of the premises*)

Yours faithfully,

....

(Owner of the premises)

NOTE: The suit may be filed for khas possession as also for damages for wrongful occupation.

Form 13

Notice by tenant to determine lease

To

....

(Name and Address of the Landlord)

Sub: Determination of tenancy in respect of Premises No. ....

Dated .... 20 ......

Dear Sir,

I hereby give you notice of my intention to determine the lease with effect from the .... day of .... when I shall quit, vacate and deliver up possession of the house and premises (or, etc.) as comprised in the deed of lease. This is in pursuance of the power, authority and liberty for this purpose reserved in my favour under and by virtue of the deed of lease dated the .... day of ....20...... and made between you, of the one part, and myself, of the other part.

Please take further notice that all our relationship also as lessor/landlord and lessee/tenant shall come to an end on that day. I shall no further remain responsible for performance or non-performance of any of the covenants, conditions and stipulations thereunder contained.

Yours faithfully,
(Name & Address of the tenant).

Form 14

Notice to a tenant informing purchase of tenanted premises

By Registered Post with AD

From Dated .... 20 ....

Sri ....
S/o ....
(State here the address)
(Name and Address of the sender)

To

Sri ....
S/o ....
(*State here Name and Address of the Tenant*)

Dear Sir,

1. Please take notice that I have purchased the premises No. .... at .... from Sri .... s/o .... residing at ...... by a sale-deed, dated .... executed by said Sri .... in my favour.

2. You are, since after date of sale, to be treated as a Tenant under me in respect of the said premises with all obligations of a Tenant.

Yours faithfully,

....

NOTES: 1. See s. 109 of the T.P. Act. Rights of Lessor's Transferee.

2. Where the Tenant receives notice of the assignment, he is bound by it and it is immaterial whether the notice is received from the assignor or from the assignee. If he has made the payment with notice actual or constructive, of the assignment, he cannot escape liability—17 CLJ 372; 19 IC 865.

Form 15

Notice seeking renewal of lease on the strength of Renewal Clause

From

Sri ....

S/o ....

(*State here name and address of the Tenant*)

To

Sri ....

S/o ....

(*State here name and address of the Landlord/Lessor*)

Sir,

I am a Tenant under you of the premises No. .... situated at .... on rent at the rate of Rs. .... per month according to English Calendar month on the strength of a lease agreement, dated .... executed between us.

2. As per terms of said agreement, dated .... the lease in respect of the aforesaid premises was created on ...... for a fixed term of .... years.

The aforesaid fixed term will be completed by the end of .... day of ...... (month), 20... ......

The aforesaid lease agreement, dated ...... contains a clause of renewal (No. ......) according to which I shall have option to get the lease/tenancy renewed on the expiry of the said fixed term of ...... years for the next term of ...... years.

3. In exercise of the aforesaid option I do hereby call upon you to renew the lease for another term of .... years from ...... (date, month and year).

Yours faithfully,

....

Tenant.

NOTES:

1. The assignee of the lease-hold can enforce a covenant for renewal—AIR 1924 Cal 346.
2. Where the lease for a certain term confers an option to the lessee for renewal of the lease, but no time is fixed within which such option is to be exercised, and the lessee after the expiry of the term continues in possession the landlord is bound to give notice to the original lessee for exercising his option of renewal—37 CWN 9.
3. If the option in a lease does not state terms of renewal, the new lease will be for the same period and on the same terms as in the original lease in respect of all essential conditions except as to the covenant for renewal—AIR 1938 Cal 724; AIR 1939 Cal 77.
4. Where there is a clause for renewal subject to such fair and equitable enhancement of rent as the lessor shall determine, the lease is not void for uncertainty, nor is the Court precluded from considering whether the enhancement is fair and equitable—AIR 1959 SC 639.

Form 16

Notice of attornment to tenant

From

Sri ....
s/o ....
r/o ....
(*Name and address of the sender*)

To

Sri ....
s/o ....
r/o ....
(*Name and address of the person to whom the notice is sent*)

Dear Sir,

I am the owner of the premises No. ...... situated at ...... which you hold and occupy as a Tenant under me at a rent of Rs. .... per month according to Bengali Calendar month.

I have sold the aforesaid premises to Sri .... s/o .... r/o .... by a registered deed of sale dated .... and because of such sale the aforesaid Sri ...... has become the owner of the said premises.

2. That I, do hereby, authorise you to become a tenant of the said premises under Sri ...... You are instructed to pay to said Sri ...... his heirs, executors and administrators, all such rent as now is or hereafter shall be payable.

Yours faithfully,

....

Form 17

Notice by the lessor to a tenant to quit

By Registered Post with AD
Dated .... 20 ....

To

....
....
(*Name and address of the tenant*)

Sir,

I hereby give you a notice to quit and deliver up unto me vacant possession of the premises, described in the Schedule below, which you hold of me as a (monthly) tenant (or, from year to year), on the expiry of (*name the month with year or give the year*).

Please take further notice that the tenancy in respect of the said premises and all relationship of landlord and tenant between myself and yourself shall stand determined with effect from the said date.

SCHEDULE OF PREMISES

Yours faithfully,

....

Landlord

NOTES: 1. In case of monthly tenancy, the period of notice is 15 days expiring with the end of a month of the tenancy and in case the tenancy is from year to year—six months expiring with the end of a year of tenancy.

2. A person in occupation of property under an unregistered lease does not become a tenant and hence a notice to quit under s. 106 is not necessary—AIR 1971 Mys 291.

3. Service of notice to a tenant in a suit for ejectment is a question of fact—Adjudication by Revisional Court under s. 115, C.P. Code is not permissible—*Suresh Chand* v *VIIth Additional District Judge, Muzaffarnagar* AIR 1992 All 295.

4. West Bengal Premises Requisition and Control (Temporary Provisions) Act.

Section 4(1)(*a*)—the word 'may' in s. 4(1)(*a*) of the said Act is mandatory in nature.

Period of 10 days from service of notice to vacate must be given. Service of notice and ordering of immediate vacation the same day is illegal and without jurisdiction—*Sambu Nath* v *State of W.B.* AIR 1991 Cal 19.

Form 18

Notice demanding possession after expiry of lease

By Registered Post with AD
Dated the ....20 ...

To
Sri ....
....
(Ex-tenant)

Dear Sir,

The lease dated the .... the day of .... 20 .... made between you, of the one part and myself, of the other part in respect of the premises described in the schedule below, expired by efflux of time on the ...... day of ...... 20... Said lease has not been renewed nor as owner of the said premises have I permitted you to continue in occupation of the said premises.

I do hereby give you notice demanding delivery of vacant possession of the said premises on or before the expiry of ...... 20...; failing compliance I shall be under painful necessity to institute a suit against you for recovery of possession, holding you responsible for *mesne profits*.

Particulars of the demised premises
....

Yours faithfully,
....
(Owner)

Form 19

Notice by the agent/lawyer on behalf of the landlord to a tenant to quit

By Registered Post with AD
Dated ...... 20 ....

To
....
(Name and address of the tenant)

Dear Sir,

As the agent of Sri .... son of .... of ...., your landlord in respect of the premises described in the Schedule below (Or, under instructions from my client Sri .... son of ...... of (*Address*) ......) I hereby give you this notice calling upon you to quit and deliver unto (said landlord or, my said client—as the case may be) the vacant possession of the premises, described in the Schedule below, which you hold under (my principal/my client as the case may be) as a tenant (from month to month or from year to year) on ...... on expiry of (state here the month and year or give the year).

Please note that your tenancy in respect of the said premises in the schedule and all relationship with my principal/client as between landlord and tenant shall stand determined with effect from said date.

SCHEDULE OF PREMISES

Yours faithfully,

....

(Agent/Advocate)

Form 20

Notice to the lessor by a tenant to quit

Dated the ...... 20 ......

To

....

(*Name and address of the landlord*)

Dear Sir,

Please take notice that I shall quit and deliver up possession of the premises, described in the Schedule below, unto you on ...... on the expiry of (*state here the month with year if the tenancy is monthly, or give the year if the tenancy is from year to year*) which I hold of you as a tenant (*from month to month or from year to year, as the case may be*).

SCHEDULE OF PREMISES

Yours faithfully,

....

Tenant

NOTE: When a defective notice is given by a tenant and the landlord accepts the same it may determine the tenancy—AIR 1968 SC 471.

Form 21

Notice to determine tenancy for breach of covenants in a lease

To

Mr. A.B.
Bonfield Lane
Kolkata ....

Dear Sir,

Please take notice that the Indenture of Lease dated the .... day of January, 20 .... made between you, of the one part, and myself, of the other part contains, *inter alia*, the following covenants to be observed and performed by you:

(*i*)
(mention the covenants)
(*ii*)

2. The said Indenture of Lease also provides for forfeiture of your interest as a lessee with consequential right of re-entry in the premises for violation of any of above covenants.

3. You have violated the covenants (*state the nature of breaches*) and have been doing so even now. I have not condoned such violations.

4. I do hereby give you a notice of determination of the lease calling upon you to deliver possession of the premises, described below, to me within 15 days of the receipt of this notice, failing which I shall exercise my right of re-entry and shall further bring a suit against you for your ejectment and for recovery of *mesne profits*, damages as may be admissible.

Particulars of the premises

Yours faithfully,
C.D.
(Landlord of the premises)

Form 22

Notice to the lessor on behalf of a tenant to quit (notice by lawyer)

To
Sri ....
....
(*Name and address of the lessor*)

Dear Sir,

As per instructions of my client Sri .... son of .... of .... I seek to inform you that my said client intends to quit and deliver up to you on .... possession of the premises, specifically described in the Schedule below, which my client now holds of you as a monthly tenant (or from year to year).

Schedule of premises

Yours faithfully,

Advocate

Form 23

Notice by a tenant to determine a lease (when lease-deed provides clause of determination)

By Registered Post with AD
Dated .... 20.......

To

Sri ....

Son of ....

N.N. Road, P.O. Raiganj

West Dinajpur

Dear Sir,

I am a monthly tenant under you in respect of the premises, described in the Schedule appended below, pursuant to a deed of lease entered into and made between you of the one part and myself of the other part on ......

In conformity with Clause No. .... of the said deed of lease, I intend to determine the lease on expiry of the month of ...... 20....

Please take notice that the lease in question shall stand determined with effect from .... on expiry of the month of .... 20... when I shall quit and deliver vacant possession of the said premises in the Schedule below.

SCHEDULE

(*State here particulars and description of the premises*)

Yours faithfully,
Signed A.B.
(Tenant)

Form 24

Notice by a tenant to the lessor for effecting repairs of the leasehold property

Dated the .... 20 ......

To

The ....

....

(*Name and address of the lessor*)

Sir,

Please take notice that you are required to effect repairs, specified in the Schedule below, of the premises which I hold of you as a tenant within 30 days from the receipt of this notice.

(*If the condition of lease provides such the same may be referred to*).

In default of your compliance I myself shall make the repairs and deduct the expenses therefor with interest admissible thereon from the rents payable to you (or I shall recover from you such expenses with interest thereon as may be admissible).

Repairs to be effected.
(Details to be given)

Yours faithfully,

....

Notes: 1. Provisions of s. 108(*f*) of T.P. Act and of s. 34 of the West Bengal Premises Tenancy Act 1956 (now ss. 35 and 36 of the Act of 1997) may be seen.

2. The lessee has to give a reasonable time to the lessor for effecting repairs.

Form 25

Notice by a landlord to a tenant for effecting repairs

Dated ....
....

To
Sri ....
Son of ....
(*Address of the tenant*)

Sir,

You have been occupying the premises, more fully described in the Schedule below, as a monthly tenant under me following an agreement of tenancy made between you, of the one part and myself, of the other part on ....

Under Clause No. ...... of the said agreement you agreed to keep the said premises in good and substantial repairs. Reportedly, the premises have been damaged substantially in the floor of etc. (*State here nature of damage*) through your negligence and misuse. You have violated the said covenant by not having effected essential repairs.

You are hereby called upon to effect and keep the premises in good and substantial repairs within three months hereof. In the event of your default, please take notice, I shall enter upon the said premises and execute works of repairs holding you liable for such expenses.

SCHEDULE

(*State here description of the premises*)

Yours faithfully,
....
(Landlord)

Form 26

Notice under s. 6(4) of the West Bengal Premises Tenancy Act 1997

By Registered Post with AD
Dated .... 20 ......

From
Mr. ....
Advocate, Cooch Behar

Notice under s. 6(4) of the West Bengal Premises Tenancy Act 1997
....

To
....
(Name & Address)

My Clients:
(Name & Address)
1. ....
2. ....
3. ....

Sir,

Under instructions of my clients named above, I address you as follows:

You were in occupation of the premises, described in the Schedule below, as a monthly tenant under one (Name) .... (since deceased) of .... paying therefor rent at the rate of Rs. .... per month according to English calendar month. Said (Name) .... having died on 22.9.20... you have been occupying the said premises as a monthly tenant/under same terms and conditions under my clients named above, they being legal heirs of erstwhile landlord (Name) ....

2. You are a habitual defaulter in payment of rent and have defaulted in payment of rent for the said premises for the period from .... to .... Deposits of rent made by you from time to time with the Rent Controller, Cooch Behar are not only invalid but also illegal. For such default you have become liable to be evicted from the tenanted premises.

My clients reasonably require the said premises for their own use and occupation and they are not in possession of any reasonably suitable accommodation.

Please take notice that you are requested to quit and deliver unto my said clients vacant possession of the said tenanted premises on 1.11.20..., after expiry of the month of October, 20.... From the said date your tenancy shall stand determined. If you fail to comply with the request made herein your occupation of the said premises shall be unlawful and you would render yourself liable to pay damages to my clients at the rate of Rs. 500 for each day of your unlawful occupation and that my clients will sue you in a competent court of law for your eviction, recovery of arrears of rent, damages and for other incidental reliefs.

SCHEDULE OF PREMISES

All that (State here description of the tenanted premises)

Yours faithfully,

....

(Advocate)

NOTE: Suit for eviction—Court can entertain a suit even in absence of a valid notice under s. 13(6) of the W.B. Premises Tenancy Act 1956 (corresponds to s. 6(4) of the W.B. Premises Tenancy Act 1997)—*Sk. Firoj* v *Sakya Sinha Mallick* AIR 1991 Cal 161. See *Subodh Ch. Sinha* v *Santosh Kumar Srimani* 68 CWN 184; *Gurudas Biswas* v *Shib Sankar* AIR 1977 Cal 110. In AIR 1991 Cal 161 it was held: It is true that a decree in a suit without such notice is assailable in Appeal but absence of notice does not take away the jurisdiction of the court either to entertain a suit or to pass an erroneous decree.

Form 27

A composite notice of suit under s. 106, T.P. Act and under provisions of a provincial Rent Control Act

Registered with AD

Dated the .... 20 ......

To

(Name and address of the tenant)

My clients: 'X' and 'Y' sons of late 'Z' of Cooch Behar Town

P.S. .... District ....

Dear Sir,

Under instructions from my clients named above and of above address I beg to inform you by this notice that you are a monthly tenant at a rate of rent of Rs. ...... per mensem according to English/Bengali/Hindi calendar month or Sambat Year under my aforesaid clients, in respect of the premises noted in the Schedule below.

It appears that you have defaulted to pay rent for six months with effect from (Kartick Sudi Navami, ... S.Y., corresponding to .... up to Baisakh Sudi Astami, ... S.Y., corresponding to ....) and have thus become liable to be ejected on ground of default.

Please take notice that you are requested to quit and vacate the said premises after expiry of Ashar Sudi Astami, ... S.Y. (corresponding to ....) and give unto my clients vacant possession thereof on Ashar Sudi Navami, ... S.Y. corresponding to .... From the said date the tenancy herein will be determined and all relationship of landlord and tenant between my clients and yourself shall absolutely cease. If you fail to comply with this notice, your occupation of the premises will be unlawful and you would be treated as a trespasser in the said premises with effect from Ashar Sudi Navami, ... S.Y. and further, you would be held liable for damages at the rate of Rs. 200 for each day of your wrongful occupation till you are ousted by a court of law and that my client will sue you in a court of law for your eviction as also for recovery of arrears of rent, damages and other incidental costs.

SCHEDULE

(*State here particulars of the demised premises*)

Yours faithfully,

....

Advocate

NOTES:
1. Reference to section or sections is not a necessity (AIR 1966 Cal 615).
2. Mere payment of rent by a particular calendar month does not, without further evidence, mean that the monthly tenancy was according to that calendar month (AIR 1971 Cal 383).
3. In view of decision reported in *Dhanpal Chettiar* v *Yesodia Ammal* AIR 1976 SC 588 and followed in *Manoranjan Dasgupta* v *Suchitra Ganguli* AIR 1989 Cal 14 notice under s. 106 of T.P. Act is not necessary.

Form 28

Notice requesting a tenant to pay arrears of rent

Registered with AD

Dated the .... 20 ...

To

....

....

(*Name and address of the tenant*)

Sir,

Under instructions from my client (*name and address of the lessor*) I hereby demand of you a sum of Rs............ being arrears of rent for .... months from the month of .... 20... ...... to ...... 20 ...... both inclusive for the premises, described in the Schedule below, which you hold as a monthly tenant under my said client at a monthly rent of Rs. .... according to English/Bengali or Samvat Lunar calendar month, (*as the case may be*) and request you to pay the same within .... days from the date of receipt of the notice.

On your failure to comply with the request made herein above, I am instructed to take legal steps against you for recovery of the same together with damages as may be admissible without further reference.

Yours faithfully,
Advocate

SCHEDULE

Description of Demised Premises
(*Give here description, locality and particulars*)

NOTE: Notice is optional under the T.P. Act.

Form 29

Notice demanding recovery of possession of tenanted premises

From ....
Sri ....
S/o ....
(*Name and address of the Landlord*)

To
Sri ....
S/o ....
(*Name and address of the tenant*)

Dear Sir,

By this notice I state that I am the owner of the premises No.......... situated at .... You had taken the ground floor portion consisting of the premises as per schedule below on rent of Rs. .... per month according to English calendar month by virtue of an Agreement of Tenancy dated .... executed jointly by us.

2. That I object to the continuance of your tenancy on the following grounds:

(*a*)

(*b*) (*State here the grounds*)

(*c*)

Accordingly, I terminate your tenancy for the said ground floor of the premises from .... and request you to deliver vacant and peaceful possession of the same in good tenantable condition on or before ...... failing which I shall be compelled to initiate legal proceedings against you for your eviction therefrom holding you liable for the costs of litigation.

Yours faithfully,
....
Landlord

Schedule

NOTE: This type of notice is not suitable for West Bengal. In West Bengal a notice must satisfy requirement of s. 6(4) of the West Bengal Premises Tenancy Act 1997.

Form 30

Notice for handing over vacant possession

Amit Kumar Dutta, Advocate
Chamber No. 6
25 Old Post Office Street
Kolkata 700 001

Registered with AD
Dated .... day of 20 ....

To

Mr. Robin Chakraborty
12 Netaji Subhas Road
Kolkata 700 001

Sir,

I, on behalf of my client Mr. Sankar Das, of No. 12 Netaji Subhas Road, Kolkata 700 001, do hereby serve upon you this legal notice, which is as under:

1. That you are a tenant in respect of 330 sq. ft. area on rear mezzanine floor, comprising of two rooms at a rent of Rs. 1,210 per month at the premises No. 12 Netaji Subhas Road, Kolkata 700 001 under my above said client who is the owner/landlord of the above said premises since its purchase vide Sale deed dated 4th February 1994.
2. That your tenancy month starts from the first day of English Calendar Month and ends on the last day of the same month.
3. That you have carried out unauthorised and illegal material alterations and additions within the tenanted portion under your occupation without the written permission and consent from my client owner/landlord of the premises. As such your above-mentioned illegal acts of material alterations and additions have diminished the value of the building of which your tenancy premises is a part. I hereby call upon you to remove the said alterations and additions in the tenancy premises and restore it to its original position within one month of the receipt of this notice.
4. That my above said client's expanding business activities necessitate and require a larger area of the said Building than the area under its occupation at the moment at 12 Netaji Subhas Road, Kolkata 700 001. In this regard it is not out of context to mention that my client's requirements for the time being are being met by taking additional premises for his office on rent. In view of this the area under your occupation is reasonably required by my client for his own use and occupation.
5. That my client does not want to keep you as a tenant any more and as such your tenancy is terminated with immediate effect. You are hereby called upon to hand over the peaceful and vacant possession of the said tenancy premises to my client on last day of your tenancy month, i.e. 30th April 20 .... after having availed one month from the service of this notice.

Please note that in the event of your failure to carry out the abovesaid requisitions, my client shall be constrained to take appropriate legal remedy against you which please note, holding you responsible for all the cost and consequences arising therefrom.

Yours faithfully,
Amit Kumar Dutta
Advocate

M: Notice 27

Form 31

Reply to the notice for handing over vacant possession

Mr. Amit Kumar Dutta, Advocate
Chamber No. 6
25 Old Post Office Street
Kolkata 700 001

Registered with AD
12th March 20..........

Dear Sir

Your Client: Mr. Sankar Das.

This is to acknowledge your letter dated 1st March 20 .... written on behalf of your aforesaid client asking me to vacate the premises under my occupation and tenancy at No. 12 Netaji Subhas Road, Kolkata 700 001.

I regret to inform you that the allegations and contentions of your client contained in your said letter are untrue and incorrect. The said letter has been caused to be written by your client on incorrect instructions.

It is wholly untrue that I have carried out any alteration or addition, material or otherwise, to my tenanted portion under my occupation as alleged or at all. Hence the question of my carrying out any unauthorized or illegal or any material alteration or addition to my said tenanted portion did not and could not, does not and cannot arise. The question of my committing any illegal act of the nature alleged or otherwise does not and cannot also arise. The question of diminishing the value of the building by my alleged illegal act also does not and cannot arise. Your call upon us to remove any alleged alteration or addition in the tenanted premises or restoring the tenanted premises to its original position is wholly unwarranted and as such I deny the same.

I deny and dispute each and every allegation and/or contention contained in paragraph 4 of your said letter. I in particular deny and dispute that the area under my occupation is at all *bona fide* required by your client as alleged or at all. Such allegation appears to us to be a pretext only to remove me, if possible, from my tenanted premises. Your call upon me to hand over peaceful and vacant possession of the said tenanted premises to your client either on 30th April 20.... or on any other date or at all is wholly unwarranted and we express regret for our inability to do so as your client is not lawfully entitled thereto.

I have never defaulted in the matter of performing my part of the obligations under the tenancy agreement and I can also assure you that I shall never fail to do so in future. I have always maintained and still wish to maintain best of my good relationship with your client. Please be informed that in spite of the aforesaid if your client resorts to any action, which is wholly unwarranted, your client will do so at his own risk and costs and I shall be at liberty to defend the same as I may be advised. I would be glad if your client is advised to immediately withdraw the said purported letter dated 1st March 20 .... to avoid any strained relationship between your client and me.

Yours faithfully,
Robin Chakraborty

Form 32

Notice for handing over vacant possession

By Registered Post with AD
Dated .... 20 ....

M/s. AB & Co.
32 Hem Chandra Street
Kolkata 700 023

Dear Sirs,

We are concerned for M/s. XY having its registered office at 53 BBD Bag (South), Kolkata 700 001 and under their instruction, write to you as follows:

1. Our client is the owner of .... sq. ft. .... of warehouse situate at 2/4 Taratala Road, P.S. South Port, Dist. 24 Parganas (South).
2. Our client is successor in interest of M/s. MN, who had let out the aforesaid warehouse to you on or about 22nd June 20 .... for a period of three years at an agreed monthly rent of Rs. .... and other terms and conditions as recorded in letter dated 22nd June 20 .... addressed by our client's predecessor-in-interest.
3. Upon expiry of the period as aforementioned, our client's predecessor-in-interest permitted you to continue in occupation of the said warehouse *inter alia*, on the same terms and conditions aforesaid save and except that the monthly rent was enhanced to Rs. ....
4. Subsequently, the lease was extended for a further period of three years, i.e. upto 30th June 20 .... on the same terms and conditions save and except that the monthly rent was enhanced to Rs. .... Thereafter the said lease was further renewed for a period of three years with effect from 11th June 20 .... *inter alia*, on the same terms and conditions save and except that the monthly rent thereof stood revised to Rs. ....
5. In view of the fact that the period of lease expired by efflux of time, on or about 10th January 20 ...., our client's predecessor- in-interest requested you to revise the monthly rent and/or vacate and make over possession of the said warehouse to our client. In spite of repeated demands, you failed and neglected to accede to such request.
6. By an order dated 27th January 20 .... passed by the Hon'ble High Court at Calcutta, the said warehouse was vested and/or transferred in favour of our abovenamed client. Due intimation in this regard was given to you by letter dated 18th June 20 ...., and in terms thereof, you accepted our client as your landlord in respect of the said warehouse and continued to occupy and possess the said warehouse *inter alia* on the same terms and conditions as stated hereinabove.
7. Subsequent to the aforesaid, our client abovenamed repeatedly called upon you to either vacate and make over possession of the said warehouse or to revise the lease rent according to prevailing market rate and enter into a fresh lease in respect of the said warehouse. However, you have avoided revision of rent and refused to make over possession of the said warehouse to our client.
8. Furthermore, you have parted with possession of portion of said warehouse and have sub-let the same without any consent in writing of our client or their predecessor-in-interest.

9. Our client states that the provisions of local Rent Act have no manner of application to the said warehouse and/or lease in respect thereof and as such our client hereby terminates the lease, on the expiry of 31st July 20 .... and calls upon you to hand over peaceful and vacant possession of the said warehouse on 1st August 20 ....

10. Please further note that despite aforesaid, if you fail and/or neglect to hand over possession of the said warehouse to our client, our client shall be entitled to recover a sum of Rs. 6,000 per diem, from you on account of damages and/or *mesne profit* for wrongful occupation thereof, which is the present reasonable letting out rent of the said warehouse.

11. In the aforesaid facts and circumstances, we hereby on behalf of client, call upon you to hand over peaceful and vacant possession of the said warehouse on 1st August 20 .... failing which our client shall be constrained to take appropriate legal proceedings against you for recovery of possession of the said warehouse along with *mesne profit* and/or damages @ of Rs. 6,000 *per diem* till handing over of possession by you.

12. It is needless to mention that if our client is compelled to take any legal action, all cost and consequence thereof shall be to your account.

Yours faithfully,

....

Partner

....

Solicitors & Advocates

Form 33

A notice for ejectment on the ground for default in payment and reasonable requirement

By Registered Post with AD

Mr. Ranjit Kumar Singh
47 Karl Marx Sarani
Kolkata 700 023

Dated .... 20 ....

Dear Sir,

Under instructions received from and on behalf of our client, Mr. Subhasis Poddar of 3/2 Rani Bhavani Road, Kolkata 700 012, we do serve upon you this notice under section 6(4) of the West Bengal Premises Tenancy Act 1997, *inter alia*, on the following amongst other grounds:

1. Our client is the owner of, *inter alia*, the premises located on the 47 Karl Marx Sarani, Kolkata 700 023 (hereinafter referred to as "the tenanted premises").

2. Since April 20 .... you are a tenant in respect of the tenanted premises under our client. Presently, the monthly rent of the tenanted premises stands at Rs. .... payable on the 7th day of every month.

3. Our client seeks to recover khas possession of the tenanted premises after evicting you therefrom on the following grounds:

    (*a*) That you have defaulted in payment of rent from and since the month of June 20 .... till date; and (*b*) That the tenanted premises is reasonably required by our client for his own use and occupation and our client is not in possession of any reasonably suitable accommodation within the area of Kolkata Municipal Corporation, in which the tenanted premises is situate, or in any other area within 10 km. from the tenanted premises for the purpose as mentioned hereinafter.

4. The tenanted premises comprises two bed-rooms with attached bathrooms, one kitchen-cum-pantry, verandah, dinning-cum-drawing room.
5. The tenanted premises is reasonably required by our client for the purpose of accommodating his only son after his marriage, which is going to be held very soon.
6. In the premises, we hereby on behalf of our client, call upon you to leave and vacate the tenanted premises on the expiry of the month of December 20 .... and deliver peaceful and vacant possession thereof to our client on the expiry of 31st December 20 ....
7. Please further note that on and from said date, your tenancy is respect of tenanted premises will stand determined and relationship of landlord and tenant between you and our client shall also cease.
8. In default of you compliance, our client shall be compelled to institute proceeding for possession of tenanted premises making you liable for *mesne profit*, damages and costs, which please note.

Yours faithfully

....

Partner

....

Solicitors & Advocates

Form 34

A notice for ejectment on the ground for default in payment and reasonable requirement

By Registered Post with AD

Dated .... 20 ....

....

....

....

Dear Sirs,

Under instruction received from and on behalf of our client, ..., having its office at ...., we do serve upon you this notice under section 6(4) of the West Bengal Premises Tenancy Act 1997, on the following amongst other grounds:

1. Our client is the owner of, *inter alia*, a flat, being .... located on the .... (hereinafter referred to as "the tenanted premises").
2. Since September 20 .... you are a tenant in respect of the tenanted premises under our client at a monthly rental of Rs. 5,000 payable on or before the 7th day of each and every month.

3. Our client seeks to recover khas possession of the tenanted premises after evicting you therefrom on the following grounds:

   (*a*) That you have defaulted in payment of rent from and since the month of June 20 .... till date.

   (*b*) That the tenanted premises is reasonably required by our client for his own use and occupation and our client is not in possession of any suitable accommodation within the area of Kolkata Municipal Corporation, in which the tenanted premises is situate, or in any other area within 10 km. from the tenanted premises for the purpose as mentioned hereinafter.

4. Our client has a liaison office of the Ministry of Health in Kolkata. Such office liaises between the patients (who are citizens of Bhutan) seeking medical attention and treatment in Kolkata and elsewhere in India, and the Doctors, Nursing Homes and Hospitals in Kolkata and elsewhere in India. Presently, such liaison office of the Ministry of Health is accommodated in and shares its office with the office of the Royal Bhutan Customs which is situate at ....

5. Our client spends over Rs. 2 crores for the medical treatment of such patients at Kolkata alone.

6. The said liaison office of the Ministry of Health presently operates from only one room in the shared office with the Royal Bhutan Customs. The liaison office has staff strength of 24 employees. The said shared accommodation of the liaison office of the Ministry of Health with the Royal Bhutan Customs is wholly inadequate. The said liaison office handles approximately 3 to 5 patients per week arriving from Bhutan. Some of such patients are required to be temporarily accommodated for medical consultation and for carrying out various medical tests both before admission and during the course of treatment in nursing homes and hospitals in Kolkata and elsewhere in India. Our client is presently not in occupation of any other premises for the purpose of accommodating these patients.

7. The tenanted premises comprises two rooms with attached bathrooms, one kitchen-cum-pantry, verandah, one large corridor, pantry and a store room and an open terrace on the western side.

8. Our client reasonably requires the tenanted premises for the occupation of the liaison office of the Ministry of Health as also for the accommodation of the said patients.

9. One room with attached bathroom of the tenanted premises is intended to be utilised exclusively by the Heath Officer for his office. The other room with attached bathroom is intended to be utilised for temporarily accommodating the patients and the attendants/relatives accompanying such patients. The large room is intended to be utilized both for installing equipments for providing emergency services to patients needing emergency care before their admission in nursing homes and hospitals as also for providing office accommodation to the said staff. The kitchen-cum-pantry and corridor, pantry are intended to be utilised for cooking food for the patients and the attendants/relatives accompanying them and also for the working staff of the liaison office. The store room is intended to be utilised for storing medicines, oxygen cylinders and other medical accessories. The open terrace is intended to be utilised for washing and drying up the clothings of the patients and their attendants.

10. Presently, our client owns 27 flats at Tivoli Court, out of which 14 flats are occupied by the following persons/departments:

....

....

None of the said 14 flats can suitably accommodate our clients' aforesaid requirement. The remaining 13 flats including the tenanted premises are in the possession of tenants and/or unauthorized occupants.

11. Our client also has a guest-house at .... which is more than 10 kilometers away from the tenanted premises. Our client does not have any other accommodation in or around the City of Kolkata.

12. In the premises, we hereby on behalf of our client, call upon you to leave and vacate the tenanted premises on the expiry of the month of May 20 .... and deliver peaceful and vacant possession thereof to our client on the expiry of 31st May 20 ....

13. Please further note that on and from said date, your tenancy in respect of tenanted premises will stand determined and relationship of landlord and tenant between you and our client shall also cease.

14. In default of you compliance, our client shall be compelled to institute legal proceeding for possession of tenanted premises making you liable for *mesne profit*, damages and costs, which please note.

Yours faithfully

....

Partner

....

Solicitors & Advocates

CHAPTER 20

Notices under the Companies Act 2013

SYNOPSIS

1 Meeting of the Board of Directors–notice
 1.1 Convening of a Board Meeting
 1.2 Notice to all the Directors
 1.3 Contents of a notice under s. 173
 1.4 Mode of service
2 General Meetings
 2.1 Rules governing the general meetings
3 Annual General Meeting
 3.1 Convening the Annual General Meeting
 3.2 Notice
 3.3 Service of notice
 3.4 Form of notice
 3.5 Contents of notice
4 Extraordinary General Meeting
 4.1 Extraordinary General Meeting convened by the Board
 4.2 Extraordinary General Meeting on Requisition
 4.3 Extraordinary General Meeting called by the Requisitionists
5 Service of notice
6 Length of notice for calling a meeting (s. 101)–General Meeting–period of notice–shorter period
7 Contents and manner of service of notice omission to give notice–interpretation of a notice–court's jurisdiction
8 Statement to be annexed to notice (s. 102)
9 Notice of application to the Central Government (s. 201)–publication in a newspaper
10 Ordinary and special resolutions–notice (s. 114)–resolutions requiring special notice (s. 115)
11 Alteration of the provisions of the memorandum of association (s. 13)
12 Notice for revocation of Licence (s. 8)
13 Alteration of Articles by Special Resolution (s. 14)
14 Prohibition on acceptance of deposits from public (s. 73)
15 Notice to Registrar of Consolidation of Share Capital, conversion of shares into stock, etc. (s. 64)
16 Date of Notice of Charge (s. 80)
17 Registered Office of Company (s. 12)
18 Notice to be given to Central Government for application under ss. 230 and 232
19 Notice to be given to the Central Government of applications under ss. 241 and 242
20 Circumstances in which company may be wound up by Tribunal
21 Passing of resolutions by Postal Ballot (s. 110)
22 Procedure

1 Meeting of the Board of Directors—notice

Meeting of the directors of a company are known as the Board meetings under s. 173 of the Companies Act 2013. Every company shall hold a minimum number of four meetings of its Board of Directors every year in such a manner that not more than one hundred and twenty days shall intervene between two consecutive meetings of the Board. This is, of course, subject to exceptions as contained in the proviso to s. 173(1).

Section 173(3) speaks of notice of Board Meetings, which reads: A meeting of the Board shall be called by giving not less than seven days' notice in writing to every director at his address registered with the company and such notice shall be sent by hand delivery or by post or by electronic means.

Section 173(4) lays down that every officer of the company whose duty is to give notice under this section and who fails to do so shall be liable to a penalty of twenty-five thousand rupees.

1.1 *Convening of a Board Meeting*

For any meeting to be valid it must first be properly convened, i.e. it must be called by proper notice given by a person duly authorised to do so. The meeting summoned without proper authority will be invalid. The Act does not provide as to who can convene a meeting. The authority to summon a meeting is generally provided in the Articles. Unless the Articles provide otherwise, any Director of a company may and the Manager or Secretary on the requisition of a Director should, at any time summon a meeting of the Board of Directors. Pursuant to the Schedule I, Table F, a Director may summon a meeting and the Manager or Secretary is obliged to summon a meeting if there is a requisition from a Director to do so. The Manager or Secretary cannot convene a meeting on his own. The Articles may contain more stringent provisions as to the authority to summon a meeting, e.g. only the Chairman or Vice-Chairman may be authorised to convene a meeting or to cause the Manager or Secretary to do so.

Notice should normally be signed by Secretary, if there is one. If there is no Secretary, the notice should be signed by the Chairman or any other person authorised by the Board.

In the case of requisitioned meeting, the requisition should be addressed to the Secretary or to the Chairman, at the Registered Office of the company and the fact that the meeting is being convened at the desire of a Director should be mentioned in the notice.

1.2 *Notice to all the Directors*

A Board Meeting to be effective must be duly convened by proper notice to its Directors and in default the meeting is irregular.[1] A meeting must be convened by giving a seven days' notice thereof to all the Directors. Section 173(3) requires that such notice should be given in writing to every Director at his address registered with the company. Such notice must be

1 *Harben* v *Phillips* [1883]23 Ch D 14.

given even to a Director who has stated that he would be unable to attend.[2] An irregular notice shall render the meeting invalid.[3] If notice of meeting is not given to all Directors, resolutions passed at such meeting would be invalid. Supreme Court in *Parameshwari Prasad Gupta* v *Union of India*[4] held that the meeting of the Board of Directors was not properly convened since notice was not given to all the Directors and as such resolution passed thereat was invalid. However, where no notice is given but all the Directors attend the meeting and do not object to the absence of notice or where the absentee Directors do not complain the want of notice, the meeting will not be rendered invalid.

The notice of the Board Meeting has to be given to all the Directors living in India. Such of the Directors who might be out of India for the time being, the notice has to be sent to their addresses in India. Notice is required to be given to Director who has gone abroad and who does not have an address in India so that even if they are unable to attend, they will be in a position to forward their views on the matters to be discussed at a meeting. A Director is entitled to a notice even if he is out of India.[5] The essential requirement is that all members entitled to notice should be given a notice of meeting and if, after due notice to all the members, some of them do not choose to appear, they are bound by the resolution passed by the majority.[6]

A Director has no power to waive his right to notice.[7] Notice should be given even to a Director who has given intimation of waiver. As to the compulsory requirement of the notice there is only one exception which has been judicially taken notice of. Thus, no fresh notice fixing time and place of the Board meeting which was adjourned for want of quorum need be given under the Act and where the Articles of Association give power to the Directors present to fix the adjourned meeting no fresh notice is necessary.[8]

1.3 *Contents of a notice under s. 173*

Coming to the contents of a notice under s. 173 of the Companies Act 2013 the notice is to mention the place, time and date of the intended meeting. Section 173(3) prescribes the mode of its service. Such notice shall be sent by hand delivery or by post or by electronic means. The day of the meeting should not be a holiday or non-working day and time should be during business hours unless otherwise agreed to by all the Directors. It may be noted here that law does not require that the notice should mention the business to be transacted at the meeting. Usually an agenda is furnished.

2 *Portuguese Consolidated Copper Mines Ltd.*, re [1889]42 Ch D 160.
3 *Homer District Consolidated Gold Mines*, re [1888]39 Ch D 546.
4 (1974)44 Comp Cas 1; AIR 1973 SC 2389; *Kuldip Singh Dhillon (Col)* v *Paragon Utility Financiers (P) Ltd.* (1988)64 Comp Cas 19 (P&H).
5 *Ebrahim Sait* v *South India Industries Ltd.* AIR 1938 Mad 962.
6 ILR (1958) AP 37.
7 *Pramod Kumar Mittal* v *Southern Steel Ltd.* (1980)50 Comp Cas 555 (Cal).
8 *Kuldip Singh Dhillon (Col)* v *Paragon Utility Financiers (P) Ltd.* (1988)64 Comp Cas 19 (P&H).

Where by an accidental omission to give due notice to any of the Directors, a meeting is rendered irregular and yet the Directors transact business, a subsequent regularly constituted Board Meeting can always ratify and confirm what was done at the prior irregular meeting and it will be valid *ab initio*.[9]

The Act does not specify any particular form in which notice should be given. However, it is necessary that notice should be in writing. Hence an oral notice either telephonically conveyed or by word of mouth is not a valid notice. The notice must be a definite notice. A contingent notice is not sufficient and is not valid.[10] If a notice of an informal type is used and no grievance is made by any of the Directors that they could not be present because of non-service of notice it cannot be held that the meeting convened by such an informal notice was not proper.[11]

Where, by provision in the Articles, the Directors are informed that there would be meeting, say, on the first Saturday of each month, it is sufficient compliance of the provisions of the Act.[12] However, notice should be given of every meeting including those meetings that are held on predetermined date or at predetermined intervals and where Directors are already aware of the date of the next meeting.

The Act does not lay down any requirement as to the period of notice but notice should be a reasonable notice.[13] What is reasonable would depend on the facts and circumstances of each case. Generally it is considered good practice to give one week's or two weeks' notice. Where any short notice is given to a Director and he does not at once object, he may be taken to have waived his objection.[14]

The notice convening a meeting should clearly specify the day and time and full address of the venue where the meeting is to be held. The mere coincidental physical presence of all Directors at one place cannot constitute a meeting. A Board Meeting can be held under informal circumstances but casual meeting at the railway station of the two Directors who constituted the full Board cannot be treated as Board Meeting.[15]

Meeting may be held on any day including a public holiday unless Articles provide otherwise. However, a meeting adjourned for want of quorum cannot, unless the Articles provide otherwise, be held on a public holiday.

9 *Portuguese Consolidated Copper Mines Ltd.*, re [1880]45 Ch D 161; *Hooper* v *Kerr, Stuart & Co.* (1900)83 LT 729; *State of Wyoming Syndicate*, re [1901]2 Ch 431.
10 *Alexander* v *Simpson* [1889]43 Ch D 139 (CA); 6 TLR 72 (CA)
11 *Sunderlal Jain* v *Sandeep Paper Mills (P) Ltd.* (1986)60 Comp Cas 77.
12 *ALARAL Arunachalam Chettiar* v *Kalesswarar Mills Ltd.* (1956)26 Comp Cas 431; AIR 1951 Mad 309.
13 *N.R. Murty* v *Industrial Development Corporation of Orissa Ltd.* (1977)47 Comp Cas 389.
14 *Browne* v *La Trinidad* [1887]37 Ch D 1 (CA).
15 *Barron* v *Potter* [1914]1 Ch 895.

A meeting adjourned otherwise than for want of quorum can be held on any day and at any time as may be decided by the Board or as is convenient to the Directors. Notice of an adjourned meeting need not be given unless the Articles provided otherwise.[16] Since an adjournment is only the continuation of a meeting, the notice of the original meeting holds good for all adjournments.[17] No new business can be introduced at an adjourned meeting unless notice thereof has been given.[18]

A Board Meeting may be held at any time. In respect of meeting of the Board there is no provision in the Act similar to that of s. 96 in respect of General Meeting which prescribes that an Annual General Meeting must commence during business hours, i.e. between 9 am and 6 pm.

Although a company may for practical considerations hold meeting at its Registered Office there is no bar against holding meeting at any other place, but it has to be within the city, town or village in which the registered office is situate.

Though not statutorily enjoined, one of the important contents of the notice is to state that the business to be transacted at the meeting. Notice of the Board Meeting has to be construed reasonably by considering what is meant to those to whom it is given.[1]

1.4 *Mode of service*

A notice relating to Board Meeting, as stated in s. 173(3) shall be sent by hand delivery or by post or by electronic means. The position that a notice is a document under the Act and notice of Board Meeting may be issued by facsimile has been upheld in *Ferruecio Sias* v *Jaimanga Ram Mukhi*.[2] Notice may even be sent through courier. However, if the Articles prescribed the method by which the notice has to be given, it should be given accordingly. If a Director has specified the mode by which notice should be given to him, the person issuing the notice should comply with such request.

2 General Meetings

General Meetings are of the following types:

1. Annual General Meeting (s. 96)
2. Extraordinary General Meeting convened by Directors:
   (*a*) Under the powers given by Articles; or
   (*b*) Upon requisition by the members (s. 100).

16 *Pramod Kumar Mittal* v *Southern Steel Ltd.* (1980)50 Comp Cas 555 (Cal).
17 *Kerr* v *Wilkie* (1860) ILT 501.
18 *R.* v *Grimshaw* [1847]10 QBD 747.
1 *Needle Industries (India) Ltd.* v *Needle Industries Newey (India) Holding Ltd.* AIR 1981 SC 1298; (1981)51 Comp Cas 743 (SC).
2 (1994)1 Comp LJ 345 (Del).

2.1 *Rules governing the general meetings*

The provisions relating to general meetings of a public company will apply to a General Meeting of a private company which is a subsidiary of a public company in the absence of any provisions in the Articles of Association or unless the Articles exclude the application. The term "General Meeting" includes all kinds of General Meetings, Annual or Extraordinary.[3]

3 Annual General Meeting

According to s. 96(1) of the Act, every company must hold in each year an Annual General Meeting. No Company except a One Person Company is exempt from this requirement. The fact that the company did not function[4] or that management was taken over by the Govt. and Books of Accounts were in possession of the custodian[5] is no excuse for not holding the Annual General Meeting. An Annual General Meeting is apart from and in addition to any other General Meeting of the company that may be held. The word 'year' is not defined in the Act. According to s. 3(66) of the General Clauses Act 1897 'year' shall mean a year reckoned according to British Calendar, i.e. 1st January to 31st December. An adjourned meeting is a continuation of the original meeting and hence where a meeting called and held on a day in one year is adjourned to a date in the next year and held on that date, the meeting held on the latter date is not a different meeting and does not satisfy the requirements of s. 96(1) in so far as it relates to the next year. In other words, in the next calendar year another Annual General Meeting has to be held. If the Annual General Meeting is not held in 'each year', company is liable to be convicted of an offence.[6] If a statute enjoins that the meeting is to be held within specified period, it follows by necessary implication that it must be completed within the said period. The flexibility in s. 96 in holding the Annual General Meeting cannot interfere with this specific requirement of section. If annual accounts are not laid at the concerned Annual General Meeting, it shall be open to the company to adjourn the Annual General Meeting to a subsequent date when the annual accounts will be ready for consideration. While the adjourned meeting must be held within the maximum time-limit allowed under s. 96, such an adjournment cannot be allowed to such an extent as to negate the provision of law.[7] There is a clear statutory duty imposed on the Directors to call the meeting whether

3 *Traco Enterprises (P) Ltd.* v *Alexander* (1964)2 Comp LJ 105; AIR 1964 Ker 273.

4 *Madan Gopal Dev* v *State of West Bengal* AIR 1968 Cal 790; (1969)39 Comp Cas 119.

5 *Hindusthan Cooperative Insurance Society Ltd.*, in re AIR 1961 Cal 443; (1961)31 Comp Cas 193.

6 *Sree Meenakshi Mills Co. Ltd.* v *Assistant Registrar, Madurai* (1938)8 Comp Cas 175; AIR 1938 Mad 640; *Harrisons and Crossfield (India) Ltd.* v *Registrar of Companies* (1980)50 Comp Cas 426.

7 *Bejoy Kumar Karnani* v *Assistant Registrar of Companies* (1958)58 Comp Cas 293 (Cal); *Subal Dutt & Sons (P) Ltd.* v *Asst. Registrar of Companies* (1986)59 Comp Cas 462.

or not the annual accounts are ready for consideration at the meeting.[8] Whether accounts are not ready or available in time to be considered at the Annual General Meeting within the time-limit fixed by s. 96, the usual practice is to hold the Annual General Meeting, transact all business other than the consideration of accounts and then to adjourn the meeting to a date when the accounts would be ready or available. In such a case, the shareholders should be notified of the intention in the notice, convening the meeting.[9] It may be noted that under the Act the Company Law Tribunals have power to call, or direct the calling of Annual General Meeting of the company in case of default in this behalf beyond the time-limit laid down in s. 96 [s. 97].[10]

3.1 *Convening the Annual General Meeting*

The power of convening the Annual General Meeting is vested in the Board of Directors. Therefore, no individual Director has power to convene the meeting without consulting other Directors.[11] In other words, a General Meeting should be convened on the authority of the Board. No Director or Secretary or the Manager or any Officer of the Company has the power to convene a General Meeting on his own. For any meeting to be duly constituted it must be duly convened—it must be called by proper notice given by a person duly authorised to do so. A meeting summoned without proper authority will be invalid, hence a resolution passed at such a meeting will also be invalid.

The authority to summon a meeting is generally prescribed in the Articles. According to s. 179(1) the Board is entitled to exercise such powers and to do all such acts and things as company is authorised to exercise but not any power to do act or thing which is required under the Act to be exercised or done by the company in General Meeting. Thus a General Meeting should be convened under the authority of the Board by passing resolution at the Board Meeting or by circulation. A notice of a General Meeting given by Secretary without the sanction of the Directors or other proper authority is invalid but such a notice may be ratified by the Directors before the meeting.[12] If a Board, which itself was not properly constituted, convenes a meeting, such meeting would be irregular and the resolution passed thereat invalid.

8 *E.I. Sombrero Ltd.*, re [1958] Ch 900; *Nungambakkam Dhanarakshaka Saswatha Nidhi Ltd.* v *Registrar of Companies* (1972)42 Comp Cas 632; *Registrar of Companies* v *Radhika Prosad Nandi* (1977) Tax LR 1610; *Dalmia Cement (Bharat) Ltd.* v *Registrar of Joint Stock Companies* AIR 1954 Mad 276.

9 *Harrison & Crossfield (India) Ltd.* v *Registrar of Companies* (1980)50 Comp Cas 426.

10 *Coal Marketing Co. Ltd.*, in re (1967)37 Comp Cas 720; *Nungambakkam Dhanarakshaka Saswatha Nidhi Ltd.* v *Registrar of Companies* (1972)42 Comp Cas 632.

11 Re, *Haycraft Gold Reduction of Mining Co.* [1900] Ch 230; *Harbon* v *Phillips* [1883]23 Ch D 14; *AL-Amin Seatrans Ltd.* v *Owners and Party Interested in Vessel M. V. Loyal Bird* (1996)1 Comp LJ 258 (Cal).

12 *Hooper* v *Kerr, Stuart & Co.* (1900)83 LT 729.

Items of business to be transacted at the meeting together with the explanatory statement in respect of items of Special Business, if any, should be approved by the Board.

3.2 *Notice*

A meeting must be convened by giving notice thereof in writing. Such notice should be sent by hand delivery or by post or through electronic mode to every person entitled to such notice. A general meeting of a company may be called by giving not less than clear twenty-one days, provided that it may be called after giving a shorter notice if consent is given in writing or by electronic mode by not less than ninety-five per cent of the members entitled to vote at such meeting. According to s. 101(3), the notice of every such meeting of the company must be sent to:

(*a*) every Member of the company, legal representative of any deceased member or the assignee of an insolvent member;

(*b*) the auditor or auditors of the company; and

(*c*) every director of the company.

The notice is served or deemed to be served on the person to whom it is addressed if the notice is posted to him by affixing postal stamp of the required value, at his address registered with the company.[13]

As it is not incumbent on the Directors to hold qualification shares, all the Directors of the company may not be members. Hence, notice should also be given to the Directors who are not Members of the Company, including to those Directors who generally reside abroad.

The notice must be given to a member even if he has waived his right to receive the notice. Notice should also be given to the practicing Company Secretary who has given the compliance certificate. If the Articles so provide, notice may be served on the joint holders named first in the register of members or in the records of the depository in respect of the shares.

3.3 *Service of notice*

Notice may be served on a company by leaving it at or sending by post (now, also by electronic mode) to the Registered Office of the company.[14] Notice may be served by the company on the persons entitled to a share in consequence of the death or insolvency of a member by sending through post in a prepaid letter addressed to them by name or by title of representatives of the deceased or assignees of the insolvent or by any like description. If no address has been supplied to the company notice has to be served as if the

13 *Kuldip Singh Dhillon (Col)* v *Paragon Utility Financiers (P) Ltd.* (1986)60 Comp Cas 1075 (P&H).

14 *Addis Ltd.* v *Berkeley Supplies Ltd.* (1964)2 All ER 753; (1964)1 WLR 943.

member has not died or insolvency has not occurred.[15] When the meeting is adjourned for 30 days or more fresh notice of the adjourned meeting should be given in the manner specified.

3.4 *Form of notice*

The Act does not specify any particular form in which notice should be given. However, it is necessary that notice should be in writing. An oral notice, whether conveyed on telephone or by word of mouth is not a valid notice. A contingent notice is not sufficient and is not a valid notice.[16] Section 101(4) provides that accidental omission to give notice to or the non-receipt of notice by any member or other person to whom it should be given shall not invalidate the proceeding of the meeting. "Accidental Omission" means omission which is neither designed nor deliberate and implies absence of intention.[17] Accidental omission to give notice to Auditors or a non-delivery of notice will not affect the validity of a notice.[18]

An omission which arises from an error as to legal position, cannot be classified as accidental.[19] In absence of *mala fide* or negligence the non-receipt of notice by any member will not affect the validity of the meeting. In a case where nine shareholders who held 101 shares out of a issued capital of 692718 shares were not given notice of the General Meeting due to the omission because the addresses of those nine shareholders had been separated from the rest. It was held that the notice of the meeting had been validly given since the omission was "accidental" and the Articles of the company provided that accidental omission to give notice would not invalidate the proceeding.[20] However, where large blocks of shareholders were inadvertently omitted to be notified about the general meeting, the advantage of the provision of s. 101(4) could not be taken. The onus of proof lies on those who claims the omission was accidental.[1] If a meeting is held without service of notice to majority shareholders, the meeting would be invalid. In situations where the company is unable to send notice to a member whose registered address is situated in enemy territory, on grounds of *force majeure*, there is no violation of requirement relating to notice. If the right of some members to receive the notice is suspended by operation of law the company can carry on its business without serving notice on such members.[2]

A private company may, by its Articles, make its own regulations in this regard in the absence of which s. 101 should be complied with.

15 *Canara Bank* v *TPR Thampi* (1972)42 Comp Cas 473.
16 *Alexandar* v *Simpson* [1889]43 Ch D 139 (CA); 6 TLR 72 (CA).
17 *Maharaja Exports* v *Apparels Exports Promotion Council* (1986)60 Comp Cas 353.
18 Re, *Maneckchowk & Ahmedabad Mfg. Co. Ltd.* (1970)40 Comp Cas 819 (Guj).
19 *Musselwhite* v *CH Musselwhite & Sons Ltd.* (1962)32 Comp Cas 804.
20 Re, *West Canadian Collieries Ltd.* [1962] Ch 370.
1 *POW Service Ltd.* v *Clare* (1995)2 BCLC 435 (*Company Law Cases*, Butterworth).
2 Re, *Anglo International Bank* [1943] Ch 233 (CA); [1943]2 All ER 88.

3.5 *Contents of notice*

The Notice convening a meeting should clearly specify the day, date, time and complete address of the venue where meeting is to be held, without which the meeting will be deemed to be invalid. Where the notice does not state exclusively the day and date of the meeting, the meeting shall be rendered invalid. Where the date of the meeting is incorrectly stated, i.e. where day of the week does not match the date and month given, the notice is bad in law.

Section 96(2) prescribes that no Annual Meeting shall be held on a national holiday. Meetings should, therefore, be held on a working day between 9 am and 6 pm and not on a national holiday. Every notice of a meeting must state a specific time at which the meeting is to commence. The meeting should commence during business hours. "Business Hours" means the normal working hours of the company, i.e. between 9 am and 6 pm [s. 96(2)]. Where the notice of the General Meeting did not specify the hour of the meeting, it was held that the notice was invalid and any resolution passed on such an invalid notice was also invalid.[3]

A notice to be valid must clearly state the nature of or type of meeting and the business to be transacted at the meeting and should give all material information to enable it to be fully understood by the members. Section 96(1) requires that notice of every General Meeting must specify that the meeting convened by the notice is an Annual General Meeting. In the case of Annual General Meeting which is convened within the extended period as granted by the Registrar of Companies under third proviso to s. 96(1), the notice should include the following information:

(*a*) the fact that such an extension of time has been sought and the reasons therefor;

(*b*) Whether meeting is being conveyed within the extended time; and

(*c*) Any other relevant information.

Every notice of annual general meeting must contain or annex financial statements and the reports of the Board of Directors, although the same are not considered to be items of "special business" in the agenda of the meeting. Every notice of meeting must contain the statement of business to be transacted at the meeting. The "Statement of Business" means the business or items proposed to be considered at the meeting. In the case of notice of an Annual General Meeting, the business to be transacted at the meeting must be divided into two parts—ordinary business and special business. According to s. 102(4), where any item of business to be transacted at a General Meeting as an item of special business, there shall be annexed to the notice of the meeting an explanatory statement. Such explanatory

3 *Pranchi Insurance Co. Ltd.* v *Chaudhary Madhusudan Das* (1964)2 Comp LJ 157 (Ori).

statement should be issued by the same person who has been authorised to issue notice and in the same manner in which he has issued the notice. The object of s. 102 is to ensure that all the material facts which have a bearing on the question on which the members have to form their judgment to their notice and they can exercise their own intelligent judgment without being persuaded to act in the manner desired by the management.[4] The provision in relation to explanatory statement is mandatory of any contravention or neglect thereof leads to nullification of the action taken in respect of that item of business.[5] The explanatory statement must be enclosed to the notice. The explanatory statement is part of notice. The explanatory statement not giving full disclosure of important facts cannot be said to comply with the spirit of law and in fact defeats the very purpose of such disclosure. A minor defect arising out of absence of strict conformity with the provisions under s. 101(2) may, however, not render the resolution null and void.[6] Where notice is required to be given within a stated period prior to the meeting, the failure to such requirement renders the meeting invalid.[7] The failure to specify and describe the business of meeting clearly and accurately will invalidate the notice and render the proceedings at the meeting void.[8] Where irregular notice has been given members may proceed to set aside the meeting so conveyed and compel the Directors to call a new meeting after giving proper notice.[9]

4 Extraordinary General Meeting

General Meetings other than an Annual General Meeting are called Extraordinary General Meetings. Companies generally provide in their Articles for convening of such meetings to deal with matters of an urgent nature or to transact business of special character of which have to be decided before the next Annual General Meeting.

The Board of Directors may, whenever it deems fit, call an extraordinary general meeting of the company. The Board shall call such meeting on a request from such number of members holding not less than one-tenth of paid-up share of the company. In the case of the company not having a share capital, such number of members having not less than one-tenth of the total voting power of all the members, the Board may call an extraordinary general meeting within twenty-one days of receipt of a valid requisition and proceed

4 *Seth Mohanlal Ganapatram* v *Shri Sayaji Jubilee Cotton & Jute Mills Co. Ltd.* (1964)34 Comp Cas 777 (Guj).

5 *Firestone Tyre & Rubber Co.* v *Synthetics and Chemical Ltd.* (1971)41 Comp Cas 377 (Bom); *Vardhaman Publisher Ltd.* v *Mathurbhumi Printing and Publishing Co. Ltd.* (1991)71 Comp Cas 1 (Ker).

6 *Joseph Michael* v *Travancore Rubber and Tea Co. Ltd.* (1986)59 Comp Cas 898.

7 *Woolf* v *East Nigel Coal Mining Co.* (1905)21 TLR 660 (KB).

8 *Lumbers* v *Fretz* (1928)4 Dominion Law Report (DLR) 269 affirmed in (1929)1 DLR 51.

9 *Mayr* v *St. Lawrence Comp* [1950]1 KB 635.

to hold such meeting on a day not later than forty-five days from the receipt of such requisition. In case the Board fails to call the meeting, the requisitionists themselves may call and hold the meeting within a period of three months from the date of requisition [section 100 of the Companies Act 2013].

4.1 *Extraordinary General Meeting convened by the Board*

The Board of Directors of a company may call an Extraordinary General Meeting whenever it may think fit. Where the Directors think fit to convene of an Extraordinary General Meeting they do so by a resolution passed at a duly convened and constituted meeting of the Board. However, if the Articles so provide, a resolution in writing signed by the Directors without a meeting (i.e. Resolution by circulation) would be as effective as a resolution passed at a meeting. The Board shall also call an extraordinary general meeting at the requisition made by the requisite number of holders of share capital or members having a right to vote, within the period as mentioned in s. 100(4) of the Act.

All business which is transacted at an Extraordinary General Meeting shall be deemed special business. The notice convening an Extraordinary General Meeting has to specify the special business to be transacted thereat and must be accompanied by explanatory statement. The statement must set out in full the reasons for the proposal of the resolution. The requisite notice for an Extraordinary General Meeting is 21 clear days.

In the case of an Extraordinary General Meeting, s. 100, unlike an Annual General Meeting, makes no provision for its holding during business hours or on a day, i.e. not a national holiday or at the registered office or at some other place within the same city, town or village limit in which the registered office of the company is situate. Therefore, an Extraordinary General Meeting can be held, subject to any specific provision in the Articles, at any time, any place and on any day. But the Directors must act reasonably in fixing the time and place of the meeting so that the members get full opportunity in exercising their rights.[10]

When the Directors wish or are bound to call an Extraordinary General Meeting they will normally do so by resolution passed at the duly convened and constituted meeting of the Board. The Secretary has no authority to convene a meeting.[11] Where, however, a meeting is irregularly convened the Board may ratify it before the meeting is held.[12]

4.2 *Extraordinary General Meeting on Requisition*

Section 100 makes detail provision for convening of an Extraordinary General Meeting on the requisition of the members. Section 100 provides that the

10 *Smith* v *Pariage Mines* [1906]2 Ch 193.

11 Re, *Haycraft Gold Reduction of Mining Co.* [1990]2 Ch 230; *Harben* v *Phillips* [1993]23 Ch D 14.

12 *Hooper* v *Kerr Stuart & Co.* (1900)83 LT 729.

Board of Directors must proceed to call an Extraordinary General Meeting on the requisition of the holders (who would have paid a call made on their shares[13]) of not less than $^1/_{10}$th of such of the paid up capital of the company as carries the right of voting in respect of the matter for which the meeting is to be called or in the case of a company not having a share capital, of members representing not less than $^1/_{10}$th of the total voting power of the members having a right to vote in regard to that matter. The requisition must state the matter for the consideration of which the meeting is held, must be signed by requisitionists and must be sent to the registered office [s. 100(3)]. It has been held that the requisitioning members must have fully paid the calls on their shares.[14]

The Board of Directors is under a legal obligation to proceed within 21 days of the receipt of the requisition to convene a meeting, which may be held within 45 days of such deposit of the requisition with the company [s. 100(4)]. The Board shall send notice within 21 days of the deposit of the requisition giving not less than 21 days' notice. Where requisition satisfies the requirement of s. 100 it cannot be rejected on the ground that some of the resolutions referred to in the requisition cannot be put to the requisitioned meeting for any reason. In other words, the Board of Directors cannot refuse to proceed with a requisition meeting on the ground that the requisition does not disclose sufficient reasons for the resolution to be put to vote at the meeting in the explanatory statement.[15]

It has been observed that if the object for which a meeting is requisitioned cannot be legally carried into effect in any manner, then the directors are justified in refusing to act on the requisition. This does not, however, relieve the directors from the obligation to comply with the requisition as to calling the meeting.[16] However, the Board is under no obligation to and cannot, in fact, call an extraordinary general meeting on the requisition of members if at the relevant time an order of a civil court restraining the company or its members from holding any meeting is pending [see Order 39, Rule 5, of the Code of Civil Procedure].[17]

A meeting requisitioned for the sole purpose of defeating a petition filed under s. 230 may not be proceeded with and the Tribunal may restrain holding of such a requisitioned meeting or giving effect to any resolution passed at such meeting.[18] However, a meeting requisitioned to enable an application to be made to the Court for modification of the scheme may be

13 *Kuldip Singh Dhillon (Col)* v *Paragon Utility Financiers (P) Ltd.* (1986)60 Comp Cas 1075 (P&H).
14 *Bradford Investment* PIC 91 BCLC 224 Ch D.
15 *Life Insurance Corporation of India* v *Escorts Ltd.* (1986)59 Comp Cas 548 (SC).
16 *Isle of Wright Railway* v *Tahourdin* [1883]25 Ch D 320.
17 *A. D. Chaudhary* v *Mysore Paper Mills Ltd.* (1976)46 Comp Cas 548.
18 *Canton Industries Alliance Ltd.* v *Pravin Kantilal Vakil* (1985)57 Comp Cas 12.

quite in order since the Court is fully empowered to grant such modification under s. 231.[19]

4.3 *Extraordinary General Meeting called by the Requisitionists*

If the Directors fail to call a meeting within 21 days from the date of the deposit of the requisition on a day not later than 45 days from the date of valid requisition, then the requisitionists may themselves call the meeting in the same manner, as far as possible, as that in which meetings may be called by the Directors, and hold it within three months from the date of the deposit of the requisition [s. 100(4) and s. 100(5)].[20] The word valid used above has no reference to object of the requisition. As to the validity of the requisition, all that is required to be seen would be to consider whether the requisition deposited was in accordance with s. 100 as to its contents, the number of signatories and similar matters and it would not be open to the Directors to refuse to act on a requisition on the ground that although such requisition was in accordance with s. 100, it was otherwise invalid.[1]

However, it has been held that Board is within its right to refuse to call and hold an Extraordinary General Meeting on the requisition of members where an order of injunction restraining the company from holding any meeting is in force.[2]

The Supreme Court has in the case of *Life Insurance Corporation of India* v *Escorts Ltd.*[3] held that every member of a company has a right to requisition an Extraordinary General Meeting in accordance with the provisions of the Act. He cannot be restrained from requisitioning an Extraordinary General Meeting and he is not bound to disclose the reasons for the resolution proposed to be moved at the meeting.

Where the Directors failed or refuse to call and hold an Extraordinary General Meeting demanded by a valid requisition, the requisitionists could themselves call and hold the meeting. They must exercise their right under s. 100(4). If for any reason it is impracticable to call a meeting under s. 100, the Tribunal may direct the calling of a meeting on its own motion or on an application of any Director or on an application of any member entitled to vote at the meeting (s. 98).

Any such requisitioned meeting duly commenced before the expiry of 3 months may be adjourned to any day after the expiry of that period, without offending the provisions of the section [s. 100(4)]. Where a Tribunal's order restraining the holding of any meeting is pending, the requisitionists are debarred from holding the meeting.

19 *Pravin Kantilal Vakil* v *Mrs. Rohini Ramesh Zava* (1985)57 Comp Cas 31.
20 *B. Sivraman* v *Egmore Benefit Society Ltd.* (1992)75 Comp Cas 198 (Mad).
1 *Cricket Club of India Ltd.* v *Madhav L. Apte* (1975)45 Comp Cas 574.
2 *A.D. Chaudhury* v *Mysore Paper Mills Ltd.* (1976)46 Comp Cas 548.
3 (1986)59 Comp Cas 548 (SC).

Where a meeting is called by the requisitionists themselves, and the registered office is not made available to them for holding the meeting, they may hold the meeting elsewhere.[4]

5 Service of notice

Section 20 of the Companies Act 2013 specifies the manner in which a notice may be served on the members.

> Section 20. (1) A document may be served on a company or an officer thereof by sending it to the company or the officer at the registered office of the company by registered post or by speed post or by courier service or by leaving it at its registered office or by means of such electronic or other mode as may be prescribed:
>
> ....
>
> (2) Save as provided in this Act or the rules made thereunder for filing of documents with the Registrar in electronic mode, a document may be served on Registrar or any member by sending it to him by post or by registered post or by speed post or by courier or by delivering at his office or address, or by such electronic or other mode as may be prescribed:
>
> Provided that a member may request for delivery of any document through a particular mode, for which he shall pay such fees as may be determined by the company in its annual general meeting.

Personal service has been recommended. Alternative mode is postal service. If the latter mode is chosen, the document (notice) had to be sent properly addressed, prepaid, although if a member desires that a notice meant for him should be sent to him by post under a certificate of posting or under the registered cover with A/D and has deposited the necessary costs for the same, the notice has to be sent in the said manner.

The notice, if sent by post, should be properly addressed, prepaid and posted. In such cases the notice is deemed to have reached the addressee by 48 hours after the posting.[5] In case of foreign nationals whose shares have become vested in the custodian of the Enemy Property under the Enemy Property Act 1968, it would be sufficient compliance of the law, if the notice has been given to the Custodian of Enemy Property.[6] If a person refuses to accept the notice sent by registered post, such tender of registered cover is a valid service.[7]

When a particular mode of 'service of notice' is provided in the Articles or the Act no other mode is permissible.

4 *M.R.S. Rathnavelusami Chettiar* v *M. S. S. Manickavelu Chettiar* (1951)21 Comp Cas 93.

5 *Nagappa Chettiar (NVR)* v *Madras Race Club* AIR 1958 Mad 831; *Balwant Singh Sethi* v *Sarder Z.H. Singh Anand* (1988)63 Comp Cas 310 (Bom).

6 *United Bank of India* v *United India Credit and Development Co. Ltd.* (1977)47 Comp Cas 689.

7 *Joginder Singh Palta* v *Time Travels (P) Ltd.* (1984)56 Comp Cas 103.

On some occasions, a notice may be advertised in a newspaper for wide circulation. A notice advertised in a newspaper is deemed to be duly served on the day on which the advertisement appears. Such newspaper must be in circulation in the neighbourhood of the registered office of the company. Such service relates to every member of the company who has no registered address in India or who did not supply to the company an address within India for the giving of notice to him.

In case of joint-holders of a share, a notice may be served on them by sending it to the person named first in the Register in respect of the said share.

Finally, in case of service of a notice to a person entitled to a share in consequence of the death or insolvency of a member, the same may be sent by post in a prepaid letter. The notice has to be addressed to him by name, or by the title of the representatives of the deceased or by any like description. Where a notice by the company to a member was sent by ordinary post though another letter of similar purport was sent previously by registered post, this by itself cannot justify a conclusion that the letter was not sent by ordinary post or was not received by that member.[8]

If the Articles prescribe the method by which notice has to be given, it should be given accordingly. Otherwise, notice may be served by hand delivery, post, facsimile, e-mail or any other electronic mode. If the notice is to be sent by post another forty-eight hours are to be added in terms of r. 35(6) of the Companies (Incorporation) Rules 2014. "Posted' is taken to mean the placing of the envelope in the post box, or delivery of the envelope to an authorised official of post office, which need not necessarily be the post box or the post office situated within the city where the registered office of the company is situated.

6 Length of notice for calling a meeting (s. 101)—General Meeting—period of notice—shorter period

> Section 101. (1) A general meeting of a Company may be called by giving not less than clear 21 days' notice either in writing or through electronic mode in such manner as may be prescribed.
>
> Provided that a general meeting may be called after giving shorter notice than that specified in this sub-section if consent, in writing or by electronic mode, is accorded thereto:
>
> (*i*) in the case of an annual general meeting, by not less than ninety-five per cent of the members entitled to vote thereat; and
>
> (*ii*) in the case of any other general meeting, by members of the company;
>
> (*a*) holding, if the company has a share capital, majority in number of members entitled to vote and who represent not less than 95

8 (1969)1 Comp LJ 144 (147) (AP).

per cent of such part of the paid up share capital of the company as gives a right to vote at the meeting; or

(*b*) having, if the company has no share capital, not less than 95 per cent of the total voting power exercisable at that meeting.

The stipulated period of notice for calling a meeting is mandatory. It can be dispensed with only by not less than ninety-five per cent of the members entitled to receive the notice; the consent only of those who are present is not sufficient for the purpose.[9] It would appear that under s. 101 a difference in the notice period has been removed whether it is for a meeting for passing special resolutions or a meeting for passing general resolutions.

Proviso to s. 101(1) specifies persons who are entitled to accord consent to a notice even for a shorter period.

7 Contents and manner of service of notice omission to give notice—interpretation of a notice—court's jurisdiction

For detailed study, we would do well to refer to relevant provisions of the Act.

Every notice of a meeting shall specify the place, date, day and hour of the meeting and shall contain a statement of the business to be transacted at such meeting [s. 101(2)].

Notice of every meeting of the company shall be given to—

(*a*) every member of the company, legal representative of any deceased member or the assignee of an insolvent member;

(*b*) the auditor or auditors of the company; and

(*c*) every director of the company [s. 101(3)].

The accidental omission to give notice to, or the non-receipt of such notice by, any member or other person who is entitled to such notice for any meeting shall not invalidate the proceedings of the meeting [s. 101(4)].

The provisions of s. 101 are mandatory and have to be complied with strictly and if one of the essentials is not complied with, the meeting is not properly held and the resolutions passed thereat will be invalid.[10] However in *Calcutta Chemical Co. Ltd.* v *Dhiresh Chandra Roy*, it was held that it cannot be urged that the provisions of s. 101 are mandatory and that short notice given to any member will render the entire meeting void and of no legal consequence even if that member has suffered no prejudice.[11]

How a notice, as contemplated herein, is to be interpreted? Shareholder having knowledge about the business to be transacted at the meeting cannot complain of insufficiency of notice.[12] But where a meeting had been held

9 *Nagappa Chettiar (NVR)* v *Madras Race Club* AIR 1951 Mad 831.

10 *Asansol Electric Supply* v *Chunilal Daw* AIR 1972 Cal 19.

11 (1985)58 Comp Cas 275 (Cal).

12 55 Ind App 174; *Parashuram Detaram* v *Tata Industrial Bank Ltd.* AIR 1928 PC 180 (185).

without due notice thereof and of the business to be transacted thereat and at the meeting a full Board of Directors was elected it was held that the election was invalid.[13] Again, if the directors issue a circular in which they refer to certain alterations and say that only alterations are with regard to cl. (*x*) of the Articles of Associations, whereas there are equally important alterations in cl. (*y*), it cannot be said that shareholders have sufficient notice of the alterations in cl. (*y*).[14]

Where a notice did not specify the hour of the meeting and a special resolution was passed at such a meeting for the transfer of registered office, the notice and the resolution are bad.[15]

8 Statement to be annexed to notice (s. 102)

Section 102 provides that a statement setting out all the material facts concerning each item of special business to be transacted at a general meeting, shall be annexed to the notice calling such meeting. Such statement is to relate to—(*a*) the nature of concern or interest, financial or otherwise, if any, in respect of each item of—(*i*) every director and the manager, if any, (*ii*) every other key managerial personnel, and (*iii*) relatives of such persons; and (*b*) any other information and facts that may enable members to understand the meaning, scope and implications of the items of business and to take decision thereon.

The explanatory statement annexed to the notice has to give material facts and not detailed particulars. Technical details of the Company's work and administration, including the question as to where certain projects were to be set up or how, were not matters to be disclosed in the Explanatory Statement.[16]

Section 102 further provides that in case of non-disclosure or insufficient disclosure in any statement made by a promoter, director, manager or other key managerial personnel, which benefits such persons or their relatives, shall have to be compensated. The Act also has penal provisions for such default or non-compliance by these persons.

The notice is mandatory, for s. 102 enacts a provision which is mandatory and not directory.[17] Provisions of s. 101 have been made expressly mandatory and for good reasons and the same must be strictly complied with to ensure

13 (1857)1 App Case 39 (53, 54).
14 *Narayanlal Bansilal* v *Maneckji Petit Mfg. Co. Ltd.* AIR 1931 Bom 354 (365).
15 AIR 1951 Mad 831.
16 *East India Commercial Co.* v *Rayman Engineering Works Ltd.* AIR 1966 Cal 232; *Bimal Singh* v *Muir Mills Co. Ltd.* AIR 1952 Cal 645. Also see *Hari Krishan Lohia* v *Hoolangooree Tea Co.* AIR 1969 Cal 912.
17 *Mohan Lal Ganpatram* v *Sayaji Jubeda Cotton Mills* AIR 1965 Guj 96; *L.C. Kapadia* v *L.C. Desai* AIR 1972 Bom 276.

the validity of resolutions placed at the meeting. Non-compliance of the said provisions would make such resolutions void and *ultra vires*.[1]

Notice of a meeting merely specifying that copies of proposed articles are deposited in the registered office for inspection is not sufficient where majority of shareholders reside at long distance from the office. Copies of new articles should be annexed to the notice.[2] The notice of the meeting to be a sufficient notice must contain all particulars that may be necessary to enable a member receiving it to decide whether in his own interest he ought to attend the meeting or not.

Knowledge of notice is imputed to a shareholder, who by his conduct shows that he knew the real effect of the work to be transacted at a meeting, cannot complain of a notice on the ground of insufficiency.[3]

It may be mentioned here that a party complaining that the notice of a meeting does not give material particulars must allege in affidavit as to what material particulars are lacking.[4] A company seeking approval of the general body of shareholders for investing capital in new undertaking need not disclose to individual shareholders the details of financial arrangement with collaborators.[5]

9 Notice of application to the Central Government (s. 201)—publication in a newspaper

Section 201 enjoins that—(1) Every application made to the Central Government under s. 196 shall be in such form as may be prescribed.

(2)(*a*) Before any application is made by a company to the Central Government under s. 196, there shall be issued by or on behalf of the Company a general notice to the members thereof, indicating the nature of the application proposed to be made.

(*b*) Such notice shall be published at least once in a newspaper in the principal language of the district in which the registered office of the company is situate and circulating in that district, and at least once in English in an English newspaper circulating in that district.

(*c*) The copies of the notices, together with a certificate by the company as to the due publication thereof, shall be attached to the application.

10 Ordinary and special resolutions—notice (s. 114)—resolutions requiring special notice (s. 115)

A special resolution has been explained in s. 114(2) of the Companies Act 2013. It reads:

1 *Asansol Electric Supply Co.* v *Chunni Lal Daw* AIR 1972 Cal 19.
2 *Bimal Singh* v *Muri Mills Co. Ltd.* AIR 1952 Cal 645.
3 *Lalita Rajya Lakshmi* v *Indian Motor Co.* AIR 1962 Cal 127.
4 *Nagaisuree Tea Co. Ltd.* v *Ram Chandra Karnani* (1966)2 Com LJ 208 (Cal).
5 *Sitaram Jaipuria* v *Banwarilal Jaipuria* AIR 1972 Cal 105.

"Section 114(2). A resolution shall be a special resolution when—

(*a*) the intention to propose the resolution as a special resolution has been duly specified in the notice calling the general meeting or other intimation given to the members of the resolution;

(*b*) the notice required under this Act has been duly given; and

(*c*) the votes cast in favour of the resolution, whether on a show of hands, or electronically or on a poll, as the case may be, by members who being entitled so to do, vote in person or by proxy or by postal ballot, are required to be not less than three times the number of the votes, if any, cast against the resolution by members so entitled and voting."

The notice, although it need not set out the terms of the special resolution in all its details, must give clear information of what is proposed to be done and also make a frank disclosure of the facts on which the shareholders will be called upon to vote. The concealment with regard to any important part of the resolution will render the proceedings invalid.[6] In other words, the notice should indicate the nature of business to be transacted at the meeting.[7]

The omission to name the meeting as an extraordinary meeting in the notice has no importance and does not vitiate the proceedings when the agenda indicated and the members had knowledge of the purpose of the meeting and did not object.[8]

The notice must be a notice of 21 clear days. Under the proviso to s. 81(2) of the Act of 1913 (corresponding to s. 114 of the present Act), the requirement as to 21 days' notice is mandatory.[9] The expression "not less than 21 days" in s. 81(2) means there should be an interval of 21 clear days and in counting this period, the date of the meeting and the date of service of the notice should be excluded.[10] The requirement of 21 days' notice may be dispensed with by an agreement of all members entitled to vote and present in person or by proxy at the meeting.[11] A meeting held without 21 days' notice and passing a resolution relating to reduction of share-capital was invalid.[12]

But when the notice is defective as regards the time of the meeting, members present at the meeting cannot waive a defect.[13] Notice stating that the point of proposed amended articles will follow shortly—draft of proposed amendments actually posted within six days of notice—notice invalid.[14]

6 (50)55 My HCR 107.
7 *Nagappa Chettiar (NVR)* v *Madras Race Club* AIR 1951 Mad 831.
8 AIR 1938 Pesh 41.
9 AIR 1951 Mad 831.
10 AIR 1951 Mad 831 at p. 839.
11 AIR 1951 Mad 831 at p. 840.
12 AIR 1956 Pat 364.
13 AIR 1951 Mad 831 (840).
14 AIR 1951 Mad 831.

Resolutions requiring a special notice are provided for in s. 115 of the Act.

11 Alteration of the provisions of the memorandum of association (s. 13)

For any alteration of the object clause, all that is required is a special resolution and the approval of the Central Government. While the companies are free to alter the provisions of the memorandum of association, the alteration has to be confined within the limits set by s. 13. Any alteration in excess of the permitted range will amount to violation of the Act. Confirmation of the Central Government on petition is necessary for inter state shifting of registered office. Rules 29, 30, 31 and 32 of the Companies (Incorporation) Rules 2014 provide that before confirming the alteration the Central Government must be satisfied (*a*) that sufficient notice has been given to every holder of the debentures of the company, and to every other person or class of persons whose interest will, in the opinion of the Central Government, be affected by the alteration; and (*b*) that with respect to every creditor who, in the opinion of the Central Government, is entitled to object to the alteration, and who signifies his objection in the manner directed by the Central Government. The Central Government shall cause service of the petition for confirmation of the alteration to be served on the Registrar.

12 Notice for revocation of Licence (s. 8)

Section 8(1) provides that where it is proved to the satisfaction of the Central Government that an association is about to be formed as a limited company for promoting commerce, art, science, sports, education, reserch, social welfare, religion, charity protection of environment or any other useful object and intends to apply its profits, if any, or other income in promoting its objects and to prohibit the payment of any dividend to its members, the Central Govt. may, by licence, direct that the association may be registered as a company with limited liability without the addition to its name of the word "Limited" or the words "Private Limited". An existing company can avail itself of the privileges under s. 8(4) by restricting its objects for non-profit making purposes as specified in sub-sec. (1) of s. 8. The Central Govt. is empowered to revoke the licence granted under sub-sec. (1). It is, however, provided that before licence is so revoked the Central Government shall give notice in writing of its intention to the concerned body and shall afford it an opportunity of being heard in opposition to the revocation. [Section 8(6)].

13 Alteration of Articles by Special Resolution (s. 14)

A Board Meeting is required to be held to decide on the changes in the articles, the time, date, venue and agenda of the general meeting and to approve the notice for calling general meeting. Notice of meeting for alteration of Articles should declare full facts and be accompanied by a copy of the proposed amendment.[15] Notice of general meeting should be issued to all the members, auditors, legal representatives of the deceased and assignees of insolvent members and to all the stock exchanges where the company is listed. An amendment to the Articles made without due notice in invalid.[16] There cannot be an alteration behind the back of member.[17] Any alteration having the effect of conversion of a public company into a private company shall not, however, take effect except with the approval of the Tribunal.

14 Prohibition on acceptance of deposits from public (s. 73)

No company shall invite, accept or renew deposits under the Companies Act 2013 from the public except in the manner provided under Chapter V of the Act and Companies (Acceptance of Deposits) Rules 2014. A company may, subject to the passing of a resolution in general meeting and subject to such rules as may be prescribed in consultation with the Reserve Bank of India, accept deposits from its members on such terms and conditions, including the provision of security, if any, or for the repayment of such deposits with interest, as may be agreed upon between the company and its members, subject to the fulfilment of certain conditions as laid down in s. 73((2) of the Act read with r. 3 of the Companies (Acceptance of Deposits) Rules 2014. In case of failure of the company to repay the deposit or interest thereon in accordance with terms and conditions of the agreement, the depositor concerned may apply to the Tribunal for an order directing the company to pay the sum due or for any loss or damage incurred by him as a result of such non-payment and for such other orders as the Tribunal may deem fit [s. 73(4)]. It may be pointed out that prior to acceptance of such deposits under s. 73(2), the company shall issue a circular to all its members by registered post with acknowledgment one or speed post or by electronic mode in Form DPT-1, and shall, in addition, publish the circular in English language in an English newspaper and in vernacular language in a vernacular newspaper having wide circulation in the State in which the registered office of the company is situated (vide r. 4 of the Companies (Acceptance of Deposits) Rules 2014). Issuance of an advertisement is equivalent to a public notice, in the absence of which a company cannot accept deposits.

15 Notice to Registrar of Consolidation of Share Capital, conversion of shares into stock, etc. (s. 64)

Section 64. (1) Where—

(*a*) a company alters its share capital in any manner specified in sub-sec. (1) of s. 61;

15 *Bimal Singh Kothari* v *Muri Co. Ltd.* AIR 1952 Cal 645; (1952) Com Cas 248.
16 *Sardar Gulabchand* v *Punjab Zamindari Bank Ltd.* (1940)10 Com Cas 188 (Lahore).
17 *Madhavramachandra Kamath* v *Canara Banking Corporation Ltd.* (1941)11 Com Cas 78; AIR 1941 Mad 354.

(*b*) an order made by the Government under sub-sec. (4) read with sub-sec. (6) of s. 62 has the effect of increasing authorised capital of a company; or

(*c*) a company redeems any redeemable preference shares,

the company shall file a notice in the prescribed form [Rule 15 and Form SH 7 of the Companies (Share Capital and Debentures) Rules 2014] with the Registrar within a period of thirty days of such alteration or increase or redemption along with an altered memorandum.

The Registrar shall thereupon record the notice and make any alteration which may be necessary in the company's memorandum.

Section 64(2) lays down that the failure to comply with the provisions of s. 64(1) may be visited with penalty.

16 Date of Notice of Charge (s. 80)

The date of execution of charge is the date of creation for the purpose of computing the time prescribed by s. 77 for registration though it may be stipulated to take effect on a later date on the happening of a later event. For the purpose of s. 80 the date of registration is the date on which the doctrine of constructive notice (deemed notice) comes into play with the effect that any person acquiring the property which has been subjected to the charge or any part thereof or any share or interest therein shall be deemed to have notice from the date of registration.[18] Though the registration of a charge constitutes notice to the whole world that a charge of a particular type exists, it does not constitute notice of the terms and conditions of the charge. In other words, there is no constructive notice of the charge.

17 Registered Office of Company (s. 12)

Section 12 inter alia provides that a company shall, as from the day on which it begins to carry on business, or as from the thirtieth day after the date of its incorporation, whichever is earlier, have a registered office to which all communications and notices may be addressed. It further provides that notice of the situation of the registered office and of every change therein shall be given within thirty days after the date of incorporation of the company or after the date of change, as the case may be, to the Registrar who shall record the same. Removal of the Registered Office from one place to another within the same city, town or village dose not, however, require any special resolution, though notice of such change also should be given to the Registrar. It is not correct to say that a Resolution

18 *English and Scottish Mercantile Investment Co. Ltd.* [1892]2 QB 700 (CA).

to change the registered office is sufficient and only effect of the failure to notify is to render the Company liable for a fine.[1] The notice of situation or change of situation of the Registered Office is to give to the Registrar on Form No. 1 NC 22 and e-form ACTIVE of the Companies (Incorporation) Rules 2014.

18 Notice to be given to Central Government for application under ss. 230 and 232

The tribunal shall give Notice of every application made to it under s. 230 or s. 232 to the Central Government and the Tribunal shall take into consideration the representations, if any, made to it by that Government before passing any order under any of these sections. A Notice to the Central Government may be given before the Court makes the order sanctioning the compromise or arrangement.[2] A notice to the Central Government is a prerequisite only at the stage of the sanction of the Scheme.[3]

19 Notice to be given to the Central Government of applications under ss. 241 and 242

The Tribunal shall give notice of every application made to it under s. 241 or s. 242 to the Central Government and shall take into consideration the representations, if any, made by it to by that Government, before passing a final order under that section. Notice to the Central Government need not be given if the petition is dismissed summarily. But if the petition is admitted for hearing the Central Government and Company both must be informed.[4]

20 Circumstances in which company may be wound up by Tribunal

On a petition under s. 272, a company may be wound up by the Tribunal in the following circumstances:

(*a*) if the company has, by a special resolution resolved that the company be wound up by the Tribunal;

(*b*) if the company has acted against the interests of the sovereignty and integrity of India, the security of the State, friendly relations with foreign states, public order, decency or morality;

(*c*) if on an application made by the Registrar or any other person authorised by the Central Government by notification, the Tribunal is of the opinion that the affairs of the company have been conducted in a fraudulent manner or the company was formed for fraudulent or unlawful purpose or the persons concerned in the formation or

1 *Jan Bazar Manna Estate Ltd.*, re AIR 1931 Cal 692.
2 *Bangeswari Cotton Mills Ltd.*, Re (1967)37 Comp Cas 195 (Cal).
3 *Vikram Organics Pvt. Ltd.* v *Anirox Pigments Ltd.*(1997)88 Comp Cas 804 (Cal).
4 *Sakhti Trading Co. (P) Ltd.* v *Union of India* (1985)57 Comp Cas 789.

management of its affairs have been guilty of fraud, misfeance or misconduct in connection therewith and that it is proper the company be wound up;

(*d*) if the company has made a default in filing with the Registrar its financial statements or annual returns for immediately preceding five consecutive financial years; or

(*e*) if the Tribunal is of the opinion that it is just and equitable that the company should be wound up (s. 271).

Any contributory or all contributories who may be the holder of fully paid shares, or the company, or the Registrar, or the Central Government or any person authorised by the Central Government, may present such petitions under s. 272 of the Act.

21 Passing of resolutions by Postal Ballot (s. 110)

This section seeks to protect the right of every member of a listed public company to vote on any important resolution. Under s. 110(1), the Central Government may by notification declare items of business that can be transacted only by postal ballot, and also in respect of any item of business other than ordinary business and any business in respect of which directors or auditors have a right to be heard at any meeting may also be transacted by postal ballot but in the prescribed manner.

It may be mentioned that notwithstanding anything contained in the provisions of the Companies Act 2013 a listed public company may get any resolution relating to any business not notified by the Central Government passed by means of postal ballot instead of transacting the business in a General Meeting.

The procedure to be followed for conducting business through postal ballot has been laid down in r. 22 of the Companies (Management and Administration) Rules 2014. Postal ballot means voting by post or through electronic means within a period of 30 days from the date of despatch of the notice. The notice shall be sent either by (*a*) Registered Post or Speed Post, or (*b*) through electronic means like registered e-mail id, or (*c*) through courier service for facilitating the communication of the assent or dissent of the shareholder to the resolution within the said period of 30 days. Also, an advertisement is required to be published at least once in a vernacular newspaper in the principal vernacular language of the district in which the registered office of the company is situated having a wide circulation, and at least once in English language in an English newspaper having a wide circulation about having despatched the ballot papers and specifying relevant facts. Similarly, the notice of the postal ballot shall be placed on the website of the company forthwith.

22 Procedure

A Board Meeting has to convened after giving notice to all the Directors of the company and to take the decision of passing a resolution or resolutions by means of a postal ballot. Every officer of the company whose duty is to give notice of the Board Meeting as aforesaid and who fails to do so will be punishable with fine.

Notice has to be sent to all the shareholders along with a draft resolution explaining the reasons therefor and requesting them to send their assent or dissent in writing on a postal ballot within a period of 30 days from the date of posting of the letter.

Notice has to be sent by registered post with acknowledgement due or under certificate of posting with an advertisement published in a leading English newspaper and in one vernacular newspaper circulating in the State where the registered office of the company is situated about having despatched the ballot papers.

The Notice shall include a postage prepaid envelope for facilitating the communication of the assent or dissent of the shareholder to the resolution within the said period.

The company may make a note below the notice of General Meeting for understanding of members that the transaction(s) at Serial No. requires consent of shareholders through postal ballot.

The Board of Directors of the company has to appoint a scrutinizer, who is not in the employment of the company, may be a retired judge or any person of repute who in the opinion of the Board of Directors can conduct the postal ballot voting procedure in a fair and transparent manner.

If a resolution is assented to by a required majority of the shareholders by means of postal ballot, it will be deemed to have been duly passed.

If a shareholder sends his assent or dissent in writing on a postal ballot and thereafter any person fraudulently defaces or destroys the ballot paper or declaration of identity of the shareholder, such person will be punishable with imprisonment for a term which may extend to 6 months or with fine or both.

"Postal ballot" includes voting by shareholders by postal or electronic mode instead of voting personally by presenting for transacting business in a General Meeting of the Company.

FORMS

Form 1

Notice intimating closure of the Register of Members (Simple Form of advertisement in newspaper)

Section 91 of the Companies Act 2013

NOTICE

XY Company Ltd.

Annual General Meeting

Notice is hereby given that the Register of Members of the Company will be closed from .... August, 20 ... to ...... August, 20 ..., both days inclusive.

(Add if necessary, for the forthcoming Annual General Meeting).

By Order of the Board
XY Company Ltd.
Sd/ ....
(Name)
Company Secretary

Registered Office
....
....
Kolkata 700 001
Dated ....

NOTES: 1. The Notice has to be published at least 7 days before the closure of the Register of members or transfer of Books in a newspaper circulated in the neighbourhood of the company concerned.

2. Section 91(1) enjoins: "A company may close the register of members or the register of the debenture-holders or the register of other security-holders for any period or periods not exceeding in the aggregate forty-five days in each year, but not exceeding thirty days at any one time, subject to giving of previous notice of at least seven days or such lessor period as may be specified by Securities and Exchange Board for listed companies or the companies which intend to get their securities listed in such manner as may be prescribed."

See also rule 10 of the Companies (Management and Administration) Rules 2014.

Form 2

Notice under s. 91 (Re: Closure of Register of Members—Form of advertisement)

Pursuant to s. 91 of the Companies Act 2013, notice is hereby given that the Company's Register of Members for equity shares will remain closed from .... 20 ... to ...... 20 ..., both days inclusive.

(*If necessary add*: The instrument of transfer together with relative share certificates and other documents, if any, received in order at the Company's Registered Office by

.... day of ... 20 ... will be considered for payment of the dividend, if approved, to the transferees).

(*If necessary add*: For the purpose of interim dividend which will be considered by the Board of Directors at a meeting to be held on .... day of ... 20 ...).

By Order of the Board

....

(Name)

Director

Registered Office:
(*Address*) ....
....
Dated the......... 20 ....

Form 3

Notice under s. 91 of the Companies Act 2013 (advertisement in a newspaper) with declaration of dividend

The XY (India) Limited
Registered Office: A.B. Road
.... New Delhi

NOTICE

Notice is hereby given under s. 91 of the Companies Act 2013, that the Register of Members will be closed from Monday, the .... day of .... to ...., the .... day of .... 20 ... (both days inclusive).

The Share Transfer Books of the Company will also remain closed for the aforesaid period.

Notice is also hereby given that the dividend for the year ended 31st March, 20 ..., if and when sanctioned, will be made payable to those shareholders whose names stand on the Register of Members of the Company on the 31st of August, 20 ....

(Or, to their mandatees).

By Order of the Board
Or, By Order of the Board of Directors

....

(Name)

Company Secretary

New Delhi
..........., 20 ....

Form 4

Notice under s. 91 for closure of Register

XY Limited

Notice is hereby given that the Register of Members and Share Transfer Register of the Company in respect of Preference and Equity Shares will remain closed from ...... day of ..., 20 ... to ...... day of ... 20 ..., both days inclusive for the Twelfth Annual General Meeting to be held on the ...... day of ...... 20..., notice and report of which are being sent to the members individually.

Sd/ ....
Company Secretary

Registered Office: ....
....
Kolkata 700 001
Dated ....

Form 5

Notice for Annual General Meeting (s. 96) (Simple Form)

XY Tea Company Limited

NOTICE

Notice is hereby given that the Annual General Meeting of the Company will be held at the Registered Office of the Company on Monday, the .... day of August 20...... at 10.30 a.m. to transact the business as detailed in the notice posted to the members of the Company.

(Or, notice of which stating the business to be transacted is being sent to shareholders).

Notice is also given that the Register of Members of the Company will remain closed from .... to .... 20... (both days inclusive)

By Order of the Board
....
(Name)
Company Secretary

Registered Office: ....
.... Old Court House Street
Kolkata 700 001
Dated .... 20 ...

Notes: 1. Year means British calendar year. The meeting should specify in the notice that it was the Annual General Meeting. 21 clear days' notice is necessary.

2. In each year there is one Annual General Meeting and not more than 15 months shall elapse between the date of one annual general meeting and that of the next [Proviso to s. 96(1)]. Provision is mandatory—AIR 1934 Cal 624.

3. For time, place and date—s. 96(2) of the Act.

4. Notice period—21 days [s. 101(1)]; shorter period—s. 101(2) of the Act.

Form 6

Notice for Annual General Meeting—advertisement in a newspaper

XY Ltd.

Notice is hereby given that the Forty-fifth Annual General Meeting of the Company will be held at the Registered Office of the Company, on Tuesday, the ...... day of ...... 20...... at ...... Kolkata 700 001 at .... p.m., to transact the following business:

(1) To receive and adopt the Audited Accounts for the year ending with the 31st day of December, ... and the Report of the Board of Directors and Auditors thereon;

(2) To elect Directors;

(3) To appoint Auditors and fix their remuneration.

(4) To transact any other Special business which may be brought before the meeting.

By Order of the Board

....

Company Secretary

Kolkata
The .... 20......

NOTES: 1. If the articles of the Company so provide a member may appoint more than one proxy. Section 105 of the Companies Act reg. provision for proxies.

2. A member entitled to attend and vote at the meeting is entitled to appoint a proxy to attend and vote in his stead and a proxy need not be a member of the Company.

Form 7

Notice of Annual General Meeting (by advertisement in a newspaper)

XY Company Limited
Notice of Annual General Meeting

The Thirty-fifth Annual General Meeting of the members of the Company will be held on Friday, the ...... 20...... at ...., Kolkata 700 001 at .... p.m.

The notice of the meeting setting out the business to be transacted thereat and the Reports of the Directors and Auditors and the statement of accounts for the year ended 31st December 20 ... have been posted to the members individually at their registered addresses.

Notice is also hereby given that the Registers of Members of the Company and the Share Transfer Books will remain closed from .... to .... 20... both days inclusive.

By Order of the Board

....

Company Secretary

Registered Office:

....

Kolkata 700 001
.... 20...

Form 8

Notice for Annual General Meeting (Detailed Notice)

XY Steel Company Limited

NOTICE

Notice is hereby given that the Forty-second Annual General Meeting of the shareholders of the X Y Steel Co. Ltd., will be held on ...... the .... 20...... at 11.00 a.m., at its registered office, at .... Street, Kolkata 700 001 to transact the following business:

1. To receive, consider and adopt the Directors' report and the audited accounts of the company for the year ended 31st December 20....

2. To declare dividend.

3. To elect Directors.

4. To appoint Auditors (and fix their remuneration).

5. To consider and if thought fit to pass with or without modification the following Resolution as a Special Resolution.

Resolved that (set out the Resolution)

....

SPECIAL BUSINESS.

6. To consider and if thought fit to pass with or without modification the following Resolution as an ordinary Resolution.

Resolved that (set out the Resolution here) ....".

Register of Members will remain closed from ...... to ...... 20... both days inclusive.

It may be noted that a member entitled to attend and vote at the meeting is entitled to appoint a proxy to attend and vote instead of himself, and that the proxy so appointed need not be a member.

Explanatory Statement for the Special Business to be passed by Ordinary Resolution is annexed to this notice.

By Order of the Board

....

Name

Company Secretary/Managing Director

Annexure: Explanatory Statement

Registered Office
Kolkata 700 001
the......... 20...

NOTE: Section 101 of the Companies Act 2013. The provision as to holding of the general meeting within the time specified is mandatory—AIR 1954 Mad 275; AIR 1934 Cal 624.

Form 9

Notice of the Extraordinary General Meeting

XY Limited

Notice is hereby given that an Extraordinary General Meeting of the above Company will be held on Saturday, the ....20... at .... 10.30 a.m., to transact the following special business:

(*i*) To consider and if thought fit to pass undermentioned Resolutions Nos. 1 and 2 as Ordinary Resolutions and Nos. 3 and 4 as Special Resolutions.

viz;

1.

2. *Set out here resolutions*

3.

4.

(*ii*) A member entitled to attend and vote at the meeting is entitled to appoint a proxy to attend and vote in his stead. A proxy need not be a member of the Company.

(*iii*) Explanatory statements.

(*Facts and grounds justifying said 4 resolutions*).

By Order of the Board
Sd/- ....
Company Secretary

Registered Office:
Kolkata 700 001
Dated .... 20...

Notes: 1. Section 100—speaks of extraordinary general meeting.

2. Section 100(1)—The Board may, whenever it deems fit, call an extraordinary general meeting.

3. Section 100(2) of the Act read with rule 17 of the Companies (Management and Administration) Rules 2014 may be seen.

Form 10

Notice of Extraordinary General Meeting convened on requisition by shareholders

XY Company Ltd.

Notice is hereby given that in pursuance of a requisition lodged at the registered office of the aforesaid Company on ...... 1981 by the undermentioned requisitionists, an Extraordinary General Meeting of the Company will be held on the ...... day of September 20... at 3.30 p.m. at .... Kolkata 700 001 at the Registered Office to consider the following matters:

(*Set out the matters here*)

By Order of the Board
Sd/- ....
Company Secretary

Registered Office:
....
Kolkata 700 001
Dated ....

Names of Requisitionists

1.
2.
3.

Notes: 1. Section 100(2) authorises the Board of Directors of Company to call an Extraordinary General Meeting of the Company, on the requisition of such number of members of the Company as is specified in sub-sec. (2) of s. 100 of the Companies Act 2013.

2. The meeting can be called by the requisitionists themselves if the Board does not within 21 days from the date of the receipt of a valid requisition proceed to call a meeting on a day not later than 45 days from the date of the receipt of the requisition [s. 100(4)].

3. A member entitled to attend and vote at the meeting is entitled to appoint a proxy to attend and vote in his stead. A proxy need not be a member of the Company.

Form 11

Notice of General Meeting by Convenors (Requisitionists)—s. 100(4) of the Companies Act 2013

XY Company Ltd.

Notice is hereby given that an Extraordinary General Meeting of the Company will be held on Saturday, the .... August 20... at 3.30 p.m. at .... (name the place) for the purpose of considering the following matters:

(*State here the matters with object for the meeting*)

As also to pass, if considered proper, the following resolution to wit:

(*State here the resolution*)

2. This notice is given by the undersigned members of the Company being the requisitionists and in exercise of their right conferred by s. 100 of the Companies Act 2013, the Directors having failed to convene a meeting within 21 days from the date of the receipt of the requisition signed by the requisitionists at the Registered Office of the Company in accordance with the abovementioned section.

Sd/- ....

....

Convenors

Registered Office:

....

Kokata 700 013

Dated ....

NOTE: (*a*) A meeting called under sub-sec. (4) of s. 100 by the Requisitionists shall be called in the same manner as nearly as possible, as that in which meetings are to be called by the Board, but

(*b*) A meeting shall not be held after the expiration of three months from the date of the requisition.

(*c*) A Member entitled to attend and vote at the meeting is entitled to appoint a Proxy to attend and, on a poll, to vote instead of himself and Proxy need not be a Member of the Company. Proxies, in order to be effective, must be received at the Registered Office of the Company not less than forty-eight hours before the time fixed for the Meeting.

Form 12

Notice of change of address of the Registered Office of a Company

XY Co. Ltd.

Notice is hereby given that the Registered Office of the above-named Company has been shifted from .... Avenue, Kolkata 700 021 to .... Street, Kolkata 700 001 with effect from the 1st day of September 20....

By Order of the Board

Sd/- ....

Company Secretary

Registered Office:

....

Kolkata 700 001

Dated ....

NOTE: Section 12(4), Notice of the change of the Registered Office is to be given to the Registrar of Companies within 30 days of the change. For shifting Regd. Office from one State to another, a special Resolution is necessary, but no company shall change the place of its registered office from the jurisdiction of one Registrar to the jurisdiction of another Registrar within the same State unless such change is confirmed by the Regional Director on an application made in this behalf by the company in the prescribed manner [s. 12(5)].

Form 13

Notice of Adjourned General Meeting/Adjourned Extraordinary General Meeting

XY Limited

Notice is hereby given that the Thirty-first Annual General Meeting/Extraordinary General Meeting of the above-named Company, convened for ...... day of July 20..., has been adjourned to the ...... day of September 20..., at 11.00 a.m. and would be held at ....(place)

The business to be transacted thereat:

(Set out the business as in the notice of the original meeting)

By Order of the Board
Sd/- ....
Company Secretary

Registered Office:

....

Kolkata 700 013
Dated .... 20....

N.B.– A member entitled to attend and vote at the meeting is entitled to appoint a proxy to attend and vote in his stead. A proxy need not be a member of the Company.

NOTES: 1. Regulation 49 of Table F to Sch. I of the Act provides for adjournment. It reads:

(*i*) The Chairperson may, with the consent of any meeting at which a quorum is present, and shall, if so directed by the meeting, adjourn the meeting from time to time and place to place.

(*ii*) No business shall be transacted at any adjourned meeting other than the business left unfinished at the meeting from which the adjournment took place.

(*iii*) When a meeting is adjourned for 30 days or more; notice of the adjourned meeting shall be given as in the case of an original meeting.

(*iv*) Save as aforesaid and as provided in s. 103 of the Act, it shall not be necessary to give any notice of an adjournment or of the business to be transacted at an adjourned meeting.

Question of adjournment is generally provided for by the Articles of the Company, when the meeting is adjourned, for 30 days or more a 21 days' notice is to be given.

Form 14

Notice by a member to the Company for removal of a Director

By registered post with A/D

Cooch Behar
August 6, 20...

To
The Secretary,
X Y Co. Ltd.,
....
Kolkata 700 001

Take notice that I, a shareholder in the aforesaid Company, intend to move, at the next Annual General Meeting of the said Company, a resolution that Mr. A, a director of the said Company, be removed from his office and that Mr. B be appointed a director in his place.

All queries and correspondences should be addressed to X Y Co. Ltd.

Sd/- ....
Member

NOTES: 1. Section 169. A Company may, by ordinary resolution, remove a director, not being a director appointed by the Tribunal.

2. A special notice is required for a resolution removing a director or to appoint somebody in place of the removed director.

Form 15

Special Notice by a member to remove a Director of the Company—14 days' notice

By registered post with A/D

....
Dated ...... 20...

To
The Directors, X Y Co. Ltd.
....
Kolkata 700 001

I hereby give special notice pursuant to s. 169 of the Companies Act 2013 that I would move the undermentioned resolutions as ordinary resolutions at the next Extraordinary General Meeting of the Company scheduled to be held on .... 20.......

1. That Mr. A.B., be and is hereby removed from his office of Director in the Company.
2. That Mr. C.D., be and is hereby appointed a Director in the Company in place of Mr. A.B., for the unexpired term of Mr. A.B.

Sd/- ....
Member

NOTES: 1. Section 169 speaks of removal of a director.

2. Section 169(2) of the Act provides for resolutions requiring special notice. Notice of the intention to move the resolution shall be given to the Company not less than 14 days before the meeting at which it is to be moved, exclusive of the day on which the notice is served or deemed to be served and the day of the meeting.

Form 16

Company's notice in case of voluntary winding up—Notice under s. 312 to the Registrar of Companies

NOTICE

Name of Company
Nature of Business

To
The Registrar ....
....

We .... of .... and .... of .... hereby give notice that we have appointed Liquidators of XY Co. Ltd., by the special resolution dated of the said Company.

(or by resolution by Creditors of the Company) dated .... 20....

Dated, Kolkata
the .... July 20 ......

Sd/- ....
Sd/- ....
(Directors)

NOTES: 1. Members' voluntary winding up—If the Company passes a special resolution to that effect a Company may be wound up voluntarily—s. 304(*b*). Again, when a Company was formed for a particular period, on expiry of the period the company may be wound up. Or, when Articles provide that the Company would be wound up on happening of an incident, the incident occurred and the Company in general meeting passes a resolution to that effect [s. 304(*a*) of the Act].

2. For powers and duties of Liquidators in voluntary winding up—see s. 314.

Form 17

Notice under s. 201 of the Companies Act to the Members for making application to the Central Government

.... Company Ltd.

Notice under s. 201 of the Companies Act 2013

Notice is hereby given that applications are being made by the Company to the Central Government under s. .... of the Companies Act 2013 for their approval to the appointment of and payment of remuneration to .... and .... Directors of the Company.

For .... Co. Ltd.
Sd/- ....
Name ....
Director

....
Regd. Office ....
Kolkata 700 001
Dated .... 20......

Form 18

Notice under s. 201 of the Companies Act–advertisement in a newspaper for payment

XY Company Ltd.

Notice under s. 201 of the Companies Act 2013

Notice is hereby given that the Company intends to apply to the Central Government for its approval pursuant to s. .... of the Companies Act 2013, for payment of Rs. .... per month to M/s. P Q Company Ltd., in partial reimbursement of the expenses incurred by them on Sri .... who is concurrently the Managing Director of both the Companies.

By Order of the Board

....

(Name)
Company Secretary

Registered Office:
.................., Kolkata
Dated .... 20....

Form 19

Notice under s. 201–for varying terms of remuneration of a Director

XY Tea Co. Ltd.

Notice under s. 201 of the Companies Act 2013

Notice is hereby given that the Company intends to apply to the Central Government for its approval for varying the terms of remuneration of Mr. A.B., Managing Director of the Company, for the period from .... 20 ...... to .... 20 ....

By Order of the Board

....

(Name)
Company Secretary

Registered Office:
....................., Kolkata
Dated .... July, 20 ....

Form 20

Notice under s. 201–for continuance of a Director–Advertisement in a newspaper

XY Limited

Pursuant to s. 201 of the Companies Act 2013, notice is hereby given that the Company intends to apply to the Central Government for its approval for the continuance of Mr. A.B., as Managing/Wholetime Director of the Company and to the remuneration paid/payable to him with effect from ...... 20 ..., same as under the agreement of service dated ...... between the Company and said Mr. A.B.

By Order of the Board

....

(Name)
Company Secretary

Registered Office:
....................., Kolkata
Dated .... July, 20 ....

Form 21

Notice under s. 201

XY Company Ltd.

Notice is hereby given under s. 201 of the Companies Act, 2013 that the Company intends to apply to the Central Government for its approval to the appointment of Mr. A.B., as Wholetime Director of the Company for a period of three years with effect from .... August, 20 ..., or such other date as may be approved by the Central Government.

Or,

Under the applicable provisions of the Companies Act, 2013, to the re-appointment of Mr. A.B. as Managing Director for a period of four years with effect from .... 20 ... on existing remuneration (or, on increased remuneration).

Or,

For the appointment of Sri A.B. as the Managing Director of the Company for a period of five years with effect from ...... 20 ... in terms of resolution passed by the shareholders at the Annual General Meeting held on ...... June, 20 ....

Or,

To the reappointment of Mr. A.B. and Mr. C.D. who are wholetime employees of the Company as the alternate Directors respectively for Mr. P. and Mr. Q, Directors during their absence from the State of West Bengal with effect from ...... and for a period of three years.

By Order of the Board

....

Company Secretary

Registered Office:

....

Kolkata 700 017
Dated ...... July, 20...

Form 22

Notice of the Board Meeting

XY Co. Ltd.

Mr. ....
Director,
New Delhi

Dear Sir,

A meeting of the Board of Directors of the Company will be held on .... (day of the week), the .... (date) .... (month) .... (year) at .... (a.m./p.m.) at the Registered Office of the Company. The Agenda of the business to be transacted at the meeting is enclosed/will follow.

You are requested to make it convenient to attend the Meeting.

Yours faithfully,
Signature
Name
Designation

Enclo: Agenda.

AGENDA

1. Confirmation of the minutes of the previous Board Meeting held on ....
2. Leave of absence, if any.
3. Notice under section 164 of the Companies Act 2013.
4. Confirmation of the minutes of the Audit Committee.
5. Matters arising out of the previous minutes.
6. Approval of draft advertisement of unaudited results for the quarter ended 30th June, ...
7. Statutory Auditor's Report on the unaudited results for the quarter ended on 30th June, ...
8. Any other matter arising with the permission of the chair.

NOTES: 1. Regulation 67(*ii*) of Table 'F' to the First Schedule of the Companies Act 2013 enjoins:

'A director may and the Manager or Secretary on the requisition of a director shall, at any time, summon a meeting of the Board.'

2. Section 173(3) provides for giving of the notice. The notice shall have to be given in writing.
3. The notice has to give a reasonable period, not less than seven days to every director at his address registered with the company, and to send by hand delivery or by post or by electronic notice.
4. A meeting of the Board may be called at shorter notice to transact urgent business subject to the condition that at least one indefendent director, if any, shall be present at the meeting.

Form 23

Notice of demand for poll

Date: .... 20 ....

To

The Chairman of the Second Annual General Meeting of CAR Limited being held on Monday, 27th September 20 .... at 11 a.m. at .... (address).

We the undersigned, being holders of an aggregate of .... equity shares of Rs. 10 each of the Company, as per the details set out below against our respective names, demand that, pursuant to the provisions of section 109 of the Companies Act 2013, a poll be taken in respect of the Resolution proposed at Item No. 4 of the Notice dated 25th August 20 .... of the fourth Annual General Meeting of the Company on which the voting is yet to be taken on a show of hands.

Or

on which voting on a show of hands has been taken but the result thereof is yet to be announced

Or

Which was declared carried on voting by show of hands.

Sr. No.	Name of Member	Folio No./ Client ID No.	No. of shares held

Form 24

Notice of an Extraordinary General Meeting

XYZ Limited

Registered Office ....

Notice is hereby given that an Extraordinary General Meeting of the Members of XYZ Limited will be held on Friday, 25th October 20 .... at 11.00 a.m. at .... (address) to transact the following special business:

SHIFTING OF REGISTERED OFFICE

1. To consider and, if thought fit, to pass the following Resolution as a Special Resolution:

"Resolved that, pursuant to the applicable provisions, of the Companies Act 2013, and subject to the approval of the Company Law Board, the Registered Office of the Company be shifted from the State of Delhi to the State of Haryana.

"Resolved further that clause II of the Memorandum of Association of the Company be altered by substitution of the words 'National Capital Territory of Delhi' with the words 'State of Haryana'.

"And resolved further that the Board of Directors of the Company be and is hereby authorised to file the necessary petition(s) before the National Company Law Tribunal, Northern Region Bench at New Delhi for confirmation of the alteration of clause II of the Memorandum of Association of the Company as aforesaid and to carry out all other acts and deeds as are necessary in connection therewith, including compliance of directors, if any, of the order of the National Company Law Tribunal, Northern Region Bench at New Delhi."

COMMENCEMENT OF NEW BUSINESS

2. To consider and, if thought fit, to pass the following Resolution as a Special Resolution:

"Resolved that, pursuant to section 11 and other applicable provisions, if any, of the Companies Act 2013, consent of the Company be and is hereby given for commencement of a new business as contained in sub-clause IIIC of the Objects Clause of the Memorandum of Association, as reproduced hereunder.

(*iv*) To carry on the business of general manufacturers, importers and exporters, traders and dealers in any raw material and store, minerals, metals, chemicals, apparatus, plants, machinery, electrical engineering and hydraulics and articles of all kinds."

By order of the Board of Directors
SCP
Company Secretary

Place: New Delhi
Date: .... 20.......

Form 25

Explanatory Statement

As required by section 102 of the Companies Act 2013, the following explanatory statement sets out all material facts relating to the business mentioned under Item Nos. 1 and 2 of the accompanying Notice dated 30th September 20 ......

ITEM NO. 1

The Registered Office of the Company is situated in New Delhi since the incorporation of the Company. The business of the Company has increased manifold since incorporation and it is expected that such growth trends will be maintained in future.

The employee strength of the Company has also increased manifold and the Company needs an area of around 50,000 square feet to accommodate the entire staff and to carry out its growing business activities efficiently. However, expansion at the present location is not possible and prevailing rents in New Delhi render it unviable to look for additional premises in the vicinity of the Registered Office.

The Board of Directors have identified suitable premises at Chandigarh in the State of Haryana, not very far from the present Registered Office. Acquiring such premises, situated close to New Delhi, is advantageous for the Company to carry on its business more conveniently, economically and efficiently.

There also then is no need for retaining the present Registered Office accommodation and hence the Company has commenced preliminary negotiations for termination of the lease agreement.

In view of these advantages, the Board of Directors has decided to shift the Registered Office of the Company from the State of National Capital Territory of Delhi to the State of Haryana subject to necessary approvals.

A copy of the Memorandum of Association is available for inspection at the Registered Office of the Company on all working days of the Company between 11.00 a.m. and 1.00 p.m. upto the date of the Meeting and at the venue of the Meeting for the duration of the Meeting.

The Board commends the passing of the Resolution at Item No. 1 as a Special Resolution.

None of the Directors is concerned or interested in the proposed Resolution.

ITEM NO. 2

Under the Export-Import Policy of the Government of India, in order for the company to become an Eligible Export House, the Company is required to make exports to the extent specified in the Policy from time to time. On acquiring and retaining the status of an Eligible Export House, the Company becomes entitled to avail of Import Licences and other benefits.

Accordingly, the Company proposes to export various products, including goods of other manufacturers. It is, therefore, necessary to seek the approval of the Members in terms of section 11 of the Companies Act 2013, to the undertaking of all such business as an Export House and an Indenting/Import House can undertake. The Company has the necessary authority to undertake such business in terms of clause III of the Objects Clause of its Memorandum of Association.

A copy of the Memorandum of Association is available for inspection at the Registered Office of the Company on all working days of the Company between 11.00 a.m. and 1.00 p.m. upto the date of the Meeting and at the venue of the Meeting for the duration of the Meeting.

The Board commends the passing of the Resolution at item No. 2 as a Special Resolution.

None of the Directors is concerned or interested in the proposed Resolution.

By order of the Board of Directors
SCP
Company Secretary

Place: New Delhi
Date: .... 20........

Notes: 1. A Member entitled to attend and vote at the Meeting is entitled to appoint a Proxy to attend and, on a poll, to vote instead of himself and the Proxy need not be a Member of the company. Proxies, in order to be effective, must be received at the Registered Office of the Company not less than forty-eight hours before the time fixed for the Meeting. A Proxy form is enclosed.

2. The Explanatory Statement pursuant to section 102 of the Companies Act 2013, relating to special business to be transacted at the meeting is annexed.

Form 26

Notice by Requisitionists Convening an Extraordinary General Meeting

Notice is hereby given that the persons named below, who are Members, of XYZ Limited, having its Registered Office at ...., and who have requisitioned the convening of an Extraordinary General Meeting of the Company, hereby, in exercise of the powers and rights conferred by section 100 of the Companies Act 2013, give notice that the said requisitioned Meeting shall be held on .... day, ... the .... 20 ... at .... a.m. at .... (address) to consider the following proposal:

(*state the proposal*)

Or

for considering and, if though fit, passing the following Ordinary/Special Resolution:

Reproduce the Resolution.

Names of requisitionists:
1. ....
2. ....
3. ....
4. ....

NOTE: A Member entitled to attend and vote at the Meeting is entitled to appoint a Proxy to attend and, on a poll, to vote instead of himself and the Proxy need not be a Member of the Company. Proxies, in order to be effective, must be received at the Registered Office of the Company not less than forty-eight hours before the time fixed for the Meeting.

Form 27

Notice of an Extraordinary General Meeting called on the Requisition of Members

NOTICE

XYZ Limited

Registered Office ....

Notice is hereby given that, pursuant to a valid requisition under section 100 of the Companies Act 2013, lodged at the Registered Office of the Company by the Members whose names are annexed hereto, an Extraordinary General Meeting of the Company will be held on Tuesday, the 30th July 20......, at 10.30 a.m. at the Registered Office of the Company to consider the following proposal put forth by the requisitionists:

"Resolved that ....

....

...."

The Board of Directors have considered the abovementioned Resolution in its Meeting held on 4th July 2002 and submits the following observations thereon for the consideration of the Members:

....

....

(after stating the observations, it should also be stated whether the Board supports or does not support the proposal of the requisitionists contained in the aforesaid Resolution.)

By order of the Board of Directors
PQR
Company Secretary

Place: New Delhi
Date: .... 20 ....

NOTE:
1. A Member entitled to attend and vote at the Meeting is entitled to appoint a Proxy to attend and, on a poll, to vote instead of himself and the Proxy need not be a Member of the Company. Proxies, in order to be effective, must be received at the Registered Office of the Company not less than forty-eight hours before the time fixed for the Meeting (see s. 105).
2. The requisition dated 1st July 20......., referred to above, signed by the requisite number of Members in terms of section 100 of the Companies Act 2013, is available for inspection by any Member at the Registered Office of the Company on any working day of the Company between the hours of 11.00 a.m. and 1.00 p.m.
3. All documents referred to in the Notice are open for inspection at the Registered Office of the Company on all working days of the Company between 11.00 a.m. and 1.00 p.m. upto the date of the requisitioned meeting and at the venue of the Meeting for the duration of the Meeting.

Form 28

Notice of Postponed Annual General Meeting

XYZ Limited

Registered Office

....

Members are hereby informed that, due to unforeseen and unavoidable circumstances, the ...... th Annual General Meeting of the Company, which was to have been held on Tuesday, the 24th September 20......., will now be held on .... 20 ......, at .... p.m. at the Registered Office of the Company, to consider the business mentioned in the Notice dated 26th August 20 .... which had been sent to Members in connection with the Meeting originally scheduled to have been held on 24th September 20 ....

A member entitled to attend and vote at the Meeting is entitled to appoint a Proxy to attend and, on a poll, to vote instead of himself and the Proxy need not be a Member of the Company. Proxies, in order to be effective, must be received at the Registered Office of the Company not less than forty-eight hours before the time fixed for the Meeting.

By order of the Board of Directors
SCP
Company Secretary

Place: New Delhi
Date: .... 20..........

Note: Members may please immediately intimate any change in their address.

Form 29

Notice in Newspapers regarding Postponement of Annual General Meeting due to Postal Strike

NOTICE

Members are hereby informed that, due to the continuing total suspension of postal services throughout the country, it has not been possible for the Company to post to the Members the Notice convening the .... th Annual General Meeting of the Company, which was scheduled to be held on .... 20......, together with the Annual Report and Accounts for the year ended 31st March 20......, within the stipulated time-limit prescribed by the Companies Act 2013.

Accordingly, and in view of the fact that resumption of normal postal service is not likely in the immediate future, the Board of Directors of the Company has decided to postpone the said Annual General Meeting, which now is convened on .... 20......... Notice and other documents, if any, relevant to the re-convened Meeting will be despatched to Members on resumption of postal service throughout the country.

A Member entitled to attend and vote at the Meeting is entitled to appoint a Proxy to attend and, on a poll, to vote instead of himself and the Proxy need not be a

Member of the Company. Proxies, in order to be effective, must be received at the Registered Office of the Company not less than forty-eight hours before the time fixed for the Meeting.

By order of the Board of Directors
SCP
Company Secretary

Place: New Delhi
Date: ....20.........

Form 30

Notice in Newspapers of Annual General Meeting

XYZ Limited

Registered Office ....
....
....

Notice is hereby given that the Second Annual General Meeting of the Company will be held on Tuesday, the 24th September 20....... at 3.30 p.m. at .... (address) to transact the business as set out in the Notice dated 26th August 20......... a copy of which, along with the relative explanatory statement, has been posted to the Members of the Company at their address registered with the Company, together with the Annual Report and accounts for the year ended 31st March 20......

The Register of Members and the Share Transfer Books will remain closed from Tuesday, the 17th September 20......... to Tuesday, the 24th September 20....... (both days inclusive) for the purpose of the Annual General Meeting and payment of dividend, if declared at the Meeting.

Dividend, if declared, will be payable to those Members whose names appear on the Register of Members of the Company on 24th September 20.......... In respect of shares held in electronic form, dividend will be payable on the basis of beneficial ownership as per details furnished on 24th September 2002 by NSDL/CDSL.

A member entitled to attend and vote at the Meeting is entitled to appoint a Proxy to attend and, on a poll, to vote instead of himself and the Proxy need not be a Member of the Company. Proxies, in order to be effective, must be received at the Registered Office of the Company not less than forty-eight hours before the time fixed for the Meeting.

By order of the Board of Directors
SCP
Company Secretary

Place: New Delhi
Date: .... 20.........

Form 31

Notice demanding payment of the sum due and, alternatively, for winding-up of the debtor-company

By registered post with A/D

M/s. Pradip Plantation & Engineering Industries Limited
45 Ganesh Chunder Avenue
Ground Floor
Kolkata 700 013

Dear Sirs,

Under instruction received from and on behalf of our client M/s. AB having its registered office at 4 Camac Street, Kolkata 700 017 we do hereby serve upon you this firm and final notice of demand *inter alia*, on the following grounds:

(1) Our client is owner of 'Madhu Mala Building' situate at No. 45 Ganesh Chunder Avenue, Kolkata 700 013.

(2) You are a tenant under our said client in respect of .... sq ft. area on the Ground floor of the said Madhu Mala Building at 45 Ganesh Chunder Avenue, Kolkata 700 013 on the terms and conditions as recorded in letters dated 20th April 1979, 2nd November 1989 and 28th December 1996 addressed by our client to you and duly accepted by you. Some of the agreed terms are as follows:

(*i*) You will pay rent @ Rs. ...... per sq ft. for the area (...... sq. ft.) under your occupation per month with effect from 01.05.20......., with the proviso that the rate would be increased by 10% every 2 years and after 4 such successive increase, and on expiry of 10 years from 30.04.1999 the rate will be revised by mutual discussions and if by mutual agreement, the revision of rent is not possible, you agree to vacate the space and give us vacant and peaceful possession.

(*ii*) The monthly rent will be payable within 10th of every month in advance failing which your tenancy will stand terminated and you shall hand over the vacant and peaceful possession of the demised premises.

(*iii*) You will reimburse to our client abovenamed the occupier's share of Corporation Taxes including Surcharge. Urban Land Tax and Building Tax proportionate to the extent of area mentioned above at the existing rate and all future increases therein also and such other Taxes as may be imposed hereafter either by the Corporation of Calcutta, the Government or any other competent authority. You will also reimburse any future increase in the owner's share of Calcutta Corporation Taxes, including Surcharge, due to enhancement of rate and/or valuation which may be levied on the aforesaid premises over the level of such taxes being paid on the date of the Agreement.

(3) Our client further states that your tenancy commenced on the aforesaid terms on 1st May 20...... and is due to terminate on 30th April 20 .... Prior to 1st May 20 ...., you occupied the aforesaid area as tenant under our client, *inter alia*, on the terms and conditions recorded in letters dated 2nd November 20 .... and 20th April 20 .... addressed by our client to you and duly accepted by you.

(4) Our client further states that although, in accordance with the terms and conditions of your tenancy, you were obliged to reimburse our client with the corporation taxes you have failed, neglected and defaulted to do so for the period commencing 1st April 1988 to 31st December 20 .... and a sum of Rs. .... as per particulars given hereunder has become due and payable by you to our client:

Period	*No of Qrs.*	*Bill No.*	*Date*	*Amount* (Rs.)
...	...	...	...	...
...	...	...	...	...
...	...	...	...	...
			Total	......

(5) Apart from the aforesaid, you have also failed, neglected and defaulted to make payment of the monthly rent payable in terms of the aforesaid agreement at the rate of Rs.......... per month for the months of August 20 ...., September 20 ...., October 20 ...., November 20 .... and December 20 .... aggregating to Rs. ....

(6) In terms of aforesaid, our client is entitled to receive a sum of Rs. .... from you as per particulars given hereunder:

PARTICULARS

1. Outstanding corporation taxes as detailed above ... Rs. ....
2. Outstanding rent for the months of August 20 ..... to December 20 ...... as aforesaid ... Rs. ....

Total: Rs. ....

(7) Our client has repeatedly demanded payment of the aforesaid sum from you but you have failed, neglected and defaulted to make payment thereof and/or any portion of the same.

(8) Our client is entitled to claim and claims interest @ 24% per annum on the said outstanding dues from the respective due dates till the date of payment. Please treat this as notice under the Interest Act 1970.

(9) Our client reasonable believes that you are in involved circumstances and are unable to pay your debts.

In the aforesaid facts and circumstances, you are hereby firmly and finally called upon to make payment of the aforesaid sum of Rs. .... along with accrued interest thereon @ 24% per annum as stated above within 21 days from date of receipt of this notice failing which we shall be constrained to file an appropriate application for you winding up in the National Company Law Tribunal at Kolkata making you liable for all cost and consequences thereof.

Yours faithfully,

....

Partner

Form 32

Notice of Consolidation, Division, etc./Increase in Share Capital/ Increase in Number of Members

[Pursuant to section 64 of the Companies Act 2013 and Rule 15 of the Companies (Share Capital and Debentures) Rules 2014]

FORM NO. SH 7

The Companies Act, 2013

Registration No. ....

Nominal capital Rs. ....

Name of the company ....

....

Notice is hereby given–

*1. In accordance with section 64 of the Companies Act 2013, that**

....

....

*2. In accordance with section 64 of the Companies Act 2013, that by ordinary resolution/ special resolution of the company, dated the day of .... 20...........

(*i*) the authorised share capital of the company has been increased by the addition thereto of the sum of Rs. .... by and the present authorised capital of Rs. ....

(*ii*) that the number of members in the company has been increased by the addition thereto of .... members beyond the present registered number of ....

*3.(*i*) In accordance with sub-section (3) of section 61 of the Companies Act 2013, that the share capital of the company has been increased beyond the present authorised capital of Rs. .... by Rs. .... consequent upon an order dated .... of the Central Government under section 62 on an application made to it by .... [here mention the name of the financial institution] for conversion of debentures/loans into shares].

(*ii*) a copy of the aforesaid order was received by the company from the Central Government on ....

4. The additional capital is divided as follows:

No. of shares	*Class of shares*	*Nominal amount of each share*
(1)	(2)	(3)
....	....	....
....	....	....
....	....	....

The conditions (e.g. voting rights, dividend rights, winding-up rights etc.) subject to which new shares have been issued are as follows (if any of the new shares are preference shares state whether they are redeemable or not).

Signature
Name
(in Block Capitals)
Designation

Dated the .... day of .... 20. ......

* Strike out which is not applicable.

** Here enter particulars of the case failing under cls. (*a*), (*b*), (*c*) of sub-sec. (1) of s. 64. If a case falls under more than one of these clauses, specify the portion falling under each clause separately.

Form 33

Notice of Situation/Change of Situation of Registered Office

[Pursuant to section 12]

FORM NO. INC 22

The Companies Act, 2013

Registration No. ....

Nominal capital Rs. ....

Name of the company ....

Notice is hereby given that–

1. (*a*) the registered office of the company is situated .... with effect from (date) ....

(*b*) the situation of the registered office of the company was changed from .... to .... with effect from (date).

2. Situation of registered office, falls under the jurisdiction of .... (name of police station).†

‡ Enclosure:

Signature
Name
(in Block Capitals)
Designation

Dated the .... day of.................... 20 ....

† State address of nearest police station with district and tehsil.

‡ Any of the following documents:

(*a*) Registered document of the title of the premises of the registered office in the name of the company; or

(*b*) the notarized copy of lease or rent agreement in the name of the company along with a copy of rent paid receipt not older than one month;

(*c*) the authorization from the owner or authorized occupant of the premises along with proof of ownership or occupancy authorization, to use the premises by the company as its registered office; and

(*d*) the proof of any utility service like telephone, gas, electricity, etc. depicting the address of the premises in the name of the owner or document, as the case may be, which is not older than two months.

[Vide r. 25 of the Companies (Incorporation) Rules 2014].

CHAPTER 21

Notices under the Consumer Protection Act 2019

SYNOPSIS

1 Prefatory note—statement of objects and reasons

2 Broad-based objects and reasons

3 Issue and service of notice

The Consumer Protection Act 1986* originally was enacted for better protection of consumers. The Supreme Court in *India Photographic Co. Ltd.* v *H.D. Shourie*[1] observed as under:

> "The Consumer Protection Act 1986 was enacted as a result of widespread consumer protection movement. On the basis of the report of the Secretary General on Consumer Protection dated 27th May 1983, the United Nations Economic and Social Council recommended that the world Governments should develop, strengthen and implement a coherent consumer protection policy taking into consideration the guidelines set out therein. The Governments were to further provide adequate infrastructure including the bodies as well as financial facilities to develop, implement and monitor consumer protection policies. The introduction of new products in the developing countries was to be assessed in relation to the local conditions having regard to the existing production, distribution and consumption patterns of the country or region concerned. With reference to the consumer movement and the international obligations for protection of the rights of the consumer, provision has been made in the said Act with the object of interpreting the relevant law in a rational manner and for achieving the objective set forth in the Act. A rational approach and not a technical approach is mandate of law."

* It has been replaced by the Consumer Protection Act 2019 (Act 35 of 2019).

1 (1999)6 SCC 428; AIR 1999 SC 2453.

The preamble of the Act of 2019 shows that it is intended to provide for better protection of the interests of consumers. It reads:

PREAMBLE

> An Act to provide for protection of the interests of consumers and for the said purpose to establish authorities for timely and effective administration and settlement of consumers' disputes and for matters connected therewith or incidental thereto.

1 Prefatory note—statement of objects and reasons

The Consumer Protection Act 2019 seeks to provide for the establishment of an executive agency to be known as the Central Consumer Protection Authority (CCPA) to promote, protect and enforce the rights of consumers; make interventions when necessary to prevent consumer detriment arising from unfair trade practices and to initiate class action including enforcing recall, refund and return of products, etc.

2. It seeks, *inter alia*, to promote and protect the rights of consumers such as—

(*a*) the right to be protected against the marketing of goods which are hazardous to life and property;

(*b*) the right to be informed about the quality, quantity, potency, purity, standard and price of goods to protect the consumer against unfair trade practices;

(*c*) the right to be assured, wherever possible, access to variety of goods at competitive prices;

(*d*) the right to be heard and to be assured that consumer's interests will receive due consideration at appropriate forums;

(*e*) the right to seek redressal against unfair trade practice or restrictive trade practices or unscrupulous exploitation of consumers; and

(*f*) the right to consumer education [vide s. 2(9) of the Act of 2019].

2 Broad-based objects and reasons

The Consumer Protection Act 2019 was enacted to provide for protection of the interests of consumers and for the said purpose, to make provisions for establish authorities for timely and effective administration and settlement of consumer disputes and matters connected therewith. The working of the redressal agencies set up under the Act helped to arouse the expectations of the people and also brought to focus certain inadequacies in the coverage of the Act. Accordingly the present Act (2019) *inter alia*, seeks to provide for following:

(*i*) to enable the consumers to file class action complaints where such consumers have a common interest and to file complaints relating to restrictive trade practices adopted by a trader;

(*ii*) to enable the consumers who are self-employed to file complaints before the redressal agencies where goods bought by them exclusively for earning their livelihood, suffer from any defect;

(*iii*) to provide for product liability action on account of harm caused to consumers due to a defective product or by deficiency in service;

(*iv*) to provide for Mediation as an alternative dispute resolution mechanism;

(*v*) to provide for simplifying the consumer dispute adjudication process of the consumer dispute redressal agencies.

In several decisions the Supreme Court expanded the scope of the Act of 1986. The Supreme Court held that the adjudicatory bodies are like quasi-judicial tribunals and not courts intended to supplement the existing judicial system.[2] These quasi-judicial bodies are required to observe the principles of natural justice and have been empowered to give relief of a specific nature and to award, wherever appropriate, compensation to consumers. Penalties for non-compliance with the orders given by the quasi-judicial bodies have also been provided.[3]

In *Lucknow Development Authority* v *M.K. Gupta,*[4] the Supreme Court on an analysis of Preamble and Statement of Objects and Reasons ascertained the legislative intention and held that Government bodies would be held liable under the Act for any deficiency in services to those who purchase their services for consideration and the officers-in-charge would be held personally liable if they cause any harassment to the users of the services.

In *Lucknow Development Authority*,[5] the Supreme Court emphasised the need for construing the provisions of the Act in favour of the consumer to achieve the purpose of the enactment as it is a social benefit oriented legislation. One of the questions before the court was whether housing or building services were within the meaning of the definition of "service" as contained in s. 2(1)(*o*) of the 1986 Act [now s. 2(42)]. The definition proceeded to say that "service" means service of any description which is made available to potential users and then specified certain services which it would include and housing was not mentioned. Yet the Supreme Court held that "housing" would be a service within the meaning of the Act. That this was the right interpretation was borne out by the fact that the definition was amended in 1993 and it now specifically includes "housing construction".

2 *Laxmi Engineering Works* v *P.S.G. Industrial Institute* (1995)3 SCC 583.
3 *J.J. Merchant (Dr.)* v *Srinath Chaturvedi* (2002)6 SCC 635.
4 (1994)1 SCC 243; AIR 1994 SC 787.
5 (1994)1 SCC 243; AIR 1994 SC 787.

The judgment of the Supreme Court in *Spring Meadows Hospital* v *Harjol Ahluwalia*[6] is again sounding the same note:

> "Being a beneficial legislation, the Act should receive a liberal construction".

The court reiterated the objects, purposes and reasons for which the Act was passed.

The Act is intended to protect the consumer. The expression "consumer" is defined in s. 2(7) of the Consumer Protection Act 2019 as follows:

Section 2(7) "Consumer" means any person who,—

(*i*) buys any goods for a consideration which has been paid or promised or partly paid and partly promised, or under any system of deferred payment and includes any user of such goods other than the person who buys such goods for consideration paid or promised or partly paid or partly promised, or under any system of deferred payment when such use is made with the approval of such person, but does not include a person who obtains such goods for resale or for any commercial purpose; or

(*ii*) hires or avails of any service for a consideration which has been paid or promised or partly paid and partly promised, or under any system of deferred payment and includes any beneficiary of such services other than the person who hires or avails of the services for consideration paid or promised, or partly paid and partly promised, or under any system of deferred payment, when such services are availed of with the approval of the first mentioned person but does not include a person who avails of such services for any commercial purpose;

Explanation. For the purposes of this clause—(a) the expression "commercial purpose" does not include use by a person of goods bought and used by him exclusively for the purpose of earning his livelihood by means of self-employment;

(b) the expressions 'buys and goods' and 'hires or avails any services' includes offline or online transactions through electronic means or by teleshopping or direct selling or multi-level marketing.

The word 'consumer' is a comprehensive expression. It extends from a person who buys any commodity from a shop, business house, corporation, store, fair price shop to use it for private use or consumption and not for a commercial purpose. The comprehensive definition aims at covering every person who pays money as the price or cost of goods and services.[7]

6 (1998)4 SCC 39; AIR 1998 SC 1801; see also *H.N. Shankara Shastri* v *Asst. Director of Agriculture* (2004)6 SCC 230; *State of Karnataka* v *Vishwabharathi House Building Co-operative Society* (2003)2 SCC 412; AIR 2003 SC 1043; *J.J. Merchant (Dr)* v *Srinath Chaturvedi* (2002)6 SCC 635; AIR 2002 SC 2931.

7 See *Lucknow Development Authority* v *M.K. Gupta* (1994)1 SCC 243; *Morgan Stanely Mutual Fund* v *Kartick Das* (1994)4 SCC 225.

It is necessary to refer to the definitions of 'defect' and 'deficiency' as enumerated in s. 2(10) and s. 2(11) respectively of the Act of 2019.

2(10) "defect" means any fault, imperfection or shortcoming in the quality, quantity, potency, purity or standard which is required to be maintained by or under any law for the time being in force or under any contract, express or implied, or as is claimed by the trader in any manner whatsoever in relation to any goods or product and the word "defective" shall be construed accordingly.

2(11) "deficiency" means any fault, imperfection, shortcoming or inadequacy in the quality, nature and manner of performance which is required to be maintained by or under any law for the time being in force or has been undertaken to be performed by a person in pursuance of a contract or otherwise in relation to any service and includes—

(*i*) any act of negligence or omission or commission by such person which causes loss or injury to the consumer; and

(*ii*) deliberate withholding of relavant information by such person to the consumer.

A consumer may make complaint about the defect or deficiency to the goods or services. Section 2(5) of the Act of 2019 define "complainant" whereas [now s. 2(6) of the Act of 2019] defines 'complaint'.

Section 2(5) "Complainant" means—

(*i*) a consumer; or

(*ii*) any voluntary consumer association registered under any law for the time being in force; or

(*iii*) the Central Government or any State Government; or

(*iv*) the Central Authority; or

(*v*) one or more consumers, where there are numerous consumers having the same interest; or

(*vi*) in case of death of a consumer, his legal heir or legal representative; or

(*vii*) in case of a consumer being a minor, his parent or legal guardian.

Section 2(6) "Complaint" means any allegation in writing made by a complainant for obtaining any relief provided by or under this Act, that—

(*i*) an unfair contrct or unfair trade practice or a restrictive trade practice has been adopted by any trader or service provider;

(*ii*) the goods bought by him or agreed to be bought by him suffer from one or more defects;

(*iii*) the services hired or availed of or agreed to be hired or availed of by him suffer from any deficiency;

(*iv*) a trader or a service provider, as the case may be, has charged for the goods or for the services mentioned in the complaint, a price in excess of the price—

(*a*) fixed by or under any law for the time being in force; or

(*b*) displayed on the goods or any package containing such goods; or

(*c*) displayed on the price list exhibited by him by or under any law for the time being in force; or

(*d*) agreed between the parties;

(*v*) the goods which will be hazardous to life and safety when used, are being offered for sale to the public,—

(*a*) in contravention of standards relating to safety of such goods as required to be complied with, by or under any law for the time being in force;

(*b*) where the trader knows that the goods so offered are unsafe to the public;

(*vi*) the services which are hazardous or likely to be hazardous to life and safety of the public when used, are being offered by a person who provides any service and who knows it to be injurious to life and safety;

(*vii*) a claim for product liability action his against the product manufacturer, product seller or product service provider as the case may be.

3 Issue and service of notice

The manner and the validity of service of notice have been provided in s. 65 of the Consumer Protection Act 2019 as follows:

> 65. *Service of notice, etc.* (1) All notices, required by this Act to be served, shall be served by delivering or transmitting a copy thereof by registered post acknowledgment due addressed to opposite party against whom complaint is made or to the complainant by speed post or by such courier service, approved by the District Commission, the State Commission or the National Commission, as the case may be, or by any other mode of transmission of documents including electronic means.
>
> (2) Without prejudice to the provisions contained in sub-section (1), the notice required by this Act may be served on an electronic service provider at the address provided by it on the electronic platform from where it provides its services as such and for this purpose, the electronic service provider shall designate a nodal officer to accept and process such notices.
>
> (3) When an acknowledgment or any other receipt purporting to be signed by the opposite party or his agent or, as the case may be, by the complainant is received by the District Commission, the State Commission or the National Commission, as the case may be, or postal article containing the notice is

received back by such District Commission, State Commission or the National Commission, with an endorsement purporting to have been madeby a postal employee or by any person authorised by the courier service to the effect that the opposite party or his agent or complainant had refused to take delivery of the postal article containing the notice or had refused to accept the notice by any other means specified in sub-section (1) when tendered or transmitted to him, the District Commission or the State Commission or the National Commission, as the case may be, shall declare that the notice has been duly served on the opposite party or the complainant, as the case may be:

Provided that where the notice was properly addressed, pre-paid and duly sent by registered post acknowledgment due, a declaration referred to in this sub-section shall be made notwithstanding the fact that the acknowledgment has been lost or misplaced, or for any other reason, has not been received by the District Commission, the State Commission or the National Commission, as the case may be, within thirty days from the date of issue of notice.

(4) All notices required to be served on an opposite party or to complainant, as the case may be, shall be deemed to be sufficiently served, if addressed in the case of the opposite party, to the place where business or profession is carried on, and in case of the complainant, the place where such person actually and voluntarily resides.

Regulation 10 of the Consumer Protection (Consumer Commission Procedure) Regulations 2020 deals with issue of notice. It runs thus:

10. *Issue of notice.* (1) Whenever the Consumer Commission directs the issuance of a notice in respect of a complaint, appeal or revision petition, as the case may be, to the opposite party (ies)/respondent(s), ordinarily such notice shall be issued for a period of 30 days and depending upon the circumstances of each case, even for less than thirty days.

(2) When there is a question of raising presumption of service, 30 days' notice shall be required.

(3) Whenever notices are sought to be effected by a courier service, it shall be ascertained that the courier is of repute.

(4) While appointing the courier for the purpose of effecting service, security deposit may also be taken.

(5) Along with the notice, copies of the complaint, memorandum of grounds of appeal or petitions as the case may be, and other documents filed shall be served upon the opposite party(ies)/respondent(s).

(6) After the opposite party or respondent has put in appearance, no application or document shall be received by the Registrar unless it bears an endorsement that a copy thereof has been served upon the other side.

The notices under the Act are to be served according to the established mode, viz. delivery or transmission of a copy of notice by registered post acknowledgment due to the addressee by speed post or an approved courier service or by electronic means. Such notice may be served upon an electronic service provider at the address provided by it on the electronic platform from where it provides its services as such. The electronic service provider shall designate a nodal officer to accept and process such notices. When such notices are received by the Commission with an endorsement purporting to have been made by a postal employee or by a person authorised by the courier service to the effect that the opposite party or his agent or complainant had reposed to take delivery of the postal article containing the notice, when tendered or transmitted to him, the Commission shall declare that the notice has been duly served. It may be noted that where the notice was properly addressed, pre-paid and duly sent by registered post acknowledgment due, the Commission shall declare due service of the notice after thirty days' from the date of issue of notice, notwithstanding the fact that the acknowledgment has been lost or misplaced. Sufficient service of notice would also be deemed if the notice is addressed to the place where the opposite party carries on his business or profession, and the place where the complainant actually and voluntarily resides.

The present Act, therefore, appear to plug the loop-holes in the service of notices experienced by the parties and the court over a long time.

Section 35 of the Act of 2019 contains the provisions regarding making of complaint and its manner. The said provisions are as under:

> Section 35. *Manner in which complaint shall be made.* (1) A complaint in relation to any goods sold or delivered or agreed to be sold or delivered or any service provided or agreed to be provided, may be filed with a District Commission by—
>
> (a) (*i*) the consumer,—to whom such goods are sold or delivered or agreed to be sold or delivered or such service is provided or agreed to be provided; or
>
> (*ii*) who alleges unfair trade practice in respect of such goods or service;
>
> (*b*) any recognised consumer association, whether the consumer to whom such goods or sold or delivered or agreed to be sold or delivered or service is provided or agreed to be provided or who alleges unfair trade practice in respect of such goods or service, is a member of such association or not;
>
> (*c*) one or more consumers, where there are numerous consumers having the same interest, with the permission of the District Commission, on behalf of, or for the benefit of, all consumers so interested; or
>
> (*d*) the Central Government or the Central Authority or the State Government, as the case may be:
>
> provided that the complaint under this sub-section may be filed electronically in such manner as may be prescribed.
>
> *Explanation.* For the purposes of this sub-section "recognized consumer association" means any voluntary consumer association registered under any law for the time being in force.

(2) Every complaint filed under sub-section (1) shall be accompanied with such fee and payable in such manner including electronic form, as may be prescribed.

Section 36 of the Consumer Protection Act 2019 states as follows:

36. *Proceedings before District Commission.* (1) Every proceeding before the District Commission shall be conducted by the President of that Commission and atleast one member thereof, sitting together:

Provided that where a member, for any reason, is unable to conduct a proceeding till it is completed, the President and the other member shall continue the proceeding from the stage at which it was last heard by the previous member.

(2) On receipt of a complaint made under section 35, the District Commission may, by order, admit the complaint for being proceeded with or reject the same:

Provided that a complaint shall not be rejected under this section unless an opportunity of being heard has been given to the complainant:

Provided further that the admissibility of the complaint shall ordinarily be decided within twenty-one days from the date on which the complaint was filed.

(3) Where the District Commission does not decide the issue of admissibility of the complaint within the period so specified, it shall be deemed to have been admitted.

Section 38 of the Act of 2019 deals with the procedure on admission of complaint. Section 69 of the Act of 2019 deals with the period of limitation. It provides that no complaint shall be admitted by the District Commission, State Commission or the National Commission unless such complaint is filed within two years from the date on which the cause of action has arisen. It is also provided that a complaint may be entertained after the expiry of the period of limitation provided the complainant satisfies the District Forum or the State Commission or the National Commission that he had sufficient cause for not filing the complaint within such period, provided that no such complaint shall be entertained unless the District Commission, the State Commission or the National Commission, as the case may be, records its reasons for condonation of such delay [proviso to s. 69(2)].

Section 38(2)(*a*) provides that a copy of the admitted complaint shall be referred to opposite party within 21 days from the date of its admission directing him to give his version of the case within a period of 30 days or such extended period not exceeding 15 day as may be granted by the District Commission. It may be mentioned that registered notice not received back will have the presumption that the notice is duly served.

It has to be noted that the provisions of this Act (Special Act) provides an additional remedy summary and speedy in nature and accordingly s. 80

of the CPC cannot be grafted in this Act when the legislature has not intended to do so.

The present Act of 2019 has introduced the alternative dispute resolution mechanism of mediation with the object of settling certain consumer disputes in a cheat and speedy manner. It is now provided that at the first hearing of the complaint after its admission or at any subsequent stage, if the District Commission is of the opinion that there exists elements of a settlement which may be acceptable to the parties it may direct the parties to give in writing their consent within five days for reference of the dispute to mediation (s. 37).

Forms

Form 1

Notice before filing a complaint

Name and address ....

....

(of the trader, dealer, firm, company, etc.)

In re: (Mention the goods/services complained of giving details)

....

Dear Sir,

This is to bring to your kind notice that I had purchased .... from your .... for a consideration of Rs. .... paid in cash *vide* your Cash Memo/Receipt/Invoice No. ....or paid through cheque No. .... dated .... drawn on .... bank).

The said goods are suffering from the following defects:

(*i*) ....

(*ii*) .... etc.

I have reported the above matter to you several times (give reference of earlier letters, if any) but despite all my pleadings you have not made good the defect in the goods (or deficiency in services) which is indeed regrettable and highly unbusiness like. On account of your aforesaid dereliction of duty and failure and neglect to rectify the same I have suffered losses/incurred expenses .... (give details) which you are liable to compensate to me.

You are hereby finally called upon to—

(*i*) remove the said defects in the goods, and/or

(*ii*) replace the goods with new goods, and/or

(*iii*) return the price/charges paid,

(*iv*) pay compensation for financial loss/injury/interest suffered due to your negligence .... (give details) in the sum of Rs. .... with interest @ ....% *per annum* within .... days of the receipt of this notice failing which I shall be constrained to initiate proceeding against you for redressal of my aforesaid grievances and recovery of the aforesaid amount such proceedings, both civil and criminal as are warranted by law, besides filing a complaint under the statutory provisions of the Consumer Protection Act exclusively at your own risk, cost, responsibility and consequences which please note.

Place ....

Dated .... (Signature)

Form 2

Complaint for defective goods

In the Ld. District Consumer Disputes Redressal Commission at ....

Consumer Case No. .... of 20.......

AB .... S/o .... R/o .... *Complainant*

Versus

(1) .... Machine Appliances Co., at .... *Opposite Party*

(2) G.K. Machinery .... at ....

In the matter of an application under s. 35 of the Consumer Protection Act 2019.

The complainant above-named states as follows:

1. That M/s. Machine Appliances Co., (opposite party No. 1) is a proprietorship concern and is presently engaged in carrying on business dealing in domestic appliances.
2. That the opposite party No. 2 is manufacturer of washing machine with brand name .... The opposite party No. 1 is a dealer of O.P. No. 2.
3. That the complainant purchased a washing machine from opposite party No. 1 .... for rupees .... on (cash memo No. ......) of .... (date). A copy of cash memo is annexed herewith as annexure 'A' herein.
4. That the said washing machine has been guaranteed for defect-free working for a period of 18 months from the date of purchase. The xerox copy of the guarantee card issued by the opposite party is annexed hereto as annexure 'B'.
5. That the complainant found the spinner of the said washing machine to be defective and as such the complainant could not use the machine within three months of its purchase. The written complaint regarding the defect was made to the opposite parties, Nos. 1 and 2 and the receipt of which has been acknowledged by the opposite parties. The said copies are annexed hereto as annexure 'C'.
6. That after expiry of two weeks from the date of complaint an engineer of the company visited the premises of the complainant and checked the said washing machine but was not able to remove the defect. He assured the complainant to come back again to do the needful.

7. That on .... after the expiry of 20 days the complainant had to visit the premises of the opposite party to complain that nothing has been done to remove the defects in the washing machine. The opposite party promised to send the engineer again for the removal of the defect.

8. That the complainant had been waiting for three months from the date of his visit to the premises of opposite party but no steps had been taken by OPS for the removal of the defect of the said washing machine.

9. That being aggrieved from the non-cooperative attitude of the opposite party the complainant had no option but to approach this Ld. Commission for redressal of his grievance.

10. That the opposite parties miserably failed to discharge their obligations in terms of the guarantee given to the complainant at the time of the purchase of the said washing machine.

11. That the defect in the washing machine is a result of poor workmanship of the manufacturer for which the complainant has suffered loss and damage. The opposite party was under the obligation to keep the washing machine in perfect working order for a period of 18 months from the date of purchase by the complainant which they have failed to perform.

12. That the opposite parties have failed to set the machine right and as such the complainant has suffered loss and injury and is entitled to compensation.

13. That unless necessary directions are made to OP parties to set the machine right and to provide the trouble-free working of washing machine the very purpose of filing this complaint would be frustrated.

14. That the complainant was unable to use the washing machine for more than 7 months despite the fact that he paid a sum of rupees .... for purchasing the machine.

15. That in the interest of justice the opposite parties should be directed to pay the complainant as under:

    1. Rupees .... being price of the washing machine.
    2. Rupees 5,000 as compensation for the harassment, inconvenience and mental agony suffered by the complainant.
    3. Rupees 500 towards the costs of the proceeding.

Prayer

It is therefore respectfully prayed that the opposite parties be directed to pay the complainant the compensation as set forth in paragraph 15 together with the cost of the machine and the cost of proceeding. Any other relief deemed fit by this Hon'ble Forum may kindly be granted.

Date:
Place:

Affidavit

Form 3

Notice for defects in goods

Dated ....

To

....

....

....

....

Dear Sir,

Re: Defects in goods so purchased from your Shop on ....
vide Bill No. .... on payment of cash.

I regret to inform you that a 16" Colour TV of .... Brand so purchased by me from your shop on .... upon payment of cash but it has failed to provide satisfactory service from the date of its installation and in spite of repeated complaints over phone, till date you have not taken any steps to set the same right. Since the TV carries warranty for a period of one year, you are duty bound to take steps to set the same right. I have waited long but now I am unable to wait any longer.

In view of the foregoing circumstances I hereby finally call upon you to set my TV right within 10 (ten) days from receipt hereof, failing which I shall have no other option but to take recourse to law without any further reference. Be it noted that in such circumstances I shall not only claim compensation for my harassment but also claim cost of proceeding which please note.

Yours faithfully,

NOTE: There is no hard and fast rule for drafting of a complaint before Consumer District Commissions. The complainant shall state specially what is the complaint, whether it is within period of limitation etc.

Form 4

Complaint in letter form

Consumer Case No. ...... of 20......

To

The Learned President

.... District Consumer Redressal Commission

....

Re: Complaint under s. 35 of
Consumer Protection Act 2019

Respected Sir,

I crave your Honour's leave to forward you herewith my complaint for your immediate intervention and necessary orders. Kindly treat my complaint under s. 12 of Consumer Protection Act 2019.

Name & Address of the Petitioner :

Name & Address of the Opposite Party :

Grievances :

Cause of Action :

Arose on :

Reliefs sought for :

Yours faithfully,

Affidavit

Form 5

Before the Learned District Consumer Dispute Redressal Commission

at ....

Or

Before the Hon'ble State Consumer Dispute Redressal Commission at ....

Or

Before the Hon'ble National Consumer Dispute Redressal Commission, Janpath Bhawan, 'A' wing, 5th Floor, New Delhi 110 001.

Complaint No. .... of 20......

In the Matter of:

An application under s. 35 (under s. 49 and under s. 59 of the Consumer Protection Act 2019).

and

In the Matter of:

Full particulars of the petitioner/petitioners with complete address

.... Complainant(s)/Petitioner(s)

versus

Full particulars of Opposite Party/Parties with complete address

.... Opposite Party/Parties

The humble petition of the complainant(s)/petitioner(s) above named

Most respectfully sheweth:

1. Introduction (State how the petitioner(s) is/are consumer(s) and can maintain his/her/their complaint(s) as consumer dispute).
2. Grievances in details.
3. The nature of defect or deficiency in service.
4. The details of documents upon which the complaint(s)/petitioner(s) will rely upon at the hearing.

5. Jurisdiction.
6. Relief sought for.
7. Prayer portion.

Affidavit

Form 6

Model Forms of Written Statement objectives to be filed by the Opposite Party(s)

Before the Learned District Consumer Dispute Redressal Commission at ....

Or

Before the Hon'ble State Consumer Dispute Redressal Commission at ....

Or

Before the Hon'ble National Consumer Dispute Redressal Commission, Janpath Bhawan, 'A' Wing, 5th Floor, New Delhi 110 001.

Complaint No. .... of 20 ....

Complainant(s)/
Petitioner(s)/
Applicant(s)

versus

.... Opposite Party/Parties

Written Statement on behalf of the Opposite Party/Parties

1. Kindly put forward your reply on the basis of the paragraphs made in the complaint.
2. State why the OP is not liable or if liable explain to what extent the OP is liable.
3. Prayer portion.
4. Model Form of Affidavit.

[Cause title will remain same as aforesaid]

Affidavit

...., Deponent 1............................., son of .... residing at .... aged ...., by faith ...., do hereby solemnly affirm and state as follows:

1. That I am the complainant/opposite party in the aforesaid proceeding and am fully conversant with the facts and circumstances thereof. This is true to my knowledge.
2. That the copies of the documents annexed along with my complaint written statement being annexures .... to .... are all received by me in due process of law and these are genuine in all respect and I aver that no pan of the same as received by me has subsequently been fabricated anywise for getting relief from this Learned Commission/Hon'ble Commission this is true to my knowledge.

3. That the facts and circumstances stated in my accompanying petition complaint objective are all true and correct to my knowledge.

...... day of 20 ....

Known to me and
identified by me. Deponent
Advocate.

Form 7

Model Form—Appeal

Before the Hon'ble State Consumer Dispute Redressal Commission at ....

Or

Before the Hon'ble National Consumer Dispute Redressal Commission, Janpath Bhawan, 'A' wing, 5th Floor, New Delhi 110 001.

Case No. .... of 20 ....

Appeal under s. 41/s. 51 of the Consumer Protection Act 2019.

(Form the Order dated ....
in Case No. .... of 20 ....)

And

In the Matter of:

.... Appellant(s)

versus

.... Respondent(s)

Most Respectfully sheweth:

1 That being aggrieved by and dissatisfied with the Order/Judgment so passed by .... in case No. .... on ...., the appellant(s) craves/crave leave to prefer the present appeal which has arisen out of the following facts:

2. Facts

3. That the impugned Order/Judgment dated .... so passed by the Learned District Commission/Hon'ble State Commission at .... is liable to be set aside/modified on the following amongst other.

Grounds

....

....

(The appellant should challenge the impugned order both on factual aspects as well as on legal aspects if necessary)

4. That the appellant herein submits that he has not preferred any other appeal against the impugned order or judgment before this Hon'ble Commission or has not preferred any writ petition challenging the legality and validity of the order so passed.

5. That the present appeal is filed within the prescribed time-limit as per s. 15/ s. 19 of COPRA.

NOTE: If the appeal is being filed beyond specified time it should be accompanied by an application for condonation of delay.

Form 8

Deficiency in Services—Air Services

In the Ld. District Consumer Disputes Redressal Commission at ....

Consumer Case No. .... of 2005

AB .... S/o .... R/o .... *Complainant*

versus

M/s. .... (*Opposite party*)

In the matter of an application under s. 35 of the Consumer Protection Act 2019.

To

The Ld. President and his companion Ld. members of District Commission ....

That the complainant above-named states as follows:

1. That the complainant, is an advocate and he had to visit New Delhi, to attend Hon'ble Supreme Court of India in connection with the hearing of an SLP (Civil).
2. That the complainant purchased a ticket on .... from the office of the opposite party No. 1 for travelling by air from Calcutta to Delhi for flight No. .... scheduled to depart at 8.35 a.m. from Netaji Subhas Airport at Dum Dum at Kolkata on Sunday.
3. That at about 7 a.m., the complainant made an inquiry about the departure of the flight. It was a surprise to note that the opposite party informed him that the flight has been cancelled.
4. That afterwards, the complainant rushed to the Howrah Railway Station to purchase a ticket for Rajdhani Exp. There too he was not able to get the train due to non-availability of the reservation.
5. That the opposite party was grossly negligent in discharging their duties as it was the duty of the opposite party to inform him about the cancellation of the flight, as the opposite party had recorded the local address and telephone number of the complainant.
6. That there was no specific reason about the cancellation of the Air flight on account of any unavoidable circumstances such as bad weather etc. or any technical snag.
7. That this Ld. Commission has territorial and pecuniary jurisdiction to entertain this complaint.
8. In the above facts and circumstances the complainant prays for the following reliefs:

   (1) Refund of the price of ticket No .... amounting to Rs. ....

   (2) Damages for mental agony and physical discomfort Rs. 5,000.

(3) Costs of the proceedings Rs. 5,000.

Further any other relief or reliefs as the complainant may be entitled to may kindly be granted.

Annexures

(1) Copy of the original ticket purchased by the complainant for the Air flight.

(2) Copy of the original bill showing payment of money by cash.

Place:
Date:

Affidavit

Form 9

Banking Service

In the Ld. District Consumer Disputes Redressal Commission at ....

Consumer Case No. .... of 20 ....

AB .... S/o .... R/o .... Complainant

versus

The Bank .... (Opposite party)

In the matter of an application under s. 35 of the Consumer Protection Act 2019.

To

The Ld. President and his Ld. companion members of
District Commission at ....

The complainant above-named states as follows:

1. That the complainant owns a savings account No. .... in ....in .... at ....
2. That the complainant is having Rs. .... in his aforesaid Bank account ....
3. That on .... the complainant deposited a draft of Rs. .... along with an application for the allotment of the shares of the company (Name) .... in.
4. That the Bank had sent the draft of the complainant No. .... to where only a sum of Rs. .... was remitted and rest of the money was returned, but for the allotment of the shares the sum of Rs. .... was required.
5. That due to negligence and dereliction of the duty on the part of the opposite party, the allotment of the share could not be made to the complainant on account of non-transmission of the requisite amount.
6. That the opposite party Bank is guilty of negligence and had been deficient in discharge of his duties which caused loss and mental agony to complainant.
7. That this Hon'ble Commission has the jurisdiction to entertain the present complaint since the Branch of the concerned Bank is situated within the territorial jurisdiction of this Ld. Commission.

8. That in view of above facts and circumstances the following claims may kindly be granted to the complainant:
   (1) The compensation due to non-crediting of the required amount for the allotment of the share .... Rs. ....
   (2) The compensation for mental agony and harassment Rs. ....
   (3) The costs of the legal proceedings Rs. ....

Any other relief which this Ld. Commission deems fit and proper may be granted to the complainant.

Place:

Date:

Affidavit

Form 10

Housing Problems

In the Ld. District Consumer Disputes Redressal Commission at ....

Consumer Case No. .... of 20 ....

.... S/o .... R/o .... Complainant

versus

.... Development Authority at ....

In the matter of an application under s. 35 of the Consumer Protection Act 2019 and the Rules made thereunder.

To

The Ld. President and his companion Ld. members of District Commission at ....

The above-named complainant states as follows:

1. That the complainant applied for a house of LIG category in .... Sector at Dist. .... and has deposited a sum of Rs. 1,00,000 with .... Development Authority on .... as registration amount.
2. That according to the terms of brochure the above Development Authority would provide to the complainant a LIG house of estimated price of Rs. 18.75 lakh with the area of 1000 sq. ft. in addition to other details.
3. That the complainant in response to the directions of .... Development Authority deposited the money in five equal instalments.
4. That after depositing the amount by instalments the petitioner came to know that .... Development Authority has increased the amount of the cost of the house and a sum of rupees one lakh had been charged in excess from the complainant towards the price of the house.
5. That the complainant also made the request to the .... Development Authority not to charge a sum of rupees one lakh in excess, but the .... Development Authority refused the request of the complainant and as a result

the petitioner had to pay the said amount to the .... Development Authority.

6. That according to the allotment letter the possession of the house was to be delivered to the complainant on .... but the same was delivered on ...., i.e., after one year from the estimated period which was provided in the brochure.
7. That the complainant has obtained a loan of Rs .... from .... (bank) for purchase of the house on payment of interest 14% per annum.
8. That the house which was delivered to the complainant has many defects and has not been finished as assured.
9. That the complainant sent the letters to .... Development Authority for removal of the defects from the house but .... Development Authority did not pay any heed to the same.
10. That the .... Development Authority is thus deficient in rendering the service to the complainant and is liable to compensate the complainant for the same.
11. That this Ld. Commission is competent to decide the present complaint as the Commission has territorial and pecuniary jurisdiction.
12. That in the interest of the justice the .... Development Authority should be directed to pay the compensation amounting to Rs. .... to the complainant and should also be directed:
    (1) To remove the defect for the house within one month so that the complainant can start living in the house.
    (2) To provide completion certificate of Municipality.
    (3) That the .... Development Authority should be directed to pay to the complainant the interest at the rate of 18% per annum on the amount which was deposited by the complainant for delay in delivery of house for a period of one year.
    (4) That the .... Development Authority should be directed to return to the complainant the excess amount (Rs. one lakh) which the OP collected upon escalating the cost.
    (5) That the sum of Rs. 50,000 as compensation should be granted to the complainant.
    (6) That a sum of Rs. 5,000 may kindly be granted to the complainant as the costs of proceeding.

To such further or other order as the nature of the case demands.

Prayer

It is therefore respectfully prayed that the present complaint be kindly allowed and amount of rupees .... as claimed above should be granted to the complainant within 30 days from the date of order of the Ld. Commission.

Affidavit

Form 11

Insurance Claim

In the Ld. District Consumer Disputes Redressal Commission at ....

Consumer Case No. .... of 20 ....

.... S/o .... R/o .... Complainant

versus

.... Insurance Company ....

In the matter of an application under s. 35 of the Consumer Protection Act 2019.

To

The Ld. President and his companion Ld. members of District Consumer Disputes Redressal Commission.

The above-named complainant states as follows:

1. That the complainant is a company mainly dealing with .... the .... manufacturing of textile yarn.
2. That the opposite party is an Insurance Company having its branch office at .... within the territorial jurisdiction of the Ld. Commission.
3. That the complainant had taken a fire policy on .... from the said .... Insurance Company for a sum of rupees .... for stock of raw material goods, and products and rupees .... for furniture, fixtures, fittings including complete electrical installation. The said policy was valid for one year from .... to ....
4. That the fire broke out in the factory on .... and the complainant lodged FIR on .... with the Police Station ....
5. That the complainant informed the opposite party Insurance Company on .... about the fire and filed a claim in connection therewith.
6. That the opposite party Insurance Company appointed the surveyors to verify the claim. The surveyors visited the company and examined the loss on ...., later on the surveyor made verification and demanded various papers, invoices including sale invoices, purchase invoices, process bills etc. which had been accorded by the complainant, but the claim did not materialise for two years.
7. That the opposite party was grossly negligent and deficient in its service in not settling the claim for a period of two years which resulted in heavy loss by closure of factory.
8. That this Ld. Commission has territorial and pecuniary jurisdiction to entertain the complaint.
9. That aggrieved by the inaction of the opposite party in settling the claim for the last two years which resulted in huge loss the present complaint is preferred for following claims:

   (*a*) Total loss on account of the fire at the factory premises in terms of the insurance policy 10 lac.

   (*b*) Interest on the amount from the date of the claim to the filing of complaint Rs. 5 lac.

(c) Damages on account of loss of profit, business as quantified Rs. 800 per day from the date of the claim to the filing of the complaint Rs. 1,60,000.

In the above facts and circumstances the complainant prays for the following reliefs:

(1) Payment of the money as claimed above.

(2) Damages for mental agony and harassment Rs. 2 lac.

(3) The costs of the proceeding Rs. 5,000.

(4) Any other relief as deemed fit by this Ld. Commission.

ENCL.
Copy of:

(1) The original Insurance Policy.

(2) The FIR.

(3) The letter given to the Insurance Company informing about the fire.

(4) The assessment of Surveyor assessing the loss.

Place:
Date:

Affidavit

Form 12

Medical Negligence

In the Ld. District Consumer Disputes Redressal Commission

Consumer Case No. .... of 20...

.... S/o .... R/o .... Complainant

versus

1. .... S/o .... R/o ....

2. .... nursing home at .... represented by its proprietor named ....

In the matter of an application under s. 35 of the Consumer Protection Act 2019.

To

The Ld. President and his companion
Ld. members of District Consumer
Disputes Redressal Commission ......

The above-named complainant states as follows:

1. That the complainant was having pain in abdomen since 20 .... and he consulted the opposite party (Doctor) and paid a sum of Rs. 500 as consultation fee on ....

2. That the opposite party Doctor advised certain laboratory tests, which were complied with by the complainant on ....

3. That the complainant showed the test reports to the opposite party on ....

4. That on examination of the test reports and on physical examination, the opposite party (Doctor) was of the view that the complainant was suffering from appendicitis and the complainant was advised to undergo operation.
5. That the opposite party (Doctor) prescribed him some medicines and instructed him to come after one week.
6. That after 10 days when the complainant again wanted to consult the opposite party he was advised to get admitted in the nursing home of the opposite party for the operation.
7. That the complainant asked the opposite party to conduct some tests like ultrasonography etc. to ascertain the disease but the opposite party told the complainant that these tests are not required.
8. That on the next day the complainant got himself admitted in the nursing home of the opposite party and after four hours from the admission, the complainant was taken to the operation theatre for operation and he was operated on ......
9. That after the operation the complainant had high temperature and pain, which caused lot of discomfort to the complainant.
10. That after 6 days when the temperature could not subside the complainant had to go for some pathological tests, which were found normal and did not show any other ailment except the infection.
11. That after 7 days from the date of the operation the complainant again was taken to the operation theatre on .... on the pretext of removing the stitches but there the second operation was performed without the consent of the complainant and the opposite party did not inform any reason why the second operation was performed.
12. That after the second operation too the complainant was having fever and after four days he was discharged from the hospital with the prescription of some oral medicines and was told that after some time the pain and temperature would subside.
13. That after few days when the pain and fever continued the petitioner-complainant consulted a second Doctor and only then he came to know that the OP doctor failed to perform the operation properly, i.e. to say what he had done, should not have been done and what was not done should have been done.
14. That these opinions of the second doctor are crystal clear from the contemporaneous medical literature, the copy of which are annexed hereto as Annexure 'O'.
15. That the opposite party was deficient in discharging his duties which necessitated further surgery which caused physical and mental harassment, financial loss and discomfort to the complainant.
16. That the Ld. Commission has jurisdiction both pecuniary and territorial to entertain the present complaint.
17. In the above facts and circumstances the complainant prays for the following reliefs:

    (1) Rupees 2,25,000 for the expenses of the operation, stay in nursing home, investigations and medicines.

(2) Rupees 20,000 for the expenses which the complainant incurred to obtain the opinion of surgeon and doctors, further investigations and to get the treatment for pain and fever and subsequent surgery.

(3) Rupees 30,000 for mental agony, stress and pain caused due to the negligence of the Doctor in performing the operations, as compensation.

(4) Rupees 5,000 as costs of legal proceedings.

Any other reliefs which this Ld. Commission may deem fit and proper.

Date: Complainant
Place:

ENCLO:

Copy of:

(*a*) The bills of the payments made for treatment and operation in the nursing home of the opposite party.

(*b*) The bills in respect of the purchase of medicines.

(*c*) The bills of the pathological and other investigations.

(*d*) The opinion of the surgeon and physician consulted after the operation along with the medical bills, investigations and medicines.

Affidavit

Forms 13

Deficiency of Postal Services

Before Ld. District Consumer Disputes Redressal Commission at ....

Consumer Case No. .... of 20...

..........................S/o .... R/o .... Complainant

versus

Post Master of .... (Branch & Place)

In the matter of an application under s. 35 of the Consumer Protection Act 2019 and the Rules made thereunder.

To

The Ld. President and his companion
Ld. members of Ld. District Consumer
Disputes Redressal Commission.

The complainant above-named states as follows:

1. That the complainant had sent the money order of Rs. 1,000 by speed post money order from .... to .... on ....
2. That the said amount was sent by the complainant to his mother for her treatment.
3. That the complainant's mother did not receive the said amount and had to wait for one month to get the amount.
4. That after two months when the money order was not received the complainant sent representation to both the Post Offices at .... and .... on ...., and

he also gave representation to the Post Office at .... as he made the money order from the Post Office .... but no relief was granted by the Postal Authorities till date.

5. That the opposite party was guilty of deficiency-in-service which caused loss of money, harassment and mental agony to the complainant as the money was needed urgently to the complainant's mother for her treatment.
6. That this Ld. Commission has the jurisdiction to entertain the complaint as the cause of action occurred within the local limits of its jurisdiction and the value of the claim is within the statutory limit as prescribed in the Act.
7. In the above mentioned facts and circumstances the complainant prays for the following reliefs:
    (1) The return of the money which was sent through money order on .... Rs. 2,000.
    (2) The damages for mental harassment and inconvenience as the complainant could not continue her treatment due to the non-availability of money Rs. 5,000.
    (3) The cost of the legal proceedings .... Rs. 500.

Such further or other relief which this Ld. Commission may deem fit and proper.

Affidavit

Form 14

Services of Railways

In the Ld. District Consumer Disputes Redressal Commission ....

Consumer Case No. .... of 20 ....

S/o .... R/o .... Complainant

versus

1. General Manager Eastern Railways
2. Chief Operation Superintendent Eastern Railways

In the matter of an application under s. 35 of the Consumer Protection Act 2019.

To

The Ld. President and his companion Ld. members of District Consumer Disputes Redressal Commission.

The above-named complainant states as follows:

1. That the complainant purchased a 1st class ticket along with a berth reservation for the journey dated .... from .... to .... on .... by train No. ....
2. The number of ticket was ....
3. That the ticket was booked from Howrah Railway Station whereas the complainant had to catch the train from Asansol Railway Station. At the Railway Station Asansol on the day of journey, it was found that there was no first class compartment attached to the train.

4. That on inquiry from the Guard of the train it transpired that the 1st class compartment is not attached to the train and issued the certificate to the complainant.
5. That the complainant had to undergo stress and strain in locating the compartment and had to run up and down at the platform of Asansol and ultimately he had missed the train.
6. That the opposite party was grossly negligent and was deficient in rendering the service to the complainant.
7. That the Ld. District Commission has territorial and pecuniary jurisdiction to decide the complaint.

Hence it is prayed that following reliefs may kindly be granted–

(1) Compensation for the loss of reputation of efficiency of the complainant Rs. 20,000.

(2) Compensation for the harassment and mental agony Rs. 5,000.

(3) The refund of the amount of ticket (first class) Rs. 850.

(4) The costs of legal proceeding Rs. 500.

Any other relief which this Ld. Commission deems fit and proper.

Affidavit

Form 15

Notice for deficiency-in-service in providing medical treatment

Dated: ....

To

Dr. ....

....

....

....

Re: Failure to provide proper Medical treatment to ....of ....

I regret to inform you, that my .... who was admitted at .... Nursing Home at Premises No. .... under you for gall-bladder operation which has not been provided with proper service though I have paid the entire bill so raised by the Nursing Home authority.

With high hope I admitted my .... under you upon payment of your fees so that the patient gets appropriate treatment, but now it has transpired that you failed to provide proper treatment which was the need of the hour. From the treatment sheet of the Nursing Home it is crystal clear that the treatment and action of yours was not as per accepted medical practice and what was done should not have been done and that what was not done should have been done. In any case, I hereby reserve my right to urge the same with documentary evidence in appropriate fora if at all the situation calls for so in near future.

In view of such circumstances I demand from you the entire treatment cost of my .... together with the cost of his physical and mental harassment and cost of proceeding, i.e. in all Rs. 4 lakh (Rupees four lakh) within 10 (ten) days from receipt hereof failing which I shall be obliged to take up the matter with appropriate fora for any relief and redressal.

Yours faithfully,

Form 16

Medical Negligence

Before the Hon'ble State Consumer Disputes Redressal Commission, ... (Please put the name of the State)

(Original Jurisdiction)

State Commission Case No. ....

Petitioner/Complainant

versus

In the matter of:

An application under section 47 of the Consumer Protection Act 2019.

The petitioner/complainant above name states as follows:

1. Fact of the case ....

i.e., when 1st contacted the doctor or nursing home for treatment, what was the initial diagnosis, what amount you paid and thereafter state in details about the treatment so provided to the patient.

(Important to note: Please make a list of dates of treatment and annex the Prescription or Bed-Head Ticket to show what sort of treatment was provided to the patient.

2. State in details about the hassles, the patient had suffered due to wrong treatment.

(Important to note: 'As per the settled law on medical negligence it has to be alleged as to which action of the doctor was not as per accepted medical practice, and what was done should not have been done and what was not done should have been done. This has to be supported by Expert evidence or available medical literature on the subject' ... Case ref. 2004 CTJ 175 (NC).

3. Kindly state in details about the actual loss the Petitioner has suffered with proper documents as to quantification of damages where-from the Commission will be able to adjudicate as to the extent of injury suffered and the manner in which and the extent to which the monetary loss has been caused thereby to the Petitioner/Complainant.

4. State in details about the cause of action.

5. Prayer:

Enclosures:

Affidavit

CHAPTER 22

Notices under the Code of Criminal Procedure 1973

SYNOPSIS

1 Summons
2 Warrant of arrest
3 Proclamation and attachment
4 Miscellaneous

1 Summons

The word summon is derived from the Latin word *summoneas* which means a writ of summons. The writ of summons is used to denote the judicial process by which one is ordered to appear before a court of law. A summons is the process by which a proceeding is commenced or by which (generally) a step therein is taken.[1] Chapter VI of the Code of Criminal Procedure deals with processes to compel appearance. Chapter VI deals with (*a*) summons, (*b*) warrant of arrest, (*c*) proclamation & attachment and (*d*) other rules regarding processes.

Sections 61 to 69 of the CrPC deal with summons. Sections 61, 62(1) and 70 deal with forms of summons and warrant of arrest. Section 61 deals with form of summons and provides that every summons issued by a court under the CrPC shall be in writing, in duplicate, signed by the Presiding Officer of such court or by such other officer as the High Court may, from time to time, by rule direct, and shall bear the seal of the Court. A summons under s. 61 may be sent to—

(*i*) the accused;

(*ii*) a witness;

(*iii*) a person to show cause against some order; and

(*iv*) the person proceeded against under s. 125.

1 Stroud's *Judicial Dictionary of Words and Phrases*, 8th Ed., vol. 3, p. 2884.

Section 61 is not limited to service of summons against an accused person only but provides for the issue of every summons under the Code.

When an application is made for a process to compel the appearance of witness, it is the duty of the Court to pass an order either granting the prayer or refusing it. Under the law, a verbal prayer for summons on the accused person is sufficient.

A summons should be clear and specific in terms. If the legal formalities are not duly observed, a conviction for non-attendance in obedience to the summons cannot be sustained.[2]

Every person on whom a summons is to be served shall be described therein as full a manner as possible so as to identify that person clearly. The summons should also state the particulars of the offence charged. A summons issued by a Magistrate which does not contain the particulars prescribed by the statute (section 61 read with the Form given in Schedule II of the Code) if objected to must necessarily be invalid.[3] It has to be noted that the summons must bear the seal of the Court. When a person legally bound to attend the Court in obedience to a summons intentionally disobeys the same, he is liable to be punished under s. 174, IPC.

Section 62 deals with the procedure of service of summons. It provides that service should be effected by a police officer or an officer of the Court or other public servant who should see that a summons is served in the manner provided in the Code and who shall be able to report to the Court as to the actual manner of service. Section 62 also provides that the summons shall, if practicable, be served personally on the person summoned by delivering or tendering to him one of the duplicates of the summons. Section 62 further provides that the serving officer may be authorised to obtain a signed acknowledgment of the service which should ordinarily be treated as a very cogent evidence of service.[4] Where the word 'service' or 'served' are technical terms, implying a definite process of the law and where they are used, this process has to be carried out. The expression 'served upon' is of wider impact than the words "delivered to". The term service has the implication of personal service. The tender of the copy is sufficient service. The service of summons by post is irregular and where such summons against the accused is returned unserved no inference can be drawn against the accused. However, s. 69 provides for service of summons by registered post on a witness only as an alternative measure. It has been held that no notice on the respondent in the maintenance case issued under s. 126 can be served by registered post,[5] or by publication in a newspaper.[6] Under s. 62

2 *Ram Saran* (1882) ILR 5 All 7.
3 *Lalchand* v *Emperor* AIR 1934 Oudh 370; 35 CrLJ 1161.
4 *Sudhir Kumar Dutt* v *The King* AIR 1949 FC 6; 50 CrLJ 294.
5 *Bhimappa* v *Indira Bai* 1981 CrLJ (NOC) 8 (Kant).
6 *Dhani* v *State* 1974 CrLJ 1234 (All).

personal service may be made either by delivering or by tendering, but the tender must be a real tender of a document which is understood by the person to be served and he must have voluntarily waived actual delivery and indicated in some way that the tender was sufficient.

But if the person to be served runs away and shuts himself in his house the summons can be served on him either by delivery or by tender.[7] The fact of a subpoena being entrusted to a process server does not give him a general right of entry in any house without obtaining the permission of the owner or the person in charge. The mere showing of a summons to the person summoned is not sufficient service. However, if the person refuses to take the summons, the mere tendering is sufficient service.[8] The principles laid down for the service of summons in civil cases cannot be applied to service of summons in criminal cases. When a summons has been issued by registered post and the same has been returned with the endorsement 'refused', it is no service of summons.[9]

Section 63 deals with service of summons on corporate bodies and societies. The 'Explanation' to s. 63 clarifies that corporation means—an incorporated company or other body corporate and includes a society registered under the Societies Registration Act 1860. An incorporated company is a legal entity and there is nothing to prevent the issue of summons against the company itself.[10] When the summons is issued against the company some competent representative like the secretary, local manager or other principal officer must be described both by name and designation as representing the company and there must be evidence of his representative character.[11]

Section 64 provides for service when persons summoned cannot be found. Where the person summoned cannot, by the exercise of due diligence, be found, the summons may be served by leaving one of the duplicates for him with some adult male member of his family residing with him and the person with whom the summons is so left shall, if so required by the serving officer, sign a receipt therefor on the back of the other duplicate. Explanation to s. 64 provides that a servant is not a member of the family within the meaning of s. 64. It must be shown by affidavit of the person entrusted with the service of summons that he made his best endeavour to effect personal service on the accused and that the accused evaded service and that he could not be found by the exercise of due diligence. Where no attempt has been made to serve the accused personally and there has been want of reasonable diligence in that behalf, a substituted service of summons is not valid.[12] To justify such service, it should be proved that proper efforts were made to find

7 *Budhu* v *Emperor* AIR 1928 All 188; 29 CrLJ 263.
8 *P.T.B. Menon* v *Govind Krishnan* AIR 1959 Mad 165; 1959 CrLJ 483.
9 *U.P. Shivanna* v *Bhadramma* 1993 CrLJ 418 (Kant).
10 *Sudhir Ranjan Rai* v *N.K. Majumdar* AIR 1944 Pat 210; 11 BR 136.
11 *Commissioner, South Dum Dum Municipality* AIR 1956 Cal 237.
12 *Monmohan Pande* v *Calcutta Corporation* AIR 1932 Cal 62; 35 CWN 868.

the person summoned.[13] If the person summoned cannot be found the summons may be served on an adult male member of his family. The service of summons on the mother of the accused is not warranted by s. 64. Where personal service can be effected the law permits service on some adult male member of the family but not a servant. To this end it is to be shown that proper efforts were made to find the person summoned.[14] If at the request of the accused the summons was served upon her husband, such service was bad. It is only when the person to be summoned is not found it can be tendered to an adult male member of the family and not otherwise. Where a conditional Order drawn in proceedings under s. 133 against a party was not served on her but service was made on her brother-in-law, the proceeding drawn up against her under s. 188 of the IPC is illegal and is liable to be quashed and as no attempt was made to serve the lady with the conditional order with due diligence and service on her brother-in-law could not be held to be the service on the adult male member of the family of the lady.[15]

Section 65 deals with service of summons by affixation. It provides that where service mentioned in ss. 62, 63 and 64 cannot after exercise of due diligence be made personally as prescribed by s. 62 or s. 63 or on an adult male member as provided in s. 64, such service can be effected by affixation. The service by affixation cannot be resorted to in the office of the person sought to be served with the summons. The affixation of one of the duplicates of the summons as provided in s. 65 must be in some conspicuous part of the residence of the said person.[16] The expression 'ordinarily resides' occurring in s. 65 connotes a quality of permanence and continuity more than what is involved in residence. Any summon on a person who is employed abroad cannot be served by affixture in his house. Court can in such a case send the summon to be served through embassy officials.[17]

Section 69 deals with service of summons on witness by post. It provides that to cut out delay in the service of summons on witness the service may be effected by post in addition or simultaneously with the issue of summons in the usual way. It may be mentioned that s. 69 applies to witness only. Service of summons by certificate of posting in addition to service by speed post and courier service can be treated as an alternative mode of service.[18]

Section 69(2) provides that when an acknowledgment purporting to be signed by the witness or an endorsement purporting to be made by a postal employee that the witness refused to take delivery of summons has been received, the court issuing the summons may declare that the summons has been duly served. Where there is no endorsement of 'refusal' made by the

13 *Hemendra Nath* v *Archana* AIR 1971 Cal 244; 1971 CrLJ 817.
14 *Hemendra Nath* v *Archana* AIR 1971 Cal 244; 1971 CrLJ 817.
15 *Munni* v *State* 1983 All LJ 513.
16 *Hemendra Nath* v *Archana* AIR 1971 Cal 244; 1971 CrLJ 817.
17 *E. Chattu* v *P. Gopalan* 1981 CrLJ 691.
18 *Mesh Trans Gears Pvt. Ltd.* v *Dr. R. Parvathreddy* 2013 CrLJ (NOC) 585 (Kar).

postal peon on the envelope containing the summons it cannot be said that the summons has been duly served.

Order issuing summons may be recalled

Summoning an accused is an interim order and not a judgment. When an accused applies for recalling of summons on showing good cause, the Magistrate cannot refuse to entertain such application on the ground that the court does not have the power to recall or review the summoning order.[19]

Summons—quashing of

The dictionary meaning of the word 'quash' is 'annul, cancel; declare null and void; invalidate; nullify; make void; abate; vacate; set aside'.[20] If a Magistrate issues summons against two accused persons but the higher court found that issuance of summon against one of the accused persons is factually incorrect, the summon issued against that accused is directed to stand quashed.[1]

2 Warrant of arrest

Warrant of arrest means a written order which is made on behalf of the State and is based upon a complaint issued pursuant to statute and/or court rule and which commands a law enforcement officer to arrest a person and bring him before Magistrate.[2] Under s. 70, every warrant of arrest issued by a court under CrPC shall be in writing, signed by the Presiding Officer of such court and shall bear the seal of the court. Every such warrant shall remain in force unless it is cancelled by the court which issued it or until it is executed. The expression 'warrant of arrest' has not been defined in the Code, but ss. 70 to 81 grouped under the sub-heading 'Warrant of Arrest' in Chapter VI deal with arrest in execution of warrant issued by the Court under this Code.[3] In Schedule II, Form No. 2 is given and it is clear from this that warrant is an order addressed to person(s) to arrest the accused, to take him into custody and bring him before the Court issuing the warrant. The conditions under which and the grounds on which warrant of arrest may be issued are given in ss. 87, 107 to 110 and s. 204 of the Code. An arrest made under a warrant of arrest amounts to deprivation of personal liberty of the person arrested within the meaning of Art. 21 of the Constitution.[4] Accordingly, warrant should be issued in strict compliance with the law. Section 70(1) applies to preventive detention also.[5]

Section 72 provides that a warrant of arrest shall ordinarily be directed to one or more Police Officers, but the court issuing such a warrant may,

19 *Prakash Industries Ltd.* v *State* 2004 CrLJ 744 (Del).
20 Mitra, *Legal & Commercial Dictionary*, 6th Ed., p. 720.
1 *B. Chandrika* v *Santosh* (2014)13 SCC 699.
2 Mitra, *Legal & Commercial Dictionary*, 6th Ed., p. 892.
3 *Ajib Singh* AIR 1953 SC 10.
4 *Jugal Kishore More* v *C.P. Magistrate* AIR 1968 Cal 220; 1968 CrLJ 604; 71 CWN 508.
5 *Talkeshwari Devi* v *Ram Ran Bikat Prasad Singh* (1972)1 SCC 536; AIR 1973 SC 639.

if its immediate execution is necessary and no Police Officer is immediately available, direct it to any other person or persons and such person or persons shall execute the same. Section 73 provides that the Chief Judicial Magistrate or a Magistrate of the first class may direct warrant to any person within his local jurisdiction for the arrest of any escaped convict, proclaimed offender or of any person who is accused of a non-bailable offence and is evading arrest. Under s. 75, the Police Officer or other person executing a warrant of arrest shall notify the substance thereof to the person to be arrested and, if so required, shall show him the warrant.

3 Proclamation and attachment

Proclamation means 'a formal public' announcement made by the Government.[6] Section 82 read with s. 83 shows that even in summons cases and against the witness a proclamation may be issued. Forms No. 4 and 5 of the Schedule II make this clear. But for the issuance of the proclamation under s. 82 with an accompanying Order of Attachment under s. 83 requires compliance with the provisions of law relating to the issue of warrant in a case where summons is an ordinary mode of enforcing attendance.

Section 82(1) reads as under:

> 82(1). *Proclamation for person absconding.* If any court has reason to believe (whether after taking evidence or not) that any person against whom a warrant has been issued by it has absconded or is concealing himself so that such warrant cannot be executed, such court may publish a written proclamation requiring him to appear at a specified place and at a specified time not less than thirty days from the date of publishing such proclamation.

The processes of attachment and proclamation are not to issue whenever a warrant fails of its effect. Before issuing a proclamation the officer sent to serve the warrant of arrest must be examined as to the measures adopted by him to serve it. If on his evidence or in any other manner the Magistrate is satisfied that the accused is absconding or concealing, then only the processes of proclamation and attachment may be issued. The processes under ss. 82 and 83 cannot be issued unless a warrant had already been issued against the person wanted and that person was absconding. Warrant of Arrest and Warrant of Proclamation cannot be issued simultaneously. It is only after the warrant of arrest has been issued the proclamation can be issued where the concerned person has absconded or he is hiding.

Section 82(2) provides the modes of publishing a proclamation.

> Section 82(2). The proclamation shall be published as follows:—
>
> (*i*) (*a*) it shall be publicly read in some conspicuous place of the town or village in which such person ordinarily resides;

6 Black's *Law Dictionary*, 8th Ed.

(*b*) it shall be affixed to some conspicuous part of the house or homestead in which such person ordinarily resides or to some conspicuous place of such town or village;

(*c*) a copy thereof shall be affixed to some conspicuous part of the Court-house;

(*ii*) the Court may also, if it thinks fit, direct a copy of the proclamation to be published in a daily newspaper circulating in the place in which such person ordinarily resides.

The provisions of sub-sec. (2) as to the mode of publishing a proclamation are perfectly clear and explicit and failure to comply with them will vitiate the subsequent attachment and sale.[7] Where the provisions of cl. (*i*)(*a*) were not complied with at all and although the provisions of cls. (*i*)(*b*) and (*c*) were complied with, the proclamation does not specify a place and time for the appearance of the absconder, the proclamation is bad, not being according to law.[8] The three sub-cls. (*a*) to (*c*) are conjunctive and unless all the three modes of publication are proved there would be no valid publication.[9]

The most important part of the publication is the publishing of the proclamation in the accused's place of residence and it is from the date of such publication that 30 days should be counted. The time of 30 days has to be counted not from the date of issue of publication but from its publication. The rules prescribed by s. 82 with regard to time and place are imperative.

> Section 82(3). A statement in writing by the Court issuing the proclamation to the effect that the proclamation was duly published on a specified day, in the manner specified in clause (*i*) of sub-section (2), shall be conclusive evidence that the requirements of this section have been complied with, and that the proclamation was published on such day.

Presumption in s. 82(3) can only apply to a proclamation which is otherwise a legal proclamation. No presumption under s. 114, Illustration (*e*) of the Evidence Act 1872 can be drawn that the requirements of the section have been duly observed and the proclamation published as provided therein.

Section 82 of the CrPC has been amended in 2005 and after sub-sec. (3) the following sub-sections have been inserted:

> (4) Where a proclamation published under sub-section (1) is in respect of a person accused of an offence punishable under sections 302, 304, 364, 367, 382, 392, 393, 394, 395, 396, 397, 398, 399, 400, 402, 436, 449, 459 or 460 of the Indian Penal Code, and such person fails to appear at the specified place and time required by the proclamation, the court may, making such inquiry

7 *Mian Jan* ILR 27 All 572.

8 *Abdullah* ILR 22 All 216.

9 *Pawan Kumar Gupta* v *State of West Bengal* 1973 CrLJ 1368 (Cal).

as it thinks fit, pronounce him a proclaimed offender and make a declaration to that effect.

(5) The provisions of sub-sections (2) and (3) shall apply to a declaration made by the court under sub-section (4) as they apply to the proclamation published under sub-section (1).

Section 83 deals with attachment of the property of the person absconding. It reads as under:

Section 83. *Attachment of property of person absconding.* (1) The Court issuing a proclamation under section 82 may, for reasons to be recorded in writing, at any time after the issue of the proclamation, order the attachment of any property, movable or immovable, or both, belonging to the proclaimed person:

Provided that where at the time of the issue of the proclamation the Court is satisfied, by affidavit or otherwise, that the person in relation to whom the proclamation is to be issued,—

(*a*) is about to dispose of the whole or any part of his property, or

(*b*) is about to remove the whole or any part of his property from the local jurisdiction of the Court,

it may order the attachment simultaneously with the issue of the proclamation.

(2) Such order shall authorise the attachment of any property belonging to such person within the district in which it is made; and it shall authorise the attachment of any property belonging to such person without such district when endorsed by the District Magistrate within whose district such property is situate.

(3) If the property ordered to be attached is a debt or other movable property, the attachment under this section shall be made—

(*a*) by seizure; or

(*b*) by the appointment of a receiver; or

(*c*) by an order in writing prohibiting the delivery of such property to the proclaimed person or to any one on his behalf; or

(*d*) by all or any two of such methods, as the Court thinks fit.

(4) If the property ordered to be attached is immovable, the attachment under this section shall, in the case of land paying revenue to the State Government, be made through the Collector of the district in which the land is situate, and in all other cases—

(*a*) by taking possession; or

(*b*) by the appointment of a receiver; or

(*c*) by an order in writing prohibiting the payment of rent on delivery of property to the proclaimed person or to any one on his behalf; or

(*d*) by all or any two of such methods, as the Court thinks fit.

(5) If the property ordered to be attached consists of live-stock or is of a perishable nature, the Court may, if it thinks it expedient, order immediate

sale thereof, and in such case the proceeds of the sale shall abide the order of the Court.

(6) The powers, duties and liabilities of a receiver appointed under this section shall be the same as those of a receiver appointed under the Code of Civil Procedure 1908 (5 of 1908).

Purpose of attachment

The purpose behind the issuing of the order of attachment is to compel the appearance of the accused against whom proclamation has been issued.[10] It is penalty for his non-appearance notwithstanding the proclamation.[11] He can also be liable for prosecution under s. 174, CrPC for disobedience of the proclamation. Without having issued any proclamation under s. 82, CrPC attachment of property is illegal. It can also be treated as invalid when the accused was not absconding.[12] Before issuing proclamation Court must have reason to believe that the accused is absconding or concealing himself to avoid execution of warrant.[13] The object of s. 83 is not to punish the absconder but to compel him to appear. Section 83 does not authorise simultaneously to issue of order of proclamation and attachment. Only in the circumstances mentioned in the proviso to sub-sec. (1) the court is authorised to issue the order of proclamation and of attachment simultaneously. Where, however, the proclamation issued under s. 82 is invalid no valid attachment of property under s. 83 can be made.[14]

87. *Issue of warrant in lieu of, or in addition to, summons.* A Court may, in any case in which it is empowered by this Code to issue a summons for the appearance of any person, issue, after recording its reasons in writing, a warrant for his arrest—

(*a*) if, either before the issue of such summons, or after the issue of the same but before the time fixed for his appearance, the Court sees reason to believe that he has absconded or will not obey the summons; or

(*b*) if at such time he fails to appear and the summons is proved to have been duly served in time to admit of his appearing in accordance therewith and no reasonable excuse is offered for such failure.

In a summons case cognizance and warrant of arrest without giving any finding that the accused has either absconded or would not obey the summons is not permissible. In such a case, coercive process of warrant of arrest in a summons case cannot be resorted to without recording the reasons in

10 *Peterson* v *Forbes* AIR 1963 SC 692.
11 *Siddanyouda* v *State of Mysore* 1972 CrLJ 289 (Mys).
12 *Ratish* v *Mahesh* 1985 CrLJ 94 (Gau).
13 *Deep Narayan Singh* v *State of Bihar* 1981 CrLJ 1672.
14 *Siddangouda* 1972 CrLJ 289.

writing.[15] Non-bailable warrant against the accused will be issued when police is inefficient in executing bailable warrant.[16]

> 113. *Summons or warrant in case of person not so present.* If such person is not present in Court, the Magistrate shall issue a summons requiring him to appear, or, when such person is in custody, a warrant directing the officer in whose custody he is to bring him before the Court:
>
> Provided that whenever it appears to such Magistrate, upon the report of a police officer or upon other information (the substance of which report or information shall be recorded by the Magistrate), that there is reason to fear the commission of a breach of the peace, and that such breach of the peace cannot be prevented otherwise than by the immediate arrest of such person, the Magistrate may at any time issue a warrant for his arrest.

Section 113 is applicable only to the stage prior to the service of the preliminary order under s. 111 and it can have no application as a preventive means after the person proceeded against has appeared to show cause.[1] An order must be passed under s. 111 before a Magistrate issues warrant under s. 113. To issue a warrant without an order under s. 111 is breach of a mandatory provision of law.

Before taking any steps for arrest of the opposite party in security proceedings, the Magistrate must have reasons to apprehend the commission of breach of peace and it must also appear to him that such breach of peace cannot be prevented otherwise than by immediate arrest of the opposite party. In such a case, it is also incumbent on the part of the Magistrate to record an order in writing showing satisfaction for the steps taken under the Proviso to s. 113, CrPC.[2]

> 128. *Enforcement of order of maintenance.* A copy of the order of maintenance or interim maintenance and expenses of proceeding, as the case may be, shall be given without payment to the person in whose favour it is made, or to his guardian, if any, or to the person to whom the allowance for the maintenance or the allowance for the interim maintenance and expenses of proceeding, as the case may be, is to be paid; and such order may be enforced by any Magistrate in any place where the person against whom it is made may be, on such Magistrate being satisfied as to the identity of the parties and the non-payment of the allowance, or as the case may be, expenses, due.

The only conditions laid down in respect of the enforcement of the order under s. 128 are the identity of the parties and non-payment of the allowance due. If any such thing occurs as may be fit to vacate the order, the proper procedure for the husband is to apply to the court and get the order cancelled.

15 *G. Sagar Suri* v *State* 2004 CrLJ 212 (Del).
16 *Pushpanjali Sahu* v *State of Orissa* (2013)1 SCC (Cri) 676; (2012)11 SCC 433.
1 *Hampaiah,* in re AIR 1944 Mad 575.
2 *Dibakar Naik* v *Puspalata Patel* (1997)3 Crimes 107 (Ori).

So long as the order stands it is capable of being enforced though in the case of a woman living with a husband it would remain suspended for the period during which she lives with her husband.

A person, having an obligation to maintain his wife and daughter, his mere filing of a suit for declaring himself an insolvent is no ground for not discharging the said obligation. Even an insolvent who is physically fit has to pay the maintenance.[3]

4 Miscellaneous

> 134. *Service or notification of order.* (1) The order shall, if practicable, be served on the person against whom it is made, in the manner herein provided for service of a summons.
>
> (2) If such order cannot be so served, it shall be notified by proclamation, published in such manner as the State Government may, by rule, direct, and a copy thereof shall be struck up at such place or places as may be fittest for conveying the information to such person.

In case of service of a conditional order under s. 133, the procedure which is provided by s. 65 cannot be made use of unless the service in the manner mentioned in ss. 62, 63 and 64 cannot be effected by the exercise of due diligence. If personal service is not practicable the order may be affixed to the house of the defendant. It is not open to resort to the procedure laid down in s. 134(2) when no attempt was made to serve the order through any adult male member of his family residing with him as laid down in s. 64 or by affixing to the person's house as laid down in s. 65. The terms of the section are directory and ought to be followed, but an omission to follow its provisions is a mere irregularity and does not nullify the order.[4] The non-service of notice does not invalidate the order if the parties admit that they knew of the existence of the notice. Where the parties had information of the order it is immaterial that the mode in which it was brought to their notice was not in strict compliance with the provisions of this section.[5]

A conditional order passed under s. 133, CrPC has to be duly served upon the opposite party and has the right to appear and to show cause. When the conditional order was made absolute without giving any opportunity to the opposite party by issuing notice, it is illegal.[6] Only on compliance with the provision of issuing show cause notice under s. 134, CrPC the Magistrate has the jurisdiction to proceed with the matter under s. 137 and s. 138, CrPC.[7]

3 *Chandra Bhan* v *Sudha Rani* 2005 CrLJ 1978 (All).
4 *Parbatty* ILR 15 Cal 9.
5 *Nurjan* 1900 PR 2.
6 *Narayan* v *S.D.M., Jaipur* 1986 CrLJ 102 (Ori); *Mohammed Rafiq* v *State* 1986 CrLJ 44 (Raj).
7 *T.P. Rajeevan* v *S.D.M.* 1986 CrLJ 693 (Ker).

141. *Procedure on order being made absolute and consequences of disobedience.* (1) When an order has been made absolute under section 136 or section 138, the Magistrate shall give notice of the same to the person against whom the order was made, and shall further require him to perform the act directed by the order within a time to be fixed in the notice, and inform him that, in case of disobedience, he will be liable to the penalty provided by section 188 of the Indian Penal Code (45 of 1860).

(2) If such act is not performed within the time fixed, the Magistrate may cause it to be performed, and may recover the costs of performing it, either by the sale of any building, goods or other property removed by his order, or by the distress and sale of any other movable property of such person within or without such Magistrate's local jurisdiction and if such other property is without such jurisdiction, the order shall authorise its attachment and sale when endorsed by the Magistrate within whose local jurisdiction the property to be attached is found.

(3) No suit shall lie in respect of anything done in good faith under this section.

Any order made under s. 136 making the conditional order absolute without notice under s. 133(1) being sufficient is bad in law and must be held to be void. In such a case any consequential order under s. 141 is also illegal and without jurisdiction.[8] Sub-section (1) is mandatory, sub-sec. (2) is merely directory. If the Magistrate's order is reasonable and proper the Magistrate is bound to make the order absolute (s. 138) and is bound under s. 141(1) to require the party to carry out the order within certain time in spite of the fact that the party has filed a civil suit and obtained a temporary injunction. The Magistrate has no discretion in the matter. But when the second stage contemplated in sub-sec. (2) is reached, the Magistrate has a discretion and can, after taking into consideration all the circumstances of the case, decide whether he would give the direction referred to in sub-sec. (2) or whether he thinks it expedient to leave the matter where it is until conclusion of the civil suit.[9]

Section 141(3) says that no suit shall lie in respect of anything done in good faith under this section. A conditional order made under s. 133 cannot be questioned by a civil suit but no bar exists to an absolute order under s. 141 being questioned in a civil court.

142. *Injunction pending inquiry.* (1) If a Magistrate making an order under section 133 considers that immediate measures should be taken to prevent imminent danger or injury of a serious kind to the public, he may issue such an injunction to the person against whom the order was made, as is required to obviate or prevent such danger or injury pending the determination of the matter.

---

8 *Nurjan* 1900 PR 2.

9 *Narayan Sahu* 1986 CrLJ 102 (Ori).

(2) In default of such person forthwith obeying such injunction, the Magistrate may himself use, or cause to be used, such means as he thinks fit to obviate such danger or to prevent such injury.

(3) No suit shall lie in respect of anything done in good faith by a Magistrate under this section.

Section 142 is not an independent section, but is controlled in its effect by s. 133. An order under s. 142 can be passed only if an injury or danger specified in s. 133 is apprehended and not otherwise.[10] Section 142 intends the order to meet an immediate danger or injury and its object is to prevent that injury pending the determination of the case under s. 133 or s. 137. An interim order of the injunction under s. 142 may be made at any stage of enquiry. A notice before issuing injunction order under s. 142 is ordinarily to be issued in very extreme cases and where the delay will frustrate the whole object of issuing the injunction and would result in dangerous consequences by way of injury to the public.[11]

The interim injunction pending enquiry can be issued only where a valid conditional order has been made under s. 133, CrPC. Such an order will be invalid if the initial order is peremptory instead of a conditional order and does not specify the date and other relevant particulars when the opposite party may appear and file objection against such conditional order. Moreover, the conditional order itself is not sufficient for the Magistrate to issue the injunction order. The Magistrate must satisfy himself that immediate measures have to be taken to prevent imminent danger or injury of a serious kind to the public. Such satisfaction must appear from the order itself or from the file that the Magistrate has been satisfied which must contain the reasons for such satisfaction.[12]

144. *Power to issue order in urgent cases of nuisance or apprehended danger.* (1) In cases where, in the opinion of a District Magistrate, a Sub-divisional Magistrate or any other Executive Magistrate specially empowered by the State Government in this behalf, there is sufficient ground for proceeding under this section and immediate prevention or speedy remedy is desirable, such Magistrate may, by a written order stating the material facts of the case and served in the manner provided by section 134, direct any person to abstain from a certain act or to take certain order with respect to certain property in his possession or under his management, if such Magistrate considers that such direction is likely to prevent, or tends to prevent, obstruction, annoyance or injury to any person lawfully employed, or danger to human life, health or safety, or a disturbance of the public tranquillity, or a riot, or an affray.

10 *Panchanan* 53 CWN 907.
11 *Chamvaay* 1979 CrLJ NOC 151.
12 *Mangal* v *State of UP* 1977 CrLJ 1036 (All).

(2) An order under this section may, in cases of emergency or in cases where the circumstances do not admit of the serving in due time of a notice upon the person against whom the order is directed, be passed *ex parte.*

(3) An order under this section may be directed to a particular individual, or to persons residing in a particular place or area, or to the public generally when frequenting or visiting a particular place or area.

(4) No order under this section shall remain in force for more than two months from the making thereof:

Provided that, if the State Government considers it necessary so to do for preventing danger to human life, health or safety or for preventing a riot or any affray, it may, by notification, direct that an order made by a Magistrate under this section shall remain in force for such further period not exceeding six months from the date on which the order made by the Magistrate would have, but for such order, expired, as it may specify in the said notification.

(5) Any Magistrate may, either on his own motion or on the application of any person aggrieved, rescind or alter any order made under this section, by himself or any Magistrate subordinate to him or by his predecessor-in-office.

(6) The State Government may, either on its own motion or on the application of any person aggrieved, rescind or alter any order made by it under the proviso to sub-section (4).

(7) Where an application under sub-section (5), or sub-section (6) is received, the Magistrate, or the State Government, as the case may be, shall afford to the applicant an early opportunity of appearing before him or it, either in person or by pleader and showing cause against the order, and if the Magistrate or the State Government, as the case may be, rejects the application wholly or in part, he or it shall record in writing the reasons for so doing.

An order under s. 144 is in the interest of maintenance of 'Public Order', some of the objects for securing it being "to prevent obstruction, annoyance, injury" etc. The power conferred by this section is not arbitrary, nor it is unlimited; it is to be reasonable. It is only where the emergency of the gravest character is made out that a court would be justified in the exercise of its power under this section to make an order which would have the effect of interfering with the exercise of the private right of individuals. When a breach is anticipated, action is to be taken against the potential lawbreakers. It is not permissible for a Magistrate under the cover of an order under s. 144 to dispossess a particular individual of certain property to deliver possession of it to another. This section does not entitle a Landlord to secure the eviction of a tenant through the intervention of a criminal court. It is also an abuse of the process of the court to invoke the help of this section for the remedy of a civil wrong. Before proceeding under this section the Magistrate should hold an enquiry and record the urgency of the matter.[13] For the purpose of s. 144 it is only necessary that the Magistrate issuing the order should believe that apprehension of nuisance or danger exists. No proof of such apprehension is necessary. An order under this section must be based upon proper evidence. An order passed by the Magistrate under s. 144 is not a judicial order but an executive order.[1] The following preconditions are required to be observed:

(*a*) The order must be in writing;

(*b*) The order must be an order which is absolute and definite in terms; s. 144(1) and (2) do not contemplate the passing of a conditional order to be made absolute later on;[2]

(*c*) The order must contain a statement of the material facts which the Magistrate considers to be facts of the case and upon the footing of which he passes his order;[3]

(*d*) The order must be specific and definite in terms;

(*e*) The thing or act which is prohibited must be clearly stated;

(*f*) The duration of the order must be co-extensive with the emergency;

(*g*) Except where the order is addressed to the public generally under sub-sec. (3), the persons against whom the order is directed must be specified;

(*h*) The terms of the notice must follow the terms of the order in pursuance of which the notice is issued.

The order must be served in the manner provided by s. 134, that is, served personally. If it is not served personally and brought to the notice of the accused, the conviction under s. 188, IPC for disobedience of the order is illegal.[4]

Any party being aggrieved by any order under s. 144, CrPC may apply for rescinding it under sub-sec. (5) or (6) of s. 144, CrPC. He may file a revision[5] or challenge it by invoking writ jurisdiction of the High Court.[6] A petition under Art. 32 of the Constitution may also be filed before the Supreme Court where a fundamental right has been affected by invoking writ jurisdiction of the High Court.[7]

13 *Kamini* ILR 38 Cal 876.
1 *Gulam Abbas* v *State of U.P.* AIR 1981 SC 2198.
2 *Bholagiri* 40 CWN 640.
3 *Renu* v *State* 85 CWN 623.
4 *Kalipada* v *State* AIR 1951 Cal 207; 51 CrLJ 1575 (Cal).
5 *Purna* v *Saogat* AIR 1960 Cal 715.
6 *Gulam* v *State of UP* AIR 1981 SC 2198.
7 *Madhu Limaye* v *S.D.M.* AIR 1971 SC 2486; *Dange* v *State of UP* (1970)3 SCC 218.

In Chapter X of the Code of Criminal Procedure, under sub-heading "C—Urgent cases of nuisance or apprehended danger", after s. 144, the following section has been *inserted*, namely:

> 144A. *Power to prohibit carrying arms in procession or mass drill or mass training with arms.* (1) The District Magistrate may, whenever he considers it necessary so to do for the preservation of public peace or public safety or for the maintenance of public order, by public notice or by order, prohibit in any area within the local limits of his jurisdiction, the carrying of arms in any procession or the organising or holding of, or taking part in, any mass drill or mass training with arms in any public place.
>
> (2) A public notice issued or an order made under this section may be directed to a particular person or to persons belonging to any community, party or organisation.
>
> (3) No public notice issued or an order made under this section shall remain in force for more than three months from the date on which it is issued or made.
>
> (4) The State Government may, if it considers necessary so to do for the preservation of public peace or public safety or for the maintenance of public order; by notification, direct that a public notice issued or order made by the District Magistrate under this section shall remain in force for such further period not exceeding six months from the date on which such public notice or order was issued or made by the District Magistrate would have, but for such direction, expired, as it may specify in the said notification.
>
> (5) The State Government may, subject to such control and directions as it may deem fit to impose, by general or special order, delegate its powers under sub-section (4) to the District Magistrate.
>
> *Explanation*. The word "arms" shall have the meaning assigned to it in section 153AA of the Indian Penal Code (45 of 1860).

Principles of natural justice—effect of notice on person having representative capacity

(A) NOTICE UNDER S. 145, CRPC—PRINCIPLES OF NATURAL JUSTICE. When direction in preliminary order is for giving notice thereof to certain specified persons, the failure to do so will invalidate further proceedings as offending the principles of natural justice as no order having civil consequences can be made against a person without giving him an opportunity of being heard.[8]

(B) EFFECT OF NOTICE ON PERSON HAVING REPRESENTATIVE CAPACITY. When a notice was served on a person who truly represented and acted as representative of the party, no objection can be raised by the person on

8 *Thounaojam Munal Singh* v *Karam Iboyaima Singh* AIR 1971 Manipur 1.

whom such notice was served or by those whom such person represented, especially when no prejudice was caused.[9]

(c) Affixation of a copy of notice on the land—presumption—duly served.[10]

145. *Procedure where dispute concerning land or water is likely to cause breach of peace.* (1) Whenever an Executive Magistrate is satisfied from a report of a police officer or upon other information that a dispute likely to cause a breach of the peace exists concerning any land or water or the boundaries thereof, within his local jurisdiction, he shall make an order in writing, stating the grounds of his being so satisfied, and requiring the parties concerned in such dispute to attend his Court in person or by pleader, on a specified date and time, and to put in written statements of their respective claims as respects the fact of actual possession of the subject of dispute.

(2) For the purposes of this section, the expression "land or water" includes buildings, markets, fisheries, crops or other produce of land, and the rents or profits of any such property.

(3) A copy of the order shall be served in the manner provided by the Code for the service of a summons upon such person or persons as the Mgistrate may direct, and at least one copy shall be published by being affixed to some conspicuous place at or near the subject of dispute.

(4) The Magistrate shall then, without reference to the merits or the claims of any of the parties to a right to possess the subject of dispute, peruse the statements so put in, hear the parties, receive all such evidence as may be produced by them, take such further evidence, if any, as he thinks necessary, and, if possible, decide whether any and which of the parties was, at the date of the order made by him under sub-section (1), in possession of the subject of dispute:

Provided that if it appears to the Magistrate that any party has been forcibly and wrongfully dispossessed within two months next before the date on which the report of a police officer or other information was received by the Magistrate, or after that date and before the date of his order under sub-section (1), he may treat the party so dispossessed as if that party had been in possession on the date of his order under sub-section (1).

(5) Nothing in this section shall preclude any party so required to attend, or any other person interested, from showing that no such dispute as aforesaid exists or has existed; and in such case the Magistrate shall cancel his said order, and all further proceedings thereon shall be stayed, but, subjects to such cancellation, the order of the Magistrate under sub-section (1) shall be final.

(6)(*a*) If the Magistrate decides that one of the parties was, or should under the proviso to sub-section (4) be treated as being, in such possession

---

9 AIR 1925 All 316; *Thounaojam Munal Singh* v *Karam Iboyaima Singh* AIR 1971 Manipur 1.

10 *Thounaojam Munal Singh* v *Karam Iboyaima Singh* AIR 1971 Manipur 1.

of the said subject, he shall issue an order declaring such party to be entitled to possession thereof until evicted therefrom in due course of law, and forbidding all disturbance of such possession until such eviction; and when he proceeds under the proviso to sub-section (4), may restore to possession the party forcibly and wrongfully dispossessed.

(*b*) The order made under this sub-section shall be served and published in the manner laid down in sub-section (3).

(7) When any party to any such proceeding dies, the Magistrate may cause the legal representative of the deceased party to be made a party to the proceeding and shall thereupon continue the inquiry, and if any question arises as to who the legal representative of a deceased party for the purposes of such proceeding is, all persons claiming to be representatives of the deceased party shall be made parties thereto.

(8) If the Magistrate is of opinion that any crop or other produce of the property, the subject of dispute in a proceeding under this section pending before him, is subject to speedy and natural decay, he may make an order for the proper custody or sale of such property, and, upon the completion of the inquiry, shall make such order for the disposal of such property, or the sale-proceeds thereof, as he thinks fit.

(9) The Magistrte may, if he thinks fit, at any stage of the proceedings under this section, on the application of either party, issue a summons to any witness directing him to attend or to produce any document or thing.

(10) Nothing in this section shall be deemed to be in derogation of the powers of the Magistrate to proceed under section 107.

Section 145 is intended only to provide a speedy remedy for the prevention of breaches of peace arising out of disputes relating to immovable property by maintaining one or other of the parties in possession.[11] The object of this section is to enable a Magistrate to intervene and pass a temporary order in regard to the possession of the property in dispute, having effect until the actual right of one of the parties has been determined by a competent civil court.[12] The Magistrate can find out who is in actual possession but not right or title.[13] The proceedings under s. 145 are *quasi* judicial and *quasi* administrative in nature and their object is to prevent a breach of the peace and maintain tranquility. The Magistrate must be satisfied on the two conditions before initiating proceedings, viz.:

(*i*) a dispute regarding immovable property exists, and

(*ii*) such a dispute is likely to cause a breach of the peace. Where the dispute is not on the right to possession but on the question of

11 *Tarapada* ILR 32 Cal 1039.
12 *Bhinka* v *Charan Singh* AIR 1959 SC 960; 1959 (Supp) 2 SCR 798.
13 *Bhinka* v *Charan Singh* (Supra).

possession, the Magistrate is empowered to take cognizance under s. 145.[14]

Parallel proceedings in civil and criminal court should not be permitted to continue and in the event of a decree of civil court the criminal court should not be allowed to invoke its jurisdiction.[15]

The jurisdiction of a Magistrate to proceed under this section arises from the fact that he has received certain information and that he is satisfied as to the truth of that information. If the proceedings are initiated under this section without passing any preliminary order, proceedings are liable to be quashed. The Magistrate after issuing preliminary order can implead a person as a party. An interested party, if not impleaded, can invoke s. 145(5) and proviso to s. 146(1) but cannot claim relief under s. 482. A Magistrate's order in instituting proceedings under the section ought to set out the grounds on which he is satisfied that a dispute likely to cuase a breach of peace exists.[16]

A copy of the order stating the grounds of the Magistrate's satisfaction must be served on the parties, for it is the intention of the law, not only that Magistrate should have sufficient grounds for proceeding under this section but that he should inform the parties concerned of the grounds on which the proceeding had been instituted. Under s. 145, it is mandatory upon the Magistrate to record the grounds of his belief. If without giving any reason and without even stating that he is satisfied there is any apprehension of a breach of the peace, the Magistrate gives an order under s. 145(1), the order is without jurisdiction.[17]

The Magistrate ought to satisfy himself that the copy of the order has been duly served on the parties alleging the non-receipt of the notice, and the Magistrate's omission to do so vitiates all subsequent proceeding.[18] In a proceeding under s. 145, when no summons was affixed to the house, or served upon the opposite party personally or upon an adult male member of his family, there was no service of any kind upon him. No *ex parte* proceedings are possible in cases where there has been no service. Where one of the parties denies the service of the order, written return of the serving peon is not sufficient proof of the service. The Magistrate should examine the serving peon. If the party professing to be aggrieved has full knowledge of the proceedings, the omission to serve the notice will not render the proceedings void, if the parties were present and no prejudice was caused.

14 *Prakash* v *State* (1994)1 SCC 471.
15 *Ram Sumer* v *State* AIR 1985 SC 472; (1985)1 SCC 427.
16 *Jagmohan* ILR 28 Cal 416.
17 *Gobind Chandra* ILR 20 Cal 520.
18 *Sripati* 8 CWN 66.

A suit has already been filed by the sons and daughters against their father, the respondent for permanent injunction restraining the defendant from dispossessing the plaintiff from the house in question and also restraining him from entering into any dealing relating to property. The respondent initiated a proceeding under s. 145, CrPC complaining apprehension of the breach of peace occasioned by dispute as to possession of the property. Such a dispute is a civil dispute pure and simple which has been given colour of a criminal case. So, the proceedings under s. 145, CrPC have been quashed.[19]

> 147. *Dispute concerning right of use of land or water.* (1) Whenever an Executive Magistrate is satisfied from the report of a police officer or upon other information, that a dispute likely to cause a breach of the peace exists regarding any alleged right of user of any land or water within his local jurisdiction, whether such right be claimed as an easement or otherwise, he shall make an order in writing, stating the grounds of his being so satisfied and requiring the parties concerned in such dispute to attend his Court in person or by pleader on a specified date and time and to put in written statements of their respective claims.
>
> *Explanation.* The expression "land or water" has the meaning given to it in sub-section (2) of section 145.
>
> (2) The Magistrate shall then peruse the statements so put in, hear the parties, receive all such evidence as may be produced by them respectively, consider the effect of such evidence, take such further evidence, if any, as he thinks necessary and, if possible, decide whether such right exists; and the provisions of section 145 shall, so far as may be, apply in the case of such inquiry.
>
> (3) If it appears to such Magistrate that such rights exist, he may make an order prohibiting any interference with the exercise of such right, including, in a proper case, an order for the removal of any obstruction in the exercise of any such right:
>
> Provided that no such order shall be made where the right is exercisable at all times of the year, unless such right has been exercised within three months next before the receipt under sub-section (1) of the report of a police officer or other information leading to the institution of the inquiry, or where the right is exercisable only at particular seasons or on particular occasions, unless the right has been exercised during the last of such seasons or on the last of such occasions before such receipt.
>
> (4) When in any proceedings commenced under sub-section (1) of section 145 the Magistrate finds that the dispute is as regards an alleged right to user of land or water, he may, after recording his reasons, continue with the proceedings as if they had been commenced under sub-section (1);

19 *Mahar Jahan* v *State of Delhi* (2004)13 SCC 421.

and when in any proceedings commenced under sub-section (1) the Magistrate finds that the dispute should be dealt with under section 145, he may, after recording his reasons, continue with the proceedings as if they had been commenced under sub-section (1) of section 145.

A proceeding under this section is a *quasi*-judicial proceeding. If, therefore, the question at issue between the parties has already been the subject-matter of suit in the civil court, the trying Magistrate has no jurisdiction to institute the proceeding. The dispute contemplated by this section must at any rate be some substantial dispute necessitating the interference in some way or other of the criminal authorities. There must not only be a dispute regarding an alleged right of user of any land or water but under s. 147(3) it must also appear to the Magistrate that such right exists. There should be a present dispute and a present fear of disturbance and this section will not apply to state of things indicating that there may be a breach of peace in future.[20] The section applies to the disputes as to the right to use any land or water as distinct from disputes as to title or possession of the land itself for which provision is made in section 145. For initiating a proceeding under s. 147, CrPC two essential ingredients must be there: (*i*) there should be a *bona fide* dispute regarding user of any land or water; and (*ii*) that dispute is likely to cause breach of peace.[1]

204. *Issue of process.* (1) If in the opinion of a Magistrate taking cognizance of an offence there is sufficient ground for proceeding, and the case appears to be—

(*a*) a summons-case, he shall issue his summons for the attendance of the accused, or

(*b*) a warrant-case, he may issue a warrant, or, if he thinks fit, a summons, for causing the accused to be brought or to appear at a certain time before such Magistrate or (if he has no jurisdiction himself) some other Magistrate having jurisdiction.

(2) No summons or warrant shall be issued against the accused under sub-section (1) until a list of the prosecution witnesses has been filed.

(3) In a proceeding instituted upon a complaint made in writing, every summons or warrant issued under sub-section (1) shall be accompanied by a copy of such complaint.

(4) When by any law for the time being in force any process-fees or other fees are payable, no process shall be issued until the fees are paid and, if such fees are not paid within a reasonable time, the Magistrate may dismiss the complaint.

(5) Nothing in this section shall be deemed to affect the provisions of section 87.

20 *Jagabandhu* 4 CWN 351.
1 *Supriya Sen* v *State of Jharkhand* 2013 CrLJ 1750.

This section comes into play where the Magistrate does not dismiss the complaint under s. 203 but is of opinion that there is sufficient ground for proceeding and commences proceedings against the accused by compeling his attendance before the court. Section 204 relates to the procedure for effecting such attendance. Section 204 provides that the proceeding before the Magistrate commences upon taking cognizance of the offence and the issue of process to the accused.

Summoning of an accused in a criminal case is a serious matter. Criminal law cannot be set into motion as a matter of course. The order of the Magistrate summoning the accused must reflect that he has applied his mind to the facts of the case and the law applicable thereto.[2] So before issuing process the court should be satisfied that the accused was *prima facie* legally responsible for the offences charged. Whether he is liable or what are the defences open to him hardly matters for consideration at this stage.[3]

Once the case is committed to the court of session, it is not open to the Magistrate to issue summons to other person in exercise of power under s. 204(1)(*b*) of CrPC.[4]

> 205. *Magistrate may dispense with personal attendance of accused.* (1) Whenever a Magistrate issues a summons, he may, if he sees reason so to do, dispense with the personal attendance of the accused and permit him to appear by his pleader.
>
> (2) But the Magistrate inquiring into or trying the case may, in his discretion, at any stage of the proceedings, direct the personal attendance of the accused, and, if necessary, enforce such attendance in the manner hereinbefore provided.

Although this section speaks of issue of summons, it is not confined to summons cases only. In a warrant case also, a Magistrate may in his discretion under s. 204 issue a summons instead of a warrant and in that case he can dispense with the personal attendance of the accused. The section applies only where summons has been issued to the accused; if, however, a warrant is issued to compel his attendance his personal appearance cannot be dispensed with unless he is too ill to attend the court.

> 206. *Special Summons in cases of petty offence.* (1) If, in the opinion of a Magistrate taking cognizance of a petty offence, the case may be summarily disposed of under section 260 or section 261, the Magistrate shall, except where he is, for reason to be recorded in writing of a country opinion, issue summons to the accused requiring him either to appear in person or by pleader before the Magistrate on a specified date, or if he desires to plead

2 *Pepsi Foods Ltd.* v *Special Judicial Magistrate* AIR 1998 SC 128; (1998)5 SCC 749.

3 *Anil* v *State of Bihar* 1996 CrLJ 408 (Pat); *Sharma Thakur* v *State of Bihar* 2007 CrLJ (NOC) 55 (Pat).

4 *Ram Chandra Verma* v *State of Jharkhand* 2012 CrLJ 2906.

guilty to the charge without appearing before the Magistrate, to transmit before the specified date, by post or by messenger to the Magistrate, the said plea in writing and the amount of fine specified in the summons or if he desires to appear by pleader and to plead guilty to the charge through such pleader, to authorise, in writing, the pleader to plead guilty to the charge on his behalf and to pay fine through such pleader:

Provided that the amount of the fine specified in such summons shall not exceed one thousand rupees.

(2) For the purposes of this section "petty offence" means any offence punishable only with fine not exceeding one thousand rupees but does not include any offence so punishable under the Motor Vehicles Act 1939 (now Motor Vehicles Act 1988) or under any other law which provides for convicting the accused person in his absence on a plea of guilty.

(3) The State Government may, by notification, specially empower any Magistrate to exercise the powers conferred by sub-section (1) in relation to any offence which is compoundable under section 320 or any offence punishable with imprisonment for a term not exceeding three months, or with fine or with both where the Magistrate is of opinion that, having regard to the facts and circumstances of the case, the imposition of fine only would meet the ends of justice.

This section enables the accused to plead guilty without appearing in court to remit the predetermined fine. This section should be made applicable to trial of petty offences particularly those under local and special laws. This provision is similar to s. 208 of the Motor Vehicles Act 1988 (corresponding to s. 130 of the Act of 1939).[5]

209. *Commitment of case to Court of Session when offence is triable exclusively by it.* When in a case instituted on a police report or otherwise, the accused appears or is brought before the Magistrate and it appears to the Magistrate that the offence is triable exclusively by the Court of Session, he shall—

(*a*) commit, after complying with the provisions of section 207 or section 208, as the case may be, the case to the Court of Session, and subject to the provisions of this Code relating to bail, remand the accused to custody until such commitment has been made;

(*b*) subject to the provisions of this Code relating to bail, remand the accused to custody during, and until the conclusion of, the trial;

(*c*) send to that Court the record of the case and the documents and articles, if any, which are to be produced in evidence;

(*d*) notify the Public Prosecutor of the commitment of the case to the Court of Session.

The commitment inquiry has been dispensed with under the present code in places exclusively triable by the court of sessions and only some

5 *Ram Dial* v *State of Punjab* (1965)2 SCR 853; AIR 1965 SC 1518.

provision is made under this section for performing certain preliminary functions by the Magistrate, such as granting copies, preparing the records, notifying the public prosecutor etc.

The limited jurisdiction conferred on the Magistrate is only to verify the nature of offence.[6] The Magistrate committing the case to the court of session becomes *functus officio* after passing the order of the commitment under s. 209, CrPC. He cannot again take cognizance of the same offence which would include summoning of any other persons.[7]

> 310. *Local inspection.* (1) Any Judge or Magistrate may, at any stage of any inquiry, trial or other proceeding, after due notice to the parties, visit and inspect any place in which an offence is alleged to have been committed, or any other place which it is in his opinion necessary to view for the purpose of properly appreciating the evidence given at such inquiry or trial, and shall without unnecessary delay record a memorandum of any relevant facts observed at such inspection.
>
> (2) Such memorandum shall form part of the record of the case and if the prosecutor, complainant or accused or any other party to the case, so desires, a copy of the memorandum shall be furnished to him free of cost.

Local inspection is no substitute for evidence and a Judge who converts himself into a witness for the defence by holding local inspection for using it as evidence, exceeds his jurisdiction.[8] Similarly, local inspection cannot be used by the prosecution for the purpose of proving its case. When the property involved is movable property which can very well be brought before the court, no question arises for praying before the court for local inspection.[9]

> 356. *Order for notifying address of previously convicted offender.* (1) When any person, having been convicted by a Court in India of an offence punishable under section 215, section 489A, section 489B, section 489C or section 489D or section 506 (in so far as it relates to criminal intimidation punishable with imprisonment for a term which may extend to seven years or with fine or with both) of the Indian Penal Code (45 of 1860) or of any offence punishable under Chapter XII or Chapter XVI or Chapter XVII of that Code, with imprisonment for a term of three years or upwards, is again convicted of any offence punishable under any of those sections or Chapters with imprisonment for a term of three years or upwards by any Court other than that of a Magistrate of the second class, such Court may, if it thinks fit, at the time of passing a sentence of imprisonment on such person, also order that his residence and any change of, or absence from, such residence after release be

6 *Rattiram* v *State of MP* (2012)4 SCC 516.
7 *Sri Niwas Prosad* v *State* 2007 CrLJ 4498 (Pat).
8 *Keisam* v *State of Manipur* AIR 1958 SC 1664; (1985)3 SCC 676; 1986 CrLJ 17.
9 *State of Maharashtra* v *Dayaram Tukaram Raut* 1998 CrLJ 1333 (Bom).

notified as hereinafter provided for a term not exceeding five years from the date of the expiration of such sentence.

(2) The provisions of sub-section (1) with reference to the offences named therein, apply also to criminal conspiracies to commit such offences and to the abetment of such offences and attempts to commit them.

(3) If such conviction is set aside on appeal or otherwise such order shall become void.

(4) An order under this section may also be made by an Appellate Court or by the High Court or Court of Session when exercising its powers of revision.

(5) The State Government may, by notification, make rules to carry out the provisions of this section relating to the notification of residence or change of, or absence from, residence by released convicts.

(6) Such rules may provide for punishment for the breach thereof and any person charged with a breach of any such rule may be tried by a Magistrate of competent jurisdiction in the district in which the place last notified by him as his place of residence is situated.

443. *Power to order sufficient bail when that first taken is insufficient.* If, through mistake, fraud, or otherwise, insufficient sureties have been accepted, or if they afterwards become insufficient, the Court may issue a warrant of arrest directing that the person released on bail be brought before it and may order him to find sufficient sureties, and on his failing so to do, may commit him to jail.

446. *Procedure when bond has been forfeited.* (1) Where a bond under this Code is for appearance, or for production of property, before a Court and it is proved to the satisfaction of that Court, or of any Court to which the case has subsequently been transferred, that the bond has been forfeited,

or where, in respect of any other bond under this Code, it is proved to the satisfaction of the Court by which the bond was taken, or of any Court to which the case has subsequently been transferred, or of the Court of any Magistrate of the first class, that the bond has been forfeited,

the Court shall record the grounds of such proof, and may call upon any person bound by such bond to pay the penalty thereof or to show cause why it should not be paid.

Explanation. A condition in a bond for appearance, or for production of property, before a Court shall be construed as including a condition for appearance, or as the case may be, for production of property before any Court to which the case may subsequently be transferred.

(2) If sufficient cause is not shown and the penalty is not paid, the Court may proceed to recover the same as if such penalty were a fine imposed by it under this Code.

Provided that where such penalty is not paid and cannot be recovered in the manner aforesaid, the person so bound as surety shall be liable, by order of the Court ordering the recovery of the penalty, to imprisonment in civil jail for a term which may extend to six months.

(3) The Court may, after recording its reasons for doing so, remit any portion of the penalty mentioned and enforce payment in part only.

(4) Where a surety to a bond dies before the bond is forfeited, his estate shall be discharged from all liability in respect of the bond.

(5) Where any person who has furnished security under section 106 or section 117 or section 360 is convicted of an offence the commission of which constitutes a breach of the conditions of his bond, or of a bond executed in lieu of his bond under section 448, a certified copy of the judgment of the court by which he was convicted of such offence may be used as evidence in proceedings under this section against his surety or sureties, and, if such certified copy is so used, the court shall presume that such offence was committed by him unless the contrary is proved.

Two kinds of bonds are contemplated under s. 446: bond for appearance or for production of property before a court and other bonds. Under s. 446 action can be taken only when the bond is taken by the court under the provisions of this Code. This section clearly shows that a bond for the production of the property seized by the police must be executed before the court although a bond for the appearance of any person before the court can be taken by the police. This section also clearly enjoins that a bond can be forfeited only if it is executed before a court, or before a Magistrate of the first class. Section 446 requires the court to record grounds of the proof that the bond has been forfeited and a bond for the appearance is forfeited when the accused does not appear, but it does not require the court to issue notice to show cause why the bond should not be forfeited. The section shows that before a surety becomes liable to pay the amount of the bond forfeited, it is necessary to give notice why the amount should not be paid and in case he fails to show sufficient cause, only then the court can proceed to recover the money. Where no opportunity has been given to a surety to show cause why he should not be made to pay the amount of the bond, the proceeding cannot be said to be in accordance with law and should, therefore, be quashed.[10] The notice issued before the bond is forfeited is illegal. Notice has to be given to show cause why the penalty should not be executed. This section does not require a notice to surety to show cause why the bond should not be forfeited. If the party appears to show cause he should be allowed an opportunity to cross-examine the witnesses upon whose evidence the rule to show cause was issued.

When the accused was present in court in the morning but left the court due to illness, it is not a fit case for forfeiture of the bond because there was no wilful absence from court. So the prosecution of the sureties without

10 *Ghulan Mehdi* v *State of Rajasthan* AIR 1960 SC 1185.

issuing proper show cause notice and imposition of penalty straightway is not proper.[11] The accused was regularly attending the court but on the date of judgment he ran away from the premises of the court before judgment and since then he was absconding. So the forfeiture of the bond has been held to be proper without any show cause notice.[12]

> 476. *Forms.* Subject to the power conferred by Article 227 of the Constitution, the forms set forth in the Second Schedule, with such variations as the circumstances of each case require, may be used for the respective purposes therein mentioned, and if used shall be sufficient.

FORMS

Form 1

Summons to an accused person

(*See* section 61)

To

.... (*Name of accused*)
of .... (*address*).

WHEREAS your attendance is necessary to answer to a charge of (*state shortly the offence charged*), you are hereby required to appear in person (*or* by pleader, *as the case may be*) before the (*Magistrate*) of ......, on the .... day of .... Herein fail not.

Dated, this .... day of ...., 20.......

(*Seal of the Court*) Signature of Judge/Magistrate

Form 2

Warrant of arrest

(*See* section 70)

To

.... (*Name and designation of the person or persons who is or are to execute the warrant*).

WHEREAS (*name of accused*) of (*address*) stands charged with the offence of (*state the offence*), you are hereby directed to arrest the said .... and to produce him before me. Herein fail not.

Dated, this .... day of ......, 20......

(*Seal of the Court*) Signature of Judge/Magistrate

11 *Rajan* v *State* 2007 CrLJ 257 (Ker).
12 *Sahab* v *State* 2006 CrLJ 348 (MP).

(*See* section 71)

This warrant may be endorsed as follows:

If the said .... shall give bail himself in the sum of rupees .... with one surety in the sum of rupees ....(*or* two sureties each in the sum of rupees ......) to attend before me on the ...... day of ...... and to continue so to attend until otherwise directed by me, he may be released.

Dated, this ...... day of ......, 20 ......

(*Seal of the Court*) Signature of Judge/Magistrate

Form 3

Bond and Bail-bond after arrest under a warrant

(*See* section 81)

I, ... (*name*), of ...... , being brought before the District Magistrate of ......(*or as the case may be*) under a warrant issued to compel my appearance to answer to the charge of......, do hereby bind myself to attend in the Court of ......on the......day of......next, to answer to the said charge, and to continue so to attend until otherwise directed by the Court; and in case of my making default herein, I bind myself to forfeit, to Government, the sum of rupees...........

Dated, this ...... day of......, 20......

(Seal of the Court) Signature

I do hereby declare myself surety for the above-named......of ......, that he shall attend before......in the Court of......on the......day of......next, to answer to the charge on which he has been arrested, and shall continue so to attend until otherwise directed by the Court; and, in case of his making default therein, I bind myself to forfeit, to Government, the sum of rupees...........

Dated, this......day of ......, 20......

Signature of the surety

Form 4

Proclamation requiring the appearance of a person accused

(*See* section 82)

WHEREAS complaint has been made before me that (*name, description and address*) has committed (*or* is suspected to have committed) the offence of ......, punishable under section...... of the Indian Penal Code, and it has been returned to a warrant of arrest thereupon issued that the said (*name*) cannot be found, and whereas it has been shown to my satisfaction that the said (*name*) has absconded (*or* is concealing himself to avoid the service of the said warrant);

Proclamation is hereby made that the said......of......is required to appear at (*place*) before this Court (*or* before me) to answer the said complaint on the......day of......, 20......

Dated, this......day of......, 20......

(*Seal of the Court*) Signature of Judge/Magistrate

Form 5

Summons to witness

(*See* sections 61 and 244)

To

.... of ....

WHEREAS complaint has been made before me that .... (*name of the accused*) of .... (*address*) has (*or* is suspected to have) committed the offence of (*state the offence concisely with time and place*), and it appears to me that you are likely to give material evidence or to produce any document or other thing for the prosecution;

You are hereby summoned to appear before this Court on the .... day of .... next at ten o'clock in the forenoon, to produce such document or thing or to testify what you know concerning the matter of the said complaint, and not to depart thence without leave of the Court; and you are hereby warned that, if you shall without just excuse neglect or refuse to appear on the said date, a warrant will be issued to compel your attendance.

Dated, this .... day of ...., 20 ....

(*Seal of the Court*)

Signature of Judge/Magistrate

Form 6

Order of attachment to compel the appearance of a person accused

(*See* section 83)

To

.... (*Name and designation of the person or persons who is or are to execute or the warrant*).

WHEREAS complaint has been made before me that (*name, description and address*) has committed (*or* is suspected to have committed) the offence of .... punishable under section .... of the Indian Penal Code, and it has been returned to a warrant of arrest thereupon issued that the said (*name*) cannot be found; and whereas it has been shown to my satisfaction that the said (*name*) has absconded (*or* is concealing himself to avoid the service of the said warrant) and thereupon a proclamation has been or is being duly issued and published requiring the said......to appear to answer the said charge within......days; and whereas the said.........is possessed of the following property, other than land paying revenue to Government, in the village (*or* town), of .... in the District of .... *viz* ...., and an order has been made for the attachment thereof:

You are hereby required to attach the said property in the manner specified in clause (*a*), or clause (*c*), or both* of sub-section (2) of section 83 and to hold the same under attachment pending further order of this Court and to return this warrant with an endorsement certifying the manner of its execution.

Dated, this......day of ......, 20 ......

(*Seal of the Court*) Signature of Judge/Magistrate

* Strike out the one which is not applicable, depending on the nature of the property to be attached.

Form 7

Order of attachment to compel the attendance of a witness

(*See* section 83)

To

The Officer-in-Charge of the police station at ....

WHEREAS a warrant has been duly issued to compel the attendance of (*name, description and address*) to testify concerning a complaint pending before this court, and it has been returned to the said warrant that it cannot be served; and whereas it has been shown to my satisfaction that he has absconded (*or* is concealing himself to avoid the service of the said warrant); and thereupon a proclamation has been or is being duly issued and published requiring the said .... to appear and give evidence at the time and place mentioned therein;

This is to authorise and require you to attach by seizure the movable property belonging to the said .... to the value of rupees .... which you may find within the District of .... and to hold the said property under attachment pending the further order of this Court, and to return this warrant with an endorsement certifying the manner of its execution.

Dated, this ...... day of ......, 20......

(*Seal of the Court*) Signature of Judge/Magistrate

Form 8

Proclamation requiring the attendance of a witness

(*See* sections 32, 87 and 90)

WHEREAS complaint has been made before me that (*name, description and address*) has committed (*or* is suspected to have committed) the offence of (*mention the offence concisely*) and a warrant has been issued to compel the attendance of (*name, description and address of the witness*) before this court to be examined touching the matter of the said complaint; and whereas it has been returned to the said warrant that the said (*name of witness*) cannot be served, and it has been shown to my satisfaction that he has absconded (*or* is concealing himself to avoid the service of the said warrant);

Proclamation is hereby made that the said .... (*name*) is required to appear at (*place*) before the court of .... on the .... day of .... next at .... o'clock, to be examined touching upon the offence complained of.

Dated, this .... day of ...., 20.....

(*Seal of the Court*) Signature of Judge/Magistrate

Form 9

Warrant to search after information of a particular offence

(*See* section 93)

To

....

(*Name and designation of the police officer or other person or persons who is or are to execute the warrant*).

WHEREAS information has been laid (*or* complaint has been made) before me of the commission (*or* suspected commission) of the offence of .... (*mention the offence concisely*), and it has been made to appear to me that the production of .... (*specify the thing clearly*) is essential to the inquiry now being made (*or* about to be made) into the said offence (*or* suspected offence);

This is to authorise and require you to search for the said .... (*the thing specified*) in the .... (*describe the house or place or part thereof to which the search is to be confined*), and, if found, to produce the same forthwith before this Court returning this warrant, with an endorsement certifying what you have done under it, immediately upon its execution.

Dated, this .... day of .... 20, ...

(*Seal of the Court*)

Signature of Magistrate

Form 10

Warrant to search suspected place of deposit

(*See* section 94)

To

....

(*Name and designation of a police officer above the rank of a constable*).

WHEREAS information has been laid before me, and on due inquiry thereupon had, I have been led to believe that the .... (*describe the house or other place*) is used as a place for the deposit (*or* safe) of stolen property (*or if for either of the other purposes expressed in the section, state the purpose in the words of the section*);

This is to authorise and require you to enter the said house (*or other place*) with such assistance as shall be required, and to use, if necessary, reasonable force for that purpose, and to search every part of the said house (*or other place, or if the search is to be confined to a part, specify the part clearly*), and to seize and take possession of any property (*or* documents, *or* stamps, *or* seals, *or* coins, *or* obscene objects, *as the case may be*), (*add, when the case requires it*) and also of any instruments and materials which you may reasonably believe to be kept for the manufacture of forged documents, *or* counterfeit stamps, or false seals *or* counterfeit coins or counterfeit currency notes (*as the case may be*), and forthwith to bring before this Court such of the said things as may be taken possession of, returning this warrant, with an endorsement certifying what you have done under it, immediately upon its execution.

Dated, this .... day of ...., 20 ....

(*Seal of the Court*)

Signature of Magistrate

Form 11

Bond to keep the peace

(*See* sections 106 and 107)

....

WHEREAS I, ... (*name*) inhabitant of .... (*place*), have been called upon to enter into a bond to keep the peace for the term of .... or until the completion of the inquiry in the matter of .... now pending in the Court of ...., I hereby bind myself not to commit a breach of the peace, or do any act that may probably occasion a breach of the peace, during the said term or until the completion of the said inquiry and, in case of my making default therein, I hereby bind myself to forfeit to Government the sum of rupees ....

Dated, this .... day of ...., 20 .....

(Seal of the Court) Signature

Form 12

Bond for good behaviour

(*See* sections 108,109 and 110)

....

WHEREAS I, ... *(name)* inhabitant of .... *(place)* have been called upon to enter into a bond to be of good behaviour to Government and all the citizens of India for the term of ....*(State the period)* or until the completion of the inquiry in the matter of .... now pending in the Court of ...., I hereby bind myself to be of good behaviour to Government and all the citizens of India during the said term or until the completion of the said inquiry; and, in case of my making default therein, I hereby myself to forfeit to Government the sum of rupees ....

Dated, this .... day of ...., 20 .....

(Seal of the Court) Signature

(Where a bond with sureties is to be executed, add ....)

We do hereby declare ourselves sureties for the above-named .... that he will be of good behaviour to Government and all the citizens of India during the said term or until the completion of the said inquiry; and, in case of his making default therein, we bind ourselves, jointly and severally, to forfeit to Government the sum of rupees ....

Dated, this .... day of ...., 20 .....

(Seal of the Court) Signature

Form 13

Summons on information of a probable breach of the peace

(*See* section 113)

To

.... of ....

WHEREAS it has been made to appear to me by credible information that .... (*state the substance of the information*), and that you are likely to commit a breach of the peace (*or* by which act a breach of the peace will probably be occasioned), you are hereby required to attend in person (*or* by duly authorised agent) at the office of the Magistrate of .... on the .... day of 20 .... at ten o'clock in the forenoon, to show cause why you should not be required to enter into a bond for rupees .... [*when sureties are required, add*, and also to give security by the bond of one (*or* two, *as the case may be*) surety (*or* sureties) in the sum of rupees .... (*each if more than one*)], that you will keep the peace for the term of ....

Dated, this .... day of .... 20 ....

(*Seal of the Court*) Signature of Magistrate

Form 14

Warrant to enforce the payment of maintenance by attachment and sale

(*See* section 125)

To

....

(*Name and designation of the police officer or other person to execute the warrant*).

WHEREAS an order has been duly made requiring .... (*name*) to allow to his said wife (*or* child *or* father *or* mother) for maintenance the monthly sum of rupees .... and whereas the said .... (*name*) in wilful disregard of the said order has failed to pay rupees ...., being the amount of the allowance for the month (*or* months) of ....;

This is to authorise and require you to attach any movable property belonging to the said .... (*name*) which may be found within the district of ...., and if within ....(*state the number of days or hours allowed*) next after such attachment the said sum shall not be paid (or forthwith), to sell the movable property attached, or so much thereof as shall be sufficient to satisfy the said sum, returning this warrant, with an endorsement certifying what you have done under it, immediately upon its execution.

Dated, this .... day of ....., 20 ....

(*Seal of the Court*)

Signature of Magistrate

Form 15

Order for the removal of nuisance

(*See* section 133)

To

....

(*Name, description and address*).

WHEREAS it has been made to appear to me that you have caused an obstruction (*or* nuisance) to persons using the public roadway (*or other public place*) which, etc., ... (*describe the road or public place*), by etc., ... (*state what it is that causes the obstruction, or nuisance*) and that such obstruction (*or* nuisance) still exists;

Or

WHEREAS it has been made to appear to me that you are carrying on, as owner, or manager the trade or occupation of .... (*state the particular trade or occupation and the place where it is carried on*), and that the same is injurious to the public health (*or* comfort) by reason .... (*state briefly in what manner the injurious effects are caused*), and should be suppressed or removed to a different place;

Or

WHEREAS it has been made to appear to me that you are the owner (*or* are in possession of *or* have the control over) a certain tank (*or* well *or* excavation) adjacent to the public way (*describe the thorough fare*) and that the safety of the public is endangered by reason of the said tank (*or* well *or* excavation) being without a fence (*or* insecurely fenced);

Or

WHEREAS, etc. etc. (*as the case may be*);

I do hereby direct and require you within .... (*state the time allowed*) .... (*state what is required to be done to abate the nuisance*) or to appear at .... in the........... Court of .... on the .... day of .... next, and to show cause why this order should not be enforced;

Or

I do hereby direct and require you within (*state the time allowed*) to cease carrying on the said trade or occupation at the said place, and not again to carry on the same, or to remove the said trade from the place where it is now carried on, or to appear, etc.;

Or

I do hereby direct and require you within (*state the time allowed*) to put up a sufficient fence (*state the kind of fence and the part to be fenced*); or to appear, etc.;

Or

I do hereby direct and require you, etc. etc. (*as the case may be*).

Dated, this......day of ...... , 20 ......

(*Seal of the Court*)

Signature of Magistrate

Form 16

Magistrate's notice and pre-emptory order

(*See* section 141)

To

.... (*Name, description and address*)

I hereby give you notice that it has been found that the order issued on ...... day of .... requiring you (*state substantially the requisition in the order*) is reasonable and proper. Such order has been made absolute, and I hereby direct and require you to obey the said order within (*state the time allowed*), on peril of the penalty provided by the Indian Penal Code for disobedience thereto.

Dated, this .... day of ...., 20 ....

(*Seal of the Court*)

Signature of Magistrate

Form 17

Injunction to provide against imminent danger pending inquiry

(*See* section 142)

To

.... (*Name, description and address*).

WHEREAS the inquiry into the conditional order issued by me on the .... day of .... 20 ...., is pending, and it has been made to appear to me that the nuisance mentioned in the said order is attended with such imminent danger or injury of a serious kind to the public as to render necessary immediate measures to prevent such danger or injury, I do hereby, under the provisions of section 142 of the Code of Criminal Procedure 1973, direct and enjoin you forthwith to .... (*state plainly what is required to be done as a temporary safeguard*), pending the result of the inquiry.

Dated, this .... day of ...., 20 ....

(*Seal of the Court*) Signature of Magistrate

Form 18

Magistrate's order prohibiting the repetition, etc., of a nuisance

(*See* sections 133 and 144)

To

.... (*Name, description and address*)

WHEREAS it has been made to appear to me that, etc., ... (*state the proper recital, guided by* Form No. 20 *or* Form No. 24 *as the case may be*);

I do hereby strictly order and enjoin you not to repeat or continue, the said nuisance.

Dated, this .... day of ...., 20 ....

(*Seal of the Court*)

Signature of Magistrate

Form 19

Magistrate's order to prevent obstruction, riot, etc.

(*See* section 144)

To

.... (*Name, description and address*)

WHEREAS it has been made to appear to me that you are in possession (*or* have the management) of .... (*describe clearly the property*), and that, in digging a drain on the said land, you are about to throw or place a portion of the earth and stones dug-up upon the adjoining public road, so as to occasion risk of obstruction to persons using the road.

or

WHEREAS it has been made to appear to me that you and a number of other persons (*mention the class of persons*) are about to meet and proceed in a procession along the public street, etc., (*as the case may be*) and that such procession is likely to lead to a riot or an affray;

or

WHEREAS etc., etc., (*as the case may be*);

I do hereby order you not to place or permit to be placed any of the earth or stones dug from land on any part of the said road;

or

I do hereby prohibit the procession passing along the said street, and strictly warn and enjoin you not to take any part in such procession (*or as the case recited may require*).

Dated, this .... day of ...., 20 ......

(*Seal of the Court*) Signature of Magistrate

Form 20

Magistrate's order declaring party entitled to retain possession of land, etc., in dispute

(*See* section 145)

It appears to me, on the grounds duly recorded, that a dispute, likely to induce a breach of the peace, existed between .... (*describe the parties by name and residence, or residence only if the dispute be between bodies of villagers*) concerning certain .... (*state concisely the subject of dispute*), situate within my local jurisdiction, all the said parties were called upon to give in a written statement of their respective claims as to the fact of actual possession of the said .... (*the subject of dispute*), and being satisfied by due inquiry had thereupon, without reference to the merits of the claim of either of the said parties to the legal right of possession, that the claim of actual possession by the said ..... (*name or names or description*) is true, I so decide and declare that he is (*or* they are) in possession of the said .... (*the subject of dispute*) and entitled to retain such possession until ousted by due course of law, and do strictly forbid any disturbance of his (*or* their) possession in the meantime.

Dated, this .... day of ...., 20 ....

(*Seal of the Court*)

Signature of Magistrate

Form 21

Special summons to a person accused of a petty offence

(See section 206)

To

....

Name of the accused

of .... *(address)*

WHEREAS your attendance is necessary to answer a charge of a petty offence .... (*state shortly the offence charged*), you are hereby required to appear in person (*or by pleader*) before .... (Magistrate) of .... on the .... day of .... 20 ...., or if you desire to plead guilty to the charge without appearing before the Magistrate, to transmit before the aforesaid date the plea of guilty in writing and the sum of .... rupees as fine, or if you desire to appear by pleader and to plead guilty through such pleader, to authorise such pleader in writing to make such a plea of guilty on your behalf and to pay the fine through such pleader. Herein fail not.

Dated, this .... day of ...., 20 ....

(*Seal of the Court*)

Signature of Magistrate

NOTE. The amount of fine specified in this summons shall not exceed one hundred rupees.

Form 22

Notice of commitment by Magistrate to public prosecutor

(See section 209)

The Magistrate of .... hereby gives notice that he has committed one .... for trial at the next Sessions; and the Magistrate hereby instructs the Public Prosecutor to conduct the prosecution of the said case ....

The charge against the accused is that, etc., (*state the offence as in the charge*).

Dated, this...... day of......, 20 ......

(*Seal of the Court*) Signature of Magistrate

Form 23

Magistrate's or Judge's warrant of commitment of witness refusing to answer or to produce docunment

(See section 349)

To

.... (*name and designation of officer of Court*).

WHEREAS .... (*name and description*), being summoned (*or* brought before this Court), as a witness and this day required to give evidence on an inquiry into an alleged offence, refused to answer a certain question (*or* certain questions) put to him touching the said alleged offence, and duly recorded, or having been called upon to produce any document has refused to produce such document, without alleging any just excuse for such refusal, and for his refusal has been ordered to be detained in custody for .... (*term of detention adjudged*);

This is to authorise and require you to take the said .... (*name*) into custody, and him safely to keep in your custody for the period of .... days, unless in the meantime he shall consent to be examined and to answer the questions asked of him, or to produce the document called for from him, and on the last of the said days, or forthwith on such consent being known, to bring him before this Court to be dealt with according to law, returning this warrant with an endorsement certifying the manner of its execution.

Dated, this .... day of ...., 20 ....

(*Seal of the Court*)

Signature of Judge/Magistrate

Form 24

Warrant for recovery of fine

(See section 421)

To the Collector of the district of ....

WHEREAS .... *(name, address and description of the offender)* was on the .... day of ... 20........, convicted before me of the offence of .... *(mention the offence concisely),* and sentenced to pay a fine of rupees ....; and

WHEREAS the said .... *(name),* although required to pay the said fine, has not paid the same or any part thereof;

You are hereby authorised and requested to realise the amount of the said fine as arrears of land revenue from the movable or immovable property, or both, of the said .... *(name)* and to certify without delay what you may have done in pursuance ol this order.

Dated, this .... day of ...., 20....

(Seal of the Court) Signature of Magistrate

Form 25

Warrant to discharge a person imprisoned on failure to give security

(*See* section 442)

To

The Officer-in-Charge of the Jail at ....
(*or other officer in whose custody the person is*)

WHEREAS .... (*name and description of prisoner*) was committed to your custody under warrant of this Court, dated the .... day of ......, and has since with his surety (*or* sureties) duly executed a bond under section 441 of the Code of Criminal Procedure.

This is to authorise and require you forthwith to discharge the said .... (*name*) from your custody, unless he is liable to be detained for some other matter.

Dated, this......day of...... , 20......

(*Seal of the Court*) Signature of Magistrate

Form 26

Warrant of attachment to enforce a bond

(*See* section 446)

To

The Officer-in-Charge of the police station at...........

WHEREAS .... (*name, description and address of person*) has failed to appear on .... (*mention the occasion*) pursuant to his recognizance, and has by default forfeited to Government the sum of rupees .... (*the penalty in the bond*); and whereas the said .... (*name of person*) has, on due notice to him, failed to pay the said sum or show any sufficient cause why payment should not be enforced against him;

This is to authorise and require you to attach any movable property of the said .... (*name*) that you may find within the district of ...., by seizure and detention, and, if the said amount be not paid within .... days, to sell the property so attached or so much of it as may be sufficient to realise the amount aforesaid, and to make return of what you have done under this warrant immediately upon its execution.

Dated, this......day of...... , 20......

(*Seal of the Court*) Signature of Magistrate

Form 27

Notice to surety on breach of a bond

(*See* section 446)

To

.... of.........

WHEREAS on the ...... day of......, 20......, you became surety for (*name*) of (*place*) that he should appear before this Court on the......day of ...... and bound yourself in default thereof to forfeit the sum of rupees.........to Government; and whereas the said (*name*) has failed to appear before this Court and by reason of such default you have forfeited the aforesaid sum of rupees.........

You are hereby required to pay the said penalty or show cause, within ......days from this date, why payment of the said sum should not be enforced against you.

Dated, this......day of...... , 20......

(*Seal of the Court*) Signature of Magistrate

Form 28

Notice to surety of forfeiture of bond for good behaviour

(*See* section 446)

To

.... of ....

WHEREAS on the.........day of ......, 20 ......, you became surety by a bond for (*name*) of (*place*) that he would be of good behaviour for the period of .... and bound yourself in default thereof to forfeit the sum of rupees..............to Government; and whereas the said (*name*) has been convicted of the offence of (*mention the offence concisely*) committed since you became such surety, whereby your security bond has become forfeited;

You are hereby required to pay the said penalty of rupees.........or to show cause within......days why it should not be paid.

Dated, this......day of...... , 20 ......

(*Seal of the Court*)

Signature of Magistrate

Form 29

Warrant of attachment against a surety

(*See* section 446)

To

.... of ....

WHEREAS (*name, description and address*) has bound himself as surety for the appearance of (*mention the condition of the bond*) and the said (*name*) has made default, and thereby forfeited to Government the sum of rupees .... (*the penalty in the bond*).

This is to authorise and require you to attach any movable property of the said (*name*) which you may find within the district of ...., by seizure and detention; and, if the said amount be not paid within .... days, to sell the property so attached, or so much of it as may be sufficient to realise the amount aforesaid, and make return of what you have done under this warrant immediately upon its execution.

Dated, this......day of......, 20 ......

(*Seal of the Court*)

Signature of Magistrate

Form 30

Warrant of commitment of the surety of an accused person admitted to bail

(*See* section 446)

To

The Superintendent (*or Keeper*) of the Civil Jail at.................

WHEREAS .... (*name and description of surety*) has bound himself as a surety for the appearance of .... (state the condition of the bond) and the said .... (*name*) has therein made default whereby the penalty mentioned in the said bond has been forfeited to Government; and whereas the said .... (*name of surety*) has, on due notice to him, failed to pay the said sum or show any sufficient cause why payment should not be enforced against him, and the same cannot be recovered by attachment and sale of his movable property, and an order has been made for his imprisonment in the Civil Jail for .... (*specify the period*);

This is to authorise and require you, the said Superintendent (*or Keeper*) to receive the said .... (*name*) into your custody with this warrant and to keep him safely in the said Jail for the said .... (*term of imprisonment*), and to return this warrant with an endorsement certifying the manner of its execution.

Dated, this ...... day of ......, 20......

(*Seal of the Court*)

Signature of Magistrate

Form 31

Notice to the principal of forfeiture of bond to keep the peace

(*See* section 446)

To

.... (*name, description and address*)

WHEREAS on the ...... day of......, 20......, you entered into a bond not to commit, etc., ... (*as in the bond*), and proof of the forfeiture of the same has been given before me and duly recorded;

You are hereby called upon to pay said penalty of rupees.........or to show cause before me within......days why payment of the same should not be enforced against you.

Dated, this ...... day of ......, 20 ......

(*Seal of the Court*) Signature of Magistrate

Form 32

Warrant to attach the property of the principal on breach of a bond to keep the peace

(*See* section 446)

To

.... (*Name and designation of police officer*), at the police station of ....

WHEREAS .... (*name and description*) did, on the......day of......, 20......, enter into a bond for the sum of rupees.........binding himself not to commit a breach of the peace, etc., (*as in the bond*), and proof of the forfeiture of the said bond has been given before me and duly recorded; and whereas notice has been given to the said ....(*name*) calling upon him to show cause why the said sum should not be paid, and he has failed to do so or to pay the said sum;

This is to authorise and require you to attach by seizure movable property belonging to the said .... (*name*) to the value of rupees........., which you may find within the district of ......and, if the said sum be not paid within......, to sell the property so attached, or so much of it as may be sufficient to realise the same; and to make return of what you have done under this warrant immediately upon its execution.

Dated, this......day of...... , 20 ......

(*Seal of the Court*) Signature of Magistrate

Form 33

Warrant of imprisonment on breach of a bond to keep the peace

(*See* section 446)

To

The Superintendent (or Keeper) of the Civil Jail at.................

WHEREAS .... proof has been given before me and duly recorded that .... (*name and description*) has committed a breach of the bond entered into by him to keep the peace, whereby he has forfeited to Government the sum of rupees.........; and whereas the said .... (*name*) has failed to pay the said sum or to show cause why the said sum should not be paid, although duly called upon to do so, and payment thereof cannot be enforced by attachment of his movable property, and an order has been made for the imprisonment of the said (*name*) in the Civil Jail for the period of .... (*term of imprisonment*);

This is to authorise and require you, the said Superintendent (or Keeper) of the said Civil Jail to receive the said .... (*name*) into your custody, together with this warrant, and to keep him safely in the said Jail for the said period of .... (*term of imprisonment*), and to return this warrant with an endorsement certifying the manner of its execution.

Dated, this .... day of ......, 20......

(*Seal of the Court*) Signature of Magistrate

Form 34

Warrant of imprisonment on forfeiture of bond for good behaviour

(*See* section 446)

To

The Superintendent (or Keeper) of the Civil Jail at.................

WHEREAS .... (*name, description and address*) did, on the day of ...., 20......, give security by bond in the sum of rupees .... for the good behaviour of .... (*name, etc., of the principal*) and proof of the breach of the said bond has been given before me and duly recorded, whereby the said .... (*name*) has forfeited to Government the sum of rupees........., and whereas he has failed to pay the said sum or to show cause why the said sum should not be paid although duly called upon to do so, and payment thereof cannot be enforced by attachment of his movable property, and an order has been made for the imprisonment of the said .... (*name*) in the Civil Jail for the period of .... (*term of imprisonment*);

This is to authorise and require you, the Superintendent (or Keeper), to receive the said .... (*name*) into your custody, together with this warrant, and to keep him safely in the said Jail for the said period of .... (*term of imprisonment*), returning this warrant with and endorsement certifying the manner of its execution.

Dated, this......day of...... , 20 ......

(*Seal of the Court*) Signature of Magistrate

Form 35

Warrant of attachment and sale on forfeiture of bond for good behaviour

(*See* section 446)

To

The Officer-in-Charge of the police station at..............

WHEREAS .... (*name, description and address*) did, on the......day of......, 20 ......, give security by bond in the sum of rupees.........for the good behaviour of .... (*name, etc., of the principal*), and proof has been given before me and duly recorded of the commission by the said .... (*name*) of the offence of .... whereby the said bond has been forfeited; and whereas notice has been given to the said .... (*name*) calling upon him to show cause why the said sum should not be paid, and he has failed to do so or to pay the said sum;

This is to authorise and require you to attach by seizure movable property belonging to the said .... (*name*) to the value of rupees .... which you may find within the district of........, and if the said sum be not paid within..........., to sell the property so attached, or so much of it as may be sufficient to realise the same, and to make return of what you have done under this warrant immediately upon its execution.

Dated, this ....day of ...... , 20......

(*Seal of the Court*) Signature of Magistrate

Form 36

Form of General Notice under s. 30(2) of the Police Act 1861

(Act V of 1861)

[Regulation 135]

WHEREAS I .... District/Assistant/Deputy Superintendent of Police .... District, am satisfied that it is intended by persons interested in the religious festival/industrial dispute between .... and there employees to convene or collect an assembly on a public road and to form a procession in the public streets or thoroughfares at ....

And whereas in the judgment of the District/Sub-divisional Magistrate such assembly or procession, if held during the period .... to .... during the continuance of the abovementioned religious festival/industrial dispute, and if uncontrolled, would be likely to cause a breach of the peace;

Now, therefore, in exercise of the power conferred by sub-section (2) of section 30 of the Police Act 1861 (Act V of 1861). I do hereby require any such persons to submit to me, at least .... days before any date that may be fixed for such assembly or procession, an application for a licence and to state therein the reason for such assembly and procession, the times of such assembly and procession, the place at which such assembly will meet or from which such procession will start, the route by which such procession will pass and the number of persons who are likely to attend such assembly or to take part in such procession, together with all other details required to be included in such licence.

Date .... 20 ....

Superintendent/
Assistant Superintendent/
Deputy Superintendent of Police

Form 37

Notice regarding apprehended breach of peace

[Regulation 252]

To ....

Owner

Occupier

At village .... Police Station .... District ....

Sir,

Information has reached me of the likelihood of a breach of the peace in respect of a dispute regarding* .... situated at and bounded as below in which you are interested as owner or occupier. I have therefore to request you to use all lawful means in your power as required by section 154, Indian Penal Code, to prevent any breach of the peace. In order to impress upon you your responsibility under the provision of the said section it is reproduced on the back for ready reference.

Boundaries of the place on which/about which breach of the peace is apprehended:

1. North– 3. East–

2. South– 4. West–

Sub-Inspector of Police

Police Station ....

District ....

* Here enter the matter or right in dispute.

Form 38

Postcard intimation to informants of cases of the action taken by police station officers

(Regulation 257)

From

The Officer-in-Charge,

.... police station

To

....

....

Sir,

The case under section .... reported by you on .... has been registered in this police station as case No. .... dated .... As there are not sufficient grounds for entering on an investigation the police do not propose to investigate the case.

I have, etc.

Signature

CHAPTER 23

Notices under the Securities and Exchange Board of India Act 1992 (SEBI)

SYNOPSIS

1 Corporate Governance
2 Conditions for continued listing (Clause 40A)
3 Disclosures by insiders

The Securities and Exchange Board of India Act 1992 provides for the establishment of a Board (SEBI) with a view to protecting the interest of the investors in securities and to promoting the development of the stock market as well as to regulating the securities market and connected matters.

Section 55A of the Companies Act 1956 was inserted by the Companies (Amendment) Act 2000 with effect from 13th December 2000.

Section 24 of the Companies Act 2013 which is corresponds to s. 55A of the Companies Act 1956.

Section 24 of the Act of 2013 reads as follows:

"24. *Power of Securities and Exchange Board to regulate issue and transfer of securities, etc.* (1) The provisions contained in this Chapter [Chapter III Prospectus and Allotment of Securities], Chapter IV [Share Capital and Debenture] and in section 127 shall—

(*a*) in so far as they relate to—

(*i*) issue and transfer of securities; and

(*ii*) non-payment of dividend,

by listed companies or those companies which intend to get their securities listed on any recognized stock exchange in India, except as provided under this Act, be administered by the Securities and Exchange Board by making regulations in this behalf;

(*b*) in any other case, be administered by the Central Government.

Explanation. For the removal of doubts it is hereby declared that all powers relating to all other matters relating to prospectus return of allotment, redemption of preference shares and any other matter specifically provided in this Act, shall be exercised by the Central Government, the Tribunal or the Registrar, as the case may be.

(2) The Securities and Exchange Board shall, in respect of matters specified in sub-section (1) and the matters delegated to it under proviso to sub-section (1) of section 458, exercise the powers conferred upon it under sub-sections (1), (2A), (3) and (4) of section 11, sections 11A, 11B and 11D of the Securities and Exchange Board of India Act 1992 (15 of 1992)."

The object of the changes made *inter alia* in s. 24 is to provide that the Securities and Exchange Board of India be entrusted with powers with regard to all matters relating to public issues and transfers including power to prosecute defaulting companies and their Directors (s. 439). It will be evident from the provisions that these relate to three matters namely (*i*) issue of securities; (*ii*) transfer of securities and (*iii*) non-payment of dividend. A listed public company is a public company which has its securities listed on any recognized stock exchange.

A public company as defined under s. 2(71) of the Companies Act 2013 desirous of getting its shares listed on a recognized stock exchange shall apply for this purpose to the Stock Exchange with documents and particulars as prescribed under Securities Contracts (Regulation) Act.

Section 40 of the Companies Act 2013 provides for compulsory listing of public issues. Two pre-conditions for valid allotments are specified:

(*i*) minimum subscription (s. 39); and

(*ii*) listing permission (s. 40).[1]

It has been clearly provided in the Act that if a Single Stock Exchange out of the Stock Exchanges applied for refuses to grant permission, the entire allotment becomes void unless, of course, the refusal of the Stock Exchange is set aside on appeal.[2]

In the event of the application for listing being granted such listing shall be subject to rules and bye-laws of the exchange from time to time and the company will comply with such further listing requirements as may be promulgated by the Exchange as a general condition for new listing. A listing agreement must be executed by and between the Stock Exchange and the Company and the company is required to strictly comply with the listing agreement.

1 Corporate Governance

Clause 49 of the listing agreement deals with Corporate Governance. Clause 49 as originally framed has been amended by SEBI in or about

1 *Rich Paints Ltd.* v *Vadodara Stock Exchange Ltd.* (1998)15 SCL 128 (Guj).

2 *Rishyashringa Jewllery Ltd.* v *Stock Exchange, Bombay* (1996)85 Comp Cas 479; AIR 1996 SC 480; *Rich Paints Ltd.* v *Vadodara Stock Exchange Ltd.* (1998)15 SCL 128 (Guj).

October 2004. Clause 49 supplements s. 173 of the Companies Act 2013 to the extent that it specifically states that the Board shall meet at least four times a year with a maximum time gap of three months between any two Board Meetings of a listed company. For such Board Meeting at least seven days' notice have to be given. Similarly seven days' notice is required to be given for holding meeting of Audit Committee, Remuneration Committee and Shareholders Committee.

2 Conditions for continued listing (Clause 40A)

Clause 40A of the listing agreement deals with the conditions for continued listing. In the event of the application for listing being granted by the Exchange, the Company shall maintain on a continuous basis, the minimum level of non-promoter holding at the level of public shareholding as required at the time of listing. Where the non-promoter holding of an existing listed company as on 1st April 2001 is less than the limit of Public shareholding as required at the time of initial listing, the Company shall within one year raise the level of non-promoter holding to at least 10%. In case the Company fails to do so, it shall buy-back the public shareholding in the manner prescribed in the SEBI (Buy-back of Securities) Regulations 1998 as amended in 2017. The following shall also be the condition for continued listing:

(*a*) When any person acquires or agrees to acquire 5% or more of the voting rights of any securities, the acquirer and the Company shall comply with the relevant provisions of the SEBI (Buy-back of Securities) Regulations 1998 as amended in 2017.

(*b*) When any person acquires or agrees to acquire any securities exceeding 15% of the voting rights in any Company or if any person who holds securities which in aggregate carries less than 15% of the voting rights of the company and seeks to acquire the securities exceeding 15% of the voting rights, such person shall not acquire any securities exceeding 15% of the voting rights of the Company without complying with the relevant provisions of the SEBI (Buy-back of Securities) Regulations 1998 as amended in 2017.

SEBI (Buy-back of Securities) Regulations 1998 as amended in 2017

In exercise of the powers conferred by sub-secs. (1) and (2) of s. 11 and s. 30 of the Securities and Exchange Board of India Act 1992 read with cl. (*f*) of sub-sec. (2) of s. 68 of the Companies Act 2013, the Board made the Securities and Exchange Board of India (Buy-back of Securities) Regulations 1998 (as amended, later in 2017).

A company may buy-back its shares or other specified securities by any one of the following methods:

(*a*) from the existing security-holders on a proportionate basis through the tender offer;

(*b*) from the open market through—

(*i*) book-building process,

(*ii*) stock exchange;

(*c*) from odd-lot holders:

Provided that no offer of buy-back for fifteen percent or more of the paid-up capital and free reserves of the company shall be made from the open market. [Regulation 4(1)]. The company shall not make any buy-back offer within a period of one year from the date of closure of the proceeding buy-back offer [Regulation 4(4)]. A company is obliged to pass a special resolution in a general meeting in this behalf and to file a copy of the resolution with the Board and the stock exchanges listing the specified securities within two working days of the passing of the resolution. [Regulation 5A]. The company shall also make a public announcement, within two working days from the date of the special resolution in at least one English National Daily, one Hindi National Daily and a Regional language daily and the announcement shall contain all material information as specified in Schedule II, Part A. [Regulation 8(1)].

As per Regulation 7, the explanatory statement annexed to the notice for the general meeting for the purpose of giving, buy-back offer by the company (mandatory under Regulation 5) has to contain the disclosures as specified in Schedule II, Part A. The said statement shall also make the following (additional) disclosures:

(*a*) the maximum price at which the buy-back of shares or other specified securities shall be made and whether the Board of Directors of the Company are being authorised in the general meeting to determine subsequently the specific price at which the buy-back may be made at the appropriate time;

(*b*) if the promoter intends to offer their shares or other specified securities—

(*i*) the quantum of shares or other specified securities proposed to be tendered, and

(*ii*) the details of their transactions and their holdings for the last six months prior to the passing of the special resolution for buy-back including information of number of shares or other specifier securities acquired, the price and the date of acquisition.

According to Regulation 11, the company shall complete the verifications of offers received and make payment of consideration to those security holders whose offer has been accepted or return the shares or other specified securities to the security-holders within seven working days of the closoure of the offer. The company shall furnish a certificate to the Board certifying compliance of the Regulation No. 12.

FORMS

Form 1

Information to the Stock Exchange to be sent at least 7 days before the meeting

Dated .... 20.......

The Secretary
The Calcutta Stock Exchange Association Ltd.
7 Lyons Range
Kolkata 700 001

Dear Sir,

Sub: Approval of un-audited results for the quarter ended on 31.3.20 .... as per Clause 41 of the Listing Agreement - Board Meeting.

We have to inform you that the accounts for the year ending on 31.3. 20 .... will be approved in the Board Meeting scheduled to be held on 30.4.20 ...... at 4 p.m. along with other regular agenda.

On approval, the audited results for the quarter ended on 31.3.20 ...... shall be published pursuant to Clause 41 of the listing agreement.

Please acknowledge.

Yours faithfully,

For XYZ Company Ltd.

....

Company Secretary

Form 2

Notice to be published in the newspaper at least 7 days before the meeting

NOTICE

XYZ Company Ltd.
Regd Office
....
....

NOTICE is hereby given that a meeting of the Board of Directors of the Company will be held on .... at the registered office of the Company at 4 p.m. *inter alia* to consider and take on record the Unaudited Results of the Company for the quarter ended on 31st March, 20 ....

Yours faithfully,

For XYZ Company Ltd.

....

Company Secretary

Place: Kolkata
Date:

Form 3

Format contents of the Public Announcement

1. The Public Announcement shall be dated and signed on behalf of the Board of Directors of the company by its manager or secretary, if any, and by not less than two directors of the company one of whom shall be a managing director where there is one.

2. A full and complete disclosure of all material facts including the following shall be made:

Disclosures under Regulations 5(1) and 8(1)

(*i*) Date of the Board meeting at which the proposal for buy-back was approved by the Board of Directors of the company;

(*ii*) Necessity for the buy-back;

(*iii*) Maximum amount required under the buy-back and its percentage of the total paid up capital and free reserves;

(*iv*) Maximum price at which the shares or other specified securities are proposed be bought back and the basis of arriving at the buy-back price;

(*v*) Maximum number of securities that the company proposes to buy-back;

(*vi*) Method to be adopted for buy-back as referred to in sub-regulation (1) of regulation 4;

(*vii*) (*a*) the aggregate shareholding of the promoter and of the directors of the promoters, where the promoter is a company and of persons who are in control of the company as on the date of the notice convening the General Meeting or the Meeting of the Board of Directors;

(*b*) aggregate number of shares or other specified securities purchased or sold by persons including persons mentioned in (*a*) above from a period of six months preceding the date of the Board Meeting at which the buy-back was approved till the date of notice convening the general meeting;

(*c*) the maximum and minimum price at which purchases and sales referred to in (*b*) above were made along with the relevant dates;

(*viii*) Intention of the promoters and persons in control of the company to tender shares or other specified securities for buy-back indicating the number of shares or other specified securities, details of acquisition with dates and price;

(*ix*) A confirmation that there are no defaults subsisting in repayment of deposits, redemption of debentures or preference shares or repayment of term loans to any financial institutions or banks;

(*x*) A confirmation that the Board of Directors has made a full enquiry into the affairs and prospects of the company and that they have formed the opinion—

(*a*) that immediately following the date on which the General Meeting or the Meeting of the Board of Directors is convened there will be no grounds on which the company could be found unable to pay its debts;

(*b*) as regards its prospects for the year immediately following that date that, having regard to their intentions with respect to the management of the company's business during that year and to the amount and character of the financial resources which will in their view be available to the company during that year, the company will be able to meet its liabilities as and when they fall due and will not be rendered insolvent within a period of one year from that date; and

(*c*) in forming their opinion for the above purposes, the directors shall take into account the liabilities as if the company were being wound up under the provisions of the Companies Act 1956 (including prospective and contingent liabilities);

(*xi*) A report addressed to the Board of Directors by the company's auditors stating that–

(*i*) they have inquired into the company's state of affairs;

(*ii*) the amount of the permissible capital payment for the securities in question is in their view properly determined; and

(*iii*) the Board of Directors have formed the opinion as specified in clause (*x*) on reasonable grounds and that the company will not, having regard to its state of affairs, will not be rendered insolvent within a period of one year from that date.

Form 4

Format disclosure under the SEBI (Buy-back of Securities) Regulation 15(*d*)

In addition to the disclosures in Part A, the following disclosures shall be made:

(*i*) Date of shareholders approval for buy-back, if applicable;

(*ii*) Minimum and maximum number of securities that the company proposes to buy-back, sources of funds from which the buy-back would be made and the cost of financing the buy-back;

(*iii*) Proposed time table from opening of offer till the extinguishment of the certificates;

(*iv*) Process and methodology to be adopted for the buy-back;

(*v*) Brief information about the company;

(*vi*) Audited Financial information for the last 3 years and the lead manager shall ensure that the particulars (audited statement and un-audited statement) contained therein shall not be more than 6 months old from the date of the public announcement together with financial ratios as may be specified by the Board;

(*vii*) Details of escrow account opened and the amount deposited therein;

(*viii*) Listing details and stock market data:

(*a*) high, low and average market prices of the securities of the company proposed to be bought back, during the preceding three years;

(*b*) monthly high and low prices for the six months preceding the date of the public announcement;

(*c*) the number of securities traded on the days when the high and low prices were recorded on the relevant stock exchanges during the period stated at (*a*) and (*b*) above;

(*d*) the stock market data referred to above shall be shown separately for periods marked by a change in capital structure, with such period commencing from the date the concerned stock exchange recognises the change in the capital structure, (e.g. when the securities have become ex-rights or ex-bonus);

(*e*) the market price immediately after the date of the resolution of the Board of Directors approving the buy-back; and

(*f*) the volume of securities traded in each month during the six months preceding the date of the public announcement along with high, low and average prices of securities of the company, details relating to volume of business transacted should also be stated for respective periods;

(*ix*) Present capital structure (including the number of fully paid and partly paid securities) and shareholding pattern;

(*x*) The capital structure including details of outstanding convertible instruments, if any post buy-back;

(*xi*) Aggregate shareholding of the promoter group and of the directors of the promoters, where the promoter is a company and of persons who are in control of the company;

(*xii*) Aggregate number of shares or other specified securities purchased or sold by persons mentioned in clause (*xi*) above during a period of twelve months preceding the date of the public announcement; the maximum and minimum price at which purchases and sales referred to above were made along with the relevant dates;

(*xiii*) Management discussion and analysis on the likely impact of buy-back on the company's earnings, public holdings, holdings of NRIs/FIIs etc., promoters holdings and any change in management structure;

(*xiv*) Details of statutory approvals obtained;

(*xv*) Collection and bidding centres;

(*xvi*) Name of compliance officer and details of investors service centres;

(*xvii*) Such other disclosures as may be specified by the Board from time to time by way of guidelines.

Form 5

Format disclosure to be made in the Letter of offer under the SEBI (Buy-back of Securities) Regulation 8(4)

The letter of offer shall be dated and signed on behalf of the Board of Directors of the company by its manager or secretary, if any, and by not less than two directors of the company one of whom shall be a managing director where there is one.

The letter of offer shall, *inter alia*, contain the following:

(*i*) Disclosures in Schedule II;

(*ii*) Disclaimer Clause as may be specified by the Board;

(*iii*) Record date and ratio of buy-back as per the entitlement in each category.

SEBI (Prohibition of Insider Trading) Regulations 2015

In exercise of the powers conferred by s. 30 read with cl. (*g*) of sub-sec. (2) of s. 11 and cl. (*d*) and cl. (*e*) of s. 12A of the Securities and Exchange Board of India Act, the Board made the SEBI (Prohibition of Insider Trading) Regulations 2015.

An insider means any person who is: (*i*) a connected person; or (*ii*) in possession of or having access to unpublished price sensitive information [Regulation 2(1)(*g*)]. A connected person, according to Regulation 2(1)(*d*), means any person who is or has during the six months prior to the concerned act been associated with a company, directly or indirectly, in any capacity including by reason of frequent communication with its officers or by being in any contractual, fiduciary or employment relationship or by being a director, officer or an employee of the company or holds any position including a professional or business relationship between himself and the company whether temporary or permanent, that allows such person, directly or indirectly access to unpublished price sensitive information or is reasonably expected to allow such access. An immediate relative of such connected persons shall be deemed to be a connected person. Similarly, a concern, firm, trust Hindu undivided family, or association of persons wherein a director of a company or his immediate relative or banker of the company has more than ten per cent of the holding or interest is deemed to be a connected person.

3 Disclosures by insiders

The disclosures to be made by any insider shall include those relating to trading by such person's immediate relatives and by any other person for whom such person takes trading decisions. These regulations are primarily aimed at prevention of abuse by trading by persons when in possession of unpublished price sensitive information. These disclosures are to be made at two stages: initial and continual.

As per Regulation 7(1), every promoter, key managerial personnel and director of every listed company shall disclose his holding of securities of the company as on the date of effect of these Regulations to the company within thirty days of these Regulations taking effect. Also, every person on appointment as a key managerial personnel or upon becoming a promoter shall disclose his holding of securities of the company as on the date of appointment or becoming a promoter, to the company within seven days of such appointment or becoming a promoter.

Continual disclosures are laid down in Regulation 7(2). Every promoter, employee and director of every company shall disclose to the company the number of such securities acquired or disposed of within two trading days of such transaction if the value of the securities traded, whether in one transaction or a services of transactions over any calendar quarter, aggregates to a traded value in excess of ten lakh rupees. Every company then shall notify the particulars of such trading to the stock exchange on which the securities are listed, within two trading days of receipt of the disclosure or from becoming aware of such information.

Form 1

Securities and Exchange Board of India (Prohibition of Insider Trading) Regulations 2015

[Regulation 7(2)]

Regulation 7(2) - Details shares held by Director or Officer of a Listed Company

Name & Address of Director/ Officer	*Date of assuming office of Director/ Officer*	*No. & % of shares/voting right held at the time of becoming Director/ Officer*	*Date of intimation to company*	*Mode of acquisition (market purchase/ public/ rights/ preferential offer, etc.)*	*Trading member through whom the trade was executed with SEBI Registration No. of the TM*	*Exchange on which the trade was executed*	*Buy quantity*	*Buy value*

Form 2

Securities and Exchange Board of India (Prohibition of Insider Trading) Regulations 2015

[Regulation 7(2)]

Regulation 7(2) - Details of change in shareholding of Director or Officer of a Listed Company

Name & Address of Director/ Officer	*No. & % of shares/voting right held by the Director/ Officer*	*Date of receipt of allotment advice/ acqui-sition/ sale of shares/ voting rights*	*Date of intimation to Company*	*Mode of acquisition (market purchase/ public rights preferential offer, etc.)*	*No. & % of shares/post acquisition/ voting rights sale*	*Trading member through whom the trade was executed with SEBI Registration No. of the TM*	*Exchange on which the trade was executed*	*Buy quantity*	*Buy value*	*Sell quantity*	*sell value*

CHAPTER 24

Notices under the Industrial Disputes Act 1947

SYNOPSIS

1 'Notice of change' of conditions of service in an industrial employment (s. 9A)
2 Conditions of service for change of which a 'Notice of change' is to be given
3 Notice for strike and lock-outs (s. 22)—strike in public utility services—r. 71 of the Central Rules
4 Strike in public utility services—what is a strike?
5 On whom notice of strikes and lock-outs to be given—Industrial Disputes (Central) Rules in that behalf
6 Lay-off by employer–right of workmen–notice of lay-off—closure and lay-off—difference
7 Notice of lay-off–form of notice—commencement and termination of lay-off—r. 75A of the Industrial Disputes (Central) Rules 1957
8 Notice of retrenchment—conditions precedent to retrenchment of workmen (s. 25F)—State Rules (W.B.I.D. Rule No. 77—Central Rule No. 76)
9 Notice to workmen on transfer of undertaking (s. 25FF)
10 Notice to workmen on closure
11 Compensation to workmen in case of closing down of undertakings–notice to workmen (s. 25FFF)

1 'Notice of change' of conditions of service in an industrial employment (s. 9A)

The Industrial Dispute Act 1947 is a piece of legislation calculated to ensure social justice to both employers and employees and advance progress in industries by bringing out harmony and cordial relationship between the parties.[1]

The object of s. 9A is that conditions of service in force when workman entered service should not be changed to his prejudice.[2] Change in the conditions of service is not prohibited but the service of a notice is a condition precedent.

We may note here the relevant law as embodied in s. 9A of the Industrial Disputes Act 1947.

1 *Dindigal Skin Merchants' Association* v *Industrial Tribunal* AIR 1953 Mad 102.
2 AIR 1968 Mad 280 (283).

"9A. *Notice of change*. No employer, who proposes to effect any change in the conditions of service applicable to any workman in respect of any matter specified in the Fourth Schedule, shall effect such change,—

(*a*) without giving to the workmen, likely to be affected by such change, a notice in the prescribed manner of the nature of the change proposed to be effected; or

(*b*) within 21 days of giving such notice:

Provided that no notice shall be required for effecting any such change—

(*a*) where the change is effected in pursuance of any settlement or award; or

(*b*) where the workmen likely to be affected by the change are persons to whom the Fundamental and Supplementary Rules, Civil Services (Classification, Control and Appeal) Rules, Civil Services (Temporary Service) Rules, Revised Leave Rules, Civil Service Regulations, Civilians in Defence Services (Classification, Control and Appeal) Rules or the Indian Railway Establishment Code or any other rules or regulations that may be notified in this behalf by the appropriate Government in the Official Gazette, apply.

The notice of change to workmen is necessary when workmen are likely to be affected prejudicially by such change. There are three stages for effecting a change. It starts with the proposal by the employer to effect a change. The second stage is the time when the notice is given. The third stage is when the change is given effect to on the expiry of 21 days (42 days in case of West Bengal)[3] from the date of the notice. The conditions of service will change when only the new conditions of service are actually introduced.

Fourth Schedule of the Industrial Disputes Act 1947 provides matters in respect of which prescribed notice of change is required which includes the following:

(1) Wages, including the period and mode of payment;

(2) Contribution paid, or payable, by the employer to any provident fund or pension fund or for the benefit of the workmen under any law for the time being in force;

(3) Compensatory and other allowances;

(4) Hours of work and rest intervals;

(5) Leave with wages and holidays;

(6) Starting, alteration or discontinuance of shift working otherwise than in accordance with standing orders;

(7) Classification by grades;

3 West Bengal Act 57 of 1980 (s. 4).

(8) Withdrawal of any customary concession or privilege or change in usage;

(9) Introduction of new rules of discipline, or alteration of existing rules, except insofar as they are provided in standing orders;

(10) Rationalisation, standardisation or improvement of plant of technique which is likely to lead to retrenchment of workmen;

(11) Any increases or reduction (other than casual) in the number of persons employed or to be employed in any occupation or process or department or shift, not occasioned by circumstances over which the employer has no control.

If any change which is proposed by the employer does not relate to any matter as provided in the Fourth Schedule, the provisions of s. 9A of the Industrial Disputes Act will not be attracted.[4]

If working hours is not shown to be a condition of service, the increase in working hours will not attract the provisions of s. 9A. Increase within limits of law is within competence of management.[5] In *Kerala Electricals and Allied Engineering Company Ltd. Workers Congress* v *District Labour Officer*[6] it was held that an employer cannot enhance the working hours merely by giving a notice under s. 9A of the Industrial Disputes Act 1947.

Whether any particular practice or allowance or concession or compensatory allowance[7] had become a condition of service would always depend upon the facts and circumstances of the each case.[8] Non-payment of wages amounts to alteration in conditions of service.[9]

The change of weekly off-day without loss of wages will not amount to change of conditions of service, so no notice in this regard will be necessary.[10] Changing declared the date of Diwali holiday to next date on request of majority of workers. This is not an alteration in conditions of service within s. 9A or s. 33(2)(*a*) of the Act.[11]

The action of a management in giving a notice of change under s. 9A of the Act in so far as payment of overtime to staff car drivers is concerned, is not justified for the reason that the management of the project entered into

4 *L. Robert D'Souza* v *Executive Engineer* AIR 1982 SC 854; (1982)1 LLJ 330; 1982 Lab IC 811.
5 *Oil & Natural Gas Commission* v *The Workmen* AIR 1973 SC 968; (1973)3 SCC 535.
6 2002 LLR 68 (Ker).
7 *The Management of Indian Oil Corporation Ltd.* v *Workmen* (1975)2 LLJ 319.
8 *Hindustan Lever Limited* v *Ram Mohan Roy* AIR 1973 SC 1156; (1973)4 SCC 141.
9 *Ibid*, p. 1162.
10 *Bajaj Tempo Ltd.* v *Bhartiya Kamgar Sena* 2002 LLR 644 (Bom).
11 *Assam Match Co. Ltd.* v *Bijoy Lal Sen* AIR 1973 SC 2155.

the settlement with the car drivers on a mistaken belief under the provisions of the Motor Transport Workers Act 1961.[12]

Change in weekly off day on the sole ground of shortage of material—giving notice to Inspector and putting notice on Display Board cannot be dispensed with.[13] Voluntary retirement scheme approved under s. 10(10C) of the Income Tax Act 1961 will not make the scheme void *ab initio* for absence of notice to employees. Notice, however, must be given at or before the offer date.[14] Circulars of State Bank of India directing local Head Offices to obtain undertaking from employee that in case he is elected in election, he will immediately resign from banks service circulars are not violative of s. 9A.[15]

If an *ad hoc* employment was given as a humanitarian measure even for a short period and it was put to an end after negotiation of contract of labour with the society formed by workers themselves s. 9A of the Industrial Disputes Act 1947 is not applicable.[16]

2 Conditions of service for change of which a 'Notice of change' is to be given

Notice is not necessary for any and every change. But if the intended change relates to any of the items in the Schedule, the above notice is necessary.

Unilateral action of management including Saturday and Sunday in holiday amounts to change in condition of service, there being loss of working day absence of notice is violative of statutory provision.[17]

Rule 34 of the Industrial Disputes (Central) Rules 1957, enjoins:

> "Any employer intending to effect any change in the conditions of service applicable to any workman in respect of any matter specified in the Fourth Schedule to the Act shall give notice of such intention in Form 'E'.
>
> The notice shall be displayed conspicuously by the employer on a notice board at the main entrance to the establishment in the Manager's office:
>
> Provided that where any registered trade union of workmen exists, a copy of the notice shall also be served by registered post on the Secretary of such union."

Where a notice of change is mandatory, its failure makes the change *ultra vires* and inoperative.

12 *Workmen of the Rajasthan Power Project* v *Management* (1976)1 LLJ 271 (SC).
13 *Hartex Tubes Pvt. Ltd.* v *Asst. Commissioner of Labour* 1998(1) Lab IC 1790 (Bom).
14 *KEC International Ltd.* v *Kamani Employees Union* 1998(2) Lab IC 2604 (Bom).
15 *General Manager, (Operation) State Bank of India* v *State Bank of India Staff Union* (1998)1 LLJ 1063 (SC); 1998(1) Lab IC 1390 (SC).
16 *International Airport Authority of India* v *International Air Cargo Workers' Union* (2009)13 SCC 374.
17 *Voltas Volkart Employees Union, Madras* v *Voltas Limited* 2000 Lab IC 917.

Section 9A and item (8) of the 4th Schedule—change in weekly days of rest from Sunday to some other day—omission to give notice of change to workmen. *Held*, change is ineffective.[18]

Whenever an employer unilaterally proposes to effect any change in respect of any of the matters specified in the Fourth Schedule, he ought to give notice as provided by this section. The provision safeguards the interests of the employees in that it prohibits an employer from taking any action in the specified matters without notice. When a notice is given to the employees, they can take such steps as the law permits them to take before the changes proposed by the employer are brought into effect by his unilateral action.[19]

We have noticed above that a notice is not a must in all cases. Notice held not necessary—Change in the conditions of service of workmen sought to be done in pursuance of settlement between the employer and the employee—notice under s. 9A is not required for effecting such change.[20]

Notice of change will not be necessary when the retrenchment of a workman is not because of rationalisation.[21]

Provision of s. 9A not complied with by the employer before ordering a change in the day of rest—order unlawful—workmen not turning up for work on the original day of rest do not go on strike.[22]

Merely declaring certain categories of posts to constitute a cadre and transferable within the cadre does not amount to classification by grades—Hence without prior notice to employees is not violative of s. 9A.[23]

3 Notice for strike and lock-outs (s. 22)—strike in public utility services—r. 71 of the Central Rules

Strikes[1] and lock-outs[2] are very common in an industrial set-up. But there should be certain restrictions.

18 AIR 1972 SC 1917.

19 *Krishnarajendra Mills Workers' Union* v *Asst. Labour Commissioner* AIR 1968 Mys 49.

20 73 CWN 381.

21 *Engineering and Ancillary Manufacturers* v *Salim Khan* 2004 LLR 685 (Bom).

22 AIR 1967 Pat 397.

23 *Orissa State Warehousing Corporation Ltd.* v *Employees Union* 1994 SCC (L&S) 1031; 1994 Supp (2) SCC 486.

1 'Strike' means a cessation of work by a body of persons employed in any industry acting in combination, or a concerted refusal, or a refusal, under a common understanding, of any number of persons who are or have been so employed to continue to work or to accept employment [s. 2(*q*) of the I.D. Act].

2 'Lock-out' means the temporary closing of a place of employment, or the suspension of work, or the refusal by an employer to continue to employ any number of persons employed by him [s. 2(*l*) of the I.D. Act].

The intention of the legislature in enacting s. 22 is to provide sufficient safeguards in matters of public utility services[3] as, otherwise great inconvenience to the society and the general public would result. The section does not restrain the worker from going on strike but only requires him to fulfil certain conditions before doing so.[4]

We quote below the provision contained in s. 22 of the Industrial Disputes Act 1947.

> "22. *Prohibition of strikes and lock-outs.* (1) No person employed in a public utility service shall go on strike, in breach of contract—
>
> (*a*) without giving to the employer notice of strike, as hereinafter provided, within six weeks before striking; or
>
> (*b*) within 14 days of giving such notice; or
>
> (*c*) before the expiry of the date of strike specified in any such notice as aforesaid; or
>
> (*d*) during the pendency of any conciliation proceedings before a Conciliation Officer and seven days after the conclusion of such proceedings.
>
> (2) No employer carrying on any public utility service shall lock-out any of his workmen—
>
> (*a*) without giving them notice of lock-out as hereinafter provided, within six weeks before locking-out; or
>
> (*b*) within 14 days of giving such notice; or
>
> (*c*) before the expiry of the date of lock-out specified in any such notice as aforesaid; or
>
> (*d*) during the pendency of any conciliation proceedings before a Conciliation Officer and seven days after the conclusion of such proceedings.

---

3 'Public utility service' means—

(*i*) any railway service or any transport service for the carriage of passengers or goods by air;

(*ia*) any service in, or in connection with the working of, any major port or dock;

(*ii*) any section of an industrial establishment, on the working of which the safety of the establishment, or the workmen employed therein depends;

(*iii*) any postal, telegraph or telephone service;

(*iv*) any industry which supplies power, light or water to the public;

(*v*) any system of public conservancy or sanitation;

(*vi*) any industry specified in the First Schedule which the appropriate Government may, if satisfied that public emergency or public interest so requires, by notification in the Official Gazette, declare to be a public utility service for the purposes of this Act, for such period as may be specified in the notification:

Provided that the period so specified shall not, in the first instance, exceed six months but may, by a like notification, be extended from time to time, by any period not exceeding six months, at any one time, if in the opinion of the appropriate Government, public emergency or public interest requires such extension [s. 2(*n*) of the I.D. Act].

4 *State of Bihar* v *Deodar Jha* AIR 1958 Pat 51.

(3) The notice of lock-out or strike under this section shall not be necessary where there is already in existence a strike or, as the case may be, lock-out in the public utility service, but the employer shall send intimation of such lock-out or strike on the day on which it is declared, to such authority as may be specified by the appropriate Government either generally or for a particular area or for a particular class of public utility services.

(4) The notice of strike referred to in sub-section (1) shall be given by such number of persons to such person or persons and in such manner as may be prescribed.

(5) The notice of lock-out referred to in sub-section (2) shall be given in such manner as may be prescribed.

(6) If on any day an employer receives from any person employed by him any such notices as are referred to in sub-section (1) or gives to any persons employed by him any such notices as are referred to in sub-section (2), he shall within five days thereof report to the appropriate Government or to such authority as that Government may prescribe, the number of such notices received or given on that day."

4 Strike in public utility services—what is a strike?

To constitute strike, it is necessary that there should be cessation of work, but it is not necessary that there must be total suspensions of work because partial stoppage of work would be strike. Cessation of work even for a few hours as a result of the concerted action of the workers amounts to a strike.[5] Again, refusal under a common understanding to continue to work is a strike and, if in pursuance of such common understanding the employees entered the premises of the employer and refused to take their pens in their hands that would no doubt be a strike under s. 2(*q*) of the Act.[6]

A strike which does not contravene restrictions imposed by the Act is legal. Section 24 enumerates situations where a strike would be illegal:

(1) A strike or a lock-out shall be illegal if— (*i*) it is commenced or declared in contravention of s. 22 or s. 23; or (*ii*) it is continued in contravention of an order made under sub-sec. (3) of s. 10 or sub-sec. (4A) of s. 10A.

(2) Where a strike or lock-out in pursuance of an industrial dispute has already commenced and is in existence at the time of the reference of the dispute to a Board, an arbitrator, a Labour Court, Tribunal or National Tribunal, the continuance of such strike or lock-out shall not be deemed to be illegal, provided that such strike or lock-out was not at its commencement in contravention of the provisions of this Act or the continuance thereof was not prohibited under sub-sec. (3) of s. 10 or sub-sec. (4A) of s. 10A.

5 *Buckingham & Carnatic Mills* v *Workmen* AIR 1953 SC 47; (1953)1 LLJ 181.
6 *Punjab National Bank* v *All India PNB Employee's Federation* AIR 1960 SC 160.

(3) A lock-out declared in consequence of an illegal strike or a strike declared in consequence of an illegal lock-out shall not be deemed to be illegal.

We, therefore, would note that the right to strike is an inherent right of every worker and the same could not be abridged or taken away except in conformity with statutory provisions.[7] Workers have right to strike but they should not obstruct others not-striking workers.[8] In a Patna case, the right to resort to strike was upheld and it was held: 'In India, every strike is not illegal because the workers enjoy a fundamental right to resort to strike whenever they are so pleased in order to express their grievances or to make certain demands. Under the Indian law, strikes are only illegal when penalties have been imposed for them for contravention of the provisions of ss. 22, 23 and 24'.[9]

Law is, however, different with respect to 'public utility services' and 'non-public utility services'.

In a public utility service, strike is prohibited—

(*i*) without giving notice [s. 22(1)(*a*)];[10]

(*ii*) during pendency of conciliation proceedings before the Conciliation Officer [s. 22(1)(*d*)];

(*iii*) during adjudication or arbitration proceedings or conciliation proceedings before a Board [ss. 23(*a*), 23(*b*), 23(*bb*)];

(*iv*) during the period in which the settlement or award is in operation in respect of any of the matters covered by the settlement or award [s. 23(*c*)].

In a non-public utility service, a strike without a notice is not illegal. It would be illegal when it contravenes the general prohibition of strikes and lock-outs in s. 23 of the Act.

For our limited study on the law, we are concerned with the notice. A strike resorted to without giving a notice as required by the Standing Orders cannot be justified in law whatever may be the grievances which led to it.[11] A strike resorted to without giving a notice as required by s. 22 is an illegal strike. Whether the strike was provoked or not is immaterial.

Lock-out

Lock-out means the temporary closing of a place of employment or the suspension of work, or the refusal by an employer to continue to employ any

7 *Andhra Pradesh State Road Transport Corporation Employee's Union* v *APSRTC* 1970 Lab IC 1225 (AP).

8 *T.C.M. Ltd.* v *District Collector* 1998 LLR 302 (Ker).

9 *State of Bihar* v *Deodar Jha* AIR 1958 Pat 51.

10 *U.P. State Bridge Corpn. Ltd.* v *U.P. Rajya Setu Nigam* 2004 (SCI) GSX 0129 C SC.

11 AIR 1958 Raj 202.

number of persons employed by him.[12] While lock-out is the closure of the place of business, lay-off is failure, refusal or inability of an employer to give employment to one or more workmen for reasons stated in sub-sec. (*kkk*) of s. 2 of the Act including circumstances enumerated in s. 25E(*iii*) of the Act, i.e. strike or slowing-down of production on the part of the workmen in another part of the establishment. Suspension of work due to trade reasons cannot be treated as lock-out.[13]

Under Rule 72 of the Industrial Disputes (Central) Rules, the notice of lock-out to be given by an employer carrying on a public utility service shall be in Form "M".[14]

In case of lay-off, the employer may be liable to pay compensation as provided in ss. 25C, 25D and 25E of the Act; but the liability of the employer to pay wages in case of lock-out would depend upon whether the lock-out was justified and legal or not.

The notice of strike to be given by workmen in a public utility service, under Rule 71 of the Industrial Disputes (Central) Rules, shall be in Form 'L'.[15]

5 On whom notice of strikes and lock-outs to be given—Industrial Disputes (Central) Rules in that behalf

A notice of strike is to be given by the workmen or their union to the employer in Form L.[16] And a notice of lock-out is to be displayed by the employer in Form M on a notice board at the main entrance to the establishment and in the Manager's office. But where a registered trade union exists, a copy of such notice shall also be served on that registered trade union.[17]

Under Rule 74 of the Industrial Disputes (Central) Rules 1957, a report of notice of a strike or lock-out to be submitted by the employer under sub-sec. (6) of s. 22, shall be sent by registered post or given personally to the Assistant Labour Commissioner (Central) appointed for the local area concerned, with copy by registered post to—

(1) The Administrative Department of the Government of India concerned,

(2) the Regional Labour Commissioner (Central) for the zone,

12 Section 2(*l*) of the Industrial Disputes Act 1947.

13 *Gordon Woodroffe Ltd.* v *Govt. of Tamil Nadu* (1997)2 LLJ 64 (Mad).

14 As to Form of notice of a lock-out see Forms *infra*.

15 For cognate legislation—Rule 73 of the Industrial Disputes (Bihar) Rules 1961 in Form L.
Rule 52(1) of the Hyderabad Industrial Disputes Rules 1950—Form E. Rule 73 of the W.B. Industrial Disputes Rules 1957, no particular form is prescribed.

16 Rule 71 of the Industrial Disputes (Central) Rules 1957.

17 Rule 72 of the Industrial Disputes (Central) Rules 1957.

(3) Chief Labour Commissioner (Central),

(4) Ministry of Labour of the Government of India,

(5) Labour Department of the State Government concerned, and

(6) the District Magistrate concerned.

Lock-out does not fall under the definition of lay-off in s. 2(*kkk*) so as to entitle the workers to claim lay-off compensation under s. 25C.[18]

6 Lay-off by employer—right of workmen—notice of lay-off—closure and lay-off—difference

In s. 2(*kkk*) lay-off has been defined as: Lay-off (with its grammatical variations and cognate expressions) means the failure, refusal or inability of an employer on account of shortage of coal, power or raw materials or the accumulation of stocks or the breakdown of machinery or natural calamity or for any other connected reason to give employment to a workman whose name is borne on the muster rolls of his industrial establishment and who has not been retrenched.

Lay-off is a temporary refusal or inability of an employer for the reasons mentioned in the sub-section to give employment to workmen. The conditions under which a workman shall be deemed to have been laid off have been given in the 'Explanation' to this sub-section. The unemployment has to be on account of a cause which is independent of every action on the part of the workmen themselves.[19]

Closure and lay-off

The term 'closure' has not been defined in the Industrial Disputes Act. Expressions 'closure' and 'lay-off' are not interchangeable. 'Lay-off' as defined in the Act is the failure, refusal or inability of an employer due to reasons beyond his control to give employment to workmen. The conditions under which a workman shall be deemed to have been laid-off have been precisely stated in the 'Explanation' below the cl. (*kkk*) of s. 2 of the Act. But 'closure' is simply the closing of business permanently or temporarily for an indefinite period by the management.

7 Notice of lay-off—form of notice—commencement and termination of lay-off—r. 75A of the Industrial Disputes (Central) Rules 1957

Rule 75A of the Industrial Disputes (Central) Rules enjoin:

> "Rule 75A. (1) If any workman employed in an industrial establishment as defined in the Explanation below section 25A (not being an industrial

18 *Management of Kairbetta Estate, Kotagiri P.O.* v *Rajamanickam* AIR 1960 SC 893; (1960)2 LLJ 275.

19 *Central India Spinning Wvg. and Mfg. Co. Ltd.* v *State Industrial Court* (1959)1 LLJ 468.

establishment referred to in sub-section (1) of that section) is laid-off, then, the employer concerned shall give notices of commencement and termination of such lay-off in Forms O-1 and O-2[20] respectively within seven days of such commencement or termination, as the case may be.

(2) Such notices shall be given by an employer in every case irrespective of whether, in his opinion, the workman laid-off is or is not entitled to compensation under section 25C."

Barely mentioning that the closure of the factory "will lead to a large-scale unemployment" is not enough to issue a notice of lay-off and, as such notices issued to different petitioners are, therefore, declared to be null and void.[1]

8 Notice of retrenchment—conditions precedent to retrenchment of workmen (s. 25F)—State Rules (W.B.I.D. Rule No. 77—Central Rule No. 76)

Section 2(*oo*) of the Industrial Disputes Act provides the meaning of retrenchment as:

'Retrenchment' means the termination by the employer of the service of a workman for any reason whatsoever, otherwise than as a punishment inflicted by way of disciplinary action but does not include—

(*a*) voluntary retirement of the workman; or

(*b*) retirement of the workman on reaching the age of superannuation if the contract of employment between the employer and the workman concerned contains a stipulation in that behalf; or

(*bb*) termination of the service of the workman as a result of the non-renewal of the contract of employment between the employer and the workman concerned on its expiry or of such contract being terminated under a stipulation in that behalf contained therein; or

(*c*) termination of the service of a workman on the ground of continued ill-health.

Retrenchment may be justified under certain circumstances as an industrial policy. The Industrial Disputes Act does not contain any provision for penalizing lay-off and retrenchment. Though the Act provides for sixty days' notice by the employers prior to closing down an establishment employing upto 300 (now 100) persons it does not provide for any prior scrutiny of the reasons for such closure. The employers have an unfettered right to close down an establishment subject to the provision of sixty days' notice.

20 For Forms: See *infra*.

1 *Indian Nut Products* v *Union of India* (1994)4 SCC 269.

In the case where 300 (now 100) or more workmen are employed under the new amendment by inserting chapter V-B in the Act, prior approval of the appropriate Government is necessary.[2]

The management can retrench its employees only for proper reasons, which means that it must not be actuated by any motive of victimisation or any unfair labour practice. It is for the management to decide the strength of its labour force. If the number of employees exceeds the reasonable and legitimate needs of the undertaking, it is open to the management to retrench them. Workmen may become surplus on the ground of rationalisation or economy reasonably or *bona fide* adopted by the management or on the ground of other industrial or trade reasons, and the right to effect retrenchment cannot normally be challenged, but when there is a dispute about the validity of retrenchment, the impugned retrenchment must be shown as justified on proper reasons, i.e. that it was not capricious or without rhyme or reason.[3]

'Retrenchment' means discharge of a workman on grounds of surplusage.[4] Retrenchment means 'to end, conclude cease'.[5] Therefore, discharge of a workman on grounds of health,[6] or on any other ground is not retrenchment. Termination of service on superannuation[7] is not retrenchment.

Section 25F enjoins: "No workman employed in any industry who has been in continuous service[8] for not less than one year under an employer shall be retrenched by that employer until—

(*a*) the workman has been given one month's notice in writing indicating the reasons for retrenchment and the period of notice has expired, or the workman has been paid in lieu of such notice, wages for the period of the notice;

(*b*) the workman has been paid, at the time of retrenchment, compensation which shall be equivalent to 15 days' average pay for every completed year of continuous service or any part thereof in excess of six months; and

(*c*) notice in the prescribed manner is served on the appropriate Government or such authority as may be specified by the appropriate Government by notification in the Official Gazette."

2 *Workmen of Minakshi Mills* v *Minakshi Mills Ltd.* (1992)2 LLJ 294.
3 *Parry & Co. Ltd.* v *P.C. Pal* AIR 1970 SC 1334.
4 AIR 1962 SC 1363.
5 *State Bank of India* v *N. Sundara Mony* (1976)1 SCC 82.
6 *National Garage* v *J. Gonsalves* AIR 1962 Bom 152; *Hindalco Industries Ltd.* v *Labour Court, Varanasi* (2001)9 SCC 178.
7 *British India Corporation Ltd.* v *Industrial Tribunal* AIR 1962 Punj 154.
8 Continuous service—defined in s. 25B of the Industrial Disputes Act 1947.

Before we proceed on to the question of notice, the word 'retrenchment', as explained judicially, has to be seen. Termination of service in accordance with the service rules is not retrenchment.[9] Termination of service on the *bona fide* closure or transfer of business is not retrenchment.[10]

Section 25F(*a*) requires one month's notice, stating reasons for retrenchment, on the workman:

(*i*) notice to be in writing;

(*ii*) retrenchment to take effect after expiry of the notice period;

(*iii*) in lieu of notice, wages for the period of notice have been paid to the workman.

The provision of s. 25F is mandatory. Requirements prescribed under s. 25F(*b*) is a condition precedent for the retrenchment of workmen. Failure to comply with the provisions of s. 25F(*b*) would render the impugned retrenchment invalid.[11]

Clauses (*a*) and (*b*) prescribe conditions precedent to a retrenchment. The requirement of cl. (*c*) is also a mandatory requirement and the same must be complied with even though it may not be a condition precedent.[12]

Notice of retrenchment is not necessary where the employer pays salary for the notice period.[13] (Rule 77 of the W.B. Industrial Disputes Rules 1958).

Under the proviso to Rule 77(1) of the West Bengal Industrial Disputes Rules 1958, when the employer retrenches an employee with immediate effect by paying him wages in lieu of notice, he shall, immediately after such retrenchment, give notice thereof to the Labour Commissioner and the Conciliation Officer.

When the notice of retrenchment was not given immediately after the retrenchment, but two days before it, although payment of wages was made, the company had substantially complied with the requirement of the proviso to sub-rule (1) of r. 77 of the West Bengal Industrial Disputes Rules.[14]

Non-compliance with s. 25F renders the retrenchment invalid.[15]

9 *Sujit Kantha Neogi* v *Union of India* AIR 1970 Ass 131.

10 AIR 1965 Ker 112.

11 *State of Bombay* v *Hospital Mazdoor Sabha* AIR 1960 SC 610 and inoperative *Beni Bhuj Sahu* v *Chief Engineer, Hirakud Dam Project* AIR 1970 Ori 9; *Workmen of Subong Tea Estate* v *The Outgoing Management of Subong Tea Estate* AIR 1967 SC 420.

12 *Bombay Union of Journalists* v *State of Bombay* AIR 1964 SC 1617.

13 AIR 1964 Ass 66.

14 *Parry & Co. Ltd.* v *P.C. Lal* AIR 1970 SC 1334; (1970)2 LLJ 429.

15 AIR 1967 SC 420.

Notice calling upon an employee to receive payment subsequent to retrenchment cannot be regarded as payment and the retrenchment would be illegal.[16]

Under r. 76[17] of the Industrial Disputes (Central) Rules:

> 76. If any employer desires to retrench any workman employed in his industrial establishment, who has been in continuous service for not less than one year under him (hereinafter referred to as "workman" in this rule and in Rules 77 and 78), he shall give notice of such retrenchment as in Form 'P' to the Central Government, the Regional Labour Commissioner (Central) and Assistant Labour Commissioner (Central) and the Employment Exchange concerned, and such notice shall be served on that Government, the Regional Labour Commissioner (Central), the Assistant Labour Commissioner (Central) and the Employment Exchange concerned by registered post in the following manner—
>
> (*a*) where notice is given to the workman, notice of retrenchment shall be sent within three days from the date on which notice is given to the workman;
>
> (*b*) where no notice is given to the workman and he is paid one month's wages in lieu thereof, notice of retrenchment shall be sent within three days from the date on which such wages are paid; and
>
> (*c*) where retrenchment is carried out under an agreement which specifies a date for the termination of service, notice of retrenchment shall be sent so as to reach the Central Government, the Regional Labour Commissioner (Central), the Assistant Labour Commissioner (Central), and the Employment Exchange concerned, at least one month before such date:
>
> Provided that if the date of termination of service agreed upon is within 30 days of the agreement, the notice of retrenchment shall be sent to the Central Government, the Regional Labour Commissioner (Central), the Assistant Labour Commissioner (Central), and the Employment Exchange concerned, within three days of the agreement.

9 Notice to workmen on transfer of undertaking (s. 25FF)

The ownership of the management of the entire undertaking should be transferred before s. 25FF comes into operation.[18] The term 'undertaking' is not defined in the Act. Undertaking is a concept narrower than Industry. It carries a restricted meaning.[19]

> Section 25FF. Where the ownership or management of an undertaking is transferred, whether by agreement or by operation of law, from the employer in relation to or that undertaking to a new employer, every workman who has

16 *National Iron & Steel Co. Ltd.* v *Third Industrial Tribunal* AIR 1964 Cal 525.

17 For West Bengal see r. 77 and Form 'P' relating to the notice of retrenchment of W.B. Industrial Disputes Rules.

18 AIR 1964 SC 645.

19 *S.M. Nilajkar* v *Telecom Dist. Manager, Karnataka* (2003)1 SCW 2196.

been in continuous service for not less than one year in that undertaking immediately before such transfer shall be entitled to notice and compensation in accordance with the provisions of section 25F, as if the workman had been retrenched:

Provided that nothing in this section shall apply to a workman in any case where there has been a change of employers by reason of the transfer, if—

(*a*) the service of the workman has not been interrupted by such transfer;

(*b*) the terms and conditions of service applicable to the workman after such transfer are not in any way less favourable to the workman than those applicable to him immediately before the transfer; and

(*c*) the new employer is, under the terms of such transfer or otherwise, legally liable to pay to the workman, in the event of his retrenchment, compensation on the basis that his service has been continuous and has not been interrupted by the transfer.

Where business changes hands from one management to another, but the employees continue in the same business, they continue to be entitled to all the rights and privileges acquired by them by reason of past services even after the transfer of business, provided there is continuity of service and there is identity of business.[1]

When a Government undertaking is taken over by a company, employees working in the undertaking are also taken over. They become employees of the company and cease to be employees of the Government. Since employees are covered by the definition of workman under the Industrial Disputes Act, in those cases, on the transfer of the undertaking, the provisions of s. 25FF of that Act, will apply.[2]

10 Notice to workmen on closure

The period of notice, contemplated in s. 25FFA, is 60 days. The notices has been prescribed by the State Government.

25FFA. *Sixty days' notice to be given of intention to close down any undertaking.* (1) An employer who intends to close down an undertaking shall serve, at least 60 days before the date on which the intended closure is to become effective, a notice, in the prescribed manner, on the appropriate Government stating clearly the reasons for the intended closure of the undertaking:

Provided that nothing in this section shall apply to—

(*a*) an undertaking in which—

(*i*) less than fifty workmen are employed, or

1 AIR 1958 Bom 133.

2 *D.R. Gurushanthappa* v *Abdul Khuddus Anwar* AIR 1969 SC 744; *Karnataka Power Transmission Corporation Ltd.* v *Amalgamated Electricity* (2001)1 LLJ 556.

(*ii*) less than fifty workmen were employed on an average per working day in the preceding twelve months,

(*b*) an undertaking set up for the construction of buildings, bridges, roads, canals, dams or for other construction work or project.

(2) Notwithstanding anything contained in sub-section (1), the appropriate Government may, if it is satisfied that owing to such exceptional circumstances as accident in the undertaking or death of the employer or the like it is necessary so to do, by order, direct that provisions of sub-section (1) shall not apply in relation to such undertaking for such period as may be specified in the order.

Section 30A of the Industrial Disputes Act provides for the penalty for closure without notice which runs as follows:

Section 30A. Any employer, who closes down any undertaking without complying with the provisions of s. 25FFA, shall be punishable with imprisonment for a term which may extend to six months, or with fine which may extend to five thousand rupees, or with both.

11 Compensation to workmen in case of closing down of undertakings—notice to workmen (s. 25FFF)

The Amending Act (Act 18 of 1957), by incorporating s. 25FFF in the main Act, gives statutory right to the workman to get compensation even for closure of an undertaking for any reason whatsoever except in respect of closure coming within the proviso to sub-sec. (1) of s. 25FFF.[3]

Section 25FFF. (1) Where an undertaking is closed down for any reason whatsoever, every workman who has been in continuous service for not less than one year in that undertaking immediately before such closure shall, subject to the provisions of sub-section (2), be entitled to notice and compensation in accordance with the provisions of section 25F, as if the workman had been retrenched:

Provided that where the undertaking is closed down on account of unavoidable circumstances beyond the control of the employer, the compensation to be paid to the workman under clause (*b*) of section 25F, shall not exceed his average pay for three months.

Explanation. An undertaking which is closed down by reason merely of—

(*i*) financial difficulties (including financial losses); or

(*ii*) accumulation of undisposed of stocks; or

(*iii*) the expiry of the period of the lease or licence granted to it; or

(*iv*) in case where the undertaking is engaged in mining operations, exhaustion of the minerals in the area in which operations are carried on,

3 1959 Ker LR 762.

shall not be deemed to be closed down on account of unavoidable circumstances beyond the control of the employer within the meaning of the proviso to this sub-section.

(1A) Notwithstanding anything contained in sub-section (1), where an undertaking engaged in mining operations is closed down by reason merely of exhaustion of the minerals in the area in which such operations are carried on, no workman referred to in that sub-section shall be entitled to any notice or compensation in accordance with the provisions of section 25F, if—

(*a*) the employer provides the workman with alternative employment with effect from the date of closure at the same remuneration as he was entitled to receive, and on the same terms and conditions of service as were applicable to him, immediately before the closure;

(*b*) the service of the workman has not been interrupted by such alternative employment; and

(*c*) the employer is, under the terms of such alternative employment or otherwise, legally liable to pay to the workman, in the event of his retrenchment, compensation on the basis that his service has been continuous and has not been interrupted by such alternative employment.

(1B) For the purposes of sub-sections (1) and (1A), the expressions "minerals" and "mining operations" shall have the meanings respectively assigned to them in clauses (*a*) and (*d*) of section 3 of the Mines and Minerals (Regulation and Development) Act 1957 (67 of 1957).

(2) Where any undertaking set-up for the construction of buildings, bridges, roads, canals, dams or other construction work is closed down on account of the completion of the work within two years from the date on which the undertaking had been set-up, no workman employed therein shall be entitled to any compensation under clause (*b*) of section 25F, but if the construction work is not so completed within two years, he shall be entitled to notice and compensation under that section for every completed year of continuous service or any part thereof in excess of six months.

Closure of business and lock-out

In the case of a closure, the employer does not merely close down the place of business but he closes the business itself finally and irrevocably. A lock-out, on the other hand, indicates the closure of the place of business and not closure of the business itself.[4]

The closure has to be genuine and *bona fide* in the sense that it should be a closure in fact and not a mere pretence of closure.[5]

4 *Management of Express Newspapers* v *Workers* AIR 1963 SC 569; *Tatanagar Foundry* v *Their Workmen* AIR 1970 SC 1960.

5 *Tatanagar Foundry* v *Their Workmen* AIR 1970 SC 1960.

The motive behind the closure is immaterial.[6] Under s. 25FFF of the Act, the closure of an undertaking cannot be limited or restricted only to financial, economic, or other considerations of a like nature.[7] The motive of the employer cannot be enquired into.[8]

Section 25FFF is designed to bring a workman within the term 'retrenchment' provided other conditions laid down in the section are satisfied and he is entitled to compensation.[9]

Section 25FFF has nothing to do with retrenchment as such. The section creates a new right in the employees for compensation in case of closure.[10]

The workmen cannot question the motive of the closure. Once the closure has taken place in fact, the matter may be different if under the guise of the closure the establishment is being carried on in some shape or form or at a different place, and the closure is only a ruse or pretence. Once the Court comes to the conclusion that there is a closure of an undertaking, the motive of the employer ordinarily ceases to be relevant. No employer can be compelled to carry on his business if he chooses to close it in truth and reality for reasons of his own.[11]

The closure of business can take place by stages and termination of service of workmen by batches is not illegal. In *Workmen* v *Straw Boards Mfg.*,[12] it was *held* that there is nothing wrong for an employer, who has decided to close an establishment, to follow the step of the closure by stages. It may be in the nature of a business to take recourse to such a mode which cannot ordinarily and *per se* be considered as unfair or illegitimate. Therefore, the termination of services of the first batch of workmen on account of the closure is not unjustified.

Closure of a distinct (DISTINCT) venture though a part of business complex (e.g. housing project of a steel plant) incurs retrenchment compensation nonetheless than the closure of the entire works.[13]

Under s. 11, the plea of infirmity of retrenchment notice is required to be specific. A general plea that grounds of retrenchment were false is not specific and precise enough to enable the employer to meet it.[14]

6 *Andhra Prabha* v *Secretary, Madras Union of Journalists* AIR 1967 SC 1869; *Kalinga Tubes Ltd.* v *Their Workmen* AIR 1969 SC 90; *Tatanagar Foundry* v *Their Workmen* AIR 1970 SC 1960.

7 *Kalinga Tubes Ltd.* v *Their Workmen* AIR 1969 SC 90 (95).

8 *Indian Hume Pipe* v *Their Workmen* AIR 1968 SC 1002.

9 AIR 1958 Punj 210.

10 67 CWN 1037.

11 *Workmen* v *Straw Boards Mfg.* AIR 1974 SC 1132.

12 AIR 1974 SC 1132.

13 *Workmen of Indian Leaf Tobacco* v *Management* AIR 1970 SC 860; *Parry & Co. Ltd.* v *P.C. Lal* AIR 1970 SC 1334; *Management of Hindustan Steel Ltd.* v *The Workmen* AIR 1973 SC 878.

14 *Management of Hindustan Steel Ltd.* v *The Workmen* AIR 1973 SC 878.

FORMS

Form 1

Notice of change in the conditions of service–proposed by an employer

Name of employer .... Dated the .... day of .... 20 ...
Address ....

In accordance with s. 9A of the Industrial Disputes Act 1947, I/We hereby give notice to all concerned that it is my/our intention to effect the change/changes specified in the annexure, with effect from ...... in the conditions of service applicable to workmen in respect of the matters specified in the Fourth Schedule to the said Act.

....
Signature
(Designation)

ANNEXURE

(here specify the change/changes intended to be effected).

Copy forwarded to:–

1. The Secretary of the Registered Trade Union, if any.
2. Assistant Labour Commissioner (Central)
   (here enter office address of the Asstt. Labour Comm. (Central) in the local area concerned).
3. Regional Labour Commissioner (Central) .... Zone.
4. Chief Labour Commissioner (Central), New Delhi.

NOTE: Vide Rule 34 of the Industrial Disputes (Central) Rules 1957.

Form 2

Notice of a strike to be given by union/workmen in a public utility service (vide Central Rules)

Name of Union
(Name of 5 elected representatives of workmen)
Address

Dated the .... day of .... 20 ...

To

....
(Name of the employer)

Dear Sir/Sirs,

In accordance with the provisions contained in sub-sec. (1) of s. 22 of the Industrial Disputes Act 1947, I/We hereby give you notice that I propose to call a strike on .... We propose to go on strike on ......20 .... for the reasons explained in the annexure.

Yours faithfully,
Sd/- ....
Secretary of the Union
(5 representatives of workmen duly elected at a meeting held on (date) vide resolution attached)

ANNEXURE

Statement of the case

Copy forwarded to:–

1. Assistant Labour Commissioner (Central).
2. Regional Labour Commissioner (Central),...... Zone.
3. Chief Labour Commissioner (Central), New Delhi.

NOTE: See Rule 71 of the Industrial Disputes (Central) Rules 1957.

Form 3

Notice of lock-out to be given by an employer carrying on a public utility service–vide s. 22(2) & (5) of the Act read with Rule 72 of the Central Rules

Name of employer ....
Address ....

Dated the ...... day of ...... 20 ......

In accordance with the provisions of sub-sec. (2) of s. 22 of the Industrial Disputes Act 1947, I/we hereby give notice to all concerned that it is my/our intention to effect the lock-out, in ...... department(s)/section(s) of my/our establishment with effect from ...... for the reasons explained in the annexure.

....
Signature
(Designation)

ANNEXURE

Statement of reasons

Copy forwarded to:–

1. The Secretary of the Registered Union, if any.
2. Assistant Labour Commissioner (Central).
   (State here office address of the A.L.C. (Central) in the local area concerned).
3. Regional Labour Commissioner (Central), ... Zone.
4. Chief Labour Commissioner (Central), New Delhi.

Notes: 1. See Rule 72 of the Industrial Disputes (Central) Rules 1957.

2. Where there is a registered Trade Union copy of the Notice shall be served on the Secretary of the Union.

Form 4

Notice under the Industrial Disputes Act 1947 –Notice of lay-off (commencement)

To

The Regional Labour Commissioner (Central)
(Here specify the region concerned)

Sir,

Under Rule 75A of the Industrial Disputes (Central) Rules 1957, I/we hereby inform that I/we have laid-off (number) out of total of[1] ...... workmen employed in the establishment with effect from[2] .... for the reasons explained in the annexure.

2. Such of the workmen concerned as are entitled to compensation under s. 25C of the Industrial Disputes Act 1947, will be paid compensation due to them.

Yours faithfully,[3]

Copy forwarded to:–

The Assistant Labour Commissioner (Central)

(Here specify the address of the Assistant Labour Commissioner (Central) of the local area concerned).

1. Here insert the number of workmen.
2. Here insert the date.
3. Here insert the position which the person who signs the letter holds with the employer issuing the letter.

ANNEXURE

Statement of reasons

NOTES: 1. Workmen employed in an industrial establishment, if laid-off, the employer is required to give notice of commencement of such lay-off in Form O-1 within 7 days of such commencement.

2. The notice is to be given in every case whether in the opinion of the employer the workmen laid-off is entitled to compensation under s. 25C or not.

Form 5

Notice under the Industrial Disputes Act 1947—Notice of lay-off (end of lay-off)

To

The Regional Labour Commissioner (Central) Dated .... 20 .....
(Here specify the region concerned)

Sir,

As required by Rule 75A of the Industrial Disputes (Central) Rules 1957, and in continuation of my/our notice, dated[1] .... in Form O-1, I/we hereby inform you that the lay-off in my/our establishment has ended on[1] ....

Yours faithfully,

(...........)[2]

Copy to:–

The Assistant Labour Commissioner (Central)

(Here specify the region concerned)

1. Here insert the date.
2. Here insert the position which the person who signs the letter holds with the employer issuing the letter.

NOTES: 1. When workmen are laid-off, the employer is required to give notice of termination of lay-off in Form O-2 within seven days of such termination.

2. The notice is obligatory, whether or not the workmen laid-off, in the opinion of the employer, is entitled to compensation under s. 25C of the Act.

Form 6

Notice of retrenchment to be given by an employer under cl. (c) of s. 25F of the Industrial Disputes Act 1947

Name of employer ....
Address ....

Dated the .... day of .... 20 ....

To

The Secretary to the Government of India

Ministry of Labour, New Delhi

Sir,

Under cl. (*c*) of s. 25F of the Industrial Disputes Act 1947 (14 of 1947) I/we hereby inform you that I/we have decided to retrench[1] .... workmen with effect from[2] .... for the reasons explained in the annexure.

2. The workmen concerned were given on the[2] .... 20... one month's notice in writing as required under cl. (*a*) of s. 25 of that Act, retrenchment is being effected in pursuance of an agreement, a copy of which is enclosed. The workmen were given on the[2] .... 20...... one month's pay in lieu of notice as required under cl. (*a*) of s. 25 of that Act.

3. The total number of workmen employed in the industrial establishment is[1] .... and the total number of those who will be affected by the retrenchment is given below.

Category and designation of workmen to be retrenched	*Number of workmen*	
	Employed	*To be retrenched*
(1)	(2)	(3)
....	....	....
....	....	....

4. I/We hereby declare that the workman/workmen concerned has/have been/will be paid compensation due to them under s. 25F of the Act on[2] ...... before the expiry of the notice period.

Yours faithfully,

.....................[3]

ANNEXURE

Statement of reasons

Copy to:–

1. Assistant Labour Commissioner (Central)
   (Here enter office address of the Assistant Labour Commissioner in local area concerned).
2. Regional Labour Commissioner (Central) .... Zone.

NOTES:

1. Here insert the total number of workmen employed in the industrial establishment.
2. Here insert the date.
3. Here insert the position which the person who signs the letter holds with the employer issuing the letter.

CHAPTER 25

Notices under the Factories Act 1948

SYNOPSIS

1 Notice to the Chief Inspector by occupier (s. 7)
2 Notice of certain accidents (s. 88)
3 Display of notices
4 Notice of periods of work for adults
5 Notice of periods of work for children
6 Modes of service of notice

1 Notice to the Chief Inspector by occupier (s. 7)

The Factories Act 1948 is a piece of social legislation with a view to ensuring safety, security and beneficial conditions of service of workmen engaged in a factory. Section 7 of the Act enjoins:

"The occupier shall, at least 15 days before he begins to occupy or use any premises as a factory, send to the Chief Inspector a written notice containing—

(*a*) the name and situation of the factory;

(*b*) the name and address of the occupier;

(*bb*) the name and address of the owner of the premises or building (including the precincts thereof) referred to in section 93;

(*c*) the address to which communication relating to the factory may be sent;

(*d*) the nature of the manufacturing process—

(*i*) carried on in the factory during the last 12 months in the case of factories in existence on the date of the commencement of this Act, and

(*ii*) to be carried on in the factory during the next 12 months in the case of all factories;

(*e*) the total rated horse power installed or to be installed in the factory, which shall not include the rated horse power of any separate stand-by plant;

(*f*) the name of the manager of the factory for the purposes of this Act;

(*g*) the number of workers likely to be employed in the factory;

(*h*) the average number of workers per day employed during the last 12 months in the case of a factory in existence on the date of the commencement of this Act;

(*i*) such other particulars as may be prescribed.

(2) In respect of all establishments which come within the scope of the Act for the first time, the occupier shall send a written notice to the Chief Inspector containing the particulars specified in sub-section (1) within 30 days, from the date of the commencement of this Act.

(3) Before a factory engaged in a manufacturing process which is ordinarily carried on for less than 180 working days in the year, resumes working, the occupier shall send a written notice to the Chief Inspector containing the particulars specified in sub-section (1) at least 30 days before the date of the commencement of work.

(4) Whenever a new manager is appointed, the occupier shall send to the Inspector a written notice and to the Chief Inspector a copy thereof within seven days from the date on which such person takes over charge.

(5) * * *"

Now, who is this occupier?

Section 2(*n*) states: 'Occupier' of a factory means the person who has ultimate control over the affairs of the factory.

Under s. 7(1) a written notice is required to be given to the Chief Inspector, disclosing the name of the occupier at least 15 days before he occupies or begins to use any premises as a factory.[1]

Looking to the provisions of the section, the occupier is required to state, by way of notice, the address, location of a factory, nature and quantum of power to be used and the number of workmen employed or to be employed in the factory. In other words, the Government should know particulars of a factory to check and prevent any illegality.

Failure of an occupier of the factory to give a written notice of occupation as required under s. 7(1) of the Act is not a continuing offence and, as such, a prosecution for such an offence filed after more than three months is barred by limitation under s. 106 of the Act.[2]

Under s. 7(1)(*f*) the notice by occupier shall include the name of the Manager of the factory for the purposes of the Act.

1 *J.K. Industries Ltd.* v *Chief Inspector of Factories and Boilers* (1997)1 LLJ 722.
2 AIR 1955 Bom 161.

Person having power to employ or dismiss persons working in the factory and empowered to give promotions or inflict fines on them is the manager.[3] In the case of company, which owns a factory, it is only one of the Directors of the company who can be notified for the purpose of the Act.

2 Notice of certain accidents (s. 88)

In the field of industry, where workmen have to use power, sophisticated plants and machinery, happening of accidents is not ruled out. There may occur injury to the workman, even death following an accident and the question of compensation to the victim comes up. Section 88 of the Act is there to avoid suppression of the fact.

Section 88(1): 'Where in any factory an accident occurs which causes death, or which causes any bodily injury by reason of which the person injured is prevented from working for a period of 48 hours or more immediately following the accident, or which is of such nature as may be prescribed in this behalf, the manager of the factory shall send notice thereof to such authorities, and in such form and within such time, as may be prescribed.'

Section 88(2) reads: Where a notice given under sub-section (1) relates to an accident causing death, the authority to whom the notice is sent shall make an inquiry into the occurrence within one month of the receipt of the notice or, if such authority is not the Inspector, cause the Inspector to make an inquiry within the said period.

Section 88A deals with notice of certain dangerous occurrences. Where in a factory any dangerous occurrence of such nature as may be prescribed occurs, whether causing any bodily injury or disability or not, the manager of the factory shall send notice thereof to such authorities, and in such form and within such time, as may be prescribed.

Under r. 96, a form of notice of accident or dangerous occurrence has been prescribed. The notice has to be sent forthwith to the Inspector of Factories.

Report of accident of worker sent to Inspector—does not constitute knowledge of offence under s. 21(1)(*iv*)(*c*).[4]

Even though more persons than one are injured as a result of a single accident, a single notice of the accident is contemplated to be given to the authorities. Contravention of this rule is a single offence which cannot be split up into as many offences as the number of casualties.[5]

3 Display of notices

All notices required by or under the Factories Act to be displayed in a factory shall be in English and in a language understood by the majority of the

3 1961 Lab LJ 335 (All).
4 *P.D. Jambhekar* v *State of Gujarat* AIR 1973 SC 309.
5 *Wazirchand* v *Emperor* AIR 1930 Lah 658.

workers in the factory, and shall be displayed at some conspicuous and convenient place at or near the main entrance to the factory, and shall be maintained in a clean and legible condition. (Section 108(2) of the Factories Act 1948).

4 Notice of periods of work for adults

(1) There shall be displayed and correctly maintained in every factory in accordance with the provisions of sub-section (2) of section 108, a notice of periods of work for adults, showing clearly for every day the periods during which adult workers may be required to work.

(2) The periods shown in the notice required by sub-section (1) shall be fixed beforehand in accordance with the following provisions of this section, and shall be such that workers working for those periods would not be working in contravention of any of the provisions of sections 51, 52, 53, 54, 55, 56 and 58.

(3) Where all the adult workers in a factory are required to work during the same periods, the manager of the factory shall fix those periods for such workers generally.

(4) Where all the adult workers in a factory are not required to work during the same periods, the manager of the factory shall classify them into groups according to the nature of their work indicating the number of workers in each group.

(5) For each group which is not required to work on a system of shifts, the manager of the factory shall fix the periods during which the group may be required to work.

(6) Where any group is required to work on a system of shifts and the relays are not to be subject to predetermined periodical changes of shifts, the manager of the factory shall fix the periods during which each relay of the group may be required to work.

(7) Where any group is to work on a system of shifts and the relays are to be subject to predetermined periodical changes of shifts, the manager of the factory shall draw up a scheme of shifts whereunder the period during which any relay of the group may be required to work and the relay which will be working at anytime of the day shall be known for any day. (Sub-sections (1) to (7) of s. 61 of the Factories Act 1948).

5 Notice of periods of work for children

(1) There shall be displayed and correctly maintained in every factory in which children are employed, in accordance with the provisions of sub-section (2) of section 108 a notice of periods of work for children, showing clearly for every day the periods during which children may be required or allowed to work.

(2) The periods shown in the notice required by sub-section (1) shall be fixed beforehand in accordance with the method laid down for adult workers in section 61, and shall be such that children working for those periods would not be working in contravention of any of the provisions of section 71.

(3) The provisions of sub-sections (8), (9) and (10) of section 61 shall apply also to the notice required by sub-section (1) of this section." (Section 72 of the Factories Act 1948).

6 Modes of service of notice

Usual modes of service by personal tender and/or by post are suggested.

Section 109 of the Act speaks that the State Government may make rules prescribing the manner of the service of orders under this Act on owners, occupiers or managers of factories.

FORMS

Form 1

Notice of change of Manager

(Prescribed under Rule 12A)

Form No. 3

To

The Inspector (concerned)

....

1. Name of factory with current licence number ....
2. Postal address ....
3. Name of out-going Manager ....
4. Name of new Manager with postal address of his residence and telephone number, if installed ....
5. Date of appointment of the new Manager with parentage ....

.... Signature of the new Manager	.... Signature of occupier

Date ....

Place ....

c.c. to the Chief Inspector (concerned).

NOTE: Under s. 7(4) of the Factories Act whenever a new Manager is appointed, the occupier shall send to the Inspector a written notice and to the Chief Inspector a copy thereof within 7 days from date on which such person takes over charge.

Form 2

Notice of accident or dangerous occurrence

(Prescribed under Rule 96)

This space to be completed by Inspector of Factories

District ....

Date of Receipt ....

Account No. ....

Industry No. ....

Causation No. ....

Sex (M.W.B. or C.) ......

Other particulars (e.g., fatal, leg injury, arm injury etc.) ....

Date of Investigation ....

Result of Investigation ....

1. Name of factory ....
2. Address of works where accident
   or dangerous occurrence happened ......
3. Name of Industry.........
4. Branch or Department and exact place
   where the accident or dangerous occurrence happened ....
5. Injured person's name and address
   (*a*) ....
   (*b*) ....
   (*c*) ....
6. (*a*) Sex ....
   (*b*) Age (last birthday)
   (*c*) Occupation of the injured person ....
7. Date and hour of accident or dangerous occurrence ....
8. Hour at which he started work on day of accident. ....
9. (*a*) Cause or nature of accident or dangerous occurrence ....
   (*b*) If caused by machinery ....
      (*i*) Give name of machine and part
      causing the accident (*b*) (*i*)
      (*ii*) State whether it was moved by
      mechanical power at that time–(*b*) (*ii*)
   (*c*) State exactly what injured person
   was doing at the time–(*c*)

10. Nature and extent of injuries (e.g., fatal, loss of finger, fracture of leg, scald, scratch followed by sepsis) ....

11. If accident is not fatal, state whether injured person was disabled for 48 hours or more ....

12. Name of Medical Officer in attendance on injured person ....

I certify that to the best of my knowledge and belief the above particulars are correct in every respect.

(Signature of Occupier or Manager)

Date of despatch of report ....

CHAPTER 26

Notices under the Employee's Compensation Act 1923

SYNOPSIS

1 Notice of accident on employer—urgency of notice
2 Want of notice or any defect or irregularity in a notice—effects
3 Contents of a notice under s. 10 of the Employee's Compensation Act—language of the notice—on whom to be served
4 Provision for a Notice Book
5 Provisions relating to employees abroad of companies and motor vehicles
6 Mode of service of a notice of accident—entry in the Notice Book

1 Notice of accident on employer—urgency of notice

Section 10. *Notice and claim.* (1) No claim for compensation shall be entertained by a Commissioner unless the notice of the accident has been given in the manner hereinafter provided as soon as practicable after the happening thereof and unless the claim is preferred before him within two years of the occurrence of the accident or, in case of death, within two years from the date of death.

The word 'claim' referred to in s. 10(1) does not refer to a claim made on the employers but denotes a formal claim made before the Commissioner.[1] Demand for compensation to a superior fellow workman like Foreman is no claim under s. 10 of the Act. Claim is to be made to some higher authority who can have it brought to the notice of the branch charged with administration of matters arising out of the Act.[2]

A claim is required to be made under s. 10 and no particular form is prescribed.[3] The words 'notice of accident' appearing in s. 10 does not mean 'notice of the details of the accident'. A wide and unnecessary extension to

1 AIR 1960 Ori 39.
2 AIR 1938 Cal 348.
3 AIR 1950 Ass 188.

the word 'accident' which might defeat the claim of compensation ought not to be lightly given.[4]

2 Want of notice or any defect or irregularity in a notice—effects

The ultimate object is to compensate an injured employee. Failure to give notice or some defect in the notice cannot frustrate the object. Proviso to s. 10(1) of the Act enjoins that the want of or any defect or irregularity in a notice shall not be a bar to the entertainment of a claim—

(*a*) if the claim is preferred in respect of the death of an employee resulting from an accident which occurred on the premises of the employer, or to any place where the employee at the time of the accident was working under the control of the employer or of any person employed by him, and the employee died on such premises or at such place, or on any premises belonging to the employer, or died without having left the vicinity of the premises or place where the accident occurred; or

(*b*) if the employer or any one of several employers or any person responsible to the employer for the management of any branch of the trade or business in which the injured employee was employed, had knowledge of the accident from any other source at or about the time when it occurred:

Provided further that the Commissioner may entertain and decide any claim to compensation in any case notwithstanding that the notice has not been given, or the claim has not been preferred in due time as provided in this sub-section, if he is satisfied that the failure so to give the notice or prefer the claim, as the case may be, was due to sufficient cause.

Accident trivial at first but becoming serious—notice is to be given when serious consequences ensue.[5] The proviso to cl. (*b*) of s. 10(1) gives jurisdiction to the Commissioner to entertain and decide any claim to compensation in any case notwithstanding that the notice has not been given.[6]

Under s. 10(1), notice has to be given 'as soon as practicable' after the happening of the accident.

No cast iron rule can be laid down in regard to what is meant by 'as soon as practicable'.[7] A notice of accident given within a week was held as given 'as soon as practicable' after the happening of the accident.[8] Where the

4 AIR 1946 Bom 169.
5 AIR 1941 Bom 296.
6 AIR 1960 Ori 39.
7 AIR 1960 MP 313.
8 AIR 1928 Bom 1.

accident occurred in the presence of the employer, notice held not necessary.[9] When the Commissioner is satisfied that the failure to give notice was due to sufficient cause, such want of notice will not be a bar to entertain the claim.[10]

Employer used to employ more than 40 employees for agricultural operation. Employer would have knowledge of accident through other employees working in paddy field. It has been held that failure of employee to issue notice of accident is not fatal—claim for compensation is maintainable.[11] Notice is not mandatory when employer has information of the accident.[12]

The Commissioner is the sole judge as to whether want of or defect in a notice,[13] shall bar proceedings. Omission to state in notice the causes of injury is not material when the manager of the factory is already aware of it.[14]

Notice under s. 10 is not necessary where an employee does not voluntarily leave service of the employer and the want of a written notice can also be excused if there is sufficient cause for failure to give notice or to institute a claim.[15]

Reference may be made of five cases where there was 'sufficient cause' for not giving the notice earlier:

(*i*) A notice given a month after the accident may, if the victim of the accident is continuously in the hospital, be held to be given as soon as practicable.[16]

(*ii*) A workman employed as a coolie in a factory met with an accident on the 23rd February 1927. On the 28th March 1927, when he was admitted to a hospital as an indoor patient, he sent a notice addressed to the solicitors of the proprietors of the company. This letter was received by them on 21st April 1927. *Held*, that having regard to the ignorance of and serious nature of the injury received by the workman, the notice of the accident was given as soon as

9 AIR 1959 All 586.

10 *Makhanlal Marwari* v *Audh Beharilal* AIR 1959 All 586; *MP Mining Corporation, Sama* v *Munda Kol* 1990(61) FLR 9 (MP).

11 *T.N. Narayanaswamy* v *Pattusamy* (1997)2 LLJ 23 (Mad).

12 *State of J&K* v *Amar Chand* (1999)3 LLJ 371 (J&K); *Divisional Forest Officer, Gwalior* v *Baijnatibai* 1994 Lab IC 2561; *Deep Metal Industries* v *B.D. Gaikwad* (1995) Lab IC 1002 (Bom).

13 AIR 1933 Nag 272.

14 AIR 1933 Nag 272 at p. 273.

15 AIR 1933 Bom 109.

16 AIR 1960 MP 313.

practicable after the happening thereof within the meaning of s. 10(1).[17]

The Commissioner can condone the delay provided he is satisfied that there was sufficient cause.[18]

Once the Commissioner has condoned the delay, he cannot dismiss the case as time-barred without giving sufficient opportunity to the applicant.[19]

(*iii*) Where the injured workman considers his injury to be trivial and one for which he is not entitled to compensation, sufficient cause is made out for failure to give notice under s. 10.[20]

(*iv*) Where an injured workman did not realise until a particular date that he had permanently lost sight of one eye, it is sufficient cause for his not giving notice earlier.[1]

(*v*) The fact that after his discharge from the hospital the man had been ill and was a complete wreck is sufficient cause for delay in giving notice.[2]

Where the non-service, non-delivery or absence of notice cannot be ignored or condoned, the employee cannot claim compensation.[3]

3 Contents of a notice under s. 10 of the Employee's Compensation Act—language of the notice—on whom to be served

Sub-section (2) of s. 10 of the Employee's Compensation Act enjoins: "Every such notice shall give the name and address of the person injured and shall state in ordinary language the cause of the injury and the date on which the accident happened, and shall be served on the employer or upon any one of several employers, or upon any person responsible to the employer for the management of any branch of the trade or business in which the injured employee was employed."

The notice may not contain details of the accident.[4] That is wide and unnecessary extension of the word 'accident'. The expression "notice shall state in ordinary language the cause of the injury" does not mean that notice must state in language to the same effect as application before the

17 AIR 1929 Bom 400.
18 AIR 1960 All 283; AIR 1950 Bom 424; AIR 1957 Cal 660.
19 AIR 1942 Mad 116.
20 AIR 1933 Bom 197.
1 AIR 1933 Nag 272.
2 AIR 1938 Mad 485.
3 AIR 1950 Cal 261.
4 AIR 1946 Bom 169.

Commissioner.[5] The notice shall be served on the employer,[6] or the person directly responsible to the employer. Notice to the fellow employee is not valid.

4 Provision for a Notice Book

In the premises, where workmen are employed, there should be kept by the employer a notice book for making entries, if any, of the accident.

Sub-section (3) of s. 10 speaks:

> "The State Government may require that any prescribed class of employers shall maintain at their premises, at which employees are employed a notice book, in the prescribed form, which shall be readily accessible at all reasonable times to any injured employee employed on the premises and to any person acting *bona fide* on his behalf."

The notice book shall be maintained by a prescribed class of employers in a prescribed form and certainly at a place in the workhouse which shall be readily accessible to an injured employee to keep note of the accident. This provides an additional reference/record to injury or death, as the case may be, which the Commissioner of the Employee's Compensation, may call for his satisfaction.

5 Provisions relating to employees abroad of companies and motor vehicles

Section 15B(*ii*)(1) of the Employee's Compensation Act 1923 states that the notice of the accident and the claim for compensation may be served on the local agent of the company, or the local agent of the owner of the motor vehicle, in the country of accident, as the case may be.

6 Mode of service of a notice of accident—entry in the Notice Book

Where a notice is prescribed by a Central Act to be served by a registered post—the course as provided for in s. 27 of the General Clause Act should be adhered to.

Sub-section (4) of s. 10. 'A notice under this section may be served by delivering it at, or sending it by registered post addressed to, the residence or any office or place of business of the person on whom it is to be served, or, where a notice book is maintained, by entry in the notice book'.

Notice addressed to the employer's office at the business place and sent by registered post coming back with endorsement 'left' is a valid notice.[7]

5 AIR 1933 Cal 130.
6 AIR 1941 Bom 296.
7 AIR 1929 Bom 490.

FORMS

Form 1

Notice of accident under s. 10(1) by the Employee or L.R. of the deceased

By registered post with AD.

....

Dated the .... 20 ....

To

M/s. ....

(Name & address: office or place of business of the Employer).

Or, (Name of the person responsible to the Employer)—See s. 10(2) of the Act.

....

(State here address—office or place of business)

An accident in the ...... room of the Factory godown at the premises of ...... occurred on ...... due to short circuit of the electric installation and in the said accident Sri .... (name) .... son of ...... of .... (address) ...... an employee of the said Factory died while in the course of his employment in the Factory godown. (If necessary add, in the presence of .... Manager etc.).

Please take notice that you are hereby requested to raise the matter before the Commissioner of Employee's Compensation ...... having jurisdiction for making an Award of compensation as may be admissible.

L/R's of deceased

Notes:
1. No particular form of notice is prescribed (AIR 1950 Ass 188). Notice does not mean a notice of details of the accident (AIR 1946 Bom 169).
2. In spite of failure to give notice the Commissioner has jurisdiction to entertain the claim in certain circumstances (AIR 1960 Ori 39).
3. Where non-service, non-delivery or absence of notice cannot be condoned, the employee cannot claim compensation (AIR 1950 Cal 261).
4. The notice shall state in ordinary language the happening of the accident.

Form 2

Report of fatal accident prescribed under the Employee's Compensation Rules, 1924

(s. 10B of the Act)

To

....

....

Sir,

1. I have the honour to submit the following report of an accident which occurred on ...... (date) at ...... (here enter details of premises)...... and which resulted in the death of the employee/employees whose particulars are given in the statement annexed.

2. The circumstances attending the death of the employee/employees were as under:

(*a*) Time of the accident

(*b*) Place where the accident occurred

(*c*) Manners in which deceased was/were employed at the time

(*d*) Cause of the accident

(e) Any other relevant particulars

I have etc.,

....

Signature and designation of the person making the report.

STATEMENT

Name	*Sex*	*Age*	*Nature of employment*	*Full postal address*

NOTE: This is Form EE—See s. 10B of the E.C. Act, and Rule II of the Workmen's Compensation Rules.

Form 3

Notice by the Commissioner under rule 39

Where a claim for compensation has been made by .... applicant, against .... and the said ...., has claimed that you are liable under section 12(2) of the Employee's Compensation Act 1923, to indemnify him against any compensation which he may be liable to pay in respect of the aforesaid claim, you are hereby informed that you may appear before me on .... and contest the claim for compensation made by the said applicant or the claim for indemnity made by the opposite party. In default of your appearance you will be deemed to admit the validity of any awards made against the opposite party and your liability to indemnify the opposite party for any compensation recovered from him.

Dated .... 20 ....

....

Commissioner

Form 4

Notice by the Commissioner under rule 38

Whereas a claim for compensation has been made by .... applicant, against .... and the said .... has claimed that .... is liable under section 12(2) of the Employee's Compensation Act 1923, to indemnify him against any compensation which he may be liable to pay in respect of the aforesaid claim, and whereas the said .... on notice served has claimed that you .... stand to him in the relation of a contractor from whom the applicant .... could have recovered compensation, you are hereby informed that you may appear before me on ...., and contest the claim for compensation made by the said applicant or the claim for indemnity made by the opposite party .... In default of your appearance you will be deemed to admit the validity of any award made against the opposite party ....', and your liability to indemnify the opposite party .... for any compensation recovered from him.

Dated .... 20 ....

....

Commissioner

Form 5

Notice by the Commissioner under rules 49 and 50

Take notice that registration of the agreement to pay compensation is said to have been reached between .... and .... on the .... 20 .... has been refused for the following reasons, namely:

....

....

Dated .... 20 ....

....

Commissioner

CHAPTER 27

Notices under the Industrial Employment (Standing Orders) Act 1946

SYNOPSIS

1 Introductory–object of the Act and the application–submission of draft Standing Orders
2 Standing Orders to cover subjects in the Schedule–certificate of Standing Orders–effects thereof
3 Item (8) of the Schedule–termination of service–item (9) of the Schedule–suspension or dismissal for misconduct
4 Departmental proceedings–stages–notices therefor
5 Resignation and termination of service–notice therefor
6 Discharge simpliciter–notice therefor

1 Introductory—object of the Act and the application—submission of draft Standing Orders

The preamble to a statute which is often described as a key to its understanding may legitimately be consulted to solve an ambiguity or to ascertain and fix the meaning of words in their context which otherwise bear more meanings than one. If may afford useful assistance as to what the statute intends to reach, but if the enactment is clear and unambiguous in itself then no preamble can vary its meaning. While construing a statute, one has also to bear in mind the presumption that the legislature does not intend to make any substantial change in the existing law beyond what it expressly declares or beyond the immediate scope and object of the statute.[1] With the advent of trade unions and collective bargaining, new problems of maintaining industrial peace and production for the society were created. It was then considered that the society had a vital interest in the settlement of terms of employment of industrial labour, and thus the settlement of labour problems became tripartite and the State, representing the society,

1 *A.C. Sharma* v *Delhi Administration* (1973)1 SCC 726.

entered on the scene. To give effect to the new ideology, the Industrial Employment (Standing Orders) Act 1946, came to be enacted.[2]

This is an Act 'to require employers in industrial establishments to define with sufficient precision the conditions of employment under them and to make the said conditions known to workmen employed by them'. In other words, the object of the Act is to require employers to define with certainty the conditions of service in their establishments and to reduce them to writing and to get them compulsorily certified with a view of avoiding unnecessary industrial disputes.[3]

The object of the Act is to have uniform Standing Orders providing for matters enumerated in Schedule I to the Act and it is not intended that there should be different conditions of service for those who are employed before and those employed after the Standing Orders come into force. Once the standing orders come into force, they bind all those presently in the employment of the concerned establishment as well as those who are appointed thereafter.[4]

Standing Orders framed after following the provisions of the Act bind even those employees who have entered service before the framing of the standing orders inasmuch as such employees would be workmen presently employed at the time when the Standing Orders are certified.[5]

Under sub-sec. (3) of s. 1 of the Act, it applies to every industrial establishment wherein 100[6] or more workmen are employed, or were employed on any day of the preceding 12 months, and to such class or classes of other industrial establishments too as the appropriate Government may from time to time, after giving not less than two months' notice of its intention to do so, by notification in the *Official Gazette*, apply, the provisions of the Act to any industrial establishment employing such number of persons less than one hundred as may be specified in the notification.

Submission of draft Standing Orders

The standing orders form part of the contract between the management and everyone of its employees. They take the place of the service rule relating to Government servants,[7] to ensure security of employment.[8]

2 *Western India Match Co.* v *Workmen* AIR 1973 SC 2650.
3 AIR 1959 SC 513.
4 *Agra Electric Supply Co.* v *Sir Alladin* AIR 1970 SC 512.
5 *Dunlop India Ltd.* v *Their Workmen* AIR 1972 SC 2326.
6 For the States like Maharashtra, Karnataka, Gujarat and West Bengal it is 50. But in Uttar Pradesh and Tamil Nadu it is less than 100. The Act does apply not to Madhya Pradesh.
7 AIR 1959 Mad 479.
8 AIR 1959 Mad 479 at p. 481.

Standing Orders cannot be ignored and they are binding and effective between the parties.

If the establishment engages less than 100 workmen, it will not be necessary to pass any Standing Orders as contemplated by s. 3. It follows that the terms of service in such establishment will be governed according to the agreement, direct or implied, or may be by practice prevailing in similar establishments.[9] We would remember that in the absence of any standing orders or rules, law of master and servant governs relationship between the employer and the employee.[10]

Section 3 of the Act prescribes submission of draft Standing Orders:

(1) Within six months from the date on which this Act becomes applicable to an industrial establishment,[11] the employer shall submit to the Certifying Officer[12] five copies of the draft Standing Orders proposed by him for adoption in his industrial establishment.

(2) Provision shall be made in such draft for every matter set out in the Schedule which may be applicable to the industrial establishment, and where model Standing Orders have been prescribed shall be, so far as is practicable, in conformity with such model.

(3) The draft Standing Orders submitted under this section shall be accompanied by a statement giving prescribed particulars of the workmen employed in the industrial establishment including the name of the trade union, if any, to which they belong.

(4) Subject to such conditions as may be prescribed, a group of employers in similar establishments may submit a joint draft of standing orders under this section.

The language in s. 3(2) is imperative.[13] But that does not mean that model prescribed Standing Orders have to be copied blindly; for this provision in s. 3(2) is merely calculated to help and guide the employers in framing

9 AIR 1959 Tripura 8.

10 *Management of M/s. Shiva Flour Mills* v *The Workmen* AIR 1970 Pat 273.

11 Industrial establishment means—

- (*i*) an industrial establishment as defined in cl. (*ii*) of s. 2 of the Payment of Wages Act 1936, or
- (*ii*) a factory as defined in cl. (*m*) of s. 2 of the Factories Act 1948, or
- (*iii*) a railway as defined in cl. (4) of s. 2 of the Indian Railways Act 1890, or
- (*iv*) the establishment of a person who, for the purpose of fulfilling a contract with the owner of any industrial establishment, employs workmen.

12 Section 2(*c*) of the Act—"Certifying Officer" means a Labour Commissioner or a Regional Labour Commissioner, and includes any other officer appointed by the appropriate Government, by notification in the Official Gazette, to perform all or any of the functions of a Certifying Officer under this Act.

13 AIR 1955 Bom 363.

their draft standing orders and does not necessarily mean that they must incorporate and copy the model standing orders in that draft.[14]

Again, when sub-sec. (2) of s. 3 of the Act states that the draft standing orders shall be, so far as is practicable, in conformity with the model standing orders, it simply means that the model standing orders furnish the pattern which the draft should try to resemble or imitate. It cannot mean that the draft should copy the model verbatim. The model standing orders are no more than a model. They do not have the force of a statutory rule which has to be obeyed without in any manner altering its contents.[15] Certifying Officer has power to permit departure from model standing orders—Employer cannot insist upon inclusion of any particular item outside the Schedule to the Act.[16]

2 Standing Orders to cover subjects in the Schedule—certificate of Standing Orders—effects thereof

THE FIRST SCHEDULE[17]

The Schedule enumerates the following matters to be provided in Standing Orders under this Act:

(1) Classification of workers, whether permanent, temporary, apprentices, fixed term employment workman, probationers or *badlis* or

(2) Manner of intimating to workers periods and hours of work, holidays, pay-days and wage rates.

(3) Shift working.

(4) Attendance and late coming.

(5) Conditions of, procedure in applying for, and the authority which may grant, leave and holidays.

(6) Requirement to enter premises by certain gates, and liability to search.

(7) Closing and reopening of sections of the industrial establishment, and temporary stoppages of work and the rights and liabilities of the employer and workers arising therefrom.

(8) Termination of employment, and the notice thereof to be given by employer and workers.

(9) Suspension or dismissal for misconduct, and acts or omissions which constitute misconduct.

14 AIR 1949 All 504.
15 AIR 1959 Mys 235.
16 AIR 1966 SC 1471.
17 For Schedule see Note 2.

(10) Means of redress for workers against unfair treatment or wrongful exactions by the employer or his agents or servants.

(11) Any other matter which may be specified by the appropriate Government by notification.

It is now well settled that the employer cannot enter into an agreement with a workman which is inconsistent with the standing orders and would prevail over the corresponding terms in the contract of service.[18] Again, there can be no different conditions of service for different employees depending upon the point of time when they came to be employed.[19]

3 Item (8) of the Schedule—termination of service—item (9) of the Schedule—suspension or dismissal for misconduct

Standing Orders are to cover matters concerning termination of employment and notice thereof to be given by the employer to the workmen.

Standing Orders framed under the Industrial Employment (Standing Orders) Central Rules 1946.

> "13. *Termination of employment.* (1) For terminating employment of a permanent workman, noti'ce in writing shall be given either by the employer or the workman; one month's notice in the case of monthly rated workmen, and two weeks' notice in the case of other workmen; one month's or two weeks' pay, as the case may be, may be paid in lieu of notice.
>
> (2) Subject to the provisions of the Industrial Disputes Act 1947, no temporary workman whether monthly rated, weekly rated or piece rated, and no probationer or badli or fixed term employment workman in apparel manufacturing sector, as a result of non-renewal of contract or employment or on its expiry, shall be entitled to any notice or pay in lieu thereof, if his services are terminated:
>
> Provided that the services of a temporary workman shall not be terminated as a punishment unless he has been given an opportunity of explaining the charges of misconduct alleged against him in the manner prescribed in paragraph 14.
>
> (3) Where the employment of any workman is terminated, the wages earned by him and other dues, if any, shall be paid before the expiry of the second working day from the day on which his employment is terminated.[20]
>
> 14. *Disciplinary action for misconduct.* (1) A workman may be fined upto two per cent. of his wages in a month for any of the following acts and omissions, namely ....
>
> ....

18 *Western India Match Co.* v *Workmen* AIR 1973 SC 2650.
19 *V.P. Electric Supply Co.* v *T.N. Chatterjee* AIR 1972 SC 1201.
20 For the State of Bombay after item No. 10 '10A. Age for retirement or superannuation'.

[NOTE: Specify the acts and omissions which the employer may notify with the previous approval of the .... Government or of the prescribed authority in pursuance of s. 8 of the Payment of Wages Act 1936.]

(2) A workmen may be suspended for a period not exceeding four days at a time, or dismissed without notice or any compensation in lieu of notice, if he is found to be guilty of misconduct.

(3) The following acts and omissions shall be treated as misconduct:

(*a*) wilful insubordination or disobedience, whether alone or in combination with others, to any lawful and reasonable order of a superior,

(*b*) theft, fraud or dishonesty in connection with the employer's business or property,

(*c*) wilful damage to or loss of employer's goods or property,

(*d*) taking or giving bribes or any illegal gratification,

(*e*) habitual absence without leave or absence without leave for more than 10 days,

(*f*) habitual late attendance,

(*g*) habitual breach of any law applicable to the establishment,

(*h*) riotous or disorderly behaviour during working hours at the establishment or any act subversive of discipline,

(*i*) habitual negligence or neglect of work,

(*j*) frequent repetition of any act or omission for which a fine may be imposed to a maximum of 2 percent of the wages in a month,

(*k*) striking work or inciting others to strike work in contravention of the provision of any law, or rule having the force of law,

(*l*) sexual harassment which includes such unwelcome sexually determined behaviour (whether directly or by implication) as—

(*i*) physical contact and advances; or

(*ii*) demand or request for sexual favours; or

(*iii*) sexually-coloured remarks; or

(*iv*) showing pornography; or

(*v*) any other unwelcome physical, verbal or non-verbal conduct of sexual nature.

Provided that where there is a complaint of sexual harassment within the meaning of cl. (*l*) of sub-paragraph (3), the Complaints Committee constituted under sub-paragraph (3B) in each establishment for inquiring into such complaints, shall, notwithstanding anything contained in paragraph 15, be deemed to be the inquiring authority appointed by the employer for the purpose of these rules.

When the services of a workman are terminated in accordance with the Standing Orders no enquiry is called for.

In case of discharge of a workman, standing orders empower the company to take disciplinary action against an employee by proceeding in the prescribed manner—delegation of power by the company to one of its officers. Nothing in Articles of Association barring delegation of powers—orders of discharge by workman passed by a delegate of company—it falls under cl. 20 of the Standing Orders and is legal.[1]

The clause termination of employment in item (8) of the Schedule cannot be equated with the word 'superannuation'. Superannuation is a process.......... There is no volition in the act............... Termination is a positive act by which one party even against the desire of the other can bring about the end to an employment.[2]

The two processes are essentially different and there is hardly any room to equate one with the other.

The termination of service in pursuance of the service rule of agreement is different from dismissal or removal.[3]

(For dismissal—discharge *simpliciter*—punitive discharge etc., see Notes below).

In any case, Standing Orders and other service rules enjoin that whether it is termination, discharge, removal or dismissal there should issue notice. The words 'notice thereof to be given by employer and workmen' in item (8) should not be read as qualifying, limiting and colouring scope of expression 'termination of employment.' They should be read disjunctively. Termination of employment would be the principal or primary subjects—Notices in relation thereto would form ancillary or subsidiary subject.[4]

Section 5 of the Act provides for certification of Standing Orders and notice inviting objections.

The whole purpose of making the Standing Orders and getting them certified from the Labour Commissioner is that conditions of service of employment must be regulated by the same. The manner in which the standing orders are made and certified suggests that the standing orders, when certified, will be binding on the employees, who are at the time in service of the employers.[5]

1 *Jabalpur Electric Supply Co. Ltd.* v *Sambhu Prasad Shrivastav* AIR 1966 SC 1288.
2 AIR 1970 Ori 126.
3 AIR 1959 All 643; AIR 1953 SC 250; AIR 1958 SC 36; AIR 1954 SC 375 and AIR 1958 SC 232.
4 AIR 1961 Mad 107.
5 (1959)1 Lab LJ 639 (Punj).

Section 5. (1) On receipt of the draft under s. 3, the Certifying Officer shall forward a copy thereof to the trade union, if any, of the workmen, or where there is no such trade union, to the workmen in such manner as may be prescribed, together with a notice in the prescribed form requiring objections, if any, which the workmen may desire to make to the draft Standing Orders to be submitted to him within 15 days from the receipt of the notice.

(2) After giving the employer and the trade union or such other representatives of the workmen as may be prescribed an opportunity of being heard, the Certifying Officer shall decide whether or not any modification of or addition to the draft submitted by the employer is necessary to render the draft Standing Orders certificable under this Act, and shall make an order in writing accordingly.

(3) The Certifying Officer shall thereupon certify the draft standing orders, after making any modifications therein which his order, under sub-sec. (2) may require, and shall, within seven days thereafter send copies of the certified standing orders authenticated in the prescribed manner and of his order under sub-sec. (2) to the employer and to the trade union or other prescribed representatives of the workmen.

While it was open to the employers to frame Standing Orders for their concerns, orders framed by them have to be certified by the Certifying Order. Section 4 of the Act enjoins upon him to adjudicate upon the fairness and reasonableness of the provisions of the Standing Orders framed and while so doing he is directed to consider and weigh the social interest in the claims of the employer and in the demands of the workmen.[6]

Standing Orders framed under the Act have the force of law.[7] Draft Standing Orders cannot relate to matters outside the Schedule. As the certified Standing Orders have force of law, even a private party or a company may be compelled by *mandamus* to perform the duties imposed upon it by statute.[8]

Not only the Certifying Officer and the appellate authority have jurisdiction to alter or amend the standing orders which are not in conformity with the model standing orders, but it is incumbent upon those authorities to insist upon the standing orders conforming to the model Standing Orders unless the employer can satisfy them that it is not practicable for him to do so.

4 Departmental proceedings—stages—notices therefor

(Readers are referred to Chapter 17 Notices under the Constitution of India—(Art. 311), Laws on wrongful dismissal).

A departmental enquiry is not the direct result of provisions under Art. 311 of the Constitution or requirements of industrial laws. It owes its

6 *Western India Watch Co.* v *Workmen* AIR 1973 SC 2650.

7 AIR 1967 Raj 145.

8 *Abani Bhusan Biswas* v *Hindustan Cables Ltd.* AIR 1968 Cal 124.

origin to the common law of hearing a man before he is condemned. This principle of common law (a principle of natural justice) has been codified in Art. 311 of the Constitution and other legislations touching the matter including the industrial establishments, irrespective of the fact whether the post is temporary or permanent. Coming in particular to cases of disciplinary action, contemplated under the Industrial Employment (Standing Orders) Act 1946 we would do well to refer to the Industrial Employment (Standing Orders) Central Rules which was framed under the said Act.

Rule 17 speaks of disciplinary action. It reads—

> Rules 17. *Disciplinary action for misconduct*. A workman may be suspended by the employer pending investigation or departmental enquiry and shall be paid subsistence allowance in accordance with the provisions of section 10A of the Act. The employer shall normally complete the enquiry within 10 days. The payment of subsistence allowance shall be subject to the workmen not taking any employment elsewhere during the period of suspension.
>
> The following shall denote misconduct:
>
> (*a*) theft, fraud or dishonesty in connection with the employer's business or property;
>
> (*b*) taking or giving of bribes or an illegal gratification whatsoever in connection with the employer's business or his own interests;
>
> (*c*) wilful in-subordination or dis-obedience, whether along or in conjunction with another or others, or of any lawful or reasonable order or a superior. The order of the superior should normally be in writing;
>
> (*d*) habitual late attendance and habitual absence without leave or without sufficient cause;
>
> (*e*) drunkenness, fighting or riotous, disorderly or indecent behaviour while on duty at the place of work;
>
> (*f*) habitual neglect of work;
>
> (*g*) habitual indiscipline;
>
> (*h*) smoking underground or within the mine area or in places, where it is prohibited;
>
> (*i*) causing wilful damage to work in progress or to property of the employer;
>
> (*j*) sleeping on duty;
>
> (*k*) malingering or slowing down work;
>
> (*l*) acceptance of gifts from subordinate employees;
>
> (*m*) conviction in any court of law for any criminal offence involving moral turpitude;
>
> (*n*) continuous absence without permission and without satisfactory cause for more than ten days;
>
> (*o*) giving false information regarding one's name, age, father's name, qualification or previous service at the time of the employment;

(*p*) leaving work without permission or sufficient reason;

(*q*) any breach of the Mines Act 1952, or any other Act or any rules, regulations or bye-laws thereunder, or of any standing orders;

(*r*) threatening, abusing or assaulting any superior or co-worker;

(*s*) habitual money-lending;

(*t*) preaching of or inciting to violence;

(*u*) abetment of or attempt at abetment of any of the above acts of misconduct;

(*v*) going on illegal strike either single or with other workers without giving 14 days pervious notice;

(*w*) disclosing to any unauthorised person of any confidential information in regard to the working or process of the establishment which may come into the possession of the workman in the course of his work;

(*x*) refusal to accept any charge-sheet or order or notice communicated in writing;

(*y*) failure or refusal to wear or use any protective equipment given by the employers;

(*z*) (*i*) sexual harassment which includes such un-welcome sexual determined behaviour (whether directly or by application) as—

(*i*) physical contact and advances; or

(*ii*) a demand or request for sexual favours; or

(*iii*) sexually coloured remarks: or

(*iv*) showing pornography; or

(*v*) any other un-welcome physical, verbal or non-verbal conduct of sexual nature.

Provided that where there is a complaint of sexual harassment within the meaning of clause (*z*) of sub-paragraph (*i*), the Complaints Committee constituted under sub-paragraph (iB) in each establishment for inquiring into such complaints, shall, notwithstanding anything contained in paragraph 18, be deemed to be the inquiring authority appointed by the employer for the purpose of these rules.

(iA) The Complaints Committee shall hold the inquiry unless separate procedure has been prescribed for the Complaints Committee for holding such inquiry into the complaints of sexual harassment, as far as practicable, in accordance with the procedure laid down in these rules.

(iB) The Complaints Committee shall consist of—

(*a*) a Chairperson who shall be a woman;

(*b*) two members representing Non-Governmental Organisation (NGO) or any other body which is familiar with the issue of sexual harassment or nominees of the National or State Human Rights Commission or the National or State Commission for Women familiar with the issue of sexual harassment,

to be nominated by the employer;

Provided that one of the members of the Complaints Committee shall be woman.

(iC) The Complaints Committee shall make and submit every year an annual report, to the appropriate Government, of the complaints and action taken.

(iD) The employers or their agents shall report, to the appropriate Government, on the compliance of the guidelines issued by the Central Government in pursuance of the directions of the Supreme Court in Writ Petition (Criminal) Nos. 666-670 of 1992 (*Vishaka* v *State of Rajasthan*) including the reports of the Complaints Committee.

(*ii*) No order of punishment under Standing Order No. 17(*i*) shall be made unless the workmen concerned is informed in writing of the alleged misconduct and is given an opportunity to explain the allegations made against him. A departmental enquiry shall be instituted before dealing with the charges. During the period of enquiry, the workman concerned may be suspended. The workman may take the assistance of a co-worker to help him in the enquiry, if he so desires. The records of the departmental enquiry shall be kept in writing. The approval of the owner, agent or the chief mining engineer of the employer or a person holding similar position shall be obtained before imposing the punishment of dismissal. A copy of the enquiry proceedings shall be given to the workmen concerned on the conclusion of the enquiry, on request by the workmen.

(*iii*) If a workman is not found guilty of the charges framed against him, he shall be deemed to be on duty during the full period of his suspension and he shall be entitled to receive the same wages as he would have received if he had not been suspended.

(*iv*) In awarding punishment under this standing order, the authority awarding punishment shall take into a account the gravity of the misconduct the pervious record, if any, of the workmen and any other extenuating or aggravating circumstances that may exist. A copy of the order passed by the authority awarding punishment shall be supplied to the workmen concerned.

In Chapter 17 *ante*, the procedural laws/rules/regulations of departmental proceedings have been discussed. Rules are more or less identical: the principle of *audi alteram partem* (i.e., hear the other side), a principle of natural justice, has been followed everywhere.

We would, in the next paragraph refer to various stages of departmental proceedings. And for an exhaustive treatment, we would refer to cognate legislations[9] where necessary.

From the above it transpires that a disciplinary action proceeds through certain stages. Once the employer contemplates or starts disciplinary action against workman in the circumstances stated in Rule 17, he may place the workman under suspension, of course with subsistence allowance. He will be charge-sheeted with opportunity to show cause and, when found guilty, with another reasonable opportunity of making representation on the penalty proposed.

Thus, the stages of a disciplinary action are:

- Issue of charge-sheet with opportunity to show cause.
- Order of suspension.
- Enquiry.
- Second opportunity to the delinquent to submit representation against punishment tentatively decided.
- Order of acquittal/discharge/dismissal etc.

We would hereunder refer to the said stages:

Charge-sheet

The standing orders, as we have seen hereinbefore, regulate the relation of the employer and the employee. By item (9) of the Schedule, the Standing Orders enjoins that misconduct of the workman is punishable. But before punishment is actually inflicted, the employer has to investigate the alleged offences, and to find if the employee really offended. Law enjoins that the employer has to inform the employee in writing the allegations against him. These allegations or charges, when reduced to writing, are to be sent to the employee as the charge-sheet.

The principle of natural justice would have to be read into the standing orders. In case of a standing order granting three days' margin within which the workman is required to return and offer satisfactory explanation of his reasons for his absence or inability to return after the leave is held to have the element of natural justice built in the body of standing orders.[10]

9 (A) Civil Service Regulations:
Article 191. A member of the Indian Civil Service is entitled, when under suspension, to the subsistence allowance of his rank, and a military officer in the civil employ to the pay and allowances of his rank.
(Article 192, 193, 193A, 194, 194A, 194A(6) and 195 may be seen).
(B) Conduct and Discipline Rules for Railway Servants Section III—Suspension—Rule No. 1706.
(C) Central Civil Services (Classification, Control and Appeal) Rules 1965—Rule 10.
(D) Fundamental Rules—Rule 54.
(E) The Railway Servants (Discipline and Appeal) Rules 1968—Rules 4, 5.
(F) West Bengal Services (Classification, Control and Appeal) Rules 1971—Rule 7.

10 *Lakshmi Precision Service Ltd.* v *Ram Bhagat* (2002)6 SCC 552.

Grounds other than those in the charge-sheet: where the employee is not charged with the acts of insubordination, which would readily justify the employer-company in dismissing him from its employ, the company cannot take advantage of the same even though these acts can be brought home to him. The company cannot be allowed to justify its action on any other grounds than those contained in the charge-sheet.[11]

Simultaneous enquiry and criminal proceedings: scope of misconduct is wider than that of a criminal offence, such as theft. The mere fact that the case was sent to the criminal court could not bar a domestic enquiry.[12]

The primary object of issuing a charge-sheet to the employee is to inform the delinquent that there are complaints against him and to know how he proposes to answer those. Rules of natural justice require that nobody should be condemned unheard. Therefore, the delinquent should be granted all reasonable opportunity to speak in his defence.

FORM

There is no prescribed form of a charge-sheet under labour laws. If it satisfies the two tests, a charge-sheet is all right. The tests are:

(*i*) offences charged against are sufficiently and clearly stated;

(*ii*) the delinquent is given a reasonable time to show cause against charges levelled.

The charge-sheet must be specific and set out all the necessary particulars. It is no excuse to say that regard being had to be made to previous proceedings, the delinquent should be taken to have known all about the charges.[13]

The time and date of incident should be mentioned in the charge-sheet. The purpose of the charge-sheet is that it should give an employee a fair idea of the case which he is to face and the validity of the charge must in each case should be determined by application of this test. If the charge is too vague regarding commission of the offence, the employee is deprived of the opportunity to make defence of *alibi*.[14]

If the charge is vague, there is no reasonable opportunity to show cause.[15]

In respect of the language of a charge-sheet, it may simply be said that the language of a charge-sheet should be such as is commonly understood. If the accused is given notice or statement of allegation in a language which he cannot understand and he asks for it in a language which he can understand, his request should be complied with.[16]

11 AIR 1957 SC 7.
12 *New Victoria Mills Co. Ltd.* v *Presiding Officer, Labour Court* AIR 1970 All 210.
13 *Amullya Ratan Mukherjee* v *Eastern Railway* AIR 1961 Cal 40.
14 AIR 1963 SC 1696.
15 *Ananthanarayanan* v *Gen. Manager, Southern Rly.* AIR 1956 Mad 220.
16 *Harikishan* v *State of Maharashtra* AIR 1962 SC 911.

SERVICE OF CHARGE-SHEET

Normally where there is a prescribed mode in Standing Orders, the notice containing the charge-sheet has to be served that way. In the absence of mention of any particular mode, the charge-sheet should be sent by registered post with AD.

Presumption of service will arise when the employee's charge-sheet comes back with endorsement 'refused'.[17]

Order of suspension

Relevant rules for placing a workman under suspension under r. 14(4) of the Industrial Employment (Standing Orders) Central Rules 1946, have been quoted earlier.

The meaning of the word "suspend" has been given in the dictionary as to debar usually for a time from the exercise of a function or employment or a privilege, specially to deprive temporarily of one's office.[18] Suspension of an employee does not amount to dismissal.[19] He continues to be in employment.[20]

When during the pendency of a departmental enquiry a workman is kept out of the office, it is an administrative reason and not a punitive order. The appointing authority or the punishing authority can place the workman under suspension. It is doubtful if the authority can be delegated. But when somebody else issues the order of suspension with the approval of the competent authority, the order is not bad.[1]

Even before initiation of a departmental enquiry a workman can be placed under suspension, but when rules provide that a workman can be placed under suspension during enquiry after the charges are framed, then charges must precede the suspension order.[2]

Placing in suspension of a workman may be justified as well as unjustified according to the facts and circumstances. When three charges out of four were dropped earlier and even if enquiry could be started in respect of the 4th charge, the suspension order was not justified. 'Where a substantial part of the suspension order is irrelevant, the order must be set aside'.[3] At times suspension becomes justified and in most cases it happens so when a workman or a servant proceeded against is a man of influence and position. In order to avoid embarrassment to the delinquent, as also to his colleagues, as also against an apprehended obstruction of fair trial, the delinquent is kept out of office.

17 AIR 1964 SC 152. Also see *Ayisabeevi* v *Aboobacker* AIR 1971 Ker 231 and *Puwada Venkaitaswara Rao* v *Chidamana Venkata Ramana* AIR 1976 SC 869.
18 *Abid Md. Khan* v *State of MP* AIR 1958 MP 44.
19 AIR 1946 Nag 347.
20 AIR 1956 Mad 95.
1 AIR 1957 All 671.
2 AIR 1959 All 230.
3 AIR 1961 Mys 31.

Before passing on to the actual hearing of a disciplinary action, we may note here that suspension with retrospective effect is not always illegal. This means that, generally speaking, an order of suspension with retrospective effect is bad in law. But when service rules or Standing Orders permit suspension with retrospective effect, that is valid.

Dismissal with effect from the date of suspension—a retrospective dismissal is not valid.[4]

But the trend of legal opinion is otherwise. We may cite the case of *Omprakash Gupta* v *State of UP*.[5] Dismissal in that case was effective from the date of order of suspension.

In a case in which the instructions contained in various letters and circulars of Central Government were allegedly not strictly followed before the lodging of the FIR, it was held that the failure to follow the instructions fully, *per se* would not invalidate the suspension order under r. 7(3) of All India Services (Discipline and Appeal) Rules 1955.[6]

Enquiry

Departmental enquiries may be described as quasi-judicial in nature.[7] But the procedural laws of a judicial proceeding do not strictly apply to a departmental enquiry. In other words, it is not governed by the provisions of the Evidence Act or the Code of Civil Procedure.[8]

Where Standing Orders provide a departmental enquiry, the requirements of standing orders have to be complied with. Standing Orders framed and certified under the Industrial Disputes (Standing Orders) Act have the force of Law.[9]

Where there are statutory rules, those should be followed in holding an enquiry.

Enquiry starts truly when the delinquent is charge-sheeted with specific charges and he is called upon to show cause. The workman should be informed about the name and designation of the Enquiry Officer before whom he is to appear and submit his defence or explanation with specific mention of date, time and place of enquiry. Notice of enquiry may be verbal as well.[10] If the notice for appearing in enquiry is vague about the date, time and place, another notice should be sent with correct particulars.[11] In all cases, the workman should be informed ahead of the date, time and place of enquiry sittings. It is not right that the worker can be called on any day at any time

4 *Sudhir Ranjan Haldar* v *State of West Bengal* AIR 1961 Cal 626.
5 AIR 1955 SC 600.
6 *D.D. Suri* v *A.K. Barren* AIR 1976 SC 1069.
7 AIR 1963 Cal 316; AIR 1950 All 607; AIR 1964 SC 364.
8 AIR 1960 Ker 63.
9 AIR 1965 SC 439.
10 AIR 1962 SC 666.
11 AIR 1960 Punj 41.

without previous intimation and enquiry can be started straightway. In case of adjournment of the hearing, a fresh notice should be issued to the workman. If, on the other hand, the enquiry proceeds without notice to the workman, the rules of natural justice are offended.

Even if the workman fails to attend a particular stage of enquiry, he can enter appearance at a subsequent stage and may demand his right to cross-examine witnesses already appearing and examined.

Ordinarily, the rule is that personal hearing should be granted to the workman though personal hearing is not a must-feature of principles of natural justice.[12] But the situation becomes different when the delinquent asks for personal hearing. In a case of refusal to grant personal hearing when asked for, an order terminating service is liable to be set aside.[13]

If the workman refuses to attend the enquiry, the enquiry may proceed *ex parte*. If he intentionally fails, he cannot complain that enquiry was against the principles of natural justice.[14] The conduct of an employee in deliberately not appearing goes against the employee that he had no opportunity to defend.[15] If the workman withdraws at a subsequent stage of enquiry, the enquiry should proceed and be completed.

Absence of the workman during the inquiry proceedings may be justified on grounds of health, personal ground, etc. Enquiry has to be adjourned in such case.

A delinquent cannot ask for the services of a lawyer or a union officer to represent him before the Enquiry Officer unless statutory rules so provide or the same is granted by the Enquiry Officer in the interest of justice.

Departmental enquiry conducted in accordance with Rule 1730 of Railway Establishment Code, Vol. I—delinquent Railway officer is not entitled to services of a professional lawyer in view of Note 3 to the said Rule..[16]

DOUBLE ENQUIRY IF BARRED?

Departmental enquiry on the same allegations as in previous enquiry does not operate as a bar. If an enquiry is held at a particular stage, possibly to determine whether regular proceedings would be drawn up or started, it does not debar a departmental trial after framing a charge.[17]

After the enquiry is over, the Enquiry Officer is to hold specific findings on each charge, and to send it to the disciplinary authority.

Opinion is divergent whether the workman is entitled to a copy of the Enquiry report. Where Standing Orders provide that the workman should

12 *A.K. Gopalan* v *State of Madras* AIR 1950 SC 27; *Shivji Nathubhai* v *Union of India* AIR 1960 SC 606.

13 *Miss Eva Rout* v *State of Orissa* AIR 1969 Ori 293.

14 AIR 1957 SC 12.

15 *H. Moitra* v *Calcutta Improvement Tribunal* AIR 1970 Cal 154.

16 *H.C. Sarin* v *Union of India* AIR 1976 SC 1686.

17 *R.C. Sharma* v *Union of India* AIR 1976 SC 2037.

be supplied with a copy of findings after completion of the enquiry, failure to supply violates the rules. Where rules are silent, failure to supply a copy of the findings does not violate principles of natural justice.

The punishing authority has to apply his mind to the record of enquiry proceedings. He may concur, he may disagree. If the punishing authority agrees, he is not required to state specifically that he agrees.[18]

If, on the other hand, the punishing authority differs from the Enquiry Officer the authority states the reason and seeks for further explanation by the second show-cause notice which is usually the notice to show cause against the penalty. If this is not followed, the punishment is liable to be set aside.[19]

Second show cause notice

The second show-cause notice is not just a requirement of the principle of natural justice. Article 311(2) of the Constitution makes a scope for the contemplated notice for the second time. Is it a must in all cases? If the employee is governed by Art. 311 or by Civil Services (Classification, Control and Appeal) Rules or cognate legislation providing therein provision for the second notice—it is a must.

This is not, and need not be, extended to private workmen if there be no rules to that effect in service rules or Standing Orders.

The second opportunity to make representation on the penalty proposed:

A second notice to show cause within a specified period as to why the proposed punishment of dismissal should not be inflicted, is required to be given not as a mere idle formality; it has a meaning and purpose. It is intended to provide an opportunity to the workman to show cause against the proposed punishment of dismissal. The workman may show that the findings of the Enquiring Officer are not justified on the evidence on record or that even if the findings are justified, they do not warrant the extreme penalty of dismissal from service having regard to the nature and gravity of the misconduct, the past record of the workman, and any other extenuating circumstances. The notice must, therefore, give a reasonable opportunity to the workman. That is a condition precedent which must be satisfied before an order of dismissal can be validly passed by the employer.[20]

Next comes the final stage of the enquiry—the punishment.

Dismissal

The word 'dismissal' has come to acquire a specific meaning of termination of service on punitive grounds. The words 'dismissal' and 'removal' are not merely totologus but are 'technical words' or 'words of art' and have acquired special significance.[1]

18 *State of Assam* v *Promod Kumar* AIR 1963 SC 1612.
19 *Manoranjan Das* v *Commr., Residency Division* AIR 1970 Cal 179.
20 *M/s. Laxmirattan Mills Ltd.* v *Workmen* AIR 1975 SC 1689.
1 *Khem Chand* v *Union of India* AIR 1958 SC 300.

There is, however, a difference between dismissal and termination of service. In dismissal, a slur is cast on the workman, while there is no such slur when services are merely terminated.

5 Resignation and termination of service—notice therefor

Termination of service in pursuance of service rule or agreement is different from dismissal or removal.

In Art. 311 of the Constitution, the expression 'dismissal or removal' has been used. The word 'removal' under the said Article means 'removal from service by way of punishment and not removal by way of termination of service. Article 311 is, therefore, not applicable to simple termination of service which is not punitive in character.

Where the service rules provide for limitation of service in certain contingencies and the service is terminated in accordance with service rules and this is also mentioned in the order of termination, then, it is not punitive.[2]

Where there is no provision in the service contract that the services of workman can be terminated by one month's notice, then the termination of service on notice would amount to punishment since the employee had a right to hold the post.[3]

6 Discharge simpliciter—notice therefor

The authority to issue an order of discharge *simpliciter* must be based either on Standing Orders or some service rules, otherwise the power cannot be exercised.

If there is no indication in the order that it is in terms of contract of service and, on the contrary, there is indication of misconduct or fault, then mere mention of 'in terms of contract' will not be discharge *simpliciter*.[4] If the workman is discharged from service in accordance with the terms of his agreement, be cannot make a grievance that provisions of s. 240 of the Government of India Act have not been followed.[5]

If discharge is due to misconduct of the workman, it is punitive and an enquiry is called for. In a case the company terminated services of a workman for taking personal loans from the wholesalers and denying them and filing criminal complaints against them which were mentioned as acts of misconduct'. In the written statement the company pleaded that it preferred to punish him by discharge instead of dismissing him. It cannot be said that the order was one of discharge *simpliciter*.[6]

2 *Union of India* v *Kartar Singh* AIR 1966 P&H 106.
3 *Pushkar Dutta* v *Union of India* AIR 1963 All 441.
4 AIR 1960 MP 294.
5 *Gopal Krishna Potney* v *Union of India* AIR 1954 SC 632.
6 *Brooke Bond India (P) Ltd.* v *Chandranath Chowdhury* AIR 1969 SC 992.

FORMS

Form 1

Notice of change

Name and address of the establishment

Take notice that following changes have taken place with effect from .... in the particulars furnished by me in notice dated .... on Form "A".

Name:

Address:

Name of the Employer:

Nature of business:

Place
Date

(Signature of the Employer with
name and designation)

NOTE: Such a notice has to be sent to the Controlling Authority of the area within 30 days of any change in the name, address, employer or nature of business.

Form 2

Notice of closure

Take notice that it is intended to close down the establishment with effect from .... The other details are furnished below:

1. Name and address of the establishment
2. Name and address of the Head Office, if any
3. Name and designation of the employer
4. Number of persons in employment
5. Number of employees entitled to gratuity
6. Amount of gratuity involved

Place
Date

(Signature of the Employer with
name and designation)

To
The Controlling Authority.

NOTE: This notice has to be served on the Controlling Authority at least 60 days before the intended closure.

Form 3

Notice (containing a charge-sheet)—case of misconduct

.... Dated the .... 20 ....

....

No. ......

To

....

(Name)

....

(Address)

Whereas it has been reported against you that you on .... at .... had committed .... (*state allegations*) and thereby misconducted yourself.

You are hereby directed to show cause within .... days from the date of receipt of this notice as to why appropriate action shall not be taken against you.

The acts, as above alleged to have been committed by you come within the purview of (major) misconduct as per clause .... of Certified Standing Orders or Service Rules of the company.

Your explanation in writing should reach this office within the period allowed hereinabove; in default it would be presumed that you have no explanation to offer and the matter will be disposed of without further reference.

(*If necessary add*: since the allegations are grave you are hereby placed under suspension with immediate effect. During the period of suspension you will be entitled to .... % of your pay as subsistence allowance).

Receipt of this letter may be acknowledged.

Sd/- ....

(Authority)

NOTE: Where the provisions of the Standing Orders cannot be cited, the particular type of misconduct has to be stated in details.

Form 4

Notice containing a charge-sheet for absence from duty

Dated the ... . 20...

....

....

To

....

....

Whereas you have been absenting yourself from duty with effect from the .... day of .... 20...... without prior intimation and permission.

Whereas your such unauthorised absence is injurious to the institution/factory .... resulting in dislocation of the work, or, thereby creating bottleneck in the smooth running of the work.

You are hereby called upon to explain in writing within 72 hours from receipt of this notice as to why disciplinary measures shall not be taken against you.

You are further directed to resume your duty forthwith.

In the event of your failure the Management may be constrained to take disciplinary measures without further reference to you.

....

....

Manager/Employer/Authority

Form 5

Notice (containing a charge-sheet) for insubordination

To Dated the .... 20 ....

....

....

Whereas you, while on duty at the factory premises, on .... were instructed by Superintendent/Chargeman/Manager (the person in authority) to .... and you, reportedly, flatly refused to do the same.

Whereas such behaviour on your part was highly reprehensible and amounted to wilful insubordination and breach of discipline.

You are hereby instructed to show cause, within 7 days from the date of receipt of this charge-sheet, as to why disciplinary action should not be taken against you.

Should you fail to submit your explanation it would be presumed that you have no explanation to offer and the matter would be disposed of without further reference.

Employer/Authority

Form 6

Notice (containing a charge-sheet) for unauthorised absence from duty—when leave refused

To

....

....

Whereas you absented yourself from duty for the period from ...... to ...... both inclusive, in spite of the fact that your application for leave dated ...... was rejected by the authority on account of exigencies.

Whereas your such unauthorised absence constitutes a misconduct as defined in cl. (*x*) of the Standing Order/Service Rules.

You are, therefore, directed to submit your explanation, within 48 hours, from receipt of this notice, as to why disciplinary action shall not be taken against you.

Sd/- ....

(Employer)

Form 7

Notice containing a charge-sheet for fraud, misappropriation etc.

To Dated the .... 20 ....

Whereas

(state here the allegations)

2. Since the aforesaid charges against you are of a serious nature, you are hereby required to submit your explanation to said charges within 10 days from receipt of this charge as to why disciplinary action shall not be taken against you.

(SEE EARLIER FORMS) Sd/ ....

(Employer/Authority)

Form 8

Charge-sheet for joining an illegal meeting

To Dated the .... 20 ....

That on ...... you along with some other workmen joined a meeting at ...... p.m. within the factory premises/within the premises of the establishment.

You had knowledge or reasons to believe that the said meeting was prohibited by the management. By joining the said meeting you committed a breach of rules of discipline.

You are hereby directed to show cause to the said charges within 10 days from receipt of this notice as to why disciplinary action shall not be taken against you.

(as in previous forms)

Sd/- ....

(Employer/Authority)

Form 9

Charge-sheet for late attendance

To Dated .... 20 ....

It has come to the notice of the management that you are coming late to your duty for the last .... days from .... This offends clause .... of Standing Orders of the Factory.

The above acts/omissions on your part make you liable for disciplinary action.

You are hereby directed to submit your explanation to said charges within 10 days from receipt of this charge as to why disciplinary action shall not be taken against you.

Sd/- ....

(Employer/Authority)

Form 10

Charge-sheet for negligence of duty

To Dated the .... 20 ....

Whereas you were detailed for duty on ....

(state the duty)

And on .... name the materials of the factory were stolen by some unknown culprits causing a loss of the factor to the tune of Rs. 10,000.

And, whereas the theft occurred because of your connivance or gross negligence.

And, whereas your act/omission make you liable for .... (as in previous forms) are directed to submit your explanation etc.

Sd/- ....

(Employer/Authority)

Form 11

Charge-sheet for resorting to strike

To Dated the .... 20 ....

....

....

Whereas you along with others stopped the work in the said Establishment on .... at .... and resorted to strike in support of your claims mentioned in your Charter of Demands dated ....

Whereas you know and/or had reasons to believe that the above matter was pending before the Conciliation Officer/Labour Court/Industrial Tribunal and that the said strike would be illegal.

Whereas the said illegal strike is a misconduct under the Industrial Employment Standing Orders of their Establishment.

Your are hereby ....

(as in previous forms)

Sd/-........................

Manager/Employer

Form 12

Notice of suspension pending enquiry

To Dated the .... 20 ....

(*State here the name of the Employee*)

Whereas you have been charge-sheeted for charges of gross misconduct and indiscipline by this Establishment/Company by its letter/Est. Order No. ...... dated ...... sent to you.

And, whereas for proper conduct of the enquiry the management feels it necessary that you should stay away from office (or feels it desirable that you should be placed under suspension). (Or, and whereas for proper conduct of the enquiry and in the interest of the establishment it is desirable that you should stay away from office).

Your are hereby placed under suspension from your service pending enquiry against you.

2. During the period of suspension you would be entitled to a subsistence allowance at the admissible rate/or at the rate of Rs. ...... per month/or as per clause .... of the Standing Orders/Service Rules.

3. You are warned not to leave the station without prior permission of the authority.

Sd/- ....
(Employer/Authority)

Form 13

A Notice for holding an enquiry against a delinquent workman
(Another form)

By registered post with AD
Dated the .... 20 ....

(Name of the Office/Company/Concern with address)

To

Sub:—Disciplinary proceedings No.

Ref:—Charge-sheet dtd....... No. ......

Your show-cause reply dated. ....

Your reply dtd. .... to the charges levelled against you by the charge-sheet dated ...... was received in the Office on .... The same does not appear to be convincing and it has been decided to hold an enquiry into the said charges.

2. Sri .... has been appointed by the Management as the Enquiring Officer to hold and conduct the enquiry.

3. You are instructed to appear before the said Enquiring Officer as may be directed by him from time to time.

4. Papers/documents forming the basis of allegations have been lying with him which you may inspect in his presence or as may be directed by him.

Sd/- ....
Manager

By registered post with AD
Dated the .... 20 ....

Copy to

Copy along with connected papers relevant to the proposed enquiry are sent herewith. He is requested to hold the enquiry, granting the delinquent reasonable opportunity to defend himself, and to submit his report after completion of the Enquiry.

Sd/- ....
(Manager)

Form 14

Appointment of Enquiry Officer

Dated the .... 20 ....

To

Whereas Sri ...., an employee of this establishment has been charge-sheeted by Order No. .... dated. .... and the authority intends to hold an enquiry into the said charges.

You are hereby appointed and authorised to hold the enquiry into the said charges, giving the delinquent employee all reasonable opportunities in defending himself.

You are requested to complete the enquiry by .... and submit your report to the undersigned soon thereafter.

The charge-sheet, explanation of the delinquent and all connected papers are enclosed. The same should be returned along with your report.

This may please be acknowledged.

Sd/-

Manager/Or, Authorised persons

Form 15

Notice of the termination of service of an employee

Regd. Post with AD

Dated the .... 20 ....

To

Sri ....

(*State here name, address and designation of the employee*)

Dear Sir,

Please take notice that you were appointed in the post of .... in the (name of the establishment) on the strength of a letter of appointment No. ...... dated .... issued by ....

The said appointment letter contains a condition to the effect that your services may be terminated at any time after giving one month's notice or one month's salary in lieu thereof.

Since your services are no longer required in the aforesaid (name the establishment) this notice may please be treated as one month's notice prior to termination of your service.

Yours faithfully

Sd/- ....

(Employer)

CHAPTER 28

Notices under the Municipalities, Municipal Corporations and other Body-corporates

SYNOPSIS

1 Notice before institution of a suit against a municipality or corporation

2 Corporation—if notice is required

1 Notice before institution of a suit against a municipality or corporation

Under s. 326(1) of the UP Municipalities Act 1916, a notice has to be given to a municipal board before filing a suit against it. Section 233 of the Ajmere Merwara Municipalities Regulation, s. 384 of the City of Nagpur Corporation Act, s. 407 of the West Bengal Municipal Act 1993, and s. 167A of the Bombay District Municipal Act, amongst others, prescribe a similar provision.

Section 407 of the West Bengal Municipal Act 1993 enjoins:

"(1) No suit shall be instituted in any court having jurisdiction against any municipal authority or any officer or other employee of the municipality or any person acting under the direction of any municipal authority or any officer or other employee of the municipality in respect of any act done or purporting to be done under this Act or the rules or the regulations made thereunder until after the expiration of one month next after a notice in writing has been delivered or left at the office of such authority or at the residence of such officer or other employee or person, stating—

(*a*) the cause of action,

(*b*) the name and residence of the intending plaintiff, and

(*c*) the relief which such plaintiff claims.

(2) [Omitted].

(3) If the municipal authority at the office of which, or the officer or the other employee of the municipality or the person acting under the direction of any municipal authority or any officer or other employee of the municipality at the office or the residence of whom, a notice has been delivered or left under sub-section (1), satisfies the court having jurisdiction that the relief claimed was tendered to the plaintiff before the institution of the suit, the suit shall be dismissed.

(4) Nothing in the foregoing provisions of this section shall apply to any suit instituted under section 38 of the Specific Relief Act."

This provision is a *verbatim* reproduction of s. 586 of the Kolkata Municipal Corporation Act 1980, although sub-sec. (2) of the West Bengal Municipal Act has since been deleted.

The object of such a notice is to give an opportunity to the Municipal Board to examine its position and give it time to decide whether the matter should be settled out of court[1] to reconsider the legal position and if their course is justified to make amends or to settle the claim out of court.[2]

It may be pointed out that if the intended suit is one for perpetual injunction, no notice under this section is required to be given.

A notice under s. 407 of the West Bengal Municipal Act 1993, has to be interpreted in the similar way as a notice under s. 80 of the Code of Civil Procedure.

But a notice under s. 326(1) of the UP Municipalities Act 1916, is required to contain:

(*i*) cause of action;

(*ii*) name and place of abode of the intending plaintiff;

(*iii*) nature of relief; and

(*iv*) amount of compensation claimed.

Obviously item No. (*iv*) is merged in item No. (*iii*) and is redundant.

Difference from a notice under s. 80 of the Code of Civil Procedure is manifest in the additional requirement of 'description' of the intending plaintiff along with his name and place of residence which is not required in a notice of suit against a municipality.

1 AIR 1962 All 211.
2 AIR 1965 SC 11.

Service of notice under s. 326 of the UP Municipalities Act is not restricted to cases arising out of contract only. Notice under the section is obligatory in every kind of suit.[3] If the act threatened to be injuncted relates to some past act or order, notice under s. 326 of the UP Municipalities Act will be necessary.[4]

For acts and omissions which are beyond the jurisdiction of the municipality or its officers, no notice is necessary under s. 407 of the West Bengal Municipal Act but when the act complained of is not in exercise of jurisdiction which is inherently absent, notice is mandatory.[5]

If a suit is to be instituted in respect of any act done but prohibited by the Municipal Act or by any other provision, no notice is necessary.

Where a notice correctly states the facts on which the suit is subsequently based and the board had ample notice of the nature of the plaintiff's claim, the mere slip or inaccuracy in starting the date of the cause of action in the notice does not render the notice defective so as to invalidate the suit because it does not go to the root of the suit.[6]

Goa, Daman and Diu Municipalities Act (Act 7 of 1969)—s. 78. Suit to restrain officers from implementing no-confidence motion on ground of want of notice to certain members—notice under s. 80 of the Code of Civil Procedure to officers is necessary.[7]

2 Corporation—if notice is required

The fact that the capital of a Corporation was provided by the Central Government or that its working was supervised or directions were issued by the Central Government does not make it a Government within meaning of s. 80, CP Code. Although the expression 'Government' has not been defined in the Code of Civil Procedure, it cannot include a 'corporation' constituted under an Act of Parliament.[8]

Where the officers of the corporation are in service and pay of the corporation and are paid out of the funds of the corporation, they are not public officers within the meaning of s. 80. Notice of suit under s. 80, CPC is not required.

3 *Dargahi Lal Nigam* v *Cawnpore Municipal Board* AIR 1952 All 382; *Babu Khan* v *Nagar Mahapalika, Lucknow* AIR 1973 All 111.
4 *Municipal Board* v *Edward Medical Hall* AIR 1976 All 349.
5 AIR 1966 SC 242.
6 AIR 1962 All 211.
7 *Jairam Ramchandra Sirsat* v *Baburao Munguesh Karikar* AIR 1973 Goa 1.
8 *Kanta Prasad Singh* v *Regional Manager, FCI* AIR 1974 Pat 376.

FORM

Form 1

Notice of suit

By registered post with AD

To

The Commissioners of the .... Municipality,
Through the Chairman ..... of the .... Municipality
P.O. ....
District ....

Dear Sir,

Please take notice that my client Sri ..... son of .... residing at .... P.S. ... District .... (when plaintiff himself issues the notice), intends to sue the Commissioners of the .... Municipality in a competent court of law after expiry of one month after service of this notice unless proper and satisfactory amends are made in the meantime.

The cause of action for the intended suit arose under the following circumstances:

(State here the cause of action).

Yours faithfully,

A./B.

NOTES:

1. Notice period is one month.
2. Notice should state name, place and above of the notice-giver. (Description as in s. 80, Code of Civil Procedure is not wanted in West Bengal).
3. Notice to be left at the office of the Commissioners of the Municipality. Law does not mention whom the notice is to be addressed to.
4. Under s. 15(2) of the Act the suit is to be filed against the Commissioners of the Municipality.

CHAPTER 29

Notices under the Labour Laws

SYNOPSIS

(A) NOTICE UNDER THE EMPLOYEES' STATE INSURANCE ACT 1948

1 Notice of accident with appropriate particulars (Reg. 65)
2 Notice, otherwise than by an entry in the Accident Book–duty of the employer to make an entry (Reg. 67)
3 Notice for dependants' benefit on death of an employee (insured) (Reg. 81)
4 Notice of pregnancy–certificate of pregnancy (Reg. 87)
5 Notice of resumption of work by an insured female employee (Reg. 91)

(B) THE MINES ACT 1952

1 Notice regarding mining operations
2 Notice of accident–consequence of failure to give notice–penal provisions (s. 23)
3 Notice about certain diseases connected with mining operations (s. 25)
4 Notices regarding hours of work (s. 36)

(C) THE CHILD AND ADOLESCENT LABOUR (PROHIBITION AND REGULATION) ACT 1986

1 Prohibition of child labour and regulation of adolescent labour
2 Notice to inspector

(A) NOTICE UNDER THE EMPLOYEES' STATE INSURANCE ACT 1948

This Act is a social security legislation meant to provide certain benefits to employees in case of sickness, maternity and employment injury and to make provisions for certain other matters in relation thereto.

Section 3 of the Act provides for setting up of a corporation to be known as the Employees' State Insurance Corporation for administration of the scheme of the Employees' State Insurance. The Act itself does not make any provision for issuance of a notice. Under s. 97 of the Act, some regulations have been framed named the Employees' State Insurance (General) Regulations.

These relate, amongst others, to benefits. Section 50 of the Act relates to maternity benefit; s. 51 to disablement benefit and s. 52 of the Act relates to dependants' benefit. The benefits are, however, not to be combined (s. 65).

Regulations No. 65, 67, 81 and 87 are relevant for our study.

1 Notice of accident with appropriate particulars (Regulation 65)

Regulation No. 65 deals with notice of an accident. Every employee sustaining an injury in the course of his employment in a factory or establishment is required to give a notice, either orally or in writing, of the accident as soon as practicable after the happening of the accident.

The meaning of the expression 'as soon as practicable' means that there should not be unreasonable delay. The expression has been used in s. 10 of the Employee's Compensation Act.

(See under Employee's Compensation Act, Note 2).

It means 'as soon as possible'.[1]

The notice has to be served on the employer, or to a person in authority under whom the employee had been working at the material time. The notice has to contain appropriate particulars.

By 'appropriate particulars' relevant information as to nature and cause of accident, identity of the employee injured, identity and authority of the notice-giver, evidence of accident are sought for.

As in the Employee's Compensation Act 1923 [vide s. 10, sub-sec. (3) of the Act] there is a similar provision for maintaining a notice book (vide Regulation No. 66 of the said Regulations) wherein also the appropriate particulars of an accident may be entered.[2] If such an entry is made 'as soon as practicable' after happening of the accident, that entry would constitute a sufficient notice of the accident.

2 Notice, otherwise than by an entry in the Accident Book—duty of the employer to make an entry (Regulation 67)

Regulation No. 67 speaks of notice otherwise than by an entry in Accident Book.

In Note 1 we have seen that the provision for a notice of accident may be avoided by making an entry in the Accident Book.

If no entry has been made by the injured employee or by any person on his behalf in the Accident Book and a notice has been given to the employer, the employer is required to make an entry in the book immediately after receipt of the notice. If any other person is authorised to be served with a notice, he is likewise required to make the entry.

Where the notice is not in writing, contents of the report orally submitted should be read over, when reduced to a writing in the book, and signature or thumb impression of the reporter should be taken in the book.

1 AIR 1950 Pat 228.
2 *Regional Director, FSI Corporation* v *Francis D' Costa* 1993 (Supp) 4 SCC 100.

3 Notice for dependants' benefit on death of an employee (insured) (Regulation 81)

Regulation No. 81 is meant for dependants' benefit where the employee was insured and died.

A claim has to be made to the appropriate regional office for dependants' benefits whereupon the regional office has to issue a notice by registered post to persons who might appear entitled to dependants' benefits but did not submit any claim.

The contents of notice shall invite submission of claims, within 30 days from the date of receipt of the notice, for the dependants' benefits showing title to the claim. It would also indicate the procedure for submission of claims.

4 Notice of pregnancy—certificate of pregnancy (Regulation 87)

Regulation No. 87 provides for a notice of pregnancy.

This notice has to be given by an insured female employee before confinement in Form 17 appended to the said Regulation to the appropriate local office by post or otherwise and should submit together with such notice a certificate of pregnancy in Form 17 appended to the Regulation.

5 Notice of resumption of work by an insured female employee (Regulation 91)

Regulation No. 91 enjoins that a notice to work for remuneration shall have to be given in Form 19 by every insured female who claims benefits of maternity under the foregoing Regulation.

FORMS

Form 1

Notice of pregnancy together with certificate of pregnancy (Regulation 87)

Registered post

Signature or thumb impression of the Insured Woman

Employer's Code No. ....

Book No. ....

Serial No. ....

Insured Woman's Name ....
Insurance No. ....
Wife/Daughter of ....

Stamp of the dispensary

Certified that I have examined the abovementioned Insured Woman today and that in my opinion she is pregnant and her pregnancy appears to be .... weeks old.

....
Signature of midwife, if any

Any other remarked ....
Date ....

M: Notice 40

....

Signature or counter-signature of the Insurance Medical Officer

....

Name in block letters and Rubber Stamp

I, ... Insurance No. .... wife/daughter of .... hereby give notice of pregnancy.

Present address ....

Present/last employer ....

Date ....

....

Signature or thumb impression of the Insured Woman

Form 2

Notice by an insured female for resuming work after confinement

Maternity Benefit
Notice to work

Insurance No. ....

I, ... Wife of/Daughter of ...., do hereby give notice that I have taken/shall take up work for remuneration with effect from the .... day of ...., 20 .... I have drawn maternity benefit up to the .... day of .... 20 ....

....

(Signature or thumb impression)

Dated .... 20....

Present address ....

....

Form 3

Notice of accident
(Regulation No. 65)

To

....

....

(Name of the employer or the person in authority under whom the employee had been working at the material time)

I, ... son of ...., Hindu male aged .... years of .... (address), a fitter of the .... department of the .... Factory lost my right eye in an accident on .... at 10-45 a.m., in the Factory premises while on duty.

Sri .... son of .... of the .... Wing and Sri .... son of ...... of the .... Wing, both fitters in the .... Wing of the said .... Factory were present at the spot when the accident happened.

The policy of Insurance bears No. ....

....

(Signature or thumb impression)

Dated .... 20....

Present address ....

....

(B) The Mines Act 1952

1 Notice regarding mining operations

This Act relates to the regulation of labour and safety in mines.

Section 16 of the Mines Act 1952, enjoins:

(1) The owner, agent or manager of a mine shall, before the commencement of any mining operation, give to the Chief Inspector, the Controller, Indian Bureau of Mines and the District Magistrate of the district in which the mine is situate, notice in writing in such form and containing such particulars relating to the mine as may be prescribed.

(2) Any notice given under sub-sec. (1) shall be so given as to reach the persons concerned at least one month before the commencement of any mining operation.

The provisions of the section are obligatory. A notice must reach the named authorities at least one month before the commencement of any mining operation.

2 Notice of accident—consequence of failure to give notice—penal provisions (section 23)

(1) Whenever there occurs in or about a mine—

(*a*) An accident causing loss of life or serious bodily injury, or

(*b*) an explosion, ignition, spontaneous heating, outbreak of fire or eruption or inrush of water or other liquid matter, or

(*c*) an influx of inflammable or noxious gases, or

(*d*) a breakage of ropes, chains or other gear by which persons or materials are lowered or raised in a shaft or an incline, or

(*e*) an overwinding of cages or other means of conveyance in any shaft while persons or materials are being lowered or raised, or

(*f*) a premature collapse of any part of the workings, or

(*g*) any other accident which may be prescribed,

the owner, agent or manager of the mine shall give notice of the occurrence to such authority in such form and within such time as may be prescribed, and he shall simultaneously post one copy of the notice on a special notice board in the prescribed manner at a place where it may be inspected by

Trade Union officials, and shall ensure that the notice is kept on the board for not less than 14 days from the date of such posting.

Consequences of failure to give a notice of accident are detailed in s. 70 of the Act; under sub-sec. (2) of s. 23, it has been stated that where a notice given under sub-sec. (1) relates to an accident causing loss of life, the authority shall make an inquiry into the occurrence within two months of the receipt of the notice and, if the authority is not the Inspector, he shall cause the Inspector to make an enquiry within the said period.

Sub-section (2) requires only the commencement of the enquiry within the period of two months from the date on which the notice under sub-sec. (1) has been received. It does not prescribe any period within which such enquiry should be completed.[3]

The penal provision for failure to give notice under s. 23(1) is contained in s. 70 of the Act which enjoins:

> Section 70(1). Whoever in contravention of the provision of sub-section (1) of section 23 fails to give notice of any accidental occurrence or to post a copy of the notice on the special notice board referred to in that sub-section and to keep it there for the period specified shall be punishable with imprisonment for a term which may extend to three months, or with fine which may extend to five hundred rupees, or with both.

3 Notice about certain diseases connected with mining operations (section 25)

Section 25. Where any person employed in a mine contracts any disease notified by the Central Government in Official Gazette as a disease connected with mining operations, the owner, agent or manager of the mine, as the case may be, shall send notice thereof to the Chief Inspector and to such other authorities, in such form and within such time as may be prescribed.

The owner or the agent of the owner or the manager of the mine, has to send the notice to the Chief Inspector and to other authorities as may be required. The form of notice and the time within which the notice has to be sent shall be as per law as may be prescribed in that behalf.

4 Notices regarding hours of work (section 36)

Section 36(1). The manager of every mine shall cause to be posted outside the office of the mine a notice in the prescribed form stating the time of the commencement and of the end of work at the mine and, if it is proposed to work by a system of relays, the time of the commencement and of the end of work for each relay. Rule 48 of the Mines Rules 1955 further enjoins that a copy of the notice shall be affixed on the first page of the registered maintained in the office.

Form A

Notice of commencement and end of work

Name of the Mine ....

Owner ....

It is hereby notified that persons employed at this mine shall begin and end their periods of work between the hours set out below.

Serial No.	Class or kind of employment	Sex	#[***]	Place of work Above ground/ Open cast working below ground	Set or Relay Number (A, B, C, etc.)	1. Set or Relay	A	B	C	D	Etc.
						2. Shift	1 2 3	1 2 3	1 2 3	1 2 3	
1	2	3		##[4]	##[5]	Period of work					
						3. Begins	A.M./P.M.				
						Ends*	A.M./P.M.				
						*Interval for rest, if any					
						4. Begins*	A.M./P.M.				
						Ends*	A.M./P.M.				
						5. System of change of shifts					
						6. Date on which this notice was first exhibited					

Note:*The words and letters not required shall be scored out.

Signature of Manager

Date ....

Column 4 omitted by G.S.R. 316, dated 14.4.1986 (w.e.f. 16.1.1986).

Columns 5 and 6 renumbered as columns 4 and 5 by G.S.R. 316, dated 14.4.1986 (w.e.f. 16.4.1986).

(C) THE CHILD AND ADOLESCENT LABOUR (PROHIBITION OF REGULATION) ACT 1986

1 Prohibition of child labour and regulation of adolescent labour

The Act is intended to prohibit the engagement of children in all occupations and to prohibit the engagement of adolescents in hazardous occupations and processes and to regulate the conditions of service of adolescents.

A child means a person who has not completed his fourteenth year of age, while an adolescent means a person who has completed his fourteenth year of age but has not completed his eighteenth year.

No child shall be employed or permitted to work in any occupation or process [s. 3(1)]. Of course, nothing in sub-sec. (1) shall apply to any family or family enterprise other than any hazardous occupations and processes, subject to prescribed conditions and safety measures and not affecting the school education of the child [s. 3(2)].

No adolescent shall be employed or permitted to work in any of the hazardous occupations or processes set forth in the Schedule to the Act [s. 3A].

2 Notice to inspector

An occupier, in relation to an establishment or a workshop, means the person who has the ultimate control over the affairs of the establishment or the workshop [s. 2(*vi*)].

Every occupier in relation to an establishment in which an adolescent is employed or permitted to work shall within a period of thirty days send to the inspector within whose local limits the establishment is situated a written notice containing:

(*a*) the name and situation of the establishment;

(*b*) the name of the person in actual management of the establishment;

(*c*) the address to which communications relating to the establishment should be sent; and

(*d*) the nature of the occupation or process carried on in the establishment. [s. 9(1)].

Failure to give such notice attracts penalty under sub-sec. (3) of s. 14 of the Act.

CHAPTER 30

Notices under other Central Acts

SYNOPSIS

1 Administrator-General's Act 1963–notice of suit (s. 40)–s. 80 of the CPC—when not attracted
2 The Explosives Act 1884–notice of accidents (as amended in 1945–s. 8)
3 The Dissolution of Muslim Marriage Act 1939–service of notice to the heirs of the husband–a condition of suit
4 The Police Act 1861–notice of suit–limitation
5 The Special Marriage Act 1954–notice of intended marriage
6 Marriage not solemnized within three months of notice
7 The Births, Deaths and Marriage Registration Act 1886–notice of birth–notice of death
8 The Indian Christian Marriage Act 1872–notice of intended marriage–notice of intended marriage in a private dwelling–when one party is minor–contents of notice–penalty for false notice
9 Notices under the Merchant Shipping Act 1958–notice of day of sailing–notice of loss of ship-wrecked vessel–notice by Receiver–notice of proceedings in respect of foreign ship
10 The Indian Ports Act 1908–manner of service of notice
11 The Foreign Marriage Act 1969–notice of intended marriage–contents of a notice
12 Notice under the Insurance Act 1938–notice to policy-holders–application of the Act to the Life Insurance Corporation by the Life Insurance Corporation Act 1956
13 Official Trustees Act 1913–notice of suit (s. 16)–s. 80 of the CPC when not attracted
14 Sea Customs Act 1878–notice of proceedings (s. 198)
15 Customs Act (*i*) notice of seizure–(*ii*) notice of refund
16 Notice under Gold Control Act– s. 79
17 Giving of Notice–what it means
18 Notice under the Carriage of Goods by Sea Act (XXVI of 1925)
19 Notice under the Carriage by Air Act 1972
20 Indian Treasure-Trove Act 1878–notice on the Collector by a finder of treasure (s. 4)
21 Waqf Act 1995—notice of suit by parties (s. 89)—notice of pending suits by courts to the Waqf Board (s. 90)
22 Notice of suits by courts
23 Notice under Evidence Act–presumption of service of notice (s. 114)
24 Land Acquisition Act (1894), s. 9(3)–notice under
25 Publication of preliminary notification and power of officers thereupon
26 Notice to persons interested
27 Notice for sale of utilities of licensees
28 Disconnection of supply
29 Notice to telegraph authority
30 Notice of accident under the Electricity Act
31 Form for Reporting Electrical Accidents
32 No liability for loss of certain goods
33 Carriage of goods of dangerous or hazardous nature to human life

1 Administrator-General's Act 1963—notice of suit (s. 40)—s. 80 of the CPC—when not attracted

Section 40 of the Administrator-General's Act 1963 dispenses with notice of suit in certain cases. It lays down: "Nothing in s. 80 of the Code of Civil Procedure 1908, shall apply to any suit against the Administrator-General in which no relief is claimed against him personally."

Provisions in ss. 91 and 92 of the Code of Civil Procedure relating to public nuisances and public charities, empower the Advocate General to institute or intervene in proceedings in Civil Courts.

2 The Explosives Act 1884—notice of accidents (as amended in 1945—s. 8)

Section 8 of the Act enjoins: "Whenever there occurs in or about, or in connection with any place in which an explosive is manufactured, possessed or used, or any aircraft, carriage or vessel either conveying an explosive or on or from which an explosive is being loaded or unloaded, any accident by explosion or by fire attended with loss of human life or serious injury to person or property, or of a description usually attended with such loss or injury, the occupier of the place, or the master of the aircraft or vessel or the person in charge of the carriage, as the case may be shall within such time and in such manner as may be by rule prescribed give notice thereof and of the attendant loss of human life or personal injury, if any, to the Chief Controller of Explosives and to the officer-in-charge of the nearest police station."

The section is comprehensive and requires every person concerned with handling of explosives at the material time of accident to issue a notice as contemplated. Failure to issue the notice is saddled with penalty of fine and imprisonment or with both, according to circumstances of the case.

The law enjoins that the time and the manner of service of notice under s. 8 of the Act may be prescribed by rules under the Act. To attract the provision of the section, the explosion must be "accidental". Therefore, if the explosion was designed, the obligation to give notice under s. 8 of the Act does not arise,[1] even if the explosion resulted in serious injury to property.

Failure to give notice must be an intentional failure to attract the penalty under s. 176 of the Indian Penal Code.

Two notices are contemplated—one to the Chief Inspector of Explosives of India and the other to the officer-in-charge of the nearest police station.

3 The Dissolution of Muslim Marriage Act 1939—service of notice to the heirs of the husband—a condition of suit

A woman married under the Muslim law shall be entitled to obtain a decree for the dissolution of her marriage on various grounds contained in s. 2 of

1 16 CrLJ 622.

the said Act. One of such grounds is that the whereabouts of the husband have not been known for a period of four years [vide s. 2(*i*) of the Act].

Under s. 3 of the Act in a suit for dissolution on the ground in s. 2(*i*) of the Act, a notice of suit has to be served on persons who would have been the heirs of the husband under the Muslim law if he had died on the date of filing of the plaint.

4 The Police Act 1861—notice of suit—limitation

Section 42 of the Police Act 1861, enjoins limitations of actions against police personnel. The section reads:

> "All actions and prosecutions against any person, which may be lawfully brought for anything done or intended to be done under the provisions of this Act, or under the general police powers hereby given shall be commenced within three months after the act complained of shall have been committed, and not otherwise; and notice in writing of such action and of the cause thereof shall be given to the defendant, or to the District Superintendent or an Assistant District Superintendent of Police of the district in which the act was committed; one month at least before the commencement of the action."

'Action, means civil action. No notice under s. 42 of the Act is required for criminal prosecution.[2]

Special limitation of three months for commencement of an action is ruled out by general provisions of the Limitation Act 1963.

5 The Special Marriage Act 1954—notice of intended marriage

Section 5 of the Special Marriage Act 1954, empowers:

> "When a marriage is intended to be solemnized under this Act, the parties to the marriage shall give notice thereof in writing in the Form specified in the Second Schedule to the Marriage Officer of the district in which at least one of the parties to the marriage has resided for a period of not less than 30 days immediately preceding the date on which such notice is given".

The notice has to be addressed to the Marriage Officer of the district concerned and has to be signed by the parties to the marriage.

Section 5 of the Special Marriage Act provides that a notice of intended marriage is to be given to the Marriage Officer of the district in which at least one of the parties to the marriage has resided for a period of not less than 30 days immediately preceding of the date of notice; the marriage is to be solemnized at least one month after the notice and within three months

2 AIR 1934 Nag 206.

thereof. The effect of solemnization before the Marriage Registrar of the district where none of the parties resided is that the marriage is null and void.[3]

Contents of notice relating to description, residence and age of parties are not essential but formalities. Misdescription in the notice does not invalidate the notice.[4] Question of notice under s. 5 of the Act cannot be raised after issuance of certificate of marriage as the certificate of marriage is conclusive proof of a valid marriage.[5]

The non-compliance of the requirement contemplated under s. 5 of the Special Marriage Act is not by itself fatal but is an irregularity which does not go to the root of the matter and cannot be taken to nullify a marriage in fact evidenced by the certificate of marriage and other facts and circumstances.[6]

FORM

Form 1

Notice of intended marriage

To
The Marriage Officer for the .... District

We hereby give you notice that a marriage under the Special Marriage Act 1954, is intended to be solemnized between us within three calendar months from the date hereof.

Name	*Condition*	*Occupation*	*Age*	*Dwelling place*	*Permanent dwelling place if present dwelling place not permanent*	*Length of residence*
A.B.	Unmarried Widower Divorcee					
C.D.	Unmarried Widow Divorcee					

Witness our hands this .... day of .... 20 ....

(Sd.) A.B.

(Sd.) C.D.

3 *Sadhan Kumar Ray* v *Saraswati Ray* AIR 1989 NOC 94 (Cal); 1988(1) Cal HN 301.
4 *Re Butter, Donaldson* v *Rutter* [1907]2 Cg 592.
5 *Purabi Banerjee* v *Basudeb Mukherjee* AIR 1969 Cal 293 (DB).
6 *Nirmal Dass Bose* v *Mamta Gulati* AIR 1997 All 401.

6 Marriage not solemnized within three months of notice

Section 14 of the Special Marriage Act provides for a fresh notice after lapse of statutory period of three months from the date of notice under s. 5 of the Act. A new notice is required to be given in the following cases:

(*i*) Wherever a marriage is not solemnized within three calendar months of the date of the notice as required by s. 5 of the Act.

(*ii*) Where an appeal has been filed under s. 8(2) of the Act, within three months from the date of the appellate decision of the district court.

(*iii*) Where record of a case has been transmitted to the Central Government under s. 10, within three months from the date of the decision of the Central Government.

In the above cases the notice and all other proceedings arising from the original notice are deemed to have lapsed, and as such a new notice as required by s. 5 starts proceedings *de novo*. A new notice cannot revive the old proceedings, but it simply initiates fresh proceedings for solemnization of the intended marriage.

FORMS

Form 1

Notice of marriage

To .... a Minister (or Registrar) of ....

I, hereby give you notice that a marriage is intended to be had, within three calendar months from the date hereof between me and the other party herein named and described (that is to say):

Names	*Condition*	*Rank or Profe-ssion*	*Age*	*Dwelling place*	*Length of residence*	*Church, chapel or place of worship in which the marriage is to be solemnized*	*District in which the other party resides, when the parties dwell in different districts*
James Smith	Widower	Carpenter	Of full age	16, Clive Street	23 days	For Church of Scotland Ch-urch, Calcutta	
Martha Green	Spinster		Minor	20, Hastings Street	More than a month		

Witness my hand, this, ... day of ....

(Signed)
James Smith

Form 2

Certificate of Receipt of Notice

I, ... do hereby certify that, on the day of ...., notice was duly entered in my Marriage Notice Book of the marriage intended between the parties herein named and described, delivered under the hand of .... one of the parties (that is to say)–

Names	*Condition*	*Rank or Profe-ssion*	*Age*	*Dwelling place*	*Length of residence*	*Church, chapel or place of worship in which the marriage is to be solemnized*	*District in which the other party resides, when the parties dwell in different districts*
James Smith	Widower	Carpenter	Of full age	16, Clive Street	23 days	For Church of Scotland Church Calcutta	
Martha Green	Spinster		Minor	20, Hastings Street	More than a month		

and that the declaration, or oath required by section 17 or section 41 of the Indian Christian Marriage Act, 1872, has been duly made by the said

(James Smith).

Date of notice entered
Date of certificate given

The issue of this certificate has not been prohibited by any person authorised to forbid the issue thereof.

Witness my hand, this day of

Signed.

This Certificate will be void, unless the marriage is solemnized on or before the day of ....

7 The Births, Deaths and Marriage Registration Act 1886—notice of birth—notice of death

Section 19 of the Act presupposes that notice has to be issued by a competent person to the Registrar of Births and Deaths within the prescribed time and in the prescribed mode.

Five classes of persons are authorised to give notice of birth. They are classified in s. 20 of the Act and are:

(*i*) the father or mother of the child;

(*ii*) any person present at the birth;

(*iii*) any person, occupying, at the time of the birth, any part of the house wherein the child was born and having knowledge of the child having been born in the house;

(*iv*) any medical practitioner in attendance after the birth and having personal knowledge of the birth having occurred;

(*v*) any person having charge of the child.

Any of the five classes of persons may issue the notice of birth.

Persons who are authorised to give notice of death are listed in s. 21 of the Act. They are:

(*i*) any relative of the deceased having knowledge of any of the particulars required to be registered concerning the death;

(*ii*) any person present at the death;

(*iii*) any person occupying, at the time of death, any part of the house wherein the death occurred and having knowledge of the deceased having died in the house;

(*iv*) any person in attendance during the last illness of the deceased;

(*v*) any person who has seen the body of the deceased after death.

Any of the persons may give the desired notice.

There is no prescribed form in the Act. The notice-giver may use language of his choice but that should intimate the birth or death as the case may be. Section 36 of the Act empowers a State Government to frame rules prescribing the time within which and the mode in which persons authorised under this Act may give notice of a birth or death to a Registrar of Births and Deaths.

8 The Indian Christian Marriage Act 1872—notice of intended marriage—notice of intended marriage in a private dwelling—when one party is minor—contents of notice—penalty for false notice

(*i*) Notice of intended marriage to be solemnised by Minister of Religion (s. 12);

(*ii*) Notice of intended marriage before the Marriage-Registrar (s. 38);

(*iii*) Notice of intended marriage in private dwelling house (s. 14);

(*iv*) Penalty for false notice (s. 66);

(*v*) Form of notice;

(*vi*) Authority to issue notice;

(*vii*) Fresh notice (s. 52).

(*i*) *Notice of intended marriage (s. 12)*—Whenever a marriage is intended to be solemnized by Minister of Religion licensed to solemnize marriages under this Act, one of the persons intending marriage shall give notice in writing, according to the form contained in the first Schedule hereto annexed, or to the like effect, to the Minister of Religion whom he or she desires to solemnize the marriage.

Section 5 of the Act names persons who are competent to solemnize Christian marriage under the Act in India. A Minister of Religion licensed under the Act to solemnize marriages is competent.

(*ii*) *Notice of intended marriage in private dwelling:* Section 14 of the Indian Christian Marriage Act 1872, enjoins: "If it be intended that the marriage shall be solemnized in a private dwelling, the Minister of Religion, on receiving the notice prescribed in s. 12, shall forward it to the Marriage Registrar of the district, who shall affix the same to some conspicuous place in his own office".

Intention is wide publication of the intended marriage to be solemnized in a private dwelling.

(*iii*) *When one party to the intended marriage is a minor*—Under s. 15 of the Act provision has been made for onward transmission of a notice of intended marriage to the Marriage Registrar of a district.

Section 15 reads: "When one of the persons intending marriage is a minor, every Minister receiving such notice shall, unless within twenty-four hours after its receipt he returns the same under the provisions of s. 13, send by the post or otherwise a copy of such notice to the Marriage Registrar of the district, or, if there be more than one Registrar, of such district, to the Senior Marriage Registrar." A minor, for the purposes of this Act, is a person who has not completed the age of twenty-one years and who is not a widower or a widow [vide s. 3].

(*iv*) Contents of a notice under s. 12.

A notice of an intended marriage under the Indian Christian Marriage Act 1872, shall contain—

(*a*) the name and surname, and the profession or condition, of each of the persons intending marriage;

(*b*) the dwelling place of each of them;

(*c*) the time during which each has dwelt there, and

(*d*) the church or private dwelling in which the marriage is to be solemnized:

Provided that, if either of such persons has dwelt in the place mentioned in the notice during more than one month, it may be stated therein that he or she has dwelt there one month and upwards.

FORM

Form 1

Notice of marriage

a Minister [or Registrar] or

To

I hereby give you notice that a marriage is intended to be had, within three calendar months from the date hereof, between me and the other party herein named and described (that is to say)–

Names	*Condition*	*Rank or Profe-ssion*	*Age*	*Dwelling place*	*Length of residence*	*Church, chapel or place of worship in which the marriage is to be solemnized*	*District in which the other party resides, when the parties dwell in different districts*
James Smith	Widower	Carpen-ter	Of full age	16, Clive Street	23 days	For Church of Scotland Church Calcutta	
Martha Green	Spinster		Minor	20, Hastings Street	More than a month		

Witness my hand, this .... day of .... seventy two.

(Signed)

James Smith

9 Notices under the Merchant Shipping Act 1958—notice of day of sailing—notice of loss of ship-wrecked vessel—notice by Receiver—notice of proceedings in respect of foreign ship

Notice of day of sailing (s. 238)—notice of loss of ship (s. 351)—wrecked vessel—notice by Receiver (s. 397)—notice of proceedings in respect of foreign ship (s. 446);

(*i*) Notice of day of sailing (s. 238)—Notice of day of sailing of pilgrim ship (s. 278):

> "The master, owner or agent of a special trade passenger ship or a pilgrim ship so departing or proceeding shall give notice to an officer appointed in this behalf by the Central Government that the ship is to carry special trade passengers or pilgrims and of her destination and of the proposed time of sailing."

Section 238 further provides that the notice shall be given—

(*a*) in the case of a special trade passenger ship, not less than 24 hours before that time;

(*b*) in the case of a pilgrim ship at the original port of departure, if in India, and in any other case at the first port at which she touches in India, not less than three days, and at all other ports not less than 24 hours, before that time.

(*ii*) Notice of loss of ship: Section 351 of the Act enjoins:

"If the owner or agent of any Indian ship has reason, owing to the non-appearance of the ship or to any other circumstance, to apprehend that the ship has been wholly lost, he shall, as soon as conveniently may be, send to the Central Government notice in writing, of loss and of the probable cause thereof stating the name of the ship, her official number, if any, and her port of registry".

(*iii*) Wrecked vessel notice by receiver (s. 397).

The receiver of wreck shall, as soon as may be after taking possession of any wreck, publish a notification in such manner and at such place as the Central Government may, by general or special order, direct, containing a description of the wreck and the time at which and the place where it was found.

(*iv*) Notice of proceedings in respect of foreign ship (s. 446).

Section 446. "If any ship other than an Indian ship is detained under this Act, or if any proceedings are taken under this Act against the master, owner or agent of any such ship, notice shall forthwith be served on the consular officer of the country in which the ship is registered at or nearest to the port where the ship is for the time being, and such notice shall specify the grounds on which the ship has been detained or the proceedings have been taken."

10 The Indian Ports Act 1908—manner of service of notice

Section 67. "Any written notice of a direction given under this (I.P.) Act, left for the master of any vessel with any person employed on board thereof, or affixed on a conspicuous place on board the vessel, shall, for the purposes of this Act, be deemed to have been given to the master thereof."

11 The Foreign Marriage Act 1969—notice of intended marriage—contents of a notice

"Section 5. *Notice of intended marriage*. When a marriage is intended to be solemnized under this (Foreign Marriage) Act, the parties to the marriage shall give notice thereof in writing in the form specified in the First Schedule to the Marriage Officer of the District in which at least one of the parties to the marriage has resided for a period of not less than thirty days immediately preceding the date on which such notice is given, and the notice shall state that the party has so resided."

Before the marriage is solemnized under this Act, the parties and three witnesses shall, in the presence of the Marriage Officer, sign a declaration in the form specified in the Second Schedule, and the declaration shall be countersigned by the Marriage Officer (s. 12).

FORM

Form 1

Notice of intended marriage

To

The Marriage Officer,

for .... (District)

We hereby give you notice that a marriage under the Foreign Marriage Act 1969 is intended to be solemnized between us within three months from the date hereof.

Name & Father's name	*Condition*	*Occupation*	*Date of birth*	*Dwelling place*	*Permanent dwelling place & present dwelling place if not permanent*	*Length of residence in the present dwelling place*
AB	Unmarried Widower Divorcee	..	..	..	..	..
CD	Unmarried Widower Divorcee	..	..	..	..	..

Witness our hand this .... day of .... 20 ....

Sd/- AB
Sd/- CD

12 Notice under the Insurance Act 1938—notice to policy-holders—application of the Act to the Life Insurance Corporation by the Life Insurance Corporation Act 1956

Notice to the Policy-holder (s. 50)

Section 50 reads: "An insurer shall, before the expiry of three months from the date on which the premiums in respect of a policy of life insurance were payable but not paid give notice to the policy-holder informing him of the options available to him unless those are set forth in the policy".—Notice to policy-holder contemplated in s. 50 of the Insurance Act 1938, applies to the Life Insurance Corporation of India by virtue of provision of s. 43(1) of the Life Insurance Corporation Act 1956.

13 Official Trustees Act 1913—notice of suit (s. 16)—s. 80 of the CPC when not attracted

Section 16 of the Official Trustees Act lays down: "Nothing in s. 80 of the Code of Civil Procedure 1908, shall apply to any suit against the Official Trustee in which no relief is claimed against him personally".

14 Sea Customs Act 1878—notice of proceedings (s. 198)

Section 198 of the Sea Customs Act enjoins: No proceedings other than a suit shall be commenced against any person for anything purporting to be done in pursuance of this Act without giving to such person a month's previous notice in writing of the intended proceeding and the cause thereof; or after the expiration of three months from the accrual of such cause.

The notice contemplated is not a notice of suit but is a notice of proceeding under the Sea Customs Act. Thereafter, s. 108 operates as a bar to all the proceedings when a notice required under the section is not given.[7]

Second show-cause notice on identical terms issued after adjudication consequent upon the first notice is complete would be barred by principles analogous to *res judicata*—First show-cause notice on the face of it containing several errors—the second correct show-cause notice is not prohibited.[8]

15 Customs Act (i) notice of seizure—(ii) notice of refund

(i) *Notice of seizure*

Notice under s. 124 must be given within six months of the seizure of the goods. If it is not so given the goods have to be returned. Upon the expiry of six months, or any extended time under the proviso, a right for the return of the goods vests in the person from whose possession they were seized. When extension was made one month afterwards, the vested right was taken away.[9] Also see *P.T.C. Thangiah Nadar & Co.* v *A.C., Central Excise*[10]—valid notice under s. 124(*a*) was not within six months from the date of seizure.

Notice by the Assistant Collector directing a party to show cause to Additional Collector is not invalid under s. 124.[11] Notice before confiscation—six months.[12]

7 AIR 1953 Cal 753.
8 AIR 1961 Cal 195.
9 73 CWN 340.
10 AIR 1977 Mad 121.
11 *Tarak Nath Sen* v *Union of India* AIR 1975 Cal 337.
12 *Collector of Customs* v *Hindustan Motors Ltd.* AIR 1975 Cal 368.

(ii) *Notice of Refund*

In the case of erroneous refund, the notice under s. 28 is to be given within six months from the date of actual refund.

Under s. 131(3) the Central Government may of its own motion annul or modify any order passed under s. 128 or s. 130. This power is to be exercised on giving notice to the person concerned.[13]

Coming to the scope of s. 124—the section does not prescribe any time-limit for issuing the show-cause notice and it is not permissible to go into the intention of the legislature for not making provision for such a time-limit in it. Therefore, it would not be legitimate to curtail the extent and scope of s. 124 which does not contain any time-limit for issuance of show-cause notice, by saying that in view of the provisions of sub-sec. (2) of s. 110, the said notice must be issued within six months of the seizure of the goods or within the duly extended period of not more than six months thereafter.[14]

The right to restoration of the seized goods is a civil right which vests in the person concerned if notice is not given to him within the period of six months from the date of the seizure.

Giving of the notice (s. 124 of the Customs Act)—means that the notice must have been received. The giving of the notice is not complete unless and until it reaches the person concerned on its actual tender to him. Merely despatching of the notice to the address of the person does not complete the giving of the notice.

16 Notice under Gold Control Act—s. 79

The object of s. 79 being to apprise the person concerned of the grounds on which it is proposed to confiscate and/or to impose penalty and to give him a reasonable opportunity of making a representation in writing with such reasonable time as may be specified in the notice and to give him further an opportunity of being heard in the matter, if he so desires, the giving of notice is vital and a condition precedent. The objects of judicial function and administrative function are the same, namely, to do justice and decide the questions fairly and justly. The power exercised under the Chapter is quasi-judicial and at any rate one requiring a judicial approach. Further, "giving" of notice is not complete unless and until the notice reaches the person concerned or is actually tendered to him. Mere despatch of the notice to the address of the petitioner is not enough.[15]

13 *Geep Flashlight Industries Ltd.* v *Union of India* AIR 1977 SC 456.

14 *Charandas Malhotra* v *A. Collector of Customs* AIR 1968 Cal 28 rel. on *Munilal* v *Collector of Central Excise* AIR 1975 P&H 130.

15 AIR 1972 SC 689; AIR 1972 Guj 126; and AIR 1966 SC 330 rel. on *Shri Nathulal Aggarwalla* v *Deputy Collector of Central Excise* AIR 1982 Ori 258.

17 Giving of notice—what it means

"There can no longer be any dispute with regard to the meaning of "giving" used in s. 79 after the decision of the Supreme Court in *Narasimhiah* v *Singri Gowda*.[16] Das Gupta, J. observed (at pp. 332-333).

Giving of anything as ordinarily understood in the English language is not complete unless it has reached the hands of the person to whom it has to be given. In the eye of law however giving is complete in many matters where it was offered to a person but not accepted by him. Tendering of a notice is in law therefore giving of a notice even though the person to whom it is tendered refuses to accept it. Thus as soon as the person with a legal duty to give the notice despatches the notice to the address of the person to whom it has to be given, the giving is not complete.[17]

18 Notice under the Carriage of Goods by Sea Act (XXVI of 1925)

Article III, s. 6, Schedule to the Carriage of Goods by Sea Act (XXVI of 1925) provides that "unless notice of loss or damage and the general nature of such loss or damage be given in writing to the carrier or his agent at the port of discharge before or at the time of the removal of the goods into the custody of the person entitled to delivery thereof under the contract of carriage, or, if the loss or damage be not apparent, within three days, such removal shall be *prima facie* evidence of the delivery by the carrier of the goods as described in the bill of lading.

Notice in writing need not be given if the state of the goods has at the time of their receipt been the subject of joint survey or inspection.

In any event the carrier and the ship shall be discharged from all liability in respect of loss or damage unless suit is brought within one year after delivery of the goods or the date on which the goods should have been delivered.

19 Notice under the Carriage by Air Act 1972

Chapter III, r. 26 of the First Schedule to the Carriage by Air Act 1972 provides as follows:

"(2). In the case of damage, the person entitled to delivery must complain to the carrier forthwith after the discovery of the damage, and, at the latest, within three days from the date of receipt in the case of luggage and seven days from the date of receipt in the case of goods. In the case of delay the complaint must be made at the latest within fourteen days the date on which the luggage or goods have been placed at his disposal.

(3). Every complaint must be made in writing upon the document of carriage or by separate notice in writing despatched within the times aforesaid."

16 AIR 1966 SC 330.
17 *Ibid* p. 259. Also see AIR 1972 Guj 126.

20 Indian Treasure-Trove Act 1878—notice on the Collector by a finder of treasure (s. 4)

Notice, by a finder of a treasure, to the Collector of the district is an illustration of statutory notice which casts an obligation on such finder to serve a notice in writing to the Collector of the district.

Section 4 of the Act lays down:

Whenever any treasure exceeding in amount of value of ten rupees is found, the finder shall, as soon as practicable, give to the Collector a notice in writing—

(*a*) of the nature and amount of approximate value of such treasure;

(*b*) of the place in which it was found;

(*c*) of the date of finding.

The collector here refers to the Collector of the district in which such treasure may be found. No date within which the notice has to be served on the Collector has been mentioned in the Act. Early intimation has been desired by the use of the expression "as soon as practicable". No particular form of notice is necessary.

21 Waqf Act 1995—notice of suit by parties (s. 89)—notice of pending suits by courts to the Waqf Board (s. 90)

Section 89 of the Waqf Act reads:

> "No suit shall be instituted against the Board in respect of any act purporting to be done by it in pursuance of this Act or any rules made thereunder, until the expiration of two months next after notice in writing has been delivered to, or left at, the office of the Board, stating the cause of action, the name, description and place of residence of the plaintiff and the relief which he claims; and the plaint shall contain a statement that such notice has been so delivered or left."

Section 90 refers to provisions of notice by court of law when in seisin of a suit or proceeding. It lays down:

> (1) In every suit or proceeding relating to a title to or possession of a waqf property or the right of a Mutawalli or a beneficiary, the court or tribunal shall issue notice to the Board at the cost of the party instituting such suit or proceeding.
>
> (2) Whenever any waqf property is notified for sale in execution of a decree of a civil court or for the recovery of any revenue, cess, rates or taxes due to the Government or any local authority, notice shall be given to the Board by the court, Collector or other person under whose order the sale is notified.

The issue of notice to the Board under s. 89 is a condition precedent to the filing of a suit or other civil proceedings against the Board. The defect of want of notice cannot be equated to a formal one, since it is a radical defect going to the root of the claim.[18]

Again, where the notice is a mere information of an intention of filing a suit but sets out neither the cause of action nor the reliefs proposed to be claimed, it would not be a proper notice under s. 89. When notice is issued by only one of the plaintiffs and the suit is filed by him along with others, it was held that the notice was not proper.[19]

22 Notice of suits by courts

In every suit or proceeding relating to a title to or possession of a waqf property or the right of a *mutawalli* or beneficiary, the court or tribunal shall issue notice to the Board at the cost of the party instituting such suit or proceeding.[20] In absence of such notice, any decree or order passed in the suit or proceeding shall be declared void, if the Board within six months of its coming to know of such suit or proceeding, applies to the court in this behalf.[1]

Similarly, absence of notice under s. 90(2) of the Waqf Act would nullify the sale of any waqf property, if the Board of Auqaf, within one month of its coming to know of the sale, applies in this behalf to the court or other authority under whose order the sale was held [vide s. 90(4).]

23 Notice under Evidence Act—presumption of service of notice (s. 114)

Notice duly affixed on the disputed land—presumption of service will arise under s. 114(*a*) of the Act.[2]

Notice served under Certificate of Posting—presumption arises.[3]

Notice sent by terminating lease registered envelope containing correct address of the tenant shall be deemed to have been properly served on the addressee. Presumption under s. 27 of the General Clauses Act and under s. 114 of the Evidence Act can be drawn.[4] The endorsement on notice 'Refused' strengthens the presumption.

24 Land Acquisition Act (1894), s. 9(3)—notice under

The 'person known to be interested' or 'person believed to be interested' must file some record before the Land Acquisition Officer to show that he

18 *Shamsuddin* v *Tuticorin Jamia Masjid* AIR 1984 Mad 276; *M.S. Abdul Hameed* v *S.M. Sheik Mohammed* AIR 2003 Mad 179.
19 *C.A. Khaja Mohidden Sahib* v *Madras State Wakf Board* AIR 1973 Mad 104.
20 Section 90(1) of the Waqf Act.
1 Section 90(2) of the Waqf Act. See S.A. Kader, *The Law of Wakfs*, 2nd Ed., p. 349.
2 *Thounaojam Munal Singh* v *Karam Iboyaima Singh* AIR 1971 Manipur 1.
3 AIR 1970 Mys 77; *Mrs. Achamma Thomas* v *E.R. Fairman* AIR 1968 Cal 49 but see *Parshotam Lal* v *Kalayan Singh* AIR 1971 J&K 20 for requirement.
4 *Gangaram* v *Smt. Phulwati* AIR 1970 All 446.

has got interest in the land. Then only it can be said that the person is known to be interested or believed to be interested. The petitioners in the instant case filed petitions before the Land Acquisition Officer requesting him to make a reference to the civil court, but they have neither produced sufficient record nor pursued the matter stating that they are the persons known to be interested or believed to be interested. Merely filing a petition claiming that they have got some right in the land does not mean they are known to be interested or believed to be interested. It is true that s. 9(3) casts a duty on the Land Acquisition Officer to issue notice to the person known or believed to be interested. A 'person interested' does not mean a person who puts forwards his claim without any proof of how he is interested in the land. Inasmuch as the petitioners have not proved to the satisfaction of the Land Acquisition Officer by filing any documentary evidence, it cannot be said that non-issuance of notice to the petitioners under s. 9(3) is in violation of the provisions of Act.[5]

25 Publication of preliminary notification and power of officers thereupon

The Land Acquisition Act 1890 has been repealed and replaced by the Right to Fair Compensation and Transparency in Land Acquisition, Rehabilitation and Resettlement Act. Section 11 of the Act provides for the Publication of preliminary notification which runs as under:

> Whenever, it appears to the appropriate Government that land in any area is required for any public purpose, a notification to that effect along with details of the land to be acquired in rural and urban areas shall be published in the following manner, namely:
>
> (*a*) in the Official Gazette;
>
> (*b*) in two daily newspapers circulating in the locality of such area of which one shall be in the regional language;
>
> (*c*) in the local language in the Panchyat, Municipality or Municipal Corporation as the case may be and in the offices of the District Collector, the sub-divisional Magistrate and the Tehsil;
>
> (*d*) uploaded on the website of the appropriate Government;
>
> (*e*) in the affected areas, in such manner as may be prescribed.

26 Notice to persons interested

(1) The collector shall publish the public notice on his website and cause public notice to be given at convenient places on or near the land to be taken, stating that the Government intends to take possession of the land, and that claims to compensations and rehabilitation and resettlement for all interests in such land may be made to him.

5 *Rajsekhar Babu* v *Deputy Collector* AIR 1992 AP 1993.

(2) The public notice referred to in sub-sec. (1) shall state that particulars of the land so needed, and require all persons interested in the land to appear personally or by agent or advocate before the Collector at the time and place mentioned in the public notice not being less than thirty days and not more than six months after the date of publication of the notice, and to state the nature of their respective interests in the land and the amount and particulars of their claims to compensation for such interests, their claims to rehabilitation and resettlement along with their objections, if any, to the measurements made under s. 20.

(3) The Collector may in any case require such settlement referred to in sub-sec. (2) to be made in writing and signed by the party or his agent.

(4) The collector shall also serve notice to the same effect on the occupier, if any, of such land and on all such persons known or believed to be interested therein, be entitled to act for persons so interested, as reside or have agents authorised to receive service on their behalf, within the revenue district in which the land is situate.

(5) In case any person so interested reside elsewhere, and has no such agent, the Collector shall ensure that the notice shall be sent to him by post in letter addressed to him at his last known residence, address of place or business and also publish the same in at least two national daily newspapers and also on his website.[6]

The Right to Fair Compensation and Transparency in Land Acquisition, Rehabilitation and Resettlement (Compensation, Rehabilitation and Resettlement and Development Plan) Rules 2015 provides Form of Notice by Collector as follows:

FORM

Form

Notice by Collector

[*See* rule 6]

No. .... Dt. ....

Notice is hereby given that the land specified in the Schedule below and situated in the village of .... in the Taluk/Sub-division/Tehsil/Block (as applicable) .... in the District of .... is needed or is likely to be needed in accordance with the notification under s. 11(1) of the Right to Fair Compensation and Transparency in Land Acquisition, Rehabilitation and Resettlement Act 2013 (30 of 2013) published by the Collector at page .... of Part I of the (name of State/UT) Gazette, dated .... All persons interested in the land are accordingly required to file their objections before .... within sixty (60) days from the date of publication of the above preliminary notification, a statement in writing of their objection, if any, to the acquisition of the said land.

6 Section 21 of the Right to Fair Compensation and Transparency in Land Acquisition, Rehabilitation and Resettlement Act 2013.

Any objection statement which is received of after the due date or which does not clearly explain the nature of the senders interest in the lands is liable to be summarily rejected.

Objections received within the due date, if any, will be enquired into on .... at .... when the objectors will be at liberty to appear in person or by Advocate and to adduce any oral or documentary evidence in support of their objections.

SCHEDULE

Sl. No.	*Survey No.*	*Total area in hectares*	*Area in hectares under acquisition*	*Name and address of the person interested*	*Boundaries N.S.E.W.*	*Details of trees, structures, etc., if any*
1	2	3	4	5	6	7

Notice under the Electricity Act 2003

27 Notice for sale of utilities of licensees

Section 20(1)(*b*) of the Electricity Act 2003 provides preceding for notice sale of utilities of licensees and runs as follows:

> 20. *Sale of utilities of licensees* (1) Where the Appropriate Commission revokes under s. 19 the licence of any licensee, the following provisions shall apply, namely:
>
> (*a*)..........................
>
> (*b*) the Appropriate Commission may, by notice in writing, require the licensee to sell his utility and thereupon the licensee shall sell his utility to the person (hereafter in this section referred to as the purchaser) whose application has been accepted by that Commission.

28 Disconnection of supply

Section 56 of the Electricity Act 2003 lays down the procedure for disconnection of supply for non-payment of charges for electricity or any other sum due from a consumer or person. The licensee or the generating company may disconnect the supply after giving not less than clear 15 days' notice in writing to the consumers. This provision is analogous to s. 24 of the Act of 1910.

But if on the spot inspection theft or pilferage of electricity by the consumer was detected disconnection of supply without notice is not illegal.[7] However, if there is a special agreement for notice, notice to consumer is to be given even in respect of theft of electricity.[8] When disconnection is made without

7 *Usha Baltron Ltd.* v *Bihar SEB* AIR 2000 Pat 183.
8 *Municipal Corporation of Delhi* v *Ajanta Iron and Steel Co. (P) Ltd.* AIR 1990 SC 882.

giving prior notice, immediate restoraction of supply is to be directed.[9] The licensee cannot disconnect supply to the occupant on request of recorded consumer, particularly when recorded consumer had not been called upon by the licensee to bear charges of consumption. In such case disconnection of supply without prior notice violates the principles of natural justice.[10]

29 Notice to telegraph authority

Section 69 of the Electricity Act stipulates conditions for licensee to comply with for laying down or placing electric lines or electric plants or other works within 10 meters of telegraph line.[11]

(1) For new installation—

(*a*) Submission of a proposal to the authority appointed by Central Government.

(*b*) The authority should take decision within 30 days.

(2) For repair, renewal or amendment of existing works—

(*a*) Issue 10 days' notice to the telegraph authority.

(*b*) ....

30 Notice of accident under the Electricity Act

Section 161 of the Electricity Act 2003 provides for giving notice of accidents occurring in connection with the generation, transmission, supply or use of electricity or in connection with any part of electric lines or electrical plants in such form and within such time of any person as may be prescribed, to the Electrical Inspector or such other person as aforesaid and such other authorities as the Appropriate Government may by general or special order direct. This provision corresponds to s. 33 of the Act of 1910.

Non-compliance with the time limit due to impossibility of performance is excusable. When the person liable or responsible to give notice is himself injured and the notice is delayed, there is compliance of the provision.[12] For failure to give notice, the Manager or Assistant Manager of Electric Supply Co. cannot be prosecuted. The statutory duty to give notice lies on the company itself. Its director alone can be prosecuted for breach of statutory duty.[13]

9 *Ramesh Kumar* v *DESU* 1996 AIHC 1215 (Del).

10 *Ashit Kumar Palit* v *West Bengal Steel Electricity Distribution Company Ltd.* AIR 2009 Cal 1.

11 "Telegraph" means any appliance, instrument, material or apparatus used or capable of use for transmission or reception of signs, signals, writing, images, and sounds or intelligence of any nature by wire, visual or other electro-magnetic emissions, Radio waves or Hertzian waves, galvanic, electric or magnetic means:
Explanation. "Radio waves" or "Hertzian waves" means electro magnetic waves of frequencies lower than 3,000 giga-cycles per second propagated in space without artificial guide. [vide s. 3(1AA) of the Indian Telegraph Act 1885].

12 *Poona Electric Supply Co.* v *State* AIR 1967 Bom 27.

13 *State of Assam* v *R. Bose* AIR 1951 Assam 130.

31 Form for Reporting Electrical Accidents

The Intimation of Accidents (Form and Time of Service of Notice) Rules 2005 specifies a form for reporting electrical accidents which runs as follows:

Form A

Form for Reporting Electrical Accidents

1. Date and time to accident.

2. Place of accident.
(Village/Town, Tehsil/Thana, District and State).

3. System and voltage of supply [Whether Extra High Voltage (EHV)/High Voltage (HV)/ Low Voltage (LV) Line, sub-station/generation station/consumer's installations/service lines/ other installations].

4. Designation of the Officer-in-charge of the generating company/licensee in whose jurisdiction the accident occurred.

5. Name of owner/user of energy in whose premises the accident occurred.

6. Details of victim(s):

(*a*) Human

Sl. No.	*Name*	*Father's Name*	*Sex of victim*	*Full Postal address*	*Approximate age*	*Fatal/ non-fatal*
1	2	3	4	5	6	7

(*b*) Animal

Sl. No.	*Description of animal(s)*	*Number(s)*	*Name(s) of owner(s)*	*Address(es) of owner(s)*	*Fatal/ non-fatal*
1	2	3	4	5	6

7. In case the victim(s) is/are employee(s) of supplier:
   (*a*) designation of such person(s);
   (*b*) brief description of the job undertaken, if any;
   (*c*) whether such person/persons was/were allowed to work on the job.

8. In case the victim(s) is/are employee(s) of a licensed contractor,—
   (*a*) did the victim(s) possess any electric workmen's permit(s), supervisor's certificate of competency?
   If yes, give number and date of issue and the name of issuing authority;
   (*b*) name and designation of the person who assigned the duties of the victim(s).

9. In case of accident in the system of the generating company/licensee, was the permit to work (PTW) taken?

10. (*a*) Describe fully the nature and extent of injuries, *e.g.*, fatal/disablement (permanent or temporary) of any portion of the body or burns or other injuries.

(*b*) In case of fatal accident, was the postmortem performed?

11. Detailed causes leading to the accident.

(To be given in a separate sheet annexed to this form).

12. Action taken regarding first aid, medical attendance etc. immediately after the occurrence of the accident (Give details).

13. Whether the District Magistrate and Police Station concerned have been informed of the accident (if so, give details).

14. Steps taken to preserve the evidence in connection with the accident to extent possible.

15. Name and designation(s) of the person(s) assisting, supervising the person(s) killed or injured.

16. What safety equipments were given to or used by the person(s) who met with this accident (e.g., rubber gloves, rubber mats, safety belts and ladders etc.)?

17. Whether isolating switches and other sectionalizing devices were employed to deaden the sections for working on the same. Whether working section was earthed at the site of work.

18. Whether the work on the live lines was undertaken by authorised person(s)? If so, the name and the designation of such person(s) may be given.

19. Whether artificial resuscitation treatment was given to the person(s) who met with the electric accident? If yes, how long was it continued before its abandonment?

20. Names and designations of persons present at, and witnessed, the accident.

21. Any other information/remarks.

Place .... Signature ....

Time ...... Name ....

Date .... Designation ....

Address of the person reporting ....

Service of notices, orders or documents

Section 171 of the Electricity Act 2003 prescribes the mode of service of notices, orders or documents by or under the Act.

> Section 171. (1) Every notice, order or document by or under this Act required, or authorised to be addressed to any person may be served on him by delivering the same after obtaining signed acknowledgement receipt therefor or by registered post or such means of delivery as may be prescribed—

(*a*) where the Appropriate Government is the addressee, at the office of such officer as the Appropriate Government may prescribe in this behalf;

(*b*) where the Appropriate Commission is the addressee, at the office of the Appropriate Commission;

(*c*) where a company is the addressee, at the registered office of the company or, in the event of the registered office of the company not being in India, at the head office of the company in India;

(*d*) where any other person is the addressee, at the usual or last known place of abode or business of the person.

(2) Every notice, order or document by or under this Act required or authorised to be addressed to the owner or occupier of any premises shall be deemed to be properly addressed if addressed by the description of the owner or occupier of the premises (naming the premises), and may be served by delivering it, or a true copy thereof, to some person on the premises, or if there is no person on the premises to whom the same can with reasonable diligence be delivered, by affixing it on some conspicuous part of the premises.

Manner and means of delivery

(*a*) after obtaining signed acknowledgement receipt; or

(*b*) by registered post; or

(*c*) by such other means as may be prescribed.

The Means of Delivery Notice, Order or Document Rules 2004 [Gazette of India Extraordinary GSR 371(E) notified on 21st June 2004 has stipulated additional means of delivery of such notice:

(*a*) through special messenger and obtaining signed acknowledgement; or

(*b*) by telegraphic message; or

(*c*) by FAX; or

(*d*) by e-mail.

Place of delivery

(1) Where the Appropriate Government is the addressee, at the office of such officer as the Appropriate Government may prescribe;

(2) Where the Appropriate Commission is the addressee, at the office of the Appropriate Commission;

(3) Where a Company is the addressee, at the registered office of the company, in the event of the registered office of the company not being in India, at the head office of the company in India;

(4) Where any other person is the addressee, at the usual or last known place of abode or business of the person.

A notice, order or document would be deemed to be properly addressed on fulfilment of the following requirements:

(*a*) if addressed by the description or occupier of the premises, naming the premises;

(*b*) if served (*i*) by delivering it or its true copy to some person in the premises, or (*ii*) if there is no person available in the premises, by affixing it on some conspicuous part of the premises.

The Carriage by Road Act 2007

The Carriage by Road Act is an Act to provide for the regulation of common carriers, limiting their liability and declaration of value of goods delivered to them to determine their liability for loss of, or damage to, such goods occasioned by the negligence or criminal acts of themselves, their servants or agents and for matters connected therewith or incidental thereto.

Definitions

COMMON CARRIER. It has been defined in s. 2(*a*) as: "'Common carrier' means a person engaged in the business of collecting, storing, forwarding or distributing goods to be carried by goods carriages under a goods receipt of transporting for hire of goods from place to place by motorised transport on road, for all persons undiscriminatingly and includes a goods booking company, contractor, agents, broker and courier agency engaged in the door-to-door transportation of documents, goods or articles utilising the services of a person, either directly or indirectly, to carry or accompany such documents, goods or articles, but does not include the Government."

GOODS. 'Goods' includes—

(*i*) containers, pallets or similar articles of transport used to consolidate goods; and

(*ii*) animals or livestock [s. 2(*e*)].

PERSON. 'Person' includes any association or body of persons, whether incorporated or not, a road transport booking company, contractor and an agent or a broker carrying on the business of a common carrier.[14]

32 No liability for loss of certain goods

Section 12(3) of the Carriage by Road Act 2007 deals with no liability of a carrier for loss or damage to any consignment which has been detained for examination or scrutiny by a competent authority. If it is found after scrutiny that the goods entrusted was the prohibited goods or goods on which due tax was not paid or insufficiently paid by the consignor, the common carrier shall not be liable for any loss, damage or deterioration caused by such

14 Section 2(*h*) of the Carriage by Road Act 2007.

detention. However, the onus of proving that such incorrect description of goods in the forwarding note was received from the consignor shall be on the common carrier.

33 Carriage of goods of dangerous or hazardous nature to human life

According to s. 13, no goods of dangerous or hazardous nature to human life shall be carried by a common carrier except in accordance with such procedure and after complying with such safeguards as may be prescribed by the Central Government. The common carrier shall scrutinize and ensure before starting transportation of any such goods that the consignment is covered by one or more insurance policies providing relief in case of injury or death to a person or damage to any property.

Section 14 provides for power of the Central Government to prohibit carriage of certain classes of goods.

Section 15 of the Carriage by Road Act 2007 runs as follows:

> 15. *Right of common carrier in case of consignee's default.* (1) If the consignee fails to take delivery of any consignment of goods within a period of thirty days from the date of notice given by the common carrier, such consignment may be deemed as unclaimed:
>
> Provided that in case of perishable consignment, the period of thirty days shall not apply and the consignment shall be deemed unclaimed after a period of twenty-four hours of service of notice or any lesser period as may be mutually agreed to by and between the common carrier and the consignor.
>
> (2) In this case of an unclaimed consignment under sub-section (1), the common carrier may,—
>
> (*a*) if such consignment is perishable in nature, have the right to sell the consignment; or
>
> (*b*) if such consignment is not perishable in nature, cause a notice to be served upon the consignee or upon the consignor if the consignee is not available, requiring him to remove the goods within a period of fifteen days from the date of receipt of the notice and in case of failure to comply with the notice, the common carrier shall have the right to sell such consignment without any further notice to the consignee or the consignor, as the case may be.
>
> (3) The common carrier shall, out of the sale proceeds received under sub-section (2), retain a sum equal to the freight, storage and other charges due including expenses incurred for the sale, and the surplus, if any, from such sale proceeds shall be returned to the consignee or the consignor, as the case may be.
>
> (4) Unless otherwise agreed upon between the common carrier and consignor, the common carrier shall be entitled to detain or dispose off the consignment in part or full to recover his dues in the event of the consignee failing to make

payment of the freight and other charges payable to the common carrier at the time of taking delivery.

General responsibility of common carrier

A common carrier shall be responsible for the loss, destruction, damage or deterioration in transit or non-delivery of any consignment entrusted to him for carriage arising from any cause except (*a*) act of God, (*b*) act of war or public enemy, (*c*) riots and civil commotion, (*d*) arrest, restraint or seizure under legal process, or (*e*) order or restriction or prohibition imposed by the Central Government or a State Government. But the common carrier shall not be of its responsibility when it could have avoided the loss, damage, destruction or deterioration of the goods with due diligence and care in the carriage of the consignment (section 17).

Notice for institution of a suit or other legal proceedings

No suit or other legal proceeding shall be instituted against a common carrier for any loss of, or damage to, the consignment, unless notice in writing of the loss or damage to the consignment has been served on the common carrier before the institution of the suit or other legal proceeding and within one hundred and eighty days from the date of booking of the consignment by the consignor (section 16).

This provision of notice is mandatory and cannot be dispensed with, prior to the institution of a suit or any other legal proceeding. No form of notice has been prescribed, but it is obvious that all necessary particulars of the consignment are to be included in the notice. It is also imperative that the notice is to be served within one hundred eighty days from the date of booking of the consignment. The mode of service of notice has not been laid down in the Act but it is apparent that it may be sent by registered post with acknowledgment due, or through electronic media or by any other verifiable means.

FORM

Form 1

Notice of suit to a common carrier for damages for loss of goods

Dated, the .... 20 ....

To

The ....

....

(*Name of the Carrier with address*)

Sir/Gentlemen,

Under instructions from my client M/s. .... (name, description and address) I call upon you to pay to my said client, within 30 days from the date of receipt of this notice, a sum of Rs. .... detailed in the Schedule below, as compensation for the damage causing loss of .... bags of (name the material) which was entrusted to you at your office at Calcutta on .... by M/s. .... for carriage through your transport service (state the nature of service) to Cooch Behar etc., the consignee being self (or, my client as the case may be), under Con. Note/Despatch Receipt No. ...... dated .... 20 ......

The above loss is due to the misconduct and gross negligence of the aforesaid (name the carrier) and their agents and/or employees.

Please take notice that in default of your compliance with this notice a suit will be brought against (name of the carrier) for recovery of the said sum of Rs. .... together with all incidental costs after the expiry of the period hereinabove allowed.

This notice shall be treated as a notice under section 16 of the Carriage by Road Act 2007.

SCHEDULE OF CLAIM

(Detailed account of loss or damage)

Yours faithfully,
Advocate
for.............

NOTES: 1. Section 16 of the Carriage by Road Act 2007 may be seen.

2. The notice is mandatory prior to institution of suit where a common carrier has to be sued for the loss of or injury to goods entrusted to him for carriage.

3. Limitation Act (Art. 30)—The plain language of the Article has to be interpreted grammatically without extraneous or equitable considerations. The period runs from the date of booking of the consignment.

Form 2

Notice of suit to a common carrier for non-delivery of goods

To

The ....
.... (Carrier)

Dear Sir,

I hereby give you notice as under in pursuance of section 16 of the Carriage by Road Act 2007.

(1) I entrusted to you the following goods on .... (date) at .... (place/s) for being delivered to .... (consignee) at .... (address of the consignee) vide consignment Note No. .... dated ....

Description of goods

(2) It is learnt that the said goods have not been delivered to the consignee and have been lost in transit.

(3) I have suffered loss amounting to Rs. .... by reason of non-delivery of the goods to the consignee and I hereby call upon you to pay Rs. .... to me within .... days from

the date of receipt of the notice, failing which legal remedy (or a suit or any other legal proceeding) would be resorted to.

Yours faithfully,

....

Date ....
Place ....

The Competition Act 2002

The Competition Act established the Competition Commission of India for the purposes of preventing practices having adverse impact on competition, of promoting and sustaining fair competition in markets, of protecting the interests of consumers and of ensuring freedom of trade carried on by other participants in markets, in India. Under the Competition Commission of India (Procedure in regard to the Transaction of Business Relating to Combinations) Regulations 2011, the acquirer is statutorily obliged to file notice in the manner prescribed by Regulation No. 9 which reads as follows:

> 9. *Obligation to file the notice.* (1) In case of an acquisition or acquiring of control of enterprise(s), the acquirer shall file the notice in Form I or Form II, as the case may be, which shall be duly signed by the person(s) as specified under regulation 11 of the Competition Commission of India (General) Regulations 2009.
>
> Provided that in case of a company, apart from the persons specified under clause (*c*) of sub-regulation (1) of regulation 11 of the Competition Commission of India (General) Regulations 2009, Form I or Form II may also be signed by any person duly authorised by the company.
>
> (2) In case the enterprise is being acquired without its consent, the acquirer shall furnish such information as is available to him, in Form I or Form II, as the case may be, relating to the enterprise being acquired:
>
> Provided that all information required to be filed, relating to the enterprise being acquired shall be filed with the Commission within fifteen days from filing of the notice and in case the acquirer is not in a position to furnish all the required information in Form I or Form II, as the case may be, relating to the enterprise being acquired, the Commission may direct the enterprise being acquired to furnish such information as it deems fit and the time taken by the parties to the combination or the acquired enterprise, as the case may be, in furnishing the required information including document(s) shall be excluded from the period provided in sub-section (2A) of section 6 of the Act, sub-section (11) of section 31 of the Act and sub-regulation (1) of regulation 19 of these regulations.
>
> (3) In case of a merger or an amalgamation, parties to the combination shall jointly file the notice in Form I or Form II, as the case may be, duly signed by the person(s) as specified under regulation 11 of the Competition Commission of India (General) Regulations 2009:

Provided that in case of a company, apart from the persons specified under clause (*c*) of sub-regulation (1) of regulation 11 of the Competition Commission of India (General) Regulations 2009, Form I or Form II may also be signed by any person duly authorised by the company.

(4) Where the ultimate intended effect of a business transaction is achieved by way of a series of steps or smaller individual transactions which are inter-connected, one or more of which may amount to a combination, a single notice, covering all these transactions, shall be filed by the parties to the combination.

(5) The requirement of filing notice under regulation 5 of these regulations shall be determined with respect to the substance of the transaction and any structure of the transaction(s), comprising a combination, that has the effect of avoiding notice in respect of the whole or a part of the combination shall be disregarded.

The form of notice for the proposed combination, submitted in accordance with sub-sec. (2) of s. 6 of the Competition Act, is to be ordinarily filed in Form I or Form II as specified in Schedule II to the said Regulations, and to be accompanied by evidence of payment of requisite fees [Regulation 5(1) and 5(2)].

FORMS

Form I

[*See* Regulation 5(2)]

Registration No. (to be assigned by the Competition Commission of India)

Information required to be filled in by the notifying party(ies)

Part I: Basic information

1. Information about each of the party to the combination:
   - 1.1. Legal names of parties to the combination and their role:
   - 1.2. Legal status of the parties to the combination (Company/Firm/LLP/Trust etc.):
   - 1.3. Jurisdiction of incorporation/formation:
   - 1.4. Registration number (if applicable):
   - 1.5. Complete registered address/principal business address:
   - 1.6. Name of the person signing on behalf of the parties to the combination and his contract details (email address, telephone number, mobile number, including country/city/area code):
   - 1.7. Complete address and contact details in India:
   - 1.8. Website address:
   - 1.9. Relevant 4-digit National Industrial Classification of the activities of the parties to the combination:
   - 1.10. Date of pre-filing consultation, if any:

Part II: Payment of fee

[*See* clause (*a*) of regulation 11]

2. Particulars of fee deposited.

Part III: Authorisation regarding communication

3. Name, complete address and contact details of Individual(s) in India who is authorised to receive communication(s) on behalf of the notifying party(ies).

Part IV: Meeting the thresholds

[*See* section 5 of the Act]

4. Details of assets and turnover of the parties to the combination in the format given below:

Name of the parties	Assets (as on ....)			Turnover (for FY ....)		
	In India (INR crore)	Worldwide		In India (INR crore)	Worldwide	
		(USD million)	(INR crore)		(USD million)	(INR crore)
Party 1						
Party 2						
Combined						

Part V: Description of the combination

5. Describe the combination by providing information regarding the following:

5.1. Scope of the combination notified pursuant to sub-section (2) of section 6 of the Act (with reference to relevant clause under the agreement(s), as applicable):

5.1.1 Details of acquisition or merger or amalgamation, as the case may be, with reference to relevant clause of section 5;

5.1.2. Any other transaction(s) that is/are inter-connected, in terms of sub-regulation (4) and/or (5) of regulation 9 of these regulations; and

5.1.3. Right(s) acquired or arising out of or in connection with the transaction(s) referred to at 5.1.1 and 5.1.2 above.

5.2. Step(s) to give effect to the combination, along with timelines for each step(s) of the combination.

5.3. Economic and strategic purpose (including business objective and rationale for each of the parties to the combination and the manner in which they are intended to be achieved) of the combination.

5.4. Value of the proposed combination.

5.5. Foreign investment as a result of the combination (FDI, FPI, etc., if any, in INR) and country(ies) of origin.

5.6. Filing requirements and its status in jurisdictions other than India.

5.7. Non-compete obligation, if any: Duration, scope in terms of persons, product(s)/ service(s) and territory(ies) and corresponding justification.

5.8. Any other relevant information related to the combination.

Part VI: Activities of parties to the combination and sector overview

6. Details about each of the parties to the combination:

6.1. Name of the group to which the parties to the combination belong.

6.2. For each of the parties to the combination, details regarding the following:

6.2.1. Entities in India and the presence in India (for example, sales office, factory, liaison office, branch office, franchise or through any entity from outside India, etc.);

6.2.2. Trade name(s), business name(s) and the brand name(s) used in India; and

6.2.3. Overview of activities worldwide and in India, as applicable.

6.3. List/details of the products (manufactured, supplied, distributed, and/or sold) and/or services provided by the parties to the combination.

6.4. *Horizontal Overlaps*: State as to whether the parties to the combination and/or their respective group entities, directly or indirectly, produce/provide similar or identical or substitutable products or services, considering all plausible alternative(s):

Yes ☐ No ☐

If the answer is yes, furnish the following information [information shall be furnished for each of the plausible alternative relevant market]:

6.4.1. Details of the overlapping products/services and the relevant product and relevant geographic market, considering all plausible alternative(s), along with explanation for accepting and rejecting each of the plausible alternative of relevant product and relevant geographic market;

6.4.2. Estimate, indicating the relevant source and the basis of estimate, the total size of the market for last three years, in terms of value of sales (in rupees) and volume (units);

6.4.3. Sales in value (in rupees) and volume (units) along with an estimate of the market share(s) of each of the parties to the combination (including their relevant group entities), for the last three years; and

6.4.4. Name and contract details of the five largest competitors (along with their market shares for last three years), customers and suppliers.

6.5. *Vertical and Complementary Activities*: State as to whether any of the parties to the combination and/or their respective group entities, directly or indirectly, are engaged in: any activity relating to the production, supply, distribution, storage, sale and service or trade in products or provision of services which is at different stages or levels of the production chain in which any other party to the combination is involved, considering all plausible alternative(s); and/or any complementary activities:

Yes ☐ No ☐

If the answer is yes, furnish the following information [information shall be furnished for each the plausible alternative relevant market]:

6.5.1. Details of the upstream and downstream activities or the complementary activities, as the case may be, and the relevant product and relevant geographic markets, considering all plausible alternative(s), along with explanation for accepting and rejecting each of the plausible alternative of relevant product and relevant geographic market;

6.5.2. Market size for the last three years for relevant product and/or services;

6.5.3. Market share of each of the parties to the combination (including their relevant group entities) for relevant product and/or services for the last three years;

6.5.4. Market share of five largest competitors for relevant product and services for the last three years; and

6.5.5. Existing supply arrangements between the parties to the combination along with volume and value of transactions, during the previous financial year and percentage of such sales/consumption of the respective parties in relation to the total sales/consumption in each of the market(s).

6.6. Whether any of the parties to the combination or any of their group entities has direct or indirect shareholding and/or control over another enterprise(s) engaged in: (*a*) production, distribution or trading of similar/identical/substitutable products or provision of similar/identical/substitutable services; and/or (*b*) any activity relating to the production, supply, distribution, storage, sale and service or trade in products or provision of services which is at different stages or levels of the production chain in which any other party to the combination is involved; and/or (*c*) complementary activities. If yes, provide details and necessary information as per Item 6.1 to 6.5 above.

6.7. Brief overview of the sector(s) in which the parties to the combination operate. If parties to the combination are engaged in identical, similar, supplementary or complementary businesses, also provide a brief description of the market structure; regulatory framework; recent entry and exit; and any other relevant information, relating to concerned businesses.

6.8. If any of the parties to the combination was a party to any proceeding before the Commission under or pursuance to any provision of the Act or before other competition authority(ies), during the last five years, provide details of said proceeding(s).

Part VII: Green Channel

[*See* regulation 5A]

7. Whether the notice for the proposed combination is under Green Channel:

Yes ☐ No ☐

Part VIII: Attachments

8. Attach the following documents:

8.1. Authorisation for signing the notice (refer item 1.6 above).

8.2. Acknowledgement for payment of fees to the Commission (refer item 2 above).

8.3. Authorisation for receiving communication (refer item 3 above).

8.4. Annual report of the parties to the combination, for the preceding financial year.

8.5. Summary of the combination in terms of sub-regulation (1A) of regulation 13 of these regulations.

8.6. Chart depicting shareholding/extent of ownership and voting right (if different from ownership pattern) along with details of control, prior to and after the combination, of: (*a*) the parties to the combination starting from their ultimate parent entity and controlling shareholder(s); and (*b*) for the enterprises, whose structure, ownership and control will be directly or indirectly affected by the combination.

8.7. Copy of approval or agreement/documents as referred to in sub-section (2) of section 6 read with regulation 5 of these regulations.

8.8. Documents, material (including reports, studies, plan, latest version of other documents), etc., considered by and/or presented to the board of directors and/or key managerial person of the parties to the combination and/or their relevant group entities, in relation to the proposed combination.

8.9. If the notice for the proposed combination is under Green Channel, declaration in terms of Schedule IV.

Declaration

The notifying party confirms that it has furnished all the information and documents as required in Form I, read with notes thereto.

The notifying party declares and confirms that all information given in this Form and all pages annexed hereto are true, correct and complete to the best of its knowledge and belief, and that all estimates are identified as such and are its best estimates based on the underlying facts.

Signed by or on behalf of the notifying party

Signature(s)

Name (in block letters):

Designation:

Date ....

[In case there are more than one notifying parties, each party may use the same format.]

Form II

[*See* regulation 5(2)]

Form of filing notice with the Competition Commission of India under sub-section (2) of section 6 of the Competition Act 2002

Registration No. (To be assigned by the Competition Commission of India) ....

1. Summary of combination—

1.1. Give a brief statement about rationale, objectives, strategy and the likely impact of the combination.

1.2. Provide an executive summary of the proposed combination specifying: (*a*) the parties to the combination; (*b*) the nature of the combination; (*c*) the areas of activities of the parties to the combination; (*d*) the market(s) (including its structure and state of competition) in which the combination will have or is likely to have an impact; (*e*) information with reference to sub-section (4) of section 20 of the Competition Act 2002; (*f*) expected time frame for completion of various stages of the combination.

2. Purpose of the combination–

2.1 What are the business objectives of the combination and how are these intended to be achieved?

2.2 Describe the economic rationale of the combination and its impact on the economy, market(s) and consumers.

3. Details of payment–

3.1 Amount of fee deposited (provide proof) Amount (in Rs.) ....

3.2 Mode of payment

(Demand Draft/Banker's Cheque/ECS)

Number ....

Date ....

Drawn on ....

Bank Identification and Code No. ....

4. Personal details–

First applicant

Legal name of combining party: ....

Name of the person signing in terms of regulation 8 (enclose documentary proof of eligibility for signing the notice, in terms of regulation 8): ....

Son/Daughter of: ....

Principal Business address: ....

City .... Country .... Postal/Zip code ....

Telephone No. .... Country code .... City/Area code ....

Mobile No. ....

Fax No. ....Country code ...... City/Area code ....

E-mail address ....

Website address ....

(In case there are more applicants, use the same format for additional applicants)

5. Provide details (in the format in paragraph 4) of an individual located in India, who is authorized to receive communications on behalf of each of the notifying party(s) regarding this notice and related proceedings.

6. Details about the combination–

6.1 Please specify the part, sub-clause and clause of section 5 of the Act under which the combination falls.

6.2 Describe the nature of the combination being notified with the following details:

(*a*) State the exact number of shares or voting rights and percentage of shares or voting rights being acquired, directly or indirectly, by the acquirer including number of shares or voting rights and their percentage held prior to such acquisition. Whether such acquisition of shares or voting rights, directly or indirectly, leads to control or may lead to control at a later date? Explain:

(*b*) Provide details and value of assets being acquired. Whether such acquisition of assets, directly or indirectly, leads to control or may lead to control at a later date? Explain:

(*c*) Provide details of series of constituent transactions leading to the combination and the sequence [including date(s)] in which they are likely to occur.

7. Supporting documents–

7.1 Furnish date(s) of approval of the proposal relating to merger or amalgamation by the Board of Directors of the enterprise(s) concerned referred to in clause (*a*) of sub-section (2) of section 6 of the Act and/or other document executed in relation to the acquisition or acquiring of control referred to in clause (*b*) of sub-section (2) of section 6 of the Act. Attach copies of such board resolution or the agreement/other document.

7.2 Furnish copies of (*a*) analysis, reports, studies or surveys or any other document taken into account for the purpose of assessing the impact of the combination by the parties to the combination and/or (*b*) final version of any document(s) prepared or commissioned by the parties to the combination or considered by the Board of Directors, for the purposes of evaluating or assessing or analyzing, the combination with resect to market shares, competition, competitors (actual or potential), markets, potential for sales growth or expansion of products or geographic markets, rationale of the combination and indicate (if not contained in the document itself) the date of preparation, and the name and title of each individual who prepared such document(s).

7.3 Copies of memorandum and articles of association of all the parties to the combination.

7.4 Furnish copies of the most recent annual reports and accounts of:

(*a*) in case of an acquisition of an enterprise(s) under sub-section (*a*) of section 5 of the Act, the acquiring enterprise(s) and the enterprise(s) being acquired (by way of acquisition of control, shares, voting rights or assets); or (*b*) in case of an acquisition under sub-section (*b*) of section 5 of the Act, the enterprise acquiring control; enterprise whose control is being/has been acquired; and the enterprise in which the acquirer already has direct or indirect control which is engaged in similar or identical or substitutable product(s)/service(s); or

(*c*) in case of merger or amalgamation under sub-section (*c*) of section 5 of the Act, all the parties to such merger or amalgamation.

7.5 List of holders of five percent or more of voting rights or shares, directly or indirectly, of the parties to the combination.

7.6 List names of CEO/CFO/directors/partners/trustees/person in charge/persons acting in concert during the last one year. Also provide recent detailed organizational chart of each of the combining parties.

8. Information about the size of the combination–

8.1 How do the parties to the combination meet the criteria for filing notice, in terms of assets/turnover given under section 5 of the Act and the notification thereunder?

8.2 Furnish the following details, as per audited annual accounts of immediately preceding two financial years, separately, for all the parties to the combination:

Name of enterprise(s)	*Year*	*Value of assets*		*Aggregate Turnover*	
		In India (Rs. in crore)	Worldwide (US$ in million)	In India (Rs. in crore)	Worldwide (US$ in million)

8.3 Furnish the following details for the current financial year, separately, for all the parties to the combination:

Name of enterprise(s)	*Year*	*Value of assets*		*Aggregate Turnover*	
		In India (Rs. in crore)	Worldwide (US$ in million)	In India (Rs. in crore)	Worldwide (US$ in million)

8.4 Aggregate for the proposed combination–Furnish the following details as par last audited annual accounts of the immediately preceding financial year. If annual accounts for the immediate preceding financial year are not audited, furnish the following details as per the last audited annual accounts as well as for the subsequent financial years:

	Value of Assets		*Aggregate Turnover*	
For the proposed combination	*For the financial year immediately preceding the date of notice*	*For the current financial year, for the completed calendar quarters till the date of notice*	*For the financial year immediately preceding the date of notice*	*For the current financial year, for the completed calendar quarters till the date of notice*
In India (Rupees in crore) (as per audited accounts) (mention year)				
Worldwide (US$ in million) (as per audited accounts) (mention year)				
In India (Rupees in crore) (as per audited accounts) (mention year)				
Worldwide (US$ in million) (as per audited accounts) (mention year)				

8.5 Furnish the following details in case of a group, to which the entity whose control, shares, assets or voting rights have been acquired or are being acquired would belong to or the entity remaining after the merger or the entity created as a result of amalgamation would belong to after acquisition/merger/amalgamation, as the case may be, namely:

	Value of Assets		*Aggregate Turnover*	
For the proposed combination	*For the financial year immediately preceding the date of notice*	*For the current financial year, for the completed calendar quarters till the date of notice*	*For the financial year immediately preceding the date of notice*	*For the current financial year, for the completed calendar quarters till the date of notice*
In India (Rupees in crore) (as per audited accounts)				
Worldwide (US$ in billion) (as per audited accounts)				
In India (Rupees in crore) (as per audited accounts)				
Worldwide (US$ in billion) (as per audited accounts)				

9. Ownership and control—

9.1 Furnish a list of all the enterprises belonging to the same group for each of the parties to the combination and list all the enterprise(s) controlling the parties to the combination, directly or indirectly, along with the nature and means of control.

9.2 Whether the party to the combination, either singly or jointly, directly or indirectly control the affairs or management of another entity or group? If yes, please furnish the following:

(*a*) details of enterprise(s) exercising control and enterprise(s) whose affairs are being controlled;

(*b*) form and manner in which the control is exercised; and

(*c*) details of common directors/partners/coparceners/trustees.

9.3. Whether the parties to the combination and another enterprise or group referred to at 9.1 and 9.2 above, are engaged in production, distribution or trading of similar or identical or substitutable products or provision of similar/identical/ substitutable services? If yes, provide following details:

(*a*) names of similar or identical or substitutable products or services; and

(*b*) market share of each of the products or services mentioned in (*a*) above, prior to and after the combination.

9.4 Whether any of the parties to the combination is engaged in any activity relating to the production, supply, distribution, storage, sale and services or trade in products or provision of services which is at different stages or levels of production chain in which any other party to the combination is involved? If yes, provide details.

9.5 Furnish details of the intended structure of ownership and control of the acquired enterprise(s) acquirer enterprise(s)/combined enterprise(s) after completion of the combination.

10. Details about the products or services–

10.1 Furnish the following details–

(*a*) Provide separately the products (manufactured and/or sold) or services of the parties to combination.

(*b*) Characteristics and end use of products or services (Attach current selling aids and promotional material of the concerned products or services).

(*c*) Do the parties to combination produce/provide similar or identical or substitutable products or services, discussing specifically whether the parties to combination are engaged in any business activities in the same relevant market?

(*d*) Market shares of the similar or identical or substitutable products or services of the parties to combination and also of rivals/competitors for similar or identical or substitutable products or services.

(*e*) Details of in-house consumption (both in terms of quantity and value), if any.

(*f*) Existence/availability of other specialised producers/suppliers.

(Submit documents that identify specialised producers/suppliers or discuss the competitive position of specialised producers/suppliers).

(*g*) Industrial classification of products or services. (Submit documents sufficient to show how the parties to combination classify and sell their products).

10.2 Are there any regulations/laws/rules/procedures/official press notes/directions/ notifications, etc. which restrict production, supply, distribution of the similar or identical or substitutable products or services of the parties to the combination? (Submit documents sufficient to demonstrate such restraints).

10.3 Are the similar or identical or substitutable products or services subject to local specifications prescribed by Government/departments/authorities? If yes, provide details. (Submit documents and material sufficient to describe any specifications with which the parties to combination must comply).

10.4 Are there any licensing/registration requirements to set up facilities for production/ supply of the similar or identical or substitutable products or services? Does their production/supply require any special technical knowledge that is not readily available?

10.5 Are there any Government procurement policies which offer special dispensation to the parties to combination or their competitors? (Attach sufficient documents/ material).

10.6. How important/significant are "distribution facilities" of the similar or identical or substitutable products or services? Furnish details of your distribution channels and service networks (for example maintenance and repair) along with the ones that exist in the market. (Submit documents or material sufficient to show the location of all distribution facilities and any strategic plans or maps relating to distribution system of each similar or identical or substitutable product or service).

10.7 Whether the product can be transported? If yes, what are the possible modes of transportation? What is the unit cost of transportation per kilometre? What is the ratio of transportation cost to the sale price? (Submit documents sufficient to show shipping or transportation cost incurred in the distribution of the similar or identical or substitutable products or services).

10.8 State and explain (in your opinion) the scope of relevant product and relevant geographic market in relation to the proposed combination. Also provide a list of products and/or services which, in your opinion, may not fall within the scope of relevant market as mentioned above, but may pose competitive constraints.

10.9 Furnish the following–

(*a*) the manner in which the parties to combination produce, price and sell the product and/or service in the relevant market. Also submit documents pertaining to price lists, pricing plans, pricing policies, pricing strategies, pricing analysis and pricing decisions for the previous two years as well as pricing forecast, of the parties to the combination relating to the relevant products and/or services.

(*b*) details of prices of product and/or services in the relevant market relating to major competitors and imports, if any, during the last two years. (Attach copies of price-lists, alongwith the analysis, if any).

10.10 What, in your opinion, is the minimum viable scale (which means the smallest amount of production at which the average cost equals the price currently charged for the relevant product or services), the minimum and optimum plant size, capacity utilization rate, production volume and all factors required to attain any available cost savings? Provide details with supporting documents.

11. Information on the Market Structure (Demand and Supply Structure, Market Entry and Innovation)–

11.1 Provide an estimate (indicate the relevant source and basis of estimate) of the total size of the market in terms of value of sales (in rupees) and volume (units) of identical/substitutes/similar products or services produced/ distributed/supplied in India. Also provide name and contact details of five largest competitors (along with market shares), customers and suppliers.

11.2 Provide details with regard to sale in value (in rupees) and volume (units) along with an estimate of the market shares of each of the parties to the combination for identical/substitutes/similar products or services produced/distributed/supplied in India. (In case of a group same information should be given for all parties of the group).

11.3 Furnish a list of your main competitors, in your opinion, in the relevant market, with reasons and analysis.

11.4 An estimate of the market share in value (and where appropriate, in volume), of all the competitors (including importers) having at least five percent of the relevant market under consideration (in your opinion).

11.5 Describe the state of competition in the relevant market, supported by market studies, forecast, surveys, etc., (if any) and including but not limited to the following:

(*a*) relative strength/weaknesses of parties to the combination and other major players in the relevant market;

(*b*) supply and demand conditions; and

(*c*) attempts to win customers from other competitors and loss of customers to other competitors.

11.6 What is the level of concentration in the relevant market? How much will the level of concentration change after the proposed combination takes effect? (Provide number of enterprise(s) before and after the combination takes effect). For concentration levels provide an estimate of HHI (Herfindahl-Hirschman Index), along with change in the Index post-combination. (Indicate the market shares used as a basis to calculate the HHI and the source from which the same have been obtained).

11.7 How many enterprise(s) have entered or attempted to enter the relevant market in the last five years? Provide their names, addresses, telephone numbers and e-mail addresses. Is there a likelihood of entry of enterprise(s) of significant size in the relevant market in the next one to two years? (Attach sufficient documents/material in support).

11.8 How many enterprise(s) have exited or attempted to exit from the relevant market in the last five years? Provide their names, addresses, telephone numbers and e-mail addresses and reasons of exit.

11.9 If any of the parties to the combination have entered in the relevant market in last five years, provide details of barriers to entry encountered, if any, along with analysis.

11.10 Describe the various factors influencing entry into the relevant market, including but not limited to the following:

(*a*) the total costs of entry (R&D, production, establishing distribution system, promotion, advertising, servicing and so forth) on a scale equivalent to a significant viable competitor, indicating the market share of such a competitor;

(*b*) the portion of initial investment that will be permanently lost on exit;

(*c*) any legal or regulatory barriers to entry, such as government authorization or standard setting in any form, as well as barriers resulting from product certification procedures, or the need to have a proven track record;

(*d*) any restriction created by the existence of patents, know-how and other intellectual property rights (IPRs) in these markets and any restrictions created by licensing such rights. (Provide details information separately for each combining party);

(*e*) provide details of IPRs that have been developed and registered by the parties to the combination in the last five years? With reference to the relevant market(s), provide details of IPRs that are held by each of the parties to the combination;

(*f*) the importance of economies of scale in the production or distribution of products and services in the relevant market; and

(*g*) access to sources of supply, such as availability of raw materials and necessary infrastructure.

11.11 Provide details of imports (total value, volume and sources) and its proportion to the total size of the relevant market for the relevant products and services for the last three years. Also, provide details of potential imports in the next one or two years. Also provide the difference in unit selling price, if any, between the imported and domestic price of similar or identical or substitutable products or services in the relevant market.

11.12 Provide details of exports (total value, volume and sources) and its proportion to the total size of the relevant market for the relevant products and services for the last three years? Provide the names of top five exporters and their contact details.

11.13 Identify some of the largest independent suppliers to the parties to the combination and their individual shares or purchases from each of these suppliers (of raw materials or goods sued for purposes of producing the relevant products in your opinion). Mention their names, addresses and contact details.

11.14 Specify whether any of the parties to the combination, or any of the competitors have "pipeline products or services" (products or services likely to be brought to the market in the near future) or have plans to expand or contract production or sales capacity. If so, provide an estimate of the projected sales and market shares of the parties to the combination over the next three to five years.

11.15 If the parties to the combination have few large buyers for the similar or identical or substitutable products or services, furnish their names, addresses and contact details along with their individual shares in your sales/supply.

11.16 Explain the structure of demand in the relevant market, including the following, supported by the documents/data relied upon by the parties to the combination, while taking decisions in the ordinary course of business:

(*a*) role of product differentiation in terms of attributes or quality and the extent to which the products or services of the parties to the combination are close substitutes; and

(*b*) role of switching cost (in terms of time and expense) for customers when changing from one supplier to another.

11.17 Are there any obligations to comply with language requirements, if any, in respect of the products/user's manual, etc., in any part of India? If yes, provide, details. (Attach documents/material sufficient to show any impact language has on the sale or distribution of each similar or identical or substitutable product or service).

11.18 Explain the importance of R&D capabilities of an enterprise to compete in the relevant market. Explain the nature and extent of the R&D activities, if any, carried by the parties to the combination over the past few years.

11.19 State the intended R&D activities, subsequent to the combination taking effect and their likely impact on the nature of competition in the relevant market.

11.20 Have any of the parties to the combination or any other enterprise(s) in the relevant market radically affected the market conditions recently with new technology or business model or by rapid use of available capacity or by any other means? If so, give details supported by analysis.

12. Documents of compliance and filing in other jurisdictions—

12.1 Whether any order has been passed on a competition issue by any Competition Authority/Court/Tribunal/Government/Regulatory Authority in the last five years in respect of the parties to combination? If yes, provide brief details of said order, indicating the issue and the direction of the authority.

12.2 Whether any bankruptcy/winding-up application/proceedings involving any of the parties to the combination have been filed with the relevant authorities in the last five years? If yes, provide details.

12.3 Furnish details of any application/notification/intimation/information relating to the proposed combination filed in a High Court/Company Law Board/ Securities and Exchange Board of India or any other authority established under any law in India along with the status thereof and certified copies of the decision in the matter, if any.

12.4 Whether this combination is subject to filing requirements in jurisdictions other than India? If yes, list the notified, or to be notified, jurisdictions along with the certified copy(s) of the order(s)/decision(s) passed in that jurisdiction.

13. The parties to the combination are also encouraged to submit any other information that they believe could assist the Commission in assessing the proposed combination and the markets involved.

(Attach documents/reports/materials, if any, in support of the above)

Notes—(1) The parties to the combination, in providing the above information including the supporting documents, as far as possible, are required to rely on the documents/data used in the ordinary course of taking business decisions.

(2) If any third party information/estimates are being relied upon by the notifying parties, then the relevant source of such information/estimates shall be clearly indicated.

(3) If any additional information is needed by the Commission for determining whether a combination would have the effect of or is likely to have an appreciable adverse effect on competition in the relevant market, the parties to the combination may be required to furnish such additional information.

(4) For the purpose of figures in this Form the accounting standards, as notified by the Government of India, from time to time, or the International Financial Reporting Standards or the US Generally Accepted Accounting Principles shall be followed.

(5) Assets shall mean total assets and its value shall be computed in accordance with *explanation* (c) of section 5 of the Act.

(6) The turnover shall be computed in accordance with section 2(*y*) of the Act, excluding indirect taxes, if any.

(7) The rate of conversion of foreign exchange currency into Indian Rupees or US Dollars shall be based on the average spot rate of the last six months quoted by the Reserve Bank of India from the date calculated with reference to the event given in section 6(2) of the Act.

(8) Unaudited figures shall be certified by the Managing Director, Director, the Chief Executive Officer or the Chief Financial Officer of the enterprise duly authorized by the board and accompanied by a certificate of the auditor of the enterprise.

Declaration

The notifying party declares and confirms that all information given in this Form and all pages annexed hereto is true, correct and complete to the best of its knowledge and belief, and that all estimates are identified as such and are its best estimates based on the underlying facts.

The notifying party is aware of the provisions of sections 44 and 45 of the Act.

Signed by or on behalf of the notifying party

Signature(s)

Name (in block capitals)

Designation:

Date ....

(In case there are more than one notifying parties, each party may use the same format).

Chapter 31

Miscellaneous Notices

Miscellaneous

Form 1

Notice of wife's leaving husband's protection

Notice is hereby given that my wife Srimati A.B. having left my care and protection on ...... I make it known that I shall not be responsible for any debt or liability incurred by her with effect from the said date.

Date ....

....

(State here name and address of the notice-giver)

Form 2

Notice to creditors to estate of a deceased

Notice is hereby given that all persons having any claim to the estate of A.B. who died on the .... day of January, 20... are requested to send to the undersigned, the Administrator of the Estate of late A.B., full particulars of claim in writing with supporting documents within 30 days from the date of publication of the notice.

Date ....

....

(State here name, address of the notice-giver)

Form 3

Notice by Attorney prior to purchase of land (inviting objections)

Notice is hereby given that Mr. A.B. son of late C.D. of .... District .... has contracted to sell the property as described in the Schedule below to my client Sri .... son of Sri .... of ....

Any person claiming any interest in the said property or any part thereof is required to communicate the same to the undersigned, within 30 days hereof. On expiry of the said date the sale would be completed and any objection or claim shall be deemed to have been waived.

Date ....

....

(Name and address of the notice-giver)

Schedule of Property

(Description)

Form 4

Notice of sale of business

Notice is hereby given that the business, heretofore carried on by the undersigned at .... as sole proprietor, was sold to Sri .... son of .... of .... on the .... day of February, 20....

The undersigned maintains his responsibility for all debts and liabilities accrued up to the date preceding the date of transfer, in connection with the said business.

....
Lately Proprietor of ....
(State here the trade-name)

ANOTHER FORM

Form 5

Public notice of sale of business

Notice is hereby given that I, Sri .... lately proprietor of 'Lakshmi Vastralaya' of Cooch Behar have transferred the said business to M/s . ... of (*name and address of the transferee*) together with goodwill of the said business.

2. That the said M/s. .... (*name of the transferee*) will carry on the said business under the said name of 'Lakshmi Vastralaya'.

3. That the undersigned shall not be liable for any debts, or liabilities made or incurred by the said M/s .... (*name of the transferee*) from and after the said .... 20... (date of sale of the business).

Sd/- ....
(Name and address)

Dated, the ...... 20 ......

Form 6

Notice on behalf of a wife to a husband claiming alimony

By registered post with AD
Dated the .... 20 ......

Sri ....

Sir,

Under instructions from my client Sreemati .... (*name and address*) living at present in care of her father Sri ...... at latter's place at ...... to give you a notice which I hereby do and call upon you to pay to my said client a monthly sum of Rs. .... for her maintenance and support, for a term not exceeding the life of my client, as she has been living separate from you since under circumstances (*state here circumstances leading to separation*) and has had no independent income (*or sufficient income*) to maintain herself. On your failure to do so legal proceedings will be taken against you for recovery of the same.

Yours faithfully,
Advocate

NOTES: 1. For claim of alimony and maintenance—see provision of s. 125, CrPC, s. 18 of the Hindu Adoption and Maintenance Act and ss. 24 and 25 of the Hindu Marriage Act.

2. Notice is optional.

Form 7

Notice by husband denying liability for his wife's debts

TO ALL TO WHOM IT MAY CONCERN

I, A of etc., hereby give notice that I will not be liable for any debt incurred or to be incurred in future by my wife B of etc., and that she has got no authority from me to incur debts on my behalf.

Dated the .... day of .... Signature of A

Form 8

Notice to the Life Insurance Corporation of India claiming policy money

By registered post with AD

Dated the ...... 20.....

To

The Divisional Manager, Division ....
Life Insurance Corporation of India
(*Address*)

Dear Sir,

1. One .... since deceased held a Life Insurance Policy No. .... with the said Corporation for an assured sum of Rs. ....

2. Said .... died on the .... day of ...... 20... and prior to his death all premiums under the policy were fully paid and cleared.

3. That said .... nominated me as his nominee and my name stands recorded in your papers as his nominee for the assured sum.

4. That under terms of the policy contained at the back of the policy I have become entitled to the said sum of Rs. ....

5. Please take notice that you are hereby called upon to pay to me the said sum of Rs. .... due on the policy within 30 days hereof lest the matter should be agitated in a competent court of law, holding you responsible for costs.

Yours faithfully,

Sd/...............

(Name and address)

Form 9

Notice by a finder of a treasure

(Under the Treasure-Trove Act)

To

The Collector of the district of ....
P.O. .... Dist. ....

Sir,

I do hereby give you a notice that I, while excavating earth for house construction, found on .... 5 gold coins at .... (*place where found*) worth about Rs. ...... (*approximate value of such*).

2. The same are retained with me pending your instructions.

Yours faithfully,
Sd/-
(Signature of the finder)
(Name and address)

NOTES: 1. See s. 4 of the Treasure-Trove Act 1870.
2. Notice has to be served on the Collector of the district where the treasure is found.

Form 10

Notice for removal of a nuisance/obstruction

By registered post with AD
Dated the .... 20 ......

To

Sri ....
Son of ....
.... Road
P.O. .... Dist. ....

Sir,

By raising a fence on .... across the ...... road you have caused obstruction (*state details of obstruction, if required*) to ....

Please take notice that you are hereby called upon to remove the nuisance and obstruction within three days from the date of receipt of this notice; in default I shall be constrained to remove such nuisance and obstruction, holding you liable for costs therefor.

Take further notice that for such obstruction and nuisance I have suffered damage and the same is continuing. In the event of your failure I shall sue you in a competent court of law for damages and a mandatory injunction seeking removal of the same.

Yours faithfully,
Sd/-
(Name and address)

Form 11

Notice to a trespasser to vacate

(By a lawyer)

By registered post with AD
Dated the .... 20. ....

From
.... Advocate
.... (Address)

To

Md. A.B.
S/o Late ....
residing at village ....
P.S. .... P.O. .... Dist. ....

Sir,

As per instructions of my client Sri .... son of .... residing at Village .... P.S. .... Dist. ...... I do hereby issue this notice requesting you to quit and deliver unto my client vacant possession of the land described hereinbelow within three days from the date of receipt of this notice.

You have no right, title and interest in the said land and you have been possessing the same illegally since ....

Please take notice that if you fail therein my client shall sue you for recovery of the khas possession of the said land in the Schedule below with damages for unlawful occupation thereof.

SCHEDULE

(*State here description of the land*)

Yours faithfully,
Advocate.

Form 12

Notice to a licensee under permissive occupation to vacate possession

By registered post with AD

To
The ...... day of ...... 20 ....

Sri ....

.... (address)

Dear Sir,

On your seeking to occupy temporarily the premises, described in the Schedule appended below, and on your promise to vacate the same whenever asked to do so you were permitted by me to occupy the said premises with effect from ....

2. Please take notice that I require the said premises for my own use and occupation. You are hereby asked to quit and deliver unto me vacant possession of the said premises on expiry of the month of .... 20 .... from which date the licence shall stand revoked.

3. Take further notice that if you fail to comply with the terms of this notice I shall be constrained to bring a suit against you for recovery of khas possession of the said premises together with damages as may be found just and admissible.

SCHEDULE

(*State here description of the premises*)

Yours faithfully,
(Name and address)

NOTE: Licensee has no interest in the property but only a personal privilege. As such, a revocation of the licence by demand for possession is not always a precondition for institution of an eviction suit against him in such case (AIR 1959 SC 1262; AIR 1968 SC 175; AIR 1971 Cal 475).

Form 13

Notice of demand of money

(Simple Form)

By registered post with AD
Name of Place ....
Date ....

From
Sri ....
s/o ....
r/o ....
(*Name and address of the person giving the notice*)

To
Sri ....
s/o ....
r/o ....
(*Name and address of the person to whom the notice is given*)

Dear Sir,

Please take notice that I do hereby demand from you payment of a sum of Rs. ...... together with interest of Rs. ...., calculated at the rate of 18 per cent per annum due from you to me on account of the loan taken by you on .... for (*state here the occasion and purpose*) within a month from the date of receipt of this notice. In default, I shall be compelled to sue you for recovery of the same with costs without further reference.

Yours faithfully,
.... (Signature)

Form 14

Notice to pay dues under the mortgage-deed (notice by a lawyer)

By registered post with AD
Dated .... 20 ...

From
Advocate
Address..................

To
Sri ....
Son of ....
P.O. ....
Dist. ....

Dear Sir,

As instructed by my client Sri .... son of .... residing at .... P.S. .... Dist. .... I do hereby claim from you payment to my said client, within 30 days from the date of receipt of this notice, of a sum of Rs. ...... (*state here the principal money*) together with interest @ 8% per annum till date of payment, secured by a registered deed of mortgage executed by you in favour of my said client on ....

If you fail therein, please take notice, my client shall proceed to sue you in a competent court of law for the sale (and/or foreclosure) of the property mortgaged without further reference.

A copy of this notice is kept in my office for future use, if required.

Yours faithfully,

....
Advocate

Form 15

Notice of demand

By registered post with AD

Dated the .... 20 ....

To

Mr. Robin Chowdhury
107A, Vivekananda Road
Kolkata 700 006

Dear Sir,

We are concerned for M/s. International Travels Private Ltd., a company having its registered office at 15 S.P. Mukherjee Road, Kolkata and under instruction from them, we hereby serve upon you this notice of demand *inter alia* on the following amongst other grounds:

1. Our client is a reputed travel agent providing efficient, reliable and convenient personalized travel service including providing domestic and international air tickets.
2. In the usual course of business, our client was requested by you to provide air tickets as per requisition made by you from time to time *inter alia* on understanding and/or agreement that payment on account of such air tickets will be made within 15 days from the date of the bills submitted by our client. It was further agreed that in the event of the bills not being paid within 15 days, our client would be entitled to charge interest @ 24% per annum on the outstanding amount.
3. Between 27th February 20..... and 1st April 20......, you placed requisition with our client for tickets and our client duly furnished you such tickets. As per the agreement, our client submitted their bills to you on account of the tickets supplied to you and such bills were duly accepted by you for payment without any objection whatsoever. Particulars of such bills are given hereunder:

Bill No.	*Date*	*Amount*
....	....	....
....	....	....
....	....	....
	Total	....

4. From time to time between 5th March 20.......... to 27th November 20.........., our client has received payment and/or credit from you for an aggregate sum of Rs. .... leaving a balance of sum of Rs. .... due and payable by you.

5. Our client has, from time to time, requested you to arrange payment of the said sum of Rs.................. along with interest thereon at the agreed rate of 24% per annum. However, you have failed, neglected and refused to make payment of the said sum on one pretext or the other.

6. It is quite apparent from your conduct that you are unable to pay your debts and are in involved circumstances.

7. Our client has also come to know that you, with intent to defeat or delay your creditors, have secluded yourself so as to deprive your creditors of means of communicating with you and are making transfer of your property.

8. In the aforesaid facts and circumstances, we, under instructions from our client, hereby call upon you to make payment of the sum of Rs. .... along with accrued interest thereon @ 24% per annum from the respective due date of bills till the date of payment or to furnish security of payment of such amount to the satisfaction of our client within one month from the date of receipt of this notice.

9. In default of compliance hereof, our client shall be most reluctantly compelled to file an application for adjudging you an insolvent *inter alia*, on the ground that you have committed the aforesaid acts of insolvency.

10. It is needless to mention that if our client is constrained to initiate the aforesaid proceedings, you shall be liable for all costs, charges and the expenses thereto.

Yours faithfully
Sd/-..............
Advocate

Form 16

Notice demanding removal of deficiency of a car

By registered post with AD
Dated the .... 20......

From:
.... Advocate
.................Address

To

M/s. Kalinga Automobiles Pvt. Ltd.
57 Raja Rammohon Roy Sarani
Kolkata 700 009

Dear Sirs,

We are concerned for Mr. Atindra Gupta of 125/B, M.G. Road, Kolkata 700 009 and have been instructed to write to you as follows:

1. Our client abovenamed, being desirous of purchasing a trouble free car, in or about March 20...., visited your show room for the said purpose when you offered

a used Honda City (1.5 Exis) car manufactured in 20 .... at price of Rs. .... lakh. While assuring that the said car will be trouble free car, you further represented that:

(*i*) The car was in perfect running condition and did not bear any defect of any nature whatsoever.

(*ii*) The car had run only 59870 kms, in last two years and was capable of giving trouble free service.

(*iii*) The car was backed by your unconditional 3 months warranty against any defect whatsoever.

2. Being induced by the aforementioned representations and acting on the basis thereof, on 22nd March 20 ...... our client obtained delivery of the said car bearing registration No. WB 02H 1156 against payments of agreed price.

3. While driving the car from your show room, our client noticed that some unusual noise was coming from the front side of the car. Such fact was communicated over telephone by our client to your representative, who assured to make good any defect and requested the car to be brought to your office.

4. Although between 25th March 20 .... to 18th April 20 ...... our client kept on making persisting requests for rectification of the defects, our client was made to run from pillar to post and no action was taken for rectification of the defects in the said car. Ultimately on 18th April 20 .... the car was inspected by your technical staff and it was found that steering of the said car required replacement since it had worn off. Since the period of warranty, i.e. 3 months had not expired, our client reasonably expected you to make replacement at your costs. However, to the utter shock and surprise, our client was asked to make payment of the costs of such replacement stated to be around Rs. .... In this connection, your attention is invited to our client's letter dated 23rd April 20 .... to which no reply has been received till date.

5. Our client's efforts to persuade you to undertake the requisite replacement at your costs has not yielded any positive response.

6. Had our client not been induced by the representation made by you, our client would not have purchased the said Honda Car for the price offered by you.

7. In the aforesaid background, our client was constrained to contact an authorized workshop of Honda car to ascertain the nature of defect whereupon our client learned that:

(*a*) the car had run more than 1,00,000 kms, and not 59,870 kms only as represented by you.

(*b*) speedo meter and other record books of the car had been fraudulently readjusted.

(*c*) the car was in a damaged state by reason of excessive user.

8. By letter dated 23rd April 20 ...., as aforesaid our client also brought the aforesaid facts to your notice and called upon you to dispense justice to our client by making good the deficiency in the services rendered by you. Regretfully till date, you have not taken any steps to redress the grievances of our client.

9. Our client states that you have failed to render the services as assured and have thus adopted unfair practices. Moreover, our client's request to make

good the deficiency has not been acceded to for the purpose of making wrongful gains.

10. In the aforesaid facts and circumstances, we hereby firmly and finally call upon you to forthwith accept return of the said car against refund of payments already made by our clients.

11. Unless our client's aforesaid demands are acceded to within a week from the date of receipt of this letter, our client shall be constrained to initiate appropriate proceeding before the concerned authority making you liable for all costs and consequences thereof.

Yours faithfully

Sd/-...............

Advocate

Form 17

Notice of demanding reimbursement of Corporation bills

By registered post with AD

Dated the .... 20. ....

From: .... Advocate

.... (Address)

To:

Mr. AB
India House
4 Ganesh Chunder Avenue
Kolkata 700 013

Dear Sir,

Under instructions received from and on behalf of our client viz. M/s. XY Co. Limited having its registered office at 4 Camac Street, Kolkata 700 017, we do hereby serve upon you this notice of demand on the following amongst other grounds:

1. Our client is the owner of 'India House' situate at No. 4 Ganesh Chunder Avenue, Kolkata 700 013.

2. On 2nd March 20 .... our client entered into an agreement for sale with M/s. MN of 12 Middleton Street, 2nd Floor, Kolkata 700 011 whereby and whereunder our client agreed *inter alia*, to sell 490 sq. ft. of area on the 4th Floor of the said building situate at 4 Ganesh Chunder Avenue, Kolkata 700 013 on the terms and conditions recorded therein. In terms of clause 4 of the said agreement of sale, on about 3rd September 20 .... the said M/s. MN nominated you to obtain conveyance from our client in respect of 61.50 sq. ft. out of 490 sq. ft. of area pursuant to and in terms of the said agreement of sale dated 2nd March 20 .... Our client accepted such nomination.

3. It was further agreed that until the Conveyance Deeds are not executed and the mutations are not done in the records of the Kolkata Municipal Corporation, our client shall pay the Corporation Tax and Drainage and Sewerage Bills on your behalf and the same shall be reimbursed by you as and when bills are submitted by our client.

4. Pursuant to and in terms of the said agreement, our client raised bills on account of payments made for Corporation Tax and Drainage and Sewerage Bills in respect of the said area for the period upto 31st March 20 .... Such bills were duly accepted by you and payments made to our client, without any objection whatsoever.
5. Our client in accordance with the agreement as aforesaid has raised bills from time to time for the period commencing from 1st April 20 .... to 31st March 20 .... Although such bills were accepted, you have not reimbursed such bills till date.
6. Our client further states that although in accordance with the terms and conditions of the Agreement for sale you were obliged to reimburse our client in respect of the Corporation Tax and Drainage and Sewerage Bills, you have failed, neglected and defaulted to do so for the period commencing from 1st April 20 ...... to 31st March 20 ...... and a sum of Rs. .... as per particulars given hereunder has become due and payable by you to our client:

(A) Tax Bill

Period	*No. of Qrs.*	*Bill No.*	*Date*	*Amount Rs.*
...	...	...	...	...
...	...	...	...	...
...	...	...	...	...

(B) Drainage & Sewerage Bill

Period	*No. of Qrs.*	*Bill No.*	*Date*	*Amount Rs.*
...	...	...	...	...
... ...	...	...	...	
...	...	...	...	...

7. Our client has repeatedly demanded payment of the aforesaid sum from you but you have failed, neglected and defaulted to make payment thereof and/or any portion of the same.
8. Our client is entitled to claim and claims interest 24% per annum on the said outstanding due from the respective due dates till the date of payment. Please treat this also as notice under Interest Act 1970.

In the aforesaid facts and circumstances, you are hereby firmly and finally called upon to make payment of the aforesaid sum of Rs. .... along with accrued interest thereon @ 24% per annum as stated above within 10 days from date of receipt of this notice, failing which we shall be constrained to file appropriate legal proceedings against you for recovery of the aforesaid sum, making you liable for all costs and consequences thereof.

Yours faithfully

....

Advocate

Form 18

Notice demanding refund of excess payment and compensation

By Registered Post with AD

Dated the .... 20 ....

To

AB Bank
Regional Bankcard Service Centre
21 Netaji Subhash Road
Kolkata 700 001

Dear Sir,

Under instructions received from and on behalf of our client Mr. Pradip Kumar Sen at BC 64, Salt Lake, Kolkata 700 064 we do hereby serve upon you this notice of demand, on the following grounds:

Our client has settled the total dues on Cards Nos.

....
....
....

With you for total Rs. .... lakh only. The said amount has been paid in the following manner:

Date	*Mode of Payment*	*Amount*
....	....	....
....	....	....
....	....	....

From the above statements you will find that against the settled sum of Rs. .... lakh our client has paid a sum of Rs. ...., therefore the excess amount of Rs. .... (Rupees in words) is refundable by you to our client.

On 4th July 20 .... our client received an SMS asking for a payment of Rs. .... on SCGB card account No. ....

From the statement made in paragraph 2 it is clear that the payment on this card has also been made in full as the same was included in the settlement.

Our client is taking serious exception to your indulging in illegal and unauthorized means of alleged recovery when nothing is due and payable by our client. Your threat that you will call the police and put him behind the bar and sending the people at our client's residence to exercise pressure tactics.

Your such activities have put our client in serious mental and physical agony resulting in increment of his blood pressure and anxiety. Our client had to rush to the doctor for immediate medical attention.

In view of this our client is constrained to claim damages of Rs. .... on account of such torture and mental agony.

You are, therefore, directed to:

(*a*) Refrain from sending your representatives in form of gundas to the residence of our client as nothing is due and payable by our client to you.

(*b*) Refund a sum of Rs. .... already paid in excess of the settled amount within a week from the receipt of this letter.

(*c*) Pay us a compensation of Rs. .... on account of torture and mental agony to our client within 15 days from the date of receipt of this letter.

If we do not hear anything from you we have the instruction to take such appropriate action in Civil and Criminal Court of law as advised without any further reference to you.

Yours faithfully

....

Partner

.... Solicitors

Form 19

Notice demanding delivery of machine and refund of the excess payment

By registered post with AD

Dated the .... 20 ....

To

M/s. Kiran Jute Machinery Co. Ltd.
52 Kyd Street
Kolkata 700 016

Dear Sir,

Under instructions received from and on behalf of our client, Sen & Ghosh Co. Private Ltd., having its office at 22A, Strand Road, Kolkata 700 001, we do serve upon you this firm and final notice of demand, *inter alia*, on the following amongst other grounds:

1. As per your Machinery Price List dated 28th June 20 ...., our client placed an order with you on 8th May 20 .... for 2 Nos. Spinning Frames along with advance payment of Rs. ...... towards cost of payment of one No. Spinning Frame.
2. Then due to some reasons, our client had to cancel the order placed with you. This was notified to you by a letter dated 17th July 20.......... Also a refund was asked from you.
3. By a letter dated 19th July 20.........., you refunded an amount of Rs. .... but retained the balance Rs. .... as 20% advance for 2nd Spinning Frame.
4. On 20th October 20 ...., our client sent you a letter of request to transfer the order in the name of one, M/s. AB Co. Ltd. which you rejected by a letter dated 2nd November 20 ....
5. Having no other option, our client by a letter dated 8th November 20 .... asked for renewal of the order for the 2nd Spinning Frame.
6. By a letter dated 12th November 20 ...., you accepted the renewal of order and gave assurance of delivery of the goods within a time period of 8 to 10 weeks.
7. Another letter dated 19th February 20 ...., was received from you indicating delivery of Machine after receiving the balance amount.
8. On the same date, our client, sent the balance payment of Rs. ....

9. By a letter dated 4th March 20 ...., you indicated to our client that an amount of Rs. .... is due on account of rise in prices from 1st March 20 ....
10. Our client disagrees to pay this amount as it is only applicable for contracts made with you after 1st March 20 .... As such you were reminded to deliver the machine but till date the machine has been received by our client.
11. Our client, had indicated to you that on 1st March 20 .... the Excise Duty on the said machine has been waived as such our client is entitled to refund of the said sum of Rs. .... which was paid to you and mentioned in your Proforma Invoice dated 19th February 20 ....
12. In the aforesaid facts and circumstances, we, on behalf of our client, firmly and finally call upon you to make payment of the aforesaid sum of Rs. .... and the delivery of the Machine within one month of date hereof, failing which our client shall be constrained to petition against you. It is needless to mention that if our client is constrained to file such application all costs, charge and expenses shall be to your account.

Yours faithfully

....

Partner

.... Solicitors

Form 20

Notice demanding money due with interest

By registered post with AD

Dated the .... 20. ....

From: .... Advocate (Partner)
.... (Address)

Mr. Partha Sarathi Banerjee
1C, Ballygunge Circular Road
Kolkata 700 019

Dear Sir,

We are concerned for M/s. S.B. Publishers and Distributors, 3/2 Ganesh Chunder Avenue, Kolkata 700 013 and under instructions from them, hereby serve upon you this notice of demand *inter alia* on the following amongst other grounds:

1. Our client is engaged in supply and distribution of books for children such as Time Life Series.
2. In the usual course, our abovenamed client approached you for purchase of the books from the said Time Life Series and you, upon being fully satisfied with regard to the contents and quality of the said books, duly placed an order on 15th May 20 .... with our client for supply of such books on the understanding that payment on account of value of such books would be made by 18 post-dated cheques of Rs. .... each issued in favour of our client abovenamed.
3. Our client acting on the basis of the representation and assurance that the aforesaid cheques would be encashed on the respective due dates, duly supplied the books ordered by you and the same were accepted by you without any

objection whatsoever. As a matter of fact, in accordance with the aforesaid understanding, you handed over 16 post dated cheques, of Rs. .... each drawn on Punjab National Bank, New Jawahar Nagar, Jalandhar in favour of our client, the particulars whereof are set out hereunder:

Sl. No.	*Cheque No.*	*Date*	*Amount*
......	......	......	......
......	......	......	......
......	......	......	......

So far the remaining two cheques are concerned, you assured to hand over the same in due course. Despite such assurance the remaining two cheques have not been handed over till date.

4. Our client duly presented your cheques bearing Nos. .... dated ...., ..., dated ...., ... dated .... and the same were duly honoured.
5. However, your cheque No. .... dated .... and .... dated .... when presented to your bankers, the same were returned unpaid on .... respectively with remarks "Insufficient Funds". Due notice of such dishonour of the aforesaid cheques was given to you but in spite thereof you failed and/or neglected to make payment in lieu thereof on one pretext or the other. Our client continued to believe your representations and grant you further opportunities to make payment in lieu of such dishonoured cheques from time to time. Our client, as requested by you, did not present the remaining cheques in view of your assurance to make payment in cash in lieu of all remaining cheques.
6. Despite our client acceding to your request and withholding presentation of the cheques, you failed and neglected to make payment. Finding no other alternative than to present your aforesaid cheques our client was shocked to learn that the said cheques were returned unpaid on 17th March 20 .... with remarks "Account Closed". Due notice of such dishonourment of cheques was also given to you. You had also asked to present these cheques again.
7. Upon such notice of dishonour being given to you, you caused to deposit a sum of Rs. .... in our client's account with ICICI Bank on 16th April 20 .... but failed and neglected to make any further payment.
8. You will appreciate that in the facts as stated above, a sum of Rs. .... has become due and payable by you to our client abovenamed which sum you have failed, neglected and refused to pay till date.
9. You will, however, appreciate that from the course of conduct as mentioned aforesaid, it is quite apparent that you had no intention to make payment of our client's dues and had made false and frivolous representations with the sole objective of inducing our client to part with the said books. Had our client known or had reasons to believe that the cheques issued by you would not be honoured on presentation, our client would not have parted with the books.
10. Our client is further entitled to and claims interest on the aforesaid outstanding dues calculated @ 12% per annum from the respective dates of the cheques till the date of payment. Please treat this also as notice under Interest Act 1970.

11. In the facts and circumstances as aforementioned, we on behalf of our client aforementioned call upon you to forthwith make payment of the entire outstanding sum of Rs. .... along with interest @ 12% as mentioned above within seven days from the date of receipt of this letter, failing which our client shall be left with no alternative but to lodge a criminal case making you liable for all costs and consequences thereof.
12. Furthermore and without prejudice to the aforesaid, our clients shall also be constrained to initiate appropriate proceedings for realization of the aforesaid dues including filing an application for adjudging you as insolvent on the ground that you have committed the aforesaid acts of insolvent on the ground that you have committed the aforesaid acts of insolvency.
13. It is needless to mention that if our client is constrained to initiate the aforesaid proceedings, you shall be liable for all costs and consequences thereof and would be to your account.

Yours faithfully

....

Partner

.... Solicitors

Form 21

Notice requesting to liquidate a loan

By registered post with AD

Dated the .... 20. ....

From: .... Advocate

.... (Address)

To

....

....

(*Name and address of the debtor*)

Dear Sir,

Under instructions from my client ...... (*name and address of the creditor*) I hereby demand of you payment of a sum of Rs. ...... which you owe my client on account of (*state here circumstances giving rise to claim*) together with interest at the rate of Rs. .... and I request you to pay to my said client the dues within .... days from the date of receipt of this notice. If you fail, I am instructed to proceed against you in a court of law for recovery of dues as may be found admissible together with incidental costs.

Yours faithfully,

Sd/- ....

Advocate

NOTES: 1. A notice of this type is optional.

2. A schedule of A/c may be appended to the notice.

Form 22

Notice to a debtor calling upon him to pay back the loan

By registered post with AD

Dated the .... 20 ....

To

A.B.

(*Name the debtor with address*)

Dear Sir,

I hereby demand of you payment of a sum of Rs. ...... which you owe me on account of a loan taken by you on .... and request you to pay back the said amount within 30 days hereof, failing which legal proceedings will be taken against you for recovery of the same with damages and other relief without further reference.

Yours faithfully,

....

(Creditor)

(Name and address)

Form 23

Notice to a surety for payment of a debt

By registered post with AD

Dated the .... 20 ....

To

Sri P.R. Sen

.... (Address)

Sir,

One Sri A.B., son of late C.D., residing at ...... P.S. .... Dist. ...... took a loan from me on .... of Rs. .... by executing a handnote the same day in my favour agreeing to repay the said sum of Rs. ...... together with interest at 10% per annum on demand. On the occasion of advancing the said loan to said Sri A.B., you stood surety of due payment of the loan together with interest by the said A.B.

That said A.B. did not repay the loan in spite of requests made by me in that behalf.

Please take notice that you as surety of the said loans are requested to pay to me, a sum of Rs. .... due on the handnote, referred to above, within seven days from the date of receipt of this notice in default of which I shall proceed against you in a competent court of law for recovery of the same.

ACCOUNT OF CLAIM

Principal — Rs. ....

Interest — Rs. ....

Yours faithfully,

(Creditor)

(Name and address)

Form 24

Notice of auction sale

To whom it may concern

I, ... son of .... residing at ...., whose signature is hereby scribed bid the amount stated hereunder at the auction sale held on the ....day of .... 20 .... of the property mentioned hereunder and I was declared the purchaser of the said property subject to the conditions of sale which were explained and read out at the time of auction sale.

1. Particulars of the property ....
2. Amount of the highest bid ....
3. Amount of deposit received ....
4. Amount remaining due ....
5. Full name of the purchaser ....
6. Address and occupation of the purchaser ....

   ....

   ....

Dated, ... 20 ....
Place ....

....

Signature of the Auctioneer   (Signature of Purchaser)

Form 25

Notice of absolute assignment of debt

Registered post with AD

Dated the .... 20 ....

To

.... (debtor)

....

.... (address)

I .... hereby give you notice that by an assignment dated the .... day of .... 20 .... executed by me, the pronote (or, any debt particulars of which are to be stated) was transferred by me for the consideration mentioned therein absolutely to *CD* of .... and that you are required to pay to the said *CD* or, as he may direct, the said debt of Rs. .... and all interests accruing thereafter.

Sd/-

....

Creditor

Form 26

Notice for return of the Deed

By registered post with AD
Dated .... 20 ....

From:

....................., Partners
....................., Solicitors

To
The Multi Financial Service Pvt. Ltd.
3/2 Mango Lane, Kolkata 700 012

Attn: Mr. ....

Dear Sir,

We are concerned for M/s. Indrolok Properties Pvt. Ltd. of 13/7 Elgin Road, Kolkata 700 020. Under instructions from our client, we hereby write to you as follows:

1. That our client M/s. Indrolok Properties Pvt. Ltd. availed a loan for an amount of Rs. .... from you as a secured loan against mortgage and/or charge of a property of our client situated at .... and entered into a financial agreement being No. .... dated .... with you for repayment of this loan amount of Rs. .... including interest by 23 equal monthly instalments.
2. To secure repayment of the dues under the said agreement, our client was obligated to create an equitable mortgage in its property mentioned above by handing over the title deed of the same as per your directions.
3. Accordingly, our client duly paid the entire loan amount including interest thereon to you, as per the agreed terms and conditions and there is no outstanding amount payable by our client to you against the said loan agreement.
4. We repeat and reiterate that our client have already fulfilled and/or completed their obligation for repayment of their entire loan amount and in that case you are bound to issue a clearance letter immediately to our client and release the said mortgaged property forthwith.
5. However, in spite of repeated requests and reminders, you have most arbitrarily and illegally withheld our client's property, resulting in undue harassment, agony and inconvenience to our client.
6. Your such *mala fide* conduct has created a lot of financial problems to our client as they are restrained from proper utilization of the said property.
7. Your illegal withholding of the valuable papers, documents and/or title deed of the said property is causing tremendous hardship to our client. They are unable to raise further funds for their business on account of the fact that you continue to hold the said property and as a result their business is being adversely affected.
8. Had our clients known that you had no intentions of honouring your promises, they never would have availed themselves of your financial service.
9. In the aforesaid facts and circumstances, we, on behalf of our client, hereby call upon you to handover all the necessary papers and documents in respect of property situated at .... to our client after granting clearance to the said property from mortgage within 10 days from the receipt of the notice, failing which

our client shall be constrained to initiate appropriate legal action against you in the competent court of law.

10. It is needless to mention that if our client is constrained to take any action, you shall be liable for all costs and consequences thereof.

Yours faithfully

....

Partner

.... Solicitors

Form 27

Notice for passing off

By registered post with AD

Dated the .... 20 ....

From:

....................., Partners

....................., Solicitors

To

1. M/s. Mahindra & Mahindra Ltd.
   18 Jeewan Deep Building
   New Delhi 110 001
2. M/s. Bhadanta Motors
   72/1, Park Street
   Kolkata 700 017

Dear Sirs,

Under instructions received from and on behalf of Smt. Mala Sen presently residing at BC 64, Salt Lake, Kolkata 700 064, we write to you as follows:

1. In or about January 20 .... our client being desirous of purchasing a BOLERO PSAC 2WD 7STR BS IV manufactured by the addressee No. 1 and for the purpose thereof approached the addressee No. 2 inasmuch as the addressee No. 2 represented themselves to be the dealer of the addressee No. 1.
2. Our client, upon visit to showroom of the addressee No. 2 was given inspection of Bolero of the aforesaid specification and it was represented to our client that the said Bolero was a brand new jeep and was free of any defect.
3. Being induced by the aforesaid representations, our client placed an order for Bolero of the aforesaid specifications and made payment of a sum of Rs. ...... towards price thereof as shown in the invoice dated 22nd January 20 .... submitted by the addressee No. 2. Such payment was accepted by the addressee No. 2 without any objection whatsoever and on the basis of aforesaid agreement and/or understanding.
4. On or about 25th January 20 ...., the addressee No. 2 caused delivery of BOLERO stated to be a brand new vehicle with the aforesaid specifications. Our client accepted delivery thereof in good faith, without verifications inasmuch as our client proceeded on the basis that a company of reputation and status of the addressee No. 2 would not indulge in activities amounting to unfair trade practice.

5. Our client states that right from the date of receipt of the delivery, our client had been facing a number of problems. Such problems were brought to the notice of the addressee No. 2 whereupon the addressee No. 2 called for the said vehicle and stated to have undertaken the necessary steps so as to ensure that the defects do not recur. Such rectification was undertaken by the addressee No. 2 during the time the vehicle was sent to the addressee No. 2 for service. Our client acted on the basis of representations made by the addressee No. 2 from time to time.

6. Being aggrieved by and dissatisfied with the performance of the said vehicle and also not being satisfied with the services rendered by the addressee No. 2, our client scrutinized the service manual handed over by the addressee No. 2 at the time of delivery of the car in order to apprise herself as to the reason of the said vehicle not performing well. Such scrutiny brought to light the following facts:

    (*a*) The date of purchase of the vehicle was stated to be 21st July 20 .... instead of 22nd January 20 ....

    (*b*) The name of the owner appeared to have been altered and our client's name was superimposed after the name of the erstwhile owner was erased by white ink.

    (*c*) The vehicle, sold to our client, appeared to have been sent for service at the workshop of the addressee No. 2 on 15th January 20 .... i.e. prior to the date of delivery thereof to our client.

7. Our client states that the aforesaid facts amply demonstrated that the vehicle delivered by the addressee No. 2 to our client had been sold by the addressee No. 2 to some other customer and thereafter returned to the addressee No. 2 for reasons best known to the addressee No. 2. Despite aforesaid, the said vehicle was sold or delivered to our client by passing the same as a brand new vehicle although the addressee No. 2 had full knowledge of the fact that the said vehicle was not a new vehicle.

8. Our client brought the aforesaid fact to the notice of the addressee No. 2 by her letter dated 10th June 20 ...... whereupon Mr. Ranjit Das of the addressee No. 2 along with Mr. P.K. Kapoor of the addressee No. 1 and Mr. SS. Bhattacharjee visited our client's office and caused a check up of the vehicle. Upon check up of the vehicle, it was found that our client's contention was justified. In fact, by letter dated 20th June 20 ...., the addressee No. 2, *inter alia* agreed to extend the warranty by six months, refund the amount paid by our client to M/s. Friends Motors on account of paid service and rectifying the Air Conditioner of the vehicle.

9. Although, our client was not satisfied with the aforesaid, it is significant to note that the addressee No. 2 have not even honoured the aforesaid assurances.

10. Our client states that it would be apparent from the aforesaid fact that addressee No. 2 have passed off an old and used vehicle to our client as a brand new vehicle. That apart, addressee No. 2 have failed and neglected to discharge their duty and provide services after sales as represented at the time of the sale of the said vehicle.

11. Our client has been advised that the action of the addressee No. 2 as aforesaid amounts to deficiency in service and unfair trade practice within the meaning of the Consumer Protection Act 2019 thus, entitling our client to approach the concerned authorities under the said Act for redressal of her grievances.

12. In the aforesaid facts and circumstances, we on behalf of our client, hereby call upon you to exchange the said vehicle with a new one in as much as the same contains manufacturing defects as found by the addressee No. 2 during inspection and suitably compensate our client so as to provide complete relief within two weeks from the date. In default, our client shall be constrained to approach the concerned authority, without any further reference to you but however, making you liable for all costs and consequences thereof.

Yours faithfully

....

Partner

.... Solicitors

SUITS AGAINST GOVERNMENT & PUBLIC OFFICERS

Form 28

Notice of suit under s. 80, CPC for suing the State Government—Notice to the Collector of a district

(SIMPLE FORM)

Notice under s. 80, CPC

By registered post with AD

Dated the .... 20. ....

From: .... Advocate

.... (Address)

To

The Collector of the District of ....

P.O. ....

Dist. ....

Sir,

Under instructions from my client Sri .... son of .... by caste .... by occupation .... residing at .... P.O. .... P.S. .... Dist. .... I give you this notice under s. 80, CPC and state that my aforesaid client intends to sue the Government of West Bengal (or, name the State) on expiry of two months, after service of this notice, on the cause of action and for reliefs appearing hereinbelow:—

(*a*) Cause of action (*give in brief facts giving rise to cause of action*).

(*b*) Reliefs claimed (*give here reliefs which the plaintiff would sue for*).

Yours faithfully,

....

Advocate

NOTES: 1. A notice under s. 80, CPC must be in writing.

2. In the case of a suit against a State Government, the notice has to be delivered to or left at the office of (*i*) either a Secretary to that Government or (*ii*) the Collector

of the district where the cause of action arose. Notice served on any Secretary to that Government will do. But it is advisable for quick disposal to serve notice to the Secretary to the Government in that department to which the subject-matter of the intended suit relates.

3. Notice under this section may be served personally or by post. Notice to be served on the Collector may be addressed to the Collector. Similarly, a notice to be delivered to a Secretary to the Government has to be addressed to the Secretary to that Government (see Note under Chapter 11).
4. Description of the plaintiff has to be given. Description means such particulars as would be sufficient to identify the plaintiff. Place of residence has to be stated (See Notes under Chapter 11).

Form 29

Notice of suit under s. 80, CPC for suing the State Government–Notice to the Collector of a district

(ANOTHER FORM)

Notice under s. 80 of the Code of Civil Procedure

By registered post with AD

Dated the .... 20 ......

To

The Collector of the district of ....
P.O. ....
Dist. ....

Dear Sir,

Please take notice that my client .... son of .... by caste .... by occupation .... residing at .... intends to bring a suit against the State of West Bengal in a competent court of law after expiry of the two months after service of this notice under s. 80, CPC.

Facts constituting the cause of action are as follows:

(*State here facts*)

Reliefs to be sought in the intended suit are:

(*State here reliefs*)

Yours faithfully,

....

NOTES: 1. For non-compliance suit must be rejected under Or. VII, r. 11.

2. For suit by State against State—notice under s. 80, CPC must be served—AIR 1969 Cal 11: 72 CWN 95.

Form 30

Notice of suit under s. 80, CPC against the Central Government

Notice under s. 80 of the Code of Civil Procedure

By registered post with AD
Dated the ....20......

To

The Secretary to the Government of India
Department of Telecommunications, Central Secretariat
Ministry of Communications, New Delhi

Dear Sir,

By this notice under s. 80, CPC., I let you know my intention to sue the Union of India owning and representing the Department of Telecommunications, on expiry of two months after service of this notice, unless you grant within the said period reliefs sought for as detailed below:

(*a*) Name, description and the place of residence of intending plaintiff — Sri .... Son of .... by caste .... by occupation .... residing at .... P.S. .... Dist. ....

(*b*) Cause of action —

(*i*) I am a contractor. On .... I had deposited with the Department of Telecommunications .... a sum of Rs. .... only in cash being earnest money for intended tender for construction of .... at .... dated .... in the State of .... against receipt No. .... dated .... issued by said ....

(*ii*) Aforesaid tender has not been accepted. I am, therefore, entitled to refund of the said sum of Rs. ....

(*iii*) I made several requests for refund of the money but to no purpose.

(*iv*) Cause of action for the intended suit arose for withholding just dues after demand.

(*c*) Relief sought for – Refund of Rs. .... as stated above.

Yours faithfully,

....

Form 31

Notice of suit under s. 80, CPC against a Public Officer of a State Government or Central Government

By registered post with AD

Dated the .... 20......

From

................., Advocate
.... (Address)

To

....
(*Name & official designation*)
P.O. ....
Dist. ....

Notice under s. 80 of the Code of Civil Procedure

Dear Sir,

Please take notice that my client .... son of .... residing at .... intends to bring a suit against the (*state here the office the intended defendant holds*), a public officer of the Government of (state the name of the province or simply, of the Government of India, as the case may be) in a competent court of law on the cause of action stated hereinunder and for reliefs appearing below:

Cause of action for the intended suit .... (facts)

Reliefs sought for ....

Yours faithfully,

....

Advocate.

NOTE: In suit against Public Officer notice is necessary only when the act in respect of which suit is brought is purported to have been done by Public Officer in his official capacity—52 CWN 494; AIR 1969 SC 227.

Form 32

Notice of suit under s. 80, CPC to the Collector of a district, for ejectment of tenant (Government)

By registered post with AD

Dated the .... 20......

To

The Collector of the District of (*name the district*)
P.O. .... Dist. ....

Dear Sir,

Please take notice that my client (*state here name, description and address*) intends to bring a suit against the Government of West Bengal in a competent court of law after expiry of two months after the service of this notice under s. 80, CPC unless reliefs claimed hereinbelow are met to him within the said period.

Facts constituting the cause of action and reliefs to be claimed in the suit are as follows:

(1) That the State of West Bengal following an agreement in writing dated ...... took out on rent, as a monthly tenant, the premises described in the Schedule below, hereinafter called demised premises, at a rent of Rs. ... per month according to English calendar month, with effect from the 1st day of October, 20..., rent being payable immediately on the expiry of each month.

(2) That rent for the said premises for two months, namely June and July, 20... has not been paid within the contractual periods as per Cl. II of the agreement and for such default the Government of West Bengal has become liable to be evicted.

(3) That for careless use of the demised premises and for storing heavy iron materials on the floor of demised premises, a good portion of the godown, verandah within the demised premises have been materially damaged for which the tenant thereof has become liable to be evicted.

(4) That my client through his lawyer, by registered post with A/D, has served a contractual notice terminating the lease under s. 106, T.P. Act on the Collector of the district of .... determining the lease on expiry of October, 20... and asking him to deliver vacant possession of the demised premises on the 1st day of November, 20.... The notice was received by him on .... but he did not vacate the premises as instructed therein.

(5) That my client is entitled to eviction of the said tenant from the demised premises and also to recover arrear rents of two months amounting to Rs. .... and to damages of Rs. .... for four days from the 1st day of November to 4th November, 20..., and to subsequent damages as would be admissible.

(6) That the cause of action for the intended suit arose at .... for default in payment of rent for June and July, 20......, for damaging the demised premises, for not vacating the demised premises and for eviction on expiry of notice–period terminating the tenancy.

SCHEDULE

Description and particulars of demised premises

Yours faithfully,

....

Advocate

NOTES: 1. When the Government is a lessee/tenant the provisions of the West Bengal Premises Tenancy Act 1997, applies.

2. Two notices under s. 106 of T.P. Act (unless there is a contract to the contrary) and the other under s. 80, CPC would not be required to be served on the Government prior to institution of suit. One notice under s. 80, CPC will do.

3. Notice under Chapter 21 may be seen.

4. Grounds on which eviction sought need not be stated in a notice under s. 106, T.P. Act but, it is submitted, grounds which gave the landlord the right to sue, i.e., 'which constituted cause of action' should be stated in a notice under s. 80, CPC.

Form 33

Notice of suit to an Official Trustee—by an Advocate

Notice under s. 80 of CPC

By registered post with AD

Dated the .... 20......

To

The Official Trustee of the
State of West Bengal, Kolkata

Sir,

Please take notice that my client etc.,
(See notice under s. 80 of CPC *ante*)

Yours faithfully,

....

Advocate

NOTE: In a suit against the Official Trustee when no relief is claimed against him personally notice under s. 80 is not required—see s. 16 of the Official Trustees Act 1913. See *ante*.

Form 34

Notice of suit under s. 42 of the Police Act 1861

By registered post with AD

Dated the .... 20......

Notice under s. 42 of the Police Act 1861

From

....
.... (Address)

To

Sri ...., S.I. of Police
attached to the office of ....
P.O. .... Dist. ....

Or,

The Superintendent of Police, ... District
P.O. .... Dist. ....

Or,

The Asst. Superintendent of Police, ... District
P.O. .... Dist. ....

Sir,

Please take notice that you while discharging your functions as D.E.B. (Enforcement), S.I. of Police illegally, without just cause and maliciously arrested me on .... in connection with .... and thereby ....

In the premises, I have suffered damages. You are hereby called upon to pay to me a sum of Rs. .... as damages within one month hereof; in default, I shall sue you in a competent court of law for damages for Rs. .... after expiry of one month after service of this notice.

Claim for damages.

(*State particulars in support of the claim*)

Yours faithfully,

Sd/- ....

NOTES: 1. A like notice may be addressed to the police officer concerned or to the Superintendent of Police of the district or to the Assistant Superintendent of Police of the district, at the option of the notice-giver.

2. Notice period must be of one clear month.

3. Cause of action shall have to be stated in the notice. Reliefs may be added.

MONEYLENDERS ACT

Form 35

Notice of deposit to moneylender

[Section 39(2) of the Bengal Moneylenders Act
(Bengal Act X of 1940)]

In the Court of .... Case No. .... of 20 ...

(Name of moneylender)

(Address)

You are hereby informed that .... (name of the debtor) of .... (address) .... has on .... deposited in this court under s. 9(1) of the Bengal Moneylenders Act, a sum of Rs. .... (Rs. on account of principal and Rs. .... on account of interest) to your account in connection with the loan of Rs. .... which was made/ stated to have been advanced by you to him on .... You are requested to withdraw this amount at your earliest convenience/within .... days. Government accepts no responsibility for any loss which you may incur in connection with the aforesaid sum while it remains in deposit with the court.

Dated the .... 20 ...

(Seal)

Judge

Address (Seal)

....

MATRIMONIAL LAW

Form 36

Notice of Intended Marriage

(*See* section 5 of the Foreign Marriage Act 1969)

To

The Marriage Officer
for ....

We hereby give you notice that a marriage under the Foreign Marriage Act 1969 is intended to be solemnized between us within three months from the date hereof.

Name and father's name	*Condition*	*Occupation*	*Date of Birth*	*Dwelling place*	*Permanent dwelling place and present dwelling place if not permanent*	*Length of residence in the present dwelling place*
A.B.	Unmarried Widower Divorcee					
C.D.	Unmarried Widow Divorcee					

Witness our hands, this .... day of .... 20 ....

Sd. A.B.
Sd. C.D.

Declaration to be made by the Bridegroom

(*See* section 12)

I, A.B., hereby declare as follows:

1. I am at the present time unmarried (or a widower or a divorcee, as the case may be).
2. I have completed .... years of age.
3. I am not related to C.D. (the bride) within the degrees of prohibited relationship.
4. I am a citizen of ....

(to be filled up)

5. I am aware that, if any statement in this declaration is false, I am liable to imprisonment and also to fine.

Sd. A.B. (the bridegroom)

Declaration to be made by the Bride

I, C.D., hereby declare as follows:

1. I am at the present time unmarried (or a widow or a divorcee, as the case may be).
2. I have completed .... years of age.
3. I am not related to A.B. (the bridegroom) within the degrees of prohibited relationship.
4. I am a citizen of ....

(to be filled up)

5. I am aware that, if any statement in this declaration is false, I am liable to imprisonment and also to fine.

Signature

C.D. (the bride)

Signed in our presence by the above named A.B. and C.D. So far as we are aware, there is no lawful impediment to the marriage.

Sd. G.H.
Sd. I.J. } Three witnesses
Sd. K.L.

(Countersigned) E.F.
Marriage Officer

Dated the...................................... day of .... 20 ....

Form 37

Certificate of Marriage

(*See* section 14)

I, E.F., hereby certify that on the .... day of .... 20 .... A.B. and C.D. ....* appeared before me and that the declaration required by section ....** of the Foreign Marriage Act 1969, was duly made, and that a marriage under that Act was solemnized between them in my presence and in the presence of three witnesses who have signed hereunder.

Sd. E.F. Marriage Officer.
Sd. A.B. (bridegroom)
Sd. C.D. (bride)

Sd. G.H.
Sd. I.J. } Three witnesses
Sd. K.L.

Dated the...................................... day of .... 20 ....

* Herein give particulars of the parties.
** To be entered.

Form 38

Notice of an intended marriage under the Indian Christian Marriage Act 1872

(See sections 12 and 38)

To .... a Minister (or Registrar) of ....

I hereby give you notice that a marriage is intended to be had, within three calendar months from the date hereof between me and the other party herein named and described (that is to say):

Names	*Condition*	*Rank or Profession*	*Age*	*Dwelling Place*	*Length of residence*	*Church, chapel, or place of worship in which the marriage is to be solemnized*	*District in which the other party resides, when the parties dwell in different districts*
James Smith	Widower	Carpenter	Of full age	16, Clive Street	23 days	For Church of Scotland Church Calcutta	
Martha Green	Spinster		Minor	20, Hastings Street	More than a month		

Witness my hand, this, ... day of ....

(*Signed*) James Smith

[The *italics* in this Schedule are to be filled up, as the case may be, and the blank division thereof is only to be filled up when one of the parties lives in another district.]

The Indian Succession Act

Form 39

Notice to Collector of application made for Probate of Will [section 19H, clause (1) of the Court-fees Act 1870] for Letters of Administration

In the Court of ....
In the goods of ....

(deceased)

.... of thana/P.S. .... District

The Collector of ....

Notice is hereby given that an application has on this day been made in this Court by pleader/attorney for ....

of ...... thana

Probate of the will

District ...... of ....

Letters of Administration of the property and credits of the deceased abovenamed.

The amount of assets which are likely to come into the petitioner's hands is stated by the petitioner to be Rs. ....

Dated the ...... day of ...... 20 ......

District Judge or Delegate.

(Seal)

Form 40

Notice of date fixed for hearing Probate or Letters of Administration cases

(Section 276 of the Indian Succession Act of 1925)

In the Court of the District Judge of ....

(Application No. .... of ....)

NOTICE

No. .... of 20 ....

Whereas an application under the Indian Succession Act 1925, for grant of probate of the will (or, for Letters of Administration to the estate) of .... late of .... has been made by .... and whereas the .... 20 .... has been fixed for the hearing of this case, notice is hereby given that any person having any interest in the .... administration of the estate of the said deceased may, if he desires, appear in this Court on the said .... day of .... 20 ...... and see the proceedings before the grant of probate (or, of Letters of Administration).

Given under my hand and the seal of the Court, this .... day of ...... 20 ....

Judge

Seal of the Court

Form 41

Notice to creditors to deceased's estate

NOTICE IS HEREBY GIVEN:

1. That A.B. of .... died on the .... day of .... 20........

2. That the undersigned was appointed an administrator of the estate of said A.B., deceased (or, *that the undersigned is the executor named in the will by said A.B., deceased*).

3. That any person having any claim against the estate of the deceased is called upon to submit his claim within 30 days hereof.

Sd/- ....

Dated .... 20 .... (Administrator/Executor)

The Specific Relief Act

Form 42

Notice on behalf of the vendee to comply with terms of agreement for sale with threat of suit for specific performance of contract

By registered post with AD

Dated the .... 20......

To

Sri

(*Name and address of the vendor*)

Sir,

Under instructions from my client Sri .... son of .... residing at .... I hereby give you this notice as follows:

You contracted by executing on .... a *Bainanama* to sell to my client your property described in the Schedule below at a total consideration of Rs. .... and took from my client a sum of Rs. .... as advance on the occasion of execution of the said *Bainanama*. You agreed therein to complete the sale on accepting from my client the balance of consideration money within ....

My client had tendered to you the balance of the consideration on .... and required you to complete the sale. You did not accept the money and have been avoiding compliance with the terms of the agreement. My client was always ready and willing and is so even now to complete the purchase by payment of the balance of the consideration subject to performing your part of the said agreement (*Bainanama*).

Take notice that you are requested to complete the sale of the said property by executing a proper deed in favour of my client after accepting from him the balance of the consideration money within .... and register the same. In default, my client shall sue you in a court of law for specific performance of the said contract.

SCHEDULE

Yours faithfully,

....

Advocate

Form 43

Notice by vendor to complete a purchase with threat of forfeiture of 'baina' (advance) paid

By registered post with AD

Dated the .... 20 ...

To

....

Dear Sir,

As per instructions of my client Sri .... son of .... residing at ...., I hereby call upon you to pay to my said client within .... a sum of Rs. .... being the balance of the consideration for the stipulated sale of my client's property, described in the Schedule below, as contracted by him on execution of an agreement (*Bainanama*) dated .... in your favour, whereupon my client would make a conveyance of the property to you.

Take notice if you fail therein within thirty days, the agreement shall stand cancelled and my client shall not be responsible to convey the property to you under the agreement and that he will exercise the penal clause of forfeiture, as provided for in the said agreement, of the *baina* money.

SCHEDULE

Yours faithfully

Advocate

Form 44

Notice to enforce the specific performance of contract

Registered post with AD/Courier/UPC

Dated the .... 20 ...

To

Smt. ....
W/o Shri ....
1, Hem Chandra Street
Kolkata 700 023

Also at:
1, XY Colony,
....

Also at:
7A, Jhama Pukur Lane
Kolkata 700 009

LEGAL NOTICE

Madam,

Under the instructions and on behalf of my client Shri .... R/o ...., I have to serve you with the following notice:

1. That an agreement to sell (bayananama) was executed between you and my abovenamed client, dated ...., for the sale of property bearing No. ...., ..., to my

client, of which you are the owner, for a total sum of Rs. .... The earnest money of Rs. .... was also paid by my client to you in cash against a proper and separate receipt of the even date.

2. That clause 1 of the said agreement stipulated for the conversion of the property from 'leasehold' to 'freehold' by you, subject, however, to a further stipulation contained in para 6 to the effect that the expenses for such conversion would be borne by my said client. Further, my client was supposed to pay you the balance of Rs. ...., for the purpose of the execution of the sale-deed in favour of my said client within 20 days from the date of such conversion.

3. That my client has already paid you a sum of Rs....... and Rs........ towards the said conversion, in addition to the abovestated earnest money.

4. That since the payment of the abovestated amounts, you have neither informed my client as to the status of the conversion of the said property, nor you seem to be interested in the deal anymore for the reasons best known to you.

5. That my client is not only interested in the payment of the remaining amount of money but is desperate and willing to get the property registered in his name as per law after the payment of the balance-sale consideration, provided you give my client a notice of 20 days or any other reasonable notice.

6. That through reliable sources, it has come to the knowledge of my client that in the mean time, atleast at this date, you have not got your stated property converted from leasehold to freehold but you are also intending to further dispose it off to some other person.

In view of the above facts and in these circumstances, I hereby call upon you to let me or my client know the correct status of the conversion of the property in question and also the date and time on which you intend to get the sale-deed registered on payment of the balance amount, within 3 days from the date of receipt of this legal notice failing which I have been clearly instructed by my client to take appropriate legal action as per law which shall only be at your costs, risks and consequences for which please take this notice. At the risk of repetition and by way of abundant caution, I hereby call upon you not to indulge in getting the property in question transferred to some third party, as doing so would attract rigors of section 420 of the Indian Penal Code 1860, besides other provisions of law, for which you shall be held liable for imprisonment of a term which may extend to seven years and also fine.

Signature ....
(Advocate)

The Mental Healthcare Act

Form 45

Notice under the Mental Healthcare Act 2017

(Reference under section 105 of the Mental Healthcare Act 2017)

In the court of the District and Sessions Judge
at .... No. .... of 20 ....

To

The Chairperson,
Mental Health Review Board at ....

Whereas in course of trial of Sessions Case No. .... of 20 ...., one of the accused persons, namely, ... son of .... of .... has produced in this court *prima facie* proof of mental illness and whereas the prosecution has challenged the same, you are requested to cause further scrutiny in the matter and, after examination of the person alleged to have a mental illness either by the Board itself or through a committee of experts, to submit your opinion to this court on or before .... 20 ....

Given under my hand and the seal of this court this .... day of .... 20 ....

Judge
(Seal)

The Land Acquisition Act*

Form 46

Notice to claimant of date fixed for the determination of objection
(Section 20 of the Land Acquisition Act 1894)

In the .... Court of Special Judge at .... for the disposal of cases under the Land Acquisition Act 1894.

In the matter of ....
and the Land Acquisition Act 1894

To

....

Whereas objection has been taken by .... to the award made by .... in respect of .... the .... and measuring more or less .... bighas/cottahs/chataks/square-feet, the same being required for a public purpose namely for .... on the following grounds, namely: .... and whereas the matter has been referred to this Court for determination.

Take notice that the court will proceed to determine the aforesaid objection on the .... day of .... 20 ...... at ...... o'clock in the forenoon and that in default of your appearance on the said day, the case will be proceeded with in your absence.

Given under my hand and the seal of the court, this .... day ...... of ...... 20 ......

Judge
(Seal)

Form 47

Notice to Collector of date fixed for hearing his reference
(Section 20 of the Land Acquisition Act 1894)

In the .... Court of Special Judge at .... for the disposal of cases under the Land Acquisition Act 1894.

In the matter of ....
and the Land Acquisition Act 1894

* The Land Acquisition Act 1894 has already been repealed and replaced by the Right to Fair Compensation and Transparency in Land Acquisition, Rehabilitation and Resettlement Act 2013.

To

....

Take notice that the above-mentioned case, which was referred by you in your letter No. ...... dated the day of ...... 20 ...... for the determination of this court, has been set down for hearing on the ...... day of ...... 20 ...... at ...... o'clock in the forenoon, and that in default of your appearance on the said day the case will be proceeded with in your absence.

Given under my hand and the seal of the court, this .... day ...... of ...... 20 ......

Judge

(Seal)

Form 48

Notification under s. 4 of the Land Acquisition Act 1894

No. .... Dated .... 20 ....

WHEREAS it appears to the Governor of West Bengal that land is likely to be needed for a public purpose, namely, for .... (state the purpose) at public expense, and the particulars of land needed are mentioned in the schedule below.

Now, in exercise of the powers conferred by s. 4 of the Land Acquisition Act 1894, the Governor is pleased to authorize the officers for the time being to be engaged in the undertaking to enter upon and survey the land and do all other acts required or permitted by the law.

Any person interested in the said land who may have any objection to the acquisition may, within thirty days of this notification or after public notice of the substance of this notification in the locality, file an objection in writing before the First Land Acquisition Collector, ... (office address). A plan of the land is available at the said office for inspection.

By order of the Governor,
Secretary to the Government of West Bengal
Land & Land Reforms Department.

THE RIGHT TO FAIR COMPENSATION AND TRANSPARENCY IN LAND ACQUISITION, REHABILITATION AND RESETTLEMENT ACT

Form 49

Notice by Collector

[See rule 6]

No. .... Dated the .... 20 .....

Notice is hereby given that the land specified in the Schedule below and situated in the village of .... in the Taluk/Sub-division/Tehsil/Block (as applicable) .... in the District of .... is needed or is likely to be needed in accordance with the notification under section 11(1) of the Right to Fair Compensation and Transparency in Land Acquisition, Rehabilitation and Resettlement Act 2013 (30 of 2013) published by the Collector at page .... of Part I of the (name of State/UT) Gazette, dated .... All persons interested in the land are accordingly required to file their objections before .... within sixty (60) days from the date of publication of the above preliminary notification, a statement in writing of their objection, if any, to the acquisition of the said land.

Any objection statement which is received after the due date or which does not clearly explain the nature of the senders interest in the lands is liable to be summarily rejected.

Objections received within the due date, if any, will be enquired into on .... at .... when the objectors will be at liberty to appear in person or by Advocate and to adduce any oral or documentary evidence in support of their objections.

SCHEDULE

Sl. No.	*Survey No.*	*Total area in hectares*	*Area in hectares under acquisition*	*Name and address of the person interested*	*Boundaries N.S.E.W.*	*Details of trees, structures, etc., if any*
(1)	(2)	(3)	(4)	(5)	(6)	(7)

Place:

Date: Collector

Form 50

Preliminary Notification

[*See* rule 5(1)]

No. .... Dated ....

Whereas it appears to the appropriate Government that a total of .... hectares land is required in the.................. Village .... Taluk/Sub-division/Tehsil/Block (as applicable) .... District for public purpose, namely,........................... Social Impact Assessment Study was carried out by Social Impact Assessment (SIA) Unit and a report submitted/ preliminary investigation was conducted by a team constituted by Collector as laid down under rule 4. The summary of the Social Impact Assessment Report/preliminary investigation is as follows (Attach copy of SIA report):

....

A total of .... (No.) families are likely to be displaced due to the land acquisition. The reason necessitating such displacement is given below.

.... is appointed as Administrator for the purpose of rehabilitation and resettlement of the affected families. Therefore it is notified that for the above said project in the .... Village of .... Taluk/Sub-division/Tehsil/Block (as applicable) .... District a piece of land measuring .... hectares, *viz;* .... hectare of standard measurement, whose detail description is as following, is under acquisition:

Sl. No.	*Survey No.*	*Type of title*	*Type of land*	*Area under acquisition (in hectare)*	*Name and address of person interested*	*Boundaries*			
						N.	S.	E.	W.

Trees	
Variety	Number

Structures	
Type	Plinth area

This notification is made under the provisions of section 11(1) of the Right to Fair Compensation and Transparency in Land Acquisition, Rehabilitation and Resettlement Act 2013 (30 of 2013), to all whom it may concern.

A plan of the land may be inspected in the office of the Collector and .... on any working day during the working hours.

The Government is pleased to authorise Officer .... and his staff .... to enter upon and survey land, take levels of any land, dig or bore into the sub-soil and do all other acts required for the proper execution of their work as provided and specified in section 12 of the said Act.

Under section 11(4) of the Act, no person shall make any transaction or cause any transaction of land, i.e. sale/purchase, etc., or create any encumbrances on such land from the date of publication of such notification without prior approval of the Collector.

Objections to the acquisition, if any, may be filed by the person interested within 60 (sixty days) from the date of publication of this notification as provided under section 15 of the Act before Collector.

Since the land is urgently required for the project falling within the purview of section 40(2) and the same has approval of the Parliament, it has been decided not to carry out the Social Impact Assessment Study, *vide* G.O. No. .... , dated ....

(Strike if not applicable)

Encl: As above

Place:
Date: Collector

THE PAYMENT OF GRATUITY ACT

Form 51

Notice of opening

1. Name and address of the establishment ....
2. Name and designation of the employer ....
3. Number of persons employed ....
4. Maximum number of persons employed on any day during the preceding twelve months with date ....
5. Number of employees covered by the Act ....
6. Nature of industry ....
7. Whether seasonal ....
8. Date of opening ....
9. Details of Head Office/branches ....
   (*a*) Name and address of the Head Office ....
   —Number of employees ....
   (*b*) Name and address of other branches in India:—
   (1)
   (2)

(3)

(4)

I verify that the information furnished above is true to the best of my knowledge and belief.

....

Place .... (Signature of employer with name)

Date .... and designation)

To

The Controlling Authority,

....

....

Form 52

Application of gratuity by an employee

(See sub-rule (1) of rule 7)

To

....

(Give here name or description of the establishment with full address)

Sir/Gentlemen,

I beg to apply for payment of gratuity to which I am entitled under sub-section (1) of section 4 of the Payment of Gratuity Act 1972 on account of my superannuation/retirement/resignation after completion of not less than five years of continuous service/total disablement due to accident/total disablement due to disease with effect from the .... Necessary particulars relating to my appointment in the establishment are given in the statement below.

STATEMENT

1. Name in full
2. Address in full
3. Department/Branch/Section where last employed
4. Post held with Ticket No. or Serial No., if any
5. Date of appointment
6. Date and cause of termination of service
7. Total period of service
8. Amount of wages last drawn
9. Amount of gratuity claimed

I was rendered totally disabled as a result of–

(Here give the details of the nature of disease or accident)

The evidences/witnesses in support of my total disablement are as follows:–

(Here give details)

Payment may please be made in cash/open or crossed bank cheque.

As the amount of gratuity payable is less than rupees one thousand, I shall request you to arrange for payment of the sum due to me by postal money order at the address mentioned above after deducting postal money order commission therefrom.

Yours faithfully,

....

Place: Signature/Thumb-impression of
Date: the applicant employee

NOTES. 1. Strike out the words not applicable.

2. Strike out paragraph or paragraphs not applicable.

Form 53

Application of gratuity by a nominee

(See sub-rule (2) of rule 7)

To

....

(Give here the name or description of the establishment with full address)

Sir/Gentlemen,

I beg to apply for payment of gratuity to which I am entitled under sub-section (1) of section 4 of the Payment of Gratuity Act 1972 as a nominee of late .... (name of the employee) who was an employee of your .... establishment and died on the .... The gratuity is payable on account of the death of the aforesaid employee while in service/superannuation of the aforesaid employee on ..../retirement or/ resignation of the aforesaid employee on .... after completion of .... years of service/total disablement of the aforesaid employee due to accident or disease while in service with effect from the .... Necessary particulars relating to my claim are given in the statement below:

STATEMENT

1. Name of applicant nominee
2. Address in full of the applicant nominee
3. Marital status of the applicant nominee (unmarried/married/widow/widower)
4. Name in full of the employee
5. Marital status of employee
6. Relationship of the nominee with the employee
7. Total period of service of the employee
8. Date of appointment of the employee
9. Date and cause of termination of service of the employee
10. Department/Branch/Section where the employee last worked
11. Post last held by the employee with Ticket or Serial No., if any
12. Total wages last drawn by the employee

13. Date of death and evidence/witness as proof of death of the employee
14. Reference No. of recorded nomination if available
15. Total gratuity payable to the employee
16. Share of gratuity claimed

I declare that the particulars mentioned in the above statement are true and correct to the best of my knowledge and belief.

Payment may please be made in cash/crossed or open bank cheque.

As the amount payable is less than rupees one thousand, I shall request you to arrange for payment of the sum due to me by postal money order at the address mentioned above after deducting postal money order commission therefrom.

Yours faithfully,

....

Place: Signature/Thumb-impression of
Date: the applicant employee

NOTES. 1. Strike out the words not applicable.

2. Strike out paragraph or paragraphs not applicable.

Form 54

Application of gratuity by a legal heir

(See sub-rule (3) of rule 7)

To

....

(Give here name or description of
the establishment with full address)

Sir/Gentlemen,

I beg to apply for payment of gratuity to which I am entitled under sub-section (1) of section 4 of the Payment of Gratuity Act 1972 as a legal heir of late .... (Name of the employee) who was an employee of your .... establishment and died on the .... without making any nomination. The gratuity is payable on account of the death of the aforesaid employee while in service/superannuation of the aforesaid employee on the .... retirement or resignation of the aforesaid employee on the .... after completion of .... years of service/total disablement of the aforesaid employee due to accident or disease while in service with effect from the Necessary particulars relating to my claim are given in the statement below:

STATEMENT

1. Name of applicant legal heir
2. Address in full of the applicant legal heir
3. Marital status of the applicant legal heir (unmarried/married/widow/widower)
4. Name in full of the employee
5. Relationship of the applicant with the employee

6. Religion of both the applicant and the employee
7. Date of appointment and total period of service of the employee
8. Department/Branch/Section where the employee worked last
9. Post last held by the employee with Ticket or Serial No., if any
10. Total wages last drawn by the employee
11. Date and cause of termination of service of the employee (death or otherwise)
12. Date of death of the employee and evidence/witness in support thereof
13. Total gratuity payable to the employee
14. Percentage of the gratuity claimed
15. Basis of the claim and evidence/witness in support thereof

I declare that the particulars mentioned in the above statement are true and correct to the best of my knowledge and belief.

Payment may please be made in cash/open or crossed bank cheque.

As the amount payable is less than rupees one thousand, I shall request you to arrange for payment of the sum due to me by postal money order at the address mentioned above after deducting postal money order commission therefrom.

Yours faithfully,

....

Place:
Date:

Signature/Thumb-impression of the applicant employee

NOTE: Strike out the words not applicable.

THE ENVIRONMENT (PROTECTION) ACT

Form 55

Notice of intention to have sample analysed

[*See* rule 7 of the Environment (Protection) Rules 1986]

To

....

....

Take notice that it is intended to have analysed the sample of* .... which has been taken today, the .... day of .... 20 .... from* .... (Name and designation of the person who takes the sample).

(Seal)

Date ....

....

Signature

* Specify the place from where the sample is taken.

Form 56

Notice preceding filing of complaint

[*See* rule 11 of the Environment (Protection) Rules 1986]

By registered post with AD

From

Shri ....

....

To

....

....

NOTICE UNDER SECTION 19(*B*) OF THE ENVIRONMENT (PROTECTION) ACT 1986

WHEREAS an offence under the Environment (Protection) Act 1986 has been committed/ is being committed by .... (2) I/We hereby give notice of 60 days under section 19(b) of the Environment (Protection) Act 1986 of my/our intention to file a complaint in the Court against .... (2) for violation of section .... of the Environment (Protection) Act 1986.

In support of my/our notice, I am/we are enclosing the following documents (3) as evidence of proof of violation of the Environment (Protection) Act 1986.

Signature(s)

Place ....

Dated .... Signature(s)

Explanation. (1) In case the notice is given in the name of a company, documentary evidence authorising the person to sign the notice on behalf of the company shall be enclosed to this notice.

Company for this purpose means a company defined in explanation to sub-rule (6) of rule 4.

(2) Here give the name and address of the alleged offender. In case of a manufacturing/ processing/operating unit, indicate the name/location/nature of activity, etc.

(3) Documentary evidence shall include photographs/technical reports/health reports of the area, etc., for enabling enquiry into the alleged violation/offence.

Form 57

Notice under the Biological Diversity Act 2002

[*See* Rule 24(1)]

By registered post with AD

From

Shri ....

To

....

....

Sub: Notice under s. 61(*b*) of the Biological Diversity Act 2002.

WHEREAS an offence under the Biological Diversity Act 2002 has been committed/is being committed by ....

2. I/We hereby give notice of 30 days under s. 61(*b*) of the Biological Diversity Act 2002 of my/our intention to file a complaint in the court against .... for violation of the provisions of the Biological Diversity Act 2002.

3. In support of my/our notice, I am/we are enclosing herewith the following documents as evidence of the offence.

Place ....

Dated................

....

Signature

NOTES: (1) In case the notice to be given in the name of a company, documentary evidence authorising the person to sign the notice of behalf of the company shall be enclosed to the notice.

(2) Give the name and address of the alleged offender. In case of using biological resource/knowledge/research/bio-survey and bio-utilisation/the intellectual property right/patent, without the approval of the Authority, the details thereof and the commercial utilisation if any, may be furnished.

(3) Documentary evidence shall include photograph, technical report, etc., for enabling enquiry into the alleged violation/offence.

Form 58

Advocate's notice to builder for refund of amount

To

South-End Builders Private Ltd.
Suryamukhi Bhawan
22A, Barakhamba Road
New Delhi 110001

Dear Sir,

Under instructions received from and for and on behalf of my client Shrimati Kanta Basu C/o. Shri K.C. Basu, B-21 Brij Nihar, P.O. Chandra Nagar, Ghaziabad (UP), I give you this notice to the following effect:

1. That my aforesaid client had booked one ultra modern flat of 400 sq. feet offered at Rs. 2,000 per sq. feet against market rate of Rs. 5,000 per sq. feet with regard to your computerised draw held on the 15th day of June 20....., *vide* relevant application, bearing serial No. 25256 dated 4th April 20...... and cheque No. 674169 dated 4th April 20..... for Rs. 40,000 drawn on the .... Bank.

2. That my aforesaid client did not get the opportunity of the concession price offer as aforesaid.

3. That my aforesaid client by her letter dated 13th July 20.... requested you to refund the said sum of Rs. 40,000 paid by her for booking of flat in Kalyani Apartments through the said computerised lucky draw.

4. That despite such request you have not refunded to my aforesaid client the said sum of Rs. 40,000 which sum you should have refunded expeditiously on the said request of my aforesaid client.

Under the above circumstances, I, on behalf of my client request you to pay to my client the aforesaid sum of Rs. 40,000 (Rupees forty thousand only) within 4 p.m. of the 25th day of February 20..... failing which my client shall be compelled to initiate appropriate legal proceedings against you for recovery of the said sum of Rs. 40,000, and you shall in such event be entirely liable for all costs and consequences.

Yours faithfully

Sd/- ....

Dated, 10th January, 20.... Advocate

PRIVACY

Form 59

Notice for protection of privacy to house

Dear Sir/Madam

It has been found that you are shortly going to construct your house on your land adjacent to my land being plot No. .... situate on .... road at .... You are hereby required to do your construction in such a manner as to create no cause for complaint due to any invasion of privacy on my side ever in future.

Dated, ... 20..... Yours faithfully,

To

CD.,
(Address)

A.B.
(Signature)

Form 60

Notice to remove invasion of privacy

Dear Sir/Madam

WHEREAS you, Shri ...., have despite the protests of my client, *A.B.*, started constructing this day a boundary wall on the northern side of your land keeping in it three large openings.

AND WHEREAS such construction has invaded the privacy of the entire courtyard of my client and other portions of his house, lying to the northern side of your land, which are in constant use of the women of my client's house:

Take notice that, unless within seven days of receipt of this notice you completely and permanently close the aforesaid openings and increase the height of the said wall suitably so as to completely remove the said invasion of privacy and further desist from making any construction which may in any way invade the privacy of any portion of my client's said house, legal proceedings will be started against you and furthermore, you will be held liable for all costs.

Dated, ... 20......

Signature

Advocate for the said AB.

To

CD

(Address)

HINDU LAW

Form 61

Notice to karta of Hindu Undivided Family

By Registered post with AD

Ref. No. ....

Dated ....

From:

....

To,

....

Subject: Notice for settlement of claims.

Dear Sir,

WHEREAS you are the *Karta* of the Hindu Undivided Family business, carrying on under name and style ....

AND WHEREAS the undersigned, in his capacity as Managing Partner of the firm .... entered into an agreement with your Hindu Undivided Family firm above named.

AND WHEREAS, there is a breach of agreement by the said family business of which you are the *karta*.

We therefore, give you the notice on the facts and circumstances narrated below:

1. ....
2. ....
3. ....
4. ....

Please take notice that you are advised to settle the claim and make the payment of Rs. .... within 15 days from the date of receipt of this notice, failing which a civil suit shall be filed against you and your Hindu Undivided Family firm and in that case you and your Hindu Undivided Family firm shall be solely responsible for all the consequences.

Thanking you,

Yours very truly,

....

Managing partner

(Name of the firm)

Form 62

Notice by karta of Hindu Undivided Family

By registered post with AD

Ref. ....

Dated .... 20 ....

From:

G.D. Kathuria

Janakpuri, New Delhi.

To,

Messers New Timber Traders,

Paharganj, Delhi

Subject: Regarding settlement of dues.

I, as *karta* of the Hindu Undivided Family, carrying on business under the name and style 'G.D. Kathuria & Sons' at Janakpuri, New Delhi, give you the following notice:

That you purchased certain timber products from our Hindu Undivided Family establishment above named on credit *vide* our bill No. 00089 dated 13.5.20..... for Rs. 1,17,568.

You promised us at the time of purchase that the payment shall be made within 30 days, but more than two years have passed and you have not cleared the dues.

That you have been requested a number of times by letters and reminders, but neither you have acknowledged the letters nor made the payment.

However, you are given one more opportunity to clear the dues within 15 days from the date of receipt of this notice failing which the case shall be referred to the legal adviser for filing a suit for recovery in the Competent Court, and in that case you shall be totally responsible for all the expenses and subsequent consequences.

Thanking you

Yours faithfully,

For G.D. Kathuria

Karta

Form 63

Notice regarding disposal of Hindu Undivided Family Property

PUBLIC NOTICE

NOTICE IS HEREBY GIVEN that my client Shri .... son of Late .... Address .... is intent upon transferring by way of sale the joint Family property, of which particulars are given below, he being the Karta/Manager of the said Hindu Joint or Undivided Family and thus having the legal right to so dispose of the said property in the interest of the said family. Any person who may have any objection to the proposed sale may communicate such objection to the undersigned within fifteen days from the date of publication of this notice. If no objection is lodged within the said date, my above named client will take steps for causing transfer of the said property and shall transfer the said property by sale. Any objection filed after the above date will not be entertained. Particulars of the property are as follows:

Particulars:

P.K. Ray
Advocate
15, Ballygunge Place
Kolkata 700 019

Form 64

Notice in pursuance of pre-emption clause to members of a divided Hindu family to purchase share

NOTICE IS HEREBY GIVEN pursuant to clause 5 of the deed of partition dated .... executed between you and others of the one part and the undersigned of the other part, whereby each divided member had promised not to sell his divided share to any outsider without first offering his share to his divided member, that the undersigned is desirous of selling his share and in furtherance of such desire the undersigned advertised the sale of his share consisting of house No. .... situated on .... Road in the city of .... and the highest offer so far received is Rs. ....

Please take notice that pursuant to the said pre-emption clause you are given the first choice to complete the sale of the said house at the aforesaid price within a fortnight of the receipt of this notice. On your failure to do so within the aforesaid period the undersigned shall close the sale with the party offering the said price of Rs. ....

Dated, this .... day of .... 20 ....

Address ....

AB
(Signature)

To

CD etc.
other etc.
(Address)

TAXATION

Form 65

Notice to the Assessing Officer/Prescribed Authority under s. 11(2) of the Income-tax Act 1961

To,

The Assessing Officer/Prescribed Authority,
Ward No. ....

I, ..., on behalf of .... [name of the trust/institution/association] hereby bring to your notice that it has been decided by a resolution passed by the trustees/governing body, by whatever name called, on .... (copy enclosed) that, out of the income of the trust/

institution/association for the previous year(s), relevant to the assessment year 20 .....-20 .... and subsequent ....previous year(s), an amount of Rs. .... per cent of the income of the trust/institution/association/such sum as is available at the end of the previous year(s) should be accumulated or set apart till the previous year(s) ending in order to enable the trustees/governing body by whatever name called, to accumulate sufficient funds for carrying out the following purposes of the trust/association/institution:

(1) ....

(2) ....

2. Before expiry of six months commencing from the end of each previous year, the amount so accumulated or set apart has been/will be invested or deposited in any one or more of the forms or modes specified in sub-sec. (5) of s. 11.

3. Copies of the annual accounts of the trust/institution/association along with details of investment (including deposits) and utilisation, if any, of the money so accumulated or set apart will be furnished to you before the expiry of six months commencing from the end of each relevant previous year.

4. It is requested that in view of our complying with the conditions laid down in s. 11(2) of the Income-tax Act 1961, the benefit of that section may be given in the assessments of the trust/institution/association in respect of the incomes accumulated or set apart as mentioned above.

Dated ....

....
Signature

....
Designation

....
Address

NOTES: 1. This notice should be signed by a trustee/principal officer.

2. Delete the inappropriate words.

Index

Adverse possession
notice of suit obligatory—when, 111

Annual General Meeting
convening of, 422
  notice for, 422
    contents of, 425
    form of, 424
    service of, 423
notice of,
  statement to be annexed, 433

Arbitration & Conciliation Act
application of Limitation Act 1963 ... 112
appointment of arbitrator, 255
  court, through, 255
arbitration agreement with Government, 255
  notice under s. 80, CPC, 255
necessity of reference, 253
notice
  arbitrator by, 254
  computation of the period of, 253
  computation of the period of limitation, 254
  non-service of, 253
    amounting to misconduct, 253
  parties to arbitration, by, 252
  service under, 254

Arbitrator
appointment of, 255
  through court, 255
notice by, 73

Arrest
warrant of, 497

Attachment
property of person absconding, 500
purpose of, 501

Attornment
not necessary, when, 373
notice of, 373
principles of, 373

Board meeting
contents of notice, 418
convening of, 417
notice for,
  mode of service of, 420
notice to all Directors, 417
procedure, 441

Breach of peace
disputes concerning
  land, 509
  water, 509
right to use of,
  land, 512
  water, 512

Cause of action
estoppel whether, 103, 104
exclusion of period—disallowed, 109
gives right to sue for reliefs, 33, 34
means, 139
not a technical word, 32
under s. 80, CPC, 138
waiver may constitute, 104
what is, 32

Certificate of posting
a forgery, was, 57, 58
carry special sanctity, when, 119

Certificate of posting—*continued*
dispatch under,
permissible, is, 57
does not attach special guarantee, 120
does not inspire confidence, 58
easily available, 58, 119
might lead to presumption, 58, 120
notice sent under, 119
presumption, 119
raises presumption, 120
service of notice under, 57
presumption of, 57
when put in evidence, 57

Charge-sheet
form, 598
service of, 599
enquiry, 599
double, if barred, 601
order of suspension, 599

Classification of notice
directory, 8
mandatory, 8
oral or verbal, 7
statutory, 8
written, 7

Code of Civil Procedure
notice under s. 80 ... 10, 131
amendment of plaints, 163
fresh notice required, if, 163
amendments in, 148
cause of action, 22, 32, 33, 138
condition precedent to suit, 141
against Government, 141
against public officer, 141, 143
construction of, 153
defects in, 155
how far excusable, 155
exceptions, 146
application u/ss. 92A, 110A of MV Act 1939 ... 146
suit against Receiver, 147
suit in respect of property of a company, 147
suit under special statutes, 147
form and contents of, 134
fresh, when required, 27, 33

Code of Civil Procedure—*continued*
notice under s. 80—*continued*
Government,
co-defendant, when, 148
pro forma defendant, when, 148
identity of notice giver, 161
plaintiff, with, 161
inartistic and careless drafting of, 153
interpretation of, 153
name, description and address
defendant of, 137
plaintiff of, 135
proposed defendant, of, 137
need no technical, form, 26
object of, 3, 27, 131
period of, 158
computation of, 158
relief sought for, 140
requirement of law, 26, 133
return of plaint, 153
savings of limitation, 159
service of, 156
effected when, 156
mentioning in plaint, 164
State against State, notice required, if, 164
suit before expiry of two months, 159
suit during currency of notice, 159
suit for injunction
Government, against, 150
Public Officer, against, 150
unnecessary where, 10, 147, 148
variation in plaints, 164
waiver of, 156
withdrawal of suit, 163
fresh notice necessary, if, 163
question of *res judicata*, 163
public officer
co-defendant, when, 148
pro forma defendant, when, 148

Code of Criminal Procedure
attachment, 498, 500
purpose of, 501
bonds contemplated under s. 446 ... 518
effect of person having representative capacity, 508

Code of Criminal Procedure—*continued*
issue of process, 513
miscellaneous, 503
principles of natural justice, 508
effect of notice on person having representative capacity, 508
proclamation, 498
means, 498
person absconding, for, 498
service of conditional order, 503
summons, 493
warrant of arrest, 497

Common carrier
general responsibility of, 648
legal proceedings against, 648
notice for, 648
right of, 647

Companies Act 2013
alteration of provisions
articles, 436
special resolution, by, 436
memorandum of association, 436
date of notice of charge, 438
extraordinary general meeting, 426
called by the requisitionists, 429
convened by Board, 427
requisition on, 427
general meetings
annual general meeting, 420, 421
convening, 422
extraordinary general meeting, 420
rules governing, 421
mode of service of notice, 420
notice, 416, 423
contents, of, 425
form of, 424
length of, for calling a meeting, 431
meeting of the Board of Directors, 416
convening of Board meeting, 417
notice to all Directors, 417
service of, 423, 430
contents and manner of, 432
statement to be annexed to, 433

Companies Act 2013—*continued*
notice for revocation of licence, 436
notice of application to Central Government, 434
publication in a newspaper, 434
notice of ordinary and special resolution, 434
notice to
application under ss. 230 & 232, for, 439
application under ss. 241 & 242, of, 439
Central Government, 439
Registrar of Consolidation of share capital, 437
notice under s. 173 ... 418
contents of, 418
passing of resolutions by postal ballot, 440
prohibition on acceptance of deposits, 437
public form, 437
registered office of company, 438
wind up of a company by Tribunal, 439
circumstances, 439

Complaint
manner of filing, 473
procedure on receipt of, 474

Constitution of India
belated notice, 279
contents of notice, 275
under Art. 311 ... 277
defective notice, 275
double opportunity—theory of, 275
forfeiture of right to notice, 285
Government servant, 285
private servant, 285
notice
contents of, 275
contract services, in, 282
defective, 275
form of, 287
service of, 287
notice of suit, 271
Article 300 ... 271

Constitution of India—*continued*
notice to
non-Government employees, 280
private employees, 280
principles of natural justice, 280
audi alteram partem, 280
reasonable opportunity, 275
conditions required, 275
second show-cause notice, 278
show-cause notice, 280
temporary incumbent, 280
statutory show-cause notice, 272
nature of notice, 272
stages of, 272
suit against,
Governor of a State, 286
President of India, 286
termination of service, 283
reasonable notice, 283
two notices
theory of, 276
unnecessary—where, 279

Consumer Protection Act
better protection of consumers, for, 466
broad-based objects and reasons, 467
service of notice, 471
consumer—meaning, 469
period of limitation, 474
procedure on admission of complaint, 474
statement of objects and reasons, 467

Contractual notice
arbitration proceedings, 13
common illustrations, of, 13
determining partnership, 13
repair of leasehold premises, 13
revocation of agency, 13
termination of service, 13
what is, 9, 13

Corporation
requirement of notice, 613

Court of Session
commitment of case to, 515

Curator
legal, is, 71
notice by, 71

Definition
complainant, 470
complaint, 470
consumer, 469
defect, 470
deficiency, 470

Departmental proceedings
notice for, 593
charge-sheet, 597
form, 598
service of, 599
discharge simpliciter, 603
dismissal, 602
enquiry, 600
double enquiry if barred, 601
stages of proceedings, 593, 597
suspension, 599
order of, 599

Discharge simpliciter
notice therefor, 603

Draft Standing Order
submission of, 587

Employee's Compensation Act
employees abroad of companies and motor vehicles, 582
provisions relating to, 582
notice book—provision for, 582
notice of accident, 578
employer on, 578
mode of service of, 582
urgency of, 578
notice under, 578, 581
contents of, 581
defect of, 579
irregularity in, 579
language of, 581
want of, 579
whom to be served, 581

Factories Act
notice—display of, 573
notice—mode of service, 575
notice of
accidents, 573
periods of work for adults, 574
periods of work for children, 574

Factories Act—*continued*
notice to
  Chief Inspector—occupier by, 571

Forfeiture
lease determined by, 386
relief against, 377, 386
  combined notice, 377

Fresh notice
amendment of plaint, 163
death of one of co-landlords, 356
death of original tenant, 356
withdrawal of suit, 163

General meeting
annual meeting—notice for, 421
extraordinary, 426, 427
  called by requisitionists, 429
  convened by the Board, 427
  requisition, on, 427
length of notice, 431
  period of notice, 431
  shorter period, 431
notice of
  contents of, 425
  court's jurisdiction, 432
  form of, 424
  interpretation of, 432
  omission of service of, 432
  service of, 423
rules governing, 421

Indian Contract Act
notice of
  renunciation of agency, 262
  revocation, 262
  sale, 264
    determination of reasonableness, 264
   requirement, 264
notice to agent, 263
  effect thereof, 263
notice under s. 206 ... 12, 23, 28
  renunciation of agency, 12
  revocation of agency, for, 12, 28
person unqualified to make contract, 64

Indian Partnership Act
date in notice is date of dissolution, 234
modes of service of public notice, 236
notice essential for dissolution—whether, 233
notice for dissolution of partnership-at-will, 231
notice for retirement of a partner, 228
notice to an acting partner, 225
  effect of, 225
notice to changes in constitution of a firm, 235
  Registrar of firm, to, 235
notice to one of judgment debtor partners, effect, 236
public notice by a partner, on attaining majority, 226
public notice by retired partner, 229
  liabilities to third parties, 229
resolutions of partners, notice, if, 233

Industrial Disputes Act
closure of business, 564
compensation to workmen, 563
  closing down of undertaking, 563
    notice to workmen, 563
lay-off
  closure and, 557
  employer by, 557
  notice of, 557
lock-out
  means, 555
notice for
  lock-out, 552
  strike, 552
    on whom notice to be given, 556
notice of change, 548
  conditions of service, 551
  required, when, 549
  workmen, to, 549
    necessary, when, 549
notice to workman, 561
  closure on, 562
  transfer of understanding, 561
notices under, 548

Industrial Disputes Act—*continued*
prohibition of
lock-out, 553
strike, 553
public utility service, 554
strike, in, 554
retrenchment
meaning, 558
notice of, 558
strike in public utility services, 552
strike—what is, 554

Industrial Employment (Standing Orders) Act
application of the Act, 586
charge-sheet, 597
service of, 599
departmental proceedings, 593
stages, 593
notice thereof, 593
discharge simpliciter, 603
notice therefor, 603
dismissal, 602
draft standing order, 586
submission of, 587
enquiry, 600
double enquiry—barred if, 601
object of the Act, 586
order of suspension, 599
second show-cause notice, 602
service
resignation of, 603
termination of, 603
standing orders, 589
certificate of, 589
covers the subject, 589
suspension or dismissal for misconduct, 590
termination of service, 590

Injunction
pending inquiry, 504

Inspection
local, 516

Labour laws
EMPLOYEES' STATE INSURANCE ACT
certificate of pregnancy, 617

Labour laws—*continued*
death of employee, 617
notice for dependant's benefit, 617
insured female employee, 617
resumption of work, 617
notice of, 617
maternity benefits, 615
notice by an enry in Accident Book, 616
duty of the employer, 616
notice of accident, 616
appropriate particulars with, 616
notice of pregnancy, 617
social security legislation, 615
MINES ACT
notice about
certain diseases, 620
notice of accident
failure to give notice, 619
consequence of, 619
penal provision, 619
notice regarding
hours of work, 620
mining operation, 619

Lay-off
closure—difference, 557
employer by, 557
right of workman, 557
notice of, 557
form of, 557
termination of, 557

Lease
surrender of, 389

Limitation
computation of period of, 105
miscellaneous cases, 114
not a notice of suit, 108
exclusion of the period, validity, 108
period of, does not alter, when, 111
savings of, 105
notice statutory when, 105

Listing
agreement, 538
corporate governance, 538
continued, conditions for, 539
granted, 538

Lock-out
meaning, 555
notice for, 552
given to when, 556
prohibition of, 553

Maintenance
enforcement of order of, 502

Mandatory notice
notice of attornment, 11
notice of renunciation of agency, 12
notice of revocation of agency, 12
notice of transfer of an actionable claim, 11
notice u/s. 10, Carriers Act, 11
notice u/s. 54(2), Sale of Goods Act, 11
notice u/s. 80, CPC, 10
notice u/s. 106, Railways Act 1989 ... 10

Municipality
corporation, 613
notice—if required, 613
notice before institution of a suit, 611
suit against, 611
notice before, 611

Negotiable Instruments Act
dishonour of cheque, 305
insufficiency of funds, 305
notice of dishonour
bill of exchange, 299
cheque, 299
person competent to accept, 299
person competent to give, 299
mode of service of, 301
object of, 301
reasonable time for given notice, 303
unnecessary, when, 302

Notice
accident of, 578
employer on, 578
entry in Notice Book, 582
mode of service of, 582

Notice—*continued*
actual, 16
in case of, 17
means, 16
provisions of s. 3, TP Act, 16, 326
Administrator-General's Act, under, 624
notice of suit, 624
section 80 of CPC not attracted, when, 624
affixation of,
does not contemplate refusal of personal delivery, 60
not good service, when, 60
not valid service, 60
agent, by, 65
agent, to, 77
principal, to, whether, 78
agent, to, is notice to principal, 20, 78
announcement, an, 1
Arbitration & Conciliation Act, under —*see* ARBITRATION AND CONCILIATION ACT
Arbitrator, by, 73
attorney, by, 65
attornment, of, 373
authentication of, 52
benamdars, on, 93
not necessary, when, 93
Birth, Death and Marriage Registration Act, under, 628
notice of
birth, 628
person authorised to issue, 628
death, 628
person authorised to issue, 629
body corporate, by, 74
body corporate, to, 82
Carriage by Air Act, under, 636
Carriage by Road Act, under, 646
dangerous or hazardous nature, of, 647
carriage of goods, of, 647
definitions, 646

Notice—*continued*
Carriage by Road Act, under—*continued*
no liability for loss of certain goods, 646
Carriage of Goods by Sea Act, under, 636
case of minor landlord, in, 350
caution, a, 1
certain accidents, of, 573
change in weekly off day, 551
change of conditions of service, 548
increase in working hours, 550
character of, 5
should be, 5
charge of, 438
date, 438
chief officer of a club, by, 74
Child and Adolescent Labour (Prohibition of Regulation) Act, under, 622
inspector, to, 622
classification of—*see* CLASSIFICATION OF NOTICE
club, to, 82
co-heirs, on, 91
co-lessees, on, 89
co-lessors, by, 68
co-sharers, by, 68
co-trustees, by, 68
Code of Criminal Procedure, under—*see* CODE OF CRIMINAL PROCEDURE
Competition Act, under, 650
obligation to file the notice, 650
composite, 24
condition precedent
not fulfilled, 8
when, 8
condition precedent to a suit
Government, against, 141
public officer, against, 141, 142
Constitution of India, under—*see* CONSTITUTION OF INDIA
construction of, 124
constructive, 16, 17
defined as, is, 17
following circumstances, arises in, 18
known as, is, 17
registration would not amount to, when, 19

Notice—*continued*
constructive—*continued*
two fold, 18–19
Contract Act, under—*see* INDIAN CONTRACT ACT
contract service, in, 282
contractual—*see* CONTRACTUAL NOTICE
coparceners, by, 68
corporation, to, 82
counsel of the party, on, 84
court, by, 64
court-fees, on, 124
CPC under—*see* CODE OF CIVIL PROCEDURE
curator, by, 71
Customs Act, under, 634
notice of
refund, 634
seizure, 634
date of, 124
date of posting, 124
defect in, 126
defect or irregularity in, 579
effect, 579
defective, 21
determination of lease, for, 378
determination of tenancy, of, 78
determine lease, to, 378
display of, 573
Dissolution of Muslim Marriage Act, under, 624
service of notice to heirs of husband, 624
condition of a suit, 624
dissolved firm, by, 75
doctrine of, 243
Electricity Act, under, 641
accident, of, 642
disconnection of supply, 641
from for reporting electrical accidents, 643
notice to telegraph authority, 642
sale of utilities of licenses, 641
ESI Act, under, 615
accident of, 615
appropriate particulars, 616

Notice—*continued*
ESI Act, under—*continued*
accident of—*continued*
other than entry in Accident Book, 616
dependants' benefit on death, 617
pregnancy, of, 617
certificate of, 617
resumption of work by female employee of, 617
estoppel, 130
Evidence Act, under, 638
presumption of service of, 638
exceptions, 146
expectant heir, by, 73
fact, of a, 2
firm, to, 85
forms and contents of, 25
fresh,
necessary when, 356
whether necessary, 356
given to Central Govt., 439
application under ss. 391 & 394 ... 439
application under ss. 397 & 398 ... 439
giving of,
not complete, when, 121
Gold Control Act, under, 635
given of notice, 636
meaning, 636
Government, by, 72
necessary when, 377
Government not a proper authority to issue, when, 71
Government, to, 87
object, of, 87
group of persons, to, 83
guardian *ad litem*, by, 71
illiterate person, to, 87
Indian Christian Marriage Act, under, 629
notice of
contents, of, 629
false, 629
penalty for, 629

Notice—*continued*
Indian Christian Marriage Act, under—*continued*
notice of—*continued*
intended marriage, in private dwelling, 630
party minor, 630
Indian Explosives Act, under, 624
notice of accidents, 624
Indian Foreign Marriage Act
notice of intended marriage, 632
contents of a notice, 632
Indian Partnership Act, under—*see* INDIAN PARTNERSHIP ACT
Indian Ports Act, under, 632
manner of service of, 632
Indian Treasure-Trove Act, 637
collector by a finder of treasure, on, 637
individual having a trade-name, by, 74
Industrial Employment (Standing Orders) Act, under, 586
inspector, to, 622
Insurance Act, under
notice to policy holder, 633
intending to determine a lease, 374
waiver of, 374
interpretation of, 124, 126
requires commonsense, 126
intimation, an, 1
invalid, 21, 23
proceedings initiated under, 29
would be *ultra vires*, 29
invalidate, a, 23-24
when, 23-24
when not, 24
issue of like, 7
provisions of law requiring, 7
issue of second, 356
waiver of first—whether, 356
joint-receiver, by, 67
joint-tenants, on, 89
Land Acquisition Act, under, 638
person interested, 638, 639
landlord's transferees, 71
language of, 581
laws relating to, 5
adjective laws, 5

Notice—*continued*
lawyer, by, 65
legal meaning of, 1
lessee to lessor
encroachment for, 372
lessee's co-assignees, on, 92
lessor assigns, by, 71
lock-outs, for, 552
public utility services, in, 552
manager of a firm, to, 80
manager of HUF, by, 72
marriage not solemnized three months of, 627
means actual notice, 226
meeting of Board of Directors, for, 416
members of HUF, to, 81
mention of section, 25
mentioning in plaint, service of, 164
Merchant Shipping Act, under
notice by Receiver, 631
notice of
day of sailing, 631
loss of ship-wrecked vessel, 631
proceedings in respect of foreign ship, 631
Mines Act, under, 619
accident, of, 619
certain diseases, about, 620
failure to give notice, consequence, 619
penal provisions, 619
notice regarding hours of work, 620
notice regarding mining operation, 619
minor landlord in case of, 350
minor, to, 85
miscellaneous, 667
mistakes in, 126
mode of pleading of, 130
Negotiable Instruments Act, under—*see* NEGOTIABLE INSTRUMENTS ACT
non-issue of, 51
does not affect jurisdiction, 51
prejudice caused by, if, 57
non-service of, 10, 130
fatal to claim, is, 10
person competent to raise objection, 130

Notice—*continued*
object of, 2
occupier by, 571
Chief Inspector, to, 571
Official Trustees Act, under, 634
notice of suit, 634
section 80, CPC, not attracted—when, 634
old address, to, 45
one of several defendants, against, 110
exclusion allowed, 110
one of the directors, to, 84
one partner in a firm, to, 83
onus probandi of, 129
oral, 7
section 94 of the Negotiable Instruments Act provides for, 8
other body corporate, by, 74
partnership firm, on, 85
party direct, by, 65
party, to, 77
party's attorney, to, 79
lawyer, to, 79
solicitor, to, 79
period of, 105, 120
computation of, 120
exclusion of, 105
disallowed, 108
no cause of action arises, 109
miscellaneous cases where exclusion allowed or disallowed, 114
never arbitrary, is, 120
reasonable period, 120
statutory period, 120
work for adults, of, 574
work for children, of, 574
personal, 24
persons incompetent to contract, by, 76
mentally ill person, 76
minor, 76
under legal disabilities, 76
persons of unsound mind, to, 85
Police Act, under, 625
notice of a suit, 625
limitation, 625
possession amounting to, 20

Notice—*continued*
principal officer of an association, to, 81
principal, on, 84
pro forma defendant
    Government, 148
    Public Officer, 148
provision for a Notice Book, 582
publication in a newspaper, 434
purpose of, 26
quit, to, 372
    defects in, 344
        excusable when, 344
    invalid notice, 348
    must be reasonable, 22
    period in, 349
        computation of months and year, 351
    person competent to issue, 353
    person competent to receive, 354
    service of, 356
        various modes, 356
    valid notice, 348
    waiver of, 372, 380
        acts amounting to, 382
        acts not amounting to, 384
    withdrawal of, 372
Railways Act, under—*see* RAILWAYS ACT
reasonable, 21
receiver, by, 67
receiver, to, 87
recital in—*see* RECITAL IN A NOTICE
refusal of, 363
    amounts to service by implication, 363
    refused and left—distinction, 363
refused notice, 58, 128
    contents of, 58, 128
        knowledge of, 58
registered, 116
    AD receipt, without signature, 119
        mistake, through, 119
        omission, through, 119
    delivery of, 116
    non-delivery of, 116
registered firm, by, 75
registered society, to, 82

Notice—*continued*
Registrar of consolidation of share capital, to, 437
registration as, 19
registration of, 116
relating to guardianship of minor, 86
repairs of leasehold property, 371
    lessor's liability, 371
requirements in, 27
resignation and termination of service, of, 603
reversionary, by, 73
revocation of licence, for, 436
right to, 285
    forfeiture of, 285
rule of imputed, 79
    of no avail, is, when, 79
Sale of Goods Act, under—*see* SALE OF GOODS ACT
Sea Customs Act, under, 634
    proceedings, of, 634
sent under certificate of posting, 119
    presumption, 119
served in sufficient time, to be, 30
service of, 575—*see* SERVICE OF NOTICE
should contain
    name, description and address of parties, 29
solicitor, by, 65
Special Marriage Act
    notice of intended marriage, 625
stamp on, 124
State *v* State case, 164
    notice required, if, 164
statutory, 9, 24
    directory, 9
    invariably mandatory, when, 9
    mandatory, 9
strike, for, 552
    public utility services, in, 552
sub-tenant, on, 93
tenants in common, on, 88
tendering of, 4
termination of,
    tenancy, 344
    transfer of leasehold premises, 339
termination of licence for, 379

Notice—*continued*
transfer of actionable claim, 388
under s. 131, T.P. Act, 38
defective notice, 388
waiver of notice, 388
trustee, by, 68
umpire in arbitration proceedings, by, 73
under s. 161, Electricity Act, 12
under s. 148, IT Act, 11, 31
invalid, when, 31
under s. 39, TP Act, 372
under s. 106, TP Act
attornment of, 373
principles of, 373
change in position, 332
death of one of co-landlord, effect, 356
death of original tenant, effect, 356
issue of second notice, 356
karta, on, 355
quit, to, 5, 66, 327, 334, 367, 372
contract to the contrary, 333, 338
lease for a term, 334
lease for an indefinite period, 337
lease for life, 336
perpetual lease, 336
tenancy-at-will, 336
denial of tenancy, 367
form and contents of, 339, 342
determination of lease, 342
object and interpretation of, 340
holding over, 368
issue of reasonable notice, 370
issued though not required, 369
lease by Government, 365
lease by municipality, 366
sub-letting, 368
usage to the contrary, 338
waiver of, 372, 380
refusal of, 363
refused and left, distinction, 363
service of notice, 356, 363
effect of, 363

Notice—*continued*
under s. 106—*continued*
service of notice—*continued*
personal service, 357, 358
postal service, 359
vicarious service, 357
suit for ejectment, 328
combined notice, 329
under s. 114A, T.P. Act
combined notice, 386
object and contents of, 387
unnecessary, where, 10
unregistered society, to, 82
urgency of, 578
valid, 348
variation in a notice, 127, 128, 164
plaint, in, 164
verbal, 7
sufficient to determine tenancy, 7
waiver of, 126—*see* WAIVER OF A NOTICE
defects for, 126
mistake for, 126
Wakf Act, under, 11, 637
notice of pending suit, 637
under s. 56 ... 33
want of, 579
when given, 4
when is not given, 4
when issued by authorized representative, 29
when statutory, 37, 121
when voluntary, is, 123
where, not statutory, is, 7, 34
whether express or constructive, should be subsistence of the agency, 78
wider import than knowledge, 2
without containing date of appearance, 35
workmen to, 561
closure of business and lock-out, 564
closure on, 562
compensation for closure, 563
transfer of undertaking on, 561
wrong particulars, effect, 30

Notice of suit
not a, 108

Notice of suit—*continued*
notice must be a, 109
when obligatory, 111
exclusion allowed, 111

Notice to quit
defects in, 344
address, 347
clerical errors, 344
excusable when, 344
minor omissions, 344
misdescription of leasehold property, 347
signature, 347
technical defects, 344
fresh term and conditions, with, 348
notice terminating tenancy, 344
tenant's undertaking to vacate, 344
fresh notice—whether necessary, 344

Notification
notice and, 5
publication of, 5

Optional notice
allows reasonable period for compliance, 122
object of
direct, 13
indirect, 13
what is, 13, 14

Postal endorsement
did not lose effect, when, 57
not admissible, when, 56
production of, 56
sufficient proof, when, 56

Presumption
bare denial does not rebut, 47
bare denial is not sufficient, when, 49
bare denial is sufficient, when, 47
cannot be raised, when, 54
cannot be rebutted, when, 48
defined as, 46
may or may not be drawn, 58
means, 45
rebutted, when, 47, 57

Presumption—*continued*
rule of law, is, 45
same import in the field of law, 45
stands rebutted, when, 55
under s. 114 of Evidence Act, 46, 47, 48, 54, 56
under s. 27 of General Clauses Act, 49, 54
when recede, 46, 54

Private notice
illustrations
appointment of Arbitrator, for, 15
assignment of lease, of, 15
claim to debtor, of, 15
dishonour of cheque, of, 15
landlord to tenant to quit, 14
tenant, to attorn, to, 14
tenant to determine lease, 14
tenant to repair, 14
vendor, by, to complete purchase, 15
relate to interests affecting individuals, 14

Public issues
compulsory listing of, 538
conditions for valid allotments, 538

Public notice
Contract Act, under, 16
formalities in case of registered firm, 15
illustrations of,
dissolution of registered firm, 14
retirement of a partner, 14
sale of a business, 14
termination of an agent's authority, 14
invalid, when, 237
means, 14
meant to be issued, 14
when, 14
mode of giving, 15, 236
necessary—when, 237
necessary in case of unregistered firm, is, 15
when, 15
Partnership Act, under, 15, 225

Public notice—*continued*
retired partner, by, 229
sine qua non, when, 2

Railways Act
notice u/s. 80, CPC when necessary, 197
notice under s. 106 ... 10
application of s. 15(2), Limitation Act, 203
case of tortious liabilities, 211
claims to compensation for losses, 188
claims to refund of overcharges, of, 188
combind with s. 80, CPC, 196
consignment dispatched throughout-agency, 215
construing of, 199
defects in, how far excusable, 198
double charge & over charge—distinction, 211
notice u/s. 106 required if, 24
each railway involved in transit, 206
if entitled to, 206
foreign railway, 188
form and contents of, 192
contrary situations, 193
interpretation of, 199
introduction of Railway Claims Tribunal Act, 197
notice u/s. 80, CPC if necessary, 197
limitation, 200
mandatory, is, 191
mistake condoned, 198
mistake fatal, 199
mistakes in, how far excusable, 198
non-delivery, for, 195
not necessary, when, 191
object of, 3, 191
period of, 200
presumption of service by post, 216
short delivery & non-delivery—distinction, 209
short delivery, for, 195

Railways Act—*continued*
notice under s. 106—*continued*
waiver of, 195
when through traffic, one notice if, sufficient, 208
whether the notice be dispensed with, 194
whom to be sent, 203
other cases, 217
public auction of unclaimed consignment, for, 217
Railway Claims Tribunal Act 1987
introduction of, 197
whether notice under s. 80, CPC necessary, 197
Railway Establishment Code under, 216
insufficient, 216
period of, 216
service of notice
railway administration
by, 215
to, 212

Reasonable notice
meaning, 3
necessary to terminate, 12
when, 12
requirement of, 12
mandatory under s. 206, Contract Act, 12
section 206, Indian Contract Act speaks of, 23
termination of service, of, 283
what constitutes, a, 4
what is, 21
when issued, 21, 23

Reasonable opportunity
concept of, 274
conditions required for, 275
essential ingredients of, 274
under Constitution of India, 274
means, 274
principle of, 275

Receiver
can issue notice, when, 67
notice, by, 67
notice, to, 87

Receiver—*continued*
suit against, 147

Recital in a notice
cause of action—expression explained, 32
reliefs claimed, 34
  incidental reliefs, 34
  principal reliefs, 34

Relief
absence of mentioning of, 34
  not make notice defective, 34
recital of, 34
  must in notice, is, 34
  not necessary, whether, 34

Resignation
notice therefor, 603

Resolution
alteration of Article, 436
  special resolution by, 436
alteration of memorandum of association, 436
ordinary, 434
requiring special notice, 434
special, 434

Retrenchment
condition precedent to, 558
means, 558
notice of, 558

Sale of Goods Act
buyer's notice to seller, 244
  while rejecting the goods, 244
notice—doctrine of, 243
notice of stoppage in transit, 245
  unpaid seller by, 245
notice to buyer by unpaid seller, 246
  intention to re-sell, 246
notice under s. 54(2) ... 11
sale of goods by other than owner, 243

Securities and Exchange Board of India
Amendment of 2017 ... 539
conditions for continued listing, 539
corporate Governance, 538
disclosures by insiders, 545
notices under, 537

Securities and Exchange Board of India—*continued*
object of changes, 538
Regulations of 2015 ... 544

Service of notice
affixation of copy on residential house, 60
contractual mode of, 59
distinction between non-service and irregular, 50
electronic form, through, 362
illiterate person, on, 63
interpretation of terms
  'to deliver', 62
  'to give', 62
  'to issue', 62
  'to prefer', 62
  'to send', 62
  'to serve', 62
karta of HUF, on, 93
meaning, 37
means, 36
mode of, 37, 375
  contractual, 39, 59
  indirect, 39
  personal service, 38
  registered post, 42
  service by post, 38, 41
    certificate of posting, 41
    delivered to a member of the family, 44
    ordinary post, 38
    pre-requisite condition of, 44
    safe and sure, 42
  service through electronic form, 39
  statutory, 39, 59
  vicarious service, 40
personal service, 38
  may be effected, when, 40
  when cannot be served, 40
presumption of
  as to time of delivery, 53
  due delivery, 47
  endorsement by postal peon
    left, 53
    not claimed, 53
    not found, 53
    refused, 50, 53

Service of notice—*continued*
presumption of—continued
rebuttable, is, 43
rebuttal of, 43, 54
how made, 54
illustrative circumstances, 54
rebutted by denial, 49
sent by registered post, 45
provisions of s. 106, T.P. Act, 51
invoked, 51
sent by registered post
onus of proof of service, 55
sent by under certificate of posting, 57
presumption of service, 57
statutory mode of, 59
personal tender affixation of copy, 59
through electronic form, 61
acknowledgement of receipt, 61
admissibility of notice sent, 62
through phonogram, 63
under Income Tax Act, 51
under Negotiable Instruments Act, 52
under Railways Act, 52
vicarious service, 40
when effected, 40
what constitutes, 37
when proper, 42

Standing orders
certificate of, 589
effect, 589
cover subjects in the Schedule, 589
misconduct
disciplinary action for, 590, 594
dismissal for, 590
suspension for, 590
punishable, when, 597
submission of draft, 586, 587
termination of service, 590

State Rent Control Acts
Bombay Rent Control Act, 331
Delhi Rent Control Act, 331
Karnataka Rent Control Act, 332
Maharashtra Housing and Area Development Act, 331
MP Accommodation Control Act, 331

State Rent Control Acts—*continued*
Mysore Rent Control Act, 331
UP (Temporary) Control of Rent and Eviction Act, 331
West Bengal Premises Tenancy Act 1997 ... 330

Strike
notice for, 552
given to when, 556
prohibition of, 553
public utility service in, 554
right to, 554
what is, 554

Suit
withdrawal of, 163
necessity of fresh notice, 163
res judicata, 163

Summons
accused to, 493
issue of warrant, 497
meaning of, 493
order issuing, 497
quashing of, 497
service of, 494
affixation by, 496
person cannot be found, 495
special in case of petty offences, 514
witness, to, 493

Termination of service
notice therefor, 603

Transfer of Property Act
actual notice, 326
amendment of s. 106 ... 322
effect of, 322
statement of objects and reasons, 322
combined notice under s. 106 ... 329
suit for ejectment, 329
constructive notice, 326
forfeiture, 377, 386
whether notice by Government is necessary, 377
invalid notice, 348
licence, termination, 379

Transfer of Property Act—*continued*
notice intending to determine lease, 374
notice of repair of leasehold property, 371
notice on karta under s. 106 ... 355
notice to determine lease, 378
notice to quit under s. 106
  change in position, 332
  computation of period, 325
  contract to contrary, where is, 333
    lease for a term certain, 334
      statutory tenant, 335
    lease for an indefinite period, 337
    lease for life, 336
    perpetual lease, 336
    tenancy-at-will, 336
  effect of service of, 363
  form and contents of, 339
  general observations, 333
  general principles, 327
  law to contrary, where is, 338
  lease by Municipality, 366
  lease by the Government, 365
  mode of service, 325, 356, 357
  notice through telegram, 363
  object and interpretation of, 340
  object, 327, 387
  period in, 349, 351
  person competent to receive notice, 353
    agents, 353
    co-assigns, 353
    co-lessor, 353
    lawyers, 353
    lessee, 353
    lessor, 353
    receiver, 353
    trustees, 353
  person competent to receive notice, 353
    co-tenants, 355
    joint tenant, 354
    partnership firm, 355
    tenants-in-common, 354
  service of, 328
    not amount to termination, 328

Transfer of Property Act—*continued*
notice to quit under s. 106—*continued*
  suit for ejectment, 328
    notice to be pleaded, 328
  under certain circumstances, 364
  usage to contrary, where is, 338
  termination of lease, 22
  to determine a lease, 342
    contents and form, 342
  withdrawal of, 372
notice to transfer actionable claim, 388
notice under s. 39 ... 372
provisions of s. 3 ... 326
  actual notice, 326
  constructive notice, 326
relief against forfeiture, 386
right of lessor's transferee, 373
    terminate tenancy, to, 374
surrender of lease, 389
termination of licence, 379
transfer of leasehold premises, 339
  notice of termination, 339
transitory provision, 324
validation of defective notice, 325

Trustee
notice, by, 68
religious society, of, 68
  can give notice, 68

Waiver of a notice
acceptance by mistake will not be a, 96
an intentional relinquishment of known right, 94
constitute cause of action, 104
meaning, 94
mere delay did not amount to, 100
Municipal Acts, under, 103
principle of, 94, 100
  connotes issuance of notice, 94
  impossibility of compliance cannot attract, 100
quit to, 380
  acts amounting to, 382
  acts not amounting, to, 383

Waiver of a notice—*continued*
revenue law, under, 103
right to plead, 104
third party not entitled, 104
under other Acts, 104
under s. 80, CPC, 99
mandatory nature not a bar to, 95, 101
under s. 106, Railways Act 1989 ... 102, 372
under T.P. Act, 95
under W.B. Premises Tenancy Act 1956, 98

Waiver of a notice—*continued*
what amounts to, 104
when law permits, 95

Warrant
issue of, 501
in addition to summons, 501
in lieu of summons, 501

Wrongful dismissal
reasonable notice of termination of service, 283